COMPARATIVE LEGAL SYSTEMS

Dr. Anu Singla

TAP

Toronto Academic Press

COMPARATIVE LEGAL SYSTEMS

Dr. Anu Singla

Toronto Academic Press
4164 Lakeshore Road
Burlington ON L7L 1A4
Canada
www.tap-books.com

Email: orders@arclereducation.com

ISBN: 978-1-77956-929-5

ABOUT THE AUTHOR

Dr. Anu Singla is a distinguished academician and founding faculty member of Dr. A.P.J. Abdul Kalam Institute of Forensic Science and Criminology at Bundelkhand University, Jhansi. With an illustrious career spanning 24 years, she has made significant contributions to teaching and research in the domain of Forensic Science. Under her supervision, 10 doctoral scholars have been awarded Ph.D. degrees, and she had mentored over 130 dissertations. Her scholarly work is reflected in the publication of six books and more than 65 research papers in reputed national and international journals. Additionally, she has 13 patents published across diverse Forensic Science disciplines. Dr. Singla has been instrumental in the institution's growth and development since its inception. Her unwavering commitment to academic excellence and innovation continues to shape the field of Forensic Science.

Brief Contents

Table of Contents

List of Figures

PREFACE

Comparing the legal systems is both an attitude and a process. It is a set of questions regarding what types of rules various societies create to address identical issues, how they look alike as they do, and how they tend to change over time. It is more than comparing cases or statutes; it enters the institutions, the procedures, the culture, and the incentives that govern professional practice. Looking across borders, we observe how ideas move, which doctrines hold firm against change, and on which reforms flourish when transplanted to new soil. Comparison itself sharpens legal thought: it distinguishes what is universal from what is local preference, and it empowers lawyers and policymakers to judge reforms on evidence not assumption. This topic also addresses pressing practical requirements.

Predictable enforcement of contracts and judgments are needed in cross-border commerce. Climate policy, electronic government, migration, and public health all involve the coordination of jurisdictional entities with differently organized power and diverse valuation of sources of authority. Foreign case law is used by courts to interpret rights; legislators borrow templates on consumer protection, data privacy, and competition law; regulatory agencies coordinate standards to reduce friction. Comparative work illuminates not only similarities and differences, but also trade-offs lying behind them—amongst certainty and flexibility, individual rights and collective purposes, judicial discretion and legislative clarity. It explains how history, economy, religion, technology, and professional schooling influence legal choice, and how reformers can devise measures which accommodate institutional realities rather than idealized forms. ***Comparative Legal Systems*** is composed as an open, practice-oriented introduction to the structures, sources, and doctrines constituting law in important traditions. It lays out central conceptual tools first, and only then applies them to substantive areas with which lawyers will be acquainted in study and in practice.

Each chapter is thematic explanation and jurisdictional snapshot to show variation and convergence. The book favors functional questions—what issue does a rule solve, for whom, and at what expense—without compromising doctrinal accuracy. Readers will encounter illustrations and questions that encourage judgment of policy choices, institutional capability, and the downstream effects of legal design. Chapter 1 lays out the foundation of comparative law research in terms of purpose, methodology, and traps. It contrasts taxonomic (family-based) with functional approaches, establishes criteria for the selection of comparator jurisdictions, and addresses translation issues, loss of context, and spurious equivalence. The chapter concludes with ethical consideration in applying rules between unequal power settings. Chapter 2 covers comparative sources of law, surveys constitutions, statutes, regulations, case law, custom, religious norms, and transnational standards. Hierarchies of norms, interpretive communities, and approaches such as purposivism and textualism are outlined, illustrating how authority is constructed differently in civil law, common law, religious, and mixed systems. Chapter 3 addresses constitutional structures and comparative government, like federal versus unitary constitutions, separation of powers, review of legislation, emergency powers, and safeguarding rights. Individuals learn how design choices influence political responsibility and how the courts resolve conflicts between branches, especially during changes, crises, and coalition governments.

Chapter 4 addresses civil procedure across all jurisdictions, comparing pleading requirements, disclosure and evidence regimes, burdens of proof, case management, collective actions, costs, and enforcement of judgments. It records the choice between party-dominated and judge-dominated models, technological effects on filing and service, and cross-border cooperation methods.

Chapter 5 discusses criminal procedure and law, including legality principles, structures of mens rea, offense categorization, policing models, prosecutorial discretion, judicial oversight, trial design, plea or confession processes, and sentencing. Chapter 5 evaluates the protection of fairness and efficiency, evidence needed, and defendant and victim treatment.

Chapter 6 outlines contract law across legal systems, tracing formation, consideration or causa, good faith, standard terms control, interpretation, mistake, frustration, illegality, remedies, and specific performance. It compares freedom of contract with consumer and small business protection, and scans cross-border choice-of-law and choice-of-forum approaches.

Chapter 7 summarizes property regimes law, comparing concepts of ownership, possession, registration and title insurance, regulation of land use, security interests, adverse possession, and indigenous or communal tenure. It examines how property regimes address risk, facilitate credit, and balance development with social and environmental objectives.

Chapter 8 addresses comparative systems of tort law and encompasses negligence, strict liability, product liability, medical liability, defamation, tests of causation, measurement of damage, insurance structures, and loss-spreading mechanisms. It sets out how systems of deterrence and compensation adjust and how collective redress and litigation finance shift incentives.

Chapter 9 deals with family and individual status law, including marriage and dissolution, property regimes in marriage, parental rights and responsibilities, adoption, assisted reproduction, gender recognition, and guardianship. It explores the standpoints of secular, religious, and customary authorities and the intersection between individual rights and community values.

Chapter 10 consolidates labor and employment law, comparing sources of workers' protection, contract formation and its end, compensation and hours, collective bargaining, strikes, discrimination, health and safety, and gig-economy problems. It describes how enforcement capacity, unionization, and social insurance influence real-world outcomes beyond statutes' text.

Chapter 11 addresses comparative administrative law, focusing especially on delegation, rulemaking, administrative adjudication, standards of judicial review, legitimate expectations, proportionality, transparency, and accountability mechanisms. It compares centralized and decentralized control and considers the role of soft law, regulatory impact assessment, and international networks.

Chapter 12 takes a look at legal professions and judiciary, tracing paths to qualification, specialization, legal education types, ethics regimes, bar regulation, judicial selection, court administration, and alternative dispute resolution. It evaluates the influence of professional resources and incentives on access to justice and the quality of legal decision-making.

There are various audiences to whom this book is devoted.

Primary users are undergraduate and postgraduate law students pursuing comparative law, public law, or transnational practice and needing a systematic introduction connecting doctrine to function.

Practitioners working across borders—transactional lawyers, litigators, in-house lawyers, and policy advisors—will have reference for assessing risk, selecting governing law, and planning enforcement.

Judges, legislative staff, and regulators will be able to use the comparative models to stress-test reforms and anticipate institutional implications. Political scientists, economists, sociologists, international relations specialists, and area studies scholars will appreciate the careful analysis of institutions and doctrinal choices. Finally, civil society organizations and journalists wanting to observe how legal design translates into social outcomes will find the discussion accessible and grounded in real-world institutional limitations.

Chapter
1

FOUNDATIONS OF COMPARATIVE LEGAL STUDY

Contents

INTRODUCTION

Comparative study of law is of immense significance in the wider legal research arena, the ultimate aim being the understanding of diverse legal systems on the face of the earth. Comparative law has a multitude of applications such as legal education, facilitating legal reform, and facilitating cross-border harmonization of laws. By methodically studying diverse legal traditions, researchers are able to identify effective legal solutions that address socio-economic problems as well as enrich legal development. For instance, comparative patient registry analysis is centered on methodological innovation and excellence in registry science as well as highlighting different regulatory strategies employed by different jurisdictions (N/A, 2020). Furthermore, comparative law enhances the academic discourse as well as contributing directly to the progress of substantive law in practice through making suggestions for improvement and change to suit changing societal needs. Use of comparative law in practice provides a strategic advantage to legal practitioners practicing in an increasingly globalizing world. With increasingly transnational issues, like the trafficking of organs, becoming more prevalent, understanding the structures governing such issues in various jurisdictions is increasingly necessary. Comparative law educates practitioners with information that directs legislative drafting, conflict resolution, and policy formulation. Through examination and thought concerning the virtues and shortcomings of different systems of law, legal practitioners are better positioned to reflect changes that have been found to be optimally good practice overseas. Cross-fertilization of legal concepts can also create innovative legal solutions that are tailored specifically for local problems, thereby enhancing the overall efficiency of legal systems. The academic application of comparative law transcends the mere examination of law; comparative law is a critical instrument of cross-disciplinary collaboration and enhancing legal education. By the absorption of learning in auxiliary disciplines, such as sociology and political science, comparative law is made more comprehensive to provide insight into law as a social phenomenon. Comparative methods are often used by legal thinkers in an attempt to criticize and develop existing legal doctrines, as well as analyze the implications of legal structures on social behavior. Furthermore, the study of legal families, including civil law and common law systems, assists in vindicating the institutional use of comparative analysis in guiding policy decisions and legislative reform. Therefore, the in-depth examination of comparative law not only enhances scholastic research but also raises the capacity of legal institutions to address imperative matters of the current time effectively.

1.1. METHODOLOGICAL APPROACHES

The study of Methodological Frameworks in comparative legal research is crucial to the understanding of how many legal systems operate and intersect. One such popular approach is the functional approach that seeks to identify the functions and effects of legal rules rather than their expression. Pondering laws on the basis of their functions in society enables researchers to identify similar consequences in various legal systems in spite of their variance in context. For instance, domestic violence legal policies in Malaysia and Indonesia have shown how different laws over time will still try to address common social issues, as highlighted from the analysis of protective legislation for women who are victims of violence (Amiruddin et al., 2024). This functional approach facilitates a more insightful comprehension of the manner in which society's needs are fulfilled by the law and encourages the exchange of best practice between jurisdictions, reinforcing the role of comparative law in legal reform. Structural comparison is another significant technique employed within this approach, concerned with the structure and organization of legal systems rather than their actual rules (Figure 1.1).

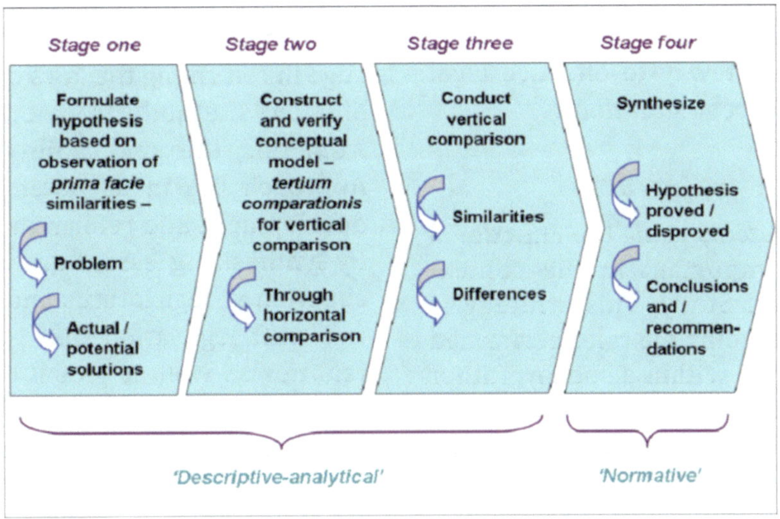

Figure 1.1. The 'ITA/WBIP' vertical comparative law method.

Source: https://www.researchgate.net/figure/The-ITA-WBIP-Ve-rtical-Comparative-Law-Method_fig2_228176741.

This kind of approach to methodology allows one to critically examine legal processes, hierarchies, and institutions. For example, research into divergent Montreal Convention implementation in Australia and Indonesia reveals the differences in the manner in which different legal systems react to international commitments (Sabrie, 2024). By situating these differences within their broader historical, cultural, and social contexts, researchers can make visible the underlying principles and barriers inhibiting national compliance. This structural approach underlines the importance of looking at legal systems in terms of their being located within specific socio-political contexts and thus making it possible to have an integrated analysis of the elements pushing legal adaptation and reform. Lastly, socio-legal methods are critical to comparative legal studies because they integrate empirical research into legal methodology. This aligns with the importance of looking at law as a social phenomenon subject to political, economic, and cultural influences. By examining lived situations of legal subjects, for example, women who fight domestic violence or passengers on aircraft navigating legal nuances in carrier liability, researchers can detect gaps between legal abstractions and actual situations (Amiruddin et al., 2024; Sabrie, 2024). This way of doing things not only improves the analysis by the addition of qualitative data but contributes to the relevance of legal scholarship to current social issues. Finally, socio-legal traditions call for the significance of interdisciplinary observations in developing a comprehensive understanding of law to allow the gateway to effective legal reforms grounded on real situations.

1.1.1. Functional Approach

The study of legal systems using the Functional Approach is most important in the context of Comparative Legal Study. This strategy is interested in understanding the roles performed by various legal norms within a society, rather than merely considering their structural or historical context. Studying the function of law allows researchers to move beyond surface-level similarities or differences and see how law rules address specific needs of society.

This methodology further allows for examination of adaptations of legal frameworks to illustrate how jurisdictions create law sufficiently responding to analogous issues. Based on studies like (Pasemko et al., 2024), the Functional Approach unravels the intricate interdependence of legal rules and the respective socio-economic environments surrounding them, and therefore context becomes indispensable to account for when researching law. Utilizing the Functional Approach enables us to gain a more comprehensive understanding of law as a tool for social engineering. Legal theorists can examine the way various systems accomplish the same objectives, such as encouraging justice, security, and social order, although having varying legal traditions. A case in point would be considering land management systems whereby comparative analysis may show the ways various countries apply property law to optimize land use and react to societal growth. By this, the Functional Approach encourages cross-legal system dialogue, as outlined in Nurmala et al. (2024), to explore the ways jurisdictions assign the same purposes to laws—enhancing efficiency, accountability, and public engagement—by different legislative mechanisms. This comparative strategy enriches legal studies as well as possesses a pragmatic edge in reforming the laws by adopting the most efficient methods from other nations. Apart from this, the applicability of the Functional Approach lies in its potential to inform legal development and reform in other jurisdictions. By synthesizing lessons drawn from comparative experience, legislatures and legal professionals can craft legislation that is informed by local realities as well as global best practices. With the background of regulatory reforms, this approach attempts to create legislation that not only succeeds within its own local legal context but also resonates with required global values such as transparency and accountability. To illustrate, as Nurmala et al. (2024) shows, Indonesia's Tapera program's ongoing reforms show the degree to which the incorporation of successful elements from Singapore's Housing Development Board can lead to more successful housing policies. Thus, understanding the functionality and intended impacts of laws becomes essential to achieving substantive legal improvement in a wide range of disparate cultural and socio-economic settings (Figure 1.2).

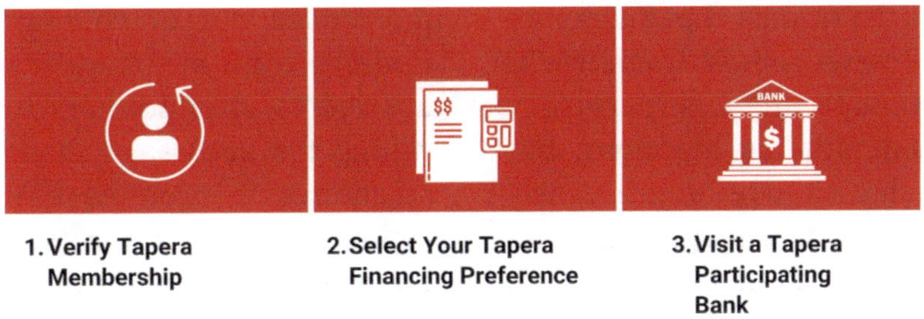

Figure 1.2. Tapera program in Indonesia.

Source: https://www.cekindo.com/wp-content/uploads/2024/06/Infographic-1024x380px-48-1024x360.png.

1.1.2. Structural Comparison

In studying the intricacies of legal systems, structural comparison is a key method in comparative legal studies. By comparing the structural elements of law in different jurisdictions, researchers become privy to information about the operation of the law structures under certain sociopolitical settings.

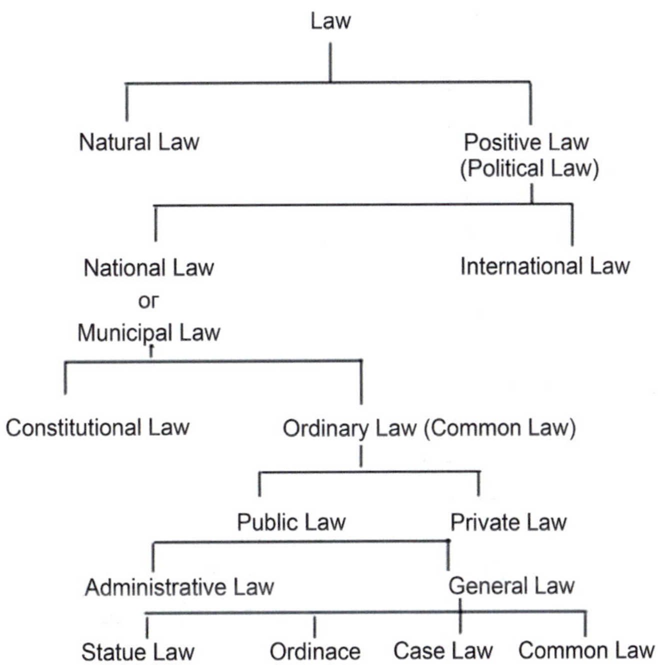

Figure 1.3. Law and its kinds.

Source: LAW notes.

As an illustration, the comparison of Southeast Asian nations' personal data protection laws shows levels of compliance and popular support depending on their institutional arrangements. Of particular interest is the finding that Singapore and the Philippines have robust frameworks underpinned by independent supervisory authorities, as recent studies highlight, but Indonesia and Malaysia are significantly hindered by weaker civil engagement and enforcement challenges (Polii et al., 2025). Such structural contrasts highlight differential responses to legal protection and provide a basis for policy recommendations aimed at harmonizing regulations across borders. Furthermore, structural comparison does not only address legal protection but also includes different spheres such as taxation systems (Figure 1.3).

A comparison of the Goods and Services Tax (GST) frameworks of Australia, Canada, and the European Union reveals significant structure-based differences that offer valuable insights on how India's GST model can be further enhanced. Each agency's taxation structure, whether Australia's simplified model, Canada's federal-provincial two-level system, or the EUs harmonized one, reflects specific administrative goals as well as cultural environments. By examining such frameworks comparatively, one is able to glean best practices, such as reducing compliance costs and enhancing inter-governmental cooperation to achieve maximum efficiency and equity in taxation (Raikwar, 2025). Such comparative analysis not only enhances academic discourse but also enables policy makers to adopt successful reforms out of international experience. Finally, structural comparison facilitates a comprehensive understanding of the underlying principles shared by diverse legal systems. While comparative legal analysis is ongoing, the realization of the study's limitations, including jurisdictional incompatibility and cultural sensitivity, arises. These highlight the importance of having a high-level and context-sensitive methodology when drawing inferences out of comparative models. The findings from structural comparisons may be utilized as vital pointers toward legal reform, calling for necessary change in existing legal structures to promote efficiency and protect rights in various jurisdictions. Drawing on the lessons of structural analysis, comparative law as an academic discipline can do much to further the development of adaptive, responsive legal systems that can keep pace with shifting imperatives of globalizing societies.

1.1.3. Socio-Legal Methods

The study of socio-legal methods deepens the overall model of comparative legal research through the integration of social backgrounds into legal analysis.

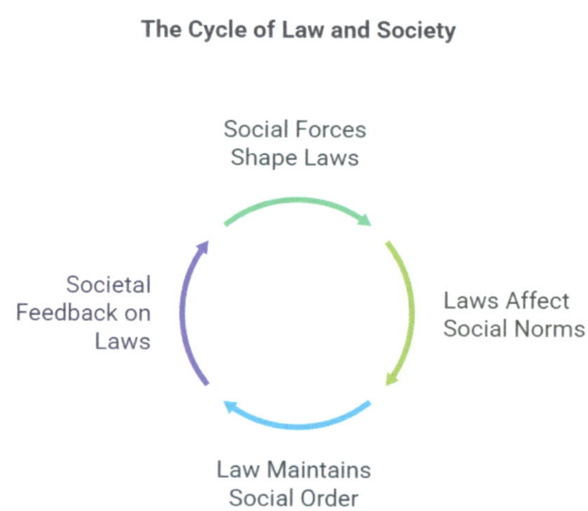

Figure 1.4. Law and sociology: How law and society influence.

Source: https://www.polisciconnect.com/wp-content/uploads/2025/03/What-is-Law-Sociology.png.

This view emphasizes that law does not exist in isolation; rather, it operates under the paradigms of a society's culture, economy, and society. By examining how legal systems influence and are influenced by social structures, researchers can identify underlying patterns that depict the effectiveness and applicability of legal principles in one jurisdiction to another. For instance, the studies conducted with the help of socio-legal methods are found to accentuate differential social views of such matters as electronic money, stressing the practices and experiences of different population groups towards the new financial tools (Абрамова et al., 2023) (Figure 1.4).

This socio-legal perspective favors a better understanding of law practice, apart from text-centric approaches, thus contributing an essential input to comparative legal analysis goals. In addition, the utilization of socio-legal analysis establishes a connection between theory and practical applications. It makes provision for a rich exploration of the manner in which legal institutions operate under varying conditions of society, illuminating the power, access, and inequality dynamics that may remain invisible to more traditional legal analysis. For example, the increased presence of medical nanorobots raises the necessity of efficient legal frameworks to address their consequences in healthcare systems. On this point, comparative law can benefit from socio-legal analysis to compare the regulatory response across different countries to the challenges presented by this new technology, such as evaluating the public sentiments and ethical concerns (Gulyaeva, 2023). For this purpose, socio-legal approaches are important in examining the loopholes in existing legal frameworks and providing suggestions that can render law more sensitive to social pressures. The insight that socio-legal approaches offer not only enhances comparative legal studies but also informs policymaking initiatives. Understanding the intricate nature of the law and society relationship enables policymakers to craft more effective governance strategies that accommodate the realities on the ground. The holistic approach is particularly relevant in regions with fast-paced technological advancement where conventional legal frameworks might not be able to match the rhythm of change in society. From the socio-legal perspectives, the intersection of law, technology, and public opinion can be meaningfully explored such that the development of regulatory environments that foster innovation but safeguard public interest is made possible. Thus, as comparative legal research evolves, the embracement of socio-legal methods will be at the forefront in facilitating enhanced understanding of legal phenomena within and across socio-cultural environments.

1.2. LEGAL FAMILIES AND CLASSIFICATIONS

Within the field of comparative legal studies, the classification of legal systems into families forms the framework through which the diversity of legal settings across the globe can be fully realized. Each legal family, such as the Civil Law and Common Law systems, possesses specific characteristics that affect the administration of justice and legislative operations within various jurisdictions. The Civil Law system is typified by codified statutes and thick legal codes, which feed into the process of judicial decision-making and greatly limit the role played by case law. The Common Law system, on the other hand, focuses on precedent, relying on previous court decisions as authoritative sources of guidance for resolving current disputes. This early categorization not only helps scholars to establish functional differences and similarities in jurisdictions but also gives practitioners information on how legal framework variation might affect international legal collaboration and adherence in transnational settings (Figure 1.5).

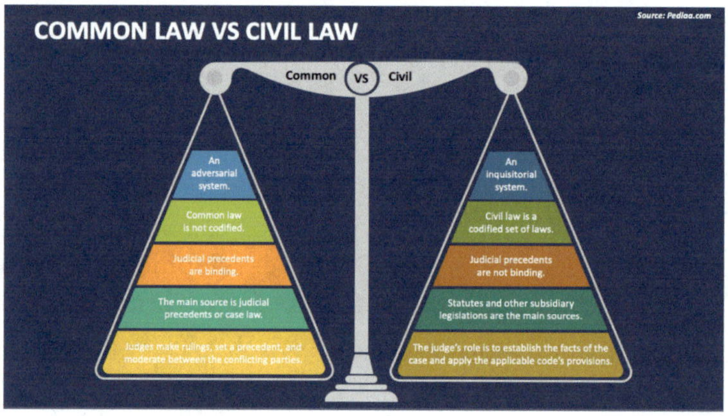

Figure 1.5. Civil law vs common law.

Source: https://lh7-rt.googleusercontent.com/docsz/AD_4nXeo9sJ13Fqiu5aeCqxxuZb4Nvf5J3ssCsqvSNDlULZqJdoaVK-cfz9LrUvIYBHNjX4U0l81BHaXLtBB_R5999u3DonZHxUiMCG3erwkbFYMq6CmYQneIygBXW89g7EzCpwlTSWJMQ?key=hZCjqtcdIGYdwmXAb_8-7RrQ.

While the comparative legal approach continues to develop, a sophisticated comprehension is necessary to examine the interaction between traditional legal families and nascent hybrid or mixed systems. These hybrids result commonly from the combination of other differing legal traditions, creating specialized frameworks that may combine features of both Civil Law and Common Law. For instance, modern legal systems can bring together codified law with the application of judicial interpretation, as a fusion of previous legacies and current demands. The analysis of such legal systems is necessary because it provides insight into how legal transplants are dealt with in states and how the convergence of different legal traditions is likely. Study of the hybrid systems extends comparative law discussion, showing how flexibility in the law fosters more comprehensive integration for member states of international organizations and groups of states, particularly in the regional cooperation context. Moreover, the classification framework applied to comparative legal study enables better understanding of the evolving nature of international law. Legal families not only reflect historical development but also enable researchers to enjoy appreciating the manner in which international trends, such as international human rights standards, are adapted in different jurisdictions. In this regard, integration processes such as those within the Eurasian Economic Union underscore the need for harmonizing legal provisions to induce regional cooperation. A comprehensive approach, with comparative legal strategies, can help to perform a significant function in effective harmonization of member states' laws, thereby developing broader legal cooperation with retention of definite national identities. The harmonization process, which is very essential for effective governance, emphasizes the significance of comparative legal studies to deal with legal harmonization and adaptation problems in an increasingly interconnected world (Chagina et al., 2024; Kashirkina, 2024).

1.2.1. Civil Law Systems

In the legal family study, civil law systems and the remaining systems differ significantly due to its development and basis. Civil law systems, which are founded on Roman law, are characterized by elaborate codes of law that regulate the rules and regulations of legal conflicts. In contrast to common law systems, which rely predominantly on case law and judicial precedents, civil law systems favor codification as the fundamental source of law. This preference guarantees predictability and certainty, which are crucial for both legal practitioners and the population as a whole. The codified form makes it possible to apply a similar case in cases, encouraging a legal system that is congruent with the stability and order of society. These characteristics highlight the necessity for comparative analysis in order to understand how different legal systems work, and most relevantly for scholars and legal practitioners as they struggle to harmonize practice between jurisdictions. Legal regimes under different civil law jurisdictions reveal an unprecedented degree of difference, highlighting the complexity of comparative legal analysis. Germany, France, and Japan provide good examples of accommodating civil law principles to the specific contexts of these nations but remaining devoted to a shared genealogical heritage. One place where these systems break down is with corporate governance structures. For instance, while German legislation encourages dualistic management structures distinguishing ownership from control, French structures lean toward a monistic system under which powers tend to be less divided.

In examining such nuances, researchers can gain useful insights into how different interpretations of building blocks influence regulatory efficacy and corporate conduct. A detailed scrutiny of such differences is indispensable to understanding not only the broad trends of the civil law system but also their implications on foreign business transactions, investment risk assessment, and international legal harmonization efforts. Further, as legal practice continues to be increasingly influenced by globalization, civil law systems are experiencing the integration of alternative dispute resolution (ADR) procedures that were previously less prevalent. Mediation, for example, has been growing in popularity in most jurisdictions, responding to the pressure of congested court systems and the quest for faster methods of resolving disputes. Jurisdictions like France and Germany have been able to incorporate mediation within their civil law with ease as a way of alleviating pressures of litigation and promoting cooperative resolutions. The analysis of the adaptive approaches of the civil laws becomes a requirement in this case, as it shows the ongoing adaptation of legal practice to address contemporary challenges. Hence, the study of how such systems embrace ADR, together with traditional litigation avenues, can contribute more to the understanding of civil laws responsiveness and adaptability in a world that is globalized, affirming the utility of comparative law studies in unveiling pioneering legal paradigms (Hamonangan, 2025; Pozov, 2025) (Figure 1.6).

Figure 1.6. Roman law was the law of the city of Rome and subsequently of the Roman Empire. The influence of Roman law on modern legal systems has been immense: several legal systems of the world (including the civil law system of Europe) have been shaped significantly, directly or indirectly, by the concepts of Roman law.

Source: https://voegelinview.com/the-contribution-of-roman-law-to-modern-legal-systems/.

1.2.2. Common Law Systems

The analysis of common law systems indicates their distinctive approach, namely the utilization of judicial precedents as a source of law. In contrast to statutory text-prevailing civil law systems, common law jurisdictions are based on case law, with the former courts' rulings playing a significant role in subsequent judgments. This application of precedent, stare decisis, ensures a dense legal tradition where continuity and adaptability exist together (Figure 1.7).

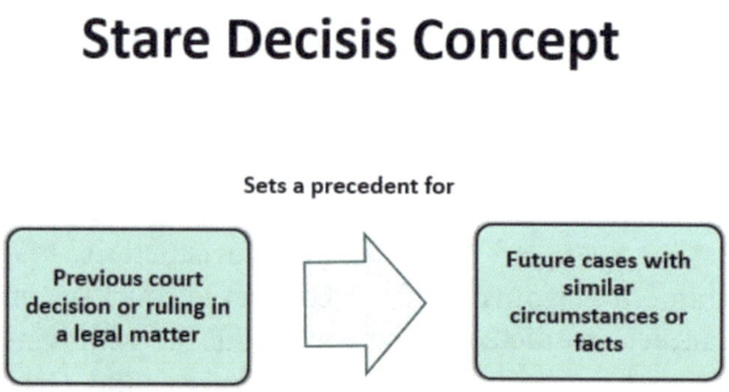

Figure 1.7. Stare decisis.

Source: https://wallstreetmojocms.recurpro.in/uploads/Stare_Decisis_8076e553bf.jpg.

The precedent-based methodology not only enhances the forcibility of judicial decisions but also amplifies the judges' role as interpreters of law with a degree of flexibility that allows the law to develop with society's changes. Thus, comparative legal examination of common law systems is informative about the historical interaction between the rules of law and judicial interpretation, which remains a governing mainstream principle in most jurisdictions (Yao, 2025).

In the context of regulating workplaces, common law systems are informative about how blended legal systems can fight modern problems effectively. For instance, the robust legal systems in the United Kingdom and the United States of America serve as the foundation for handling cases such as workplace harassment. These common law systems have developed elaborate legal remedies that allow victims, impose employer responsibility, and promote workplace safety. By making stronger protection through enunciating definitive legal standards, they unavoidably touch on both legal and social dimensions of harassment, thus positively contributing to employee mental well-being. This yields a nuanced insight, as comparative legal research demonstrates how reflective incorporation by common law systems of robust legal rules may be applied to other regimes in order to reduce equivalent challenges, especially in countries like China that can benefit from it (Tian, 2025). Moreover, comparative study between common law systems sheds light on the theory of legal transplants, in which legal structures and rules are transplanted across jurisdictions. Common law flexibility offers a model for legal borrowing, allowing jurisdictions with comparable legal issues to implement effective reforms. Under this perspective, the characteristics of traditional common law systems are to be compared to hybrid or mixed legal systems in which features of other traditions are usually combined. Analysis of the operation dynamics in such legal transplants reveals the complexities and benefits involved in legal adaptation between jurisdictions. These interactions not only enhance comparative legal research but also demonstrate how law can respond to cultural and institutional differences, thus propelling greater global legal collaboration and more unity of understanding across different legal environments (Yao, 2025).

1.2.3. Hybrid and Mixed Systems

Understanding the intricate tapestry of legal systems worldwide unveils the significant role that hybrid and mixed systems play in comparative legal studies. These systems emerge from the confluence of diverse legal traditions, typically blending elements from both civil law and common law frameworks. Consequently, they offer a rich tapestry for legal analysis, reflecting the historical interactions between different jurisdictions. The dynamics of hybrid and mixed systems often lead to innovative legal solutions that address unique societal needs while promoting stability and coherence in governance. As societies evolve, the adaptability of these systems becomes paramount, allowing them to respond to emerging challenges and opportunities in governance and law. As articulated by the OECD, the ability of democratic governance to evolve remains essential, particularly as these systems strive to protect individual rights and freedoms amidst global changes (N/A, 2022). In the realm of hybrid and mixed systems, the interplay between aspirations and capabilities further deepens our understanding of legal evolution. By framing migration within the context of social change, it is evident that hybrid systems reflect a broader human mobility dynamic shaped by both contextual opportunities and constraints. This emphasis on the aspirations and capabilities of individuals reveals how these systems can serve as conduits for legal and social transformation. As migration often illustrates the instrumental and intrinsic dimensions of human mobility, hybrid legal systems can facilitate the agency that allows individuals to choose their legal framework, depending on their circumstances. Thus, the capacity of legal systems to reconcile diverse legal traditions offers a practical reflection of societal aspirations, allowing individuals to navigate their rights and responsibilities (Hein de Haas, 2021). Examining the implications of hybrid and mixed legal systems, it becomes crucial to address the associated challenges of integration and legal borrowing. The blending of different legal traditions can elicit tensions and uncertainties, especially when striving for coherence within the legal framework. These challenges become further complicated by cultural sensitivities and the potential for jurisdictional incompatibility. Nevertheless, hybrid systems possess the potential to foster innovative legal responses that resonate with local customs and norms while adhering to global legal standards. Ultimately, this adaptability is vital for sustainable governance, reinforcing the importance of democratic frameworks that safeguard individual rights and promote social cohesion. By studying these systems, scholars and practitioners can glean valuable insights from the adaptive capacity that hybrid legal frameworks embody in the contemporary landscape (N/A, 2022) (Figure 1.8).

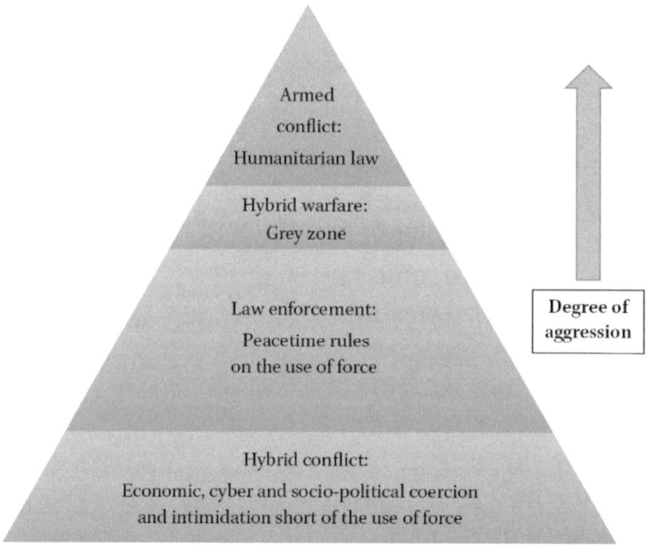

Figure 1.8. The concept of hybrid threats.

Source: https://brill.com/display/book/9789004509368/9789004509368_webready_content_m000005.jpg.

1.3. LEGAL TRANSPLANTS AND CONVERGENCE

The intricacies of legal transplants highlight the adaptive nature of legal systems and the difficulties of grafting foreign legal principles. Legal borrowing, as the activity is variously referred to, transcends legal rule transplants to require a subtle appreciation of the socio-cultural context from which the law arises. As legal principles are transplanted between jurisdictions, professionals and academics need to appreciate the potential for divergence in application and interpretation. Divergence has the potential to result in an absence of harmony, where imported laws come into conflict with prior to transplant local practice and belief. Legal transplants scholarship is, therefore, genuinely interested in the question of how to learn from foreign law, to be assimilated, adapted, and institutionalized in foreign legal systems, and points to the importance of contextual factors in deciding on the success of such transplants in the broader comparative legal scholarship enterprise. In the context of institutional acceptance of legal transplants, the success of foreign law imposition is subject to numerous variables, including political will and social preparedness. Each legal system has specific institutional characteristics that influence the manner in which new legal ideas are accepted or spurned. For instance, in a case where the traditional legal institutions are strong, the integration of foreign legal concepts may be considerably hampered by power relations and cultural biases. Convergence is achieved as the legal structures are altered through voluntary transformation and coercion.

An analysis of these dynamics sheds light on local traditions versus borrowed ideas in the law, and the broader ramifications for legal harmonization in general, and in an era marked by increasing globalization and interdependence. The challenge of integration is multifaceted, frequently finding a tension between the desire for legal conformity and preserving local legal identities. As legal transplants are subjected to various levels of scrutiny, the question of matching transplanting laws with local ethos also becomes a primary issue. Scholarly researchers demand critical models that discuss not just the efficiency of the transplanted law but also its implications on existing legal systems and societal norms. In other jurisdictions, there are colonial heritage concerns surrounding the authenticity and legitimacy of adopted legal ideas. This critical assessment is paramount in exploring the ways in which varying legal traditions are able to have productive discourse, creating a setting where there is mutual learning and adaptation. Addressing these challenges within the field of comparative law requires an interdisciplinary approach that is compatible with numerous methodologies and perspectives to intensify the conceptualization of convergence and divergence in the practice of law (Abdullah, 2018; Cherp et al., 2017).

1.3.1. Concept of Legal Borrowing

In comparative law, legal borrowing is the process that highlights a main factor expressing the interdependence of legal systems around the world. As jurisdictions frequently borrow and appropriate legal norms, the process enables the establishment of a rich and differentiated collective legal discourse. Legal borrowing facilitates the passage of ideas, institutions, and norms from one legal culture to another, making it possible to understand beyond geographical and ideological boundaries. In addition to facilitating the solution of complex legal issues, legal borrowing fosters the unity of legal doctrine across different jurisdictions. Through the mix of elements from different systems, legal borrowing captures the essence of comparative law that recognizes the imperative of interactive dialogues between clashing legal traditions toward the creation of stronger and more balanced legal systems (Figure 1.9).

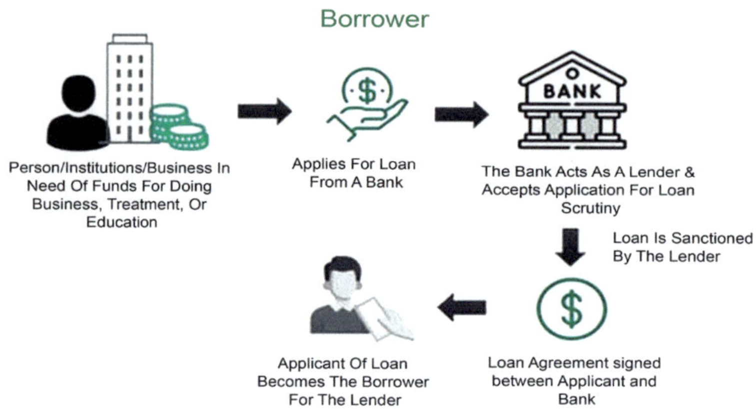

Figure 1.9. Concept of legal borrowing.

Source: https://www.wallstreetmojo.com/wp-content/uploads/2022/08/Picture1-4.jpg.

The significance of legal borrowing exceeds adaptation because it also raises questions of authenticity and contextual appropriateness of borrowed legal principles. It has been suggested that although legal concept transfer can facilitate innovation and modernity within a legal system, it may also lead to conflicts regarding the harmonization of disparate legal cultures and the respective values held. This is particularly pertinent when looking at the meaning of borrowing in legal systems with significant cultural and historical variance. In such environments, understanding the criteria for successful legal transplants becomes extremely significant as it clarifies the conditions under which norms are able to be successfully integrated into indigenous legal conduct. Legal scholars and practitioners must be guarded about the underlying motivations to borrow and carefully examine if such arrangements fulfill the objective of the law at the cost of local identity and functionality. Legal borrowing dilemmas underscore the complexities of comparative legal research. Specifically, jurisdictional incompatibility and cultural orientations can be stumbling blocks to effective implementation. Resistance may be built up by institutions that are interested in reforming entrenched legal structures or populations displaced by foreign impositions of law. Secondly, double mechanisms of external and internal constitutional influence play significant roles in shaping how borrowed legal norms are addressed and integrated into domestic systems. By subjecting these dynamics to critical analysis, researchers can offer a perspective on the broader implications of legal borrowing, towards a more evolved comprehension of how global legal discourse is shaped. This analysis is especially timely as societies increasingly want to tackle international issues through shared legal norms while being mindful of their own special cultural environments, which underscores the irresistible negotiation of the global and the local when it comes to law.

1.3.2. Institutional Reception

The intricate process of reception in comparative law illustrates how legal institutions take up and take up foreign law, as much as it is a reflection of unique social and cultural settings. It is not just a reflection of how institutions evolve but also an example of the complexity of legal transplants involved. Alteration of law at reception often leads institutions to reinterpret and impose such norms in line with existing practices and values. This dynamic implies that while an implanted legal system's fundamental principles may be maintained, the reception process is able to induce a shift that could lead to legally disparate results. These subtleties enrich the comparative study by providing more insight into how different jurisdictions apply legal principles to their respective societal conditions. This adaptive character of legal systems supports context-based understanding in the broader context of comparative law. Understanding globalization's engagement with institutional reception is more nuanced in comparative legal studies. In the increasingly globalized world, international treaties and transnational actors' legal diffusion frequently provokes a response in domestic legal systems (Figure 1.10).

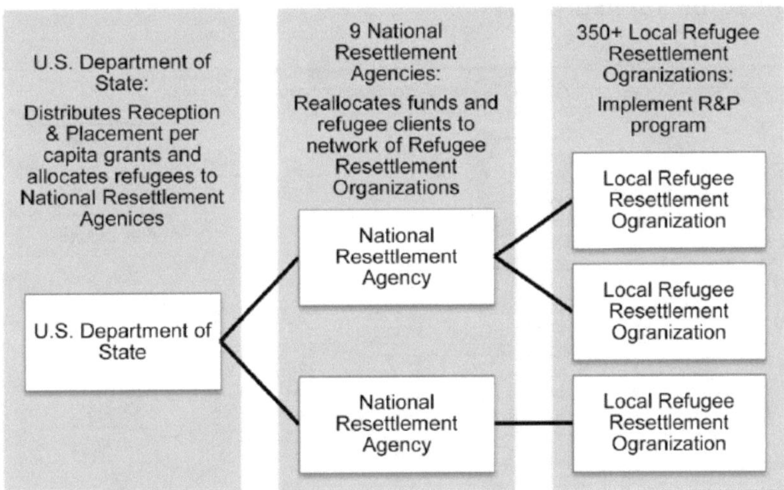

Figure 1.10. Institutional structure of reception and placement.

Source: https://www.researchgate.net/figure/nstitutional-Structure-of-Reception-and-Placement_fig1_276325451.

The ability of a jurisdiction to incorporate external legal norms can, however, be impeded by institutional resistance rooted in historical, cultural, or sociopolitical factors. As highlighted in recent discourse, the emergence of crises, such as those surrounding migration policies, can intensify institutional reception challenges. This reflects the idea that crises are not merely external shocks but are inadvertently linked to patterns of legal integration and the capacity of institutions to function effectively. Therefore, understanding these dynamics is crucial for a comprehensive examination of institutional reception within comparative legal frameworks, providing insights into how law adapts during periods of turmoil and change. Moreover, the role of legal pluralism in institutional reception is a fundamental aspect worthy of exploration in comparative law. Legal pluralism recognizes the coexistence of multiple legal systems within a jurisdiction, impacting how laws are received and interpreted. This introduces tensions not only between international norms and local legal traditions but also among different legal authorities within the same sovereign space. The challenges of aligning divergent legal frameworks can deter effective reception and implementation of legal norms. Engaging with these complexities requires a nuanced approach, as the integration of legal transplants must account for the varying degrees of acceptance and applicability that coexist within pluralistic contexts. Such complexities accentuate the importance of a thorough methodological framework in comparative legal studies, pointing to a need for tailored strategies to facilitate smoother institutional reception and harmonization among legal systems.

1.3.3. Challenges of Integration

In the evolving context of legal frameworks, the challenge of integration is a pertinent issue, particularly in the case of diverse legal systems operating within jurisdictions. Legal transplantation, where laws and principles of law are borrowed from one legal system and applied to another, is beset with issues that can interfere with productive integration. One of the chief worries arises from the inherent variability of legal traditions and cultural environments, whereby extraneous laws may be misapplied or applied poorly.

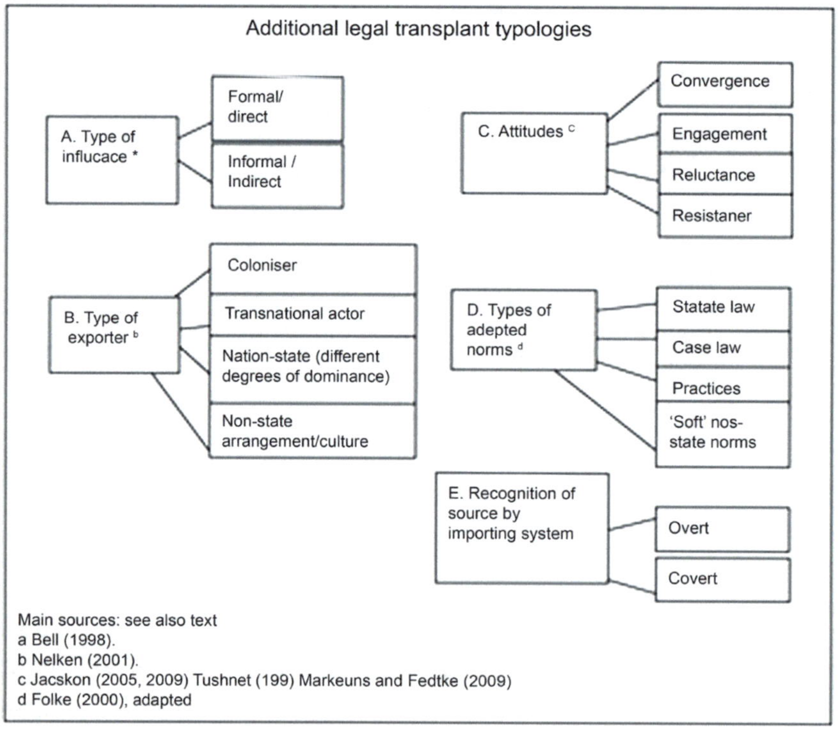

Figure 1.11. Legal transplants: A theoretical framework.

Source: https://static.cambridge.org/binary/version/id/urn:cambridge.org:id:binary-alt:20240125145119-94947-mediumThumb-png-84308fig21_4.jpg?pub-status=live.

For instance, idiosyncrasies of common law may not harmoniously integrate into the codes of civil law, revealing the value of comprehensive comparative research to understand the consequences of such integrations on the practice of law and coherence of structures. In the absence of adequate attention to such differences, the anticipated benefits of legal borrowing are undermined and create a dissonance in the law that disrupts good governance and legal certainty. The unification of heterogeneous legal systems also faces the challenge of terminological homogeneity, thus posing hurdles to understanding and application. Legal terminology has a tendency to carry articulate connotations that vary vastly from one jurisdiction to another and make the process of unification laborious. Whereas lawyers and legal scholars conduct comparative legal study, they are always confronted with the dilemma of transferring legal concepts that do not immediately find equivalents in other systems. This gap between languages always leads to misunderstanding and lack of understanding between practitioners, furthermore inhibiting the successful implementation of transposed legal norms. The essence of clear communication in legal contexts cannot be overstated since effective success in any integration within the legal context largely relies on the mutual comprehension of legal concepts and jargon. Neglect of acknowledging and answering such issues of translation can significantly hinder not only academic research, but even actual legal application. Additionally, various resistances within institutions equally pose a great impediment towards the successful integration in comparative law contexts. Institutions that are tasked with implementation and enforcement of legal norms may be hesitant to foreign laws, prioritizing established legal norms over potential valuable innovations. This may be because they are afraid of disrupting established practices or do not trust the ability of their domestic environment to accommodate foreign influences. Additionally, increasing emphasis on globalization and digitalization of legal transactions can also complicate institutional reactions. As cited in recent research, the intersection of legal, financial, and digital expertise is central to the creation of efficient legal experts in a digitally integrated economy (Владислав, 2020). Moreover, growing realization of cultural variability in responses to behavior means legal thinkers must be wary of threats from broad generalizations based on thin databases (Henrich et al., 2010). Overcoming these challenges requires not just theoretical knowledge but also practical methods of developing receptiveness to legal integration and innovation in legal settings (Figure 1.11).

1.4. LEGAL TERMINOLOGY AND LANGUAGE

The delicate dance between language and legal jargon needs to be navigated in the pursuit of comparative law. Legal systems have their own sets of terminologies that not only mirror their own history of development but also their inherent principles and associated values of society. Translatability becomes a challenge while efforts are made to fill the gaps between heterogeneous legal languages. A definition in law in one society may not be immediately comparable in another, which can create potential misunderstandings that alter the meaning and intent behind legal terminology. This complexity suggests the need for intensive study of the contextual nuances that accompany legal terms to ensure clarity and specificity. Researchers must consider that legal language is not only a medium of communication but also a medium of power that can decide legal outcomes and force the meaning of laws across jurisdictions. Terminology consistency is one main ingredient towards consistency in comparative legal research, particularly when comparing across different legal families. The inconsistency in uses and definitions of legal terms may yield great legal interpretations differences, which might obstruct cross-jurisdictional understanding. For instance, a term such as property may be meaning various rights and obligations in civil law regimes and common law regimes. These consistencies mean researchers and practitioners must cope seriously with the specific terminologies employed by various legal environments. This consistency is not just necessary for comparative legislative study but also for functional efficacy in international legal documents. Through establishing a common linguistic paradigm, stakeholders can facilitate further cooperation and openness to issues of law, therefore making easier transactions and interaction among jurisdictions.

Finally, interpretations of legal terms are significantly prone to cultural context, yet again making them challenging to employ in comparative study of law. With legal practitioners and academics dealing with various jurisdictions, cultural awareness becomes essential. Individual legal systems have varying interpretative culture, and the use of legal terminology in such environments can vary substantially. Legal vocabulary concerning data privacy and forensics, for example, in the age of the Internet of Things (IoT), presents special challenges due to the interaction between technology, law, and cultural attitudes towards privacy (Stoyanova et al., 2020). In such a situation, an understanding of how language and terminology function across various legal systems not only widens the boundaries of comparative legal studies but also raises the internal complexity of legal scholarship, promoting a more nuanced approach to the study and application of law in a globally expanding world.

1.4.1. Translatability Issues

It is only by a meticulous understanding of issues of translatability that the complexity of cross-border legal interactions can be managed and the parameters of comparative legal studies greatly defined. Legal translation does not only refer to the translation of terms from one language to another but also to the intangible connotations that such terms carry within specific structures of law. For instance, a term like contract can have contrasting connotations in civil and common law traditions, thus complicating comparative analysis. Failure to pay heed to these differences will result in misinterpretation, incorrect conclusions, and ultimately, unproductive legal practice. The language and law bridge underscores the pivotal significance of linguistic precision in the process of communicating legal concepts across jurisdictions (Figure 1.12).

Figure 1.12. Image showing intersection of language and law.

Source: https://i0.wp.com/lawnotes.co/wp-content/uploads/2024/08/download.png?resize=275%2C183&ssl=1.

This is compounded by the increasing globalization of law, with legal texts and standards also traversing linguistic boundaries, which also requires a firm foundation of understanding of the effects of such translations on legal use and interpretation, particularly in those concerning international arbitration and treaties. As an example of further indicating the effects of translatability issues, the role of bilateral investment treaties comes into view. It is possible for states to receive their consent to arbitration either explicitly in contractual conditions or implicitly in legislative bills, as discussed under international legal obligations. Here, language subtleties are the subject of major importance; the definition provided to words such as investment or dispute can play a significant role in determining the interpretation of treaties and enforceability of arbitration clauses. To that end, the move from diplomatic protection to arbitration under frameworks like the International Centre for Settlement of Investment Disputers (ICSID) brings in degrees of complexity due to varying interpretations across legal systems. Omission of such translational complexities can lead to expectation mismatches between investors and states. Hence, awareness of these aspects of language is crucial to the establishment of a harmonious and effective legal system with multilateral legal traditions and underpinning international legal cooperation. The translatability consequences extend to the area of emerging technologies, primarily via contemporary phenomena such as the digital incitement to suicide. With modern legal systems finding it difficult to respond to the challenges posed by social media and how it aids in amplifying some crime trends, the applicability of legal language is even more crucial. The variety of varying legal responses across legal jurisdictions, such as the steps taken by Saudi Arabia and France, points towards the need for terminological consistency and accuracy. Conceptual inconsistency in translations of digital crimes can hinder legal collaboration and sound policymaking. Moreover, as reiterated in the overview of current legal traditions, harmonized laws and enhanced international cooperation are urgently needed to effectively tackle digital incitement. It is not an academic exercise to settle translatability issues but an imperative to regain accountability and protect vulnerable groups within the era of the internet, emphasizing the urgent necessity for legal systems to adapt and adapt to such demands, as emphasized by emerging research in the field (Abdelaziz, 2025).

1.4.2. Terminological Consistency

The inherent complexities of comparative legal studies call for a thorough exploration of language, that is, the terminological consistency as the basis for legal discourse clarity and consistency. By analyzing the intricate levels of legal language, researchers can determine how various readings of similar terms in different legal systems can lead to misunderstandings or misapplications of law. For instance, Ma et al. (2025) focuses on how it is essential that a consistent system of legal principles, particularly the "Principle of Good Faith," is maintained where textual variations might lead astray from the original context and intent of legal provisions. Thus, an efficient consistent system for legal vocabulary becomes essential in facilitating cross-jurisdictional discourse and understanding (Figure 1.13).

Figure 1.13. Principles of utmost good faith.

Source: https://media.licdn.com/dms/image/v2/C4D12AQEXR6HZKtHSbw/article-cover_image-shrink_600_2000/article-cover_image-shrink_600_2000/0/1520097417266?e=2147483647&v=beta&t=yYlmXRH9X345HER8VtElhXI-bcdvTFAuc4-k2x09Clg.

This foundation not only allows for the proper transmission of legal concepts but also allows for a better comprehension of several legal traditions, hence comparative legal writings. As comparative law continues to unfold, the role of terminological consistency in increasingly large amounts becomes increasingly important. Definitions and meanings of legal concepts must be synchronized to enable cooperation in communications among legal scholars and legal experts across borders. Obstacles in other legal cultures can lead to ambiguities that complicate legal analysis and decision-making. For example, Spytska (2024) emphasizes the requirement of clear-cut definitions in the case of e-governance, where digital services terminology needs to have precise calibration to cater to various applications worldwide. The lessons drawn from comparative research, in return, illustrate that terminological inconsistency can hinder scholarly research and also practical implementation in legal orders in globalization pressures. In addition, terminological consistency also ensures respect and understanding among jurisdictions and thus enhances cooperation under international legal orders. The pursuit of consistency in vocabulary in comparative legal studies ultimately comes to be an effective tool for convergence of law in jurisdictions. By terms standardization, legal scholars can craft a common vocabulary that facilitates informed discussion about the points of similarity and difference between legal systems. Harmonization of this kind can drive more effective legal reform efforts, as parties will have clearer vision of the impact of importing specific principles or procedures from other nations. Developing a common language between legal frameworks, such as would be achieved through the adoption of recommendations following comparative examination, allows for smoother integration of best practice. This can in turn lead to greater coherence in law and better government. As legal experts and professionals continue to grapple with the nuances of comparative law, emphasizing uniformity in terminology will be vital to furthering the discussion and making the practical applicability of comparative research a reality.

1.4.3. Interpretation Across Systems

The intricacy of legal interpretation is usually a severe difficulty in comparative legal studies, particularly in relation to how jurisdictions interpret the same concepts. The intricacy is added by variations in language and terminology, which pose possibilities of misinterpretation and confusion. Legal terms that are translated across systems lose subtlety and create inconsistencies, making legal practice complicated. For instance, while a word of particular value in one system may lack an exact equivalent in the other and thus establish obstacles to communication among legal specialists, the challenge of translatability presented by legal terminology highlights scholars' as well as practitioners' need to be cautious when interpreting laws across systems. It underscores the importance of appreciation for context in facilitating proper use of accurate communication and application of principles of law, hence driving the necessity of a nuanced analysis of interpretation in the diverse pool of international legal systems. Legal families and classifications provide a pedestal from which interpretation can be critically analyzed. Civil law systems, common law systems, and mixed regimes each possess their own interpretive methods, and this affects the application of laws and interpretation. In civil law countries, for instance, there is usually emphasis on written law with great judicial restraint, whereas in common law systems, there is usually emphasis on judicial interpretation and case law. The nuances embedded in these systems reveal underlying features of their nature, reflecting broader socio-political realities and evolution. As shown in recent analyses of subsidiary liability under European and Ukrainian law, for example, variation of interpretation focus can be a key shift toward protection of creditors that resonates globally, tracking back to a broader pattern within legal families. Such comparative observations inform our understanding of the development of interpretative practices and how legislative changes can learn from them. For legal transplants and convergence, the trajectory towards harmonizing interpretations across systems presents opportunities alongside challenges. Legal borrowing as an idea facilitates cross-fertilization across different jurisdictions to allow for the exchange of best practices between legal systems. But this is also fraught with the danger of misapplication or abuse if context is not carefully examined. As seen in the analysis of the application of Ultra Vires Doctrines between Malaysia and Indonesia, although both countries share underlying principles, their divergent legal cultures determine how those principles are translated in actual life. The comparative analysis elucidates the strength of indigenous understanding based on historical and cultural nuances, therefore highlighting the value of cogently articulated methodologies when examining legal principles in systems. These thorough inquiries not only uphold better scholarly arguments but also facilitate more effective legal practice in a more interconnected world (Figure 1.14).

Figure 1.14. Image showing judicial interpretation.

Source: https://encrypted-tbn0.gstatic.com/images?q=tbn:ANd9GcSswVsJklz02l96Se68SNRVidcF3RjvMDG5ziFhtVszgfk5vZDOdogF5k9LqUGELfARMJs&usqp=CAU.

1.5. LIMITATIONS OF COMPARATIVE LAW

The comparative law project is often complicated by jurisdictional incompatibilities that lie within the diverse legal regimes of different nations. It is not just brought about by the alternative legal traditions—civil law and common law—but also by the distinctive socio-political contexts in which these laws operate. Jurisdictional diversity presents significant barriers to effective comparison of legal institutions and concepts. For instance, judicial reasoning and statutory interpretation may vary greatly, creating problems when attempts are made to export findings across one legal system to another. Such limitation reinforces the necessity to approach comparison with a sophisticated touch, observing that legal doctrine cannot merely be transplanted from one jurisdiction to another without considering the specific legal culture in focus. This level of comprehension is most crucial for scholars and professionals who want to apply comparative law efficiently in resolving matters of global law in an applicable manner. Another unavoidable limitation is cultural sensitivities underpinned by legal systems, whereby culture can play a serious role in distorting the findings of comparative legal research. Legal norms are deeply rooted in a society's prevailing cultural, historical, and social context and therefore are not highly amenable to external criticism or revision. Therefore, an analysis that overlooks the substratum of culture can lead to misunderstandings or oversimplifications of complexities of legal phenomena. For example, comparative law models of legal reform can break down if these do not take local traditions and values into account. Such cross-cultural dissonance not only precludes comparative applicability but also raises ethical issues regarding the imposition of one over another legal system. It therefore becomes necessary that comparative law experts bring about cross-cultural exchange so as to bring about greater insights that do not show disrespect to the unique contexts in their respective legal systems. Institutional resistance is also a significant difficulty in the comparative law context because entrenched legal institutions may be resistant to foreign legal practice-derived reforms. Legal transplants, as theoretically desirable, are typically resisted by traditional legal institutions and practitioners who may perceive such reforms to be defiance of their roles or conventional practices. This resistance is also reflected in a reluctance to conform legal models or domesticate comparative wisdom into domestic law. Institutions can also fail to have the requisite training or resources to utilize foreign notions of law properly, thereby dampening potential incentives for comparative work. As the problematics of institutional reception and integration highlight, understanding such levels of resistance is vital to each comparative law practitioner and scholar who aspires to affect meaningful change within the legal domain.

1.5.1. Jurisdictional Incompatibility

Collisions of legal structures usually take place in comparative law, particularly when defining the term jurisdictional incompatibility. It encapsulates the intricacies present when incompatible legal structures meet, and where they may collude to produce opposing laws of implementation and interpretation. Such incompatibility may be observed when variant legal traditions, for example, civil law and common law, intersect and introduce opposing interpretations and implementation of the law. These differences should be compared as they stand to blunt effective legal cooperation and complicate transnational legal processes, thereby affecting the outcome of legal disputes. Comparative legal scholars have to deal with these matters with a view to creating models that consider these jurisdictional factors that can ultimately lead to an integrated conception of legal systems and their relations as part of the international law context. Jurisdictional incompatibility is further complicated by the existence of multilateral agreements that seek to harmonize incompatible legal standards. States belonging to certain legal families prefer agreements of integration or cooperation; nonetheless, these arrangements have a tendency to inadvertently expose underlying incompatibilities. For instance, differences in degrees of recognition and enforcement of rights, such as protection of health, can find expression in ambiguous legal obligations that conflict among state parties. The comparative analysis of these structures indicates that the intent of legislations can be the same, but enforcement structures can be quite different, leaving room for judicial discretion that may have not been anticipated during negotiations. Disagreement resolution is essential for continued assertion that agreements are effective and conducive to international legal consistency that makes more predictable interactions possible across jurisdictional boundaries. Overcoming jurisdictional incompatibility typically entails increased entanglement with cultural and institutional factors that influence the effectiveness of laws in diverse environments. Comparative law scholars have emphasized the merit of grasping cultural sensitivities that form the basis for legal regimes and, therefore, condition their methods toward particular problems. Through consideration of such contextual factors, legal scholars and policymakers are better placed to navigate the intricacies of jurisdictional compatibility. For instance, when examining the implementation of e-governance models, like in the Ukrainian and other countries' cases, differences in technology readiness and legal foundation reveal significant jurisdictional problems that have to be addressed to produce winning legal outcomes (Spytska, 2024). A thorough grasp of these cultural pillars, therefore, will improve comparative legal scholarship and contribute to the development of more robust and resilient legal frameworks that respect native tradition without inhibiting international collaboration.

1.5.2. Cultural Sensitivities

In comparative legal research, cultural sensitivity cannot be overrated. Legal systems are not independent; they are inseparable from the social, historical, and cultural environment of society. This implies what may be acceptable or effective legal practice in one jurisdiction may not be so in another, particularly as far as values, beliefs, and societal values are concerned (Figure 1.15).

Figure 1.15. Cultural sensitivities necessitate that legal scholars and practitioners critically evaluate the social fabric that shapes individual legal systems, as failing to appreciate these nuances can lead to misinterpretations and ineffective legal transplants across borders.

Source: https://encrypted-tbn0.gstatic.com/images?q=tbn:ANd9GcQeDueWhF__L6qd1ZpWEwNbb5IEjoMRJcbL2w&s.

This consciousness is particularly pertinent in the age of globalization where legal dissimilarities and similarities are traditionally considered in black-and-white terms, without due regard to supporting cultural factors. An apt case in point of this observation is the manner in which governments responded to the COVID-19 pandemic, according to numerous youth organizations in OECD countries. These groups elaborated the distinct challenges undergone by young populations during the pandemic and condemned the government responses to address their distinct needs. These responses were not just legal accommodations but also an expression of the prevailing cultural inclinations towards youth, health, and politics in given societies. Entertaining these important cultural observations not only provides richer understandings of legal consequences but also assists in structuring future policy paths that are inclusive and adaptive. As emphasized, cultural sensitivity is key to ensuring that legal frameworks are relevant and operative within pluralizing environments (OECD, 2022). Second, integrating cultural sensitivities into comparative legal scholarship is also vital to recognizing the moral implications of legal practice. Legal systems around the world operate on formal and informal rules that are culture-driven, necessitating a model that honors and considers these dynamics. For instance, legal registry methods tend to be different according to cultural attitudes towards privacy, data ownership, and knowledge consent (N/A, 2020). These variations have a significant impact on the form and application of legal systems and hence need to be comprehended when conducting cross-jurisdictional research. By doing this, one can foster an appreciation of cultural sensitivities, offering lawyers and academics with the tools to deal with complexity and challenge within comparative legal contexts and creating more equitable and efficient legal solutions.

1.5.3. Institutional Resistance

Institutional and cultural frameworks are powerful forces behind the effectiveness and suitability of comparative legal studies. Occasionally, these frameworks have been known to produce what is termed institutional resistance, generally ensuring that free incorporation of new legal concepts into different jurisdictions is halted (Figure 1.16).

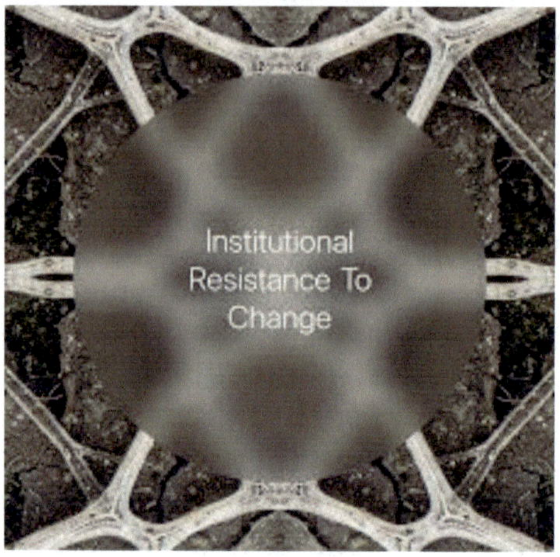

Figure 1.16. Institutional resistance manifests in various forms, such as reluctance among legal practitioners to adopt foreign legal principles or a lack of support from government entities for comparative initiatives.

Source: https://pollution.sustainability-directory.com/wp-content/uploads/2025/03/institutional-resistance-to-change-term-image.webp.

For instance, institutional structures can be predisposed to traditional practice, and therefore dismiss potential innovations that can arise from comparative analyses. Such resistance should be comprehended because it demonstrates the incongruence between theory and practice in legal structures. Such incongruence highlights the need for ongoing interaction and exchange among practitioners and scholars in law towards a more collaborative process of incorporating comparative legal viewpoints. The challenges of institutional resistance are perhaps most evident when the subject is legal transplants and legal borrowing. Foreign application of legal principles in most jurisdictions faces not only pragmatic obstacles but also instinctive distrust rooted in history and culture. Such distrust can be a stalemate, with local legal traditions opposed to innovative solutions produced with comparative analysis. The process of institutional reception, described in the context of law transplants, requires a nuanced understanding of how foreign law is understood and perceived by the local structures. In responding to these questions, researchers are able to enrich the legal integration debate and work towards bridging the gap between codified legal rules and emerging comparative methods. Institutional resistance as an enduring impediment should thus be identified so that the objectives of comparative law can be progressed. Further, the conflict between jurisdictional incompatibility and institutional resistance points to the subtleties found in comparative studies of law. Different legal frameworks are predisposed to function under different ideologies, which can cause conflict in attempting to combine or modify legal concepts for real application under different contexts. For instance, both common and civil law systems vary greatly in handling legislation and case law, making transplants of the law complicated and riddled with misconceptions. Issues of translatability and terminological consistency only add to these problems, as legal terminology lacks direct equivalents across systems. All these factors are considerations for creating a more accommodating and dynamic comparative law framework. Addressing institutional resistance from a socio-legal angle can ultimately yield productive avenues for research, furthering the overall goals of fostering legal cooperation and cross-border mutual understanding.

1.6. APPLICATIONS OF COMPARATIVE LAW

Interaction with comparative law can yield profound insight into the nuances of legal systems and their applications that impact varied fields like legislation, judicial processes, and global governance. Through comparative analysis, legal professionals and attorneys can evaluate how different jurisdictions approach similar legal issues, thereby highlighting the virtues and imperfections inherent in different legal structures. For instance, the application of the doctrine of territoriality in criminal law demonstrates how various countries deal with matters of jurisdiction. Scrutiny of the mode of application of this doctrine provides for not only the sovereignty of each nation-state but also the necessity for international cooperation within an increasingly integrated world of transnational crimes (Shermatov, 2025). By comprehending these comparative features, legal practitioners can more effectively advocate reforms that enhance justice and efficiency in their respective judicial systems. In addition, examining court decisions through the lens of jurisdictions exemplifies how comparative analysis shapes legal theory and practice. More specifically, an examination of civil law systems illustrates how differently cultures view the nature and effects of judicial judgments. In Russia, for example, scholars such as Prof. N.A. Chechina have done considerable work towards understanding court rulings in terms of the civil law tradition, aligning their analyses with the ideas under French law (Daria, 2024).

These studies not only elucidate the legal nature and validity of court judgments but also investigate broader sociological impacts, knowing legal verdicts have an influence beyond the courtroom. The comparative approach enables a better understanding of the roles of judges and implications of legal norms, resulting in practitioners to more nuanced applications of law derived from differing judicial philosophies. Finally, the problem of legal transplants and convergence is a significant topic in comparative law applications. As countries borrow legal ideas and models from each other, questions arise about the fidelity of these translations to the local environment. This process, while promising to be enriching, can cause big problems about the consistency and coherence of legal systems, as evidenced in divergent interpretations and applications. For instance, the adoption of French legal codes into Russian legislation demonstrates both the benefits of legal borrowing and challenges of different legal traditions (Daria, 2024). Through this means, working with the complexities of legal transplants, comparative law scholars can develop strategies that are attuned to local peculiarities yet allow for fruitful exchange of legal ideas in a manner which prompts law to adapt and change in terms of international issues.

1.6.1. International Law and Treaties

In examining the intricate dance of international law and treaties, one must first marvel at the initial position that treaties play in creating legal frameworks among nations. Formal treaties are binding agreements between states that intertwine a multitude of subjects from security and trade to conservation of the environment. The ratification and treaty-making process is at the core of international law, and therefore, comparative legal scholarship must seek out how jurisdictions interpret and apply these treaties (Figure 1.17).

Figure 1.17. The impact of foreign direct investment (FDI) treaties highlights significant disparities in legal protections afforded to investors across various nations, underscoring the importance of a coherent legal regime in fostering a favorable investment climate (PA D et al., 2025).

Source: https://leappakistan.com/wp-content/uploads/2025/04/1568971442488.jpg.

Through comparative analysis, specialists are in a position to ascertain best practice and regulatory frameworks that best foster global cooperation and maintain national legal cultures. A closer look into the implications of these treaties shows that their effectiveness will be greatly influenced by the robustness of domestic legal systems. States are incredibly variant in their attempts to consolidate global treaties into local law, leading to a mosaic of legal commitment and enforcement mechanisms. Some other jurisdictions may have well-developed legal institutions for enforcing provisions of international law, and some may be marked by uncertainty of regulation and poor protection for human rights. For example, Ukraine's efforts to reform its FDI regime are directly linked with the loopholes of its legal system, which may deter foreign investors (PA et al., 2025). This gap not only determines economic relations but also calls into question the enforcement of international agreements in domestic law, echoing wider motifs in comparative legal scholarship about convergence and divergence of legal systems. Furthermore, interaction between international law and domestic legal systems intersects with the environmental sphere, where pollution-fighting treaties serve to underscore regional cooperation needs. An effective response to environmental transboundary issues usually requires coordination of legal rules across boundaries, emphasizing the necessity for international legal alliances. The varying degrees of compliance with environmental conventions demonstrate the complexities involved in obtaining compliance and joint responsibility among states. By comparing legal frameworks for environmental protection and pollution, comparative analysis can distinguish both the positive and negative factors inherent therein. These results not only add to academic discussion but also offer useful guidance to policymakers who seek to enhance their nations' national legal reactions to global environmental matters with an emphasis on the pivotal position that treaties hold in shaping domestic and international law.

1.6.2. Human Rights Law

This assessment reveals how various jurisdictions interpret and implement human rights principles, with convergences as well as divergences. For instance, while most states may subscribe to principles like equality and non-discrimination, their practice is usually quite different, with cultural, religious, and historical considerations playing a role. These discrepancies become glaringly evident in hybrid legal systems where Islamic law intersects with secular legal systems. An appreciation of these nuanced understandings is vital for legal scholars and practitioners, as it foregrounds the importance of contextuality in determining human rights claims across different jurisdictions. Moving beyond reductive definitions, comparative analysis therefore serves to deepen our understanding of the way human rights are developed through different legal contexts, as evidenced by the findings of current research into Pakistan's legal system (Salam et al., 2025). In the realm of human rights law, the structural framework is crucial for deciphering how legal systems respond to global standards. Comparative studies often utilize a functional approach, allowing a thorough examination of how different laws achieve similar goals through varying means. This approach is especially relevant in regions with hybrid systems, like Pakistan, where Shari'ah and international human rights norms coexist. The existing tension between these frameworks casts doubt upon legal coherence and the success of applying human rights. Above all, judicial contradictions indicate the limits placed by cultural sensitivities and institutional resistance to change (Gul et al., 2025). By adopting a comparative approach, researchers can critically analyze the workings of these systems so as to enhance debate on the efficiency and applicability of human rights law in multijurisdictional systems. Finally, the limitations of comparative law should be known, particularly when evaluating human rights in jurisdictions. Jurisdictional incompatibilities can hamper consistent legal analysis, with differing cultural sensitivities potentially influencing the interpretation and enforcement of human rights norms. To cite an example, the efficacy of human rights law in Pakistan is undermined by incongruence among legal practitioners and institutions, with which typically results in selective implementation of rights depending on cultural paradigms. This highlights the necessity for a principled approach to legal synthesis that considers both the objectives of Shari'ah and international standards, as underscored by recent studies (Salam et al., 2025). Embracing legal pluralism, as advocated in contemporary research, offers a pathway towards enhancing human rights protections and legal accountability. Finally, a full appreciation of these limitations is crucial to the development of human rights law in comparative legal studies, allowing for a greater understanding of the issues at play (Figure 1.18).

Figure 1.18. The discourse surrounding human rights law plays a pivotal role in the field of comparative legal studies, particularly in examining the interplay between different legal systems.

Source: https://blog.ipleaders.in/wp-content/uploads/2021/05/dissertation-topics-in-human-rights-law-1.jpg.

1.6.3. Globalization and Legal Harmonization

The process of globalization has brought significant changes in legal systems around the world, presenting opportunities and challenges towards legal harmonization. As nations are increasingly integrated by trade, technology, and communications, it can be clearly seen that there is necessity for a common legal system to facilitate free interaction across borders. However, divergence in legal traditions—civil law and common law systems, for example—is a significant barrier to actual legal harmonization. To address these challenges, legal scholars must equip themselves with comparative analysis, considering how various legal cultures can best practice without undermining their unique identities. This convergence of legal systems would result in a more efficient globalized legal landscape, ultimately endorsing international trade and cooperation. Supranational institutions intensify this need even more, as these institutions have a tendency to require conformity of country laws to broader international norms. One of the central aspects of legal harmonization in light of globalization is that of legal transplants, wherein elements from a legal system are borrowed and integrated into another. This exemplifies an ongoing quest for the efficiency and effectiveness of law based on comparative law studies. Legal borrowing is not without difficulties, however; each system is entwined in an intricate relationship with its sociocultural context and institutional setup. The success of law transplantation is often contingent on domestic welcome of foreign legal concepts and demands careful juridical examination of the compatibilities between jurisdictions. When nations attempt to implement overseas law, they may encounter various degrees of institutional hostility. It must overcome such resistance through a more nuanced understanding of the local legal traditions in developing a climate-friendly environment for reform and integration to enable the newly adopted legal elements to be compatible with the prevailing legal culture and social norms. Also, the interfacing between globalization and legal harmonization involves significant policy implications, such as in entrepreneurship and sustainable development. The emergence of high-growth firms, women entrepreneurship, and social ventures can be facilitated by aligned legal systems that foster business activities across borders. Empirical evidence underscores the need for tailored legal policies to ensure inclusive economic growth by minimizing regulatory obstacles and creating fair competition regimes. As nations vie for economic development, aligning their legal systems to facilitate entrepreneurship is crucial. In addition to facilitating market fluidity, legal harmonization also assists in resolving broader issues of society, such as market failures and sustainable conduct. By including sustainability objectives within legal frameworks, countries can demonstrate dedication to economic development and social responsibility at once, compatible with the inherent interdependency between globalization and legal harmonization today (Figure 1.19).

Figure 1.19. Globalization has profoundly reshaped the landscape of legal systems worldwide, presenting both opportunities and challenges for societies navigating an increasingly interconnected world.

Source: https://swiftnlift.com/wp-content/uploads/2024/05/global-justice-law-law-hammer-with-globe_1048944-10099250-1.jpg.

SUMMARY

In exploring the origins of comparative legal scholarship, it is important to recognize that this academic pursuit is informed by a variety of purposes. Comparative study not only aids legal practitioners in the appreciation of different systems but also animates intellectual discussion by advancing a critical dialogue among different legal cultures. By studying how laws function in different jurisdictions, scholars can explain the strengths and weaknesses of various legal systems, thereby promoting reforms specific to enhance legal effectiveness. Such a mode of legal practice becomes more pertinent with the upsurge of globalization in heightening legal system interactions. By forming basic principles and quantifying how real they are in practice, for example, in comparative analysis of Mauritius and Tanzania based on derivative claims, researchers can make well-informed contributions which can go to strengthen shareholder protections, hence harmonious with the overall goals of comparative legal studies (Habiye et al., 2025).

Methodological frameworks are the cornerstones on which comparative legal studies are built, hence the ease of making systematic inquiries into legal systems. By adopting functional methods, researchers can concentrate on the real impacts of laws and determine their efficiency apart from textual analysis. Structural comparisons give researchers a platform to study the underlying framework of legal frameworks in an attempt to draw conclusions about how they operate mechanically. Socio-legal methods go an extra step by merging sociological thinking, focusing on how principles of law are influenced by social contexts and culture. For example, a study of the regimes of law that govern biomedical research ethics can comment on the tension between individual rights and social interests and point out implementation challenges between jurisdictions (Bielova et al., 2024). Adopting such different approaches, comparative legal studies can provide advanced understanding of the complex interaction among law, culture, and society, culminating in the creation of improved legal norms and institutions. Legal families and categories are at the heart of comparative legal scholarship, supplying a systematic approach to understanding diverse legal traditions. Classification of legal systems into distinct families—civil, common, and mixed—enables scholars to facilitate comparative analysis and the cross-jurisdictional transfer of principles. Transplants of law refer to the experience of transplanting legal ideas across systems, raising issues of compatibility and congruence of laws within their new contexts. This is especially relevant when looking at procedural requirements and shareholders' protection rights in various systems. Secondly, attention should be paid to language and terminological identity; differences of legal language risk obstructing communication and interpretation between systems. By engaging with these complexities, comparative legal research advances our understanding of law and enables the articulation of harmonized legal principles that resonate on an international level (Habiye et al., 2025).

A LOOK TO THE FUTURE

FUTURE DIRECTIONS IN COMPARATIVE LEGAL SCHOLARSHIP

With the face of law constantly evolving with a more globalized landscape, the future directions of comparative legal scholarship are promising as much as challenging. The emerging new paradigms for law, like the effect of technology on law and the global convergence of legal systems, require the re-examination of set comparative methods. New approaches, such as the socio-legal and functional schools, are likely to develop from the demands of contemporary society so that researchers and practitioners can better understand how laws condition each other across borders. This responsiveness of comparative legal research not only enhances academic discourse but also legal practice as it presents diverse perspectives that are significant in creating effective and culturally sensitive legal regimes capturing the complexities of global regulation. In considering the use of comparative legal research to practice law, new paths can involve further emphasis on artificial intelligence and data analysis as tools used in research. Leveraging advanced technology software will be able to enable comparative analysis, enabling further scrutiny of legal theory and systems. For instance, tools that examine legal outcome trends can unlock the adaptability of laws across different cultures. Moreover, as noted through the continued development of Agentic AI, the application of such technology can enhance legal decision-making through a comparative understanding of existing laws under different jurisdictions (Joshi, 2025). Actually, as technologies improve, they will likely affect not just techniques used in comparative legal research but even the nature of the practice of law itself. Further, a key element of future progress in comparative legal research lies in addressing the challenges of jurisdictional compatibility as well as cultural sensitivities. The increasing mobility of law ideas across borders necessitates that researchers be sensitive to surrounding contexts in which laws operate. In order to address these challenges, one requires an interdisciplinary approach incorporating cultural studies, international relations, and human rights. For instance, the UAE's cultural diplomacy shows how law and soft power are interdependent in building international relations (Dyakov et al., 2025). As comparative legal scholarship develops, understanding the dynamic interplay between legal systems and their associated culture will be crucial to make transplants of law establish themselves well and become cherished in multicultural societies.

REFERENCES

1. Abdelaziz, D. K. A. (2025). Incitement to suicide in the digital age: A comparative legal study of criminal liability. *Journal of Posthumanism*. https://www.semanticscholar.org/paper/313685638931c38730ed89f77295f15894c31841 (accessed on 9th September 2025).
2. Agency for Healthcare Research and Quality. (2020). *Registries for Evaluating Patient Outcomes: A User's Guide*. https://doi.org/10.23970/ahrqepcregistries4 (accessed on 9th September 2025).
3. Alkassaabeh, F. Y., & Al-Zoubi, M. A. K. (2024). Legal frameworks for facing environmental pollution crimes: A comparative study of Jordanian legislation and international agreements. *Journal of Law and Sustainable Development*. https://www.semanticscholar.org/paper/ba3c6ebc5af655b9bf3b36c70c439d2d6be36609 (accessed on 9th September 2025).
4. Amiruddin, M. Z., Zuhriah, E., & Zarapi, N. H. (2024). Perpetuating inequality: Barriers and legal safeguards for women in domestic violence situations. *DIKTUM: Jurnal Syariah dan Hukum*. https://www.semanticscholar.org/paper/14e43008eb56fbd96733fe41db3e8630167ab63f (accessed on 9th September 2025).
5. Assetization. (2020). The MIT Press eBooks. https://doi.org/10.7551/mitpress/12075.001.0001 (accessed on 9th September 2025).
6. Averchenkova, E., & Lozbinev, F. (2022). Management methodology of a regional socio-economic system as a theoretical and practical contribution to the management theory development. *Automation and Modeling in Design and Management*. https://www.semanticscholar.org/paper/9c06a3e38be47d7a7ddb43b634bd0a53afb34671 (accessed on 9th September 2025).
7. Bielova, M., Fridmanska, V. I., Svyshcho, V. Yu., & Leshanych, L. V. (2024). Legal regulation of biomedical research: Key principles and their implementation. *Wiadomosci Lekarskie, 77*(10), 2070–2076. https://www.semanticscholar.org/paper/12a212436960d9a2452930843d9cea3a41ea3999 (accessed on 9th September 2025).
8. Chagina, E., & Sisoev, Y. E. (2024). Administrative and criminal liability for violation of consumer rights in the legislation of the Russian Federation and the Republic of Belarus: A comparative legal study. *Юридические исследования*. https://www.semanticscholar.org/paper/42698f021d5004114203498cc068713b18dd5f2e (accessed on 9th September 2025).
9. Cherp, A., Vinichenko, V., Jewell, J., Brutschin, E., & Sovacool, B. K. (2017). Integrating techno-economic, socio-technical and political perspectives on national energy transitions: A meta-theoretical framework. *Energy Research & Social Science, 37*, 175–190. https://doi.org/10.1016/j.erss.2017.09.015 (accessed on 9th September 2025).
10. de Haas, H. (2021). A theory of migration: The aspirations–capabilities framework. *Comparative Migration Studies, 9*. https://doi.org/10.1186/s40878-020-00210-4 (accessed on 9th September 2025).
11. Dikhtiaruk, B. (2025). Constitutional and legal aspects of implementing the right to higher education under emergency legal regimes: A comparative legal study. *Uzhhorod National University Herald. Series: Law*. https://www.semanticscholar.org/paper/01df052d0687bf9d0655623b23c2be5d5a184fb2 (accessed on 9th September 2025).
12. Dvornikova, P. A. (2025). Reforming the legal regime of foreign direct investment: A catalyst for economic growth and stability. *Juridical Scientific and Electronic Journal*. https://www.

semanticscholar.org/paper/645c65ba2223ee52e1d0fd53afe0cbb4b37e7401 (accessed on 9th September 2025).

13. Dyakov, N. N., & Khusikhanov, T. R. (2025). The UAE cultural diplomacy: West, East and Russia. *Concept: Philosophy, Religion, Culture*. https://www.semanticscholar.org/paper/36f5155313c22b20e8f44416ffc01144c9acb752 (accessed on 9th September 2025).

14. Gul, S., Ahmad, R., & Rahman, S. U. (2025). Constitutional dualities: Reconciling Islamic normativity with common law principles in hybrid legal systems. *Indus Journal of Social Sciences*. https://www.semanticscholar.org/paper/aeade378ff2a328724dc8c142f8f1dcb1c53f0d1 (accessed on 9th September 2025).

15. Gulyaeva, P. S. (2023). Medical nanorobots in the focus of law. *Journal of Digital Technologies and Law, 1*, 89–122. https://doi.org/10.21202/jdtl.2023.4 (accessed on 9th September 2025).

16. Habiye, Y. L., Gunputh, R., Pudaruth, S., & Mtaki, C. K. (2025). Reflections on shareholders' protection in Tanzania through derivative claims: A comparative legal analysis with Mauritius. *International Journal of Law and Management*. https://www.semanticscholar.org/paper/a8d728c12016b84fbbbc3a2a2a4061e0310d2d5d (accessed on 9th September 2025).

17. Hamonangan, J. P. (2025). Legal form analysis of state-owned limited liability companies in Indonesia and Malaysia. *Journal of Social Research*. https://www.semanticscholar.org/paper/9f4d58a20456781458fce89675dc34f98142b2a3 (accessed on 9th September 2025).

18. Haridhi, Z., Simbolon, E. D., Sitompul, N. A. K., Pauzi, A., & Ikhwan, C. (2024). Judicial review of the application of ultra vires doctrine in Malaysia and Indonesia: A legal comparison. *Recht Studiosum Law Review*. https://www.semanticscholar.org/paper/4bcb99afa8ac76c55e1e65a569cf6d1ed277ef47 (accessed on 9th September 2025).

19. Haspelmath, M. (2010). Comparative concepts and descriptive categories in crosslinguistic studies. *Language, 86*, 663–687. https://doi.org/10.1353/lan.2010.0021 (accessed on 9th September 2025).

20. Henrich, J., Heine, S. J., & Norenzayan, A. (2010). The weirdest people in the world? *Behavioral and Brain Sciences, 33*, 61–83. https://doi.org/10.1017/s0140525x0999152x (accessed on 9th September 2025).

21. Ivanskiy, V. P., & Kovalev, S. I. (2019). The role of rationality philosophy in legal studies (Part II). *RUDN Journal of Law, 23*, 184–199. https://doi.org/10.22363/2313-2337-2019-23-2-184-199 (accessed on 9th September 2025).

22. Joshi, S. (2025). Comprehensive review of artificial general intelligence AGI, agentic AI and GenAI: Current trends and future directions. *International Journal of Multidisciplinary Research and Growth Evaluation*. https://www.semanticscholar.org/paper/1f8df7e4e46cc42008ab31e2e43473d3bd77d70e (accessed on 9th September 2025).

23. Kashirkina. (2024). Comparative legal and international legal methods in the study of the constitutional foundations of interstate integration. *Journal of Foreign Legislation and Comparative Law*. https://www.semanticscholar.org/paper/bdfa8e01b3c776b2beafde86dad54a5bc7a4c041 (accessed on 9th September 2025).

24. Kiria, G. (2024). Author's rights in musical works within contractual relationships and international legal mechanisms for their regulation (Comparative legal research based on German example). *Journal of Law*. https://www.semanticscholar.org/paper/

be23694091102a39e00b5cc58c99805e5fa8bb1f (accessed on 9th September 2025).

25. Kurochkina, D. S. (2024). The multidimensional phenomenon of judicial decision: A comparison of domestic and French approaches. *Ural Journal of Legal Research*. https://www.semanticscholar.org/paper/74f5efeff4f0e9ec69f1b8fa0d4912f20263e2df (accessed on 9th September 2025).

26. Lewin, H. A., Robinson, G. E., Kress, W. J., Baker, W. J., Coddington, J. A., Crandall, K. A., Durbin, R., et al. (2018). Earth BioGenome Project: Sequencing life for the future of life. *Proceedings of the National Academy of Sciences, 115*, 4325–4333. https://doi.org/10.1073/pnas.1720115115 (accessed on 9th September 2025).

27. Ma, X., & Zhang, Y. (2025). A study on the translation strategy of the "principle of good faith" in the contractual compilation of the Civil Code–A three-dimensional analysis based on terminological consistency, contextual adaptation and cultural differences. *Law and Humanities*. https://www.semanticscholar.org/paper/da9edd0cc7a100a7120f3df15d064b4bed99c321 (accessed on 9th September 2025).

28. McLaughlan, R., & Srivastava, N. (2014). 13 *Colonial discourse and postcolonial theory. The Year's Work in Critical and Cultural Theory, 22*, 240–270. https://doi.org/10.1093/ywcct/mbu013 (accessed on 9th September 2025).

29. Myakhanova, T. I., Erkhitueva, Z. P., & Gunzynov. (2024). Death penalty in criminal law of Russia, China and Mongolia: A comparative legal analysis with examples from the judicial practice of contemporary China. *International Criminal Law and International Justice*. https://www.semanticscholar.org/paper/55a81eb2b6445f6d65c180dc57d21c48554f0c3c (accessed on 9th September 2025).

30. Nakorchevskyj, S. (2025). The application of the institution of subsidiary liability in bankruptcy cases. *Scientific Journal of the National Academy of Internal Affairs*. https://www.semanticscholar.org/paper/51306b982c72c9212a59e4d98c9c10beaba3885d (accessed on 9th September 2025).

31. Nurmala, S. A., & Utami, I. (2024). Public housing saving program: A comparative legal analysis between Indonesia and Singapore. *Indonesian Comparative Law Review*. https://www.semanticscholar.org/paper/1538b2bbab8a81e7cdba363821909de6ecfd58dc (accessed on 9th September 2025).

32. OECD. (2022). *Building Trust and Reinforcing Democracy*. OECD Public Governance Reviews. https://doi.org/10.1787/76972a4a-en (accessed on 9th September 2025).

33. OECD. (2022). *Delivering for youth: How governments can put young people at the center of the recovery. OECD Policy Responses to Coronavirus (COVID-19)*. https://doi.org/10.1787/92c9d060-en (accessed on 9th September 2025).

34. Pasemko, G., & Shynkarenko, V. Y. (2024). Theoretical basis for managing the development of land relations in Ukraine. *Journal of Management, Economics and Technology*. https://www.semanticscholar.org/paper/1e664f9b2a267b4cb62b81adc9f7a6766823fb6e (accessed on 9th September 2025).

35. Pauer, E., Wohner, B., Heinrich, V., & Tacker, M. (2019). Assessing the environmental sustainability of food packaging: An extended life cycle assessment including packaging-related food losses and waste and circularity assessment. *Sustainability, 11*, 925. https://doi.org/10.3390/su11030925 (accessed on 9th September 2025).

36. Polii, V., Julius, D., & Banaya, C. L. (2025). Legal protection of personal data privacy in the digital era: A comparative study between Indonesia and ASEAN countries. *Hakim: Jurnal Ilmu Hukum dan Sosial*. https://www.semanticscholar.org/paper/23abd2a8da031ee8ca954646635cb8e20f5580d0 (accessed on 9th September 2025).

37. Pozov, D. (2025). Some peculiarities of the use of mediation in foreign countries: A comparative legal aspect. *Economics. Finances. Law*. https://www.semanticscholar.org/paper/cb95c26d20c0b45404163a5679de85a0a9ce1fd5 (accessed on 9th September 2025).

38. Raikwar, B. (2025). Comparative analysis of GST frameworks. *International Journal for Multidisciplinary Research*. https://www.semanticscholar.org/paper/104447f0c9779e5879ddfd9b528800a111ebd57c (accessed on 9th September 2025).

39. Rashed, T. G. E. S. (2025). Arbitration without agreement under the ICSID rules: A comparative study with Egyptian and Qatari legal systems. *Access to Justice in Eastern Europe*. https://www.semanticscholar.org/paper/f22d16080d1056001b903a500a389ee270f82c89 (accessed on 9th September 2025).

40. Russell, S. T., & Fish, J. N. (2016). Mental health in lesbian, gay, bisexual, and transgender (LGBT) youth. *Annual Review of Clinical Psychology, 12*, 465–487. https://doi.org/10.1146/annurev-clinpsy-021815-093153 (accessed on 9th September 2025).

41. Sabrie, H. Y. (2024). Implementation of the Montreal Convention in Indonesia's and Australia's air transport laws on carrier's liability. *Veritas et Justitia*. https://www.semanticscholar.org/paper/23f65b8aa583edaea86c0b3b191c4904a0e4e10c (accessed on 9th September 2025).

42. Şahin, A. (2018). Critical issues in Islamic education studies: Rethinking Islamic and Western liberal secular values of education. *Religions, 9*, 335. https://doi.org/10.3390/rel9110335 (accessed on 9th September 2025).

43. Salam, K., Baig, S., Sattar, J., & Khokhar, A. (2025). Human rights in Islam: A comparative analysis of the legal frameworks in context of Pakistan and international norms. *The Critical Review of Social Sciences Studies*. https://www.semanticscholar.org/paper/075c95f039a223675f7b531782fd75424ada34f3 (accessed on 9th September 2025).

44. Samoilenko, V. (2025). AI and Deep face influencers: The challenge of authenticity in the online space. *Universal Library of Engineering Technology*. https://www.semanticscholar.org/paper/3cf286fe1e9b64caa105322b6b74401e09c90e03 (accessed on 9th September 2025).

45. Scipioni, M. (2017). Failing forward in EU migration policy? EU integration after the 2015 asylum and migration crisis. *Journal of European Public Policy, 25*, 1357–1375. https://doi.org/10.1080/13501763.2017.1325920 (accessed on 9th September 2025).

46. Shermatov, B. (2025). Territorial application of criminal law: Theoretical foundations and comparative analysis. *The American Journal of Political Science Law and Criminology*. https://www.semanticscholar.org/paper/76edf711f713ca23e6dbeb991edeade9d6b15977 (accessed on 9th September 2025).

47. Sidorova, N., & Serikbayev, A. (2023). Comparative study of the legal regulation of international cooperation in the field of criminal justice in the Eurasian space. *Bulletin of the Karaganda University. "Law Series"*. https://www.semanticscholar.org/paper/f426b1d71a1103b3586d9739ed6f1424770e48f5 (accessed on 9th September 2025).

48. Sivokoneva, P. (2024). The right to health protection in the constitutions of the countries of

the Commonwealth of Independent States: A comparative legal study. *Legal Concept*. https://www.semanticscholar.org/paper/c6cb12d17fd5f94ffafae7d9940cf78166bd0382 (accessed on 9th September 2025).

49. Solum, L. B. (2020). *Legal Personhood for Artificial Intelligences. Routledge eBooks*. https://doi.org/10.4324/9781003074991-37 (accessed on 9th September 2025).

50. Spytska, L. (2024). E-government in Ukraine and the world: A comparative legal analysis. *Social Legal Studios*. https://www.semanticscholar.org/paper/c7667463d2703af4ebf2bd5d89c463f2198b2b33 (accessed on 9th September 2025).

51. Stoyanova, M., Nikoloudakis, Y., Panagiotakis, S., Pallis, E., & Markakis, E. (2020). A survey on the Internet of Things (IoT) forensics: Challenges, approaches, and open issues. *IEEE Communications Surveys & Tutorials, 22*, 1191–1221. https://doi.org/10.1109/comst.2019.2962586 (accessed on 9th September 2025).

52. Taqi, R. H. (2025). Alternative sanctions in criminal justice: A comparative legal study. *Academia Open*. https://www.semanticscholar.org/paper/e4a343e183764448667b1d9bfd25938917f275b9 (accessed on 9th September 2025).

53. Terjesen, S., Bosma, N., & Stam, E. (2015). Advancing public policy for high-growth, female, and social entrepreneurs. *Public Administration Review, 76*, 230–239. https://doi.org/10.1111/puar.12472 (accessed on 9th September 2025).

54. Tian, X. (2025). Enhancing China's legal response to workplace harassment and its mental health consequences: Lessons from common law systems. *Advances in Economics, Management and Political Sciences*. https://www.semanticscholar.org/paper/d45c981caa93a9a990591ec4b6194ec487f2272e (accessed on 9th September 2025).

55. Vasilieva, V. A., Stefanyshyn, N. M., & Skhab-Buchynska, T. (2019). Surrogate motherhood: Analysis of the basis of the legislation of Ukraine and foreign countries. *Journal of Advanced Research in Law and Economics*. https://www.semanticscholar.org/paper/634f7ef5f5820a7166b6a7ed063dfc15e46fb0cc (accessed on 9th September 2025).

56. Yao, Q. (2025). A comparative study of undue influence and unfair conduct in contract law using NLP and knowledge graphs: Bridging common law and Chinese legal systems through computational legal intelligence. *Applied and Computational Engineering*. https://www.semanticscholar.org/paper/24788a818a41b7b2ba78edf39def11795ca9899e (accessed on 9th September 2025).

Chapter 2

SOURCES OF LAW IN COMPARATIVE PERSPECTIVE

Contents

INTRODUCTION

The exploration of legal sources within the framework of comparative law necessitates a multifaceted approach, examining how various jurisdictions think about and prioritize these factors. One of the main features achieved in legal systems is the supremacy of the constitution, typically creating a general framework of law that sets the legal relationship between various sources of law. This aspect is critical, as it determines legislation procedure and statute order, dictating how laws are enacted and interpreted. Different jurisdictions react differently to constitutional supremacy, determining how statutory law and other sources of law relate. Such institutional determinants are key to explaining the quality and effectiveness of law in various legal systems, as charted by Hadfield in investigating legal design and institutional arrangements (Michaels et al., 2009). By examining the underlying layer, the issue of legal sources will illuminate broader comparative distinctions that define the world of law. Other than concerns of constitutionalism, precedent and case law are instrumental in deciding the sources of law in various legal traditions. These factors emphasize the function of binding authority and persuasive value given by judges and courts to earlier decisions. Understanding citation styles and the manner in which legal systems utilize such precedents has the potential to make an individual conscious of their systems of interpretation. In legal regimes where case law prevails, the evolution of law comes close to replicating pragmatic use of judicial judgment, hence influencing statutory interpretation as well as legal doctrine construction. The interaction between legislative and judicial sources is a response to a dynamic legal landscape, which varies significantly across frontiers. As noted in the conference contributions on the institutional aspects of law, such differences are an integral part of comparative analysis (Jansen et al., 2008).

Moreover, customary and religious sources provide a rich tapestry upon which legal systems borrow norms and practice, highlighting the variety of influences that form the law. Such sources often coexist with statutory and constitutional regimes, providing dilemmas and possible judicial acceptance by courts. Customary norms in other jurisdictions can be of huge normative significance, particularly where they address the values of the people. The identification and acceptance of such sources are immensely diverse, as some juridical traditions possess a more liberal attitude, while others maintain a strict segregation of secular and religious legal systems. The nuanced dynamics between such sources of law not only showcase regional applications but also illustrate the diverse cultural bases that govern legal systems throughout the globe. Such a multifaceted perspective will be important in resolving sources of law in an integrated manner in comparative contexts.

2.1. CONSTITUTION AND STATUTORY LAW

The doctrine of constitutional supremacy is the cornerstone of modern legal orders, announcing that all laws and all acts of government are subject to the Constitution. This basic maxim is foundational because it establishes a normative hierarchy within which statutes must operate. In the majority of jurisdictions, not only does the Constitution provide the framework of government but also sets out the fundamental rights of the people such that any legislation that is enacted will not contravene these rights. Supremacy clause encapsulates this principle, which at times comes in another form under different legal systems, that is to say that statutes that are inconsistent with the Constitution may be declared void. Comparative analysis illustrates that the importance of constitutional supremacy varies among states; in certain European states, direct access to constitutional courts by individual complaints boosts protections for basic rights (Gentili et al., 2012). This new practice reflects a broader trend towards strengthening constitutional frameworks, thereby creating a more robust system of government.

Figure 2.1. Image of constitution law.

Source: https://assets.thehansindia.com/h-upload/2021/12/06/1125288-cl.webp.

Closest to the creation of constitutional supremacy is the legislative process, which is the mechanisms through which legislation is created and enacted. Legislative processes vary immensely from jurisdiction to jurisdiction, and they tend to reflect the political, social, and legal nature of a given system. The complexity of legislative processes like committee review, debate, and voting procedures serves to incorporate public input as well as to provide checks and balances in governmental activity. Also, the statutory hierarchy theory forms the core of this framework as it is used to determine the relative precedence of different types of legislation. Although others prioritize provisions in the constitution over parliament acts, there are those that posit a formal hierarchy of different types of statutory law, regulations, and municipal ordinances. This multi-faceted approach highlights the different ways of ranking legal sources between jurisdictions, demonstrating the dynamic interaction between constitutional and statutory law. Statutory law construction and interpretation are increasingly beholden to the shifting patterns in judicial precedents and the development of legal doctrines. As the courts manage conflicts of statutes, particularly where discrimination and equal protection are involved, patterns emerge which indicate movement towards conformity with international best practice. The United States Supreme Court, for instance, has been typified by a shifting stance on the issue of the difference between facial discrimination and disparate impact, an approach that is aligned with the introduction of international jurisprudence into domestic law (Lau et al., 2017). Not only does integration strengthen the legal landscape but also provides scope for reform through comparative examination of the law. By studying foreign jurisdictions, which have developed advanced solutions to constitutional and statutory issues, the United States can craft a more inclusive, more equitable legal regime. This dynamic exchange underscores the significance of constitutional and statutory law as center sources of law for comparative analysis (Figure 2.1).

2.1.1. Supremacy of the Constitution

In such governments where the Constitution takes precedence, not only does it enunciate fundamental principles and rights but also announces governmental power and duty. Such supremacy is most significant where legislatures' actions or executive orders can conflict with constitutional provisions as such supremacy empowers the courts to invalidate the actions. Thus, the judiciary is responsible for interpreting the Constitution and ensuring all other laws are in keeping with its spirit. In comparative analysis, particularly in those states where there is modes of governance divergence, the concept of constitutional supremacy can cause gigantic divergence of the mode and manner of operation and interaction between legal systems, again defining how the laws come into force and are enforced in the jurisdictions. Besides, institutional driving forces for constitutional primacy differ a great deal from country to country, owing to their political, social, and historical nuances. For example, constitutional hegemony in the United States is chiefly a judicial role, as it is the Supreme Court, above all, that supports this doctrine through judicial review. In contrast, in the European Union framework, for example, there are supra-national and national laws in harmony with each other. The European Court of Justice (ECJ) and the European Commission demonstrate the manner in which EU law can override national legal systems on occasion, thereby demonstrating the delicate balance necessary between rival legal powers. This multi-contextualism underscores that constitutional supremacy is ever a conditional reality rather than an independent one, susceptible to being influenced by varied conceptions of law in individual jurisdictions and emphasizes the subtle interplay between domestic and international legal norms. The discussion of constitutional supremacy also raises the most important questions regarding government decision-making accountability and control.

This is particularly true in areas such as counterterrorism, where power delegation within government branches has the authority to influence the legitimacy of what is being done under authority. Countries such as the United States, United Kingdom, and Israel do everything else differently in managing such tensions, with the U.S. Executive having quite some discretion, while the U.K. Parliament and Israeli Judiciary play key roles in oversight and accountability. This functionalist differentiation indicates that constitutional norms superiority is not an ideal concept but an operative concept for preventing abuses of power. Therefore, analyzing those differences through comparative law analysis opens a window of understanding on how to improve mechanisms of institutions that are closer to achieving the ideals of justice and accountability under the lens of constitutional superiority (Grimmel et al., 2025; Gil et al., 2020) (Figure 2.2).

Figure 2.2. The concept of constitutional supremacy plays a pivotal role in shaping the legal framework of various nations, ensuring that the Constitution acts as the ultimate source of law.

Source: https://blogger.googleusercontent.com/img/b/R29vZ2xl/AVvXsEjopUOFugieo2PYNvq4qAT_o7mWKp-XGBp7mER6xlSZgp9lzvFZLv9hjn1UDhyphenhyphenu-OXvXY8kXhasarmHQ6RES-DtrbQ_xbuWOrwFHB543Oq4DsLPt_QkZYGugmYW_BbfcVZkmBFglU03u0o/w1200-h630-p-k-no-nu/blogger-image--1562456458.jpg.

2.1.2. Legislative Processes

Legislative processes are a central part of making and enforcing law in any jurisdiction of law, being the theoretical construct upon which statute law is based. At the core of these processes is the doctrine of constitutional supremacy, by which anything produced by the legislator must be in accordance with the overall tenets enshrined within the constitution. This hierarchical structure bestows importance on the legislative institutions, which undergo serious debate and discussion to produce bills that are indicative of what society needs. Secondly, the process is typically comprised of a number of stages, including drafting, a committee review, and voting, during which stakeholders from various segments of society provide inputs to the discussion (Figure 2.3).

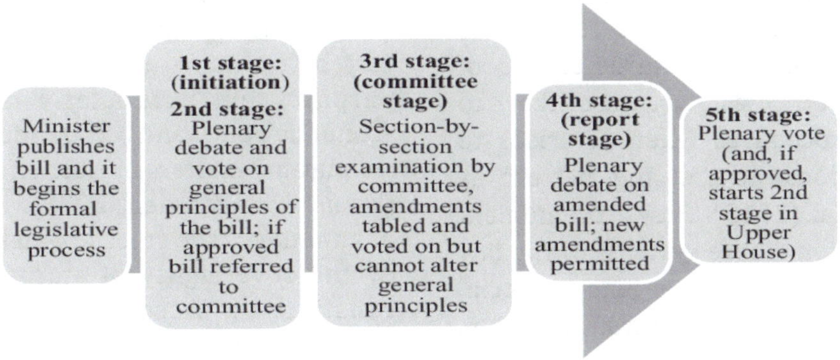

Figure 2.3. Formal legislative process.

Source: https://www.researchgate.net/publication/317831136/figure/fig2/AS:512454597804034@1499190105485/Formal-legislative-process.png.

This kind of bargaining that occurs in legislatures actually goes on to form the world of law in such a manner that not only are laws enacted, but are themselves a product of a bargaining and public participation process, and thus are legitimate and acceptable in society. The interactive nature of legislative processes has a tendency to create a duality of effect, which is best demonstrated in the subject area of labor law. Reform legislation in the majority of European countries depicts deregulation as a trend to improve the prospects of employment. As elaborate in Sitzia et al. (2016), the development of the concept of joint employment presents advancement in labor market flexibility at the expense of rigidities giving way to more universal norms on the basis of advanced aspirations rather than singular legislative prescriptions. This is symptomatic of a larger phenomenon of de-juridification across legislative frameworks by which the complexities of law can succumb to more compliant, market-sensitive adjustment. These trends suggest the range of legislative frameworks to evolve under pressure from the economy and unveil a deeper dynamic between regulation, forces of the market, and the functioning of law in modern societies. Legislative procedures otherwise come under the control of transient environments, particularly in times of crisis or emergency. Formation of norms and sources like constitutions and legislations by statute is likely to respond to extreme changes that are characteristic of stressors in society. Legislatures are likely to use expedited procedures when in crises to enable quick response to pressing matters, as argued in Ciolli et al. (2015). They are a moment of crisis intersection where systems of the law can be bent to conform to the urgency of social need but at the price of thoughtful reflection. To that extent, though, this accommodation of legislation is necessary to effective government in a state of crisis without so doing at the cost of reflections regarding long-term consequence to the rule of law and constitutional integrity. The tension between urgency and legality under such circumstances puts more weight on achieving a balance between speed of legislative action and respect for established legal tradition.

2.1.3. Statutory Hierarchies

Statutory law in most legal frameworks is not in a void; rather, it is preceded by constitutional regimes that attribute meaning to independent hierarchies of juridical authority. Supremacy of constitution constitutes a foundation, where by any legislation in conflict with constitutional norms is rendered null and void. Practitioners of law must comprehend the hierarchy because it directly affects their ability to cope with complex regulatory environments. In addition, parliamentary procedures that are fundamental to statutory interpretation vary significantly between jurisdictions and affect legislation, amendment, and repeal. These processes most commonly include openness and public participation principles and thus render statutes compliant with public values as well as responsive to evolving needs in the law. The interrelation of administrative and statutory regulations then makes statutory hierarchies more complicated, raising issues of dynamic aspects of law in a process of governance. Administrative powers can enact delegated legislation, which will offer rules or directives which will tend to accord with statutory directions. These are rules that may be crucial to the functioning of statutory purpose, and particularly in areas such as economic policy and competition policy in which technicality matters most to effective governance (Frans van Waarden, 2025). However, powers of administrative rules are rightfully controlled by the sovereignty of statutory law and the constitution. Accordingly, when there are inconsistencies between regulation and statute law, the courts must resolve the inconsistency in a manner that is consistent with the hierarchical structure. This serves to illuminate the importance of judicial control in the interest of upholding statutory hierarchies unimpaired and balanced, consistent with overall principles of law. Secondly, conflict between varying levels of statutes can be comprehended by examining the statuses and rights accorded to individuals under various regimes of law. The complexity of statutory hierarchies can best be noted where conflict between national law and state law prevails, such as in the instance of illegal immigration. Where the individuals are illegal aliens under federal law but employee unions under sub federal code, the paradox is one that requires careful scrutiny of legislative history. Using an empirically-based approach in dealing with this legislative history, researchers are able to assess the effect that inconsistencies in statutory hierarchy have on legal consequences for employees (Griffith et al., 2014). Thus, statutory hierarchies' understanding is not just augmented but the tool of interpretation in which legal theorists and practitioners researching policy within comparative legal contexts are more empowered (Figure 2.4).

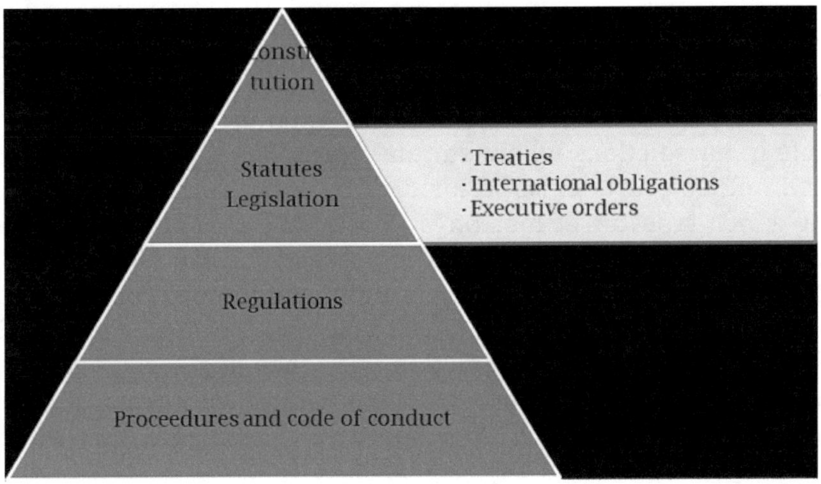

Figure 2.4. An exploration of statutory hierarchies reveals the intricate relationship between various sources of law and the principles that govern their application and interpretation.

Source: https://www.researchgate.net/profile/Hashem-Alshurafat/publication/348335044/figure/fig1/AS:977698016993282@1610112780130/The-hierarchy-of-laws.ppm.

2.2. JUDICIAL PRECEDENT AND CASE LAW

In jurisprudence, types of judicial precedent and case law are inherent aspects of legal principle development and development. Judicial precedent is the doctrine whereby previous court decisions become a model for judging similar future cases, having a foundation of consistency and predictability in the legal system. The doctrine depends on a hierarchical framework whereby decisions made at a higher court bind lower courts to follow earlier interpretations. Through compliance with such precedential authority, the courts are able to obtain a certain level of legal reliance, thereby maintaining public confidence in the judicial process. As noted by MacCormick and Summers, argument based on precedent avers that provisions of a law that have entrenched meanings must be applied uniformly in order to guarantee the rule of law (Sartor et al., 2014). In this way, this use of court rulings not only builds modern legal meanings but also shapes legislative processes and statute making. The persuasive effect of case law extends beyond simple binding authority, playing a central role in jurisdictions where statute legislation is deficient in particularity. Judges often cite decisions in other courts or superior courts in the same regime to support their own arguments, creating a rich tapestry of meanings in law that enhance overall clarity of law. Most notably perhaps in common law, such determining precedents may fill the gaps when there is no statutory provision or if there is ambiguity in statutory provisions. For example, judges will cite leading cases to justify verdicts or clarify the development of law, which sparks the controversy in the court of law. Furthermore, case law interaction with changing social values is achieved where the courts interpret statutes in accordance with contemporary norms and principles, thereby reflecting public opinion and making the law responsive to change within the boundaries set by established precedents (Sartor et al., 2014) (Figure 2.5).

Judicial Precedent

- Judicial precedent refers to sources of law where past decisions of the judges create law for future judges to follow.

- This source of law is also known as case law.
- It is a major source of law both historically and today.

Figure 2.5. Judicial precedent as a source of law.

Source: https://eclipas.top/ProductDetail.aspx?iid=90714091&pr=67.88.

In other jurisdictions, judicial precedent and citation procedures of case law are highly significant in achieving transparency and credibility of legal processes. A transparent process of citation enables judges and practitioners to make their arguments more convincingly, using well-established precedents that support their legal position. Secondly, adherence to convention for citing assists in deciding jurisdiction of judgments, which can be employed to make arguments used in court stronger. As observed in the Ukrainian case, reception of the European Court of Human Rights

(ECtHR) decisions demonstrates a growing commitment to integrating international case law into domestic legal frameworks. Thus, by possessing such an understanding of the dynamics of citing within the law courts, legal scholarship is promoted and more importantly, serves the courts since judgments can be based on a settled body of caselaw, hence further entrenching the rule of law comparatively.

2.2.1. Binding Authority

In the world of legal systems, binding authority is a significant mechanism by which courts can achieve predictability and consistency in court decisions. Binding authority is largely enforced through the doctrine of stare decisis, where lower courts are constrained by higher court-established legal precedents. The function of binding authority preserves the rule of law by ensuring that similar cases are resolved in a similar manner, promoting stability and fairness in the legal system. Moreover, this regard for precedent emphasizes the importance of judicial decisions as a source of law. The effects of binding authority extend beyond a mere compliance; they establish public trust in the legal order by illustrating that judicial decisions are grounded in already established legal rules rather than unfettered discretion. In comparison, the imposition and meaning of binding authority can greatly differ among various legal systems. In exploring typical common law jurisdictions such as the United States and England, the application of judicial precedents remains a unifying element. In civil law jurisdictions, however, codified statutes become paramount, often limiting the use of judicial decisions in establishing legal norms. This highlights the multifaceted character of binding authority, as courts in civil law jurisdictions will commonly rely on legislative intent and statutory interpretation rather than binding precedents. Hence, the identification of binding authority is a nuanced examination of each legal tradition's values and principles. As scholars appreciate, legitimacy of judicial authority tends to rest upon the publics belief that the judiciary is proceeding along common moral and legal norms, concurring with the wider social surrounding wherein these legal systems exist (Jackson et al., 2012). The impacts of binding authority also reverberate through international law, particularly where states are grappling with reconciling local and international legal norms. Binding authority is extensive enough here to encompass recognition and enforcement of international agreements under domestic law. The extent to which binding authority is embraced in international law depends on whether states subscribe to monist or dualist philosophies. It raises the issue of how binding authority in national courts affects compliance with international obligations. Lastly, the effectiveness of binding authority hinges on the interactions between national law, judicial interpretation, and international legal norms, where legal scholars and practitioners must navigate this complexity with care. As new economics theories, such as those covering Chinas transition, reinforce, the adherence to codified legal rules can also have an impact on broader-scale socio-economic dynamics (Song et al., 2011).

2.2.2. Persuasive Value

In law, the concept of persuasive value is most relevant in deciding and enforcing judicial precedent and case law. This factor goes beyond mere binding authority to examine how much the rulings of higher courts or foreign courts are likely to influence lower court holdings. The value of persuasion normally resides in the cogency and beauty of the judicial argument of such cases, and therefore become persuasive to judges who are deciding similar cases. In comparative law, the value of persuasion is identified as mobility of legal principles between jurisdictions, whereby foreign law or judicial precedents prove to be useful in shaping local jurisprudence. This dynamic interaction emphasizes the importance of legal language and how having the ability to be able to argue a point is capable of making material differences to the meanings of laws and principles of a legal system. This judicial precedent function is supplemented when courts resort to drawing on the context of society and norms within which the laws are in operation (Figure 2.6).

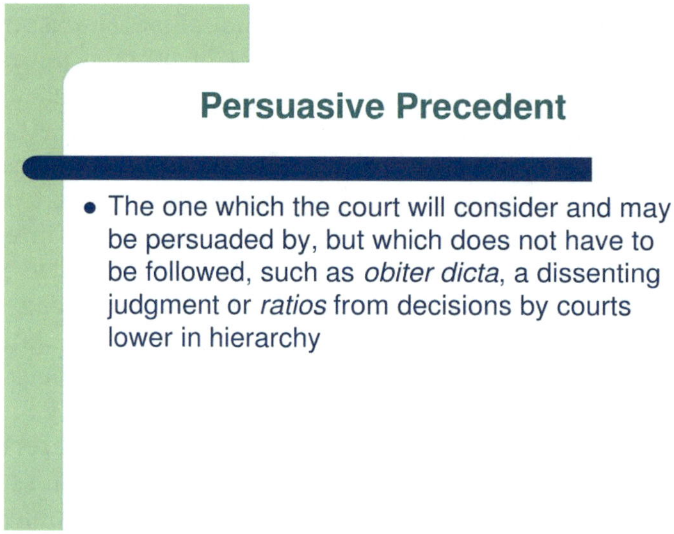

Figure 2.6. Looking at persuasive precedents, judges are encouraged to reflect upon the overarching principles of justice, equity, and social progress, which may not be fully encapsulated within local statutory law.

Source: https://image.slideserve.com/631974/persuasive-precedent-l.jpg.

This critical examination is aimed at a judiciary that is not only mechanical in enforcing the law but also more attuned to the evolving legal landscape. In line with Yogesh et al. (2022), the contemplation on persuasive value further shows the potential for the legal system's capacity to innovate and respond to contemporary social issues, thereby making the law more useful and effective. Courts are apt to borrow influencing precedents to explain the law-society interface and push the limits of law towards an equilibrium of consistency of judicial rulings. Moreover, referencing customs surrounding speech and speechwriting of influencing precedents demonstrates the extensive implications of legal thinking as a communal and community-based endeavor among legal practitioners. Judges, scholars, and lawyers frequently refer to landmark judgments to support settled principles of law but also to promote change and innovation in law. As discussed in Klein (2021), it generates a culture of debate and pluralism in judicial argumentation and a possibility of a better comprehension of legal principles. Such an environment enables courts to engage with international and regional legal standards further enhancing the ability of foreign decisions to persuade. By the use of persuasive precedents, the law becomes a dynamic living document, not stiff, and evolves through debate and cross-influence of diverse interpretations of law across jurisdictions. Last but not least, the persuasive power of case law is at the forefront of evolving and responsiveness of legal systems in comparative perspective.

2.2.3. Citation Practices

Amongst the intricate framework of legal systems, conventions for citation serve a critical function of ascertaining the cogency and consistency of judicial reasoning. The ability to refer to judicial precedents, statutory provisions, and learned writing provides a foundation on which legal arguments and court rulings are constructed. In case law and judicial precedent, citation of leading cases not just proves the legal argument but also shows adherence to legal doctrine. Through citation in this way within comparative law scholarship, differences in legal culture and methodology within various jurisdictions are identified, showing towards the way in which laws are interpreted and applied differently—a central problem with studying Sources of Law in Comparative Perspective. As legal scholars and practitioners go through the intricacies of citation patterns, there may be inconsistencies, especially when combining sources from various legal traditions (Figure 2.7).

Common Legal Citation Systems in Law

System	Used in	Description	Example
The Bluebook (U.S. Legal Citation)	United States	Comprehensive rules, common in U.S. legal practice	Smith v. Jones, 123 U.S. 456 (2020)
OSCOLA (Oxford University Standard for the Cittion of Legal Authorities)	United Kingdom	Standard for legal citation in the UK	Donoghue v Stevenson [1932] AC 562 (HL)
AGLC (Australian Guide to Legal Citation)	Australia	Guide widely adopted in Australian legal contexts	Cole v South Tweed Heads Rugby League Football Clu Ltd (2004) 217 CLR 469
McGill Guide (Canadian Guide to Uniform Legal Citation)	Canada	Cited in Canadian legal writing and courts	R v Smith, [1992] 2 SCR 915
ALWD Citation Manual (Association of Legal	United States	Alternative legal citation system in the U.S.	

Figure 2.7. Citation in law.

Source: https://doitbylaw.com/wp-content/uploads/2024/02/Common-Legal-Citation-Systems-in-Law-1024x683.webp.

For instance, some jurisdictions may emphasize the binding authority of precedents more than others, affecting their approach to citation. This divergence speaks to the broader implications of such practices, including potential challenges in cross-border legal issues and the harmonization of legal standards. To enrich scholarly discourse, researchers must be vigilant in providing comprehensive citations that reflect these complexities, ensuring that their contributions to legal scholarship are both accessible and substantiated. The interplay between citation practices and legal development is further explored in the realm of customary and religious sources which intricately intersect with formal statutes. Engaging with citation practices not only involves the mechanics of referencing but also entails a deeper understanding of the underlying principles that govern the selection of sources. For example, the acceptance of certain doctrines or customary laws in different regions often influences judicial reasoning, necessitating precise citation to avoid ambiguities. Moreover, the role of digital and social media in disseminating legal scholarship cannot be overlooked, as these platforms create new pathways for legal citation. As emphasized in recent literature, such as the collective insights provided by specialists in digital marketing, the breadth and depth of citation practices are evolving in response to technological advancements (Yogesh et al., 2020). Additionally, recognizing the behavioral implications of social media within the legal context offers an opportunity to enhance citation practices, fostering a more comprehensive legal discourse as highlighted by Kapoor et al. (2017).

2.3. CUSTOMARY AND RELIGIOUS SOURCES

A significant aspect of law within various jurisdictions lies in its customary and religious sources, which serve as foundational undercurrents for legal systems across the globe (Figure 2.8).

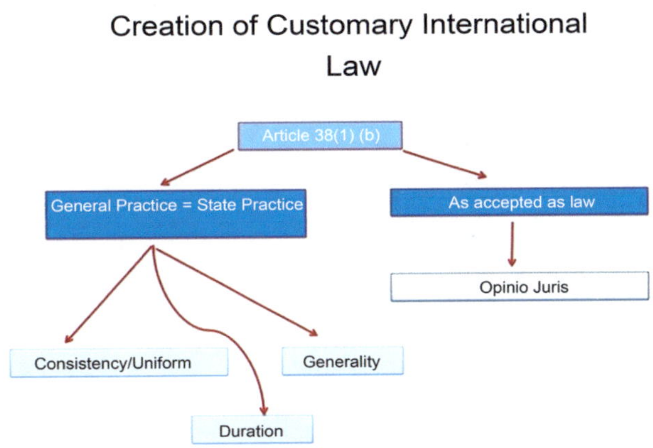

Figure 2.8. Customary law emerges from long-standing traditions and practices of communities, reflecting their social values and norms.

Source: https://ruwanthikagunaratne.wordpress.com/wp-content/uploads/2010/09/slide1.jpg?w=640.

In the majority of regions, these customs gain acknowledgment in court hearings, for they allow better adaptation to local conditions compared to strict statutory laws. Furthermore, religious codes, particularly within the context of Islamic law, have significant power over legal matters such as family, inheritance, and marriage (Khoirunnisa et al., 2025). Interestingly, customary practices can, at times, redefine the application of religious codes in some countries, providing a blend of tradition and God-given precepts. This integration indicates the dynamism of legal institutions and highlights how law evolves through the interaction between the prevailing traditions and divine revelations. The recognition and incorporation by courts of customary and religious sources further enlighten their application in legal adjudication. Courts across various jurisdictions often refer to these sources in informing their judgments, particularly where statutory law is evasive on some points. For instance, according to Islamic family law, Malaysian and Indonesian legislations diverge regarding the application of religious principles in their respective jurisdictions, which are largely based on local culture governed by traditional norms (Khoirunnisa et al., 2025). This context-based application allows one to question the degree to which legally embedded practices impact legal interpretation and outcomes. The recognition of such religious and customary influence by the courts is evidence of a more comprehensive understanding of law as not merely a technical construct but as an entity that must respond to the lived experiences of individuals in societies. The regional inceptions of customary and religious law also bear witness to the different variations of such influence in different settings. For instance, while division of inheritance according to Islamic law normally conforms to the prescribed rules laid out in the Quran, in reality, most societies blend indigenous customs that may deviate from these scriptures. This synthesis of tradition is often a result of a combination of factors like cultural identity as well as lack of religious knowledge among societies. The resulting legal system can be a source of variation in the interpretation and application of religious laws, leading to a unique hybridity of practice reflecting both codified dogma and vernacular customs. Toward that end, an investigation of such regional variation is central to a constructive examination of legal systems, highlighting the role of customary and religious sources as leading actors in the broader narrative of law.

2.3.1. Normative Practices

Of particular importance in exploring legal frameworks that underlie societies is the role of normative practices. Normative practices, such as tradition and custom that regulate behavior within a group, are an informal but effective source of law. These practices often provide the meaning and the application of official law, covering areas where statute books fall short (Figure 2.9).

Comparative analysis suggests that in most jurisdictions, such as Indonesia and the UK, these practices are embraced by courts as necessary to understand the nuances of law. According to Kharisma et al. (2022), the coexistence of statutory regulation and customary norms highlights the dynamic relationship between informal social norms and formal law, which significantly contributes to the topology of justice and legal responsibility in multiculturality. The prevalence of normative practices is particularly pertinent in discussing the way legal systems resolve conflicts and social order. In most societies, such practices not only shape common behavior but also impact judicial decisions in courtrooms. For instance, in countries where customary law is honored, judges often appeal to such normative systems in deciding legal matters to their effect to reflect the local values and societal expectations. This approach fosters legitimacy within the legal process since citizens see their customs identified by virtue of official court processes. Further, as depicted in Kharisma et al. (2022), the efficacy of these normative practices can affect the level to which citizens trust their legal systems, and therefore strengthen or deconstruct social cohesion based on whether the legal process is considered fair.

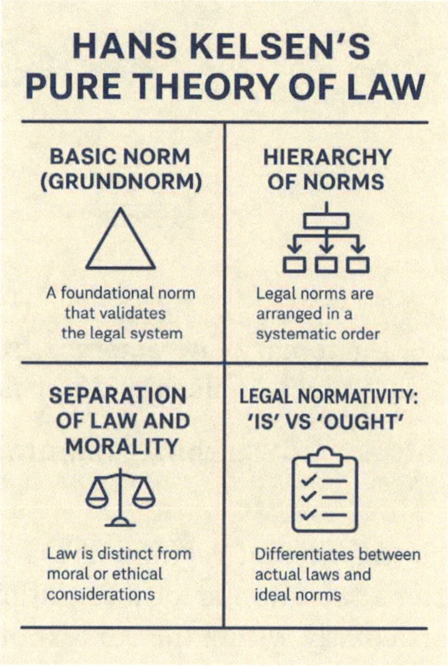

Figure 2.9. Hans Kelsen's pure theory of law.

Source: The Legal QnA.

But the integration of normative practices into law systems can also be contentious. While the practices, while raising the access to justice, at times conflict with statute law or with universal principles of human rights and thereby produce complex legal puzzles. The acknowledgment of these practices varies considerably across jurisdictions, relying on the various environments of culture and history that determine their legal contexts. For instance, when comparing legal systems, it is obvious that some states like Indonesia are faced with the complexity of adopting normative practices in a rapidly developing modernizing legal framework while others naturally incorporate them in the courts to promote social harmony. As explained in, the interaction between customs and formal law not only educates case law but also calls for continuous discourse on the development and flexibility of legal standards in multicultural societies.

2.3.2. Court Recognition

In the world of legal systems, the aspect of court recognition is a crucial intersection at which religious and customary laws merge with formal statutory systems. This recognition is evidence of the judiciary's function of sustaining social norms that may not be enshrined in codified law but are part of the common practices and identities. Courts frequently encounter cases of customary practices that are at odds with prevailing statute provisions, and the courts must strike a fine balance between adherence to settled law and respect for cultural norms. Such tolerance facilitates the dynamism of law, demonstrating that judicial decisions are not merely mechanical applications of legislations but also include an appreciation of the social realities that can influence legal determinations significantly. For instance, courts could validate customary laws over marriage or rights on property, tolerating their extended use among particular communities, thereby enriching the legal environment and promoting concordance between formal and informal legal systems. Besides, the court's validation is more than mere attesting to customs; it is part of the larger argument about rights and equality in diverse legal contexts. Judicial interpretation of customary law can empower marginalized communities since one of the primary ways of ensuring the right of these communities to access justice and preserve their cultural identity is by interpreting their customs. This process can interrupt hegemonic legal discourses, enabling a pluralistic construction of legality encompassing various perspectives. This judicial recognition can then encourage social integration and solidarity, creating an avenue for redressing grievances involving cultural violations and discrimination through the legal system. Courts are therefore placed as central umpires, having to navigate the complex interplay of local tradition and general principles of law, all to the end that jurisprudence is reactive to social complexity. Yet, challenges exist as tension and conflict in judgments are frequently the outcome of interaction between customary law and legislation. The equal protection principle under the law is sometimes at odds with traditional practices that might not conform to modern observations on human rights, especially with regard to gender and minority rights. The judges can be confronted with challenges when customary laws oppose constitutional requirements, prompting them to make hard decisions on applying specific customs. For instance, where in the legal system the traditional practice discriminates against women, the courts are confronted with balancing a respect for tradition and their role to safeguard constitutional rights. Here thus the courts' recognition operates both as a mechanism of legitimation of cultural identity and as a point of crossing for advancing the law reforms in line with evolving social values, bringing out the nuances of complexity of law from comparative law (Minow, 2021; Perju, 2011).

2.3.3. Regional Uses

In the intricate world of law, the role of regional uses could play a critical role in how legal norms are interpreted and implemented in different jurisdictions. These applications are a product of the interaction between customary, statutory, and international sources of law, attesting to the relevance of regional legal tailoring. For instance, the manifestation of law systems in specific regions is likely to be determined by the dominant social norms, history, and cultural practices in the given regions. This regional approach is more likely to give us the sense of how law functions in practice, particularly in multicultural societies where local traditions are likely to conflict with general statutory laws. An evident example of this is the situation in Southeast Asia, where countries like Indonesia are challenged with balancing customary practice against legal provisions, most notably on drug trafficking and law enforcement practices (Hidayatullah et al., 2025). Besides, the dynamic nature of regional application necessitates a robust examination of the engagement between international law and domestic law. Where international treaties are ratified by states, the dualist or monist approaches can delineate the extent to which such laws become effective in domestic jurisdictions. The transnational challenges raised by questions such as nuclear liability and environmental protection similarly highlight the necessity of creating well-integrated legal systems. Various regional treaties, such as those addressed in the context of nuclear energy, indicate the complexity of compliance and liability that nations must manage when implementing international concepts within domestic legislation (Kia et al., 2025). By favoring an integrated framework of legal sources, there is a chance to enhance cooperative mechanisms and ensure consistency between jurisdictions. Local applications transcend harmonization with international treaties; they embrace the ideological and pragmatic constructs of legal pluralism. Prescriptive practices which derive from customary law and religious materials must be recognized and brought into the mainstream legal system so that justice and equity are preserved. The courts then grapple with these contradictions, harmonizing the need to conform to stipulated laws while harmonizing local customs and practices. This tension can create progressive judicial interpretations that are both based on modern values and traditional norms. In culturally vibrant areas of the world with advanced legal traditions, like in the Middle East, the incorporation of Islamic law into codified frameworks creates a special chance for legal growth that is respectful of deeply ingrained legal traditions but responsive to contemporary legal challenges. Lastly, regional applications are necessary mediums for the domestication of international legal norms into local contexts that define every jurisdiction.

2.4. INTERNATIONAL LAW AS DOMESTIC SOURCE

The intricate relationship between international law and domestic legal systems has garnered increasing interest, particularly with respect to the way nations localize international norms within domestic legal systems. Localization often occurs through monist and dualist doctrines, which dictate the degree to which international law converges with domestic legislation. Monist systems, prevalent in the majority of legal orders, view international law inherently part of the domestic order and place treaties and customary international law directly into the domestic legal order on ratification. Dualist systems, on the other hand, require formal legislation in order to incorporate international law. This highlights varying degrees of integration and interpretation, leading to a rich ambience in which the application of international legal principles may vary significantly between states. Moreover, the complexities of treaty incorporation illustrate such dynamics and illustrate that states can assert different levels of commitment to international law based on their national structures.

One aspect of international law as a source of national origin is tensions that might arise when international obligations are inconsistent with national law. Such tensions necessitate judicial interpretation and the formulation of hierarchical norms in legal practice. Where international and domestic law conflict, courts must tread the tightrope between maintaining sovereignty and being loyal to global commitments. Such dilemmas evoke the debate regarding international law's supremacy—partially, courts might favor international undertakings at the expense of conflicting domestic statutes, as if reciting adages written into treaties or customary laws. This exchange not only identifies the actual use of international law in domestic courtrooms but also raises questions about the nature of legal authority and state functions within the international community as a whole. As legal academics move forward to settle these controversies, the effect on state sovereignty and international relations becomes prime issues. In the area of commercial law, the incorporation of international principles of law, like those in the Unidroit Principles of International Commercial Contracts, is illustrative of the applied international norms in national systems. The courts can apply these principles to interpret and fill gaps in domestic law, resulting in higher predictability and consistency in cross-border transactions. Such integration ensures international standards to influence domestic legal interpretation, which serves to assure a coherent regime of international business activity. This perspective is also in line with the proposition that customary international law (CIL), once established, imposes certain obligations upon states, as recently argued in CIL scholarship. The existing controversy regarding the authenticity of withdrawal from CIL further emphasizes the complexity of international law's role as a domestic source and invites continued examination of its impact on state practice and legislative processes, as described in recent legal writings (Bradley et al., 2010) and (Michaels et al., 2009).

2.4.1. Monist and Dualist Doctrines

The interaction between global and national law is best understood in terms of the monist and dualist theories, which outline different paradigms of ratification and domestication of international legal principles. Under monism, international law does not need national legislation to become applicable; it automatically forms part of national law upon ratification. This smooth incorporation fosters a unitary system of law, with the potential for a direct application of international treaties in national court rulings. By contrast, under dualist theory, international law is regarded as distinct from municipal law, with the need for a legislative act to apply it in the national legal framework. This splitting gives rise to significant issues of the superiority and applicability of international law in home states, leading to a highly nuanced debate about how nations respond to their international obligations while maintaining sovereignty and legal autonomy. Both doctrines illustrate divergent strategies in balancing domestic legal systems with international principles, which reveal varying degrees of flexibility. For instance, some monist jurisdictions would place greater premium on the direct applicability of international treaties and thereby establish an environment more conducive to comprehensive human rights protection and stricter observance of international obligations. However, this ideal has its conditions. The dynamic of constitutional pluralism would ensure that there is conflict potential at the border of domestic and foreign laws and that it does not always tend towards a desirable outcome. As explained in later jurisprudence on constitutional conflict, most prominently within the European Union and member states, there are instances where such conflicts lead to destructive rather than progressive legal interpretations, rendering it challenging to reconcile a country's adherence to international obligations and its constitutional standards (Bobi, 2020). Against such a background, the role of national courts is central in the sense that they work within the legal spectrum between the dualist and monist perspectives. Courts are often left to implement international law within the boundaries of domestic legal frameworks through vehicle mechanisms such as canons of interpretation and direct effect. The latter sanctions judges to interpret domestic law in alignment with international obligations while the former sanctions judges to invalidate domestic legislation that contravenes international agreements. The effectiveness of both mechanisms often hangs in the balance with the political climate and the independence of the judiciary, who have to balance adherence to international norms with potential domestic backlash (Lupu et al., 2019). This interdependence serves to underscore the manner in which monist and dualist theories are not theoretical propositions; instead, they carry important consequences for the practice of the judiciary and the very nature of legal sources within their own respective jurisdictions.

2.4.2. Treaty Incorporation

Accomplishing the legal complexities of treaty incorporation entails an appreciation of the intricate interaction between international and domestic legal frameworks. In certain states, the technique of treaty incorporation differs greatly, depending largely on whether a monist or dualist approach is utilized. Monist states, for example, view international law as a part of their legal system and thus require no additional legislative application to allow a treaty to become binding domestically. Conversely, dualist states need to be formalized by national law, evidencing a profound difference in terms of how domestic legal frameworks interface with international obligations. The contrast in practice evidences the complexity involved in reconciliation between domestic law and requirements under international treaties, highlighting the challenges facing countries in their efforts at domestic compliance with international obligations within the framework of their constitutional systems. The U.S. Supreme Court decision in Medellín v. Texas is a milestone case symbolizing the conflict between international and domestic law. The decision of the court emphasized the conflict of using treaties when domestic and international legal principles are not the same. These examples require serious debate regarding the harmony between national and international orders of law, namely how various states balance their adherence to global norms of human rights and their deeply rooted legal orders. There is debate that more fine-grained and particularized understanding of such engagements is required, noting the ways in which they vary in various jurisdictions, namely the reception of global norms of human rights into local law (Bruch et al., 2006). Moreover, the implications of such divergences are great since they bear on a nation's ability to contribute constructively to global governance and have confidence in the practice of treaty obligations and thereby determine the legitimacy of international law as a system. Comparative methodologies show how different legal traditions approach treaty incorporation and expose a variety of approaches that risk reinforcing or undermining the effectiveness of international law. For example, a collection of essays contrasting Australia, Canada, China, and the United Kingdom's practices in the context of international treaties emphasizes their individual methods of integrating international treaties into national legal systems (Telman et al., 2010). The comparative study not only shows differences in mechanisms employed by states but also emphasizes the culture and history behind their legal practices. By taking into account these varied experiences, one can better see the far-reaching implications of treaty incorporation and how these mechanisms influence legitimacy and enforcement of international law within national courts. These dynamics need to be learned so more can be debated about legal systems better being able to absorb international obligations while maintaining domestic constitutional norms.

2.4.3. Conflicts with Domestic Law

Operating through the intricacies of legal systems proves the strong impact of conflicting sources of law on government and sovereignty in states. When international law clashes with domestic legal systems, the unavoidable tension results in a full spectrum of outcomes. In monist doctrine-following states, such as most members of the European Union, international law is by its nature absorbed into domestic law, thereby allowing treaties to prevail over domestic legislation. By contrast, dualist regimes like that of the United States demand overt legislative action to incorporate international agreements into domestic law. The two differing methodologies thus underscore a central dilemma: reconciliation of divergent legal practices and traditions where they intersect, since attempts at the enforcement of international law can raise matters of constitutional supremacy and legislative authority. Such concerns need to be closely examined if one is to understand how the law reacts to balance international commitment and domestic legal principles. Underlying such tensions is, more frequently than not, a conflict over the interpretation of domestic constitutional provisions under international obligations. The judiciary has a dominant role to play here since they resolve controversies emerging from the conflict between domestic law and international accord. The courts must tread a thin line between adhering to constitutional provisions and fulfilling a nation's international obligations. As an example, in comparative environments, judgments by courts can reflect varying degrees of willingness to consider international law, typically based on historical and cultural traditions characteristic of individual legal traditions. Courts may, in some instances, place constitutional norms above conflicting international codes by supporting the sovereignty of domestic law. This dynamics of domestic dominance and devotion to international law provokes legal practitioners and scholars alike to seek avenues towards congruence in legal thought and practice in various jurisdictions, illustrating an existing debate within the discipline of law. Among the leading sources of contention regarding adherence to international obligations is in the field of human rights law, where contradictions between domestic and international law can give rise to contentious legal battles and broad societal implications. The integration of international human rights norms into domestic law can be fraught with complications, particularly when such norms are at variance with prevailing domestic legislation or mainstream cultural practices. This conflict is often apparent in court cases relating to equality and non-discrimination, where the domestic legal provisions may hold long-standing social attitudes which are incompatible with international human rights standards. The law is also often made more complex by the inconsistency with which courts apply these discrepancies, asking urgent questions regarding the function of legal systems to foster justice and equality. The internal contradictions between these legal conflicts highlight the intermeshed character of conflicting sources of law and highlight the necessity of ceaseless scholarship and legal change as states seek to harmonize domestic laws with global obligations and thus to achieve increased compliance with international legal norms (Michelle, 2012; Porta et al., 2008).

2.5. ADMINISTRATIVE REGULATIONS

The complex web of rule in any system of law commonly depends significantly on the structure created by administrative regulations, which provide crucial vessels for the implementation of statutory legislation. Legislative regimes commonly allocate power to certain agencies, enabling the establishment of specific regulations, which handle complicated administrative requirements. This reality is best observed in the context of regulatory schemes that promote specificity and efficiency over the sweeping brushstrokes of legislative texts so that a more responsive legal tool may be had (Figure 2.10).

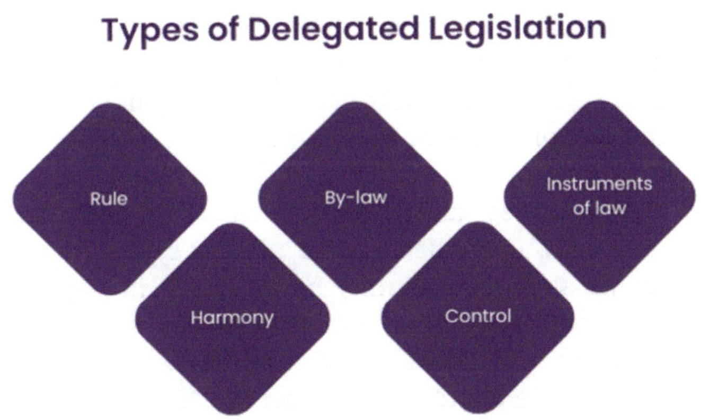

Figure 2.10. Delegated legislation plays a crucial role in this process, as it allows regulatory agencies to fill gaps left by statutes with the technical expertise required to navigate evolving societal needs and technologies.

Source: https://www.theknowledgeacademy.com/_files/images/Types_of_Delegated_Legislation.png.

Consequently, administrative regulations become pivotal in interpreting the intentions of lawmakers while adapting to real-world conditions without necessitating frequent legislative amendments (Welter, 2011). Additionally, the rulemaking procedures underpinning administrative regulations embody a structured yet flexible approach to lawmaking. Typically, these procedures involve multi-stage processes that include drafting, public commentary, and revisions before formal adoption. This participatory dimension enhances transparency and allows stakeholders to voice their concerns, thereby fostering a level of legitimacy in the regulatory environment. Agencies often provide justifications for their regulatory choices, reflecting the underlying rationale and evidence gathered during the process. Such practices also enhance the legal framework by ensuring that regulations are based on informed decision-making and reflect a diversity of interests. The complexities of rulemaking are particularly pertinent when considering the implications of these regulations in a comparative law perspective, as they reveal how different jurisdictions approach regulatory creation and public engagement (Daniel et al., 2009). Beyond their role in shaping policy, administrative regulations are subject to judicial oversight, thus functioning as a check on agency power and ensuring accountability. Courts have the authority to review regulations for compliance with statutory mandates and constitutional principles, scrutinizing whether agencies have overstepped their bounds in exercising delegated authority. Judicial oversight serves not only to protect individual rights but also to uphold the integrity of the regulatory framework, reinforcing the legitimacy of administrative agencies within the broader legal landscape. This relationship between the judiciary and administrative regulations highlights a critical balance between regulatory discretion and the rule of law, a cornerstone of democratic governance. In comparative perspectives, different nations exemplify varied approaches to this oversight, offering valuable insights into the effectiveness and efficiency of administrative law (Welter, 2011; Daniel et al., 2009).

2.5.1. Delegated Legislation

The law system in various jurisdictions comprises a number of levels of administration, which is a living illustration in the scenario of delegated legislation. The judicial process confers power upon legislative assemblies to transfer their authority to administrative bodies, enabling them to make complicated rules and regulations without introducing new legislation. With this process, parliaments can address the complexities of contemporary governance more effectively. Delegated legislation serves to keep the making of laws in line with changing societal needs and in facilitating specialized expertise by means of regulatory bodies. However, this delegation also raises issues regarding accountability and accountability as the efficiency-democratic accountability balance is generally in jeopardy in most legal systems, particularly in regions where the institutional arrangements are inherently fragile, such as illustrated in China's governance debates over its decentralized authoritarian setup (Xu, 2011). In comparing the sources of law, an understanding of the rule of law implications of delegated legislation is essential in consideration of it. Effective governance demands institutions that not only provide accountability in terms of procedural efficiency but also substantive justice.

The tension between enabling legislation and resultant regulatory frameworks created by way of delegated legislation reinforces the requirement for overall guiding principles. How much these delegated powers are held to account can have significant effects on the legitimacy of the regulatory outcomes that they produce. As explored in the accountability literature, the distinction between accountability as a virtue to be admired and accountability as a mechanistic process is a better forceful application of this concept in the context of delegated legislation (Bovens, 2010). Legal systems that embrace such perceptions can establish environments in which regulatory bodies operate effectively and openly. Furthermore, the nexus of the dynamics of delegated legislation can be examined through the lens of international law, which often demands harmonization with domestic legislative frameworks. Such a dynamic poses challenges in jurisdictions experiencing challenges in balancing local needs for regulation and international standards. Delegated legislation therefore shares a double aim: to develop an harmonization mechanism compliant with international obligations while navigating the façade of domestic government. Since, as has been noted in a number of comparative studies, the balancing of the administrative efficacy of rules and the widespread demands of accountability continues to be central to maintaining democratic principles,. To offer a guarantee of judicial examination of delegated legislation makes the rule of law more robust as well as promotes the active involvement of the public with regulatory regimes that impact their lives, making democratic forms of governance systems in various legal settings more robust.

2.5.2. Rulemaking Processes

Handling the machinery of good governance demands a clearly defined comprehension of rulemaking procedures, which constitute a critical subset of administrative rules in legal frameworks. They define how government authorities develop, change, or rescind regulations that have the force of law. It is important that these processes adhere to publicity and participation principles, in the sense that more stakeholders have been involved in rule-making that guides their lives. Procedural legitimacy of such rules has a tendency of influencing their administrative impact. In comparative law, an analysis of how multiple jurisdictions institutionalize rulemaking has the potential to explain governance style differences, participatory citizenship differences, and responsiveness of rules to the requirements of society, perhaps indicative of broader trends of political involvement in a country. Some leading methodologies influence the rulemaking process, by general category formal or informal. Rule transgressions are typically associated with formal rulemaking, with stricter institutional standards in the form of longer public comment periods and lengthy reports, representing accountability and openness. Informal rulemaking provides agencies with enhanced flexibility and discretion, which can accelerate the promulgation of mandated regulations. The differences represent not only the speed of implementing rules but also the extent to which different viewpoints are considered. Thus, analyzing these processes in various comparative contexts provides understanding of how legal cultures perceive participatory government. It also highlights that legitimacy and effectiveness of regulations are contingent upon the frameworks established for their creation and the level of stakeholder involvement in them. The effects of rulemaking extend beyond immediate production of rules and tread on other societal concerns, including the interplay between regulatory efficiency and the rights of the individual. The imposition of innovative models, like the implementation of environmental policy and energy efficiency laws, portrays the complexity of rulemaking processes. For instance, the diffusion of green energy policy globally reflects how responses at the jurisdictional level can significantly differ in promoting technological progress in response to ecological deterioration (Figure 2.11).

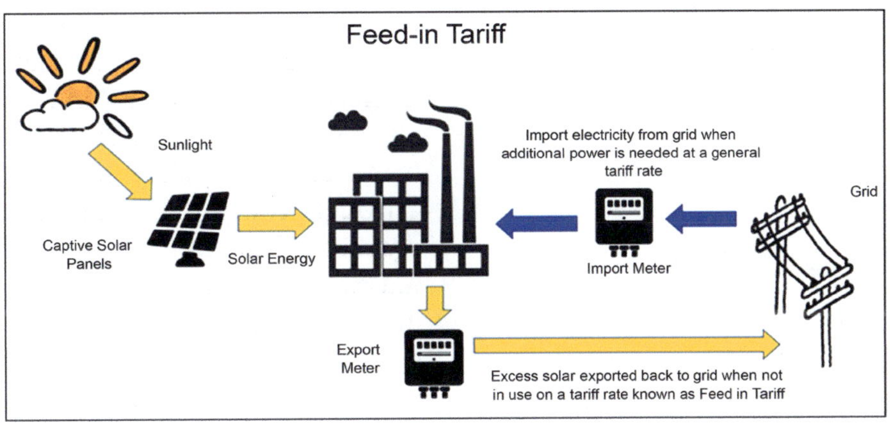

Figure 2.11. Feed-in tariffs.

Source: https://sustent.in/blog/wp-content/uploads/2020/10/image.png.

The successful application of methodologies, such as the application of feed-in tariffs to stimulate the expansion of renewable energy, proves the socio-economic impact of soundly designed rulemaking.

Therefore, through comparative analysis, it is evident that procedures on rulemaking are not merely bureaucratic actions but indispensable tools in shaping public policy and leading to a shift in the practices and conventions of society, as evident in various legal contexts globally (Yogesh et al., 2022; Lu et al., 2020).

2.5.3. Judicial Oversight

Judicial oversight is a critical mechanism in judicial systems, helping to keep the exercise of state power within limits established by legislated law and ethical guidelines. Evaluating the extent to which laws are enforced and complied with, the courts are able to influence legislative choice and administrative action. Oversight is particularly vital in democracies, where balance of power is necessary for holding individuals accountable and protecting human rights. The judiciary's role is even more important in contexts in which statutory order and constitutional primacy are threatened, encapsulating its role in enforcing and interpreting the constitution. This judicial action manifests itself in a variety of types of checks, in which courts can inspect executive action and legislative legislation to safeguard against potential abuses of power, explaining how the exercise of judicial oversight serves to ensure democratic rule and rule of law (N/A, 2022) (Figure 2.12).

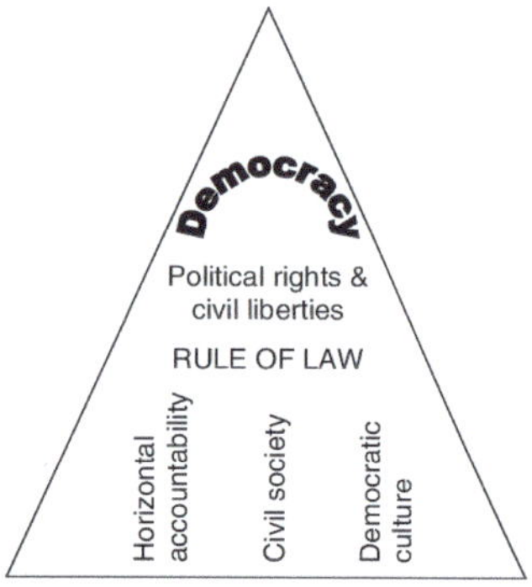

Figure 2.12. Three pillars of the rule of law and democracy.

Comparative studies on judicial oversight indicate varied practices across various countries, especially regarding the extent to which they control government actions, for example, in counterterrorism. For example, whereas the executive may play a controlling role in the United States, other countries, like Israel, grant great supervisory power to the judiciary. This divergence raises issues of accountability and institutional performance, which are examined critically from a functionalist viewpoint. The unique structural position of the judiciary often compels it to engage in the creation of legal standards that regulate and discipline government actions.

Thus, judicial institutions serve not just as legal interpreters but also as important watchdogs that confirm that government utilizes its authority responsibly and in accordance with set legal measures (Gil, 2019). Apart from legal interpretation, the demand for judicial oversight is also required to promote a culture of accountability in government institutions. Where the control is weak or absent, the executive bias was more likely to lead to discretionary choices. This would weaken the rule of justice and fairness that democratic governments are founded upon. Accordingly, legislatures are typically ineffective in becoming influential enough in altering executive decision-making, particularly in sensitive domains like counterterrorism. Through comparative institutional analysis, research has demonstrated that enhanced judicial involvement can decrease instances of unconstitutional behavior by the executive and enhance governance institutions. The inclusion of judicial oversight in legal proceedings not only enhances individual rights but also fortifies the democratic structure in general by making sure that the whole government acts within the set laws and transparent ethical standards (Gil, 2019).

2.6. DOCTRINAL WRITINGS AND LEGAL SCHOLARSHIP

Legal scholarship is extremely wide-ranging, covering a lot of activities that are highly relevant to the comprehension and use of law. Doctrinal literature in this scholarship is a specially significant source that systematically analyzes, criticizes, and interprets law. It is literature developed on the basis of established legal traditions and frames comprehension of legal concepts with contextualization that is enormously valuable for practitioners and scholars. Important as it is, doctrinal books are never sterile; they are inextricably bound up with judicial experience and legislative frameworks, so that there is a living tension between practice and theory. As a result, not only do they report the law as it exists but they also enable practitioners to search for innovations and refinements in legal norms. This is reflective of an essential aspect of the legal environment, noting the value of scholarly contribution towards the continued evolution of legal systems and principles across jurisdictions. The contributions of legal scholars in shaping the law cannot be overstated, as their work is often the basis for judicial reasoning. Through a detailed examination of statutes, case law, and custom, doctrinal scholarship illuminates various interpretative approaches to which judges can appeal. Judicial decision-making in the course of judging is usually guided by the conclusions of such scholarly research, that leads judges in their decisions, while analytic models informing them augment their understanding of relevant legal issues.

Figure 2.13. Domenico Ghirlandaio: St. Jerome in his study St. Jerome in his study, fresco by Domenico Ghirlandaio, 1480; in the church of Ognissanti, Florence.

Source: https://cdn.britannica.com/66/123166-004-87CB3F17/Saint-Jerome-in-His-Study-Domenico-Ghirlandaio.jpg?w=300.

This is particularly so in common law jurisdictions, where case law influences legal interpretation significantly. Therefore, the relationship between judicial decision-making and doctrinal texts becomes a core area of legal scholarship that creates an active discourse that not only clarifies but develops the implementation of law. The two-way relationship ultimately ensures that the law is adaptable and resilient to challenges and demands in society. Institutional acceptance of doctrinal writing further reinforces their position in the wider legal order, making them more applicable in comparative analyses. Legal systems place different values on these academic works, which affects the interpretation of legal norms and how they are applied in legal practice. For example, in some legal jurisdictions, some doctrinal works may be regarded as authoritative, significantly informing legislative reform and judicial decisions. Moreover, the dynamic character of international legal discourse calls for constant research on these writings within comparative frameworks, stressing their function of mediating differences between legal traditions. With interdisciplinary measures, researchers can interact responsibly with the divergent interpretative traditions provoked by differing legal cultures. The collision of national and international forces indicates how writings in doctrine function as ahistorical connectives to use in making law a more rewarding subject to learn and more knowledge between various legal cultures and jurisdictions to maintain their importance in the tapestry of national and international law (N/A, 2018; Taekema, 2018) (Figure 2.13).

2.6.1. Influence on Legal Development

It has been established in most research that judges both in Denmark and England demonstrate a distinguishable perception towards the mass media, which impacts considerably their decision-making roles. A study to evaluate the lower Court theft sentencing practices made it plain that judges in most cases perceived media coverage as biased and uninformed hence perceived it as a low influence on their judicial work. Such views are essential in the context of how outsiders influence legal frameworks because they capture judges confidence and regard towards numerous sources of information. As such, an appreciation of the interplay between judicial views and media influence becomes most meaningful for legal evolution, with this suggesting that informed and sound sources play a positive role in the judicial environment and guide through the intricacies of sentencing guidance in the legal environment (Lowenstein et al., 2010). The classification of legal systems into families, presented in comparative law frameworks, serves to contextualize the various influences on legal development while highlighting specific national characteristics. By examining where Scots law fits within these families, scholars can gauge how distinct legal traditions interact and evolve. Legal systems often share foundational concepts while simultaneously exhibiting divergence as a result of cultural, historical, and sociopolitical factors. This comparative perspective not only underscores the significance of historical context in shaping contemporary legal interpretations but also demonstrates how similar challenges can lead to different legal responses across jurisdictions. As legal systems absorb and modify external influences, they continually redefine the parameters of their normative frameworks, thus illustrating the fluid nature of law and the importance of scholarly discourse in bridging gaps among various legal traditions (Lowenstein et al., 2010). In comprehending the sources of law, the significance of doctrinal writings and legal scholarship is paramount. These sources not only inform judicial reasoning but also contribute to the evolution of legal principles. When scholars engage with pressing legal issues through rigorous analysis, their contributions serve to influence judicial interpretations and legislative developments. The institutional recognition of these writings as authoritative enhances their role within the legal community, highlighting their importance in shaping legal norms. Their influence may manifest in the adoption of new legal doctrines or in the refinement of existing laws, showcasing the ongoing dialogue between academia and the judiciary. Consequently, doctrinal writings are indispensable in understanding the trajectory of legal development, further emphasizing the need for an interdisciplinary approach in addressing complex legal challenges (Farran et al., 2010) (Figure 2.14).

Figure 2.14. The intricate relationship between media reporting and its influence on legal development cannot be overlooked in a comparative legal analysis.

Source: https://blog.ipleaders.in/wp-content/uploads/2021/09/media.png.

2.6.2. Role in Judicial Reasoning

The intricate relationship between judicial reasoning and various sources of law reflects a multidimensional aspect of legal interpretation in comparative legal systems. In examining this relationship, one discovers that judicial decisions often transcend mere statutory interpretation; they consider broader principles and norms that inform legal contexts. In this respect, the role of judicial precedent becomes paramount. Binding authority helps a court reach a consistency in the law by making identical cases have identical results. This practice not only upholds the rule of law but also fosters predictability in a legal context, which contributes to social order and protection of rights. The notion of persuasive value also helps courts draw rationales from other jurisdictions or legal systems to fill the gaps of judicial discourse. It is this sort of mechanism that courts make a contribution to dynamic evolution of legal frameworks, responsive to the environmental changes in the society. With changed judicial reasoning, doctrinal writings and legal scholarship have become influences that shape how the law is interpreted and applied. These scholarly contributions give a foundational understanding of legal principles, methodologies, and doctrines related to judicial decision-making. A critical examination of the doctrinal research methodology reveals its relevance not only to academic discourse but also to practical adjudication. Scholars articulate various methodological approaches, enhancing the clarity with which courts approach complex legal issues. In doing so, they bring forth the argument that judicial reasoning is not simply a mechanical application of law but an interpretive process that requires rigorous analysis and contextual understanding. This complexity has prompted calls for greater transparency in judicial reasoning, echoing sentiments in legal academia that suggest a need for deeper dialogue regarding the place of doctrinal methodologies (Hutchinson et al., 2012). Furthermore, the role of legal scholarship in judicial reasoning is particularly pronounced in systems where comparative perspectives enrich the understanding of laws application across different cultural contexts. Scholars have clarified that the non-level integration of legal sources—both international and local disturbs conventional conceptions of law as a static system. Instead, it has been described as a living organism that interacts with varied sources, including international treaties and customary law. The conversation of judicial reasoning with legal scholarship is essential in mediating possible conflicts between domestic law and international commitments. As courts integrate these perspectives into their decisions, they not only affirm their commitment to legal pluralism but also enhance their legitimacy in the eyes of the public, ultimately fostering a more comprehensive legal framework (Fritz, 2009).

2.6.3. Institutional Recognition

When examining the sources of law through a comparative lens, the concept of institutional recognition becomes increasingly significant. This recognition extends beyond the mere formal acknowledgment of laws and regulations; it encapsulates the legitimacy bestowed upon various legal frameworks by the institutions that uphold them. As legal systems evolve, the recognition of legal sources—ranging from statutory law to customary norms—plays a crucial role in their acceptance within society. For instance, the intermingling of international law with domestic legal systems is particularly illustrative of how institutions may develop hybrid systems that reflect the existence of more than one legal tradition. This blending is important to help realize how different states perceive the introduction of external legal norms into their domestic legal practice, thereby framing a more integrated legal environment that accommodates differences in sources of law. An essential aspect of institutional recognition is its impact on minority rights and the historical context of legal protections. Diverse political systems exhibit varying degrees of responsiveness to minority rights, often influenced by the legacy of colonial practices and their institutional arrangements. For example, posits that the politicization of ethnic entities during colonial governance establishes prolonged institutional legacies affecting minority rights post-independence. This balanced understanding of institutional recognition clarifies how modern legal systems are conditioned by historical processes and the different institutional approaches to ethnicity in given political settings. Thus, the recognition or denigration of minority rights can significantly alter the legal environment and impact the sustainability of democracy. As nations pursue more inclusive forms of law, the historical foundation of their law will inform their current policies and legal reforms. Building on the argument about institutional acknowledgment, the part played by scholarly work in informing legal evolution cannot be downplayed. Legal scholarship acts as a central source of inspiration, guiding not only judicial argumentation but also bolstering prevailing institutional structures. As attested by Morgera et al. (2014), interdisciplinarity in interpreting legal concepts—such as benefit-sharing—smacks out the necessity to acknowledge work from law, sociology, and political science. These insights demonstrate how institutional recognition is not merely a static endorsement of legal statutes but involves an ongoing dialogue between scholars, practitioners, and the institutions themselves. By fostering a culture of recognition among legal scholars and practitioners, jurisdictions can ensure a dynamic legal environment that adapts and responds to changing societal needs while adhering to foundational principles of justice and equity.

SUMMARY

In the analysis of the fundamental aspects of law across numerous jurisdictions, supremacy of the constitution is prominently embodied as a basic principle. Steadily, the constitution is understood as the supreme law in every legal system, outlining a framework through which the statutory laws are formulated and interpreted. Different countries have different legislative processes, through which the intended statutes are devised, debated, and enacted. The hierarchies of statutory laws further complicate this structure, where specific laws may either supersede or be subordinate to others based on their perceived authority or the context of their creation. Such dynamics explain that although all legal systems are based on a constitution, the extent of legislative power and how law is produced can differ widely between jurisdictions, thereby requiring a comparison of these sources of law to fully comprehend their specific features and implementations in practice. Judicial precedent, or case law, plays a critical role in shaping the application of statutes and guiding future legal interpretations. Binding authority holds significant weight in legal proceedings, as precedents set by higher courts dictate the outcomes in lower courts, thereby ensuring a degree of uniformity in the application of the law. Conversely, persuasive value gained from rulings in jurisdictions which are not obligatory can impact judicial reasoning, enhancing legal discourse. Citation practices also reinforce the significance of case law, as judges and attorneys draw on previous decisions to support arguments and enhance comprehension of convoluted legal principles. Thus, a close analysis of case law and judicial precedents in the context of statutory and constitutional law indicates a sharp interplay in which traditional rules are placed alongside changing legal development across various jurisdictions. Even customary and religious sources of law have significantly played a part to enhance the legal frontier found in several realms. Normative practices often reflect deeply rooted traditions or beliefs that have become integral to the legal frameworks of certain societies. Courts may recognize these customary laws, provided they align with the overarching principles of justice and equity as established by the constitution or statutory laws. Regional applications of customary law further illustrate the complexity of legal systems, where local traditions can coexist with national legislation, leading to diverse legal interpretations. This interplay accentuates the significance of understanding how cultural contexts influence the legitimacy and enforcement of laws. As such, a comprehensive comparative perspective necessitates thorough research into these customary and religious sources, highlighting their relevance in contemporary legal systems.

A LOOK TO THE FUTURE

EVOLVING SOURCES OF LAW IN COMPARATIVE LEGAL SCHOLARSHIP

Engaging with the future of comparative law scholarship involves grappling with the changing landscape of legal sources as world dynamics shift. Comparative law has historically utilized static categories like constitutional, statutory, and customary sources; yet the rapid pace of globalization calls for an update of these categories. Scholars are already venturing to introduce new approaches that include transnational legal influences, thereby broadening the conventional limits of what is considered law. The emergence of international law librarianship, for instance, exemplifies this trend by promoting a shared professional knowledge among legal researchers that transcends nationalistic borders. By fostering collaboration among law librarians, comparative law studies can respond more effectively to the diverse information needs of contemporary legal practitioners, as articulated in the notion of a communal commitment to ensure free and open access to legal resources globally (Danner et al., 2011). Within this context, an important aspect of future directions in comparative law studies is the increasing role of judicial precedents as dynamic sources of law. The examination of how different jurisdictions interpret and apply precedents reveals crucial insights into their legal systems. For example, understanding the mechanisms by which the US Supreme Court and the French Cour de cassation navigate precedent can illuminate the complexities of judicial lawmaking. These jurisdictions provide possible templates for other systems of law hoping to integrate judicial decision-making with constitutional principles. In addition, this comparative assessment highlights the importance of an overarching framework to fill gaps regarding how the European Court of Justice handles legal precedents, an issue that is still very much open to further research (Komárek et al., 2011). Framing a unitary vision of these matters will better improve the legitimacy and effectiveness of law throughout various jurisdictions. As comparative law studies move forward, scholars must also consider the impact of interdisciplinary approaches in shaping legal frameworks and doctrines. Incorporating perspectives from sociology, economics, and political science can enrich the analysis of legal sources, enabling a more holistic grasp of their implications on society. This interdisciplinary lens can aid in understanding how various sources of law, whether derived from tradition or evolving social norms, impact legal outcomes and societal well-being. Additionally, recognizing the interplay between customary norms and statutory law in different jurisdictions can provide valuable insights into the inherent adaptability of legal systems. Such explorations warrant significant attention as they can lead to innovative legal reforms that reflect contemporary needs while maintaining essential cultural values. Through this multifaceted examination of legal sources and their interconnections, comparative law studies can position itself at the forefront of understanding the diverse global legal landscape.

REFERENCES

1. Alford, R. P. (2008). Lower courts and constitutional comparativist. https://core.ac.uk/download/144223991.pdf (accessed on 9th September 2025).
2. Bature, M. M., & Sulong, J. (2024). Inheritance distribution among Muslims: A comparative analysis on the practice of some Muslim countries. *International Journal of Academic Research in Business and Social Sciences*. https://www.semanticscholar.org/paper/07e284817caed9d32fcedb14587c5012b60b6ed1 (accessed on 9th September 2025).
3. Berg, G., Ekerfelt, C., Ernerudh, J., et al. (2011). Reconsidering res judicata: A comparative perspective. https://core.ac.uk/download/62547252.pdf (accessed on 9th September 2025).
4. Bobić, A. (2020). Constructive versus destructive conflict: Taking stock of the recent constitutional jurisprudence in the EU. *Cambridge Yearbook of European Legal Studies, 22*, 60–84. https://doi.org/10.1017/cel.2020.9 (accessed on 9th September 2025).
5. Bovens, M. (2010). Two concepts of accountability: Accountability as a virtue and as a mechanism. *West European Politics, 33*, 946–967. https://doi.org/10.1080/01402382.2010.486119 (accessed on 9th September 2025).
6. Bradley, C. A., & Gulati, M. (2010). Customary international law and withdrawal rights in an age of treaties. https://core.ac.uk/download/62547263.pdf (accessed on 9th September 2025).
7. Bruch, E. M. (2006). Whose law is it anyway? The cultural legitimacy of international human rights in the United States. https://core.ac.uk/download/144549144.pdf (accessed on 9th September 2025).
8. Ciolli, I. (2015). The constitutional consequences of financial crisis and the use of emergency powers: Flexibility and emergency sources. https://core.ac.uk/download/54520034.pdf (accessed on 9th September 2025).
9. Comparative international law. (2018). Oxford University Press eBooks. https://doi.org/10.1093/oso/9780190697570.001.0001 (accessed on 9th September 2025).
10. Danner, R. A. (2011). Defining international law librarianship in an age of multiplicity, knowledge, and open access to law. https://core.ac.uk/download/62563842.pdf (accessed on 9th September 2025).
11. de Saussure, F. (2017). *Course in General Linguistics*. Macat Library eBooks. https://doi.org/10.4324/9781912281732 (accessed on 9th September 2025).
12. Dwivedi, Y. K., Hughes, L., Baabdullah, A. M., Ribeiro-Navarrete, S., Giannakis, M., Al-Debei, M. M., Dennehy, D., et al. (2022). Metaverse beyond the hype: Multidisciplinary perspectives on emerging challenges, opportunities, and agenda for research, practice and policy. *International Journal of Information Management, 66*, 102542–102542. https://doi.org/10.1016/j.ijinfomgt.2022.102542 (accessed on 9th September 2025).
13. Dwivedi, Y. K., Ismagilova, E., Hughes, D. L., Carlson, J., Filieri, R., Jacobson, J., Jain, V., et al. (2020). Setting the future of digital and social media marketing research: Perspectives and research propositions. *International Journal of Information Management, 59*, 102168–102168. https://doi.org/10.1016/j.ijinfomgt.2020.102168 (accessed on 9th September 2025).
14. Farran, S. (2010). Scots law: A system in search of a family? https://core.ac.uk/download/4150086.pdf (accessed on 9th September 2025).

15. Galdia, M. (2017). *Legal Russian in Legal-Linguistic Research.* https://core.ac.uk/download/154437474.pdf (accessed on 9th September 2025).

16. Gentili, G. (2012). *A Comparison of European Systems of Direct Access to Constitutional Judges: Exploring Advantages for the Italian Constitutional Court.* https://core.ac.uk/download/30613662.pdf (accessed on 9th September 2025).

17. Gil, E. (2019). Institutional choice and targeted killing: A comparative perspective. *SSRN Electronic Journal.* https://doi.org/10.2139/ssrn.3478525 (accessed on 9th September 2025).

18. Gil, E. D. (2020). *Institutional Choice and Targeted Killing: A Comparative Perspective.* https://core.ac.uk/download/287917930.pdf (accessed on 9th September 2025).

19. Griffith, K. L. (2014). *When Federal Immigration Exclusion Meets Subfederal Workplace Inclusion: A Forensic Approach to Legislative History.* https://core.ac.uk/download/33615399.pdf (accessed on 9th September 2025).

20. Grimmel, A. (2025). *Politics in robes? The European Court of Justice and the myth of judicial activism.* https://core.ac.uk/download/pdf/6613843.pdf (accessed on 9th September 2025).

21. Hidayatullah, S., Supriyadi, A., Purwanto, I. E. D., Aritonang, S., & Saleh, B. R. (2025). Strategic leadership model in regional cooperation to improve the effectiveness of resolving drug delivery routes in Indonesia. *Ilomata International Journal of Social Science.* https://www.semanticscholar.org/paper/fb834c8d150da25034c4c7370f416bba38b84cef (accessed on 9th September 2025).

22. Hutchinson, T., & Duncan, N. (2012). Defining and describing what we do: Doctrinal legal research. *Deakin Law Review, 17,* 83–83. https://doi.org/10.21153/dlr2012vol17no1art70 (accessed on 9th September 2025).

23. Jackson, J., Bradford, B., Hough, M., Myhill, A., Quinton, P., & Tyler, T. R. (2012). Why do people comply with the law? Legitimacy and the influence of legal institutions. *The British Journal of Criminology, 52,* 1051–1071. https://doi.org/10.1093/bjc/azs032 (accessed on 9th September 2025).

24. Jansen, N., & Michaels, R. (2008). *Introduction: Beyond the State? Rethinking Private Law.* https://core.ac.uk/download/62563157.pdf (accessed on 9th September 2025).

25. Kagame, A., et al. (2015). Reframing Kurtz's painting: Colonial legacies and minority rights in ethnically divided societies. https://core.ac.uk/download/62567472.pdf (accessed on 9th September 2025).

26. Kapoor, K. K., Tamilmani, K., Rana, N. P., Patil, P. P., Dwivedi, Y. K., & Nerur, S. (2017). Advances in social media research: Past, present and future. *Information Systems Frontiers, 20,* 531–558. https://doi.org/10.1007/s10796-017-9810-y (accessed on 9th September 2025).

27. Kaufmann, D. E., Kraay, A., & Mastruzzi, M. (2009). *Governance Matters VIII: Aggregate and Individual Governance Indicators 1996–2008.* World Bank Policy Research Working Paper. https://doi.org/10.1596/1813-9450-4978 (accessed on 9th September 2025).

28. Kharisma, D. B., & Hunaifa, A. (2022). Comparative study of disgorgement and disgorgement fund regulations in Indonesia, the USA and the UK. *Journal of Financial Crime, 30,* 635–649. https://doi.org/10.1108/jfc-01-2022-0022 (accessed on 9th September 2025).

29. Khoirunnisa, A., Dewi, R. A., Siahaan, F. Z., Samra, S., & Amri, A. (2025). Comparison of Islamic family law in Malaysia and Indonesia. *An-Nisa: Journal of Islamic Family Law.* https://www.

semanticscholar.org/paper/23cc241a1101f8025c784c325e54fa413f412e11 (accessed on 9th September 2025).

30. Kia, B., Pishrobat, S. R., & Musazadeh, M. (2025). Analysis of principles of nuclear damage compensation in international conventions and customary law. *Interdisciplinary Studies in Society, Law, and Politics*. https://www.semanticscholar.org/paper/53d53535f6a7eb1849a4a6d218dee9cbe352c45a (accessed on 9th September 2025).

31. Klein, S. (2021). Democracy requires organized collective power. *Journal of Political Philosophy, 30*, 26–47. https://doi.org/10.1111/jopp.12249 (accessed on 9th September 2025).

32. Komárek, J. (2011). *Judicial Lawmaking and Precedent in Supreme Courts*. https://core.ac.uk/download/220905.pdf (accessed on 9th September 2025).

33. La Porta, R., López-de-Silanes, F., & Shleifer, A. (2008). The economic consequences of legal origins. *Journal of Economic Literature, 46*, 285–332. https://doi.org/10.1257/jel.46.2.285 (accessed on 9th September 2025).

34. Lau, H., & Li, H. (2017). *American Equal Protection and Global Convergence*. https://core.ac.uk/download/144232668.pdf (accessed on 9th September 2025).

35. Lowenstein, M. (2010). *An Irrelevant Media When Sentencing? –Comparing the Perceptions of English and Danish Lower Court Judges When Sentencing Theft Offenders*. https://core.ac.uk/download/12681431.pdf (accessed on 9th September 2025).

36. Lu, Y., Khan, Z. A., Alvarez-Alvarado, M. S., Zhang, Y., Huang, Z., & Imran, M. (2020). A critical review of sustainable energy policies for the promotion of renewable energy sources. *Sustainability, 12*, 5078–5078. https://doi.org/10.3390/su12125078 (accessed on 9th September 2025).

37. Lukács, K. (2022). *The System of Sources of Law*. https://core.ac.uk/download/541086878.pdf (accessed on 9th September 2025).

38. Lupu, Y., Verdier, P. H., & Versteeg, M. (2019). The strength of weak review: National courts, interpretive canons, and human rights treaties. *International Studies Quarterly, 63*, 507–520. https://doi.org/10.1093/isq/sqz026 (accessed on 9th September 2025).

39. McKinley, M. A. (2012). Till death do us part: Testamentary manumission in seventeenth-century Lima, Peru. *Slavery and Abolition, 33*, 381–401. https://doi.org/10.1080/0144039x.2012.668302 (accessed on 9th September 2025).

40. Michaels, R. (2009). Preamble I: Purposes, legal nature, and scope of the PICC; Applicability by courts; Use of the PICC for the purpose of interpretation and supplementation and as a model. https://core.ac.uk/download/62563437.pdf (accessed on 9th September 2025).

41. Michaels, R. (2009). The second wave of comparative law and economics? https://core.ac.uk/download/62563265.pdf (accessed on 9th September 2025).

42. Minow, M. (2021). Equality vs. equity. *American Journal of Law and Equality, 1*, 167–193. https://doi.org/10.1162/ajle_a_00019 (accessed on 9th September 2025).

43. Morgera, E., & Parks, L. (2014). An inter-disciplinary methodology for researching benefit-sharing as a norm diffusing in global environmental law. https://core.ac.uk/download/29176504.pdf (accessed on 9th September 2025).

44. Nesterenko, P. (2012). Some issues concerning application of the practice of the European Court of Human Rights in Ukraine. *European Integration Studies*. https://www.semanticscholar.org/

paper/648356891e203dd42080b84e68e298a0458ad1ef (accessed on 9th September 2025).

45. OECD. (2022). *Building Trust and Reinforcing Democracy*. OECD Public Governance Reviews. https://doi.org/10.1787/76972a4a-en (accessed on 9th September 2025).

46. Perju, V. (2011). Impairment, discrimination, and the legal construction of disability in the European Union and the United States. *Cornell International Law Journal, 44*, 279–348.

47. Riadi, M. E. (2013). Kedudukan fatwa ditinjau dari hukum Islam dan hukum positif (analisis yuridis normatif). *Ulumuddin Journal of Islamic Legal Studies, 7*. https://doi.org/10.22219/ulumuddin.v7i1.1305 (accessed on 9th September 2025).

48. Sartor, G., Walton, D., Macagno, F., & Rotolo, A. (2014). *Argumentation Schemes for Statutory Interpretation: A Logical Analysis*. https://www.semanticscholar.org/paper/f89ee78c9f02c401f548904c634e9763133516ca (accessed on 9th September 2025).

49. Scharpf, F. W. (2009). The asymmetry of European integration, or why the EU cannot be a 'social market economy'. *Socio-Economic Review, 8*, 211–250. https://doi.org/10.1093/ser/mwp031 (accessed on 9th September 2025).

50. Sitzia, A., & Viglione, F. (2016). Comparative law and the process of de-juridification: The joint-employment law case in labor law. https://core.ac.uk/download/53525866.pdf (accessed on 9th September 2025).

51. Song, Z., Storesletten, K., & Zilibotti, F. (2011). Growing like China. *American Economic Review, 101*, 196–233. https://doi.org/10.1257/aer.101.1.196 (accessed on 9th September 2025).

52. Taekema, S. (2018). Theoretical and normative frameworks for legal research: Putting theory into practice. *Law and Method*. https://doi.org/10.5553/rem/.000031 (accessed on 9th September 2025).

53. Telman, D. A. J. (2010). Plural vision: International law seen through the varied lenses of domestic implementation. https://core.ac.uk/download/144548623.pdf (accessed on 9th September 2025).

54. Terry, L. S. (2014). Putting the legal profession's monopoly on the practice of law in a global context. https://core.ac.uk/download/144230203.pdf (accessed on 9th September 2025).

55. Twining, W. (2009). Normative and legal pluralism: A global perspective. https://core.ac.uk/download/62571364.pdf (accessed on 9th September 2025).

56. van Waarden, F. (2025). *Markets Institutions as Communicating Vessels: Deregulation and Changes Between Economic Coordination Principles*. https://core.ac.uk/download/pdf/6538411.pdf (accessed on 9th September 2025).

57. Welter, F. (2011). Contextualizing entrepreneurship—Conceptual challenges and ways forward. *Entrepreneurship Theory and Practice, 35*, 165–184. https://doi.org/10.1111/j.1540-6520.2010.00427.x (accessed on 9th September 2025).

58. Xu, C. (2011). The fundamental institutions of China's reforms and development. *Journal of Economic Literature, 49*, 1076–1151. https://doi.org/10.1257/jel.49.4.1076 (accessed on 9th September 2025).

Chapter

3

CONSTITUTIONAL STRUCTURES AND COMPARATIVE GOVERNANCE

Contents

INTRODUCTION

Constitutional government analysis reveals a complex landscape shaped by political, cultural, and historical factors. Every nation supports various forms of government—primarily presidential, parliamentary, or semi-presidential—that accommodate its unique political landscape. For example, the presidential model will emphasize a directly elected powerful executive, while parliamentary systems will distribute power more evenly between legislature and executive, yielding a different sort of accountability and cooperation. In addition, semi-presidential hybrids are attempting to balance these characteristics, with regime complexity which can affect policy-making and political stability. These are distinctions that are necessary to note, as they are the building blocks that define the arrangement of power, authority, and responsibility in various nations, highlighting different paths of democratic government and development. In understanding the primary role of separation of powers in constitutions, one needs to note the discrete entity of authority delegated to legislative, executive, and judicial branches. Legislative authority brings with it the power to pass and amend laws, articulating the will of the people. Simultaneously, executive autonomy allows presidents and prime ministers to implement policies effectively, if frequently in conflict with legislative will. There is a delicate balance between the two that avoids abuse of power and sustains democratic values. Furthermore, judicial independence ensures that the judiciary may enforce constitutional provisions and protect human rights without obstruction. Analysis of these dynamics reveals how variations in the separation of powers can have a significant impact on governance outcomes and democratic norms' observance across different jurisdictions. The procedural sophistication of constitutional review mechanisms also explains disparate governance practices globally. Judicial review mechanisms, whether they are entrusted to a constitutional court or applied by regular courts, are valuable institutions for interpreting laws and establishing constitutional validity. It is a required role in the maintenance of the rule of law and ensuring government actions are brought into conformity with constitutional provisions. Likewise, the level of review offered by different nations can enable or suppress judicial monitoring of governance matters. Thus, these review mechanisms must be attuned to the given political and social contexts of each country, both inheriting the strengths and vulnerabilities intrinsic in their constitutional frameworks. Close look at these systems reveals that while some nations develop good systems of constitutional review, others might be plagued by weaknesses hindering accountability and protection of basic rights, as one can see in local examples like Chinas, whose institutional designs are really very different from those in more democratic regimes (Xu, 2011). Moreover, emergent ideas such as collaborative innovation reflect the significance of multifactor methods in enhancing governance, and hence there has been a rethinking of traditional methods in the establishment of democratic practice (Eva Sørensen et al., 2011).

3.1. FORMS OF GOVERNMENT

In government analysis, systems classification is both sensitive and nuanced since it lays bare the innermost dynamics of power distribution in a state. Presidential systems, in which there exists a strong head of executive who is voted into office via an election, are the quintessential example of a category in which the executive branch is separate from the legislature. This arrangement allows for a clear delineation of responsibilities, theoretically enabling efficient governance and direct accountability to the electorate. However, such separation can lead to political gridlock, particularly when legislative support is lacking. Comparative research demonstrates that nations employing presidential systems are likely to be confronted with certain problems, from greater propensity for executive aggression to lower cooperative policymaking, that could further influence political culture and the efficacy of administration in such nations (David, 2015).

Figure 3.1. Shows forms of government.

In contrast, parliamentary systems show closer cooperation between the legislature and the executive and typically result in greater governmental stability and responsiveness. In this structure, the head of government, usually a prime minister, is selected from the legislative assembly, thus developing a fusion of powers. This dependence sometimes leads to more harmonious legislative processes and quicker access to popular sentiment. The danger of quick change in power, for example, government collapse and elections, characterizes a liability in this arrangement. This volatility is likely to impede long-term policy planning, particularly in times of extreme socio-economic upheavals. This element is indicative of the need for a sensitive balance of power and collaboration, necessitating institutional environments that are conducive to both stability and adaptability within governance systems (Khaunya et al., 2015). Semi-presidential hybrids also mirror the sophistication of models of governance by combining elements of both the presidential and the parliamentary model. Such a system unites a single set of powers in a unique manner, typically with a president having a prime minister to accompany him with a mandate to oversee routine matters. Such hybrids attempt to amalgamate the best from both and balance their respective disadvantages. For example, they are able to enhance democratic accountability in the form of checks on executive power through the system of dual leadership. Yet, it is always possible there might be tension and misunderstanding as to roles, and thus efficiency in making governance is always tough. When such complexities are handled by stakeholders, the efficiency of hybrid models most often depends greatly on their corresponding constitutional design and the political environment in which they operate, highlighting the role of tailor-made solutions within constitutional structures (David, 2015; Khaunya et al., 2015) (Figure 3.1).

3.1.1. Characteristics of Presidential Systems

The dynamics within presidential systems exhibit distinct characteristics that define their structure and operation, fundamentally contrasting with other governance forms such as parliamentary models. A hallmark of presidential systems is the establishment of a clear separation of powers among the executive, legislative, and judicial branches. This separation not only helps to prevent the concentration of power but also fosters a system of checks and balances that can lead to greater accountability within the government. The president, elected independently of the legislature, wields significant executive authority and is tasked with implementing laws and policy decisions. This relationship precludes the legislative assembly from directly controlling the presidency, thus allowing for a distinct executive agenda that can sometimes operate independently of legislative will. Such autonomy can lead to dynamic governance, yet it may also cultivate tensions between branches, particularly when partisan divisions arise, highlighting the delicate balance of power essential to effective governance. The interaction between executive autonomy and legislative authority often presents both opportunities and challenges within presidential systems. While the president can initiate policies without legislative approval, the necessity of obtaining legislative support for budgetary matters and significant reforms can strain presidential efficacy. The potential for gridlock becomes evident when Congress and the presidency are controlled by opposing parties, leading to prolonged stalemates on key legislative issues. This scenario raises questions about the effectiveness of government operations and the ability to respond to urgent social and economic needs. Furthermore, the nature of election cycles adds another layer of complexity; a president may focus on shorter-term goals to secure re-election, thereby potentially compromising long-term national interests. As observed in comparative governance studies, such as those utilizing qualitative analysis from varying constitutional contexts, these dynamics underscore the intricate interplay between executive power and legislative processes. In addition to the separation of powers and the interplay between the branches, the role of judicial independence in presidential systems is a vital characteristic that influences overall governance. An independent judiciary serves as a guardian of constitutional principles, affirming the rule of law and ensuring that the rights of individuals are upheld against potential governmental overreach. In presidential systems, where the executive may sometimes attempt to exert influence over judicial appointments or rulings, the robustness of the judiciary becomes crucial in safeguarding democratic processes. As noted in comparative studies of constitutional law, such as those examining the experiences of India and Indonesia, the ability of the judiciary to operate free from executive interference directly correlates with the effectiveness of governance and the promotion of human rights. Thus, judicial independence not only complements the separation of powers but also acts as a stabilizing force in the governance framework of presidential systems, ensuring that the principles of justice and equity are maintained (Figure 3.2).

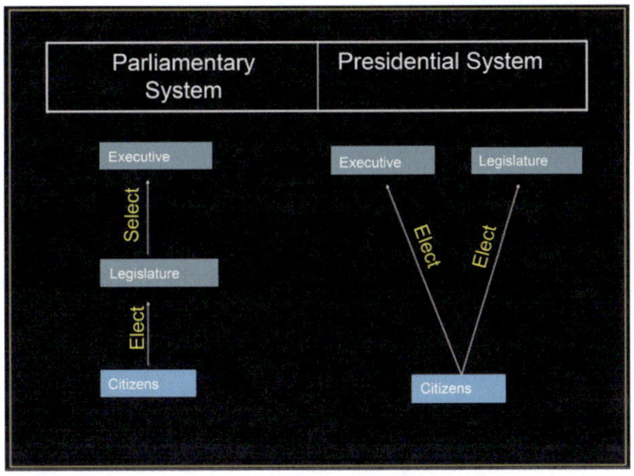

Figure 3.2. Shows presidential systems of Government.

Source: https://qph.cf2.quoracdn.net/main-qimg-bf45515ffcceb5c2b2b973586dd2be01-lq.

3.1.2. Features of Parliamentary Models

In examining the intricate landscape of governance, parliamentary models present distinct operational characteristics that set them apart from other forms of government. Central to these models is the fusion of executive and legislative functions, allowing for greater collaboration and efficiency in policymaking. The Prime Minister, often the leader of the majority party in the legislature, is directly accountable to the parliament, thus fostering a system where the executive's survival depends on legislative support. This relationship creates a dynamic environment conducive to rapid legislative action, as seen in multiple parliamentary democracies where coalitions may form to navigate political plurality. However, this close interdependence also poses risks of fragility, particularly in coalition governments, where divergent party interests may create instability, undermining governance effectiveness and leading to potential crises of confidence among citizens (Jordan et al., 2010). Another notable aspect of parliamentary models is the principle of collective responsibility, where the Cabinet must collectively engage in decision-making and subsequently take responsibility for the government's actions as a whole. This notion reinforces the idea that no single minister is solely accountable for the success or failure of policies; rather, responsibility is shared, promoting a unified front that can enhance public confidence in government decisions. However, this collective accountability contrasts with the more individualized accountability found in presidential systems, where leaders often emphasize personal leadership over group consensus. Additionally, the fluidity of party alignments within parliamentary systems can encourage pragmatic governance, as parties may collaborate to achieve legislative goals even across ideological divides (Jordan et al., 2010). Over time, this can lead to more inclusive decision-making processes but also complicate the electorate's ability to hold specific parties accountable for their governance choices (Figure 3.3). Party system power is particularly robust in parliamentary systems, as party organization and political party processes play a significant role in shaping the types of governance that are yielded. Cartel party development, which relies on the use of state resources to consolidate and crush competition, is a characteristic party organization and political competition trend for these systems (Richard et al., 2009).

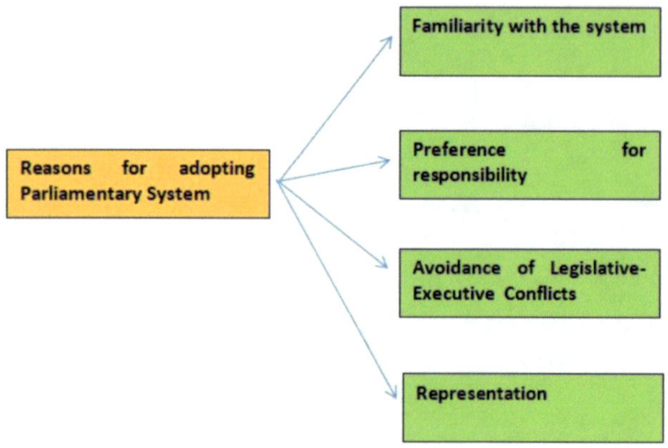

Figure 3.3. Features of parliamentary models.

Source: https://pwonlyias.com/wp-content/uploads/2024/09/unnamed-33.webp.

These forces can lead to a scenario where entrenched parties become the focal point in the political arena, with the possibility of marginalizing entrants and constraining democratic diversity. Given that parties are more inclined to pursue survivability than ideological loyalty, issues regarding voter engagement and policy responsiveness become significant research areas in comparative government. Exploring these trends offers a perspective into the complexities of parliamentary types, indicating the interaction between party politics, government stability, and the necessity for responsive political organization in addressing challenges of modern democracy.

3.1.3. Overview of Semi-Presidential Hybrids

In the study of complexities within governmental forms, semi-presidential hybrids emerge as a special subcategory that is a hybrid of both presidential and parliamentary forms. Such a model has gained popularity in many countries, reflecting varying political contexts and aspirations for effective governance. In semi-presidentialism, the executive is divided between a president and a prime minister and tends to generate a double executive system that can either reinforce and complicate the administration. The president normally has extensive powers like foreign policy and certain domestic policies, while the prime minister handles issues of day-to-day administration. Such a configuration can permit an equilibrium of power that moderates the worst aspects of either authoritarian and Highly fragmented rule, and thus the necessity of understanding the hybrid character of such regimes within the broader context of comparative governance scholarship (Figure 3.4).

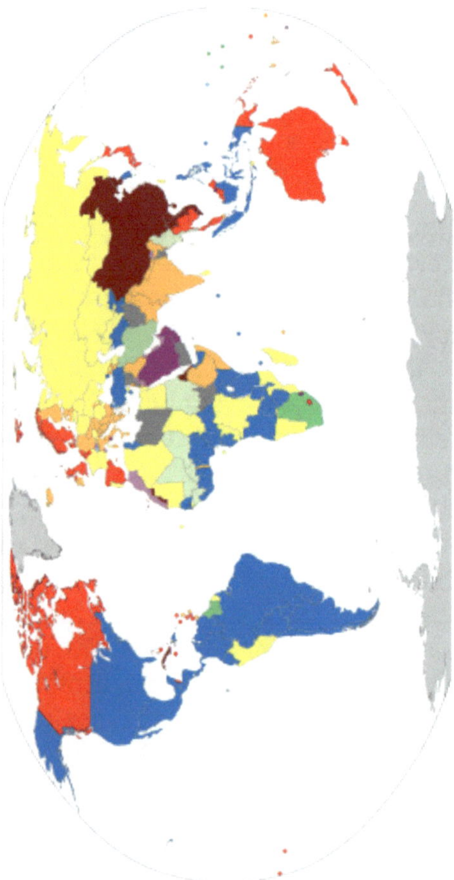

Figure 3.4. Yellow colour shows Semi-presidential republic: Executive president is independent of the legislature; head of government is appointed by the president and is accountable to the legislature.

Source: https://en.wikipedia.org/wiki/Semi-presidential_republic.

Examining how semi-presidential hybrids work means paying close attention to the interplay between legislative power and executive autonomy. In these types of systems, power sharing is an important determinant of political stability as well as efficient government performance. Having a president and a prime minister can be at odds or complementary when it comes to legislative initiative and policymaking. For example, leading academics have made the argument that having a powerful president can dominate the premiership, creating a risk of an imbalance in government where presidential power is wielded without adequate checks from parliament. This dynamic relationship gives rise to the need for robust constitutional frameworks to guarantee accountability and separation of authority, furthering discussion on how hybrid regimes adapt to suit changing political landscapes while yet observing democratic principles. In reflecting upon the stakes of semi-presidential systems, it is evident that the effectiveness of the same is not entirely dependent on the design of the institution but also on external factors such as public perception and international policy. As illustrated in situations such as the Turkish Republic of Northern Cyprus (TRNC), de facto state volatility also points to the critical juncture of governance and sovereignty issues. The TRNC, being within a separate political context, shows how the institutional functioning mechanisms of institutions in semi-presidential hybrids can shift in accordance with factors such as foreign recognition and foreign political control, and that reforms in accordance with widely accepted international democratic norms are therefore necessary. By implication, the study of such hybrid systems like the TRNCs brings into perspective the overall importance of semi-presidential systems to the democratic government system, prompting scholars to think more critically about how various contextual considerations affect the functional environment of such governance systems, thus prompting the establishment of constitutional habits under such systems (Safa, 2025; Bab Mšek et al., 2024).

3.2. SEPARATION OF POWERS

In talking about governance nuances, a key aspect comes up in terms of power distribution within political systems (Figure 3.5).

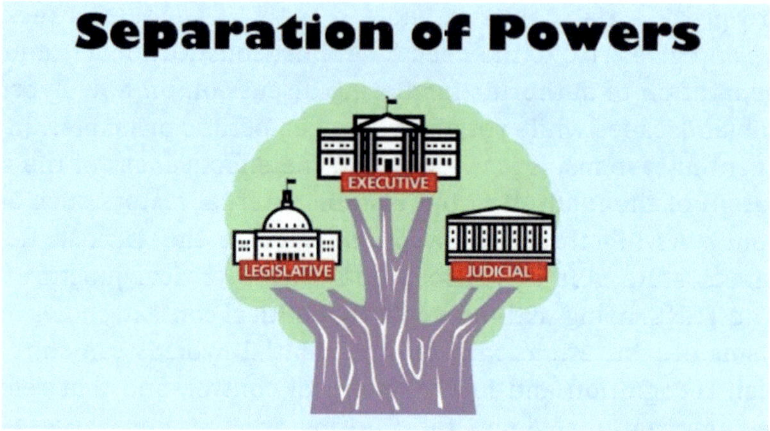

Figure 3.5. The principle of separation of powers serves as a cornerstone in many democracies, designed to prevent the concentration of authority in any single entity.

Source: https://img1.wsimg.com/isteam/ip/5e1b6983-7b30-4c56-9186-c9b0e8698cbd/1521110496Separation_of_Powers.jpg.

By distinguishing legislative, executive, and judicial functions, this model ensures a system of checks and balances that improves accountability and transparency in the work of government. Executive freedom resides with the head of state authority to enforce laws while legislative duty belongs to elected members who pass laws. Judicial independence then ensures laws are interpreted fairly and without bias, thereby safeguarding against abuse of power. This framework not only ensures individual freedoms but also strengthens democratic institutions, thus making the separation of powers a necessity in the contemporary governance landscape in the world. The mechanisms underpinning this division are, however, subject to challenges, most notably with changing socio-political environments. Current scholarly literature reports an alarming democratic backlash trend, whereby settled practices and checks of governance are gradually worn away. While political leadership is moving in the direction of authoritarian tendencies, the constitutional brakes to ensure this separation are usually found wanting. The interplay of institutions and culture is at this point paramount, with societal values and norms having a significant bearing on the effectiveness of such mechanisms. Empirical evidence has shown that cultural characteristics exert a strong influence on institutional results, with a two-way relationship between governing frameworks and societal structures suggested (Alesina et al., 2015). This engagement makes the dynamics of the separation of powers challenging, which demand a nuance appreciation of how political realities are formed by the dynamics of culture. The dangers to a dysfunctional separation of powers have significant implications for political stability and democratic values. As the United States navigates a complex socio-political reality, concerns about potential democratic backsliding increase salience. While a basis in historical strength of constitutional foundations exists, the contemporary context suggests that the risk of gradual erosion of democratic norms is great. Forms of governmental authority must be protected against incursions likely to cause authoritarian reversal or constitutional stuntedness, which threaten to destroy the balance of power (Aziz et al., 2017). Lastly, the well-being of democracy not only relies on institutional form but also on a vigilant citizenry that resists decay and is actively participating, attesting to the significance of educated public engagement in seeing that separation of powers remains strong.

3.2.1. The Role of Legislative Authority in Governance

A mature understanding of governance demands an examination deeper than that of legislative authority, which is one of the foundations on which democratic standards in various governments rest (Figure 3.6).

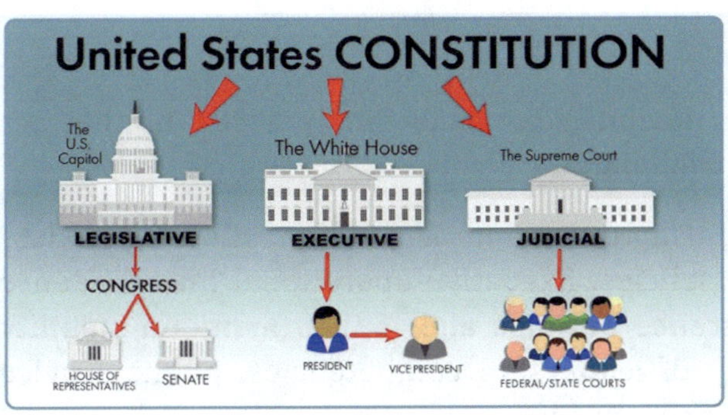

Figure 3.6. Legislative bodies, whether structured within presidential, parliamentary, or semi-presidential frameworks, play a pivotal role in shaping policies and laws that dictate the functioning of the state.

Source: https://i.ytimg.com/vi/McbuCAJUh3s/hq720.jpg?sqp=-oaymwE7CK4FEIIDSFryq4qpAy0IARUAAAAAGAElAADIQj0AgKJD8AEB-AH-CYAC0AWKAgwIABABGFsgYihlMA8=&rs=AOn4CLAV6Q5OHfb5AFbP0pK4bR4nQqfwYg.

Their function extends beyond mere lawmaking; it involves oversight of the executive, appropriation of finances, and representation of fragmented constituencies. For instance, in presidentialism, the division of powers emphasizes independence in the legislative branch so that it can enact checks and balances that limit executive power. This function is critical in maintaining democratic accountability and ensuring that governance reflects the will of the people, reasserting the role of legislative authority in promoting good governance and responsive public policy in alternative constitutional frameworks. Legislative authority also has its place within the domain of federalism, where its interaction with subnational states takes center stage in maintaining the delicate balance of power. Legislative institutions, within federated government, not only participate in national policy-making but must also deal with regional legislatures to coordinate effect.

Such cooperation can be problematic, particularly where there are overlapping jurisdictions regarding the task of competent domains or overlapping interests among states, as the structural complexities present in multi-level governance systems illustrate. The experiences of nations such as Canada and Australia illustrate how the legislative power can be utilized to enhance cooperation or exacerbate tensions in climate policy-making since they demonstrate that legislators must navigate their places within both the national and the local arenas. Lastly, the interaction of legislative power in federal systems accentuates the need for effective intergovernmental relations to achieve coherent policy-making. With the changing world scenario, the role of legislative power too has to change to address new issues, such as climate change and social control. To take an example, contemporary global climate change negotiations have put legislative branches' designs for environmental policy implementation into the spotlight, with activity coordination across multiple governments becoming more crucial than ever. The development of inclusive structures involving all relevant stakeholders can provide collaborative avenues for addressing impending issues, like climate governance issues outlined in the Copenhagen Consensus. The synergy of coercive, competitive, and collaborative modes of governance in this instance helps ensure the need for legislative interventions in developing coordinated responses. In the event of nations riding out the intricacies both domestically and internationally, the capacity of legislative power to respond appropriately in a sensitive balance between domestic and national interests assumes the limelight in facilitating effective and sustainable governance as well as responsiveness in legislation as critical analyses on the governance structure and its competence everywhere envision it (David, 2015; Xu, 2011).

3.2.2. Importance of Executive Autonomy

The subtle equilibrium between power within constitutional systems is essential to good governance, particularly that of the independence of the executive (Figure 3.7).

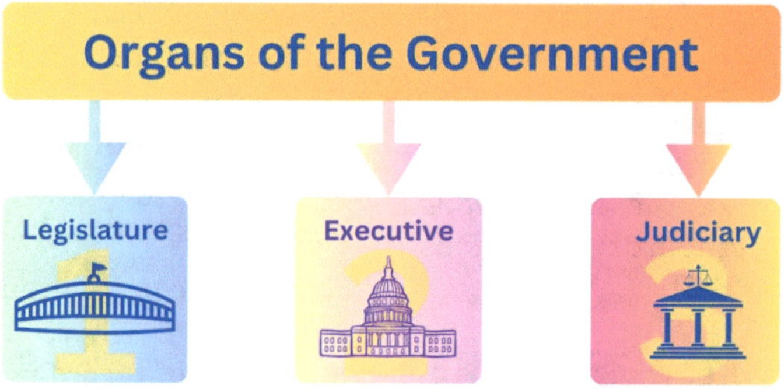

Figure 3.7. Executive autonomy affords leaders the flexibility to make timely decisions that are critical for addressing complex and dynamic policy challenges.

This independence is essential in situations requiring quick and firm action, allowing leaders to translate political mandates into efficient public policies. Executive operational independence not only shields it from excessive legislative interference but also allows it to maintain stability and continuity in government. Based on the theory of leadership competencies, public service executives need to cultivate values leadership and advanced problem-solving capacities, as elaborated in new governance theory, so that their executive functions enhance complementarily the citizens' expectations and needs (Gerson, 2020). As various forms of governance are considered, executive independence's role becomes increasingly vital. Under presidential systems, separation of powers allows for freedom from executive action, which is meant to foster successful policy implementation. Paradoxically, however, under parliamentary systems, since executive power may be more directly controlled by legislative, separation of powers remains significant to facilitate coherent decision-making and check accountability. The comparative analysis of such systems suggests that excessive legislative intrusion in the executive sphere has the potential to create an ineffective governance system, thus undermining the ability to cope with the needs of the society effectively. Hence, in such multicellular structures, it is essential that a balanced autonomy of the executive sphere be practiced to make it answerable while making the governance process efficient (N/A, 2018). Moreover, executive independence is not only an issue of effective governance; it is also a determinant for guaranteeing public trust and integrity. When the public observes that their leaders are able to ensure independence against corrupting forces, their confidence in the government system grows. Where the executive branch is subject to too much pressure from legislative or political factions, the corruption risk arises, ultimately discrediting people's trust. Legislative actions undermining executive autonomy can be an indicator of accountability and governance failure, and thereby developing effective measures that allow for both executive action and integrity is imperative. With problems highlighted in recent governance studies, adopting models that enhance executive independence while ensuring checks and balances is paramount to fostering responsible and responsive governance (Gerson, 2020).

3.2.3. Importance of Judicial Independence

The government in any democracy is wholly dependent upon the doctrine of separation of powers, a Pillar of Strength that ensures judicial independence. This doctrine ensures that the judiciary acts impartially as an arbiter, free from determinants which may contaminate its findings (Figure 3.8). The threat of government encroachment becomes more formidable when judges owe political stakeholders, rendering the courts helpless to uphold citizen rights and implement constitutional demands. Such alignments not only tarnish trust in legal systems but also discourage the potency of checks and balances crucial in democratic society. Judicial autonomy is thus crucial in maintaining the integrity of the legal system and promoting accountability in government agencies.

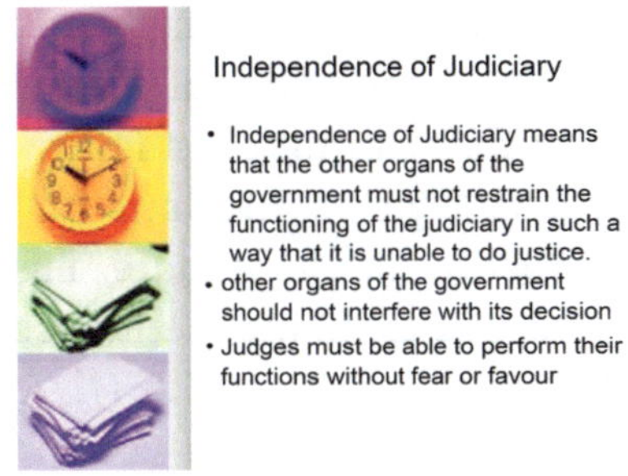

Figure 3.8. Without judicial independence, the rule of law becomes compromised, leading to a judiciary that operates more like an extension of the government than a check on its powers.

The value of judicial independence transcends merely ensuring fairness in individual cases; it is also necessary to impact broader patterns of governance and cultural norms. If the judiciary remains insulated from political pressures, it can uphold laws and precedents defending interests such as freedom of expression, equality before the law, and right to a fair trial. This guardianship function unifies the social contract among citizens and the state, affirming the judiciary's role as a champion of human rights and democracy. Moreover, robust judicial autonomy is likely to serve as an incentive towards staying clear of corruption and abuse of power, which are habitually committed by cross-cutting interests of political elites. Here, independence of the judiciary exists alongside the aim of integrity in governance, maintaining frameworks that guarantee accountability and openness, thus safeguarding the democratic values of a nation (N/A, 2022).

In comparative government, the articulation of judicial independence is uniquely varied in constitutional systems. In presidential systems, judicial independence will occasionally be subject to executive threat, necessitating strong constitutional protection against invasion. Conversely, parliamentary governments usually approach judicial independence in a different manner, occasionally encouraging government branch freedoms of interaction. Nonetheless, freedom from manipulation and external pressures is the very factor that enables governance to be enhanced by a judiciary that can independently function. Greater judicial independence not only reinforces popular faith in legal institutions but also government effectiveness through guaranteeing laws effectively execute their mandate. Lastly, as democracy continues to battle new challenges, the pursuit of strong judicial independence becomes paramount to protecting rights, maintaining order, and the political system's health (N/A, 2018).

3.3. CONSTITUTIONAL REVIEW MECHANISMS

The constitutional review institutions are the crucial checks in various governance systems, ensuring accountability and protection of fundamental rights. Judicial review is frequently part of the process, a key function where the courts decide the constitutionality of executive or legislative actions. The role is most obviously seen in systems where a supreme or constitutional court possesses the authority to undertake such reviews. These mechanisms, though differing from context to context, seek to ensure the equilibrium of power among government branches so as to avoid abuses that would be precipitated by untrammeled authority. For example, when considering the electoral system in Indonesia, one finds that the apparatus of law has been established to reinforce democratic values. Yet challenges still exist in most notably law enforcement and the settlement of election disputes, which are areas in which constitutional review mechanisms must be strengthened to ensure electoral integrity (Pradipta, 2025). In comparative constitutional review mechanisms, particularly in judicial review models, the role of constitutional courts is most centrally positioned as a defining feature. Germany and Brazil demonstrate how devoted courts can effectively exercise jurisdiction on constitutional matters, thus entrenching democratic government. Not only do these courts interpret constitution provisions, but also participate in the broader judicial discourse on the protection of freedoms and rights. For example, the epoch-making decisions rendered by the German Federal Constitutional Court are found to illustrate the dicta of the doctrine of basic structure with far-reaching implications to the practice of governance in the country. Judicial activism, on the other hand, has been faulted for entrusting judges with too much power, mirroring an extensive discussion in literature regarding the appropriate limits of judicial review as a model of governance (Vaishali et al., 2024). The scope of constitutional review has direct impact on the robustness of democratic institutions and the rule of law. By defining what is reviewable—whether it be laws, executive actions, or even constitutional amendments—these mechanisms define the character of governance. The varying scopes within each jurisdiction not only adjust to cultural and historical influences, but also reflect tensions surrounding the appropriate role of the legislature, executive, and judiciary. For instance, while the Indian Supreme Courts broad perception of its review powers has widened the scope of judicial intervention, it has also instigated probing of checks and balances between branches of government. This twofold relationship necessitates ongoing debate of enhanced judicial independence at the expense of no compromising mechanisms of review at the expense of democratic procedure (Vaishali et al., 2024).

3.3.1. Different Models of Judicial Review

Though judicial review is a core principle in the constitution governance system, its application may differ across jurisdictions. Basically, judicial review is a mechanism by which courts can examine the constitutionality of legislative and executive actions. There are two forms that have been found to be most prevalent: strong-form and weak-form judicial reviews. The strong-form model permits courts to have final jurisdiction over the interpretation of the constitution, hence nullifying laws deemed unconstitutional. This occurs in such models as that in the United States, where the Supreme Court has unlimited power to override congressional legislation that runs counter to constitutional stipulations. On the other hand, weak-form judicial review, broached in most legal treatises, calls for more cooperative interaction between the judiciary and the other two branches such that legislature adjustment would take place subsequent to judicial decisions, thus signifying an active relationship in the governance process (Tushnet et al., 2006). The consequence of these models is significant, particularly with respect to accountability and power relations among governing institutions. Strong-form judicial review is a bulwark against prospective government overreaching, but only on the condition that the rights of individuals are also protected from the whims of transient political majorities. It is also a threat to judicial overreaching, in which the courts may end up discrediting democracy. Weak-form judicial review, then, is likely to foster greater legislative imagination and responsiveness to need by allowing elected representatives to modify legislation with reference to judicial comment. This model can foster a more sustainable type of governance, where accountability and efficiency values are maximized. As such, the choice between these models is not only theoretical in scope but has very real practical consequences for the nature of constitutional democracy and governance (Tushnet et al., 2006).

Furthermore, the context of these judicial review models is generally established by the unique constitutional design and political situation of a nation. Within federal regimes, for instance, powers separation may render judicial review procedures lengthy, as courts attempt to ride the complex crosscurrents between state and national jurisdictions. Within parliamentary regimes with strong powers, legislative dominance may be more the central concern, with the prospect to circumscribe judicial action. Consequently, constitutional provisions for review arrangements have an immediate correlation with issues of governance, accountability, and rule of law. Identifying these dynamics is critical to the study of how different models of judicial review can impact not only the results in law, but also overall societal axioms contained within constitutional government (Matei et al., 2004) (Figure 3.9).

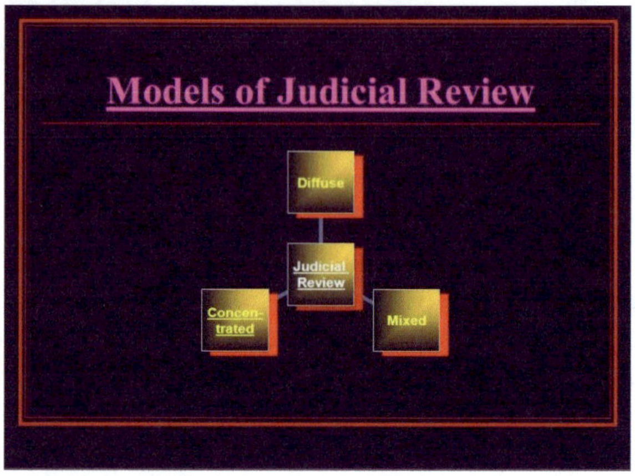

Figure 3.9. Models of judicial review.

Source: https://images.saymedia-content.com/.image/c_limit%2Ccs_srgb%2Cq_auto:eco%2Cw_700/MTc0MTc0NDU2NzU4MTUxMDM2/models-of-judicial-review.webp.

3.3.2. Function and Role of Constitutional Courts

The emergence of constitutional courts is an expression of profound influence on the governments of different political contexts (Figure 3.10).

Figure 3.10. Illustrates the role of judiciary in India.

Source: https://cdn.toprankers.net.in/images/role-of-judiciary-in-india-0282f79e651f9.png.

Working primarily as guardian institutions, these courts have the most significant responsibility of enforcing the primacy of constitutional law over discretionary rule. In most countries, including India, the recourse to the basic structure doctrine has shown the quintessential significance that constitutional courts play in safeguarding the foundational principles of democracy and the rule of law. This doctrine provides courts with the powers to invalidate laws which are in violation of the constituting governing values, thereby further reinforcing their position as judicial arbiters of political power. Second, the growth in the area of public interest litigation (PIL) has made such courts active tools which are capable of exercising judicial control, which has been extremely influential in maintaining accountability within mechanisms of governance (Mate, 2010). Constitutional courts' role as protectors of constitutional integrity under the constitution accordingly defines them as institutions of political stability and justice. Constitutional courts also express the principles of judicial independence and the separation of powers, vital components of comparative models of governance. They provide for an important check on legislatures and executives, ensuring balance in a state's governance. This division is most pronounced in systems where judicial review is a traditional practice, whereby courts have the ability to interpret legislation against constitutional norms. The disparate model of judicial review—the model varying from strict to more lenient paradigms—illustrates how jurisdictions vary judicial authority with legislative autonomy. Constitutional courts in such conditions not only decide cases but also make legal precedents that establish national policy and demarcate the boundaries of government actions. It is this feature of their role that is most important, inasmuch as it stabilizes political cultures and fosters civic faith in the rule of law, providing a procedural channel for the resolution of subtle constitutional dilemmas relevant to the governance of states (Porta et al., 2008).

Secondly, the work of constitutional courts is inescapably immersed within the broader debate regarding federalism and government. As courts at the intersection of law and policy, they play a significant role in resolving disputes arising out of federal dual powers. Through this, they help determine the spheres of national as compared to subnational governments, thus avert overreach of authority and potential violation of rights. Their interpretive jurisdiction includes evaluating emergency powers and limits, such that any restrictions of civil liberties in times of emergency are in accordance with constitutional demands. By exercising judicial oversight in these areas, constitutional courts facilitate the health of democratic processes, protecting the rights of citizens and maintaining the rule of law. Collectively, the diverse and critical functions of constitutional courts aggregate to advocate a system of governance that is robust and adaptive to the complexities of contemporary political processes.

3.3.3. Scope and Boundaries of Constitutional Review

The. multi-aspect process of constitutional review encapsulates a key feature of leadership in different political frameworks. It is a method through which the judiciary can ensure compliance of decisions taken by legislatures and executives with the ideals of the constitution. The effectiveness of such review processes, however, relies on several variables, such as the level of judicial independence along with the prevailing legal frameworks of interpreting provisions within the constitution. Judicial review has broad scope in certain legal frameworks, allowing for the courts to invalidate legislation which offends fundamental rights or exceeds legislative authority. In others, its scope is limited, often in response to deeper political issues or allegiance to the supremacy of parliament. These differences emphasize the various levels of judicial power and control over different types of governance, focusing on the inherent relationship between law and politics inherent in federal and unitary systems. The role of constitutional courts is pivotal within the broader framework of constitutional review as established institutions distinct for deciding the constitutionality of laws and acts. Such courts are likely to be the line of defense of rights, particularly in political matters where the legislature is prone to abuse of authority. The success and vulnerability of such courts are best seen in their procedural rules and the extent of their jurisdiction. Constitutional courts may be empowered to take cases on their own initiative in certain systems, whereas other systems rely on initiations by other branches of the government or citizens. This divergence in purpose and accessibility has significant implications on right guardianship and the balance of power, proving that the success of constitutional review is ultimately dependent on the institutional setup and culture of governance. Knowledge of the scope and limits of constitutional review also provokes a comparative analysis of how different judicial institutions respond to crisis and conflict. Faced with tremendous challenges, such as economic crisis or social upheaval, courts are often called upon to decide the conflict between individual rights and state interests. The tensions embedded in such rulings can result in substantial variations in judicial outcomes between jurisdictions. For instance, while the European Union promotes a degree of centralization and judicial homogenization, many member states maintain strong intergovernmental policies that can slow the extent of judicial review (Young et al., 2016). Comparative analysis such as this reveals the complex interplay between constitutional design and patterns of governance, useful in shedding light on controversies surrounding judicial power and democratic responsiveness (Kelemen et al., 2012).

3.4. FEDERALISM AND DEVOLUTION

The intricate interplay between federalism and devolution carries profound implications for the administration of multicultural societies (Figure 3.11).

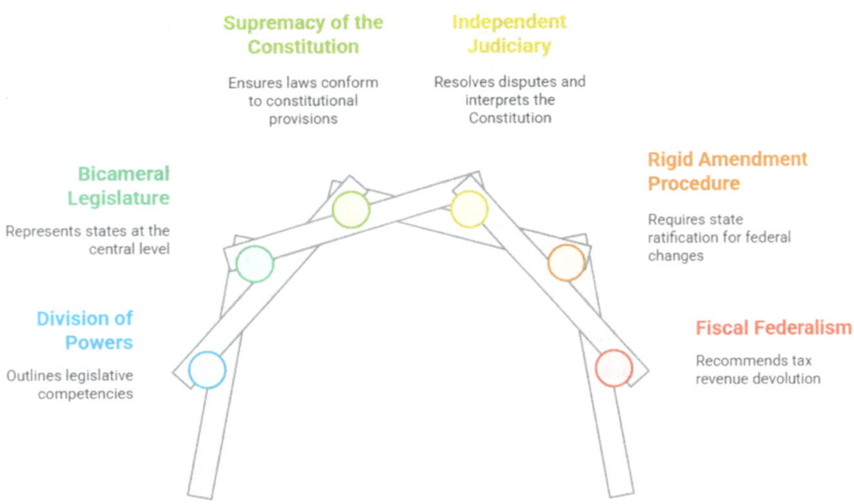

Figure 3.11. Federalism powers between central and regional governments, allows distinct entities to exercise autonomy while maintaining a unified state.

Source: https://triumphias.com/blog/wp-content/uploads/2025/06/Features-of-Indian-Federalism-visual-selection.png.

This model of governance seeks to reconcile regional identities with national unity by promoting localized governance to suit the needs of certain communities. Devolution, on the other hand, is the transfer of powers from central government to subnational units, granting them different levels of administrative autonomy. The distinction lies in the fact that while federalism grants a constitutionally embedded structure for these powers, devolution can be politically inspired and withdrawable by the center government and thereby impact the stability and efficiency of state government. The subtle interplay between them impacts the public policy regime and shapes local responses to governance matters (Hausing, 2023). Understanding the autonomy of subnational entities in federal systems is crucial to determining the efficacy of administration in complex situations. In federations, regions or states enjoy constitutionally defined powers that enable them to enact legislation and rule independently within well-defined domains, for example, education, transport, and health. Such autonomy can enhance local governance, allowing tailored solutions to regional issues, hence enhancing civic engagement and political responsibility. In contrast, devolution can be informalized, and central governments hand over powers that can be revoked at any time. The relationship can add uncertainty and instability for subnational governments, reducing their autonomy to govern effectively. The level of autonomy therefore not only symbolizes legal provisions but also recognition of distinct regional identities and efficacious distribution of competences vital to the integrity of federations (Silva, 2023). Intergovernmental relations (IGR) are quite crucial in dealing with the complexities of federalism and devolution. IGR embrace the interactions and negotiation procedures between the different levels of government that are essential to the implementation of policies and resolution of conflicts. Formal structures, such as councils and commissions, are common IGR devices utilized in federal systems for promoting cooperation and communication among the central and regional governments. However, in devolved structures, IGR could be more reliant on informal ties and political bargaining due to the lack of institution-based frameworks. This difference can have an impact on the efficiency and effectiveness of state functioning, particularly in situations that require coordinated action, such as public health crises or economic development initiatives. Therefore, the study of IGR structure and operations in devolved and federal systems is crucial to determine the wide-ranging implications of governance and public administration in complex political contexts (Hausing, 2023).

3.4.1. Allocation of Competences Among the Levels of Government

The intricacies of government have a tendency to be based on competence allocation across the various levels of government, which is paramount in understanding how responsibility and authority get allocated in a state (Figure 3.12).

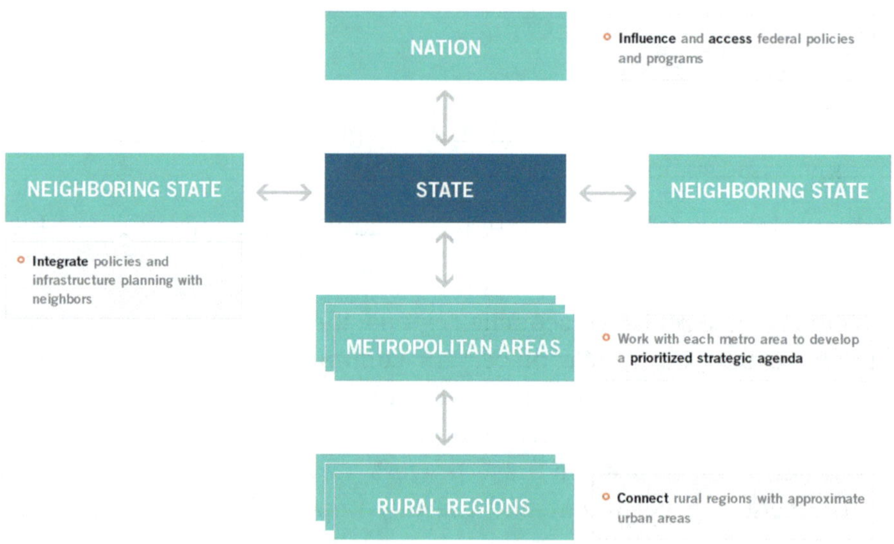

Figure 3.12. Levels of Government in federal system.

Source: https://www.isc.hbs.edu/Style%20Library/hbs/images/ced/levels-of-government.png.

In federal governments, this allocation is usually enshrined in a constitution that states the powers granted to both the subnational and national governments. This allocation directly affects the effectiveness of governance, as it stipulates which level of government deals with major issues such as education, healthcare, and infrastructure. Through comparative governance studies, one can observe that variations in this distribution across different nations lead to distinct governance outcomes, highlighting the need for a structure that balances efficiency and accountability. For instance, too much decentralization may result in fragmentation, while excessive centralization could stifle localized innovation and responsiveness. The varying frameworks of government, whether presidential, parliamentary, or semi-presidential, significantly affect how competences are distributed. In presidential regimes, the executive is likely to wield significant authority, having control over the extent of decentralization at which subnational governments can become independent. However, parliamentary regimes may provide a better organized framework where there is division of powers and collaborative governance. This comparison illustrates how institutional settings not only facilitate or limit the assignment of competences but also affect the interaction between government levels. As various case studies suggest, the relationship between central and local governments in policy-making and policy enforcement provides an opportunity for increasing the understanding of governance impacts in politics across different domains. Moreover, recent international tendencies show the complexity involved in competence distribution, particularly concerning the management of crises and state responses to civil unrest. The Arab world uprisings, according to theory in the academic literature, illustrate the interdependency of military professionalization and government institutionalization and its influence on the efficiency of governance. Whether or not institutions of governance have been inflexible or flexible in Tunisia and Egypt has explained the ability of the state to respond to popular demands efficiently. This dynamic comes to the fore in explaining how competence allocation between levels of government can exacerbate conflict or reduce governance challenges at times of crisis. Research on constitutional frameworks within comparative governance is thus necessary in observing carefully how such dynamics influence political stability and capacity of the state, particularly in the case of mass social unrest (Xu, 2011; Kraay et al., 2010).

3.4.2. Autonomy of Subnational Units in Federal Systems

In examining the federal system's structure, central and subnational government relationships are a web of governance that reflects the significance of autonomy. As federalism inevitably divides authority, autonomy entrusted to subnational governments contrasts widely among different systems depending on history, politics, and legislation. In others, such as the United States, state governments have considerable powers and duties, which allow them to initiate independent policies, producing huge regional variations in administration. But in others, for example, Argentina, the central government is more dominant, limiting the powers of provinces. This difference in autonomy captures the tension between unity and diversity in federalism, whereby the balance must be renegotiated constantly, showing the importance of constitutional design in delineating these relationships. The federal-subnational unit relationship is typically characterized by interdependence and thus needs strong intergovernmental relations. The intergovernmental dynamics can facilitate or hinder the autonomy of subnational governments to perform their role in the federal framework. This collaboration can be in the form of fiscal arrangements, legislative cooperation, and joint policy initiatives, which influence the overall governance architecture. As in the latest OECD reports, the success of governance in all its levels relies exclusively on the coordination of these relationships and how well they are being implemented, especially in a rapidly evolving world where concerns such as corruption and capacity in the public sector persist. A coordinated strategy can enhance productivity and integrity within the system as well as emphasize the value of the autonomy of the subnational units in ensuring inclusive governance (N/A, 2022). Subnational autonomy is to be judged not just on the basis of formal constitutional provisions but also on the facts of governance and the attitude of the people. The facts that face subnational governments will usually be quite different from de jure provisions, as has been indicated in much of the world where implementation of policies is being obstructed by socio-political factors such as corruption and vested interests. In Latin America in particular, a perceived lack of integrity has brought widespread popular discontent with subnational governments into question regarding their efficacy and ability to deliver their constitutional mandates. A concerted effort to counteract these challenges requires an integrated effort to enhance the quality and integrity of governance at both the subnational and national levels. Reforms must look not only to legal processes but also to the concerns and aspirations of people so that the autonomy of subnational governments remains effective and meaningful (N/A, 2018) (Figure 3.13).

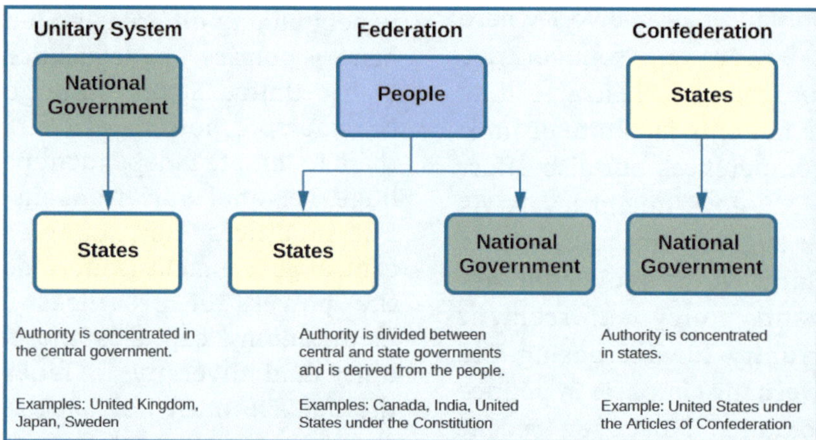

Figure 3.13. Framework of federal systems.

Source: https://vivaopen.oercommons.org/editor/images/502.

3.4.3. Dynamics of Intergovernmental Relations

The relationship between government levels forms the basis of effective governance, particularly in federal systems that experience a division of power between the central and regional levels of government. The intergovernmental relations can, in such context, play a critical role in influencing policy implementation as well as the efficiency of administration. In the same way, collaboration across government levels is often necessary for the management of complicated social issues such as health care and environmental conservation. Over time, conceptual paradigms such as Intergovernmental Law (IGL) have emerged to describe how legal rules and principles govern such interactions. The paradigm demonstrates that legal adherence is necessary due to the fact that all public action ultimately must be accountable to the rule of law, even in the usually stormy realpolitik of intergovernmental negotiations (Poirier, 2024). As a result, delving into these dynamics not only explains governance, but also delves deeper into how law influences federal practice and intergovernmental interaction. Federalism is a system in which several layers of governance interact in a way that often requires negotiation and compromise. The early construction of the American federal system demonstrated the value of intergovernmental negotiation as federal powers needed state accommodation in order to effectively pass laws. The application of federal measures in the domains of customs and coastal defence illustrated this interdependence requirement. Federal agents soon realized that their influence depended on the actions of state governments that followed, thus fostering an interdependent relationship (Grace, 2024). This doctrine, which is referred to as negotiated federalism, illustrates the way in which federal power does not exist independently but as one thread in a net of relationships between federal and subnational governments (Grace, 2024). The evolution of these interactions over time reflects a pragmatic acknowledgment that effective governance emerges out of an interdependent rather than strictly hierarchical process. To learn about intergovernmental relations also entails examination of mechanisms of accountability that sustain this nuanced equilibrium of power. In elaborating through IGL, both downstream and upstream processes are essential in managing the federal-state relationship. Constitutional precepts upstream determine the parameters of intergovernmental expectations and institutions, while downstream institutions like judicial review and parliamentary scrutiny are crucial to government accountability. Such institutions ensure that even as federal and state governments can negotiate and collaborate, they remain held accountable to legal standards. Analysis of such dynamics in intergovernmental relations underscores the need for constant exploration of the relationship between law and governance. A study of such connective tissues among laws and intergovernmental activity provides vital perspectives on how constitutional arrangements shape conduct and policy choices in federal democracies (Poirier, 2024).

3.5. EMERGENCY POWERS AND RESTRICTIONS

In reviewing the intricate balance between emergency powers and their restraints, it is apparent that the rule of law relating to such powers has a significant function in the preservation of democratic rule (Figure 3.14).

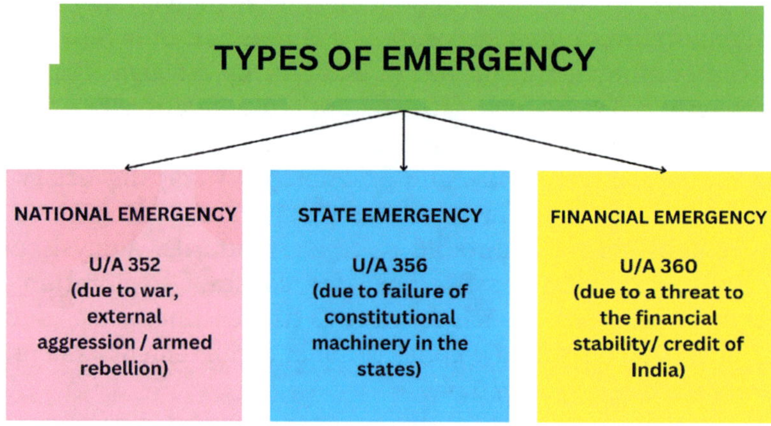

Figure 3.14. Types of emergency.

Source: https://cdn-images.prepp.in/public/image/15-09:47-FACTORS%20INFLUENCING%20 POPULATION%20GROWTH%20(3).png.

Emergency powers tend to arise in situations of crisis, requiring immediate action on the part of the government to help enforce order and respond to unexpected threats. This need, however, must be balanced against legal foundations which specify when such powers may be used, thereby preventing abuse. As an example, most constitutional frameworks demand explicitly stated definitions of emergencies so that a government cannot abuse these provisions for purposes of authoritarian control. The OECD points out that robust democratic government is crucial, particularly in times of emergency, since it forms the foundation for the protection of the rights of individuals while facilitating effective action by the state to adequately address emergencies (N/A, 2022). Thus, understanding legal boundaries in emergency powers is pivotal in navigating the narrow path between effective government and upholding democracy. Temporal and substantive limits are integral ideas in the management of emergency powers, as they set down the governing considerations of when and within what conditions these powers can be utilized. These limits have the ability to guarantee that emergency measures do not become unnecessarily prolonged past their warranted period, and hence protect democratic institutions against encroachment. For example, in Italy at the beginning of the COVID-19 pandemic, the government's handling of the crisis demonstrated the way in which unpreparedness would lead to reliance on policy institutions already in place while simultaneously defining institutional strengths and weaknesses in managing emergencies (Capano, 2020). Italy's experience underscores the significance of having clearly defined temporal boundaries that are incorporated into constitutional mandates. Additionally, imposing meaningful limitations on the scope of emergency powers is essential in preventing government overreach and thus imposing the role of checks and balances to ascertain that democracy continues to reign even in the midst of a crisis. Oversight and accountability mechanisms are the guardians when using emergency powers, so that governmental action is within parameters set by the constitution. These measures can take various forms, from legislative examination to judicial regulation, designed to ensure that public trust is not lost, and democratic values are not eroded. In most nations, it is important that emergency powers be subjected to rigorous scrutiny, because experience has shown that unchecked powers mean authoritarianism, particularly in protracted crises. The OECD recognizes that protecting democratic governance during emergency situations is among ensuring people's freedoms and institutions' stability over the long term within the country (N/A, 2022). An effective oversight system is therefore not only a safeguard mechanism but also an integral component of quality governance, attempting to hold the government accountable even when exceptional action is warranted to address pressing issues.

3.5.1. Legal Foundation of the Proclamation of a State of Emergency

The justification for the proclamation of a state of emergency can then lie in the constitutional article authorizing extraordinary government powers during unforeseen emergencies. Constitutions of most democracies authorize the limited circumstances under which a state of emergency may be established, ranging from natural disasters to extreme national security threats. These are fundamental provisions that articulate both the law and the boundaries necessary to stem abuse of power. Such legal underpinnings ensure that declarations of emergencies have to rely on facts, thus maintaining the integrity of constitutional directives, while reconciling the necessity for rapid action during a time of crisis. The distinction of these conditions not only justifies the exercise of emergency powers but also safeguards founding values of governance by necessitating obedience to legislative oversight in the face of such extraordinary circumstances. The practical implications of emergency powers reveal tensions between effective governance and the preservation of democratic values. Although acknowledging the possibility that states of emergency can vest chief executives with the authority to derogate from ordinary procedures, care should be taken to critically assess the consequences of such powers towards democratic integrity. Existing literature points towards an extensive correlation between states of emergency and democratic feature erosions, with democracies witnessing an added threat of autocratization during states of emergency. Such an association brings serious issues of direction in governance because the use of emergency powers could be extended to justify eroding democratic institutions while maintaining a cover of constitutional legitimacy. Therefore, it is essential that a cautious approach to invoking states of emergency be adopted to ensure that government action remains democratic and society's welfare-oriented. The emphasis of discussion on legal justification of emergency declarations is in the area of the theme of oversight and accountability as a critical check on the risks of such powers. Good constitutional practice is usually the case of legislation making provision for parliamentary authorization, judicial oversight, and public accountability during an emergency. These verifications are instituted to prevent potential abuses and ensure that extraordinary measures are not unjustifiably prolonged beyond their necessary duration. The dynamics between the executive and legislative branches during such moments accentuate the importance of upholding civil liberties in spite of heightened security measures. By having oversight mechanisms in place, the impact of emergency powers can be contained, thus enabling the responsive model of governance that ensures both security and protection of democratic values and enables stability in the overall constitutional framework of governance.

3.5.2. Temporal and Substantive Limits on Emergency Powers

The use of emergency powers has typically reflected the gravity of crises facing governments, but the power must be carefully circumscribed to guarantee the spirit of democratic government. Time limits for emergency powers are critical to the extent that emergency powers will not become permanent. The vast majority of constitutional frameworks give the durations by which emergency powers can be invoked, with renewals subjecting those powers to parliamentary vetting. These constraints prevent the normalization of extraordinary measures, therefore maintaining the constitutional order and protecting citizens' rights. In addition, creating a specific time limit increases transparency and accountability because governments will be compelled to justify the continued need for extraordinary measures as conditions evolve. Without the time limits, there is the risk that emergency powers could become tools of authoritarianism rather than instruments of public security. Apart from temporal restraints, there must be substantive restraints in upholding democratic values during crisis. They regulate the level at which activities can be undertaken under emergency powers, so as not to contravene entrenched rights or the rule of law. Emergency laws, for instance, can particularly exclude suspension of particular rights, so as to leave guarantees of free expression and due process intact. This act of balancing necessitates governments to balance the delicate interplay between urgency and democratic checks. In imposing substantive checks in the constitution, states enshrine the doctrine that even in exceptional situations, government has to be exercised within the realm of basic democratic principles. This not only safeguards the rights of individuals, but also helps maintain public trust as citizens are more likely to support emergency measures when they perceive them to be rational and reasonable. The challenge in contemporary governance is how to implement these time and content limitations in the appropriate context of swiftness and complexity, that is, in the era of social acceleration and changing crises. Strategies must be developed by governments to enable rapid decision-making yet not compromise democratic criteria and human rights, as comparative governance research stresses. Denmark and the Netherlands are shown with successful cases where policy interventions and digitalization for strategic reasons push the responsiveness of governance without sacrificing democratic standards (Kees van Kersbergen et al., 2022). The European Union migration policies, on the other hand, are a showcase for the conflict that arises when emergency measures conflict with established human right's needs, showing the necessity of inclusive oversight mechanisms (Jürgen et al., 2022). Lastly, the inclusion of robust constraints on emergency powers is essential in the preservation of democracy so that at times of crisis, government is grounded in constitutional values.

3.5.3. Mechanisms for oversight and Accountability During Emergencies

In terms of government reactions to crises, the rules of oversight and accountability during emergencies become important for democratic integrity. They provide assurance that though governments can gain special powers to cover exceptional situations, their actions are still under scrutiny. Oversight can be through different branches of government, such as legislative oversight and judicial interventions, which act as checks on the extended powers of executives. The relationship among the institutions has to exist; for example, it is the powerful legislature which can examine emergency provisions aggressively, ensuring openness. Good governance is not just creating these institutions but also actually using them dynamically to prevent misuse. Empowering citizens and civic groups to oversee activity raises accountability and strengthens democratic processes, thus furthering the fact that even in emergency situations, officials are responsible to the people (N/A, 2022). Separation of powers also plays a key role in preventing emergency power abuse. Though executive power is often granted more authority in emergencies, judicial independence is still a counterbalancing necessity. Courts need to review the legality of emergency measures, that they do not infringe on fundamental rights and freedoms. The challenge lies in ensuring an open and responsive judiciary, especially during heightened government activity. Moreover, comparative governance knowledge integration hastens learning regarding effective judicial review models under conditions of crises, revealing how diverse judicial structures adjust to suit constitutional demands (Abubakar et al., 2022). Beyond just ensuring the survival of a legal system during crisis, adaptability builds the legitimacy of governmental actions through acquired norms. Besides, the integration of accountability measures into emergency legal provisions can enhance public trust and strengthen government resilience. Accountability measures usually involve definite temporal and substantive limits on emergency power use, thus curbing potential misuse. For example, periodic reporting requirements for activities conducted under emergency provisions maintain citizens informed and active. Furthermore, making arrangements for phased return to usual constitutional arrangements conveys a clear signal of going back to pre-emergency levels, maintaining faith in government accountable to its people. This is a foresight needed to guarantee that emergency powers serve their objective without eroding the spirit of democratic values, eventually leading to improved health and socio-economic benefits in concerned societies (N/A, 2022).

3.6. AMENDMENTS AND CONSTITUTIONAL CHANGE

The process of constitutional change is inherently complex, reflecting the dynamism of political, social, and economic conditions within a state. In the context of governance, the distinction between rigid and flexible amendment systems plays a critical role in shaping how constitutions evolve over time. Rigid systems, such as those found in the United States, require supermajority approvals for amendments, embodying a cautious approach to constitutional change. This high threshold serves to preserve stability and continuity in governance, guarding against impulsive alterations that could undermine foundational principles. Conversely, flexible systems, commonly observed in parliamentary models, allow for easier amendments, thereby enabling rapid responses to shifting societal needs and values. However, while increased flexibility promotes adaptability, it may also heighten the risk of populist or short-sighted changes that jeopardize long-term democratic norms. The balance between these approaches ultimately shapes the resilience of constitutional frameworks across different governance models. Procedures for amendment are essential in understanding how constitutions adapt to changing societal contexts and values. Various countries implement diverse mechanisms that dictate the pathway for enacting constitutional amendments, ranging from legislative approval to referendums. For instance, in some federal states, amendments may necessitate concurrent approvals from both state legislatures and the national parliament, reflecting the delicate balance of power among different governing tiers (Figure 3.15).

18th Amendment

Further to amend the Constitution of the Islamic Republic of Pakistan WHEREAS it is expedient further to amend the Constitution of the Islamic Republic of Pakistan for the purposes hereinafter appearing;

AND WHEREAS the people of Pakistan have relentlessly struggled for democracy and for attaining the ideals of a Federal, Islamic, democratic, parliamentary and modern progressive welfare State, wherein the rights of the citizens are secured and the Provinces have equitable share in the Federation;

AND WHEREAS it is necessary that the Legal Framework Order, 2002, as amended by the Chief Executive's Order No. 29 and the Chief Executive's Order No. 32 of 2002, be declared as having been made without lawful authority and of no legal effect, and the Constitution (Seventeenth Amendment) Act, 2003 (Act No. 111 of 2003), be repealed and the Constitution further amended to achieve the aforesaid objectives; It is hereby enacted as follows:

1. Short title and, commencement: (1) This Act may be called the Constitution (Eighteenth Amendment) Act, 2010.

(2) It shall come into force at once, save as otherwise provided in this Act.

2. Repeal, etc.- Subject to Article 264 and the provisions of the Constitution (Eighteenth Amendment) Act, 2010, (a) the Legal Framework Order, 2402 (Chief Executive's Order No. 24 of 2002), the Legal Framework (Amendment) Order, 2002 (Chief Executive's Order No. 29 of 2002) and the Legal Framework (Second Amendment) Order, 2002 (Chief Executive's Order No. 32 of 2002), are hereby declared to have been, made without lawful authority and of no legal effect and, therefore, shall stand repealed; and (b) the Constitution (Seventeenth Amendment) Act, 2003 (Act No. III of 2003), is hereby repealed.

3. Amendment of Article 1 of the Constitution. In the Constitution of the Islamic Republic of Pakistan, hereinafter referred to as the Constitution, in Article 1, in clause (2), in paragraph (a), for the word "Baluchistan" the word "Balochistan", for the words "North West Frontier" the words "Khyber Pakhtunkhwa", and for the word "Sind" the word "Sindh", shall be substituted.

4. Amendment of Article 6 of the Constitution.- In the Constitution, in Article 6, (i) for clause (1), the following shall be substituted, namely: "(1) Any person who abrogates or subverts or suspends or holds in abeyance, or attempts or conspires to abrogate or subvert or suspend or hold in abeyance, the Constitution by use of force or show of force or by any other unconstitutional means shall be guilty of high treason.

(ii) in clause (2), after the word "abetting" the word "or collaborating" shall be inserted; and (iii) after clause (2) amended as aforesaid, the following new clause shall be inserted, namely:-

Figure 3.15. In Pakistan, the 18th constitutional amendment is a fine illustration of how a managed process can lead to autonomy of provincial units and the power of local government to exercise more control over education and public services (Hafeez A, 2021). All such amendments indicate the drift towards decentralization of powers, which is now increasingly considered necessary to address localized needs across areas and increase democratic participation.

Source: https://imgv2-1-f.scribdassets.com/img/document/30269950/original/53f50ac880/1?v=1.

An appreciation of these varied procedures is therefore the focus of the study of the responsiveness and effectiveness of constitutional regimes. The interpretation of amendments by the judiciary is another salient factor that affects constitutional change and its implications on governance. Judges play a crucial role in determining the validity and scope of amendments, typically acting as arbiters in disputes concerning their constitutionality. This interpretative function can have the ability to influence a state's balance of forces, particularly when courts decide how much authority they have to review constitutional amendments. In times of political polarization, for instance, as highlighted in the analysis of various countries, judicial decisions can solidify or destabilize democratic institutions (McCoy et al., 2018). Where courts invalidate widely popular amendments, tensions between majority will and judicial review have the potential to create legitimacy crises. The intersection of amendment procedures and judicial interpretation is thus a significant subfield of the broader conversation in constitutional design and comparative government.

3.6.1. Differences Between Rigid and Flexible Constitutional Systems

The political contexts of governance in most nations lean towards their constitutional frameworks that shape their political contexts. Of such frameworks, the flexibility or stiffness of constitutional systems significantly influences the flexibility of governance in changing with changing societal demands. Rigid systems, with stringent amendment processes, are reluctant to change often at the expense of stability and predictability. Such rigidity provides a defence against precipitous changes, which might lead to instability in the political context. But it can also deter responsiveness to urgent problems, as in settings where community mores change quickly, leaving earlier provisions to operate. Flexible constitutional frameworks, by contrast, permit less complicated amendment processes, so governments can modify legislation and structures to fit today's circumstances without undue bureaucratic obstruction. This flexibility is needed in volatile political landscapes where dangers of democratic backsliding and erosion of principle threaten the very foundations of the governance (Aziz et al., 2017). The scope of implications from inflexible to flexible constitutional systems extends beyond mere amendment procedures; it also extends to democratic institution health overall. In hard systems, the deeply rooted protections may stay off the deterioration of fundamental freedoms and rights, establishing an atmosphere in which democratic values reign supreme. Meanwhile, as is evident in recent studies, inflexibility would ironically drive exposure to gradual modes of erosion, such as constitutional backsliding. This happens when politicians utilize available frameworks to dismantle democratic processes without even making consequential alterations to the constitution (Aziz et al., 2017).

On the other hand, flexible systems, while permitting timely reforms, may either fail to provide the necessary checks on authoritarian drift where incessant changes compromise stability that is pivotal to democratic governance. A balance between rigidity and flexibility is therefore needed to guarantee constitutional integrity and prevent either overt authoritarian reversion or insidious erosion of democratic ideals. Another consideration in evaluating constitutional systems is the degree of governance produced by rigid and flexible frameworks. Flexibility can enable innovative policy responses, in the view of theorists who are advocating increased bureaucratic autonomy in multifaceted governance settings. However, this autonomy can be problematic in more unsettled settings where government encroachment is a major issue. Formal systems, though maybe cumbersome in amendment processes, are most likely to contribute to the stability that improves public trust in democratic institutions. Rigidity and flexibility tension also decides the viability of mechanisms that guarantee the separation of powers—a primary characteristic in contemporary leadership. Strong separation of powers will avoid the ill effects of rigid as well as flexible systems and ensure accountability, either by judicial review under the constitution or executive checks. Lastly, understanding the interaction between rigidity and flexibility gives valuable insight about the longevity and good health of democratic government in various constitutional settings (Figure 3.16).

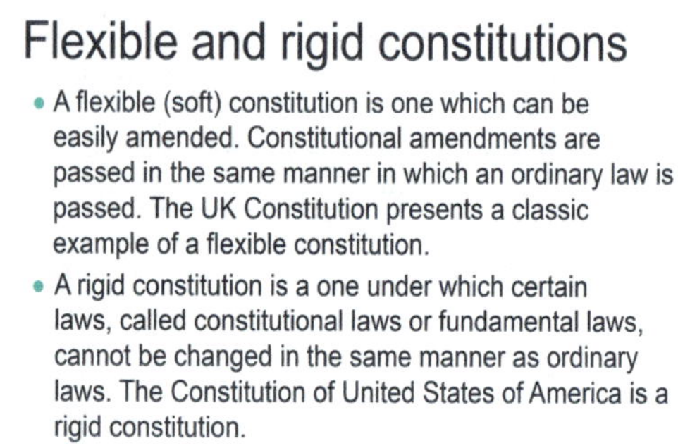
Flexible and rigid constitutions

- A flexible (soft) constitution is one which can be easily amended. Constitutional amendments are passed in the same manner in which an ordinary law is passed. The UK Constitution presents a classic example of a flexible constitution.
- A rigid constitution is a one under which certain laws, called constitutional laws or fundamental laws, cannot be changed in the same manner as ordinary laws. The Constitution of United States of America is a rigid constitution.

Figure 3.16. Flexible and rigid constitutions.

Source: https://encrypted-tbn0.gstatic.com/images?q=tbn:ANd9GcS6yLBcGGoKeCaE5sDLYjNgplumbPNTEzDzCg&s.

3.6.2. Procedures for Amending Constitutions

Amending a constitution is a serious exercise that reflects a societys active political, social, and legal climates. The process differs significantly in different countries, largely categorized as rigid and flexible systems. Rigid systems involve more demanding conditions for alterations, most commonly supermajority votes in legislatures or public referendums, which ensures that changes reflect more extensive consensus among citizens. In contrast, elastic systems provide space for smoother variations, which have the tendency to allow legislative bodies to make constitutional provisions through simple majorities. Such differences in procedural demands directly influence the flexibility of constitutional frameworks, as seen in the different approaches taken by states like India, which applies a relatively cumbersome process for amendments, as compared to the easily accessible processes employed in states like the United Kingdom. This understanding is vital to know how constitutional systems can ensure democratic governance (Kumar et al., 2025). The technicalities of constitutional amendments are further supplemented by the political landscape where they occur. In the majority of instances, the amendment process is not only a technical procedure but also a platform of political struggle and ideological engagements. For example, in times of sociopolitical crisis, ruling authorities will try to amend constitutions to consolidate power or quell opposition, leading to so-called constitutional regression. In contrast, democratic transformation campaigns will seek reforms to expand rights or expand openness. By studying the political agendas and social pressures that lead to constitutional change, researchers can discover patterns in how different types of governance manage crises. This conflict between procedural rules and political powers accounts for the complexity of constitutional development in diverse systems of government (Suratno, 2025). Ultimately, procedure success in constitutional amendment rests on its ability to broker stability and responsiveness. While adherence to stringent amendment procedures guards against spontaneous or populist reforms, it can render the constitution obsolescent in fluid geopolitical contexts. Conversely, however, flexible systems risk falling prey to manipulation by transitory majorities and thus diminishing core democratic tenets. The problem is one of formulating an amendment process that is resilient against both authoritarian incursions and destabilizing amendments. In addition, as societal values change and global challenges are formed, constitutional systems need to be able to incorporate progressive legal tenets while retaining their essentialities. They need a nuanced understanding in order to support sustainable rule and robust democratic institutions in the rapidly globalized world (Kumar et al., 2025).

3.6.3. Role of Judicial Interpretation in Constitutional Changes

The evolution of constitutional frameworks depends greatly on interpretation provided by the judiciary, which not only serve as unbiased adjudicators of legal discrepancies, but also as driving force for constitutional change. Across the centuries, judicial interpretation has altered the interpretation and enforcement of constitutional provisions, attesting to the subtle interplay between law and evolving social mores. This dynamic has a tendency to formulate a reinterpretation of ideals in constitutions, whereby the judiciary can rework original legal documents to suit contemporary contexts. For instance, various ways of judicial review are capable of illustrating the extent of judicial power involved in conceptualizing constitutional states, as courts exercise their powers to certify or invalidate legislative acts based on constitutional compliance. This dynamic dialogue underscores the judiciary's responsibility to make constitutional governance stable and flexible, highlighting judicial interpretation not merely as a case of legal reasoning but a necessary process of constitutional development. While judges do their constitutional interpretation, they are able to react and even initiate systemic cultural shifts, in turn affecting governance institutions. Identification of cultural variables is essential, as underscored by empirical findings that institutional determinants are significant in affecting outcomes. Judicial interpretation harmonized with cultural influences is capable of precipitating alterations in governance models or the institutional structure. A judiciary attuned to changing cultural norms, for instance, can precipitate alterations to the constitution by protecting rights that adjust to societal interests, thereby affecting the general precepts governing state and individual interactions. This relationship between culture and legal interpretation assumes a reciprocal influence that emphasizes the judges role as not only legal technicians, but as agents of the constitutional discourse. The implications of this shift bring to the forefront the judiciary's participation in the construction of collective ethical norms within constitutional frameworks, bridging the gap between legislative intent and social realities (Alesina et al., 2015). Besides, more complex ruling structures demand a high-level understanding of the concept of polycentricity and how it can elucidate the role of judicial interpretation in multiple centers of decision-making. Polycentricity highlights a social system with different centers of decision-making being under a single legal regime to enhance flexibility and sensitivity of governance structures. In cases of judicial interpretation, plurality within governing institutions—legislative, executive, or judicial—allows for a stronger probing of constitutional implications. By interpreting and applying constitutional ideals, the judiciary assists in a polycentric approach to governance that looks toward the future and evolves to meet changing social demands. This conversation not only reflects the judicial role in constitutional change but also points to the importance of collective rule, where different agents subsist and understand legal principles and implement them to achieve stability and responsiveness in complex social environments (Aligic et al., 2011).

SUMMARY

In comparative governance and constitutional systems, the various forms of government become fundamental aspects of political system study. The various models such as presidential systems, parliamentary models, and semi-presidential hybrids showcase the variability in the forms of governance. Each system offers unique characteristics that influence the exercise and separation of power. For instance, presidential systems normally emphasize executive power and require legislative accommodation, whereas parliamentary models combine the legislative and executive branches, with possibly more efficient governance. Semi-presidential hybrids, on the other hand, try to combine the best of both worlds, creating a challenging dynamic balancing power among the branches. Such structural frameworks form the background for the following analysis of the vital interrelationship between governance and constitutional systems as a backdrop to matters of democratic erosion (Aziz et al., 2017) and the process of culture-institution interaction (Alesina et al., 2015). The system of separation of powers is central to understanding the governance dynamics of different constitutional systems. This principle ensures that legislative power, executive autonomy, and judicial independence operate independently to prevent power concentration in a single branch. Weak separation can lead to authoritarian tendencies, weakening democratic values and institutional confidence. Moreover, the success of this separation is often at the mercy of political context, including the combination of political culture and institutional formations. States with strong separation of powers will be apt to construct healthier democratic inclinations, whereas those with weak separation will be apt to deliver extreme threats of democratic backsliding in norms and rights. Following current research, America is facing critical issues that remind us about the fragility of constitutional protections amid changing cultural environments (Aziz et al., 2017). Thus, a nuanced understanding of the separation of powers is critical in considering potential flaws in various models of governance (Alesina et al., 2015). The tools at one's disposal to undertake constitutional review are critically significant in shaping the governance landscape, particularly the protection of rights and accountability by institutions. Judicial review, constitutional courts, and their constitutive ambit of review are fundamental tools to uphold constitutional tenets. These reviews ensure that executive action and legislation are in accordance with the constitutional order, reinforcing democratic rule institutions to resist erosion. The quality and efficiency of these review processes vary extensively across countries and affect how political and legal norms are upheld in practice. A traditional judicial review process can act as a defense against incremental incursions of authoritarianism, which can be done through institutional disintegration. As highlighted, the new dangers of slippage against democratic standards necessitate special focus on the resilience of such constitutional review mechanisms, given the empirical connection between culture and institutional functioning (Alesina et al., 2015) and the need for vigorous protection against the slide towards authoritarianism (Aziz et al., 2017).

A LOOK TO THE FUTURE

THE FUTURE OF GOVERNANCE IN COMPARATIVE CONSTITUTIONAL SYSTEMS

The future of government is progressively defined by the intricacies inherent in constitutional frameworks, which provide the basic structure for different types of government. In assessing such systems, researchers observe that the nature of the governance—whether presidential systems, parliamentary forms, or semi-presidential hybrids—has important policy-making and state stability implications. Each system has an impact on the level of executive power, legislative power, and judicial independence. For instance, strict separation of powers nations can find more robust checks and balances, but they can also encounter legislative gridlock. Parliamentary democracies, by contrast, can facilitate rapid law-making but at the expense of executive accountability. These factors suggest that as countries consider their governance systems, familiarity with the interrelations within the systems will be important to creating strong, adaptive styles of governance in an interdependent world. With the evolving character of governance, collaborative frameworks become key building blocks in addressing issues of the modern world. Collaborative governance, for example, relies on convening diverse stakeholders from the government to the non-government organizations to address problems that cut across traditional boundaries. The ability to establish cross-boundary collaboration not only enhances the flexibility of governance arrangements but also facilitates policy innovation. According to the model proposed in recent studies, the interaction between such collaborative relations might determine practical implications, and thereby there is a need for intergovernmental cooperation with various stakeholders (Emerson et al., 2011). This is an indicator that suggests the significance of institutional arrangements and social learning processes, which can facilitate conflict resolution and collective decision-making. Accordingly, future governments will also have to shift towards more participatory patterns that enshrine stakeholder participation while remaining accountable and efficient institutions. Moreover, the country's background within its juridical system plays a significant role in shaping its outcomes of governance. Studies indicate that the origin of a nation's legislation is connected to its general legal system and economic performance, which, in turn, affects governance effectiveness and personality (Porta et al., 2008). This information necessitates rethinking the ways legal systems can be redesigned to provide better governance outcomes. The consequences are significant: governments might be required to undertake legal restructuring in the interests of preventing entrenched and inefficient practices that impede political and economic development. Moreover, as states pursue modernization and reform, they must navigate the entrenched legal identities while promoting progressive changes. Thus, the interplay of legal origins and governance paradigms will remain significant in designing future governance policies and strategies, with greater emphasis on refining legal principles so that they resonate with contemporary socio-economic realities.

REFERENCES

1. Abubakar, I., Dalglish, S. L., Angell, B., Sanuade, O. A., Abímbọ́lá, Ṣ., Adamu, A. L., Adetifa, I., et al. (2022). The Lancet Nigeria Commission: Investing in health and the future of the nation. *The Lancet, 399*, 1155–1200. https://doi.org/10.1016/s0140-6736(21)02488-0 (accessed on 9th September 2025).
2. Adnyani, N., Hartono, M. S., Parwati, N. P. E., & Salles, S. (2025). The constitutional law in contemporary times: Comparison of India and Indonesia. *Jurnal Suara Hukum*. https://www.semanticscholar.org/paper/624d61619124df7986066e7eda2cc9ad7c8ba1b1 (accessed on 9th September 2025).
3. Alesina, A., & Giuliano, P. (2015). Culture and institutions. *Journal of Economic Literature, 53*, 898–944. https://doi.org/10.1257/jel.53.4.898 (accessed on 9th September 2025).
4. Aligică, P. D., & Tarko, V. (2011). Polycentricity: From Polanyi to Ostrom, and beyond. *Governance, 25*, 237–262. https://doi.org/10.1111/j.1468-0491.2011.01550.x (accessed on 9th September 2025).
5. Babšek, M., Tomaževič, N., & Kovač, P. (2024). Comparative analysis of social services reform in Slovenia, Austria and Croatia: Legal-administrative perspective. *DANUBE, 15*, 321–340. https://www.semanticscholar.org/paper/2a9e30059d5029d780fca8748c81c7aee0138270 (accessed on 9th September 2025).
6. Bast, J., von Harbou, F., & Wessels, J. (2022). Human rights challenges to European migration policy. https://doi.org/10.5771/9783748926740 (accessed on 9th September 2025).
7. Capano, G. (2020). Policy design and state capacity in the COVID-19 emergency in Italy: If you are not prepared for the (un)expected, you can be only what you already are. *Policy and Society, 39*, 326–344. https://doi.org/10.1080/14494035.2020.1783790 (accessed on 9th September 2025).
8. Council of Europe. (2021). *Theory and Practice of the European Convention on Human Rights*. Nomos Verlagsgesellschaft mbH & Co. KG eBooks. https://doi.org/10.5771/9783748923503 (accessed on 9th September 2025).
9. Da Silva, M. (2023). Federalism as an institutional doctrine. *Journal of Social Philosophy, 55*, 81–105. https://doi.org/10.1111/josp.12540 (accessed on 9th September 2025).
10. Emerson, K., Nabatchi, T., & Balogh, S. (2011). An integrative framework for collaborative governance. *Journal of Public Administration Research and Theory, 22*, 1–29. https://doi.org/10.1093/jopart/mur011 (accessed on 9th September 2025).
11. Fukuyama, F. (2013). What is governance? *Governance, 26*, 347–368. https://doi.org/10.1111/gove.12035 (accessed on 9th September 2025).
12. Gerson, D. (2020). *Leadership For a High Performing Civil Service. OECD Working Papers on Public Governance*. https://doi.org/10.1787/ed8235c8-en (accessed on 9th September 2025).
13. Gordon, D. J. (2015). An uneasy equilibrium: The coordination of climate governance in federated systems. *Global Environmental Politics, 15*, 121–141. https://doi.org/10.1162/glep_a_00301 (accessed on 9th September 2025).
14. Hafeez, A. (2021). Impact of devolution of power on school education performance in Sindh

after 18th constitutional amendment. *Journal of Development and Social Sciences, 2*, 273–285. https://doi.org/10.47205/jdss.2021(2-iv)24 (accessed on 9th September 2025).

15. Hausing, K. K. S. (2023). Intergovernmental relations and the territorial management of ethnic diversity in India. *India Review, 22*, 397–432. https://doi.org/10.1080/14736489.2023.2236462 (accessed on 9th September 2025).

16. Huq, A. Z., & Ginsburg, T. (2017). How to lose a constitutional democracy. *SSRN Electronic Journal*. https://doi.org/10.2139/ssrn.2901776 (accessed on 9th September 2025).

17. Jafarova, R. F. K. (2025). Implementation of state governance in the liberated territories as one of the manifestations of Azerbaijani constitutionalism. *Futurity Economics & Law*. https://www.semanticscholar.org/paper/64dadb5904e4d5257d944aceab7c0bd16fe9a9da (accessed on 9th September 2025).

18. Jordan, A., & Lenschow, A. (2010). Environmental policy integration: A state-of-the-art review. *Environmental Policy and Governance, 20*, 147–158. https://doi.org/10.1002/eet.539 (accessed on 9th September 2025).

19. Katz, R. S., & Mair, P. (2009). The cartel party thesis: A restatement. *Perspectives on Politics, 7*, 753–766. https://doi.org/10.1017/s1537592709991782 (accessed on 9th September 2025).

20. Kelemen, R. D. (2012). The Court of Justice of the European Union in the twenty-first century. https://core.ac.uk/download/62570714.pdf (accessed on 9th September 2025).

21. Khaunya, M. F., & Wawire, B. P. (2015). Devolved governance in Kenya; is it a false start in democratic decentralization for development?

22. Khotynska-Nor, O. (2024). The model of prosecutorial self-governance in Ukraine and the Baltic countries: A comparative aspect. *Access to Justice in Eastern Europe*. https://www.semanticscholar.org/paper/ca5206207dceeb34a81ac969046d845dc4eccaed (accessed on 9th September 2025).

23. Koutnatzis, S. I. G. (2011). Verfassungsvergleichende Überlegungen zur Rezeption des Grundsatzes der Verhältnismäßigkeit in Übersee. *44*, 32–59. https://www.semanticscholar.org/paper/18c1969b649997924671900c62279051b6890da3 (accessed on 9th September 2025).

24. Kraay, A., Kaufmann, D., & Mastruzzi, M. (2010). *The Worldwide Governance Indicators: Methodology and Analytical Issues*. World Bank Policy Research Working Paper. https://doi.org/10.1596/1813-9450-5430 (accessed on 9th September 2025).

25. Kumar, R., Halder, D., & Singh, R. K. R. (2025). Navigating constitutional change: A cross-jurisdictional examination of amendment procedures in India, France, and the USA. *American Journal of Psychiatric Rehabilitation*. https://www.semanticscholar.org/paper/57376fce7d7bc3e40bb55c991d57f4296737bc91 (accessed on 9th September 2025).

26. La Porta, R., López-de-Silanes, F., & Shleifer, A. (2008). The economic consequences of legal origins. *Journal of Economic Literature, 46*, 285–332. https://doi.org/10.1257/jel.46.2.285 (accessed on 9th September 2025).

27. Lührmann, A., & Rooney, B. (2020). Autocratization by decree: States of emergency and democratic decline. *Comparative Politics, 53*, 617–649. https://doi.org/10.5129/001041521x16004520146485 (accessed on 9th September 2025).

28. Mallon, G. E. (2024). Negotiated federalism: Intergovernmental relations on the maritime

frontier, 1789–1815. *The William and Mary Quarterly, 81*, 687–720. https://www.semanticscholar.org/paper/0cdf62f165a3ef7378341f5ad961e711b0e6c518 (accessed on 9th September 2025).

29. Mate, M. (2010). Two paths to judicial power: The basic structure doctrine and public interest litigation in comparative perspective. *SSRN Electronic Journal*.
30. Matei, A. (2004). The development of the European administration: Fundamental concepts and approaches. https://core.ac.uk/download/5085664.pdf (accessed on 9th September 2025).
31. McCoy, J., Rahman, T., & Somer, M. (2018). Polarization and the global crisis of democracy: Common patterns, dynamics, and pernicious consequences for democratic politics. *American Behavioral Scientist, 62*, 16–42. https://doi.org/10.1177/0002764218759576 (accessed on 9th September 2025).
32. Organization for Economic Co-operation and Development. (2018). *Integrity for Good Governance in Latin America and the Caribbean*. OECD eBooks. https://doi.org/10.1787/9789264201866-en (accessed on 9th September 2025).
33. Organization for Economic Co-operation and Development. (2022). *Building Trust and Reinforcing Democracy*. OECD Public Governance Reviews. https://doi.org/10.1787/76972a4a-en (accessed on 9th September 2025).
34. Poirier, J. (2024). Beyond intergovernmental relations in federal systems: The concept of intergovernmental law. *Comparative Constitutional Studies*. https://www.semanticscholar.org/paper/1abb218251f2d9710e47d81ba7e95286e49f73a2 (accessed on 9th September 2025).
35. Pradipta, A. M. (2025). The position of election law in ensuring regional political justice and stability. *Journal of Law and Humanity Studies*. https://www.semanticscholar.org/paper/6b8694d2f8702af3adbff929a82431b9a57da4d1 (accessed on 9th September 2025).
36. Safa, R. (2025). Democracy practices in de facto states: A TRNC perspective. *Turkish Academic Research Review–Türk Akademik Araştırmalar Dergisi (TARR)*. https://www.semanticscholar.org/paper/5fa7ecd7552ac8b904153eb74835dd0c9d3e6462 (accessed on 9th September 2025).
37. Sarkar, T. (2025). Education & training for parliamentarians: A pathway to effective governance. *International Journal for Multidisciplinary Research*. https://www.semanticscholar.org/paper/60829e546f16b6f0fd0c27d9e755f699c7f55d59 (accessed on 9th September 2025).
38. Saxena, V., Ansari, F., & Zaheer, A. (2024). Judicial review and democratic governance: Assessing the role of the Indian Supreme Court. *International Journal for Multidisciplinary Research*. https://www.semanticscholar.org/paper/1e536f8f28e5a969f5a4c802bd946fea9e6d6435 (accessed on 9th September 2025).
39. Somuncuoğlu, İ. E. (2025). Navigating indigenous self-government in Canada: The case of Nunavut and the struggle for institutional sovereignty. *Eklektik Sosyal Bilimler Dergisi*. https://www.semanticscholar.org/paper/e4e841574fa23fe10ed22c09e9cad3be2482f54b (accessed on 9th September 2025).
40. Sørensen, E., & Torfing, J. (2011). Enhancing collaborative innovation in the public sector. *Administration & Society, 43*, 842–868. https://doi.org/10.1177/0095399711418768 (accessed on 9th September 2025).
41. Suratno, U. (2025). Constitutional law and social change: A global perspective.

Journal of Law and Social Politic. https://www.semanticscholar.org/paper/e1c02191201cbb1390dd983162f698aa2d2c34bc (accessed on 9th September 2025).

42. Tushnet, M. V. (2006). Weak-form judicial review and core civil liberties. https://core.ac.uk/download/70373766.pdf (accessed on 9th September 2025).
43. van Kersbergen, K., & Vis, B. (2022). Digitalization as a policy response to social acceleration: Comparing democratic problem solving in Denmark and the Netherlands. *Government Information Quarterly, 39*, 101707–101707. https://doi.org/10.1016/j.giq.2022.101707 (accessed on 9th September 2025).
44. Waldner, D., & Lust, E. (2018). Unwelcome change: Coming to terms with democratic backsliding. *Annual Review of Political Science, 21*, 93–113. https://doi.org/10.1146/annurev-polisci-050517-114628 (accessed on 9th September 2025).
45. Xu, C. (2011). The fundamental institutions of China's reforms and development. *Journal of Economic Literature, 49*, 1076–1151. https://doi.org/10.1257/jel.49.4.1076 (accessed on 9th September 2025).
46. Young, E. A. (2016). The European Union: A comparative perspective. https://core.ac.uk/download/62570872.pdf (accessed on 9th September 2025).

Chapter 4

CIVIL PROCEDURE ACROSS JURISDICTIONS

Contents

INTRODUCTION

The evolution of legal systems across jurisdictions illustrates a complex interplay of procedural, cultural, and historical forces shaping modern civil procedure. Various legal traditions, be they common law or civil law based, illustrate the various paths taken by various jurisdictions to administration and the dispensation of justice. The interplay of international norms and national constitutional principles has influenced the practice of civil litigation, reflecting a fundamental commitment to the rule of law. Having initially been the focus of legislative efforts to enhance multi-level governance (MLG), there remains a persistent drive to decentralize procedure, which can create innovation as much as complexity in the practice of law (Bache et al., 2017). This decentered paradigm is intended to foster accountability and adaptability in legal systems, testing the efficacy of customary hierarchical systems in an increasingly interconnected world. Civil procedure is the foundation of the justice system, facilitating the resolution of conflicts and upholding legal accountability. Its structure regulates the manner in which cases are opened, the manner evidence is led, and the roles of judges and lawyers, thereby establishing the basis for the guarantee of fair hearings. An integral aspect of civil procedure is the intricate system of filing requirement and jurisdictional constraints, that can vary significantly between jurisdictions. This disparity can cause opportunity and challenge to litigants in that the peculiarity of procedural law will hinder or facilitate the pursuit of justice (Garrett et al., 2017). Moreover, the growing emphasis on specialized courts introduces a transforming terrain, which compels jurisdictions to make legal frameworks adapt in response to handle intricate conflicts effectively. The modern civil procedure debate is worthy of attention because the need for reform and harmonization within jurisdictions is acute. As globalization encourages cross-border legal engagements, the need to comprehend varying civil procedure strategies is of priority concern to legal practitioners and scholars. The quest for increased judicial efficiency and availability has encouraged reform in many jurisdictions to provide broader remedies, in response to wrongful convictions and claims of innocence, and therefore reflect shifting social values. These reflect the necessity for the administration of law to answer not merely to ideals of justice, but to fresh evidence and social expectation. In this regard, the study of civil procedure between jurisdictions is pivotal to an understanding of the intricacies of contemporary law and its ability to evolve in a changing global environment.

4.1. COURT STRUCTURES

The intricacies of the organization of courts are fundamental to the development of civil procedure across jurisdictions. Different legal systems possess several hierarchical organizational schemes, which significantly influence the processing and adjudication of cases. For instance, common law jurisdictions possess a tier system, whereby lower courts decide first cases and superior courts decide appeals. This hierarchy enables a systematic resolution of conflicts while offering the scope of legal remedies on several levels. These setups work in comparison to the principles of multi-level governance, showing that although hierarchies can assist with accountability, they can also introduce complications and inefficiencies within the judicial system. These dynamics invite an appreciation of hierarchical frameworks in each jurisdiction as they apply to case management and procedural justice (Bache et al., 2017). Also of similar importance are jurisdictional limits delineating the scope and jurisdiction of different courts. These boundaries vary significantly across jurisdictions and decide on which court a case may be heard, with effects on access to justice and the overall effectiveness of the judicial apparatus. For example, certain courts may handle only specific types of cases, such as family law or commercial disputes, essentially funneling cases to locations optimally geared to deal with them.

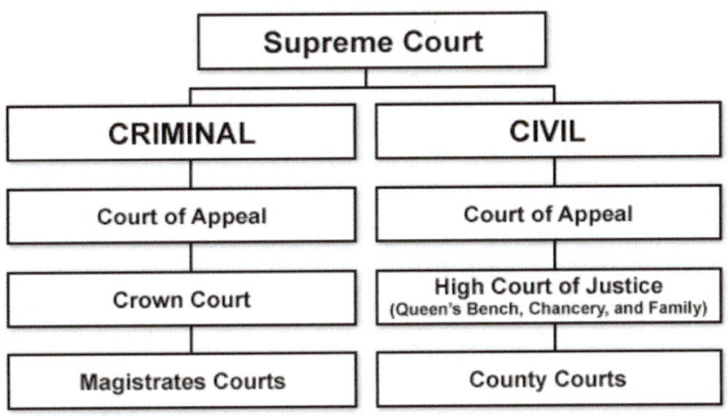

Figure 4.1. Court structure in England and Wales.

Source: https://ivypanda.com/essays/wp-content/uploads/2020/05/98308_1.png.

This specialization can yield more intelligent judgments and more efficient procedures; however, it also offers issues of overlap and potential conflicts between different legal systems. Such demarcations of jurisdiction pull out persistent controversies on how to harmonize incommensurate legal schemes better, especially in the ever-more globalized atmosphere where cross-border disputes are customary and necessitate all-encompassing solutions to problems of jurisdiction (Marshall et al., 2011). Besides, specialist courts are a significant trend in court designs aimed at enhancing effectiveness and specialization. By clustering certain legal concerns in specialist courts, jurisdictions can ensure that judges and lawyers acquire comprehensive knowledge of special fields, leading to more informed judicial rulings. Courts that specialize in areas such as tax law or administrative law are good examples of this trend, since they can manage complex legal frameworks more effectively than their generalist counterparts. However, there is a thin line between walking and falling off the edge; while specialization enhances legal understanding and accelerates the process, it can lead to isolated judicial cultures that work outside mainstream legal frameworks. Thus, the role of specialist courts adds another dimension to the study of courts in regard to structure, pushing the general account of civil procedure in several diverse legal settings (Bache et al., 2017) (Figure 4.1).

4.1.1. Hierarchical Arrangements

Sophistication in judicial systems generally emanates from court hierarchies' complex nature, which are fundamental structures of civil procedures in various jurisdictions. The hierarchical systems dictate a specific segregation of power between different levels of courts so that cases will be allocated effectively based on severity, complexity, and legal priority. At the grassroots level, lower courts will naturally handle less significant cases, whereas appellate courts are required to review judgments by such lower courts. This system not only ensures that legal doctrine is practiced equally across cases but also offers a window for appeal, thus facilitating a balance of justice and oversight within the court system. However, the effectiveness of these hierarchical frameworks is not uniform across jurisdictions since the harmonization of incentives across institutions is a critical factor in the determination of civil procedure results. The idea of collaboration among water utilities, civil society, and local government demonstrates the complexity of such collaborations. It has been shown that misaligned interests in such triad configurations will produce inefficiencies and failure of contract, as identified in the study of civil partnerships (Caplan et al., 2005). In this way, robust documentation that specifies roles, responsibility, and conflict resolution mechanisms becomes important to sustain cooperation among the actors involved. These formalized structures are instrumental in enforcing hierarchical values in civil procedure to bring about more effective judicial outcomes over the long term. An effective hierarchical system entails not only self-evident procedures but also a reflective mode of procedural compliance. The establishment of specialized courts, for instance, is a vital development in traditional hierarchies whereby more nuanced expertise can inform case determinations. The hierarchical model may then appear more adaptable as courts become more specialized, with the growing complexity of contemporary legal problems. This trend fits the importance of proper documentation in constructing cross-sectoral coalitions because poor definition of roles and expectations can create failure in coalitions in civil procedure (Evans et al., 2005). Lastly, what gives hierarchical designs strength in civil procedure is their capacity to adapt to evolving societal needs so that justice becomes accessible and equitable across jurisdictions (Figure 4.2).

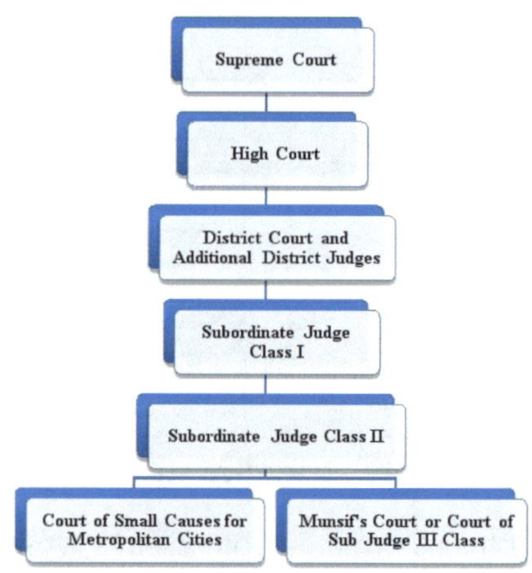

Figure 4.2. Hierarchy of courts in India.

Source: https://blog.ipleaders.in/wp-content/uploads/2019/08/c2808a.jpg.

4.1.2. Jurisdictional Boundaries

Civil procedure operates within a framework shaped by jurisdictional boundaries, which delineate the authority of courts to hear and adjudicate cases. In examining the nature of these boundaries, it becomes evident that they are not merely geographical but also conceptual, encompassing various factors like subject matter jurisdiction and personal jurisdiction. Courts function under distinct hierarchies, with jurisdiction often dictated by the level of government at which the court operates, whether local, state, or federal. The interaction between these levels can lead to complexities, especially in cases that cross state lines or international boundaries. The delineation of jurisdictional power also aligns with the need to ensure that legal processes are fair and equitable, taking into account the rights of parties involved, such as in cases involving asset restraint, which raise significant human rights concerns in accordance with Article 1 of Protocol 1 of the European Convention of Human Rights (Egan et al., 2011).

The implications of jurisdictional boundaries extend into the realm of enforcement mechanisms post-judgment. As civil disputes increasingly take on a cross-border characteristic, the enforcement of judgments can become an arduous process, often fraught with challenges stemming from a lack of universal jurisdictional standards. Different jurisdictions may apply varying thresholds for what constitutes adequate grounds for recognition and enforcement of foreign judgments, leading to potential discrepancies in legal outcomes. These disparities can manifest in instances where a party seeks to enforce a judgment obtained in one jurisdiction against assets located in another, further complicating enforcement strategies. Such complexities highlight the necessity for a coherent framework that bridges jurisdictional divides, ensuring that justice is not only obtained but effectively enforced across borders, thereby minimizing the potential for inequitable treatment due to jurisdictional discrepancies (Bookman et al., 2016). Moreover, the discussion surrounding jurisdictional boundaries cannot overlook the phenomenon of forum shopping. This practice, often criticized as unethical, allows litigants to choose a legal forum that may offer a more favorable outcome based on differing jurisdictional rules. Such strategic selection can reveal underlying flaws within civil procedures across jurisdictions, as courts may impose barriers to discourage this practice, potentially undermining access to justice. However, the concept encompasses unrecognized benefits, including facilitating private regulatory enforcement and driving legal reforms within jurisdictions striving to provide fairer legal frameworks. Understanding the dual nature of forum shopping—its potential to both hinder and promote justice—emphasizes the importance of a nuanced approach to jurisdictional governance that acknowledges these opposing facets in an interconnected legal landscape (Bookman et al., 2016) (Figure 4.3).

Figure 4.3. Jurisdictional boundaries in corporate disputes.

Source: https://mkajaipur.com/wp-content/uploads/2025/07/image-NCLT-CIVIL-COURT.png.

4.1.3. Specialized Courts

Specialized courts are an important step in the progress of the judicial system, a reflection of increased recognition of the need to deal with some problems in society more effectively.

Unlike general courts with a policy of one size fits all, specialized courts, like domestic violence courts, are designed to handle their case-loads in specially tailored strategies. Such courts generally operate according to special principles involving specially dedicated dockets and specially trained judges over the relevant legal and social issues. Established in response to the particular needs of domestic violence, these courts are indicative of the responsiveness of the courts to evolving social norms and issues such as the protection of victims and the rehabilitation of offenders that are necessary to achieve efficacy and public trust in the judicial process (Chris et al., 2009). In the grander context of civil procedure for all courts, specialized courts serve as a bridge between traditional legal structures and contemporary social expectations (Figure 4.4).

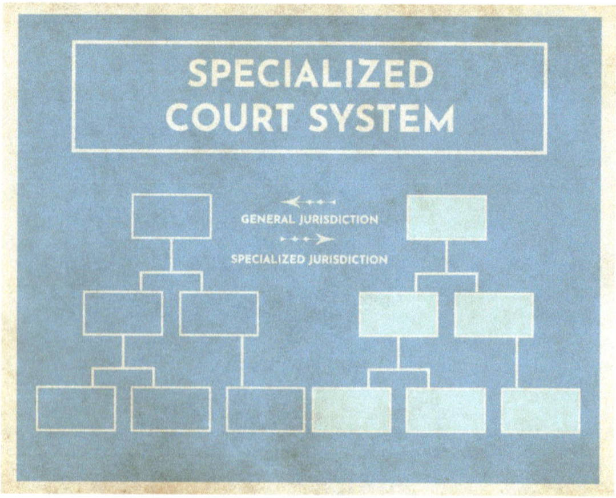

Figure 4.4. Some countries structure their specialized courts as an independent court system, with its own building, staff, and internal administrative structure. This approach is often taken when the subject matter is complex or generates a high volume of litigation.

Source: https://judiciariesworldwide.fjc.gov/sites/default/files/2023-05/Spec-Cts-System.png.

They demonstrate the shift from punitive models to a more restorative and supportive model within the justice system. The courts focus on resolving underlying problems rather than punishing, as seen in the way they handle domestic violence cases where collaborative effort among legal, social, and mental health providers becomes the utmost priority. Special courts try to combine an individualized approach to judicial processes with understanding of social forces impacting the involved persons. This model not only seeks justice, but also ensures a maximum level of procedural fairness so that courts can better respond to victims' needs and to offenders' rehabilitative needs (Chris et al., 2009). Moreover, the establishment of specialty courts has provided the door for reform in eliminating imbalances in the judicial system. As they handle specific types of cases, specialty courts can better explore experimental programs that are able to remedy the root causes of legal disputes or criminal behavior, particularly those resulting in systemic issues such as racial disproportion. Findings from empirical studies of these courts have enabled one to identify best practices and other options in such fields as plea bargaining or pretrial detention, and they suggest possible solutions to social justice issues. Finally, the integration of specialized courts with a problem-solving focus and the ideal of rehabilitation reflects a pivotal shift in civil procedure that emphasizes unique cases as well as broader societal concerns, ultimately making the judicial process more balanced.

4.2. COMMENCEMENT OF PROCEEDINGS

Filing of an action marks the beginning of the civil litigation process, paving the way for the resolution of controversies in various jurisdictions. Most legal systems require varying requirements of filing to initiate actions, with typical requirements being the filing of a complaint or petition with the respective court. These documents must plead the essential elements of the claim so that they meet jurisdictional demands and procedural requirements. For instance, in some jurisdictions, plaintiffs have to make the initial disclosures or certification that the claim is not frivolous before proceeding. The additional layer of procedural safeguards aims to screen out frivolous claims, thereby conserving judicial resources and ensuring effective case management. As such, identification of these filing requirements is critical to practitioners navigating the complexities of civil procedure, particularly in measuring the pragmatics of the obstacles to initiating proceedings in different legal systems. Once a complaint is lodged, the next pivotal step is the service of process, whereby each party is duly notified of the steps taken against them pursuant to the law. This procedural prerequisite is most crucial in terms of due process and is often overseen by stringent rules differing from jurisdiction to jurisdiction. Valid service could be personal delivery, substituted service, or publication, depending on circumstances and the rules of the jurisdiction. Invalid service may result in long delays or disqualification of the action, thus necessitating compliance with procedural prerequisites. As stressed by various works, including those on housing company refurbishments, the completeness of information regarding the mechanism of service has significant consequences for the advancement of a case and the ability of plaintiffs to receive legal remedies in time. Hence, thorough familiarity with service requirements is a significant factor in initiating proceedings in jurisdictions. The initial hearings play a decisive role in charting the path of civil proceedings. In these hearings, the court balances the strength of the claims and defenses presented, ruling on procedure that will control further phases of litigation. The function of this stage differs based on the legal framework, from preliminary injunction hearings to case management conferences intended to facilitate timeliness and speed in case advancement. Additionally, the courts are also able to address issues such as objections to jurisdiction, dismissal motions, or security for costs applications, particularly in the case of impecunious defendants as interpreted from provisions of the law by the courts (Ching et al., 2009). A successful first hearing can ease the process of litigation, which plays a significant role in the allocation of resources and sets the tone for cooperation among the warring parties. Thus, identifying the functions of initial hearings within the larger framework of civil procedure is vital to gaining insight into how proceedings begin and unfold across different jurisdictions.

4.2.1. Filing Requirements

The commencement of civil proceedings in different jurisdictions comes with the need to meet some filing requirements that differ so vastly across different legal systems. These are significant requirements that contribute to orderly court processes by ensuring cases are presented in a systematic way. In countries like the United States, for instance, the requirements could be submitting a complaint, payment of filing fees, and conformity with local rules of civil procedure. Such procedural requirements not only detail the validity of the claims, but they also stipulate the timeliness of subsequent actions. Also, such methods reflect broader jurisdictional strategies aimed at managing caseloads in an economical fashion and avoiding delay without reason and promoting judicial economy, with profound effects for access to justice and effective representation of the legal system. There is a value in having knowledge regarding the sophistication of these filing requirements, particularly considering the effects of non-compliance. In some other jurisdictions, failure to follow proper filing may result in automatic dismissal of a case, thereby depriving individuals of their right to seek redress. For example, Alaska's Civil Rule 82 contains a fee-shifting provision that will dissuade frivolous claims but at the same time dissuades rightful plaintiffs who are afraid of the monetary cost of losing a case (Rennie et al., 2012). This idea encapsulates a delicate balance between reducing frivolous lawsuits and preserving robust access to legal remedy for meritorious plaintiffs. The nuance of civil procedure from state to state adds another level of complication to the challenges litigants suffer in compliance with these requirements, which vary not only state by state but also within a single court in which one brings an action. Furthermore, the exchange of filing requirements and the fluid dynamics of civil litigation should not be underestimated. As the planet is becoming more globalized and technology evolves, legal structures are modifying to accommodate international controversies. The challenges that encompass international patent rights, for instance, underscore the call for harmony and clarity of filing processes (Loftus et al., 2011). Hence, those jurisdictions that are successful in harmonizing their filing needs can make legal proceedings more effective and enhance cooperation in cross-border situations. Last but not least, the methodology toward filing requirements reflects the legal philosophy and operational aspirations of each jurisdiction, structuring the delivery and experience of civil justice by litigants in a multiform and interdependent world (Figure 4.5).

Figure 4.5. If one needs to file a complaint in consumer Court against an Insurance company. Then they can do it with the help of various legal service providers.

Source: https://www.edrafter.in/wp-content/uploads/2025/01/file-a-consumer-complaint-in-courts.jpg.

4.2.2. Service of Process

The initiation of legal proceedings hinges significantly on the procedural steps that adhere to jurisdictional requirements, one of the most crucial being the service of process. This fundamental procedure ensures that all parties involved in a legal dispute are adequately notified, allowing them the opportunity to respond. Failure to properly serve process can result in delays or dismissals, emphasizing the importance of adherence to both local and international regulations governing service methods. As jurisdictions vary widely in their procedures, understanding the nuances is vital for effective legal practice. For instance, while some jurisdictions may allow personal service, others might recognize substituted service, which is particularly relevant in global contexts where parties reside in different countries. This variability emphasizes a critical aspect of lawyering in a globalized environment, where the boundaries of legal processes overlap and shift per jurisdiction, necessitating a comprehensive understanding of each. A deeper examination reveals the implications of service of process, particularly in how it impacts the overall efficacy of legal proceedings. The way service is executed often reflects the underlying legal structure of a jurisdiction; the efficiency or inefficiency of service can either facilitate or hinder access to justice. In jurisdictions such as the United States, service of process is a well-defined area governed by specific rules, which may differ at the federal and state levels. Conversely, in countries like France, where labor court activity is prevalent, the complexities of service can directly affect labor market flows, as noted in research highlighting the relationship between judicial outcomes and employment protections (Fraisse et al., 2025). The consequences of service of process extend beyond mere notification; they influence case outcomes and legal strategies, further complicating the procedural landscape across jurisdictions. Additionally, the service of process bears implications for the international practice of law, especially in how legal professionals communicate and operate across borders (Figure 4.6).

Figure 4.6. Learning English can be an exhilarating and rewarding journey, especially when it opens doors to diverse fields, including the intricate world of law.

Source: https://5minuteenglish.com/wp-content/uploads/2024/11/a-courtroom-in-session.webp.

With the advent of legal English as a common language of international legal discourse, the service process can be impacted by the linguistic proficiency of the parties (Künnecke et al., 2017). While professionals serve clients from different legal traditions, risk of miscommunication is enhanced, making the importance of clear and easy-to-understand procedures for serving process even more paramount. Besides, lawyers trained in a different legal tradition—common law or civil law—will need to adjust their technique when handling cross-national cases so that they can comply with an assortment of procedural requirements. The interplay of procedural requirements and communicative clarity testifies to the richness of global lawyering, in which serving process is not merely a procedural nicety but an important factor in access to justice and legal efficacy.

4.2.3. Initial Hearings

This step in procedure is very dissimilar across jurisdictions, reflecting differing legal traditions and philosophies of the courts. Under some systems, the initial hearing might be a formal session in which issues of prime concern are outlined and preliminary motions entertained. Under others, it might be an informal conference to ready a case for litigation. Prioritization of expediency and speedy determination of disputes is globally attractive, but the machinery employed in achieving such ends differs vastly, exposing the nuanced reconciliations between expediency, justice, and rights of parties under each system. An appreciation of the nature and significance of first hearings is thus essential to an understanding of more universal systems of civil procedure. Also, the initial hearings typically include critical matters such as determination of jurisdiction, determination of issues of law, and determination of defenses available. Such a procedural session can be of immense value in streamlining the issues that are to be decided by the court, thereby making the subsequent phases of litigation easier. In discovery-focused jurisdictions, the initial hearing can allocate timetables and limits for evidence disclosure, as compared to jurisdictions that like less comprehensive pre-trial disclosure tactics. The composition and conduct of first hearings can influence a party's strategy in a specific way; they might be forced to establish their sides before defining them and anticipate the judge's questions and concerns. Thus, not only are these hearings enabled procedurally, but they also engage the parties to an extent that they facilitate active legal involvement and strategic preparation within the civil justice system. The impacts of the way initial hearings are administered thus extend beyond procedure; they also shape the ground of access to justice and resource allocation. Concerns arise particularly with respect to equitable treatment of litigants, with disparities potentially leading to disproportionate outcomes between jurisdictions. In one jurisdiction, for instance, a party may benefit from a comprehensive first hearing that allows for effective interaction, while in another, a cursory process may do their case harm. In addition, preliminary hearings can provide insight into the way jurisdictions handle sophisticated cases with esoteric knowledge or border-crossing implications, as manifest in the dynamics of international litigation. Through examination of these hearings, researchers as well as practitioners are better placed to evaluate the efficiency and fairness of judicial proceedings, such as is the case in recent arguments for strengthening the civil justice system, such as those documented in the in-depth analysis of patent litigation highlighted in Huang et al. (2011) and political motive deliberations in enforcement proceedings in the Voting Rights Act quoted in Charles et al. (2007) (Figure 4.7).

Figure 4.7. In civil procedure, the initial hearing serves as a pivotal moment in the adjudication process, often setting the stage for the subsequent progression of a case.

Source: https://bonvillelaw.com/wp-content/uploads/2022/09/Preliminary-Hearing.png.

4.3. EVIDENCE AND PROOF STANDARDS

Underlying this is the admissibility of evidence, which determines what may go before the courts attention in a matter of litigation. Various jurisdictions have various thresholds for admissibility; rules on hearsay, for instance, differ widely between common law and civil law systems. These differences not only influence the caliber of evidence presented but also trickle down to trial dynamics generally. Jurisdictions with rigid admissibility rules risk unconsciously constricting the boundaries of evidence, thereby impairing litigants' chances to substantiate their claims in their entirety. Practitioners and researchers must hence understand these distinctions to navigate the procedural scaffolding that determines the course of justice in their jurisdictions. Furthermore, the requirement of proof remains a fundamental element in determining complaints and defenses in the course of civil trials. The rule prescribes which party is responsible for proving their claims at trial. Under common law systems, the burden normally is on the plaintiff to establish his case by a preponderance of the evidence, and in a few instances, such as criminal cases, the burden shifts to the defense under specified conditions.

Figure 4.8. The concept of evidence and proof standards is pivotal in establishing the integrity and legitimacy of judicial outcomes, serving as a cornerstone across various legal jurisdictions.

Source: https://blog.ipleaders.in/wp-content/uploads/2021/02/1577458404.jpg.

The such clarity as to who bears this burden can do much to alter trial strategy and outcomes. In addition, the relationship between standards of evidence and burden of proof speaks to varying levels of proving liability or innocence across jurisdictions and is a reflection of more basic philosophical underpinnings of justice in other disparate judicial systems. Practices of witness examination also provide insight into the nuances of evidence and standards of proof across jurisdictions, where methods can radically differ. In adversarial systems, such as those historically prevalent in the United States, the examination of witnesses is marked by aggressive cross-examinations that are intended to undermine credibility and the reliability of testimony. By contrast, inquisitorial systems, the standard in a vast majority of European nations, lean toward a more collaborative approach, in which judges occupy the foreground of questioning witnesses. These variations not only affect the procedural aspects of trials but also impact significantly on how evidence is viewed and evaluated. Lastly, the processes of questioning witnesses are indicative of broader legal philosophies, emphasizing the fact that legal professionals should be competent at working within these complicated frameworks with a view to delivering justice (Garrett et al., 2017; Bache et al., 2017) (Figure 4.8).

4.3.1. Admissibility Rules

These rules control the extent to which different types of evidence can be presented in court, and thereby the outcome of trials in various jurisdictions. Each legal system utilizes its own template, one that is governed by history, sociocultural, and practical considerations that are reflective of the values of due process and justice. For instance, the admission of hearsay evidence is considerably variant in that some jurisdictions accept it subject to certain conditions whereas others preclude it entirely.

Figure 4.9. In the complex landscape of civil procedure, the principles governing admissibility rules play a crucial role in maintaining the integrity of legal proceedings.

Source: https://sociallawstoday.com/wp-content/uploads/2023/08/PHOTO-3-1-551x431.png.

This inconsistency can create conflicting court rulings, alluding to the need for more examination of how these regulations interact with the overriding aims of fairness and applicability in courtroom proceedings, a concern that resonates throughout the ancient trials for the sake of doing justice amid chaos, such as the Nuremberg tribunals (Halpern et al., 2018). The nuances of admissibility are then reinforced by the conflict between standards and practice of evidence at law. Within adversarial-style jurisdictions, the burden of producing evidence and the lodging of objections to their admissibility often falls most markedly on the lawyers.

Within such regimes, stringent standards ensure that only evidence meeting criteria of relevance and reliability is placed before the jury. Judges, however, are not entirely absent from playing an active role in the examination of expert testimony based on its scientific foundation, as evidenced in judicial argument models of intertextuality. The intersection with scientific literature and legal standards demonstrates the manner in which restrictions form a tightly knit structure whereby non-legal texts rarely filter through, demarcating the boundary of knowledge within courtrooms (Bazerman et al., 2009). Thus, understanding the structures underlying admissibility rules must entail reflection both on the legal principles at stake and on general consequences for the administration of justice. As civil procedure evolves everywhere, the diversity of admissibility rules reflects a tension underlying the surface between visions of justice and procedural expediency. Judicial systems must walk that thin line between inclusiveness in admitting evidence and ensuring the rights of the accused are held intact. Though some legal jurisdictions are more liberal in their stance—enduring flexibility in rules of evidence to permit the special circumstances of civil litigations—others prefer to adhere to stricter formalities. This divergence can have a significant impact on trial outcomes, particularly where key evidence is at risk of being excluded on grounds of difference in jurisdictions. Therefore, reformers have a tendency to beg for harmonizing admissibility standards between courts so that equality and uniformity in civil proceedings can be achieved. By taking a more cohesive approach, court systems can effectively fulfill their very function of dispensing justice even in the diversified world of international law (Halpern et al., 2018) (Figure 4.9).

4.3.2. Burden of Proof

In the intricate landscape of civil procedure, the concept of the burden of proof plays a pivotal role, shaping the trajectory of litigation across various jurisdictions (Figure 4.10).

Figure 4.10. The burden of proof is defined as the obligation of a party to establish the truthfulness of its claim or defense in lawsuits. The doctrine varies extensively from one jurisdiction to another, typically based on the underlying legal traditions and culture of the relevant courts.

Source: https://criminallawstudiesnluj.wordpress.com/wp-content/uploads/2019/06/burden-of-proof.jpg.

In common law systems, for example, the burden traditionally lies on the plaintiff to prove his case on a preponderance of the evidence. In other civil law states, the judge may play a more inquisitorial role and actually decide the merits of the case, and it is challenging to apply the traditional allocation of the burden and leads to different interpretations and uses of this basic principle of law. The implications of the burden of proof extend beyond matters of procedural machinery alone; they have extremely large effects on the substantive outcomes of cases. In instances such as war crime trials, the sensitivity of evidentiary requirements can have an influence on the definition of justice and fairness. As noted in studies of the Nuremberg trials, the challenge is how to balance the need for accountability with the rights of the accused, especially where usual evidentiary rules may not apply. The introduction of hearsay evidence, for instance, raises issues of credibility and reliability which encroach on the very foundation of burden of proof. These nuances demand a nuanced understanding of how courts deal with evidentiary standards in unorthodox circumstances, and it is argued that while the burden of proof can be a trope in civil procedure, its deployment is by no means straightforward, especially under war and political turmoil pressures (Halpern et al., 2018).

Moreover, differences in burden of proof across jurisdictions reflect overarching questions of accountability and procedural justice in civil litigation. This contrast is particularly strong in comparative work, such as the comparison of the legal frameworks in nations, and they reveal the ways in which localized customs shape the pursuit of justice. A case in point is Switzerland's competition policy, which provides insight into the manner in which the interplay between procedural requirements and standards of proof may be explored, with relevance to the operation of the burden of proof in commercial cases. Understanding such differences enables legal researchers and practitioners to examine critically the effectiveness of different systems in providing fair outcomes based on their unique legal traditions (Neven et al., 2025). Thus, researching the burden of proof within the framework of civil procedure makes it clear that there is a need for adaptive and responsive practices based on the evolving context of international legal standards.

4.3.3. Witness Examination

Witness examination also falls within procedural frameworks that vary significantly across jurisdictions, influencing the dispensation of justice. For example, the United States and United Kingdom adversarial systems rely heavily on the tactic of cross-examination in order to undermine witness testimony. The process places great emphasis on lawyers' strategic abilities to the extent that they can disclose inconsistencies and prejudice within witness testimonies. Conversely, inquisitorial jurisdictions, prevalent in most of the countries in Europe, emphasize a more active approach, with an active role for the judges in questioning witnesses. Such fundamental difference in witness examination practice serves to underline the contrasting philosophies that underlie civil procedure and echo the ongoing debate regarding the efficiency and effectiveness of judicial processes. Evolution of witness questioning reflects a constant rethinking of efficiency and fairness in the justice system. Latest reforms, particularly in Australia, have been trying to minimize expert bias by innovating concurrent evidence sessions, where expert witnesses present together and directly confront one another. This new procedure not only simplifies complex expert testimony but also instills scientific temper in the courts. By curtailing adversarial posturing and receptiveness to argumentation, Australian courts establish precedent for the prevention of biases which otherwise would cloud pursuit of justice. The transformation is evidence of acceptance of the need for witness examination processes that prioritize accuracy and accessibility over more conventional, adversarial methods. These reforms are indicative of a broader trend towards enhancing procedural integrity within civil suits as well as aligning with social understandings of fairness within courtrooms (Edmond et al., 2009). The interaction between witness examination procedures and the broad principles of justice is particularly apparent in instances where war crimes trials are at issue. These processes, which too often operate under scrutiny and immense pressure, need a delicate handling of standards of proof, such as admissibility of hearsay evidence. With some of the trials held at Nuremberg and later trials, the issue of unreliable testimonies and how to provide justice has prompted judges to rethink traditional boundaries of proof. Amending the rules to render the evidence more pertinent and credible but not at the expense of defendants' rights is essential under such extraordinary circumstances. The flexibility here brings out the necessity to modify civil procedures to meet justice despite war and conflict complexities (Halpern et al., 2018). Lastly, the expansion of witness examination procedures across jurisdictions is representative of a broader commitment to ensuring that legal procedures adapt to the demands of justice in the modern era along with the specific demands of unusual circumstances (Figure 4.11).

Figure 4.11. In contemporary legal systems, the examination of witnesses plays a pivotal role in establishing the credibility and reliability of evidence presented in court.

Source: https://encrypted-tbn0.gstatic.com/images?q=tbn:ANd9GcQMESup0zHzZm4ZksXHjJyRcGX9EX4FPJJdVg&s.

4.4. ROLE OF THE JUDGE AND LAWYERS

The intricate roles played by judges and lawyers in civil procedure reflect the tension between authority and advocacy. Judges find themselves in a commanding position, often as gatekeepers to ensure the integrity of the judicial process. The role of judges varies significantly in different jurisdictions depending on whether an inquisitorial system or an adversarial system is employed. For instance, in adversarial models, the judges simply primarily preside over the court, ensuring equity but allowing lawyers to do most of the advocacy. In an inquisitorial model, the judges actively engage in the pursuit of the facts and questioning of the witnesses, which drastically changes the dynamics of legal representation. This structural difference dictates the overall objectives of civil procedure in countries, eventually affecting the administration of justice. No less significant is the role of the attorney, whose obligation extends not just to representation of their clients, but also to observance of ethical norms and procedural prudence. Attorneys are the chief advocates for their clients, employing strategies consistent with the overall framework of civil procedure. Their role is more than. Advocacy to entail serving justice and conflict resolution in a manner that preserves dignity of the courts. Proper representation is also based on local procedures and legal precedents, which require attorneys to adapt strategies through respective jurisdictions. Moreover, specialist courts can impose certain expectations on attorneys, altering the degree of their roles in ensuring proper legal proceedings. This flexibility speaks to the critical role lawyers play in navigating the complexity of civil litigation. Judicial control of proceedings is another primary characteristic defining the connection between judges and lawyers across civil jurisdictions. Judges possess authority to structure court proceedings, streamline procedures, and encourage compliance with procedural requirements. Such control is particularly critical in jurisdictions like Australia, where recent legislative changes have aimed at promoting efficiency and minimizing partisan expert evidence during civil trials. In this respect, concurrent evidence allows expert witnesses to provide evidence together, meaning an enhanced rapport between lawyers and judges, with the trend of heightened cooperation in the courtroom. These advances imply a shift away from the confrontational roles of the past, including the emphasis on reducing expert conflict and enhancing procedural justice (Edmond et al., 2009). The integration of the judge as guardian of justice and the lawyer as talented advocate is thus key to creating a civil procedure that not only decides legal contests, but also makes access to justice a reality (Edmond et al., 2009).

4.4.1. Inquisitorial vs. Adversarial Systems

The contrasting mechanisms of justice, represented by the inquisitorial and adversarial systems, highlight divergent philosophies regarding the role of judges and the pursuit of truth in legal proceedings (Figure 4.12).

This system promotes a culture of evidence-seeking jointly, with many pre-trial investigations being detailed in nature. On the other hand, the adversarial system, prevalent in common law systems, places judges as neutral referees between parties, with parties themselves searching for and submitting evidence to plead for their case. This fundamental distinction not only decides courtroom dynamics but also influences procedural efficiency, because inquisitorial paradigms are likely to emphasize speed through procedural simplification, while adversarial models are likely to lead to protracted litigation as both sides try to outsmart each other.

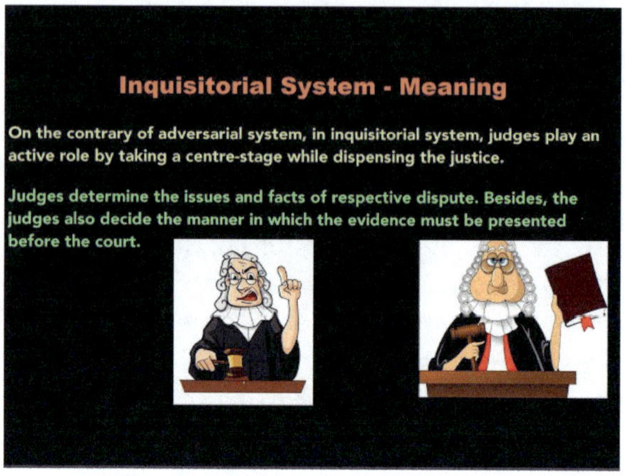

Figure 4.12. In the inquisitorial system, which is prevalent in many civil law jurisdictions, judges assume an active role in investigating the facts of a case.

Source: https://i.ytimg.com/vi/EL03Gs-s6Fs/sddefault.jpg.

The impacts of these competing paradigms resonate through evidentiary needs as well as the dynamics of examining witnesses. Under the inquisitorial system, judges personally question witnesses, thus carrying out a detailed investigation of the facts that can lead to more precise results but also raises the judges' inquiries about impartiality. The adversarial model, however, employs the method of cross-examination, where attorneys confront witnesses to challenge their credibility and the reliability of the testimony. This method, as far as it enables opponents to represent their clients assertively, creates avenues for prejudice and exploitative tactics that can obscure the truth. The orientation of these systems reflects underlying values within society, with inquisitorial systems perhaps having more emphasis on group seeking the truth and adversarial systems placing greater emphasis on individual rights and adversarial rivalry, thereby casting wider legal practices and interpretations. Further, the interplay between these systems of law can provide valuable lessons towards reforming court procedures and maximizing the efficacy of civil procedure between jurisdictions. According to observations on comparative legal traditions, a combination of aspects of the two systems could result in enhanced procedural legitimacy and citizen trust in court decisions. For instance, integration of inquisitorial regimes' rigorous fact-finding methods into an adversarial system can help curb problems of evidentiary validity, particularly in cases involving science. Solving the current crisis in scientific evidence, criticized widely on legal forums, necessitates a rethinking of how these systems work. Through the integration of the strengths of both paradigms, as argued in present debate, for instance in Bibas et al. (2010), the justice system would be in a position to enable better outcomes, with the aim of truth coming first, but still maintaining the procedural rights inherent in both paradigms, such as discussed in Sevier et al. (2014).

4.4.2. Judicial Control over Proceedings

In other court systems, control of legal proceedings by judges is a fundamental feature that heavily influences the outcomes of cases (Figure 4.13).

This oversight by the judiciary can be carried out through methods such as case management, where judges can set deadlines and procedural rules to speed up the process. By being engaged in the early stages of litigation, judges can prevent wasteful delays and attain judicial economy, particularly in complex cases requiring large amounts of evidence gathering. Besides, the potential for conflicting outcomes between courts aggravates this necessity of judicial control, as in the case of patent litigation, when litigants can have repetitive hearings in multiple nations (Huang et al., 2011). Such situations highlight the necessity of a robust and uniform methodology in handling complex legal issues, justifying the importance of a judges role in civil procedure.

Figure 4.13. Judges are not merely arbiters but also active participants in ensuring that proceedings are conducted in a fair and efficient manner.

Source: https://www.shutterstock.com/image-photo/court-law-justice-trial-proceedings-600nw-2056423637.jpg.

Apart from procedural efficiency, the extent of judicial control directly impacts the equitable administration of justice. Judges generally have the discretion to balance the far-reaching implications of their rulings, particularly in cases that involve extraterritorial implications. With judicial systems worldwide grappling with problems provoked by extraterritorial judgments and diverse procedural standards, the role of judges increasingly takes center stage. For instance, coordination efforts across the world have focused on creating uniform discovery standards to settle extraterritorial disputes that multiply the complexity of civil proceedings (Levarda et al., 1994). In this regard, judges may be used as agents of dispute settlement, facilitating interaction and cooperation among the courts towards enhancing the effectiveness of the legal system. This active judicial involvement ensures that principles of justice are not undermined by territorial distances, thus boosting the integrity of the judiciary. Judicial oversight engaging with advocates appearing on behalf of clients also underscores the complexities of civil procedure between jurisdictions. Lawyers must travel between various procedural landscapes while remaining in conformity with the peculiar expectations of various judges within different legal systems. This is an essential relationship since litigators are prone to be required to illuminate and lead in the model that is imposed by judicial guidance. In an inquisitorial style of law, for example, the judge may have a more prominent role in seeking out the facts and leading the proceedings. An adversarial model, on the other hand, relies significantly on initiative by the parties. Regardless of the system, effectiveness of judicial control ultimately hinges on cooperative relationships between legal advisors and the judiciary, working within a balanced relationship requisite for equitable conclusions. By recognizing such varied functions, legal experts can better accommodate the nuances of civil procedure and thus devise improved overall effectiveness of judicial process.

4.4.3. Counsel Responsibilities

In the intricate system of civil procedure, the functions of counsel are pivotal to keeping legal proceedings running smoothly across varied jurisdictions. Counsel must handle unbelievably intricate regulations and guidelines that often vary greatly from jurisdiction to jurisdiction. This variance demands a solid comprehension of state and federal laws as well as the respective rules governing courts. The American Bar Association (ABA) Model Rules provide a general standard, but the distinctive agency rules that govern lawyers reflect a wide variety of differences in practice. Cohen et al. (2016) emphasizes the importance of recognizing these differences, particularly with respect to regulatory lawyering, and observes that familiarity with agency rule variations can enable lawyers to make well-informed decisions that are consistent with local standards and expectations. Thus, the onus rests upon counsel to keep their wits about them, adapting their strategy and practice to the jurisdiction they find themselves in. Laying additional complexity on these tasks, ethical and legal mandates imposed upon counsel not merely control their procedural maneuvers but their overall dedication to client and justice system as well (Figure 4.14).

Figure 4.14. Counsel must maintain a consistent standard of care, which encompasses both diligence and competence in their representation.

Source: https://www.bls.gov/ooh/images/2145.jpg.

This entails a complete understanding of the evidence and proof standards, as well as the rules of admissibility in the respective courts. Adherence to these standards exhibits a lawyer's duty to uphold the integrity of the judicial process. Furthermore, counsel also have to prepare to execute effective cross-examinations of witnesses and craft persuasive arguments consistent with the burdens of proof for the court. The ethical implication of these responsibilities cannot be overstated, since a failure to obtain these standards can have dire repercussions for both client and counsel involved.

Also, the interaction between the judiciary and legal advisors emphasizes the critical role played by lawyers in the paradigm of civil procedure. Counsel must understand the nature of adversarial compared to inquisitorial systems so that they can frame their case preparation and advocacy styles in a manner consistent with the system's nature. In more controlled courts, counsels would need to alter how they advance cases, as well as represent their clients. How a judge's control is balanced by counsels' advocacy dictates the outcome of legal disputes. Thus, counselors must be able to decipher judicial signals and adapt their strategy accordingly. Flexibility is then necessary, especially as civil law procedures evolve and additional regulatory matters come to the front to obligate lawyers to stay current and attuned to change in the legal environment. Lee et al. (2017) explains how the legal responsibilities of school officials reflect broader societal interests, offering a helpful analogy for counsel as they face their own responsibilities across the heterogenous platforms of civil procedure.

4.5. APPELLATE REVIEW

The very intricate nature of review on appeal is at the heart of civil procedure in various jurisdictions, reflecting the fundamental principles of justice and legal equity (Figure 4.15).

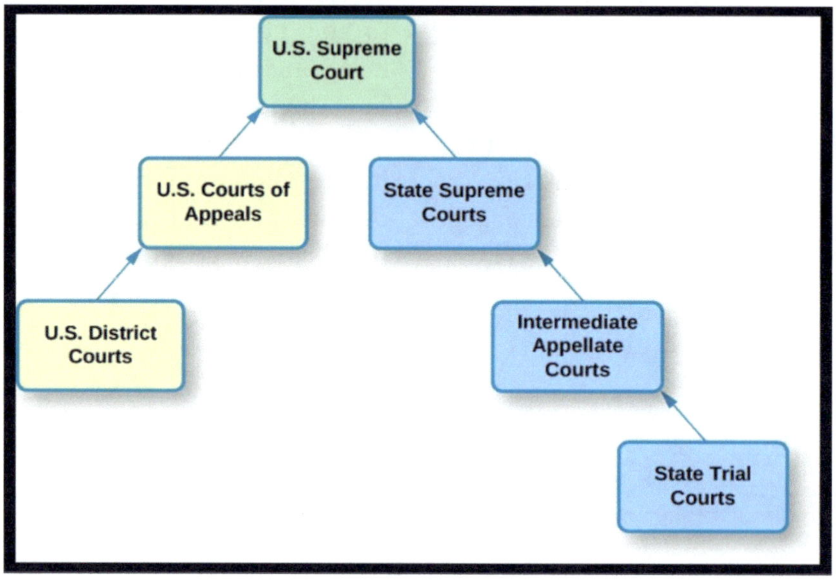

Figure 4.15. The appellate process allows a higher court to re-evaluate decisions made by lower courts, ensuring that errors in law or procedure can be rectified.

Source: https://library.fiveable.me/_next/image?url=https%3A%2F%2Fstorage.googleapis.com%2Fstatic.prod.fiveable.me%2Fsearch-images%252F%2522Direct_vs_collateral_appeals_in_US_law_highlighting_differences_in_process_and_constitutional_issues.%2522-OSC_AmGov_13_02_Structure.jpg&w=1080&q=75.

It is essential in safeguarding the rights of the litigants, especially in countries where there could be disparities that could arise from improper application of the law or inadequate representation. Notably, appellate review does not just amount to a re-testing of facts but a testing of legal interpretations and adherence to procedural norms. Such a scrutiny can lead to the establishment of legal precedents, which ultimately defines the judicial landscape. The diversity of appeal systems highlights the necessity to understand local procedure and rules, eventually based on more general principles of legal reform and access to justice (Garrett et al., 2017).

The foundation of appeal in civil proceedings is often quite diverse between jurisdictions, reflecting the diversity of legal traditions and standards of appellate courts. Common grounds may range from procedural mistakes, incorrect application of statutory law, or conclusions not adequately supported by evidence. Each ground functions as a basic basis of appeal jurisdiction, allowing parties to adequately challenge lower court rulings. Time limits in which to file an appeal are also critical, in that they may debase a party's ability to seek relief following a judgment. It is thus basic that parties seeking relief in appeal must understand the time limits and procedural complexities. The legal profession's knowledge of these parameters is significant not just for practitioners but also for researchers examining the availability and efficacy of appellate systems in the broader scheme of civil procedure (Marshall et al., 2011).

While appellate review rectifies judicial error, the rule of finality is no less a consideration than maintaining order and predictability in the legal system. The necessity of providing sufficient appellate scrutiny is often set against the need to provide finality of judgment in jurisdictions. Allowing excessive appeals may end up eroding the power of lower courts and interfering with judicial efficiency, one reason why appellate courts typically possess discretion in hearing cases. Procedural standards that underpin the process of appeal often emphasize the necessity of raising timely and brief arguments because appellate judges are only interested in legal issues as opposed to factual ones. Moreover, the burden of proof in appeals falls, for the most part, on the appellant, endorsing a system that places judicial stability first. In doing so, a lengthy picture of the relationship between appellate review and civil processes exists, ultimately impacting the administration of justice in courts (Garrett et al., 2017).

4.5.1. Grounds of Appeal

Appellate review is a core component of civil procedure that allows parties to appeal the decisions in lower courts. Through it, the importance of ensuring that justice is not only pursued but achieved as well through serious examination of legal standards is justified. Reasons for appeal are the specific legal bases on which an appellate review is sought, commonly involving errors of law, procedural errors, or errors of substance on the part of the trial judge. In the majority of the jurisdictions, such grounds are a multifaceted interrelationship of rules of law and procedure that can be quite divergent.

For instance, the court could base appeal on the absence of jurisdiction, where the lower court had crossed its legal mandate, or on the wrongful reception of evidence that had impacted the trial's outcome. Hence, the multiplicity of grounds for determining correct grounds of appeal has an important bearing on ensuring the integrity of the court system. Also, apart from these grounds addressing the faults in the judiciary, they address the need for better legal standards across jurisdictions. In cases raising international conflict, the variations of grounds for appeal complicate the process of resolution. Different legal systems will prioritize different issues, such as levels of negligence or statutory construction, that determine the grounds on which an appeal can be launched. For instance, for private international law to apply so that foreign-linked claims are suitably addressed in European Union jurisdictions, economic relationship integration is usually a stimulus for collaborative attention to both grounds of appeal and procedural modalities to ensure consistency in the adjudication of cross-border disputes. As law adapts to fit emerging contexts, the nature of grounds of appeal requires dynamic legal systems that function in multiple contexts (Oppong et al., 2006).

On top of this, the procedures and timelines associated with appealing add additional layers of complexity that interact with grounds of appeal that have been identified. The need to adhere to strict procedural standards highlights the importance of legal representation since failure to meet given timelines would make an appeal nugatory regardless of quality. To this end, parties intending to appeal must be familiar with not only the legal grounds on which they stand but also with procedural standards to pursue their appeal. This emphasizes the necessity for lawyers, who are required to navigate the intricate landscape of civil procedure in various jurisdictions. As a corrective mechanism, the appeals process not only rectifies judicial error but also keeps subordinate courts accountable, thereby enhancing the overall integrity of the legal system (Marshall et al., 2011).

4.5.2. Procedures and Timelines

In civil procedure analysis, procedural complexity and timelines are important determinants of the direction cases take in various jurisdictions. Each legal jurisdiction has idiosyncratic rules of procedure that oversee the life cycle of a case from its creation to its end. In legal frameworks such as the United States, Germany, Japan, and the United Kingdom, rules of filing and service of process significantly dictate the timing and effectiveness of court proceedings. The requirements reflect a systemic respect for the due process since all stakeholders are officially notified and given the right of response. Initial hearing schedules can vary widely, creating a framework under which legal professionals must tactfully navigate to adjust to local mindsets and procedural norms while concurrently protecting clients rights and interests. The imbedded legal culture in most jurisdictions further shapes the procedural setting, particularly review of appeal timelines. For instance, the foundation of appeal may usually differ, affecting the time for submitting appeals and, hence, subsequent procedures entailed within them. Where tight appellate timelines exist in jurisdictions, there could be pressure to adhere to procedural rules, leading to strategic decisions by attorneys on whether to appeal or settle the case in question. It is necessary to learn about these dynamics so that legal advocacy is effective because parties must deal not only with the letter of the law but also with the temporal constraints placed by the law. The processes in the appellate process, therefore, must be approached with serious planning and foresight so that shortcuts that can undermine a client's case are avoided. Additionally, rules of procedure for the enforcement of judgments add another layer to the complexities of civil procedure across jurisdictions. The time periods associated with the enforcement of a judgment can have a perceptible impact on a party's capacity to enjoy the benefits of a favorable ruling. As noted in intellectual property litigation discussions, concurrent suits in different jurisdictions can result in conflicting judgments and added expenses for patent holders who want to enforce their rights (Huang et al., 2011). This necessitates not only an awareness of the local court structure and specific timetables but also potential global consequences when seeking enforcement of orders in cross-border litigation (Huang et al., 2011). This consciousness demands streamlined processes and open timelines, which are crucial to conserve judicial resources and ensure equitable results across frontiers.

4.5.3. Finality of Judgments

The intricacies of civil procedure are likely to reveal significant differences in the handling of finality of judgments across jurisdictions. In some other jurisprudence, once a judgment is given, it is left as final, effectively stifling the basis for subsequent appeals. This rule serves to enhance judicial efficiency and ensure confidence in judicial pronouncements, creating faith in the judicial process. But this very practice also threatens the undesirable result of wrongful convictions remaining unappealed due to the emphasis on finality. In fact, historical examination indicates that this emphasis on verdict finality has brought considerable suffering to defendants when new evidence emerges after trial, thereby exposing an inherent conflict in criminal justice systems. The evolution of this attitude in contemporary legal frameworks has revealed the controversies regarding the attainment of a balance between finality and the pursuit of justice (Garrett et al., 2017).

In addition, the global controversy regarding judgments finality has witnessed reconsideration of the mechanisms of law across jurisdictions. While the presumption of innocence guarantees certain rights, the majority of countries have residual procedural limitations that make it difficult for defendants to effectively plead innocence following trial. Different jurisdictions are currently undergoing change because the availability of broader remedies allows the majority of convicted individuals to appeal verdicts upon the disclosure of fresh evidence. This accommodative aspect, increasingly observed in international law, reflects a paradigmatic shift in legal norms by adapting to modern perceptions of justice and human rights. The interplay between ensuring the holiness of final judgments and allowing corrective steps comes into play particularly against the backdrop of changing civil procedures and altering social values with regards to equity and accountability (Calliess et al., 2005). The subject of finality of judgment also overlaps with the broader subject of civil procedure and review on appeal. As the law evolves the idea of finality, appellate procedures are of particular importance since they form the foundation for concluding when and how an order may be appealed. Various jurisdictions specify specific grounds for appeal, outlining grounds like errors of law or procedural flaws that can invalidate a previous judgment. The regulations and timeframes governing appeals also differ based on varying philosophies of the law, further influencing what is understood as final. The ability of parties to interact with these complicated structures highlights the requirement for jurisdictions to find a balance between finality and opportunities for corrective actions against missteps. Lastly, this dynamic interweaves the aggregate potency and impartiality of civil procedures to yield an ongoing pursuit of how best to administer justice in varied legal cultures.

4.6. ENFORCEMENT OF JUDGMENTS

Jurisdictions are likely to be having profound differences in mechanisms and processes employed to enforce judgments based on their law traditions and circumstances. For instance, in most of the civil law systems of Europe, the process of enforcement is likely to be systematized and centralized with the potential for systemized enforcement of judgments within various regions. Conversely, jurisdictions applying common law place significant emphasis on individualism and local rule, thereby placing more of a fractured and, at times, incongruent arrangement for enforcement. These variations are likely to cause litigants enforcing judgments problems, especially in a period of globalization where transnational transactions are increasingly common, leading to the necessity for strong frameworks to facilitate effective enforcement across the board (Oppong et al., 2006). In the examination of cross-border enforcement of judgments, international relations and economic integration introduce layers of complexity. International commerce necessitates robust frameworks for adjudicating transnational disputes and making judgments obtained in a given legal system enforceable and recognized in another. Legislation such as the Recognition and Enforcement of Foreign Judgments Act attempts to break some of these barriers with stringent criteria for enforcement. However, success in such systems generally hinges on the cooperation of individual jurisdictions to move in a direction towards enforcement. Variation in standards, procedure, and juridical approach to international judgments can act as barriers, hence necessitating continuous dialogue and cooperation among nations. Thus, it is crucial to address these enforcement challenges in order to enhance the certainty of judicial decisions in the international arena (Bookman et al., 2016).

Figure 4.16. The enforcement of judgments represents a critical facet of civil procedure, particularly when delineating the variances across jurisdictions.

Source: https://thumbs.dreamstime.com/b/business-illustration-showing-concept-enforcement-foreign-judgments-business-illustration-showing-concept-110227875.jpg.

Despite the evolving process of judgment enforcement, there are enormous restraints imposed by jurisdictions on such enforcement, which are tremendous issues of fairness and legal integrity. Some jurisdictions may refuse to enforce a foreign judgment on the basis of exceptions of public policy or lack of jurisdictional power of the court of rendition. The constraints are meant to deter abuse of the judicial process and rule against forum shopping, thus reducing the integrity of cross-border litigation. The constraints would be seen to impart arbitrariness to enforcement, which may discourage international cooperation and trade. Apart from this, as the courts grapple with the interplay of an integrated legal environment, finding a balance between forestalling abuse and facilitating access to justice remains a perpetual challenge. Judicial institutions are thus required to walk cautiously through such constraints in a bid to enhance predictability and efficiency in judgment enforcement and facilitate smoother international relations in civil matters (Oppong et al., 2006) (Figure 4.16).

4.6.1. Mechanisms for Enforcement

The mechanisms for enforcing court judgments are a critical element in upholding the rule of law both inside and across various jurisdictions. Across the majority of legal systems, enforcement mechanisms consist of the interrelation between state power and procedural devices with the intention of coercing the compliance of court orders. This structure can differ substantially between jurisdictions, reflecting attendant philosophies of law and administrative capacity. Enforcement typically means judgments being translated into active orders in the appropriate contexts, either in terms of monetary penalties or orders compelling definite action. The effectiveness of such mechanisms can have direct implications for not just the immediate parties involved in such action, but also the broader public's perception of legal reliability and the integrity of the court system. Hence, a correct understanding of how these mechanisms operate is vital to practitioners and scholars alike who are interested in the comparative nature of civil procedures. In competition law, the enforcement mechanisms that are invoked in prosecuting cartels elicit nuances that serve to emphasize the merits of procedural innovation in jurisdictions. Where the government agencies make investigations, they must contend with varying legal systems governing under what circumstances evidence gathered in one context—for example, mergers and acquisitions—may be applied in the prosecution of collusion. While most jurisdictions now restrict the direct use of the same for reasons in statutes, optimal enforcement of competition law is made hard. There are suggestions to revise these obstacles to allow for the more unified approach by which intelligence from these sources is utilized to guide an entire enforcement strategy. By making such enforcement mechanisms more efficient and effective, jurisdictions can not only penalize offending parties, but also deter future offenses against competition law, ultimately promoting fair market practice (Ghosal, 2025). Enforcement mechanism reform is also on the agenda in jurisdictions such as the MENA, where significant gaps exist between secured transactions laws and enforceability of security interests in movable assets. According to debate regarding these legal systems, the MENA region is way behind in modernizing its model of secured transactions, which is detrimental to businesses, including SMEs, when accessing credit. Enforcement of security interests comprehensively is critical to fostering economic growth and stability, yet most states suffer from ineffective legal structures and lack of electronic registries. Addressing these through effective reforms can establish a more secure business environment that encourages investment and facilitates availability of credit. Therefore, focus on such enforcement mechanisms not only aligns with international best practice but is also essential to the economic development of a jurisdiction wishing to modernize its legal system (Alvarez et al., 2025).

4.6.2. Cross-Border Execution

In legal interactions within globalized structures, the cross-border enforcement principle becomes a vital matter in the procedure civil. Court structures, far from being able to harmonize in an integrated way because of incompatible legislative systems, pose challenges in enforcing judgments across the border. Complexity in jurisdictions requires a sophisticated level of understanding regarding how specialized courts function and how hierarchical frameworks influence enforcement effectiveness. Each jurisdiction tends to have its own method of recognition and enforcement of judgments, and these variations tend to cause issues when the parties try to enforce rulings across frontiers. The challenge of dealing with these varied systems becomes an aggravating factor and increased litigation expenses as litigants tend to be compelled to use multipronged strategies to law as they seek to achieve their objectives in foreign courts (Huang et al., 2011). Further, the interplay can result in inconsistent judgments, which complicate the general resolution of disputes under cross-border scenarios. Procedural issues in starting proceedings for cross-border enforcement add another layer of intricacies to civil actions. Parties and organizations must be very careful about the prerequisite filing requirements and service of process protocols that apply within each jurisdiction. For example, jurisdictions may have varying rules regarding the admissibility of evidence and may require compliance with specific procedural standards for the filing and prosecution of cases. These variations not only delay proceedings but also require legal representatives to be familiar with the intricacy of every jurisdiction's rules in detail. Failure to meet these criteria will lead to ineffective service or outright rejection of claims, and thus even more difficult foreign judgments to enforce. Where jurisdictions develop their own systems for foreign judgment recognition, the rendering of good legal representation is important in traversing these intricate procedural labyrinths (Dima Cristea et al., 2025). Moreover, enforcement of a judgment across countries is limited severely, which has to be realized in full by lawyers involved in cross-border litigation. Often, the enforceability of a foreign judgment hinges on bilateral recognition agreements between courts, which are significantly different in both scope and application. Therefore, the practitioners not only need to examine the enforcing jurisdiction's legal environment but also political and economic relations that may influence enforceability. Such a fact poses interesting challenges, particularly in intellectual property disputes where patent rights, for example, need to be adjudicated over numerous countries depending on the character of national legislations (Huang et al., 2011). Finally, the cross-border enforcement mechanisms are a reflection of the general subject of civil procedure throughout jurisdictions, where an appreciation of the interrelatedness of legal systems must be understood in order to successfully navigate the nuances of international law.

4.6.3. Restrictions on Enforcement

In civil procedure, the enforcement of judgments is central to the delivery of justice as well as ensuring the rule of law in various jurisdictions. In taking into consideration restraints on enforcement, one can observe that jurisdictional borders and the distinctive nature of court systems are significant factors. Jurisdictional borders have a way of making things more complex, particularly in international cases where parties may be located in various states. These territorial limitations can also hinder successful enforcement as a judgment procured in one jurisdiction may not be enforceable or actively enforced within another jurisdiction. The divergence of the legal standards and enforcement mechanisms complicates it further, calling for an understanding of each jurisdiction's rules of civil procedure and enforceable channels to pursue the enforcing of rights. A realistic appreciation of such limits is essential for lawyers handling transnational disputes, as it has direct implications for the client's right to seek redress and enforcement of claims. The differences in machinery of enforcement between jurisdictions highlight a fundamental contradiction in the paradigm of civil procedure. In America, for instance, reliance on public and private enforcement mechanisms exhibits a distinct solution to deterring harmful conduct. Procedural barriers, too often drawn from a business-friendly account, can significantly undermine the effectiveness of private action. Conversely, the European Union has affirmatively tried to promote private rights of action, especially in antitrust law, but it has not followed this path across all member states (Oppong et al., 2006). The lack of comprehensive private enforcement means, including claims aggregations and litigation funding, presents challenges to those seeking redress in Europe. Hence, comparative enforcement limitation analysis finds that the effectiveness of judgment enforcement varies significantly, depending on regulation policies and sociopolitical circumstances underlying each jurisdiction. Additionally, the implications of these enforcement limitations go beyond mundane procedural consequences; they ultimately dictate the experiences of affected parties of justice. In jurisdictions with aggravated enforcement difficulties, claimants may face severe hurdles in realizing their rights and compensation. This is particularly so in foreign element cases, where factors such as economic integration and mobility of capital make enforcement more challenging (Oppong et al., 2006). Perceptions of cross-border claims also have the tendency to generate uncertainty among parties, with the risk of non-enforcement or delayed enforcement of judgments exacerbating the situation. It is therefore crucial for law scholars and practitioners to explore the intersection between enforcement limitations and civil procedure further. Not only does an exploration lay bare the effects of variations in law on rights of individuals, but it also ends up placing premiums on the need for harmonization and reform of enforcement practice in jurisdictions, thereby enhancing the integrity of international legal orders.

SUMMARY

Analysis of civil procedure across jurisdictions underscores the complex interrelation between legal frameworks and the judicial institutions that administer them. In comparing different court structures, hierarchical ones and jurisdictional divisions are observed to play a fundamental role in influencing litigation pathways. Specialist courts have evolved to deal with specific types of disputes, optimizing the efficiency of the judicial process and providing access to justice for claimants. Knowledge of procedural nuances inherent in various jurisdictions, such as implications of competition policies in jurisdictions like Switzerland, is important for gaining insight into international best practices and legal practitioners' challenges across borders (Neven et al., 2025). Hence, identification of a coherent framework of civil procedure involves an in-depth understanding that addresses the idiosyncratic features of every legal system while pursuing convergence on the basis of dispute resolution principles. The commencement of judicial proceedings is yet another area of civil procedure that deserves critical analysis. Disparate filing provisions and the rule of service of process vary across other jurisdictions, with a direct bearing on commencing claims. Commencement of hearings may greatly differ, impacting the way cases are perceived and processed right from the beginning. Such diversity may result in procedural inefficiencies and inconsistencies in the disposition of comparable cases across borders that erode the canons of fairness and access to legal practices. Moreover, just as in the examination of patent litigation across various nations, the tendency towards duplicative litigation shows the costs that are transported when litigants must contend with alternative procedural realities (Neven et al., 2025). Accordingly, a harmonized system to enable more effective cross-border contacts among different legal regimes would significantly enhance the efficacy of civil procedures throughout the world. Finally, enforcement of judgments is a critical aspect of civil procedure that often faces jurisdiction problems. Enforcement procedures could differ profoundly where there is a cross-border execution involved, whereby conflicting acts and policies may discourage sound settlement. Restrictions on enforcement serve to point up variations among jurisdictions, highlighting the necessity of increased cooperation and more standardized guidelines for the recognition of foreign judgments. The incoherence of patent conflict resolution, for instance, has the effect of laying bare the challenges faced by litigants in trying to reach resolution across borders, highlighting the relevance of international legal norms (Huang et al., 2011). As a result, filling these gaps with reform and mutual agreements demonstrates an essential step toward more harmonious and equitable civil procedural practices to the advantage of all participants in the litigatory process.

A LOOK TO THE FUTURE

MODERNIZATION OF CIVIL PROCEDURE IN A GLOBALIZED LEGAL ENVIRONMENT

As the legal sphere spreads, jurisdictions worldwide are increasingly recognizing the necessity of civil procedure reforms that render it more accessible and efficient. The most significant trend is that technology is being integrated into civil proceedings, particularly in the context of digital platforms to file and conduct cases. This transition allows for a streamlined beginning of proceedings, where traditional requests for physical submissions are supplemented by electronic requests which have a greater degree of acceptance with a broader category of users. Additionally, jurisdictions are exploring the establishment of specialized courts, which apply the use of technology to settle certain types of disputes, maximizing the process of case management and reducing the backlog which tends to plague regular court systems. Refining procedural structures in this manner is aligned with aims for enhancing judicial effectiveness and strengthening equal access to justice, paving the way for civil procedures modernization across diverse legal systems (Ibrahim et al., 2025).

In addition to these technological advancements, there is a growing significant emphasis on harmonizing procedural rules so as to facilitate cross-border litigation. This demand arises from increased globalization, which has the tendency to generate conflicts that cross borders and jurisdictions. Debate among legal scholars and lawyers has, in turn, focused more on the development of standardized norms that control jurisdictional frontiers and enforcement of judgments. These efforts are designed to minimize differences in civil procedure so that the process can go on more smoothly for both litigants and courts engaged in cross-border conflicts. By fostering coordination among jurisdictions, there is a possibility of establishing mechanisms that would facilitate service of process and first hearings, reimaging civil controversies in an interdependent legal world (Palazzo et al., 2025).

Moreover, the practice of judges and lawyers is also experiencing a revolutionary shift towards collaboration instead of adversarial styles, particularly in jurisdictions adopting inquisitorial forms. This development favors control by the judiciary of proceedings, persuading judges to be more participative in case management and in guiding trials. Therefore, lawyers are more and more expected to make changes to their strategies, turning to cooperative representations stressing the effective resolution of controversies rather than using customary fight-like methods. This movement not only enhances the effectiveness of the courts but also serves to enhance the overall level of justice in proceedings, as litigants enjoy a process where clarity and cooperation take center stage. Such paradigms for civil procedure occurring in the jurisdictions represent a significant departure from conventional approaches, and they have the potential to revolutionize the face of civil litigation (Ibrahim et al., 2025).

REFERENCES

1. Alvarez de la Campa, A. (2025). Increasing access to credit through reforming secured transactions in the MENA region. https://core.ac.uk/download/pdf/6333148.pdf (accessed on 9th September 2025).
2. Bache, I., Benz, A., Citroni, G., Cowles, M. G., Domorenok, E., Domorenok, E., et al. (2017). Traps of multi-level governance: Lessons from the implementation of the Water Framework Directive in Italy. https://core.ac.uk/download/154329411.pdf (accessed on 9th September 2025).
3. Bachtler, J., Charles, D., Frangenheim, A., Granqvist, B., et al. (2013). An assessment of multilevel governance in cohesion policy, 2007–2013. https://core.ac.uk/download/29176909.pdf (accessed on 9th September 2025).
4. Bazerman, C. (2009). How does science come to speak in the courts? Citations, intertexts, expert witnesses, consequential facts, and reasoning. https://core.ac.uk/download/62553212.pdf (accessed on 9th September 2025).
5. Bibas, S., & Burke-White, W. W. (2010). International idealism meets domestic-criminal-procedure realism. https://core.ac.uk/download/62560142.pdf (accessed on 9th September 2025).
6. Bookman, P. K. (2016). The unsung virtues of global forum shopping. https://core.ac.uk/download/223119461.pdf (accessed on 9th September 2025).
7. Calliess, G. P. (2005). *Reflexive Transnational Law: The Privatization of Civil Law and the Civilization of Private Law*. https://core.ac.uk/download/14503938.pdf (accessed on 9th September 2025).
8. Caplan, K., Evans, B. E., & McMahon, J. (2005). *The Partnership Paperchase: Structuring Partnership Agreements in Water and Sanitation in Low-Income Communities*.
9. Charles, G. U., & Fuentes-Rohwer, L. (2007). The politics of preclearance. https://core.ac.uk/download/62563217.pdf (accessed on 9th September 2025).
10. Che Ibrahim, C. K. C., & Ahmad Kamal, N. (2025). A bibliometric exploration of accreditation in civil engineering education: Trends and insights. *Quality Assurance in Education*. https://www.semanticscholar.org/paper/afe6d2bb9448a6f3eff0ba28bd7c3f15aec1f065 (accessed on 9th September 2025).
11. Ching, J. (2009). The statutory ground to award security for costs against an impecunious company: Should we mourn its passing? https://core.ac.uk/download/30649427.pdf (accessed on 9th September 2025).
12. Cockburn, H., Lacey, N., & Farmer, L. (1999). Debatable land: An essay on the relationship between English and Scottish criminal law. https://core.ac.uk/download/1422349.pdf (accessed on 9th September 2025).
13. Cohen, G. M. (2016). The laws of agency lawyering. https://core.ac.uk/download/144231467.pdf (accessed on 9th September 2025).
14. Cramton, R. C., & Martin, P. W. (1995). Information technology and legal ethics: Expanding the teaching and understanding of legal ethics through the creation of a new generation of

electronic reference materials. https://core.ac.uk/download/62553701.pdf (accessed on 9th September 2025).

15. Dima (Cristea), S. M., Dima, B., Moldovan, N., Pirtea, M., et al. (2025). National legislative systems and foreign standards and regulations: The case of International Financial Reporting Standards adoption. https://core.ac.uk/download/pdf/6622139.pdf (accessed on 9th September 2025).
16. Dropkin, D. D. (2002). Linking the culpability and circumstantial evidence requirements for the spoliation inference. https://core.ac.uk/download/62548851.pdf (accessed on 9th September 2025).
17. Edmond, G. (2009). Merton and the hot tub: Scientific conventions and expert evidence in Australian civil procedure. https://core.ac.uk/download/62553218.pdf (accessed on 9th September 2025).
18. Egan, M. (2011). Non-conviction-based sanctions: The Court of Justice v. the European Court of Human Rights, who decides? https://core.ac.uk/download/228177152.pdf (accessed on 9th September 2025).
19. Evans, B. E., McMahon, J., & Caplan, K. (2005). *The Partnership Paperchase: Structuring Partnership Agreements in Water and Sanitation in Low-Income Communities.*
20. Fraisse, H., Kramarz, F., & Prost, C. (2025). Labor disputes and labor flows. https://core.ac.uk/download/pdf/6424402.pdf (accessed on 9th September 2025).
21. Garrett, B. L. (2017). Towards an international right to claim innocence. https://core.ac.uk/download/213020519.pdf (accessed on 9th September 2025).
22. Ghosal, V. (2025). The law and economics of enhancing cartel enforcement: Using information from non-cartel investigations to prosecute cartels. https://core.ac.uk/download/pdf/6634653.pdf (accessed on 9th September 2025).
23. Gramatikov, M. A., & Vriesendorp, R. D. (2025). Impact of the financial crisis. https://core.ac.uk/download/pdf/6844006.pdf (accessed on 9th September 2025).
24. Halpern, M. (2018). Trends in admissibility of hearsay evidence in war crime trials: Is fairness really preserved? https://core.ac.uk/download/213020809.pdf (accessed on 9th September 2025).
25. Huang, J., & Qian, A. X. (1995). "One country, two systems," three law families, and four legal regions: The emerging inter-regional conflicts of law in China. https://core.ac.uk/download/62547779.pdf (accessed on 9th September 2025).
26. Huang, V., & Pooley, J. (2011). Multi-national patent litigation: Management of discovery and settlement issues and the role of the judiciary. https://core.ac.uk/download/144230660.pdf (accessed on 9th September 2025).
27. Künnecke, M. (2017). English as common legal language: Its expansion and the effects on civil law and common law lawyers. https://core.ac.uk/download/151161045.pdf (accessed on 9th September 2025).
28. Lee, C. J., Lockley, S. W., Nolan, D. M., Pattison, K., et al. (2017). Law-based arguments and messages to advocate for later school start time policies in the United States. https://core.ac.uk/download/225000631.pdf (accessed on 9th September 2025).
29. Levarda, D. (1994). A comparative study of U.S. and British approaches to discovery

conflicts: Achieving a uniform system of extraterritorial discovery. https://core.ac.uk/download/144226562.pdf (accessed on 9th September 2025).

30. Loftus, D. (2011). International patent protection: Time for a fully EU functioning supra-national patent mechanism. https://core.ac.uk/download/1667526.pdf (accessed on 9th September 2025).
31. Marshall, P. D. (2011). A comparative analysis of the right to appeal. https://core.ac.uk/download/62547246.pdf (accessed on 9th September 2025).
32. Neven, D., & von Ungern-Sternberg, T. (2025). Competition policy in Switzerland. https://core.ac.uk/download/pdf/7353554.pdf (accessed on 9th September 2025).
33. O'Sullivan, C. S., Labriola, M., Rempel, M., Moore, S., & Bradley, S. (2009). A national portrait of domestic violence courts. https://core.ac.uk/download/71361444.pdf (accessed on 9th September 2025).
34. Oppong, R. F. (2006). Private international law and the African Economic Community: A plea for greater attention. https://core.ac.uk/download/68885.pdf (accessed on 9th September 2025).
35. Palazzo, S., Palazzo, F., & Zambetta, G. (2025). The role of artificial intelligence in advanced engineering: Current trends and future prospects. *Journal of Intelligent Communication*. https://www.semanticscholar.org/paper/4e46cb483ef4835270b46ee4c9ffdb9eeab3bf58 (accessed on 9th September 2025).
36. Rathod, J., & Veheesan, S. (2016). The arc and architecture of private enforcement regimes in the United States and Europe: A view across the Atlantic. https://core.ac.uk/download/72052955.pdf (accessed on 9th September 2025).
37. Rennie, D. C. (2012). Rule 82 & tort reform: An empirical study of the impact of Alaska's English Rule on federal civil case filings. https://core.ac.uk/download/62546127.pdf (accessed on 9th September 2025).
38. Rudovsky, D., Owens, E., Mayson, S., & Bibas, S. (2015). Improving fairness and addressing racial disparities in the Delaware criminal justice system. https://core.ac.uk/download/75761612.pdf (accessed on 9th September 2025).
39. Sevier, J. (2014). Redesigning the science court. https://core.ac.uk/download/56359548.pdf (accessed on 9th September 2025).

Chapter

5

CRIMINAL LAW AND PROCEDURE

Contents

INTRODUCTION

The intricate geography of criminal procedure and law is the basis for maintaining the order of society, as well as justice. Delving into the subtleties in this field can be useful for legal professionals as well as members of society whose lives are meshed with such law. Understanding the classification of crimes is fundamental; the distinction between felonies and misdemeanors offers crucial knowledge regarding the severity and penalty of various criminal activity. Additionally, an advanced appreciation of private rather than public wrongdoing brings out the nuances between responsibility in the law and social morality, affecting laws' enactment and enforcement. Inchoate offenses also illustrate the flexibility of the criminal law because they touch on behavior that is not necessarily moving towards a completed offense but merits consideration and intervention from the law. As criminal proceedings move forward, criminal investigation methods define the framework under which justice is pursued. Arrest rules, search and seizure, and detention practices establish the boundaries of law enforcement's authority and that of the citizens. All these procedures have to balance the need for public safety with the obligation to protect civil liberties, thereby securing public trust in the judiciary. Further, the subtlety of prosecutorial discretion is an important determinant of case direction, largely dictating the choice at the charging point and influencing the overall justice meted out. These should be handled with caution as they are meant to safeguard against potential abuses of power while ensuring that justice is not only pursued but also achieved reasonably too. The trajectory of trial proceedings is a milestone of criminal law, where due process and fairness issues are at the forefront. The role of the jury or bench reflects contrasting philosophies regarding the administration of justice, with the guideline of innocent until proven guilty as a pillar of defense in law. As the proceedings continue, the evidentiary standards become determinant in ensuring that evidence of guilt is obtained to a standard of reasonable doubt. Furthermore, sentencing trends both articulate the judicial discretion of judges' decision-making and mirror the policies behind punitive policy. An awareness of these steps is central in understanding not only the final outcome of trials, but also their effect on individuals who are caught up in the criminal justice process. The sophistication of these processes illustrates the significance of continued debate within the realm of criminal law and procedure, promoting ongoing debate and revision.

5.1. CLASSIFICATION OF OFFENCES

An obvious understanding of the classification of offences is at the heart of criminal law practice because it directs the legal penalties for various types of wrongdoing (Figure 5.1).

Figure 5.1. In the legal realm, offences are primarily categorized into felonies and misdemeanors, a distinction that significantly impacts the severity of punishment and the procedural process involved in prosecution.

Source: https://1.bp.blogspot.com/-crBOt5_uvBQ/X9Ywp2F4IqI/AAAAAAAABm8/yCxgXaFHbmUd7HjL6QsOVcUGoBcj3AnwwCLcBGAsYHQ/s251/Kinds%2Bof%2BOffences-%2BCognizable%252C%2BBailable%252C%2Band%2BCompoundable.jpg.

Felonies are more severe offenses, typically involving extended prison sentences, while misdemeanors are typically less serious crimes which lead to reduced incarceration or other sanctions, like payment of fines or community service. This is not only significant from a sentencing perspective but also as a means of describing the social consequences of criminal activity and the consequent criminal justice responses that attempt to rehabilitate or deter criminal activity. Therefore, by identification of the various levels of criminality, legislators can craft legal systems appropriately to respond to them, thereby establishing a more just legal environment. Another significant distinction in connection with the classification of offences is that between public and private wrongs, and this is an articulation of the public as compared to private character of crime. Public wrongs, such as serious crimes like theft, assault, or murder, are thought to be crimes against society as a whole and thus worthy of prosecution by the state for the good of public order. Private wrongs denote conduct that mainly causes damages to individual victims, such as fraud or defamation, wherein the aggrieved parties seek remedies in civil action. This difference emphasizes not only the penal implications of various offences but also indicates the state's function as a defender of public interest and illustrates the broader societal impact of criminal law. These differences matter since they decide the legal procedures and relative resources assigned to enforcement, prosecution, and victim support, and that justice ought to be delivered efficaciously in response to various categories of transgression. Further complexity in the offence categorization comes with the inclusion of inchoate offences, which are offences initiated but left unfinished.

They underscore important society interests by recognizing intent behind criminal conduct and intervening before harm is successfully accomplished. Examples of inchoate offences include conspiracy, attempt, and solicitation, which all indicate defendants criminal intent even where the act itself has not yet been done. The legal framework underlying these inchoate crimes is instrumental in the prevention of suspected criminal activity, exhibiting a proactive character in criminal law. Furthermore, classification has operational implications to criminal investigation and prosecution strategy because it enables law enforcement to shift resources towards prevention and intervention. Through not only analysis of what constitutes completed offences but also the reasons and attempts leading up to them, the legal system better understands criminality while retaining the significance of nuance classifications in criminal law (Usatii, 2025; Kostiuk, 2024).

5.1.1. Felony vs. Misdemeanor

The distinctions between felonies and misdemeanors are at the heart of understanding the criminal justice system and how it works (Figure 5.2).

Figure 5.2. Felony in Texas: Classes & penalties.

Source: texascriminaldefensegroup.com.

Usually, felonies are considered more serious offenses with heavier punishments, including over one year of imprisonment or death in extreme circumstances. The offenses bear grave implications for society, such as violent offenses, severe robberies, and severe drug offenses, which signify the need for harsh legal repercussions. Conversely, misdemeanors are more minor offenses, typically punishable by fines or a year or less in a local jail, compared to a state penitentiary. The category addresses both the seriousness of the crime and society's response to such behavior. Accordingly, the legal frameworks upon which these classifications are based, for example, jurisdictional legislation and sentencing legislation, vary widely, determining the application of justice between jurisdictions. The legal impact of felony and misdemeanor classifications goes beyond punishment; they both have significant effects on the life of convicted persons for both offenses. Felons typically have concomitant collateral consequences like disenfranchisement, restriction of employment opportunities, and finding housing. These consequences can feed patterns of recidivism and cycles of poverty, further making it more difficult for them to reintegrate into society. On the other hand, though misdemeanor offenses are not as severe, they too can result in fines, requirements for community service, and other punitive steps that impact an individual's future. The profound meaning of such classifications highlights the necessity for legally informed representation and advocacy, ensuring defendants understand the potential outcomes and long-term implications of their crimes in criminal law. Familiarity with these dynamics is essential to comprehending the nuances of legal procedures and designing effective crime prevention measures. Legislation and court rulings also determine the classification of felonies and misdemeanors, reflecting shifting social values and historical realities. For instance, the passing of legislations like the Pure Food and Drug Act (1906) and the Federal Food, Drug, and Cosmetic Act (1938) demonstrates a sudden turn in criminalizing some activities, demonstrating heightening recognition of the need for intervention concerning public health problems. Such legislation establishes specific prohibited actions, the doing of which can constitute felony or misdemeanor crimes based on the type of violation, as seen in the enforcement of the U.S. Criminal Code. Further, the laws of limitation of offenses like those defined under Article 8 of the Code of Criminal Procedure further reflect the complexity of legal classifications; they ensure that justice is ever timely and responsive with an appreciation of the uniqueness of different offenses (Maamir, 2025). Such regulations provide a legal environment that tries to achieve balance between public safety and the protection of individual rights, indicating the ongoing growth of criminal law.

5.1.2. Public vs. Private Wrongs

The distinction between public and private wrongs of criminal law is the source of defining how crimes are classified and prosecuted in the criminal justice system. Public wrongs, traditionally classified as felonies, are offenses that not only violate the law but also insult society. A few of such offenses include murder, larceny, and assault, which endanger public order and safety. It is the state, in its capacity as the representative of society's interest, which prosecutes this violation within the criminal justice system. Private wrongs are typically misdemeanors or torts and are the ones that victimize single victims as compared to society in general. They are minor assaults or vandalism, the focal point of which is the victim and not society in general. Knowledge of these distinctions clarifies the way in which statutes are enforced and administered, dictating the procedural paths adopted in varying cases. Public and private wrongs differ in ways that have implications beyond mere classification; they significantly influence the prosecutorial mechanisms and associated legal duties. Public wrongs are pursued vigorously by the state, to which resources and penal enforcement are committed in order to prevent further violations. This approach reflects the presumption that offenses to societal interests need to be resolved collectively to provide security and order.

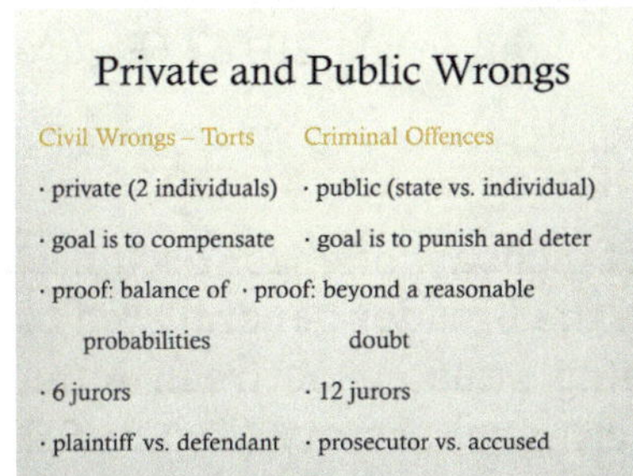

Figure 5.3. Distinction between public and private wrongs.

Source: slideserve.com.

Private wrongs, nonetheless, resolution tend to center around making amends for harm rather than punishment, with more focus on restorative justice meant to restore the victim and the offender, as opposed to punitive consequences. This differentiation demands an obvious understanding of the legal mechanisms and instruments involved, settling on expectations and outcomes for the involved parties under the justice system. Legal philosophy innovations continue to drive and develop the concept of notions of public and private wrongs, emphasizing fairness and justice functions in the criminal system. The fluidity of the law means that principles must be adaptable, in a position to embrace new social insight and technological determinants of harm and reparation. Jurisprudence has increasingly embraced the fact that boundaries between public and private wrongs may be blurred, particularly in instances of systemic wrongdoing where the conduct of the individual may reflect larger societal ills. A combative legal approach, one that encompasses distributive justice tenets, is integral to managing health equity and disparities resulting in both public and private injustices. Hence, the current debate over these two categories is a valuable piece of the greater discussion regarding criminal law and its procedure, which impacts the pursuit of equity and justice in judicial verdicts (Rajkomar et al., 2018; John et al., 2016) (Figure 5.3).

5.1.3. Inchoate Offences

The field of inchoate offences occupies a unique position in the broader general area of criminal law by being situated between intention and complete criminal activity (Figure 5.4).

Figure 5.4. Inchoate offences, characterized by an incomplete or unexecuted crime, underscore the legal system's recognition of the harm posed by criminal intent alone.

Source: pinterest.com.

This form of offence takes many forms including attempts, conspiracy, and solicitation, all which are meant to discourage individuals from getting closer to committing a larger offence. The jurisdiction for treating inchoate offences comes on the basis that even simple intent to commit an offence is a sign of a threat to security and public order. As society faces new threats, the law adapts, fortifying the script for prosecution of these crimes. This progressive focus on criminal intent raises serious questions regarding the balance between public safety and personal liberties, which must be addressed cautiously within any criminal jurisprudence. Criminalization of inchoate offences is a reflection of the ideologically driven preventive state focused on preventing risks ahead of the tangible realization of harm. The law prioritizes the risk of future offence, authorizing the state to act when people exhibit the intent for which there is a genuine threat to public safety. This prevention model is particularly pertinent in conspiracy and other pre-crime operations, as it permits law enforcement to effectively counter criminal enterprises without enduring the sting of procrastination. But such operations also involve scrutiny over implications to civil liberties and potential for abuse. The prescriptive proactive stance of the preventive state raises severe ethical issues; although it can provide greater security, it also entails risks to the effect of overly broad and coercive preventive legislation that will infringe on the rights of individuals. In heeding the appeal by the state to intervene prior to crime, a thin line has to be walked between safeguarding freedoms and liberties and assuming the protective role. In respect of inchoate offences, the doctrine of corrective justice adds additional tiers of understanding to enhance criminalization debate. Under corrective justice, criminal offending actually upsets the inter-personal relationship by encroaching on personal interests, and the reaction ought to seek to re-equilibrate. This framework provides robust grounds for consideration, particularly with respect to inchoate offences such as conspiracy and attempts. If we take such crimes to be a breach of normative expectations of interpersonal conduct, the corrective justice model provides means of responding to tensions underpinning such disruption. Secondly, it necessitates critical examination of the responsibility of individuals in the context of the social environment for thinking about duty and responsibility. Therefore, examining inchoate offences from the perspective of corrective justice not only makes them comprehensible in light of legal status but also reveals the principles on which criminal law and procedure are based, summarizing the centrality of a culpable and fair legal system responsive to prevention and reparation in response to criminal purpose (Zedner et al., 2018; Poam, 2017).

5.2. CRIMINAL INVESTIGATION

The procedural framework that is applicable to criminal investigation is required in the sense that there must be an equilibrium between the rights of the person and needs of public safety. Paramount in this undertaking is that of the arrest rules, which stipulate how police must possess probable cause in arresting a person. Due process requirement ensures that there is safeguard against arbitrary detention and that persons are not arbitrarily deprived of their liberty. Besides, in arrest scenarios, law enforcement officers are obligated to alert suspects of their rights, thus upholding the people's right to be treated fairly. In the majority of jurisdictions, such practices are rigorously vetted to prevent abuses so that the integrity of the investigation is upheld. By adhering to prescribed standards, the process ensures harmony between law enforcement agencies and the communities they serve, ultimately resulting in a better criminal justice process. Search and seizure procedures are another important element of criminal investigations, as they determine what type of evidence will be allowed at trial.

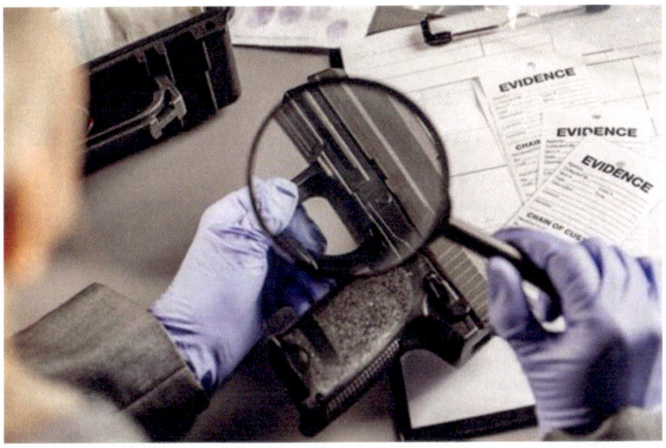

Figure 5.5. Shows evidences considered in a court of law.

Source: dkhlegacytrust.org.

The Fourth Amendment protects against unreasonable search and seizure by requiring police to secure warrants based on probable cause. Further, the procedures mandate a clear description of the scope of the search for the purpose of protecting individuals from overly intrusive government conduct. Without strict adherence to these rules, any recovered evidence would be found inadmissible, weakening the prosecution's case. In addition, the use of technology within modern investigations has brought new challenges and issues, which often confuse the borders of antiquated search and seizure doctrines. With ongoing advancement of criminal investigations alongside advancements in technology, such legal tools need to adapt to continue to function and safeguard civil liberties within changing societal parameters. Additionally, the application of detention rules is significant in ascertaining the prosecutor success of a criminal investigation. Detainees typically come to a point of critical legal representation. Such access ensures defendants are able to effectively traverse the complexity of the criminal justice system, most notably during interrogations or pre-trial hearings. Notably, procedural protections aim to hinder coercive methods of interrogation that could result in false confessions or wrongful convictions. In some jurisdictions, such as Pakistan, where the Criminal Procedure Code (CrPC) provides principles for interrogative practices, underlying system weaknesses, including ineffective training of law enforcement and socio-political corruption, can thwart fair investigations. The call for reform is urgent, with the correctly designed detention process not only protecting rights to the individual but further enhancing overall efficiency and integrity of the criminal justice system, illustrating the strong relationship between procedure and justice (Azhar et al., 2025; Bakhtiar, 2024) (Figure 5.5).

5.2.1. Arrest Procedures

In criminal justice, proper deployment of arrest procedures is essential to the preservation of the rule of law. Law enforcement officials must navigate through a sensitive framework that safeguards the necessity of public safety while upholding the constitutional rights of all.

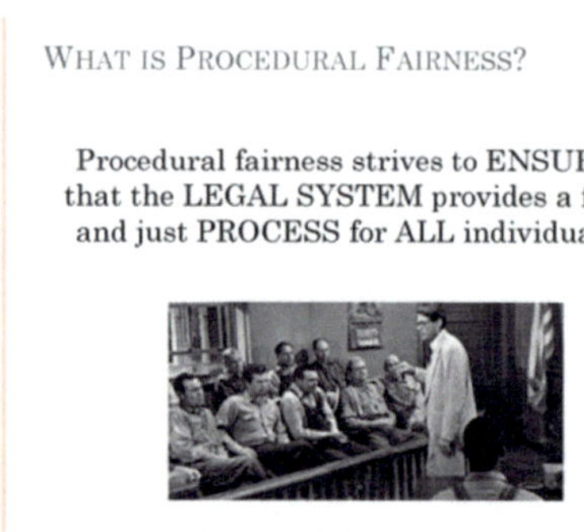

Figure 5.6. Procedural fairness is pivotal during the execution of arrest, as it significantly impacts the treatment of suspects.

Source: slideplayer.com.

Effective arrest procedures begin with law enforcement officials establishing probable cause, which guarantees an arrest to be valid and in accordance with law. This is a critical requirement that helps avoid unnecessary detainment, which can lead to the violation of civil rights. By adhering to established procedures, officers not only legitimize the criminal justice system but also maintain the integrity of evidence that may become crucial in subsequent legal proceedings. Thus, the conduct of arrests is a pivotal component in deciding on the direction of criminal investigations and the responsibility of the law enforcement practices (Figure 5.6).

Officers are required to follow specific guidelines that stipulate how an arrest should be conducted, taking into account factors such as the use of force and the rights of the individual. For example, in South Africa, legislation governs the use of force in apprehending suspected offenders, with the Constitutional Court playing a crucial role in interpreting these provisions to align with human rights standards. Around the world, similar legal frameworks emphasize the need for proportionality, requiring that any physical force employed be necessary and reasonable in the circumstances. Ensuring the proper application of these guidelines not only protects the rights of those arrested but also upholds public confidence in law enforcement agencies, which is essential for maintaining social order and respect for the law. The evolution of arrest procedures is influenced by legal reforms and societal demands for just and transparent law enforcement practices. In jurisdictions like Nigeria, there has been a push for the establishment of clear guidelines concerning plea bargains and the treatment of individuals during arrest, reflecting a growing recognition of the need for systematic oversight. The Economic and Financial Crimes Commission (EFCC) has faced scrutiny regarding its handling of cases, illuminating the complexities involved in enforcing criminal law while respecting constitutional rights. As these discussions advance, the pressing need for procedural justice within arrest protocols becomes evident, calling for comprehensive reforms. Stakeholders in the criminal justice system must ensure that arrest practices not only secure public safety but also enhance fairness and equality, thus reinforcing the foundational tenets of justice in a democratic society.

5.2.2. Search and Seizure

The intersection of technology and criminal law has transformed the landscape of search and seizure, compelling law enforcement to adapt their practices to align with contemporary digital realities. In an era where smartphones and social media applications serve as repositories of personal information, the methods for collecting evidence have become more complex.

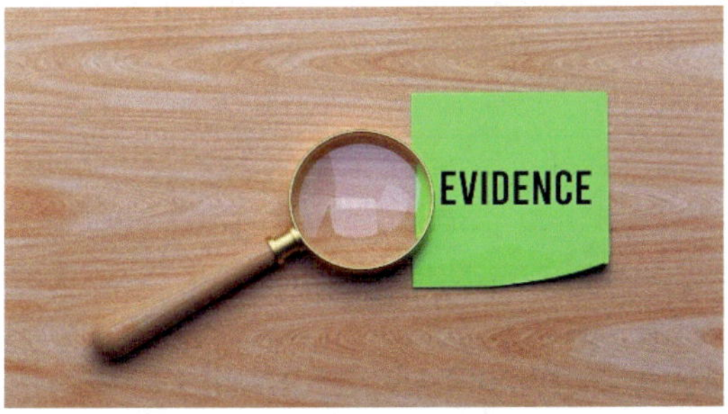

Figure 5.7. Evidence gathering is not merely about acquiring data; it is a nuanced cognitive process demanding adherence to legal frameworks designed to protect individuals rights.

Source: financialcrimeacademy.org.

Traditional approaches to finding and securing evidence now compete with the vulnerabilities associated with digital data, which may be rapidly destroyed or altered if not addressed swiftly. Recent legal developments underscore the necessity for courts to ensure that individuals under investigation are afforded the fundamental right to be present during any search and seizure procedures. However, balancing this right with the imperative of preserving evidence—particularly in urgent cases—poses significant challenges to law enforcement agencies aiming to maintain investigative secrecy while complying with legal standards (Kim et al., 2024). Understanding the principles surrounding evidence collection is crucial in the context of search and seizure (Figure 5.7).

A various definitions of "evidence collection" have been employed by scholars, focusing on facets such as discovery, segregation, maintenance, and fixation of pertinent information. Each facet comes to the forefront to see that evidence gathered in the course of a search and seizure is credible and admissible in court. This focus on evidence collection as a process also implies that law enforcers must make their process of gathering evidence more advanced. Hence, the establishment of standard practice is vital in keeping the criminal justice system intact (Dulskyi, 2024).

Among these subtleties, legislative reforms are required to make search and seizure procedures more effective without infringing upon suspect rights. Suggestions such as the imposition of data preservation regulations can provide a systematic method of safeguarding electronic evidence. By allowing law enforcement officials to request preservation of third-party data in legally defined emergent circumstances, destruction of the evidence can be minimized. Moreover, such amendments are in accordance with international standards highlighted in conventions for cybercrime. These innovations require balance between research needs and citizens' rights, ultimately developing a more effective and fair criminal procedure system capable of managing technological advancements (Kim et al., 2024; Dulskyi, 2024).

5.2.3. Detention Rules

The nuances of detention provisions are important to gaining insight into the system as a whole of criminal procedure and law. They manage the climate and treatment of those in custody, stressing the balance that must be achieved between public safety and individual rights. Detention centers have a crucial role to play, as the central point of serious contact between the state and suspects of crime and pre-trial detainees. In organized analyses conducted from successive studies, it has been documented that the enhancement of detention conditions can serve to provide improved outcomes for the subjects themselves, for example, greater hopes for rehabilitation and subsequent integration into society. This supports the findings that emphasize the necessity to adhere to established standards, as reflected in the recommendations by the European Committee for the Prevention of Torture, Inhuman or Degrading Treatment or Punishment in some of the investigations of the detention centers in various years (Sikun, 2023). Additionally, organizational structure of detention regulations displays an overall commitment to upholding safety and human rights respect within prisons. The human right to decent treatment in detention is enshrined in most international instruments, including the Mandela Rules, which offer a benchmark for assessing facility conditions and policies. The concept of regime in prisons is important in shaping a culture that facilitates positive behavioral outcomes. By establishing good-written procedures and protocols that cover security and individual rights, prisons can foster a culture of rehabilitation rather than punishment. This dual focus was emphasized in recent discussion advocating harmonization of concepts in the areas of safety, security, and broader objectives of correctional facilities (Kuznietsov et al., 2023).

Moreover, complications of engaging detained individuals in productive work reinforce the need for reform of detention legislation. Empowering prisoners to participate in purposeful work is not only better for their mental and emotional wellbeing but also prepares them for resettlement as full civic members. As made clear in various suggestions, such as those of the European Court, there is a very direct connection between prisoners' employment and their overall rehabilitation journey. New proposals that suggest offering remote work opportunities to detainees introduce new avenues to enhance engagement while addressing the age-old issue of employment opportunities shortage in detention centers (Sikun, 2023). Policy-makers are then able to reshape detention practices in accordance with international standards and improve overall performance among those engaged in the system (Figure 5.8).

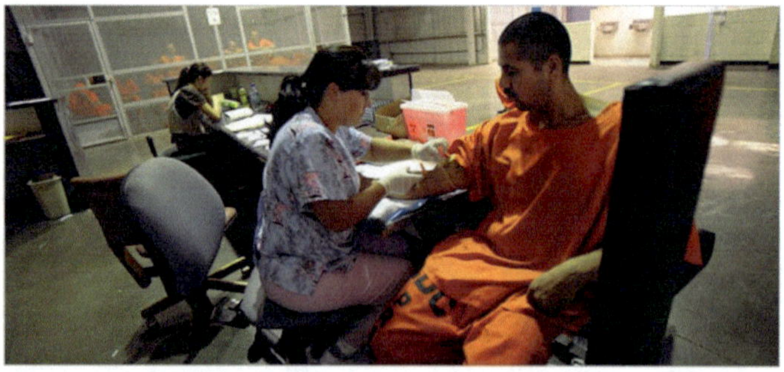

Figure 5.8. Health care in U.S. prison.

Source: glennellis.com.

5.3. PROSECUTION AND CHARGING

An understanding of the charging and prosecution complexities is at the heart of an appreciation for the broader criminal law and procedure landscape. Prosecutors are given broad discretion in terms of what cases to bring to trial, depending on the evidence at their disposal and the interests of society. It enables them to take into account such considerations as the offense severity, the defendant's history, and the likelihood of securing a conviction. Therefore, all criminal investigations do not culminate in charges being brought. The procedure illustrates the judicial systems adherence to justice and justice as it endeavors to sidestep unwarranted prosecutions that will jam up the courts and the defendants too. Additionally, ethical issues of prosecutorial discretion need monitoring at all times to ensure such powers are fairly employed, maintaining the understanding of justice being dispensed without prejudice or undue influence.

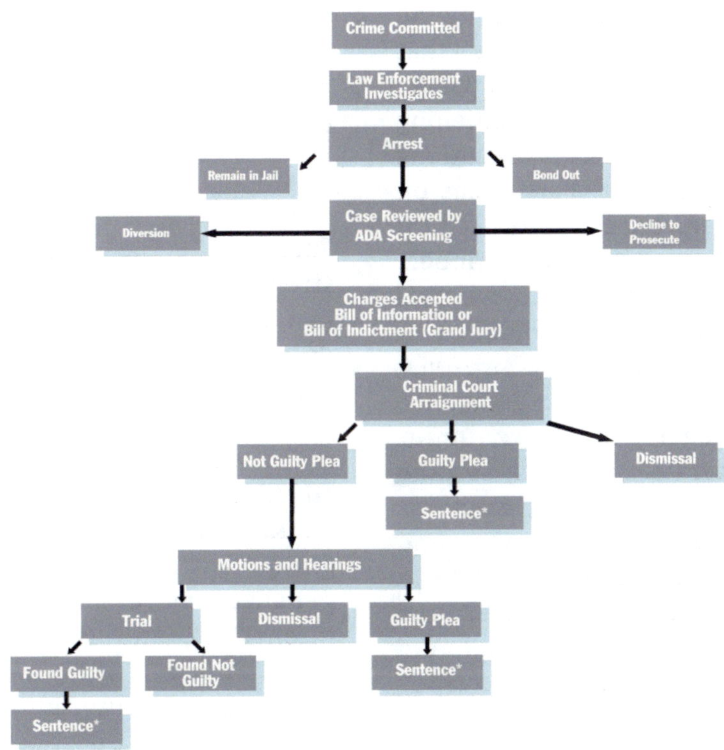

Figure 5.9. Prosecution process.

Source: https://collinsimsda.org/learning-and-resources/prosecution_process/.

Both the structure and substance of indictments are important elements of the charging process as well. Indictments are not merely formal accusations but a predicate for the entire trial process, presenting clear allegations against the defendant. The wording of an indictment can have a significant impact on follow-up proceedings, affecting such matters as jury disposition and legal strategies used by defense lawyers. Rigorous adherence to the prescribed requirements of evidence is mandatory; prosecutors must offer sufficient facts of the commission of probable cause prior to instituting charges. The requirement guarantees due process standards are in place and people are protected from illegal arrests. Lastly, an appropriate indictment on good evidence and legal principle ensures the foundation of open and fair adjudication to facilitate a fair criminal process in respect of the rights and interests of all parties concerned. Accompanying these are the dynamic nature of prosecutorial roles across different jurisdictions, particularly with emerging models of legislation. For instance, legislative amendments often seek to clarify the constitutional and procedural requirements that regulate prosecution, in society's broader vision of justice. Since the constitutional strengthening of the prosecutors role in criminal prosecutions in July 2020, there has been a sharp focus on ensuring procedural safeguards are consistent with contemporary legal norms (Kasumbek, 2024). Such a two-stage approach to criminal prosecution underscores the importance of a strict review process involving pre-trial as well as ultimate prosecutorial decisions, thus fortifying the legal framework under which prosecutors operate. Moreover, settling contradictions in criminal codes, such as those noted in the case of administrative and criminal offenses, underscores the need for a comprehensive conceptualization of prosecution and charging practices to provide maximum protection of the rights of defendants (Karpov et al., 2024). This fusion of legal principles with procedural caution seeks to promote greater accountability within the prosecution system, thereby increasing public trust in the judiciary (Figure 5.9).

5.3.1. Prosecutorial Discretion

In the context of criminal procedure and law, the discretion of prosecutors is a key determinant of legal outcomes (Figure 5.10).

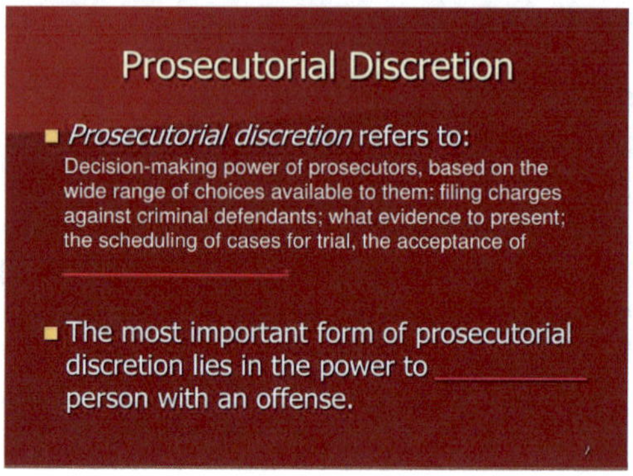

Figure 5.10. Prosecution discretion allows prosecutors to determine whether to bring charges, what charges to file, and even when to drop cases altogether. Importantly, this decision-making power can significantly affect the lives of individuals accused of crimes.

Source: Slideserve.com.

Factors like the severity of the offense, the strength of evidence, and the facts of the crime in question all play a role in a prosecutor's determination. However, the exercise of prosecutorial discretion sometimes leads to the perception of bias or disparity, especially in the existence of systemic disparities. This is added to by the increasing criticism of discretion wielded between jurisdictions, where some groups within society are disproportionately penalized more severely or prosecuted more intensively, and with corresponding social implications within the justice system. In addition, prosecutorial discretion gives rise to inherent ethical questions about accountability and integrity of processes within the justice system.

Prosecutors have broad discretion; thus, unchecked discretion may lead to potential abuses of discretion. For example, if prosecutorial office impropriety or corruption is hinted at, it erodes public trust in the entire justice system, for example, in other contexts around the world. Balance of discretion with supervision is necessary to ensure that prosecutorial discretion demonstrates both acceptable legal norms and acceptable ethical norms. Where corruption and governance issues are ingrained in the legal environment, robust systems must be established so that prosecutorial discretion is not exploited as an avenue for unfairness. Addressing these challenges head-on is essential to building public trust in the ability of legal institutions to deliver equitable and impartial justice, as corruption by nature undermines this trust, a finding made by endeavors committed to building integrity (N/A, 2018). Furthermore, prosecutorial discretion extends well beyond the immediate case, with effects on general public attitudes toward justice and legality in large. Discretion exercised inconsistently or the appearance that it is politicized and it can create public discontent and institutional distrust. This is brought home starkly in geopolitics where mechanisms of justice are pitted against the push of rule of law versus authoritarian forces. In countries experiencing competitive authoritarianism, monitoring prosecutorial behavior has the ability to reveal entrenched political bias, causing injustices in the legal system. It brings about the necessity of accountability and change in prosecutorial behavior to create a forum where justice can be achieved by all citizens regardless of social or political status. Lastly, establishing a good system of checks and balances can avoid dangers of unchecked discretion, ensuring prosecutorial decisions adhere to firm concepts of justice and fairness (Esen et al., 2016).

5.3.2. Indictment Forms

In the context of criminal law, the procedural aspect relative to types of indictments plays a crucial role in ensuring a fair trial. Indictments are formal charges that establish the prosecution of an individual, laying out the specific accusations against him/her. Comparison of types of indictments involves understanding variations between various types—for example, direct and grand jury indictments—and their varied purpose in legal proceedings. The nature of the charges, whether felonies or misdemeanors, significantly influences the format and procedures involved. As criminal processes evolve, particularly with advances in technology and information dissemination, the formats of indictments must adapt to maintain clarity and precision in articulating the offenses committed, reflecting the ongoing dialogue between legal principles and contemporary practices in law enforcement and prosecution. The increasing complexity in evidence accumulation and presentation demands a critical assessment of ways in which indictment forms can be modified to suit new types of evidence, particularly under the context of modern recording technologies. These technologies are transforming the procedural environment, as valued in admissibility disputes over private records as evidence in criminal trials. As required by powerful legal frameworks, such as Article 10(21) of the Code of Criminal Procedure, evidence integrity must be upheld in the context of such technological advances. An understanding of the types of indictment must therefore be complemented by the ability to see how evidence, either traditional or technological in form, is absorbed into criminal trials, influencing the validity and effectiveness of the trial for the prosecution. The challenge lies in reconciling the inclusion of new forms of evidence with established procedural safeguards in a way that preserves justice. Finally, the procedural intricacies entailing indictment forms raise basic questions concerning participant rights at pre-trial stages, namely legal counsel and right to confront and defend against the accusations. The existing statutory provisions in many cases do not provide for uniform procedures to ensure both the prosecution and the defense access to relevant documents as well as scope for challenging inconsistencies or ambiguity within an indictment. Such lack of uniformity would undermine the integrity of trials, as emphasized in recent studies on rights and interests of parties throughout the criminal process. Strengthening indictment templates might involve reformulating existing legislation to craft more defined structures for their preparation and submission to make sure that the legal system is dedicated to transparency, justice, and safeguarding individual rights, which are essential to integrity in the overall legal process (Maksim, 2024).

5.3.3. Evidentiary Thresholds

In criminal law, the determination of evidentiary thresholds is essential in establishing the prosecution's prerogative to bring a case. The thresholds establish the quality and quantity of evidence required to secure a conviction or secure a conviction in different classes of offenses, such as felonies and misdemeanors. The prosecution bears the burden of proof and will be required to prove the evidentiary burden necessary to persuade the judge or jurors of the defendants' guilt beyond a reasonable doubt. This is what underscores the general legal tenet that one is presumed innocent until established to be guilty, highlighting that substantial evidentiary support becomes a shield of protection for the individual against unfair conviction and arbitrariness in the system. As offenses range from minor misdemeanors to major felonies, standards of evidence follow suit and range in proportion to the severity of the offense. For instance, under felonies, higher proof is required, which necessitates robust evidence in a bid to establish guilt. The distinction reveals a significant aspect of legal processes: while the assumption of innocence operates in the same way for every case, the need to breach the threshold of evidence has a profound effect on prosecutorial strategy and the trial process as a whole. The interplay between offence categories and thresholds constitutes not only the pursuit of justice but also challenges fairness, especially regarding resources for both prosecution and defence. Within this complex setting, it is important to sustain an even system of standards for evidence in order to keep the criminal justice system credible. Additionally, evidentiary thresholds and their meanings are not simple procedural niceties; instead, they are inseparable from basic legal and social principles. The implications of the thresholds linger beyond the courtroom struggle; they touch public perceptions of the legal systems competence and fairness. For example, evidence of high evidentiary standards can serve to create trust among citizens that decisions made within the justice system are evidence-led and not predicated on conjecture or bias. Conversely, perceived failure to meet such thresholds may provoke a lower degree of trust in legal institutions and heightened popular discontent against perceived corruption or incompetence. These issues need to be discussed and reformed continually in the judicial context, as has been cited in most studies on integrity and anti-corruption policy in contexts like in Latin America, where the integrity of judicial processes matters for inclusive governance (N/A, 2018).

5.4. TRIAL PROCEEDINGS

The process of criminal trial is largely characterized by rules and procedures that ensure fairness as well as justice (Figure 5.11).

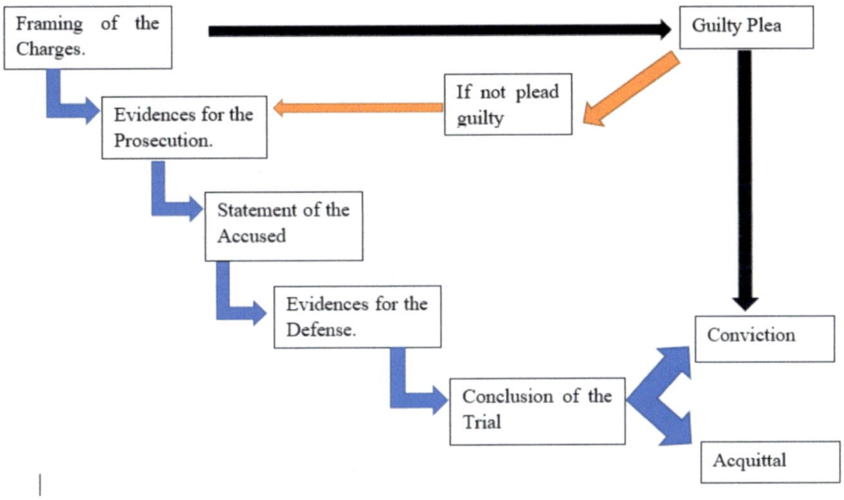

Figure 5.11. Trial stage in criminal law.

Source: iPleaders.

Trial procedures include vital elements like the right to a fair trial, the presumption of innocence, and the prosecution's burden of proof. The presumption of innocence is a cornerstone of this process in ensuring defendants are not wrongly convicted by requiring that their guilt be established beyond all reasonable doubt. This strict burden of proof, in contrast to civil cases, necessitates that the jurors or judges lean towards acquitting the accused if they have any rational doubt about the evidence presented to them. These strict standards are vital in upholding the integrity of the legal system because they reflect the society's determination to protect the rights of individuals through strict judicial scrutiny during trial proceedings. The bench or jury function in trial processes has a decisive function in determining the outcome. In jury trials, laypeople are charged with evaluating evidence and delivering a verdict, illustrating democratic virtues by making possible the involvement of ordinary people in the justice system. In bench trials, judges determine facts according to legal standards and professional interpretation of legislation. Each system has its strengths; jury trials can better reflect community attitudes and opinions, while bench trials can rush the process and reduce sources of bias. Additionally, the juror selection process, aimed at presenting a reasonable and unbiased panel, helps to underscore the importance of avoiding prejudicial influences stemming from the seriousness of criminal charges. The procedural nuances inherent in both types of trials really define the way in which justice is seen and applied within the criminal justice system. As trial proceedings unfold, the proof requirement becomes a critical element that marks what is required during litigation. The prosecutions obligation to establish guilt beyond a reasonable doubt is less a procedural nicety than a fundamental commitment to justice that derives its origins in legal traditions. This heightened standard attempts to lower the possibility of wrongful conviction, a concern that resonates strongly within criminal law debate. Furthermore, the separation of trial and sentencing in adversarial systems, as defined in Julian et al. (2025), emphasizes the complexities of ensuring equitable treatment of defendants throughout the process. This separation allows for intentful considerations during sentencing, lessening prejudice that could be caused by trial evidence. Although regulations of trial processes have the goal of safeguarding legal rights and procedural consistency, effective determination of appeals subject matter also contributes to the effectiveness of judicial review, as explained in Veronika (2025). Through these interrelated mechanisms, the system is established that will ensure promotion of justice to address the multifaceted issues of criminal law and procedure.

5.4.1. Role of Jury or Bench

The criminal justice system operates in an environment that necessitates the implementation of procedural norms, practically affecting the operation of juries and judges. The jury, as a critical component of trial procedures, operates as a symbol of the voice of society in legal matters, ensuring verdicts truly represent the values and norms of society. This community participation is what gives rise to the idea of a fair trial by peers, providing protection against potential government overreach. On the other hand, the bench, composed of judges, bears the responsibility of overseeing trial procedures, making matters of law, and ensuring evidence is presented within tolerable parameters. The union of these two functions puts to the forefront the tension between legal professionalism and community attitudes, generating a dynamic judicial system that reflects the balancing of justice and rule of law. A two-model approach is at the heart of the aim to secure a just and impartial process in the field of criminal law and procedure. The impact of juror structure and deliberation practices must not be overstated because such practices have the potential to significantly influence case outcomes. Empirical studies indicate that diverse juries deliberate more thoroughly, which leads to more comprehensive analyses of evidence and witness credibility. However, the utilization of jurors to rationalize information at times has unforeseen consequences; racial biases and assumptions can be exposed in deliberations, distorting verdicts. Still more, jurors are unable to resist allowing inadmissible data influence their capacity for making educated decisions. All of this challenges the practicality of juries in contrast to judges, who are presumed to possess training and expertise necessary to discount biased or irrelevant information when deliberating. Last but not least, conflict between the representational validity of the jury and the legal knowledge of the judges gives rise to today's controversy over each's effectiveness in the criminal justice system.

The judges have the mandate of ensuring that legal proceedings adhere to formulated laws and that they remain impartial. The psych cognitive challenges they face, such as the effect of inadmissible information, make it difficult for them to meet this mandate. Research shows that judges typically struggle to set aside prejudicial information even when told to do so, stifling their objective judgment skills. This is similar to challenges faced by juries but shows perhaps that judges are less immune to prejudice than long believed. Also, the expectation that judges are able to transcend emotional responses to evidence may be unrealistically high; thus, this is a complex dynamic in an understanding of judicial process. With an evolving justice system, such cognitive constraints can make one rethink the management of evidence and reforms defending the purity of verdicts while preserving the values of justice and equality in criminal proceedings, as defined in literature reviewing the systemic functions of legal institutions (Kutateladze et al., 2014; Guthrie et al., 2005).

5.4.2. Presumption of Innocence

This fundamental principle maintains that a defendant is innocent until proven guilty, thereby establishing a necessary benchmark of justice. It ensures that the prosecution will be burdened with proof, that is, the state will be required to present sufficient evidence for the court to decide that the defendant is guilty. This model not only symbolizes the equity inherent in democratic countries but also a vital safeguard against erroneous convictions and the corrupting effect of power that may emerge within the legal structure. Presumption of innocence tremendously enhances public confidence in the legal process and invites an unbiased approach to determining criminal charges. In analyzing the presumption of innocence, its import extends beyond procedural legitimacy and reaches to deeper human rights concerns. The principle emphasizes the right to a fair trial, through which people are provided with the opportunity to build a comprehensive defense against charges. Judicial systems must be aware that pre-trial publicity and pressure from the public have the power to undermine this presumption, which in turn goes on to influence perceptions of guilt even before the trial has begun. As reflected in much global legal standard, such protections are required to maintain not only the integrity of the legal process itself but also the dignity that lies in every human being to be accused of grave charges. Thus, maintaining the presumption of innocence is required in order to ensure respect for the accused, and to do so simultaneously with re-inforcing axiomatic notion that they are still human beings with rights and privileges regardless of what charges are leveled against them. Secondly, the observance of the presumption of innocence is crucial in the assurance of the fair administration of justice. For the enforcement of this rule to work effectively, legal professionals, that is, judges and jurors, must be vigilant in ensuring that their verdicts are not influenced by bias or pre-judgment of guilt. Emphasizing the presumption of innocence is critical in guiding jury instructions and evidence standards, and hence acts as a bulwark against unjust convictions. Legal principle not only delimits the function of the prosecution but also speaks to the wider socio-legal context in encouraging a climate within which the accused can reasonably expect their innocence to be presumed until proved to the contrary. In this regard, defining the parameters of presumption of innocence is most important to the present controversies relating to criminal law and human rights, and it underscores its position as an essential component in coming up with a fair and balanced legal system (N/A, 2021; Zulfan, 2018) (Figure 5.12).

Figure 5.12. Within the framework of criminal law, the principle of the presumption of innocence plays a pivotal role in protecting the rights of defendants throughout legal proceedings.

Source: https://charlesomole.org/wp-content/uploads/2019/12/presumption-of-innocence.jpg.

5.4.3. Standard of Proof

This standard is also crucial in upholding that the legal system itself should be ethical since it's the basis of the presumption of innocence, a principle which dictates people are presumed to be innocent until they can be shown to be guilty. In criminal prosecution, the burden of providing evidence to establish guilt beyond doubt lies with the state so that no one is unjustly convicted. This threshold for evidence is high to ensure the rights of the accused are upheld and upholds justice in accordance with the legal framework, hence validating that it is worse to sentence an innocent individual than it is to release possible criminals. The distinction between beyond a reasonable doubt and other standards of proof, such as preponderance of the evidence or clear and convincing evidence, is essential for understanding criminal procedures. The latter standards, routinely applied in civil cases, require lesser certainties, and those might lead to more convictions if used in criminal proceedings. This departure is reflective of the seriousness of the rights at stake in criminal law, where a false conviction may result in severe penalties, including incarceration. The insistence on adherence to the test of proof then serves as a safeguard against arbitrary application of the law, so that the prosecution case is enough to warrant a verdict of guilt and the accused is afforded absolute protection of the law. Further complications arise in situations where circumstantial evidence is the dominant type of evidence, hence complicating the application of the standard of proof. The jurors may find it challenging to decide whether the evidence presented is adequate to the point of beyond a reasonable doubt, especially when significant doubt exists regarding the defendant's guilt. Furthermore, as legal precedent shifts, so does understanding what reasonable doubt is under trial circumstances. As a case point, the technological innovations have raised controversy on how the digital evidence can meet evidentiary requirements. These tensions reflect the imperative of the pursuit of legal certainty and firm debate to ensure that the standard of proof continues to be effective in averting unjust convictions without jeopardizing the prosecution of valid criminal activity within our justice system (Wang et al., 2018; Ienca et al., 2017) (Figure 5.13).

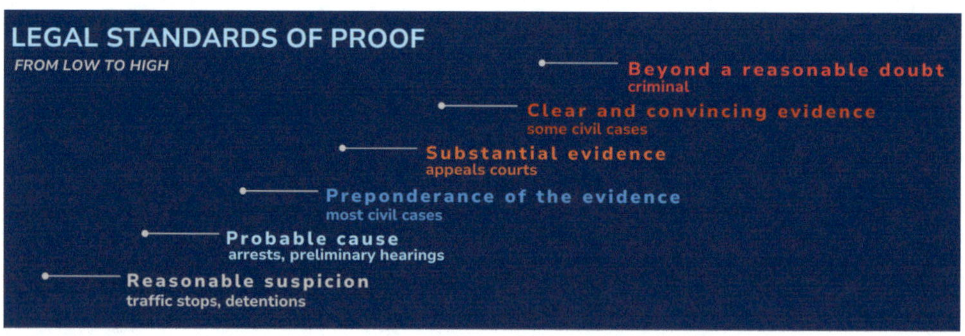

Figure 5.13. The Standard of Proof serves as a foundational element that delineates the threshold the prosecution must meet to establish a defendant's guilt.

Source: https://cimg2.ibsrv.net/cimg/www.nolo.com/1200x627_100/734/legal-standards-of-proof-2-736734.png.

5.5. SENTENCING PRACTICE

In the intricate universe of criminal procedure and law, sentencing practice is a central fulcrum that exists between theory and actual justice. Foremost to this dilemma is the categorization between various forms of punishment, which may extend from fines to incarceration, each carrying varying effects on both offender and society as a whole. The selection of an appropriate penalty depends not only upon the character and seriousness of the offence but also upon legislative needs and the discretion vested in the judges. The discretion is necessary since judges must often weigh punishment, deterrence, and rehabilitation objectives in sentencing. Safin (2024) emphasizes that while sentencing law is meant to provide guidance, the individualized facts in every case, including the history of the offender and the motivating factors, can produce variation in sentencing decisions, acknowledging the complexity of this judicial function. No less important in addressing sentencing practice are guidelines designed to make decisions consistent and reduce variations. Guidelines of sentencing are used to promote similarity in similar cases so that like offenders committing like offenses are punished alike. The functioning of the guidelines occasionally carries with it an admixture of inherent bias, as particular demographic groups are overrepresented within particular categories of crime. Notably, gender and criminal law studies show that women receive varying sentences from men, a result that shows gender assumptions are influencing court decision-making. Wang (2024) illustrates how successful sentencing reform can be the work of fully grasping such biases, complemented by targeted training of judges with an ultimate aim of promoting an even-handed approach according to justice and fairness ideals. Judicial discretion remains an integral part of sentencing practices, allowing judges to tailor sanctions to the specifics of individual cases. While this use of flexibility can produce equitable outcomes, it also lends itself to concern about the potential for arbitrary consideration or public bias to creep into sentence choices. Courts thus have the delicate responsibility of exercising discretion in a judicious manner, that it is tolerable not only according to legal standards but also according to moral standards. The trend towards embracing restorative justice approaches makes the traditional punitive models even more complicated, as it focuses on victims' needs as well as reintegration into society of the offenders. As the law keeps advancing, comprehension of the interactions between discretion, guidelines, and the overall goal of fair sentencing will be essential in shaping better and more equitable sentencing practices in the future.

5.5.1. Types of Penalties

In criminal law, the categorization of offenses has direct relevance to the application of the type of penalties. The penalties serve as deterrents, retributions, and rehabilitations meant to address various levels of criminality. More broadly, penalties are in two broad categories: custodial and non-custodial. Custodial punishments, such as confinement, are usually reserved for more severe crimes, such as felonies, which are often characterized by their capacity to cause extreme harm to people or society. Non-custodial punishments, such as fines, community work, and probation, tend to be applied to less severe crimes, such as misdemeanors. This nuanced mixture allows the judiciary to balance the goals of punishment and the need for rehabilitation, particularly in the case of first-time offenders or minor crimes. Additional reflection on custodial sentences also highlights the diversity of punitive sanctions. Of the latter, the death penalty is the most severe, with some jurisdictions adopting it as a response to particularly heinous crimes, for example, murder. The rationale for maintaining the death penalty is diverse; some argue that it deters violent crime and reflects society's moral distaste for the most heinous types of wrongdoing. That is not universal, though, as evidenced by rising calls for abolition on moral, ethical, and empirical grounds for wrongful convictions and discriminatory sentencing. Death penalty legislation in other countries also reflects this duality, with some countries upholding it while others have enacted moratoriums or abolished it, showing the cyclical nature of issues related to justice and the sanctity of life in law, as suggested by the argument over (Nopriandi et al., 2020). By way of contrast, non-custodial sentencing demands a more sophisticated sentencing mechanism that takes into account the circumstances of the offender and the offense. To illustrate, fines may be gradient-dependent with respect to the offender's financial standing such that punishments are equitable and will in fact induce compliance with the law. Community service is not merely punishment but also a tool of restitution, where the criminals are encouraged to engage well with society even as they acknowledge their criminal activities. Further, probationary measures can facilitate rehabilitation by mandated surveillance and yet allow the criminals to enjoy a feeling of autonomy. This range of non-custodial sanctions reflects a trend towards restorative justice practices, aimed at restoring damage caused by criminality and facilitating reintegration into society, transforming the concept of punishment within the framework of criminal law, particularly as societies evolve on issues of fairness and justice, in accordance with information presented in Katherine et al. (2022).

5.5.2. Sentencing Guidelines

The sentencing guidelines system is very vital in the US criminal justice process, and it offers a framework of determining penalties for crimes. Through this action, the guidelines attempt to reduce disparity in the sentences, such that the same crime has the same sentence. One of the best things about this system might be that it ensures consistency, such that defendants get a more predictable legal outcome. The authors have noted that though the intention behind the guidelines is to be equitable, sometimes they end up magnifying systemic discrimination, particularly in reference to race and socio-economic status, by laying stress on factors that may not always reflect the individual's guilt or the specifics of the offence that has been committed (Alex, 2021). Therefore, the assessment of the efficacy and impact of sentencing guidelines is paramount in understanding their role toward justice as well as society's perception of fairness. In addition to consistency, sentencing guidelines also enlist judicial discretion in an intricate dance between pre-set standards and the particular facts of each case. Judges are often granted the leeway to issue sentences beyond guideline recommendations when there are aggravating or mitigating factors emerging during the trial. Such flexibility is necessary as it allows room for consideration of the unique circumstances of every crime, as well as the background and reasons of the perpetrators. Nonetheless, this discretion can potentially be arbitrary, depending on how differently judges interpret justice and apply these interpretations in their judgments (Guidotti et al., 2018). Therefore, it is crucial that there is a constant examination of the balance between being bound by guidelines while exercising judicial discretion so that the legal system remains fair and effective in the administration of justice. The shifting face of sentencing guidelines also reflects broader shifts and perspectives in society regarding criminality and rehabilitation. As greater recognition of such factors as drug abuse, mental illness, and socio-economic determinants of crime has been forthcoming, calls have been made to update the guidelines more comprehensively to address such underlying causes. Reform efforts center on alternatives to incarceration, in resting on restorative justice strategies that aim at rehabilitation rather than merely punitive punishment. Historically, these trends constitute a significant move away from the traditionally punitive bent of the legal system, marking an imperative shift towards viewing criminal justice as a system meant to serve both public safety and rehabilitative opportunities for offenders. Ultimately, though, the value of sentencing guidelines in criminal law and process will depend on their ability to adapt in light of new information regarding crime, justice, and the needs of communities and thereby transform problems into opportunities for effective reform.

5.5.3. Judicial Discretion

In criminal justice, judicial discretion complexities play a crucial role in deciding the fate of defendants and broader legal consistency. The discretionary power gives judges a scope to interpret meanings in statutes as well as modify sentences based on the individual facts of the case. By adding flexibility to the application of statute rules, judicial discretion may serve to facilitate more just outcomes that are closer to the actualities of human beings. However, such discretion is accompanied by concern for bias and inconstancy since variations can result from personal belief and public pressure. In addition, openness of judicial decisions is paramount, with public perception of fairness of the legal process being compromised when outcomes are perceived as arbitrary or unpredictable.

Resolution of such concerns is imperative to the maintenance of the integrity of the judicial process and the enhancement of the rule of law, a situation that must be treated with care by judges. Judicial discretion is at its most apparent while sentencing, when judges are often asked to balance competing interests, for example, public safety, rehabilitation, and deterrence. Both the discretionary aspect and statutory framework decide the shape of the sentencing practice, resulting in wide differences in the outcomes. Variation in the sentences imposed on offenses that are perceived to be of similar nature demonstrates the conflict between the standard and the individualized nature of justice. Furthermore, the discretion can be informed by socio-economic status, race, and public opinion, and this raises questions of equality and fairness in the eyes of the law. For example, studies have identified that algorithmic software may introduce bias into risk assessments impacting mostly marginalized communities unevenly. Blending ensuring flexibility in sentencing with avoiding effects of bias is an important way to create a fair and equitable system of criminal justice (Corbett et al., 2017). The tension between judicial discretion and legislative constraints makes possible the dynamic nature of criminal law and procedure, particularly as shifting legal mores influence them. Discretionary power allows judges to modulate the application of law to reflect what is occurring in society at large and the development of understanding of justice, thus making the legal system more applicable. Yet this flexibility needs to be restrained lest it creates overextension or misuse of judicial authority. Parliament and legislatures try to limit judicial discretion by mandating minimum sentences or raising sentencing guidelines. However, whether such measures will prove successful remains doubtful since rigid systems could not accommodate the subtlety of singular cases. Hence, it is important to retain a continuous dialogue between legislative intention and judicial practice so that discretion exercised fulfills the core principles of justice and proportionate punishment (Andreas, 2020).

5.6. CRIMINAL APPEALS AND REVIEW

The review and appeal of criminals is an essential tool in the protection of the defendants' rights under the bigger umbrella of criminal law and procedure. Aside from being a curb against potential judicial errors, it is also an emblem of justice, where each is offered an opportunity to appeal convictions that are potentially flawed (Figure 5.14).

Figure 5.14. The right to appeal is a fundamental tenet of a fair legal system, as it allows the appellate courts to reassess trial court decisions for legal and procedural inaccuracies.

Source: https://www.rooneylawfirm.com/wp-content/uploads/2023/03/14.png.

Despite the severity of trial court processes, human error or fault is likely to occur, making a proper appeal process an imperative. The evolution of the process over the years is evidence of the process being crucial in fostering public confidence in the justice system, as it strives to fulfill the demands of justice, particularly for those wrongly convicted (Panokin, 2024). In examining the various foundations for criminal appeals, it is apparent that the proceedings can be based on a wide variety of issues, including misinterpretation of the law and the introduction of new evidence. An essential aspect of the appellate review is its ability to ascertain whether the standards of law were well applied during the trial. For example, errors in procedure, such as negligent instruction of the jury or evidentiary rulings infringing on a defendant's rights, are often the basis for appeals. The appellate courts must walk a thin line between the two competing interests of justice and finality in the law; while it is essential to reverse wrongful convictions, there is a public interest in affirming judicial decisions to maintain stability in the law. This dance of balance hints at the delicate dynamic between the expanding jurisprudence and the strict standards established in case law, as evidenced by recent Supreme Court decisions that speak to key dimensions of criminal procedure (N/A, 2023). Further, post-conviction remedies add depth to the discourse around criminal appeals and review, suggesting the layered nature of the judicial universe. These cures—in motions for new trials, claims of ineffective assistance of counsel, and habeas corpus petitions—are all necessary avenues for defendants to try to correct miscarously of justice, if any, that may have occurred after trial. These mechanisms are employed by the judiciary to acknowledge the potential for errors in past procedures, whereby further inquiry into justice is permitted. This aspect of criminal law mirrors the dynamic nature of legal protections afforded to participants in the system.

With advancing legal frameworks, the need to safeguard basic rights using effective reviewing mechanisms does not cease. These evolving standards of judicial checks and balances are a testament to an ongoing desire to build stronger integrity into the justice system and provide guarantees that ideals of fairness and equity are upheld (Panokin, 2024).

5.6.1. Rights of Appeal

Within the context of criminal procedure and law, the evolution and conceptualization of appeal rights are a significant area of emphasis toward protection of individual rights in the judicial process. The right to appeal provides defendants with an essential tool to protest against adverse judgments delivered in the process of trial proceedings, thereby upholding integrity of judgments in the judiciary. According to this model, the process of appeal guarantees that inaccuracies by lower courts can be reviewed and, thus, that injustices resulting from misapplications of law or lack of proper evidentiary considerations can be corrected. Legal analysts note that the appeal right is necessary not only to obtain fairness and justice but to uphold the rule of law itself, guaranteeing in effect that no one is unjustly punished on account of faulty reasoning or procedural flaws in the law. The right of appeal having been established, there remains controversy over the limits and procedural details that govern the appeal process. For instance, the absence of a definite list of appealable grounds, particularly on prosecutorial behavior during pre-trial proceedings, is one of such weaknesses in existing frameworks of law. Importantly, the certainty of appealable rulings has to be enhanced in order to safeguard defendants from the arbitrary exercise of prosecutorial discretion and enhance transparency in criminal procedure. As is comprehensively explained in various critiques, the lack of explicit provisions of the law to do with the scope of appealable actions may indirectly have the effect of undermining defendants' rights to further impede their ability to build sound legal complaints against prosecutorial actions and investigative tactics threatening their liberties (Andrukh, 2025). In addition, appellate rights everywhere represent the ideals of principles for a fair trial enshrined in constitutional and international law regimes. Appellate courts play a vital role in ensuring such rights by interpreting and making decisions on procedural protections that guard individuals from the misuse of government power. Nevertheless, the relationship between appellate rights and attorney-client privilege, particularly the protection of confidential communications, is full of legal complexity. For instance, current legislative framework does not expressly accommodate the nuances of attorney-client privilege in appeals context, so one wonders how such privileges are being incorporated in appeals based on evidentiary barriers. Thus, academics suggest reforms that appropriately recognize such rights to allow the judicial system to maintain its integrity without compromising on its operational standards while providing defendants with a good platform to safeguard their interests against wrongful convictions and procedural injustice (Lee, 2025).

5.6.2. Post-Conviction Remedies

The effect of a criminal conviction is normally serious personal and societal consequences, which call for mechanisms that ensure review and correction of potential miscarriages of justice. Within the realm of criminal procedure and law, post-conviction remedies are crucial mechanisms for correcting wrongful convictions and maintaining justice. Such remedies may be appeals, motions for new trial, or other forms of collateral relief filed to reverse errors in the law made at trial. The function of post-conviction remedies is particularly significant to mark the balance between the maintenance of the integrity of the judicial process and the recognition of the possibility of human error in the administration of justice, and thus safeguard individual rights from the risk of unjust legal outcomes. These reflections challenge the finality normally to be found in judicial decisions, and one is faced with a living tension between law and equity. The primary means of post-conviction relief is one of the appellate process, allowing convicted defendants to challenge the legality of convictions for stated reasons, for example, procedural error or insufficiency of evidence. The appeal will most often involve a review of transcripts at trial, evidence standards, and the application of legal principles generally, all with the ultimate objective of determining whether a fair trial was afforded to the convicted defendant. The courts are required to make a complete determination of whether constitutional rights were observed, consistent with the overall ideal of justice in the law. It is significant that the availability of this remedy highlights the importance of active judicial oversight as a check upon the finality of convictions that would otherwise not meet the test of legal rigor. The lengthy appellate process also emphasizes the necessity of good legal representation at the critical juncture of criminal prosecution. In addition, the topic of post-conviction remedies is increasingly relevant to argument about wrongful convictions and systemic flaws in the justice system. Italy, for instance, has established official legal mechanisms to address this issue in particular, confirming the need to rectify judicial errors in a formal manner. The Italian Constitution actually formulates the right to compensation for miscarriage of justice, highlighting the need for robust procedural protection to prevent such miscarriages of justice in the first place. As intimated in contemporary legal jargon, the need for post-conviction remedies is not so much to correct past errors but to enhance public confidence in the criminal justice system. Providing strong remedies can do much to ease the damaging effects of wrongful convictions, and eventually, more just outcomes, and reinforcing the social contract among citizens and the state (Lup Lària et al., 2020; N/A, 2018).

5.6.3. Clemency and Pardon

The dialogue between clemency and the formal systems of criminal justice provokes important questions regarding rehabilitation and justice. Clemency is a tool whereby executive power can mitigate the severity of punishment or, in exceptional cases, overturn convictions completely. Such power generally acts with respect to preventing potential miscarriages of justice and providing a second chance to those who may have been disproportionately punished. The role of clemency in the criminal justice system emphasizes that there needs to be a balance between retribution and mercy so that there is hope for rehabilitation and reintroduction into society. Institutions such as clemency, as they evolve, also must adapt to new challenges, including public attitudes toward crime and punishment and the subtleties of the judicial process, demonstrating the adaptability of mechanisms of justice in accordance with changing moral environments. But clemency and pardon programs often reveal holes in their availability and functioning, raising profound questions about fairness in their application. Although theoretically available, empirically studies report that its provision is spasmodic, exhibiting a difference between right and deed. Not only does it have an effect on individual cases, but it also has an influence on public views of justice at a societal level. In particular, barriers such as intricate bureaucratic process, public ignorance, and attorney services availability could discourage eligible participants from benefiting from clemency channels. Consequently, tens of millions of Americans are trapped in a second chance gap, burdened with the outcomes of previous errors because they qualify for some form of redemption under existing law. Closing these disparities is crucial to the development of a more equitable criminal justice system that actually allows for rehabilitation and reintegration. The significance of clemency and pardon extends beyond the individual case, affecting the broader criminal justice system and cultural expectations. Legislative solutions to clemency process reform, such as automatic expungement legislation, have appeared as a response to systemic inequities. These programs not only seek to simplify the application process but also to ease the ability of people to re-assert rights and opportunities upon conviction. The possible impact of the reforms to transform lives is great; nonetheless, effective implementation remains contingent on resolving foundational issues like bureaucratic ineffectiveness and public misconceptions regarding the pardon process. Reforms in these fields would enable the system to better plead for clemency and encourage restorative justice. Therefore, a close analysis of clemency and pardon processes is vital to grasp their place within the context of criminal procedure and law, indirectly influencing community attitudes toward forgiveness and justice in practice.

SUMMARY

Last but not least, the study of criminal law and procedure indicates a solid system with the aim of keeping justice in a style of equilibrium of an individual's rights and society. The legal system distinguishes crime severity and proportionate punishment by establishing the classification of offenses, dividing felonies from misdemeanors. It is crucial stratification, for it affects not only the prosecution and sentencing of the perpetrator, but also influences public opinion of legal wrongdoing. Furthermore, the separation of public and private offense, and the identification of inchoate crimes, indicate the complex mindset one must be prepared with in practice. Hence, the functional dynamics of criminal law serve as a foundation for effective legal outcomes, generating simplicity in dispensing justice in society.

Additionally, the procedural aspect of the criminal justice system, that is, the investigation, prosecution, trial, and appeals process, exhibits observance of due process. The guarantee that the procedure in arresting, the statutes of search and seizure, and detention directives are enforced vigorously is essential to safeguarding individual freedoms. The discretion in charging exercised by the prosecution reflects the difficulty in balancing the tightrope between justice and management of resources. With trials unfolding in courtrooms, the presumption of innocence continues to be an unshakeable tenet that demands an impeccable burden of evidence prior to one being convicted. These procedural safeguards, including the right of appeal and post-conviction relief, amplify the importance of fairness and accuracy in legal rulings to the integrity of the criminal justice system. Lastly, victim protection offers a reason why criminal laws application shall play a central role in society. The legal responsibilities of the providers, such as midwives, can have severe consequences when care standards are violated, which points to the aspect of accountability in healthcare environments (Irawan et al., 2025). Furthermore, the protection of victims and witnesses is important in developing public trust for the justice system; Law Number 31 of 2014 provisions are an example of the legal elements required that are targeted towards ensuring their security and support (Uyun, 2024). In short, the richly textured levels of criminal law and procedure combined illustrate an imperative social requirement for justice, accountability, and the safeguarding of individual rights, making necessary constant reforms and realignments within the ever-evolving context of law.

A LOOK TO THE FUTURE

TRANSFORMATIONS IN CRIMINAL JUSTICE IN THE AGE OF TECHNOLOGY

Criminal law and procedure are at a crossroads, subject to the influence of social change and technological advancement. One of the most significant trends shaping the future is redefinition of traditional distinctions of crime in a way that the dichotomy between felony and misdemeanor is being challenged. Traditionally defined in terms of severity, the distinctions can be redefined with restorative justice making headway. In addition, the emergence of inchoate offenses indicates an increasing acknowledgement of different levels of culpability and intention, and with it comes an expected change towards more subtle systems in the formulation of criminal liability. This shift is especially pertinent in nations such as Ukraine, where legislative change is already responding to the pressing necessity for a more humane approach in criminal law (Yermak, 2021). As legal systems mature, they will continue to evolve towards adopting restorative justice concepts in the attempt to harmonize punishment and rehabilitation as they adapt to the needs of society. In the field of criminal investigation, the use of technology presents challenges and opportunities for criminal law and procedure in the future. Enhanced surveillance, data analysis, and artificial intelligence software are altering arrest processes and decision-making around search and seizure, promising more efficient investigatory processes. But these advancements carry with them critical concerns around privacy, due process, and the potential for algorithmic biases in making decisions. The balance between public safety and protection of civil liberties has become more fragile, necessitating stringent requirements governing the application of technological assistance to investigations. Hence, as AI becomes further entrenched within the procedures of law, legal systems must reform so that the rights of the people are upheld in the presence of these technology advances (Putera et al., 2021). The future will be characterized by a redefinition of traditional procedures such that law enforcements technological gains are brought in terms of constitutional rights.

Trial proceedings to await transformation, underpinned fundamentally by shifting expectations of society and technological advances. The traditional roles of juries and judges can increasingly incorporate digital technology to support proceedings and increase access to victims and defendants alike. In pursuing greater efficiency from courts, the assumption of innocence will remain the basis of justice, but the principle must prevail in the context of novel evidence and testimony introduced through the application of cutting-edge analytics and surveillance technologies. Furthermore, the criminal threshold of proof of guilt could be reconsidered to fit the increased complexity of evidence in a world where there is more data. The judicial systems will need to reconcile the maintenance of judicial integrity and embracing innovations that can disrupt traditional practices (Yermak, 2021). Lastly, the future of criminal procedure and law hangs in the balance of the ability to balance the quest for justice with technology's relentless pace of development.

REFERENCES

1. Amirbekov, K. I. (2024). The constitutional law nature of criminal prosecution implemented by the Prosecutor's Office of the Russian Federation: The conceptual approach. *Constitutional and Municipal Law*. https://www.semanticscholar.org/paper/c70c539d7ff1bfe0d915c16d98a7c3745b017c83 (accessed on 9th September 2025).
2. Andrukh, V. (2025). Problematic issues of regulatory approach of appealing actions or inaction of the prosecution in pre-trial criminal proceedings. *Analytical and Comparative Jurisprudence*. https://www.semanticscholar.org/paper/f2705dbec5b87d622291b61811a835ef62a5b9ea (accessed on 9th September 2025).
3. Artamonova, E. A. (2024). Representation of a minor victim in criminal proceedings: Analysis of federal and regional (Stavropol) legislation. *Pravosudie / Justice*. https://www.semanticscholar.org/paper/c1116b7690da6a11f4b1df9c3426c333bf62c1e6 (accessed on 9th September 2025).
4. Azhar, S., Arshad, S., Rizvi, A., & Asghar, U. (2025). Criminal Procedure Code in Pakistan: Evaluating the process and challenges in investigating crimes. *The Critical Review of Social Sciences Studies*. https://www.semanticscholar.org/paper/dec48687bf9488db147ef8a28faac0710b819be1 (accessed on 9th September 2025).
5. Bakhtiar, H. S. (2024). Legal regulation of forensic autopsies in the criminal investigation process: A study of concepts and legal reform. *Journal of Law, Politic and Humanities*. https://www.semanticscholar.org/paper/b485c8757577197204bfa0b1b8e780476a861ae1 (accessed on 9th September 2025).
6. Belov, M. V. (2024). On systematicity of procedural guarantees on the stage of termination of various pre-trial investigation types. *Russian Investigator*. https://www.semanticscholar.org/paper/3b7e6999a9252e8d0ca86b0870ec2f46b8f0cf65 (accessed on 9th September 2025).
7. Berzina. (2025). Socio-historical prerequisites for the criminalization of acts that infringe on the established procedure for drugs circulation under US criminal law. *Analytical and Comparative Jurisprudence*. https://www.semanticscholar.org/paper/675f458900ff4475a5da0e8d6fd19a615813397c (accessed on 9th September 2025).
8. Bespalko. (2024). Peculiarities of the proof process in Japanese criminal procedure. *Uzhhorod National University Herald. Series: Law*. https://www.semanticscholar.org/paper/f2b45ffcd7449173167cb4d2d0f732bf44a945b7 (accessed on 9th September 2025).
9. Chien, C. V. (2020). America's paper prisons: The second chance gap. *Michigan Law Review*. https://doi.org/10.36644/mlr.119.3.america (accessed on 9th September 2025).
10. Cole, G. F., & Smith, C. E. (2020). *Criminal Justice in America*. https://doi.org/10.5040/9798216963394 (accessed on 9th September 2025).
11. Corbett-Davies, S., Pierson, E., Feller, A., Goel, S., & Huq, A. Z. (2017). Algorithmic decision making and the cost of fairness. https://doi.org/10.1145/3097983.3098095 (accessed on 9th September 2025).
12. Dulskyi, O. (2024). The concept of gathering evidence by parties of criminal proceedings. *Uzhhorod National University Herald. Series: Law*. https://www.semanticscholar.org/paper/a86a7adce8988704188cb1320f43facc4a9f1fba (accessed on 9th September 2025).
13. Esen, B., & Gümüşçü, Ş. (2016). Rising competitive authoritarianism in Turkey. *Third World*

Quarterly, 37, 1581–1606. https://doi.org/10.1080/01436597.2015.1135732 (accessed on 9th September 2025).

14. Farrington, D. P., Loeber, R., & Howell, J. C. (2012). Young adult offenders. *Criminology & Public Policy, 11*, 729–750. https://doi.org/10.1111/j.1745-9133.2012.00842.x (accessed on 9th September 2025).
15. Feld, B. C. (2020). *The Evolution of the Juvenile Court*. New York University Press eBooks. https://doi.org/10.18574/nyu/9781479856664.001.0001 (accessed on 9th September 2025).
16. Føllesdal, A. (2020). Survey article: The legitimacy of international courts. *Journal of Political Philosophy, 28*, 476–499. https://doi.org/10.1111/jopp.12213 (accessed on 9th September 2025).
17. Gabbiani, L. (2013). Insanity and parricide in late imperial China (eighteenth–twentieth centuries). *International Journal of Asian Studies, 10*, 115–141. https://doi.org/10.1017/s147959141300003x (accessed on 9th September 2025).
18. Guidotti, R., Monreale, A., Ruggieri, S., Turini, F., Giannotti, F., & Pedreschi, D. (2018). A survey of methods for explaining black box models. *ACM Computing Surveys, 51*, 1–42. https://doi.org/10.1145/3236009 (accessed on 9th September 2025).
19. Guthrie, C., & Rachlinski, J. J. (2005). Can judges ignore inadmissible information? The difficulty of deliberately disregarding. *University of Pennsylvania Law Review, 153*, 1251–1251. https://doi.org/10.2307/4150614 (accessed on 9th September 2025).
20. Ibn, A., Hakami, O., Saleh, Y., Dahāmi, H., & Ali, L. (2025). The impact of blocking pretexts on the relationship between the investigator and the judiciary and investigation results from the Saudi Criminal Procedure Law. *Journal of Information Systems Engineering and Management*. https://www.semanticscholar.org/paper/4e45eee19a7637185b31022077085f2a259aaa4c (accessed on 9th September 2025).
21. Ienca, M., & Andorno, R. (2017). Towards new human rights in the age of neuroscience and neurotechnology. *Life Sciences Society and Policy, 13*. https://doi.org/10.1186/s40504-017-0050-1 (accessed on 9th September 2025).
22. Irawan, H. H., Sanusi, S., & Indraswari, S. P. (2025). Legal responsibility of midwives for delivery assistance in the efforts of material and child health. *Hermeneutika: Jurnal Ilmu Hukum*. https://www.semanticscholar.org/paper/1dde285c77620d77a5fff676c169046bf03771d3 (accessed on 9th September 2025).
23. Karpov, V., & Sinkov, D. (2024). On the issue of criminal prosecution of persons previously brought to administrative responsibility within the framework of the current norms of the Criminal Procedure Code of the Russian Federation and the Code of Administrative Offenses of the Russian Federation. *Siberian Criminal Process and Criminalistic Readings*. https://www.semanticscholar.org/paper/83219d95dbde2b83d3edde0434d49388127b3a70 (accessed on 9th September 2025).
24. Kim, M., & Lee, K. L. (2024). A study on measures to guarantee the right to be present for the actual person subject to search and seizure: Focusing on notification during search and seizure, and data preservation orders or reques. *The Korean Association of Criminal Procedure Law*. https://www.semanticscholar.org/paper/1a8b05b514de14949ac6c2b4acf6c48c806a925c (accessed on 9th September 2025).

25. Kore-Okiti, E. T. (2023). Reconceptualizing plea bargain as a prosecutor tool in Nigeria. *Kampala International University Law Journal*. https://www.semanticscholar.org/paper/65bafe39a83d84e06e2178626ec2b5a42b48ad70 (accessed on 9th September 2025).

26. Kostiuk. (2024). Forensic classification of military criminal offences and the place of abuse of power or authority by a military official. *Ûridičnij Časopis Nacìonal'noï Akademìï Vnutrìšnìh Sprav*. https://www.semanticscholar.org/paper/2b96b680b6c345400a98561d10addc756661cb70 (accessed on 9th September 2025).

27. Kraschel, K. L., Chen, A., Turban, J. L., & Cohen, I. G. (2022). Legislation restricting gender-affirming care for transgender youth: Politics eclipse healthcare. *Cell Reports Medicine, 3*, 100719–100719. https://doi.org/10.1016/j.xcrm.2022.100719 (accessed on 9th September 2025).

28. Kutateladze, B. L., Andiloro, N. R., Johnson, B. D., & Spohn, C. (2014). Cumulative disadvantage: Examining racial and ethnic disparity in prosecution and sentencing. *Criminology, 52*, 514–551. https://doi.org/10.1111/1745-9125.12047 (accessed on 9th September 2025).

29. Kuznietsov, O. O., Kyriienko, A. I., & Yesypenko, O. (2023). Some aspects of formation of a new model of ensuring security, regime and security of penal institutions and remand prisons, taking into account the requirements of international regulatory and legal acts. *Scientific Herald of Sivershchyna. Series: Law*. https://www.semanticscholar.org/paper/ee70bd9f5633835dd79244efcc2c8dba0be28b08 (accessed on 9th September 2025).

30. Lee, S. (2025). Attorney-client privilege and the criminal evidence. *Institute for Legal Studies, Chonnam National University*. https://www.semanticscholar.org/paper/aad9263ebf670128fbdfae17f5897a0ac6dcdedd (accessed on 9th September 2025).

31. Lopotenko, V. S. (2025). Some aspects of determining the subject of a criminal procedural appeal in pre-trial proceedings. *Теория и практика общественного развития*. https://www.semanticscholar.org/paper/064e45577bb9e9b20c7addfd22627591be7800ec (accessed on 9th September 2025).

32. Lupària Donati, L., & Pittiruti, M. (2020). Post-conviction remedies in the Italian criminal justice system. *Erasmus Law Review, 13*, 73–86. https://doi.org/10.5553/elr.000185 (accessed on 9th September 2025).

33. Maamir, H. (2025). Statute of limitations in lawsuits concerning forgery of official documents in light of Algerian law and judicial precedent. *Science of Law*. https://www.semanticscholar.org/paper/45ac7c84899a888b2422f700f312d1ffa20348fe (accessed on 9th September 2025).

34. Matis, J. (2024). Legality and admissibility of evidence in criminal proceedings. *Uzhhorod National University Herald. Series: Law*. https://www.semanticscholar.org/paper/4adddc7d5e4c462dc15a0017c3f2dcc5394d24bd (accessed on 9th September 2025).

35. McChesney, R. (2024). The wrongful arrest theory: Justice for individuals with diabetes in criminal law procedure. *The Undergraduate Law Review at UC San Diego*. https://www.semanticscholar.org/paper/59007a13aed8395e0a691cbbe1c22d03f63c739f (accessed on 9th September 2025).

36. N/A. (2021). *Theory and Practice of the European Convention on Human Rights. Nomos Verlagsgesellschaft mbH & Co.* KG eBooks. https://doi.org/10.5771/9783748923503 (accessed on 9th September 2025).

37. N/A. (2023). A study of Supreme Court decisions on criminal procedure in 2022. *Kyung Hee Law Journal*. https://www.semanticscholar.org/paper/2ba2aec34e2c328464ba7604211503 4c3f5dccb2 (accessed on 9th September 2025).

38. Nicholson, P. (2017). The death penalty and its reduction in Asia: An overview. *Asian Law Centre Briefing Papers*. https://doi.org/10.46580/11343.241739 (accessed on 9th September 2025).

39. Nopriandi, T., & Ardhiansyah, R. F. (2020). Paradigm of death penalty (comparative study in Indonesia, Saudi Arabia and China). *Lampung Journal of International Law, 2*. https://doi.org/10.25041/lajil.v2i1.2032 (accessed on 9th September 2025).

40. Organization for Economic Co-operation and Development. (2018). *Integrity for Good Governance in Latin America and the Caribbean*. OECD eBooks. https://doi.org/10.1787/9789264201866-en (accessed on 9th September 2025).

41. Panokin. (2024). Criminal appellate proceedings through the prism of a social project: Synergy of the society's request and legislative regulation. *Lex Russica*. https://www.semanticscholar.org/paper/227fff0e5b79fa504be03a7f3e6d436d87eb499d (accessed on 9th September 2025).

42. Piquero, A. R. (2021). The policy lessons learned from the criminal justice system response to COVID-19. *Criminology & Public Policy, 20*, 385–399. https://doi.org/10.1111/1745-9133.12562 (accessed on 9th September 2025).

43. Poamă, A. (2017). Corrective justice as a principle of criminal law: A prolegomenon. *Criminal Law and Philosophy, 12*, 605–623. https://doi.org/10.1007/s11572-017-9447-4 (accessed on 9th September 2025).

44. Putera, N. S. F. M. S., Saripan, H., Abu Hassan, R., & Abdullah, S. M. (2021). Artificial intelligence for construction dispute resolution: Justice of the future. *International Journal of Academic Research in Business and Social Sciences*. https://www.semanticscholar.org/paper/4d92278 4ef9cf44aaa10f001f2a6dc786b0ffada (accessed on 9th September 2025).

45. Puzyrov, M. (2025). The concept and content of the normative and legal support for the activity of the State Bureau of Investigation as a subject of preventing military criminal offenses under martial law. *Scientific Journal Criminal and Executive System: Yesterday. Today. Tomorrow*. https://www.semanticscholar.org/paper/8b816cc126ba20146f9ba51dde622923 3b14b05f (accessed on 9th September 2025).

46. Rajkomar, A., Hardt, M., Howell, M., Corrado, G. S., & Chin, M. H. (2018). Ensuring fairness in machine learning to advance health equity. *Annals of Internal Medicine, 169*, 866–866. https://doi.org/10.7326/m18-1990 (accessed on 9th September 2025).

47. Roberts, J. V., & Petzsche, A. (2025). Sentencing procedures under the adversarial and inquisitorial models of justice: A comparative analysis. *Criminal Law Forum*. https://www.semanticscholar.org/paper/5c485556035fcd131a2900303452c5af2df29a0e (accessed on 9th September 2025).

48. Safin, L. (2024). A critical analysis of the general principles of sentencing under the criminal law doctrine and their application by the Supreme Court of the Russian Federation. *Uchenye Zapiski Kazanskogo Universiteta. Seriya Gumanitarnye Nauki*. https://www.semanticscholar.org/paper/f04a2f504f7412f753cd2157ae7f86b9c24e271a (accessed on 9th September 2025).

49. Shaughnessy, J. J., & Zechmeister, E. B. (2016). *Research Methods in Psychology*. https://doi.org/10.24926/8668.2201 (accessed on 9th September 2025).

50. Sikun, A. (2023). Current state of implementation of the right to work by prisoners in detention centers. *Scientific Herald of Sivershchyna. Series: Law*. https://www.semanticscholar.org/paper/a4325e0a55082252ba6824a00e2daeac5433168f (accessed on 9th September 2025).

51. Smanaliev, K., & Salybekova, T. (2024). Criminal liability of legal entities in the Kyrgyz Republic and the specifics of the application of criminal law terms. *Bulletin of Science and Practice*. https://www.semanticscholar.org/paper/3d02af2d396d83a8f1e5d1094ea21614928c0ca7 (accessed on 9th September 2025).

52. Tkacheva, N. V. (2025). Conciliation procedures in criminal proceedings in courts of first instance in Russia. *Revista Brasileira de Alternative Dispute Resolution*. https://www.semanticscholar.org/paper/c1023ab71d18feabcce43d8197fd400fe7e9ed97 (accessed on 9th September 2025).

53. Usatii, V. (2025). Forms of specialist knowledge applied in the criminal investigation of offences in the field of economic activity. *Bulletin of Kharkiv National University of Internal Affairs*. https://www.semanticscholar.org/paper/9e9c827ea1230da6faff303719836b679c5610eb (accessed on 9th September 2025).

54. Uyun, A. (2024). Analysis of the protection needs of witnesses and victims in criminal cases. *Al-Qanun: Jurnal Kajian Sosial dan Hukum Islam*. https://www.semanticscholar.org/paper/c0ec524e5b3013fc8b84773feb4119ae26711afe (accessed on 9th September 2025).

55. Walt, T. V. D. (2017). The use of force in effecting arrest in South Africa and the 2010 bill: A step in the right direction? *Potchefstroom Electronic Law Journal, 14*, 137–162. https://www.semanticscholar.org/paper/b89a13a667f812f7a9af84dc47fe7e49d94d0373 (accessed on 9th September 2025).

56. Wang, Y., Han, J. H., & Beynon-Davies, P. (2018). Understanding blockchain technology for future supply chains: A systematic literature review and research agenda. *Supply Chain Management: An International Journal, 24*, 62–84. https://doi.org/10.1108/scm-03-2018-0148 (accessed on 9th September 2025).

57. Wang, Z. (2024). Gender and criminal sentencing: A comparative analysis of global judicial biases and reform efforts. *Journal of Education, Humanities and Social Sciences*. https://www.semanticscholar.org/paper/7a9a4a625b4ab10cdc8e25585c713ea58a0a2900 (accessed on 9th September 2025).

58. Yermak, O. (2021). Current state and prospects of legislative regulation development of measures of criminal legal influence on juveniles. *Scientific Herald of Sivershchyna. Series: Law*. https://www.semanticscholar.org/paper/f645a54c8034fb2736ce9ab88ba1583547775ccf (accessed on 9th September 2025).

59. Zedner, L., & Ashworth, A. (2018). The rise and restraint of the preventive state. *Annual Review of Criminology, 2*, 429–450. https://doi.org/10.1146/annurev-criminol-011518-024526 (accessed on 9th September 2025).

60. Zgoliński, I. (2025). Nodal issues of criminal liability on the level of public procurement. *Europejski Przegląd Prawa i Stosunków Międzynarodowych*. https://www.semanticscholar.org/paper/dd868169d5565d636decbbb43b41f23a85fc5449 (accessed on 9th September 2025).

Chapter 6

CONTRACT LAW ACROSS LEGAL SYSTEMS

Contents

INTRODUCTION

In the context of globalization of legal systems, the relationship between convergence and divergence of contract law is a highly significant field of research, particularly in analyzing how such legal principles operate in various nations. Contract law is significant based on its fundamental purpose of enabling transactions to occur and to govern the relationship between parties. This essay examines these principles comparatively in order to discover the nuance of contract formation, validity, and obligations under various legal traditions. As international business becomes increasingly sophisticated, it is essential that legal practitioners and scholars acquire an appreciation of these variations. With globalization more and more redefining the legal context, the implications for contract law become progressively vital to identify, particularly as legal frameworks are confronted with various practices and expectations, which may eventually shape the manner in which legal harmonization is approached. The intricacy of contract formation, including offer and acceptance, consideration, and requirements of formality, demonstrates differential paradigms cultural and legal within contract law. Systems which contrast with one another, that is, common law and civil law systems, have varying demands on the components of an enforceable contract. For instance, while common law accepts verbal contracts as enforceable in certain situations, civil law tends to insist on writing to fully sanction a contract. Moreover, these fundamental elements pose key issues regarding the legal capacity of contracting parties and the nature of consent in contract formation. It explains the wider relevance of contract law and opens the debate for potential areas of reform, unification, and adaptation in the wake of growing cross-border transactions that characterize the modern economic environment (Michaels et al., 2018). Contractual obligations beyond formation and validity are also significant to establish the obligations of parties and remedies for breach. The doctrines of performance standards, risk distribution, and third-party rights set the stage for enforcement and dispute resolution under contracts. These terms are compounded by the expectations imposed in international commercial contracts, where governing law provisions, choice of forum, and arbitration provisions come into play. The adoption of legal English as a global lingua franca further complicates the mix, requiring close scrutiny of the ways in which language and legal vocabulary impact negotiation and enforcement of contracts (Künnecke et al., 2017). As such, the imperative for flexible yet consistent knowledge of contract law within various legal regimes is critical to providing useful legal practices in a quickly changing global economy.

6.1. CONTRACT FORMATION

In the complex world of contract law, understanding the nuance of offer and acceptance within the context of contract formation is essential. An offer is an indication to be bound to a legally enforceable contract, with terms for acceptance. The acceptance by the offeree of these terms has to be unqualified, with little room for ambiguity or revision. However, cultural contexts play a major role in determining the meaning of offers and acceptances in various legal systems. Therefore, while the common law is formal about adhering to the mirror image rule, there are civil law regimes that allow a more expansive interpretation that also includes a broader sense of agreement. In addition, the rapid dissemination of legal English as a lingua franca highlights diverse international negotiation practices, which highlight the importance of transparency and understandability in contract formation processes (Künnecke et al., 2017).

Figure 6.1. Contract formation.

Source: Cody.

Furthermore, no less critical within the framework of contract law is the comprehension of consideration and cause since it forms the foundation for enforcing obligations under contract. Consideration is the value exchanged between the parties, while cause—especially in civil law systems—is the underlying rationale justifying a contract. Legal traditions vary significantly in their treatments of these doctrines. Common law, for example, requires consideration for a binding contract, while some civil law systems emphasize the intent of the parties and the inherent purpose of the contract, hence permitting reliance on non-monetary considerations. This variation complicates cross-border transactions since parties may hold varying perceptions of what constitutes adequate consideration and cause. Increased insight into these variations can assist in guaranteeing that worldwide agreements are formulated with the aim of meeting the legal obligations of involved jurisdictions, thus enhancing compliance and reducing conflict (Michaels et al., 2018). Lastly, the role of formalities in making a contract cannot be emphasized enough, especially when it comes to jurisdictions with particular statutory requirements for enforceable contracts. Certain contracts require written form or certain procedural formalities, like notarization or registration, for the sake of validating the contract. However, other juridical systems may be less restrictive and are more amenable to accepting verbal contracts as having binding effect. This divergence of formalistic demands can raise mountainous obstacles for players of cross-border contracts, especially where there is disparity of expectations. The internationalization of legal practices, amidst an explosion of world trade and business relationships, demands a delicate understanding of local formalities in order to evade inadvertent disputes. Therefore, the addition of knowledge of appropriate formalities at the formation of contracts can significantly enhance the legal standing of agreements within various legal systems, in accordance with global business norms and legal requirements (Künnecke et al., 2017) (Figure 6.1).

6.1.1. Offer and Acceptance

In the intricate universe of the law of contract, offer and acceptance are key pillars upon which binding contracts are established. How these ingredients work within legal systems marks the extent of strategy variety and serves to minimize uncertainty in contractual interactions. An offer is generally a positive intention to be bound by certain terms, and an acceptance is the positive agreement to those terms. The nuances of these definitions vary significantly across jurisdictions; Common Law jurisdictions, for example, will require a mirror image acceptance and the acceptance follows the offer closely. Civil Law traditions, on the other hand, may permit less formal negotiation, with acceptances that are not entirely different from original propositions. This comparative analysis reveals that, while the supporting doctrines are standardized, application and interpretation can differ substantially, influencing enforceability of contracts and providing practitioners with degrees of predictability in contract formation (Lang, 2024).

Adding to the dynamics of offer and acceptance are the advances of electronic contracts, which have transformed traditional thinking in consideration of digital transactions. As more and more companies engage in e-commerce, the means of making offers and writing acceptances have evolved, giving rise to new legal compliance issues. For instance, the act of creating an electronic offer may be through an email or click-through agreement that is a modern method very dissimilar from older handwritten contracts. Researchers have referred to the need for a rigorous analysis of these electronic changes, advocating for an integrated legal framework to serve the doctrines of offer and acceptance under electronic conditions. This is demonstrated by hybrid regulatory measures experienced within jurisdictions around the world, where some nations have welcomed specialist legislation while others apply prevalent legal frameworks to govern electronic contracts. Hence, the challenge remains for legal frameworks to reconcile these developments with established principles of contract law (Milash, 2024).

There can be no underestimation of the demand for clear definitions and standards in offer and acceptance procedures, especially with globalization still impacting contract practice. Harmonized legal frameworks must not only address traditional contractual arrangements but also be able to manage the intricacies introduced through global trade. The varying definitions of offer and acceptance can have far-reaching effects on cross-border contract enforceability. With companies doing business across borders, understanding how each legal culture understands such building blocks is more relevant than ever.

For example, the CISG establishes rules that harmonize aspects of offer and acceptance to promote international commerce consistency. Such initiatives highlight the need for distinguishing between these terms through clear definitions, hence enhancing legal predictability and avoiding conflict. Therefore, with the evolution of contract law, a deep understanding of offer and acceptance across different legal systems will be vital for effective negotiation and enforcement in more complex commercial settings (Lang, 2024) (Figure 6.2).

Offer and Acceptance

- An offer is a proposal by one party to another to enter into a legally binding agreement
- The person making the offer is known as the offeror, proposer, or promisor and the person to whom it is made is called the offeree or proposee
- When the offeree accepts the offer, he is called the acceptor or promisee
- A contract emerges from the acceptance of an offer
- Acceptance is the act of assenting by the offeree to an offer
- An offer when accepted becomes a promise

Figure 6.2. Offer and acceptance.

Source: The Lawyers & Jurists.

6.1.2. Consideration and Cause

In analyzing the intricate interaction between consideration and cause in contract law, it is evident that these doctrines constitute pillars in the various legal systems (Figure 6.3).

Essentials of consideration

- Consideration must move at the desire of the promisor.
- Consideration may move from promisee or any other person.
- Consideration may be past, present or future.
- Consideration need not be adequate.

Figure 6.3. Consideration, generally understood as the value exchanged between parties, confirms the binding nature of agreements.

Source: https://blogger.googleusercontent.com/img/b/R29vZ2xl/AVvXsEjtprayKegwNkR7DL8RPkpCbdWV3hzbtfLhAi7KmWGN9ILYZOo57qk18y7kgBKO79IencLznOVmNEaM79El2-at4-LILuxkdwzeDpm6UUL_Wuk3kw_CTi0z50R2-slOZj4U8akwCctKJMc/w0/Consideration-Contract+Law.jpg.

Consideration is the quid pro quo which makes otherwise promises binding contracts, satisfying the principle that something valuable must be received in exchange for the promise. In contrast to this, the concept of cause, which is typically analyzed in civil law jurisdictions, addresses the intent behind the contract. While this distinction may seem to be fine, it has significant implications for contract enforcement, particularly in cases of non-standard contracts and emerging legal devices. Further, such knowledge informs us about how different traditions of law deal with the complexities of obligations, and hence calls for an evaluative approach to contract law that is inclusive as well as context sensitive. The contemporary environment of contract law has been highly influenced by developments in technology, which pose threats to traditional notions of consideration and cause. One such example is the development of smart contracts, which are automatic agreements operated through the application of blockchain technology. These contracts often do not incorporate direct common consideration, which would make their classification under the traditional legal framework difficult. Here, cause's very nature is most important; comprehending the underlying intent behind these contracts is what is necessary to secure them a place in law and in practice. Those jurisdictions that have started to cope with such challenges have shown degrees of accommodation that vary according to different perspectives on consideration and cause. Consequently, comparative examination of these changing perceptions further explains the dynamic relationship between contract law and legal theory in contemporary contract law. As legal systems continue to struggle with dealing with the challenges brought about by advanced contractual arrangements, consideration and cause must be redetermined in a broader regulatory framework. The emergent dominance of artificial intelligence and other digital technologies means that the foundational principles that form the basis of contracts need to be reconsidered. Particularly, the lack of physical touch in certain transactions, for example, those conducted via smart contracts, necessitates legislative intervention that respects how settled legal principles must be adjusted to accommodate new realities. Research indicates that there are grave loopholes in the regulation of such new-age deals, necessitating it even more urgently that progressive action gets to reconcile technological developments with the strength of legal systems. By the integration of experience from various jurisdictions, including comparative examination of the way countries like Iran and India address these issues, the law of consideration and cause can be advanced. Ultimately, developing a discourse that integrates technological intricacies will mean that the law of contracts remains robust and effective in an evolving world, as discussed in conclusions on smart contracts and AI (Nazarov, 2024; Houshmand et al., 2024).

6.1.3. Formalities

The formalities theory in contract law is a vital element that transcends diverse legal systems, impacting the way agreements are formulated and enforced. The long-standing practice of preferring written contracts is primarily to ensure that parties stipulate their obligations and intentions in clear terms. Formality in the form of signatures, notarization, or specific terms imbues legitimacy and is an authoritative determinant in cases of disputes. Various jurisdictions have varying degrees of formality when it comes to such formalities; they may even reject claims that do not indicate compliance with these specifications, effectively nullifying agreements. Realizing the significance of formality thus helps to clarify why some contracts succeed while others fail. As a quintessential case in point, noncompliance with formalities set in acquiring titles results in convoluted legal disputes and raises significant issues about the legitimacy of imposed agreements (Levitin et al., 2013). While formalities are there to ensure clarity and intention, their application can differently influence the parties' rights under a contract. For the majority of legal frameworks, the rigid application of formalities can serve to protect parties, particularly those with inferior bargaining positions. By way of example, contract law often employs formalities to shield weaker creditors from other organizations that can otherwise avoid liability with fig-leafed complexity in corporate structuring or financing behavior. It can particularly be seen in veil-piercing cases, where courts might reexamine formalities to allocate responsibility for tort creditors on the basis of an advanced weighing of strict compliance with legal form and practical justice (Peterson et al., 2017). So, the legal systems are confronted with the challenge of ensuring enforcement of strict formalities while having sufficient flexibility to maintain the spirit of contractual agreements. Commercial conduct has further complicated the role of formalities. Developments in technology and globalisation have given rise to innovative ways of contracting that significantly avoid traditional formal requirements, particularly in international trade. So, for instance, electronic contracts and digital signatures become ever more the norm. The transformation raises questions of a fundamental nature about the sufficiency of formal rules to modern methods. The tension between the necessity to maintain formal standards and the flexibility of evolving methodologies highlights the need for an integrated approach to formalities within contract law that adapts to the commercial realities of modern times. This kind of a path can bring about transparency and ease in contractual transactions with the assurance that basic legal concepts remain enforced, thereby increasing overall market trust.

6.2. VALIDITY AND CAPACITY

At the heart of this is the capacity of parties in law, that is, the capability of people to enter into a contract. The law generally takes into consideration that parties must possess the required mental capacity and age so as to consent to binding obligations. For instance, minors and persons with mental incapacity may lack the required legal capacity required to form enforceable contracts, hence affecting their enforceability. One must clearly understand these principles since, as can be observed through different regulatory systems that seek to protect vulnerable groups from abusive contracts, such protections underscore the need for statutory intervention that not only permits a contract to be entered into but also ensures that the parties entering into these contracts are healthy. Will and consent are also at the forefront of determining the validity of contracts across legal systems since they involve the nature of the agreement between the parties. A valid contract mandates that all parties agree voluntarily, free from coercion, undue influence, or misrepresentation. This aspect is dealing with the broader examination of vitiating factors, which are situations that will render a contract invalid, such as fraud or mistake.

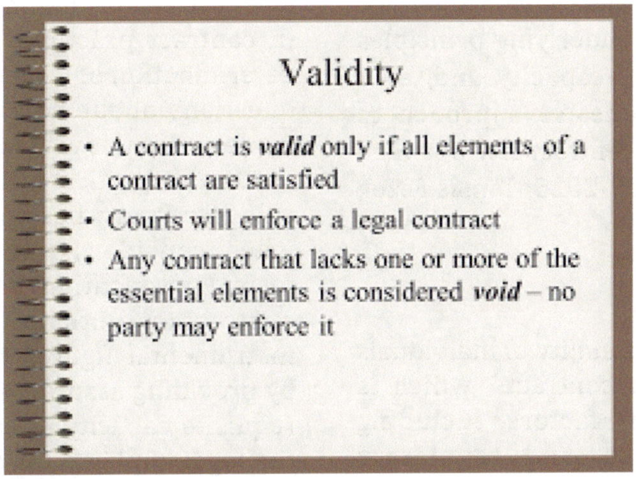

Figure 6.4. In exploring the multifaceted subject of contract law, one must consider the critical dimensions of validity and capacity, which underpin the enforceability of agreements across various legal systems.

Source: https://encrypted-tbn0.gstatic.com/images?q=tbn:ANd9GcRUm51lR5Zx4fzBCcW8WDEYAnTPn3nkysVlzQ&s.

Against this backdrop, the Principles of European Contract Law (PECL) specifically addresses issues of invalidity and consent with the underlying focus lying on informed consent as the key to contract formation. The PECL structure also gives important insight into the many factors that may result in contract invalidity, thus serving as a critical point of reference towards contract law harmonization across the multitude of jurisdictions. Here, then, the relationship between vitiating factors, capacity, and consent becomes the focal point of understanding the intricacies of contract validity in a globalized legal system. Moreover, the consequences of invalidity under contract law are an expression of the strength of complexity among various legal systems. The concerns with respect to contract validity, particularly the legal capacity and consent, become the cause for stringent regulatory frameworks. With this, it can be seen that the examination of contract law legislation shows that various jurisdictions have differing methods to these questions. For instance, there are some nations with a precise meaning for capacity and consent, which means they tend to produce varied results in contractual obligation disputes. Legislative instruments, for example, those found in the licensing schemes of health laboratories, illustrate the significance of administrative procedural law and of substantive law to control such capacities effectively in order to limit the threat of invalidity of contracts. These differences emphasize the need for an internationally accepted standard to bridge gaps in comprehension of the underlying principles that support validity and capacity and, as a result, create a more cohesive approach to this foundational area of contract law between systems of law (Huber et al., 2025; Tamás Fézer, 2022) (Figure 6.4).

6.2.1. Legal Capacity of Parties

Legal capacity refers to the ability of individuals or entities to enter into contracts, which is contingent upon various factors, including age, mental competence, and regulatory compliance. For instance, minors generally lack the capacity to contract, thus rendering agreements voidable at their discretion. This limitation aims to protect young individuals from exploitation while recognizing their burgeoning autonomy. Additionally, parties deemed mentally incapacitated, either due to psychological conditions or substance abuse, may also be incapable of executing contracts effectively. Therefore, legal systems establish criteria that delineate when and how parties can engage in contractual commitments to safeguard their rights and interests, ultimately fostering fairness and justice in contractual dealings. Furthermore, the concept of legal capacity varies significantly across jurisdictions, influencing the principles that govern contract law. In civil law countries, for example, the age of majority is a pivotal determinant of legal capacity, with statutes explicitly outlining the conditions under which minors can enter into binding agreements. Conversely, common law jurisdictions tend to adopt a more flexible approach, where courts may assess the specific circumstances surrounding each case. This divergence underscores the necessity for understanding local regulations and norms when navigating contract law. Moreover, as society evolves, contemporary legal frameworks increasingly address issues such as digital contracts and remote transactions, where traditional measures of capacity may not apply seamlessly. The integration of technological advancements in contract practices further complicates the determination of legal capacity, raising pressing questions about how these systems adapt to modern realities while ensuring the protection of vulnerable parties. In addition, the complexities of legal capacity become even more pronounced when considering the role of notaries and formal verification procedures in enhancing contractual authenticity. Notaries serve as instrumental figures in various legal systems by providing assurance that parties possess the requisite capacity to consent and are aware of the legal implications of their agreements. The evolution of notarial law, particularly in the context of burgeoning digital platforms, presents both opportunities and challenges in ensuring reliable contract validation. As highlighted in recent research, advances in technologies could streamline notarial processes and improve risk assessment related to contractual agreements (Basyarudin, 2024). However, these developments also prompt discussions regarding security concerns, fraud prevention, and the preservation of the notary's traditional role amidst these changes. As such, a thorough examination of legal capacity and the functions of notaries is crucial for understanding the dynamic interplay between contract formation and enforceability in diverse legal landscapes (Figure 6.5).

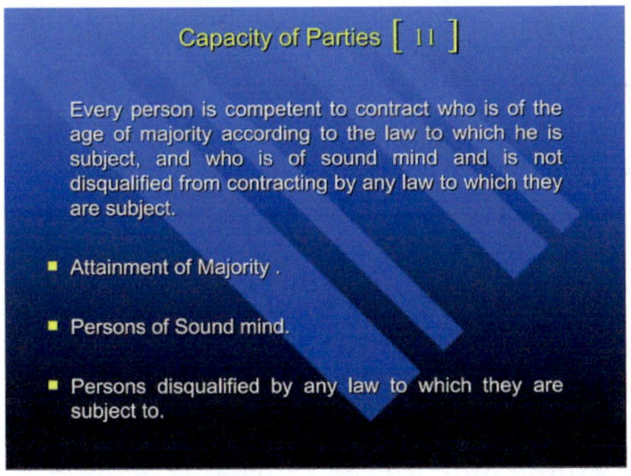

Figure 6.5. Understanding the legal capacity of parties engaged in contract formation is essential to ensuring that agreements are valid and enforceable across various legal systems.

Source: https://cdn.slidesharecdn.com/ss_thumbnails/capacity-of-parties-to-enter-in-to-contract-1291807242-phpapp01-thumbnail.jpg?width=640&height=640&fit=bounds.

6.2.2. Consent and Will

Fundamental to understanding contract formation, consent ensures that parties enter agreements of their own volition, which aligns with the principles of autonomy and intention. In jurisdictions that uphold strict adherence to these principles, the absence of genuine consent may lead to the classification of a contract as void or voidable. This ambiguity is particularly evident in cases involving duress or undue influence, where a party's ability to consent is compromised. The variability of consents interpretation across legal contexts highlights its scalar nature, ranging from strong to weak consent. The implications of this spectrum necessitate an examination of the conditions under which consent is deemed adequate, ultimately shaping the legal landscape of contract validity (Raza et al., 2025). The challenges surrounding consent are not limited to contract law; they also resonate prominently within fields such as medical ethics. In medical contexts, the concept of consent is paramount and often categorized as a multi-faceted obligation that requires the patient to be fully informed and competent to make decisions. This becomes particularly significant when discussing topics like organ donation, where consent mechanisms can often be convoluted and fraught with ethical dilemmas.

The call for a model that disaggregates consent highlights the necessity to consider varying degrees of understanding, autonomy, and capacity. This model can serve to refine the consent process, ensuring that the plurality of values embedded in consent is acknowledged and respected. By applying such frameworks to both legal and ethical dilemmas, the broader implications for contract law become considerably clearer and more comprehensive (Raza et al., 2025). As technology evolves, so too does the interpretation of consent within contract law, particularly concerning innovative instruments such as smart contracts. These digital contracts, which function autonomously based on pre-defined conditions, present significant challenges regarding traditional notions of consent and will. The integration of smart contracts into existing legal frameworks necessitates a thorough examination of their compatibility with established principles of contract law. Vitiating factors such as lack of mutual assent or undeclared limitations in capacity raise questions about the enforceability of these technological instruments. Moreover, the ongoing discourse illustrates a pressing need for regulatory frameworks to adapt in order to address these gaps effectively. Addressing these issues could lead to the harmonization of smart contracts with civil law principles, ultimately reinforcing the importance of explicit consent and the foundational role it plays across legal systems (Figure 6.6).

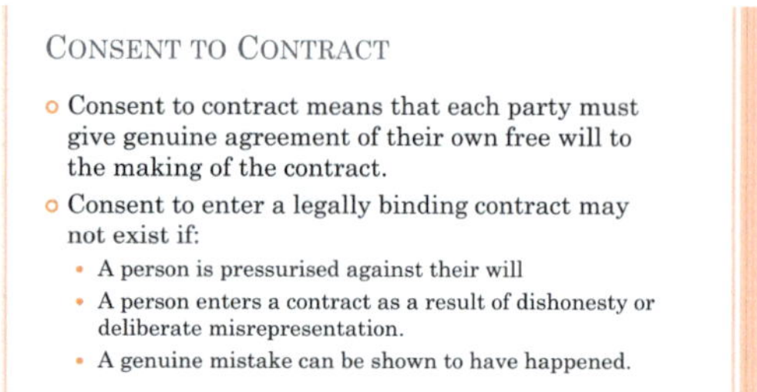

Figure 6.6. The concept of consent emerges as a foundational element, influencing the validity and enforceability of agreements across different legal systems.

Source: https://image1.slideserve.com/1556663/consent-to-contract-l.jpg.

6.2.3. Vitiating Factors

In the realm of contract law, the enforceability of agreements often hinges on the presence of certain vitiating factors that can undermine the validity of a contract (Figure 6.7).

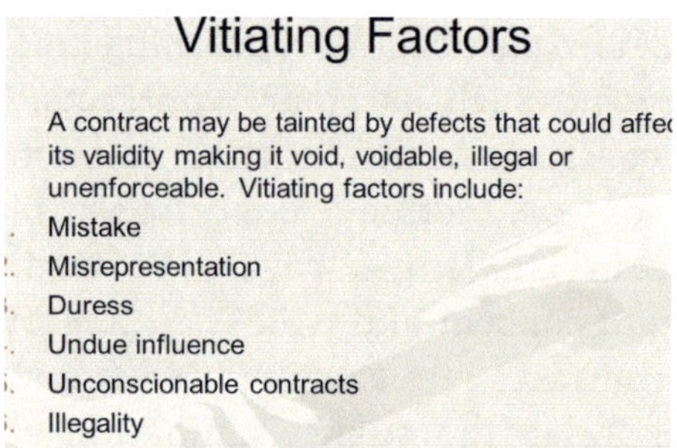

Figure 6.7. Vitiating factors include misrepresentation, duress, undue influence, and mistake, all of which can compromise the genuine consent of the parties involved.

Source: https://theintactone.com/wp-content/uploads/2019/04/topic-2.jpg.

For instance, a contract made under coercion lacks the voluntary consent that is necessary in contract formation, and thus is voidable. Similarly, misrepresentation destroys trust and validity in contractual relations since it induces one of the parties to make choices based on untruthful information. Correction of such issues is important in ensuring that contracts reflect the actual intentions and capacity of parties and thus avoid exploitation or unjust advantage in business deals. Furthermore, legal stipulations defining and describing vitiating factors vary across legal systems, which indicate the complexity of contract law globally. Each jurisdiction formulates its own tests for ascertaining whether and in what manner such factors exist and impact these factors. For instance, common law jurisdictions attach particular importance to clear intention and voluntary agreement in contracts, while civil law systems may attach more importance to the rules codified under obligations and liabilities. This divergence, expressed in varying legal models, complicates matters for cross-border contracts, under which contracting parties may be exposed to different understandings of what will vitiate. It is essential for legal professionals to understand these differences to serve their clients' better interests and to facilitate compliance with applicable laws. The expanding influence of technology and electronic communication has also introduced new elements to the issue of vitiating factors in the law of contract. The development of electronic contracts and new ways of communication, like emojis, are challenging classical notions of consent and intention. For example, research has begun to explore the legal implications of emojis on contract formation, debating whether or not virtual signs can be employed in forming an offer or acceptance based on classical principles of contract law (Hassan et al., 2025). This inquiry is indicative of the need for modification in legal provisions to accommodate the evolving context of contractual agreements. Additionally, with technology revolutionizing the manner in which parties interact with one another, understanding vitiating factors is vital in helping to ensure that contracts remain enforceable and valid under different legal systems, especially when considering the use of such platforms as artificial intelligence in automating contract risk assessment (Poornima et al., 2025).

6.3. CONTRACTUAL OBLIGATIONS

Central to contractual obligations is the standard of performance, one that varies across legal systems but has some common traits. In all the jurisdictions, contracting parties are required to perform according to terms of the contract, which could be quality and promptness of performance. The determination of whether there has been adequate performance often invokes good faith and fair dealing standards that serve to promote good faith in contract relations. For instance, from the areas of English, German, and French law, the unifying theme is the determination of good faith performance as a root principle for which the resolution of disputes regarding uncertain or indefinite terms should aim to be administered. Such a crossing point proves both the divergences and the convergences of legal frameworks as they tackle the complexity of performance of contractual obligations as they balance underlying doctrines in their domains (Russi et al., 2009).

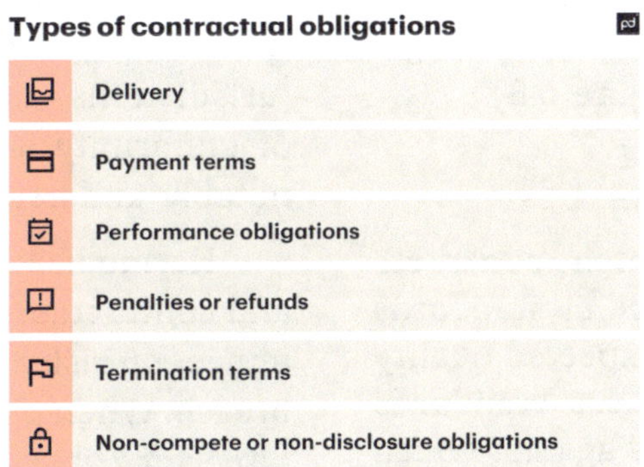

Figure 6.8. Types of contractual obligations.

Source: https://public-site.marketing.pandadoc-static.com/app/uploads/sites/3/INF_Contractual-obligation_2-1024x770.png.

Apart from frivolous performance standards, risk distribution regarding contractual obligations is another compounded aspect of contract law in legal systems. Parties frequently negotiate provisions that define liability in the case of unexpected events that may influence heavily their exposures relative to each other throughout the life of the contract. Distribution of risk may not only mirror the relative bargaining positions of the parties but also the prevailing norm of the law in different jurisdictions. For example, the Convention on Contracts for the International Sale of Goods (CISG) seeks harmonization when it comes to the distribution of risks but loses sight of that goal when jurisdictions interpret its provisions in varying ways. Without harmonious application, uncertainty threatens, eroding the predictability essential for effective commercial transactions. It is thus critical to understand these variations in assisting parties engaged in international transactions to successfully navigate their contractual agreements (Blair et al., 2011). Apart from this, third-party rights under contract have received increased recognition across legal systems, making wide-ranging implications to the enforceability of contracts. Traditionally, the privity doctrine insisted that only parties to a contract were entitled to enforce the contract, but today legal trends have moved towards conferring third parties certain rights under certain conditions. This evolution is particularly observed in the United Kingdom by virtue of the Contracts (Rights of Third Parties) Act of 1999, whereby third-party beneficiaries may enforce contract terms intended for their benefit. Similarly, comparative principles from civil law jurisdictions illustrate a variety of third-party rights and look towards the imperative of an informed approach within the creation of contracts. As such principles of law evolve further, they bring to the fore the necessity of not just considering the primary contracting entities but also potential third parties, thereby beefing up the discourse on contractual obligation in the globalized legal context (Russi et al., 2009) (Figure 6.8).

6.3.1. Performance Standards

The environment within which contracts operate is significantly influenced by standards of performance, which are the expected quality of commitments of parties. These standards serve as the points of reference against which contractual obligations can be measured, and the parties are held responsible to perform their obligations effectively. In various legal traditions, varying understandings of such performance standards are applied, thereby affecting the enforceability and expectations of contract relationships.

These differences underscore the necessity for specificity and clarity in writing contracts as indeterminateness in standards of performance would lead to conflict. Of special importance is that the role of performance standards transcends compliance; they induce stability and confidence in business transactions as a foundation of ensuing relations in multi-jurisdictional contexts. Above all, the existence of performance standards in contracts cannot be separated from the legal regimes that govern them. Various jurisdictions will have varying attitudes to delivering acceptable performance, informed by cultural assumptions and legal traditions. For instance, whereas some legal systems take a strict approach to adhering to the terms agreed upon, others will allow scope for some adaptability in performance on grounds of good faith or reasonableness. This flexibility may be troublesome, particularly in cross-border contracts where parties to a contract with diverse legal backgrounds may have disparate perceptions of acceptable performance. In these respects, the CISG attempts to harmonize performance expectations among contracting parties, but all too often the effectiveness of its efficiency is undermined by variations in interpretation and application among jurisdictions, as revealed in the examination of uniformity and flexibility under the treaty, notably underscored in Blair et al. (2011).

Harmonization of standards of performance and contractual terms thus has a wide-ranging impact on risk and liability allocation in case of breach. When parties fail to meet the standards of performance established, the legal remedies can range from monetary penalties to rescission of contract, depending on the governing law. Because performance standards entail subjective meanings, they are essential in determining the amount of liability that remains in cases of breach, something that has a broad range of variations across legal systems. In addition, the intricacies of quantifying performance in multiple jurisdictions underscore the imperative of careful risk management and legal acumen. Analysis of labor market flexibility in a wide range of contexts, as offered in Santos et al. (2009), further demonstrates the manner in which the relational aspect of contractual promises crosses over with measurements of performance, indicating the multifaceted aspects of compliance and enforcement cutting across wide legal regimes.

6.3.2. Risk Allocation

The complexities of risk management under contractual agreements identify an essential element of the legal system across the world. Effective risk allocation not only establishes legitimate responsibility among parties but is also a system through which disputes over claims arising from unforeseen circumstances are minimized. In certain jurisdictions, risk distribution practices reflect divergent legal cultures and values. For example, negotiated risk appreciation is emphasized by common law systems under which the parties will commonly attempt to shift the risk to the party most able to manage it. Civil law systems can be more distributive and emphasize equal sharing of risk by parties.

The difference mirrors how fairness and responsibility perceptions vary across cultures and shape contract practices and injects these into the development of risk-based legal doctrines in different legal contexts. An appreciation of these nuances is essential to international contract law practitioners and theorists as well as risk management strategies. Additionally, the advent of modern technology and the rapid growth of commercial transactions enhance the sophistication of traditional assumptions of risk allocation. The intersection of Artificial Intelligence and machine learning platforms, such as Legal T5, has revolutionized contract negotiation and analysis. These advanced systems enhance the risk detection by employing automation to browse as well as applying advanced algorithms in highlighting pertinent contract terms that may initiate liabilities. These technology advancements have a significant role in addressing contemporary challenges, especially in sectors that are exposed to high-speed alteration, such as technology and cybersecurity. As observed by recent studies, the potential for risk analysis to be optimized with automation not only increases efficiency but also improves overall understanding of contractual requirements and risk implications, a testament to dynamic contract law evolution in practice (Poornima et al., 2025).

Distribution of risk is also further codified in digital contracts. The emergence of cyber threats necessitates reconsideration of the traditional models of contract, given that contracting parties must consider how to share risk in case of data breaches or service interruption. Court rulings in common and civil law regimes have already begun to include the importance of certain clauses concerning cybersecurity in formal contracts. Regulatory frameworks like the GDPR and CCPA also influence how risks are allocated, with emphasis on bolstering data protection obligations in contractual structures. After reading extensively upcoming trends in cyber contractual liability, it is evident that legal framings of risk allocation are evolving, conforming to the complexity of today's digital landscape (Khan et al., 2025). Such a shift has immense implications for legal professionals drafting new contracts, highlighting the requirement for keen sensitivity to risk management in a more connected world.

6.3.3. Third Party Rights

The idea of third-party rights in contract law is an astonishing evolution of the comprehension of contractual obligations under various legal systems. Traditionally, contracts were deemed agreements between the contracting parties themselves, with little consideration given to strangers. But the perception that third parties can derive benefits from contractual commitments has also gained traction, especially under civil law systems. For instance, in certain nations like France, recent updates to the Civil Code particularly acknowledge third parties' right to benefit from contractual obligations. This update allows for more comprehensive contract structures with room for possible third-party beneficiaries, thereby making contracts more functional and inclusive in modern legal systems. These advancements are particularly well-suited to international commercial transactions, whereby contracting parties might desire to provide security and guarantees to third parties who are indirectly not on the contract, hence making it more predictable and easier for trade (Mamouri et al., 2024). Third-party rights' analysis also gives differing approaches among legal traditions. For common law jurisdictions, the initially restrictive notions on the transferability of contractual rights have radically transformed. English courts, as well, have evolved their approach since the early days, moving from a drastic exclusion of third-party benefits to a liberal approach allowing third-party claims in some cases. This evolution mirrors the attempt by the court to reconcile the purity of original bargains with commercial realities of modern times. A comparative study emphasizes the significance of understanding the way different systems understand and enforce third-party rights as a reflection of deeper societal values and economic imperatives. With global trade increasingly dependent on complex contractual arrangements, it is important to recognize the diverse legal regimes regulating third-party rights if parties are to transact across borders (Mamouri et al., 2024). Finally, the effect of the recognition of third-party rights also extends to contract enforcement effectiveness and efficiency. Directly vesting rights in third parties, contracts are more likely to be robust, encouraging greater involvement in the economy and fostering greater confidence among participants. This judicial transformation addresses the modern subtleties of business transactions, where the stakeholders may comprise other parties indirectly committed to the agreement. Lawmakers and practitioners are thus faced with the task of molding legal systems to suit these rights appropriately. Furthermore, it is necessary to provide for such recognition not to make contracting parties face unintended liabilities. With the evolving global economy, the role of third-party rights must be examined in order to enhance consistency of contract laws across different jurisdictions and create an integrated global legal framework.

6.4. REMEDIES FOR BREACH

The effectiveness of remedies against breach of contract is very important in safeguarding the interests of contracting parties in legal contracts. This is particularly true when comparing the distinction between specific legal systems. Under common law systems, remedies such as damages focus on monetary compensation intended to place the aggrieved party in a position it would have been in, had the breach not occurred. In contrast, some civil law systems adopt specific performance as a central remedy, and the enforcement of promise rather than monetary compensation. The Iranian system is a good example where the specific performance would be the principal means for contractual breach solutions. This divergence in cures highlights the underlying philosophy governing contractual relations and raises questions on the efficacy of compensation over strict performance of the contract, thereby influencing judicial rulings in various legal systems.

Damages and penalties form a universal blue print for handling breach of contract in most legal systems to deter misuse and compel compliance. However, computation of damages varies substantially across legal systems. Common law principles place stress on actual loss incurred, commonly in terms of the damages foreseen, subject to the rule of abatement of loss. Such alternatives as found in some civil law jurisdictions may encompass punitive damages, as reflecting an expansive definition of contractual fidelity. And, too, as revealed in practices of law regarding contracts for personal property, the awarding of mental anguish as damage remains controversial. The discrepancy in awarding or rejecting such claims demonstrates the adaptability of legal standards, whereby remedies must align with the nuances of impairments suffered by the non-breaching party in different situations, thus influencing the rights and liabilities of parties to a contract (Xu, 2024).

Other than traditional money remedies and specific performance, rescission is also a fundamental remedy in contract law. This legal doctrine allows a contract to be set aside and returns parties to their pre-contractual positions. Availability of rescission can be contingent on a variety of factors, including the nature of the breach and whether there are vitiating factors such as misrepresentation or fraud. Its application is a recognition of the inherent relational nature of contracts, where the sanctity of the agreement is of highest concern. However, rescission can also be complex, particularly where personal property is in question, as the termination of the agreement may not always address the emotional or psychological impact experienced by the parties. Considering this, the rationale for invoking rescission must be duly measured against the necessity of sufficient remedies that uphold the dignity and contractual rights of individuals in varying juridical systems (Shakiba et al., 2022).

6.4.1. Specific Performance

In explaining the intricacies of contract law, the different remedies for breach of contract need to be considered. Among these remedies, specific performance stands out as a special and much-debated remedy. This quality of mutual obligation necessitates the defaulting party to specifically perform their contractual obligation rather than merely paying compensatory damages to the aggrieved party. While specific performance is generally preferred under civil law systems, where such relief is considered normal, common law legal systems are more strict. There, courts tend to prefer damages as relief and reserve specific performance for special cases. Apertome of this divergence sheds light on the general principles that underpin remedial routes in different legal systems, paving the way for more interesting discussion around enforceability and the nature of obligations in contractual obligations (Rñoz et al., 2011).

The significance of specific performance is further emphasized when taking into account its use in all arbitration contexts. Arbitrators need to navigate through conflicting legal regimes and their accompanying inclinations towards ordering specific performance. Arbitrators may order specific performance in the majority of situations, provided the underlying grounds of authority support such exercise. As arbitration is increasingly becoming a preferred instrument of disputants, it is important to understand the manner in which specific performance is integrated into such an instrument. This overlap makes possible a more situational and responsive approach to contractual conflict, since arbitrators can order specific performance even in courts traditionally resistant to such relief. In addition, examining cases where arbitrators have issued more advanced orders illustrates how they can, in effect, redefine the parties' relations in the future, thereby treating not only prior violation but also future compliance issues within contractual contracts (Goossens et al., 1989). In the end, the enforcement of particular performance begs fundamental questions about contractual loyalty and legal obligations. The distinction between civil and common law systems illustrates a basic tension over enforcement of promises under contract. Under civil law, the reliance on particular performance is consistent with the philosophy of law stressing sanctity of contract and exact observance. By contrast, common law's reluctance to enjoin specific performance other than for extraordinary reasons is concerning in its implications regarding the enforceability of contractual promises and potential uncertainty. This analysis demands closer scrutiny of whether legal machinery in various systems can catch parties' intentions when they enter contracts and maintain the sanctity of contractual relationships, thereby highlighting the importance of critical analyses of specific performance in cross-jurisdictional settings (Rñoz et al., 2011).

6.4.2. Damages and Penalties

The subtlety of the law of contracts reveals a variety of remedies for parties injured, one of which is assessing damages and penalties. Central to this regime is the distinction between compensatory damages to restore the injured party to where they would have been if the contract had been completed and punitive damages to deter future misconduct. This distinction identifies the philosophical assumptions of alternative legal frameworks that emphasize restoration over retribution. The imperative of definition and demarcation is particularly urgent, as application of damages varies significantly between jurisdictions, generating inconsistencies in judicial decisions. Knowledge of these nuances is crucial for organizations entering into contracts that traverse multiple legal jurisdictions, especially as they face nuances intrinsic to cross-border transactions. In addition to compensatory and punitive damages, legal systems also embrace foreseeability as an underlying consideration in determining the extent of recoverable damages. Foreseeability requires that damages are a natural consequence of the breach, imposing limits of liability on the party in breach. This is incorporated in various international instruments, including the Vienna Sales Convention (CISG), which prioritizes predictability in contractual dispute resolutions. These strategies enable prospective liabilities to be understood in the early stages, rendering international commercial relations easier. The legal terminology employed in reference to foreseeability reflects its evolution and complexity across contexts, a tacit attempt to counteract unintended outcomes and ensure the stability of contractual relations.

Furthermore, the dialogue between damages and penalties reflects the broader complexities of contract law enforcement. Even while sanctions can be designed to sanction wrong, their enforceability could invite judicial doubt, particularly in civil law countries where restorative justice is the focus. Variations in language and interpretation between legal cultures may complicate enforcement steps, calling for precise distinctions in meaning to be a requirement. This is the case where there would be no direct equivalents for certain legal notions. For instance, the functional equivalent principle functions in this bridging function, enabling effective conveyance of the legal terminology among diverse legal systems (Aliyev, 2025). Ultimately, the quest for accuracy in the definition of penalties and damages is still the final longing for effectuating just remedies that communicate loud and clear throughout the extent and reach of international legal traditions (Quynh, 2024).

6.4.3. Rescission

This solution is premised on the principles of justice and equity, enabling parties to rescind contracts found to be tainted with vices such as misrepresentation, undue influence, or coercion. It is rooted in the belief that it is essential to maintain contractual consent purity; thus, when a party is tricked or compelled into a contract, rescission acts as a rectification. In other traditions of law, the method of imposition of rescission would also differ, based on cultural and juridical variation in the conceptualization of equitable justice. For instance, in certain jurisdictions, the acknowledgment of judicial discretion to order rescission would be more expressed, whereas in others, tighter requirements need to be met by the aggrieved party in order to have the contract voided, thus justifying the varying application of this remedy (Poornima et al., 2025). In addition, rescission serves a two-fold function: not just does it void an unproductive contract, but it also returns the parties to their original position, as though the contract never took place. This principle of restitution is the underlying basis for the broader objective of contract law to ensure that parties are not unjustly enriched at the loss of another party. The nature of rescission as a remedy is actually capable of influencing business transactions and legal obligations within different jurisdictions, thereby calling for an extensive understanding of the respective legal frameworks. The complexity of rescission procedures also highlights its importance in legal disputes as the party seeking rescission often must show the existence of a vitiating factor that justifies rescission. This aspect is particularly relevant in transnational commercial contracts, wherein higher stakes are involved and the chances of disputes are enhanced through differing interpretations of contract validity (Basyarudin, 2024). The exploration of rescission under the said subject contract law reveals its adaptability and applicability under varying situations, especially in the case of electronic contracts as well as prevailing technological trends. The arrival of electronic contracts gives rise to new problems, especially with respect to consent and the capability to make an informed choice. Electronic signatures and virtual sites, although offering ease and convenience, also raise the issue of fraud or misrepresentation and consequently necessitate clear rules of rescission in such cases. With evolving legal infrastructures, there is greater need to ensure that traditional conceptions of rescission remain adequately suited for dealing with problems in modern times. For instance, the use of computer-based contract analysis through software such as Legal T5 has been beneficial in bringing out risks incorporated in contractual agreements, which can be used to analyze grounds for rescission. By integrating traditional legal principles with emerging technologies, law can still remain topical in a fast-developing complicated contractual sphere (Poornima et al., 2025) (Figure 6.9).

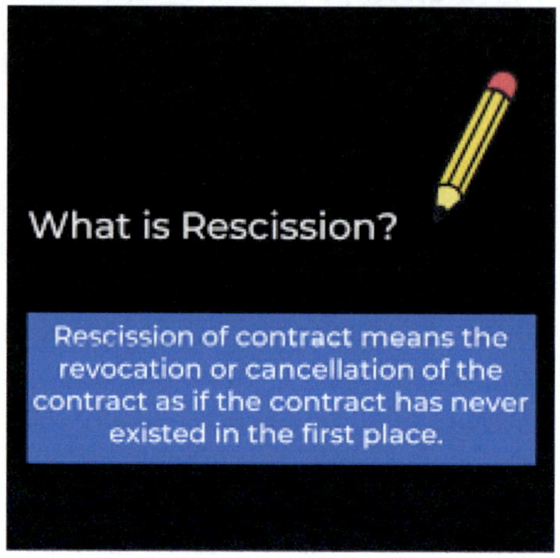

Figure 6.9. The concept of rescission serves as a crucial mechanism within contract law, allowing parties to void an agreement under specific circumstances.

Source: https://encrypted-tbn0.gstatic.com/images?q=tbn:ANd9GcTcpntyRsttfqFIBTtV0XpmOvv3B0HHzf8_jQ&s.

6.5. TERMINATION AND DISCHARGE

The fulfilment of a contractual agreement could be in various modes of termination and release that eventually amount to the mutually consented or legislatively accepted termination of obligations. Termination by mutual agreement is the most frequent mode of contract termination through parties consenting to discharge each other from the contractual obligations. This voluntary termination needs to be communicated clearly and shared with mutual understanding of the intention to cancel, stressing mutual assent as a fundamental aspect of contract law. All legal systems around the world identify this maxim, which underscores its basis in respect for the parties' autonomy and intentions. These agreements may be documented in writing to ensure clarity and prevent later disagreements regarding terms of contract termination. A second significant feature of discharge and termination is the doctrine of frustration of purpose, which states that unexpected events rendering nugatory the very basis of the contract, hindering its performance.

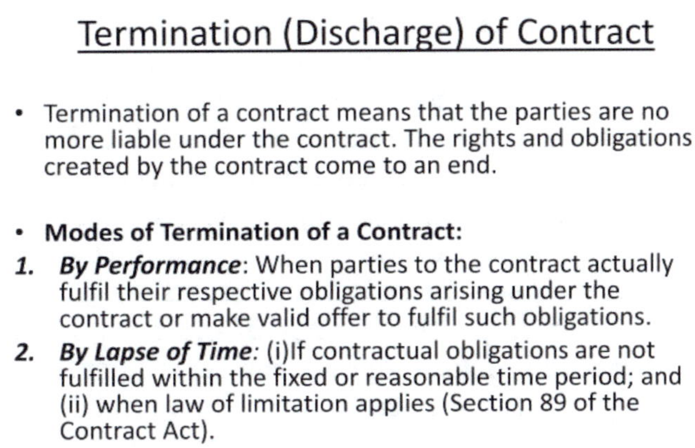

Figure 6.10. Termination (discharge) of contract.

Source: https://cdn1.slideserve.com/2075135/termination-discharge-of-contract-n.jpg.

The doctrine provides a judicial remedy where unexpected events beyond the control of the parties make it impossible to perform the contract. For example, if a natural calamity erupts and prevents the commodity delivery as envisaged, courts will allow for the discharge of the contract on frustration grounds. Recognition of this doctrine by different legal regimes shows how crucial it is in protecting parties against liability where unexpected issues prevent their performance, and it encourages a fair balance in contract performance under diverse circumstances. Also, provision under the law typically stipulates the specific grounds for termination, including the situation where a party is failing to perform in line with the contract. The aforementioned provisions under law vary by jurisdiction and shape the contractual remedies and rights landscape. For instance, some jurisdictions have notice provisions or grace periods prior to termination being invoked, but others provide for immediate discharge upon breach. The effect of specific legislation, say governing water supply contracts in civil law states, illustrates the way in which the laws can be so niche. Examining these various approaches, particularly in remedies for breach as exhibited in comparative formats such as Lang (2024), provides a more advanced understanding of the way discharge and termination function in contract law in different legal systems (Figure 6.10).

6.5.1. Mutual Agreement

The establishment of mutual agreements is a cornerstone in the domain of the law of contracts with the goal of establishing the consent necessary for binding contractual relationships. The principle relies on the offer and acceptance principles, where one party issues terms the other must irrevocably agree on to establish a contract. Significantly, the phrase mutual agreement can cross over cultural and jurisdictional boundaries and manifest differently across various legal systems. For instance, for international commercial contract parties, a delicate awareness of the specific legal regimes is essential to prevent contract validity disputes arising from conflicting interpretations. By necessity, the specificity of mutual agreement acts as a preventive control for potential misunderstanding, exemplifying the importance of contractual negotiation and documentation precision. In the law of contracts, mutual agreement also is influenced substantially by the capacity and consent of parties. Legal capacity defines the capability of parties to enter into contracts and focuses on parties possessing an awareness of the commitments they are entering into. Vitiating factors such as duress or undue influence could vitiate the purity of mutual agreement, resulting in a deviation from consent that is informed. Such factors differ considerably from one system to another, with some states placing more stringent requirements on capacity or vitiation than others. Such identification not only takes account of the varying connotations of mutual agreement but also operates to protect vulnerable parties to contracts so that contracts are founded on a foundation of genuine understanding and purpose. Dissolving contracts by mutual assent exemplifies the flexible nature of contractual relationships. Termination by mutual assent allows parties to mutually consent to terminate their obligations, balancing their interests such that independence of contract principle is ensured. This is particularly necessary in commercial contexts, where fluctuating market conditions may render it impracticable to keep contracts going. Such voluntarily initiated termination fosters flexibility and facilitates peaceful solutions, an aspect that has been observed in several legal frameworks. Moreover, the legal consequences following a mutual agreement to end a contract vary extensively, mainly depending on earlier provisions in regard to terminations as well as redressal measures. Comprehension of such divergence between legal systems underlines astute contractual tactics that allow smoother exits, thereby underscoring the value of agreement in the dynamic environment of contract law.

6.5.2. Frustration of Purpose

Frustration of Purpose is a significant legal principle that addresses situations where unexpected events render the essential purpose of a contract impossible. The principle relies on the natural expectation that things will not change and establishes the discharge of contractual obligations whenever outside elements render the sought purpose nugatory. In other jurisprudence, the doctrine defines varied approaches to the enforcement of contracts, highlighting the conflict between blanket compliance with contractual terms and the necessity for flexibility in the presence of changing realities. The legal analysis of these cases suggests that while different jurisdictions try to put strict controls on the acknowledgment of frustration, there are others that are lax in approach, thus the different legal cultures and frameworks that affect contract law. What follows therefore is this contrast that spawns critical debate about the impact of imposing contractual will vis-a-vis the acknowledgment of unforeseen disruption. In common law jurisdictions, the frustration doctrine has emerged in judicial case law in order to free the parties from their obligations that they are no longer capable of performing with the purpose of avoiding unjust enrichment. Historically, the courts looked for whether the frustrating event was sufficient to eliminate the gist of the contract with regard to foreseeability and allocation of risk. The relevance of the doctrine becomes particularly clear in international business, where the parties often encounter unexpected changes of circumstances due to political turmoil, natural disasters, or legislative changes. Here, the need for legal elasticity is imperative, when commercial parties seek to re-negotiate their arrangements on the basis of changed circumstances. Frustration is therefore not just a safety valve for parties out of contractual contracts but also an indication of the dynamic character of contracts in today's globalized world. Different legal systems impose different demands on determining and applying Frustration of Purpose. For instance, while Anglo-American legal traditions emphasize a strong objective approach founded on common law roots, civil law traditions can favor the parties' mutual intention in contracts. This discrepancy is likely to indicate various levels of protection for parties facing unforeseen events, significantly affecting business dealings and contracting negotiations. Furthermore, as international trade increases and increasingly more businesses that operate beyond borders, uniformity in the law in relation to the concept of frustration becomes increasingly necessary. Mitigating such inequalities through international legal regimes can encourage fairness and predictability in contract law and encourage sustainable commercial relations. As has been brought out by continuing scholarship, understanding these complications also helps towards creating a more balanced basis for the creation of contract law, as it grapples with issues of freedom and responsibility within commercial activity (Hoàng, 2025; Sebastián, 2025).

6.5.3. Legal Provisions

The dynamics between law and contract law with other provisions illustrate the intricate interplay between law and economic practice, influencing the formation and enforcement of contracts across different legal systems. Knowledge of the nuances of contract formation, particularly the major concepts of offer and acceptance, is crucial. The fundamental rules will determine whether a contract can be defined as a binding contract. Although some jurisdictions concentrate on mutual assent, others include additional conditions into the process of contract formation, such as consideration or form requirements for validity. As highlighted by the adoption of Collective Action Clauses (CACs) for sovereign bonds of the Eurozone, the quality of the legal system has the potential to make significant contributions to perceptions and market action, suggesting that comprehensive legal systems enhance the relative efficiency of protection in contracts (Carletti et al., 2014). Therefore, interpretation and enforcement of such clauses are critical in supporting contractual relationships across diverse jurisdictions. As pertinent to legal provision discourse is the doctrine of legal capacity and consent. Both parties to a contract must be of legal capacity to enter into an agreement, which varies significantly across legal systems. Vitiating factors such as duress, undue influence, or misrepresentation may invalidate consent, thus making contracts unenforceable. Different jurisdictions might structure and handle such factors differently, thus generating inconsistencies in how the contract obligations are fulfilled and the redress remedies sought in case of breach. Such acknowledgment shapes the intricacies of international commercial contracts because parties must navigate complex regimes of law that govern their contracts. This sophistication is further augmented by public resource management considerations, which suggest that the way in which governments manage public contracts can also come to represent and influence the effectuation of perceived private contractual effectiveness (Huang et al., 1995). The apportionment of duties and risks in contracts reflects the overall implications of provisions in legislation defining the way parties function under legislation. Both systems share similar standards of performance and breach remedy that can fundamentally affect contractual relations. Whether a remedy of specific performance or damages is available, for instance, varies, affecting how contracting parties word their contracts and allocate risk. The contrast is even more striking when it comes to international contracts, where governing law provisions and arbitration clauses take center stage. Such legal instruments not only provide certitude and certainty to the contracting parties but also highlight the need for effective legal protections within the realm of global trade. As such, it is crucial to identify how legal provisions operate in various systems to guarantee the fulfillment and enforcement of contractual promises.

6.6. INTERNATIONAL COMMERCIAL CONTRACTS

In international commercial contracts, the complexity of contract formation plays a decisive role in ensuring legal enforceability in various jurisdictions. Principles of offer and acceptance form the foundation, with the one side having to respond to a definite offer with the other side's definite acceptance, which is usually governed by cultural and legal considerations. In addition, the principle of consideration—transferring something of value between parties—is interpreted differently by jurisdiction. Whereas common law has historically insisted upon consideration, civil law may emphasize cause more. The formality that must be fulfilled prior to a contract being enforceable may also differ significantly, with some states asking for a specific form or registration, so a thorough knowledge of applicable legal systems is necessary to avoid pitfalls in cross-border transactions. Lastly, attention to these factors is crucial for the practitioner who engages in international trade as he or she navigates through the intricate web of international contract law, underscoring the need for clarity and knowledge. Validity and capability of parties to contract are also critical determinations in international contracts. Legal capacity varies from jurisdiction; for example, minors or mentally incapacitated individuals might be bound by restrictions that will render a contract void. Also, the concepts of will and consent will be vital since vitiating factors such as duress, fraud, and undue influence can vitiate a party's ability to validly consent to contractual terms. The subjective and personal nature of consent demands an astute awareness of cultural forces and legal hermeneutics that color perceptions and expectations in commercial interactions. Unless these factors are properly understood, legal practitioners unknowingly expose their clients to controversy or enforceability problems. Making sure all the parties have full legal capacity and have given informed consent is thus crucial to reduce risk and protect the integrity of international commercial contracts. A major aspect of international commercial contracts consists of risk distribution and performance of obligations in a specific manner, and this is further compounded by varying interpretations in jurisdictions. Standards of performance have the implication of laying down the standards of quality and timing for performance of contractual obligations and are influenced by the law of governing parties as stipulated in governing law clauses. In cross-border transactions, parties often turn to arbitration provisions to resolve disputes efficiently, as they offer a neutral forum and flexibility unavailable in traditional court systems. The choice of forum also bears significant weight, as differing legal environments can impact dispute outcomes dramatically. To further navigate these complexities, understanding industry standards and employing comprehensive contractual provisions can significantly enhance the enforcement and interpretation of obligations. Therefore, harmonization of these factors within the broader paradigm of international trade is necessary for effective risk management and dispute resolution, highlighting the critical interface of business strategy and law in international trade (Zheng, 2025; Sun et al., 2024).

6.6.1. Governing Law Clauses

In the multifaceted context of contract law, governing law clauses have a fundamental role in determining the governing law for contractual commitments. The clauses are significant for the purposes of expressing expectations of parties as well as ensuring stability and certainty in international agreements. By clearly specifying what legal system shall apply to the contract, parties can minimize the uncertainties created by varied legal interpretations across jurisdictions. To this end, the governing law clause is therefore very important in international trade contracts where competing legal systems can cause complications in enforcement and compliance. It is this very feature which allows the parties to far more easily manage future disputes because they are in advance agreed upon the legal regime which shall apply between them and guide their conduct and settlements. Furthermore, the efficiency of governing law clauses is underscored by the fact that they can decide not only the substance of contractual rights and obligations, but also procedural matters such as jurisdiction as well as methods of settling disputes. By harmonizing specific principles like contract formation and capacity, parties minimize the frequency of disputes that could occur from differing interpretations across jurisdictions. Such harmonization complements a unified approach to key elements such as offer and acceptance and standards of performance, hence strengthening contractual security. The importance of these provisions is especially urgent when one reflects on the implications of default, since parties may well be burdened with unforeseen liabilities if they engage in material transactions without an unmistakable governing system. Such prescience operates in international transactions, making clear the critical role governing law provisions play in contemporary contract law. The necessity for effective risk management is also heightened when looking at regulatory challenges related to managing law clauses in the light of novel technologies such as smart contracts. Since legal frameworks are finding it difficult to accommodate new legal frameworks, the intersection of new technologies and old principles of contracts in laws calls for reframing in terms of current practices. The complexity of this interface unavoidably reveals deep gaps in today's legal doctrines, particularly regarding performance and enforcement of contract under electronic conditions. Bridging these gaps requires legal experts to acquaint themselves with the traditional tenets of contract law, yet evolve them in a manner to incorporate novel techniques such as smart contracts. This twofold complexity highlights the need for ongoing legal development, as parties have to stay updated with both governing law provisions and how they relate to current legal technology to effectively limit possible disputes (Poornima et al., 2025; Javokhir, 2025).

6.6.2. Choice of Forum

In contract law, the selection of a venue in which to resolve disputes forms a critical part of international commercial contracts. The location of litigation can be a difference maker in the outcome of a case, particularly in an era dominated by heterogenous legal systems. Different jurisdictions may produce varying interpretations of contractual terms, raising the stakes for worldwide parties seeking to enforce their rights. Choice of forum is also inextricably linked with the underpinning law principles of the contract, such as those of offer and acceptance or consideration and cause. With increasing transnationality of contracts, implications of jurisdiction become even more acute, prompting parties to scrutinize carefully forum selection clauses to determine whether they suit their strategic necessities and serve to restrict legal risk. Because jurisdictions are not only heterogeneous in procedural demands but also in substantive law, the implications of forum choice move into the realm of enforcement complexities and compliance difficulties. This divergence also challenges legal capacity of the parties, particularly regarding how different legal systems address issues of consent and will. Disparities in how courts assess vitiating factors, which may disaffirm a contract, show the importance of coming to know the machinery of local law in the chosen forum. Beyond that, increasing use of electronic transactions underscores the importance of specific choice of forum clauses since the facility of cross-border contract formation does not erase the requirement for predictability of adjudication. Therefore, stakeholders must navigate the subtleties of potential forums so as not to face unintended legal issues that undermine contractual settlements. The interplay of forum selection also emphasizes the role played by arbitration clauses in international agreements, which increasingly are resorted to as a preferred alternative for court litigation. Arbitration offers a compact process of resolution of disputes that could beam through conventional court adjudication. However, the effectiveness of arbitration relies on the enforceability of arbitration provisions and the recognizability of arbitral awards across jurisdictions. In such a case, governing law provisions and definite choice of forum clauses become focal points to determine the procedural context. It is critical to address these subtle issues when companies transact international business, where interfaces of different legal systems can generate efficiencies or magnify issues. The interaction between these factors finally determines risk distribution and performance needs, underlining the pervasive influence of forum choice on the contracting process within the international market.

6.6.3. Arbitration Provisions

Drafting arbitration clauses in international business contracts is important for efficient handling of disputes across various legal systems. Transacting parties across borders can face various legal hurdles that render conventional litigation inefficient. Arbitration offers a good alternative by providing an impartial platform for dispute resolution, thereby mitigating against jurisdictional bias or foreign legal landscapes. The enforceability of arbitration clauses is crucial since provisions allow contracting parties to select the seat and law of arbitration, reflecting their own will and risk preference. Moreover, modern arbitration models, such as the Uncitral Model Law, provide a globally consistent model that enhances predictability and efficiency in the arbitral process and enhances international traders' confidence in resolving their legal disputes well without resorting to domestic courts. In examining the legal foundations of arbitration provisions, it is critical to contrast them with the law of consent and contractual agreements. The terms should be clear and not obscure so that they reflect a shared agreement of the parties on the desirable means of dispute resolution. A well-effective arbitration provision can preclude future conflicts regarding the scope of arbitration, accurately defining the parameters of what is arbitrable. In the majority of jurisdictions, maintenance of parties' autonomy in making arbitration clauses supports the contractual approach, where parties voluntarily agree to refer their disputes to arbitration. This consent is central because it emphasizes parties inherent legal capacity and volition to apply alternative dispute resolution mechanisms, subjecting the core pillars of contract law in the majority of systems (Kamil, 2025). In addition, contextualizing arbitration provisions within other mechanisms of dispute resolution is important. Judicial mediation and other alternative methods often overlap with arbitration, so having a complete understanding of how these processes can coexist with each other is needed. In contemporary legal research, the debate over legislative gaps in relation to arbitration and mediation is responding to the evolving face of contract law. Marriage of these techniques can enhance procedural efficiency, reduce expenses on litigation, and ultimately lead to quicker resolutions. By comparing systems that have used these innovative approaches successfully, legal professionals are better placed to build a wider approach to dispute resolution for the good of all parties involved. Hence, this comparative analysis highlights the importance of legislative development and change to reinforce the role of arbitration as a pillar in modern contract law (Ahmad et al., 2025).

SUMMARY

As the analysis of contract law in various legal systems draws to a close, it is clear that the intricacies of such systems are instrumental to understanding domestic and international contracts equally. Every system possesses its unique characteristics that govern how contracts are formed, executed, and enforced. For instance, the difference between England and Germany regarding need for offer and acceptance highlights the significance of how cultural forces and history influence legal processes. Additionally, the application of formality, such as written agreement or notarization, also illustrates the variety of ways through which nations utilize in recognizing and institutionalizing contract relationships. Through examination of these core elements, it becomes clear that improved understanding of such differences will promote legal fairness and predictability and allow parties to cope with the intricacies of contractual obligations in a proper manner. Moving on to obligations and remedies for breach of contract, it is apparent that every jurisdiction has its own set of rules on non-performance and enforcement. The comparative examination of approaches to risk allocation and performance standards reveals considerable disparity that can have the consequence of greatly shaping contractual relationships. Legal systems, for instance, such as civil law based on principles of good faith, emphasize a mutual basis of performance of contract, while others are likely to be more subject to strict liability for non-performance. In addition, the remedies of redress available to aggrieved parties, from specific performance to damages, demonstrate the extent of remedies to be given consideration while framing international agreements. Knowledge of these nuances is critical for legal professionals aiming to design sound contracts that consider probable disputes and meet the needs of participating parties. With the diverse frameworks outlined, note should be taken of the practical effects of contract law on international commerce and the need for transitional approaches to harmonization. As world trade increases, the interaction of the different legal traditions necessitates sorgfältige negotiation and an understanding of underlying principles shared across boundaries. The conclusions from the comparative analysis not only enhance the drafting of international commercial contracts but also point to the necessity of such frameworks as the CISG, which aim at achieving uniformity in international sales law. The call for a more standardized legal regime is a call for realization of heightened cross-border transaction complexities and the necessity to establish legal certainty with the objective to facilitate interaction within the global marketplace better. In meeting this evolving requirement, legal regimes can make sure that they are attuned to the demands of contemporary commercial reality (Kovalenko, 2025; Lang, 2024).

A LOOK TO THE FUTURE

DIGITAL TRANSFORMATION AND THE EVOLUTION OF CONTRACT LAW

The advent of digital technology is revolutionizing the landscape of contract law, with new technologies unfolding as the signature of its future. Automated contracts, smart contracts, executed via blockchain technology are one such instance that negates mediaries and makes transactions more efficient. With legal systems of the world lagging behind incorporating such technologies, issues are being raised regarding their compatibility with current legislation. Significantly, the integration of smart contracts within civil law systems raises significant questions of contract formation and enforceability that need to be carefully considered in relation to the relevance of classic principles like offer and acceptance within this new framework. Jurisdictions increasingly recognize the importance of making their contract legislations relevant to accommodate these technological advancements, which will ultimately require regulatory changes towards harmonizing cross-border legal practices, making the effective operationalization of smart contracts and other digital contracts feasible (Tao et al., 2025).

Furthermore, the role of international organizations in coordinating the contract law towards harmonization will increasingly be essential as globalization gathers momentum. The Hague Conference on Private International Law embodies this endeavor, addressing the standardization of international legal norms in a manner that facilitates cross-border trade. The power of the organization lies in the fact that it will work to overcome the disparity in legal systems, with countries cooperating to make contract issues easier. Particularly now with countries like China being heavily involved in negotiating Hague Conventions, the ability for cross-jurisdictional legal systems grows. Such interactive dynamism not only enhances Chinas international governance role but also signifies a rise in acknowledgment of the imperative for cooperation in private international law. Therefore, future trends of contract law will hence be tied directly to the prolongation of growth within international legal developments and collaborative activities of states in establishing an enhanced collective global legal framework (Tao et al., 2025). Looking ahead, the direct participation of artificial intelligence (AI) in contract negotiation and administration is another front for future contract law. AI tools have the ability to scan huge volumes of data, automate contract generation, and based on historical data, make predictions, thereby transforming traditional methods of contract management. However, this advancement raises significant questions regarding accountability and responsibility in instances where algorithms produce agreements. While attorneys seek to take leverage from the capabilities brought about by AI, they must navigate through the complexities of ensuring that autonomous systems conform to existing legislations and moral guidelines. Thus, the law of future contracts will understandably require the formulation of new regulatory standards that expressly cover AIs involvement in contract enforcement and execution, giving rise to a rich dynamic interplay between technology, legal standards, and ethics that will govern future contractual relations across jurisdictions (Javokhir, 2025).

REFERENCES

1. Al Dalaien, A. A., & Aladaseen, M. A. (2025). Judicial mediation and the governance of administrative contract disputes: The legal possibilities under Jordanian and UAE legislation. *Corporate Law and Governance Review*. https://www.semanticscholar.org/paper/d71b2bce22a2b3450a854ec5bb6ad4022a6ac5f7 (accessed on 9th September 2025).
2. Aliyev, C. (2025). Functional equivalence in the translation of legal terms: Insights from Arabic and Azerbaijani. *Porta Universorum*. https://www.semanticscholar.org/paper/3d8969d2fe19601e10c3226a06427f73ed0c6b71 (accessed on 9th September 2025).
3. Basyarudin, B. (2024). The evolution and significance of notarial law in modern legal systems. *Law and Business, 4*, 39–44. https://www.semanticscholar.org/paper/82795d418a47c4084a3e9962a6ee7d8d9d5d6724 (accessed on 9th September 2025).
4. Blair, H. A. (2011). Hard cases under the Convention on the International Sale of Goods: A proposed taxonomy of interpretative challenges. https://core.ac.uk/download/62547257.pdf (accessed on 9th September 2025).
5. Carletti, E., Colla, P., Gulati, M., Ongena, S., et al. (2014). The price of law: The case of the Eurozone's collective action clauses. https://core.ac.uk/download/62571295.pdf (accessed on 9th September 2025).
6. Dorskaya, A. (2024). Evolution of the comparative method in Russian historical and legal research. *Journal of Foreign Legislation and Comparative Law*. https://www.semanticscholar.org/paper/f253030d0b5dcf93201081dd93328482b6184e3d (accessed on 9th September 2025).
7. Dubé, È., Vivion, M., & MacDonald, N. E. (2014). Vaccine hesitancy, vaccine refusal and the anti-vaccine movement: Influence, impact and implications. *Expert Review of Vaccines, 14*, 99–117. https://doi.org/10.1586/14760584.2015.964212 (accessed on 9th September 2025).
8. Eshonkulov, J. (2025). The role of smart contracts in civil law and issues of legal regulation. *Uzbek Journal of Law and Digital Policy*. https://www.semanticscholar.org/paper/900febff3fee994bd9a28672f003f00ce6dcfabb (accessed on 9th September 2025).
9. Fézer, T. (2022). The invalidity in the principles of European contract law–Common cores and alternate ways. *European Integration Studies*. https://www.semanticscholar.org/paper/58ca2b729de8b76bf159df4b292188745b77d92e (accessed on 9th September 2025).
10. Goossens, K., Larsson, E., & Vermeulen, B. (1989). Deciding disputes: Factors that guide Chinese courts in the adjudication of rural responsibility contract disputes. https://core.ac.uk/download/62554315.pdf (accessed on 9th September 2025).
11. Hale, T., Angrist, N., Goldszmidt, R., Kira, B., Petherick, A., Phillips, T., Webster, S., et al. (2021). A global panel database of pandemic policies (Oxford COVID-19 Government Response Tracker). *Nature Human Behaviour, 5*, 529–538. https://doi.org/10.1038/s41562-021-01079-8 (accessed on 9th September 2025).
12. Hassan, S. A. M., & Younes, A. S. (2025). Emojis as expressions of will in contract law: Legal challenges and judicial perspectives. *Journal of Lifestyle and SDGs Review*. https://www.semanticscholar.org/paper/3af959b7e80bf4835f11849e208859f256f0f94c (accessed on 9th September 2025).

13. Hoàng, T. H. (2025). Vietnamese law on the limitation of freedom of contract for sustainable development purposes. *Journal of Law and Sustainable Development*. https://www.semanticscholar.org/paper/b1cc56ef4c03c1b8191ee76fcc11d45a5777ff0b (accessed on 9th September 2025).

14. Houshmand, S., Piroozi, P., Monavari, H., & Mazloum Rahani, A. (2024). Challenges in the implementation of smart contracts in the legal systems of Iran and India. *Legal Studies in Digital Age*. https://www.semanticscholar.org/paper/a10cc3894c451500d69889d0936333324d5e3caf (accessed on 9th September 2025).

15. Huang, J., & Qian, A. X. (1995). "One country, two systems," three law families, and four legal regions: The emerging inter-regional conflicts of law in China. https://core.ac.uk/download/62547779.pdf (accessed on 9th September 2025).

16. Huber, M., Andreyeva, M., Presser, L. D., & Salvi Le Garrec Zwetyenga, J. (2025). Health laboratory licensing: A policy and best-practice analysis. *Bulletin of the World Health Organization, 103*, 383–391. https://www.semanticscholar.org/paper/a7f3cf19f4ecd5f964632acec33b7c13339072ab (accessed on 9th September 2025).

17. Jones, C. (2021). Understanding the Belt and Road in EU-China relations. *Journal of European Integration*. https://www.semanticscholar.org/paper/7c267f3dc63eb6fa23a6441b2ff9e1438df876b5 (accessed on 9th September 2025).

18. Kamil, I. M. R. (2025). Provisions governing the formation of an individual employment contract in light of Palestinian law: Analytical study. *International Journal of Judicial Law*. https://www.semanticscholar.org/paper/3586ba1b3089d3dbe748d6027806aa8bb2208233 (accessed on 9th September 2025).

19. Ker, A., Libecap, G., Brewer, J., & Glennon, R. (2006). Transferring water in the American West: 1987–2005. https://core.ac.uk/download/75783400.pdf (accessed on 9th September 2025).

20. Khan, M. N. I., & Goswami, D. (2025). Cybercrime and contractual liability: A systematic review of legal precedents and risk mitigation frameworks. *Journal of Sustainable Development and Policy*. https://www.semanticscholar.org/paper/6295510073a083998d0a9f79a69f0a929788e2d1 (accessed on 9th September 2025).

21. Kovalenko, M. (2025). Contractual regulation of surrogacy in the legal systems of Ukraine and EU member states: A comparative analysis. *Uzhhorod National University Herald. Series: Law*. https://www.semanticscholar.org/paper/dcb0549b75f901923d2d60f1f54b638276598e3d (accessed on 9th September 2025).

22. Künnecke, M. (2017). English as common legal language: Its expansion and the effects on civil law and common law lawyers. https://core.ac.uk/download/151161045.pdf (accessed on 9th September 2025).

23. Kurchinskaya-Grasso, N., Goryacheva, E., Popov, I., Abramova, A., & Pechkurov, V. A. (2021). Legal regulation of property insurance and law enforcement problems. *SHS Web of Conferences*. https://www.semanticscholar.org/paper/8887bbeeb5d72cbc91f73aa6b2ab48628a7b1132 (accessed on 9th September 2025).

24. Lang, Y. (2024). Comparative analysis of contractual frameworks: Insights from England, Germany, Norway, Italy, and the CISG. *Science of Law Journal*. https://www.semanticscholar.org/paper/afdd0bf54ceb4b67f851c86be6aa3bded233ed77 (accessed on 9th September 2025).

25. Levitin, A. J. (2013). The paper chase: Securitization, foreclosure, and the uncertainty of mortgage title. https://core.ac.uk/download/62560288.pdf (accessed on 9th September 2025).

26. Mamouri, M. S., & Amini, M. (2024). Non-conformity of contracting parties in the performance stage of debt and claim transfer contracts: A comparative study in the legal systems of France, Germany, and England. *Comparative Studies in Jurisprudence, Law, and Politics*. https://www.semanticscholar.org/paper/1e1f292a86a5e13734bc9a2c1a7101efe34e0d71 (accessed on 9th September 2025).

27. Mavlekeev, I. (2024). Legal data: Ontology of the syndicated loan agreement. *Public Administration*. https://www.semanticscholar.org/paper/c6acddbf7fba3ff17d76a83711d7d4e6e40e1caf (accessed on 9th September 2025).

28. Michaels, R. (2014). The UNIDROIT Principles as global background law. https://core.ac.uk/download/62569847.pdf (accessed on 9th September 2025).

29. Michaels, R. (2018). How Asian should Asian law be? –An outsider's view. https://core.ac.uk/download/213020784.pdf (accessed on 9th September 2025).

30. Michaels, R., & Pauwelyn, J. (2011). Conflict of norms or conflict of laws? Different techniques in the fragmentation of public international law. https://core.ac.uk/download/62547229.pdf (accessed on 9th September 2025).

31. Milash, V. S. (2024). Selected aspects of contractual regulation in the context of digitalization of the economy. *Law and Innovations*. https://www.semanticscholar.org/paper/ab0d8eee57367b615e4cf28dd8dc457ae3e1c6ab (accessed on 9th September 2025).

32. Nazarov, A. (2024). Legal nature and classification of smart contracts in crypto exchanges: Challenges to traditional contract law. *International Journal of Law and Policy*. https://www.semanticscholar.org/paper/3d6bde831c7a9abda9a6384efad4250fc8da9791 (accessed on 9th September 2025).

33. Organization for Economic Co-operation and Development. (2018). *Oslo Manual 2018: The Measurement of Scientific, Technological and Innovation Activities*. https://doi.org/10.1787/9789264304604-en (accessed on 9th September 2025).

34. Peterson, C. W. (2017). Piercing the corporate veil by tort creditors. https://core.ac.uk/download/153518165.pdf (accessed on 9th September 2025).

35. Poornima, A., Nagaraja, K. V., & Venugopalan, M. (2025). Legal contract analysis and risk assessment using pre-trained Legal-T5 and Law-GPT. *2025 3rd International Conference on Integrated Circuits and Communication Systems (ICICACS)*. https://www.semanticscholar.org/paper/766154f8d8a7e8a6bc8682cfbb2db9a9109b5f5a (accessed on 9th September 2025).

36. Quynh, T. N. (2024). Comparing foreseeability in contractual damages under the CISG, UNIDROIT Principles and Principles of European Contract Law. *Pázmány Law Review*. https://www.semanticscholar.org/paper/b3a740b2a50f2ed288cbfc56583fc7d38870c0e7 (accessed on 9th September 2025).

37. Ramos Muñoz, D. (2011). The power of arbitrators to make pro-futuro orders. https://core.ac.uk/download/29402453.pdf (accessed on 9th September 2025).

38. Raza, F., Herring, J., Neuberger, J., Quiroga, I., Engelmann, C., Ryder, E., & Berg, T. (2025). Strong or weak consent in medical law? Identifying the values protected in transplantation

medicine in Europe. *European Journal of Health Law*. https://www.semanticscholar.org/paper/dc869528254ffa96044d228852a62e14f4c983ed (accessed on 9th September 2025).

39. Richman, B. D. (2004). Firms, courts, and reputation mechanisms: Towards a positive theory of private ordering. https://core.ac.uk/download/62562245.pdf (accessed on 9th September 2025).

40. Rivero-Silva, S. (2025). The blockchain DAO as an evolution of the North American trust: Legal and philosophical aspects. *DICERE Revita de Derecho y Estudios Internacionales*. https://www.semanticscholar.org/paper/f9fc5e4eee323cf5ef8a25e1d1f62d920c455d9d (accessed on 9th September 2025).

41. Russi, L. (2009). Substance or mere technique? A precis on good faith performance in England, France and Germany. https://core.ac.uk/download/9323672.pdf (accessed on 9th September 2025).

42. Rybak, S., & Ponezhin, M. (2024). Water supply contract in the context of environmental safety: Features of legal regulation. *BIO Web of Conferences*. https://www.semanticscholar.org/paper/ab28b4f1c09d7453d6d5648ba4524ea080315f50 (accessed on 9th September 2025).

43. Santos, A. (2009). Labor flexibility, legal reform and economic development. https://core.ac.uk/download/70373779.pdf (accessed on 9th September 2025).

44. Shakiba, A. H., & Qasmi, M. (2022). An investigation into the specific performance remedy for breach of contracts: A comparative study of the Islamic Iranian legal system and common law. *Journal of Shariah Law Research*. https://www.semanticscholar.org/paper/2c17fcf11a399293e4943559e4b01a77b8546b04 (accessed on 9th September 2025).

45. Stoyanova, M., Nikoloudakis, Y., Panagiotakis, S., Pallis, E., & Markakis, E. (2020). A survey on the Internet of Things (IoT) forensics: Challenges, approaches, and open issues. *IEEE Communications Surveys & Tutorials, 22*, 1191–1221. https://doi.org/10.1109/comst.2019.2962586 (accessed on 9th September 2025).

46. Sun, L., & Xu, J. (2024). Global commerce and the law: A comparative exploration of international commercial and intellectual property law. *Lecture Notes in Education Psychology and Public Media*. https://www.semanticscholar.org/paper/e5d72fa3dc75d0b4d805ed16cd42d0b2376844f2 (accessed on 9th September 2025).

47. Tao, D., & Lu, W. (2025). The impact of the Hague Conference of Private International Law on China: Past, present and future. *Chinese Journal of Transnational Law, 2*, 82–101. https://www.semanticscholar.org/paper/aa268bf9f0468ca58dd7a6e6351f6981a967dd91 (accessed on 9th September 2025).

48. Tehrani, H. R. R., Abbaslou, B., & Ziyazi, H. S. (2024). Comparative study of compensation for breach of technology transfer contracts in the legal systems of Iran, Canada, and France. *Comparative Studies in Jurisprudence, Law, and Politics*. https://www.semanticscholar.org/paper/e374dec47328e1a564241f4eb81d13eaae5762ec (accessed on 9th September 2025).

49. Xu, R. (2024). A study on the compensation for mental damage in the breach of personhood property contracts. *Frontiers in Humanities and Social Sciences*. https://www.semanticscholar.org/paper/815fec38870e0e11f1d4d5198c92823779f14d9d (accessed on 9th September 2025).

Chapter

7

PROPERTY LAW SYSTEMS

Contents

INTRODUCTION

Property law regimes form the very bedrocks of social organization, establishing how individuals and institutions relate to physical and non-physical property. Independent legal regimes categorize property into different types, say movable and immovable properties, each with their respective set of rules and regulations. The differentiation is significant, as it establishes ownership rights, transferal processes, and the effects of possession. Additionally, property rights are divided into public and private property, where the former underscores common usage as well as state interests, while the latter underscores the rights of individuals to ownership. Understanding these classification is important because they affect the various levels of control and benefit property owners have under legal regimes, resulting in sophisticated arguments about rights in rem and protection for owners of property in differing circumstances (Khan, 2025).

The intricate relationship between possession and ownership necessarily creates controversies over rules of title transfer and concepts such as adverse possession. While ownership constitutes the legal right to possess property, possession sometimes subsists apart from ownership, drawing attention to legal nuances. For instance, adverse possession doctrine allows one to claim the rights of ownership through continuous and sole possession in a specific time frame. Similarly, co-ownership arrangements compel legal jurisdictions to specify distinct statutes delineating the rights and obligations of more than one owner, which may vary significantly across jurisdictions. This dynamic interplay not only highlights the complexities of property law but also reflects broader socio-economic determinants on ownership, tenancy structures, and long-standing controversy regarding equitable access to property rights (Journal of Law and Review C, 2022).

With property law continuing to be dynamic, land use control is an essential area of focus where zoning, eminent domain, and building codes are essential. Zoning ordinances regulate land uses permitted, controlling urban development and property value. Furthermore, the eminent domain authority in governments allows them to acquire private property for public use, necessitating equitable equations between community needs and individual liberties. Building codes also regulate building practice, mandating safety and compliance with community standards. These paradigms of regulation do not only illustrate the complexity embedded in property law systems but also exhibit the perpetual conflict between regulation and property rights. An ultimate understanding of property law systems is thus necessary for overcoming and reacting to issues of ownership, use, and liability in contemporary socio-legal contexts (Khan, 2025).

7.1. TYPES OF PROPERTY RIGHTS

In the appreciation of property rights' nuances, the dichotomy between movable and immovable property is a core part in the property law systems. Movable property comprises objects such as vehicles, personal effects, and machinery that are easy to transport without deconstruction of their value or use. Unlike immovable property, which predominantly entails property in land and real estate, with possession entailing a more complex legal system due to attachment and permanence considerations. These categorizations find their influence over many legal doctrines such as taxation, zoning, and right of inheritance. For instance, the transfer of immovable property is likely to involve conditions such as writing and registration, thereby providing more legal protection to the proprietors. Therefore, understanding the implication of the property classification is essential to know the rights and obligations entailed in the ownership, be it for personal ends or commercial activities. Moreover, property rights come in the form of public and private rights, which recognize their different roles played on behalf of the public in society. Public property, owned by government agencies, is intended for common use and benefit, including parks, roads, and public buildings.

Figure 7.1. Visualize property rights.

Source: https://wallstreetmojocms.recurpro.in/uploads/Property_Right_62cbd23ec2.jpg.

Private property, owned by individuals or firms, has another set of rights and duties. The distinction reveals the underlying conflict between individual ownership and public social interests, especially with reference to land use and environmental harmony. For instance, private ownership rights may conflict with public interests in land development that threatens ecological harmony. In addition, some legal systems, such as those in socialist regimes, may provide for controls on private ownership for the sake of advancing public interests (Chung, 2025). Hence, being aware of these boundaries is crucial to understanding the complexity of how social and economic relations are established through property rights. Another critical aspect of property rights is in relation to rights in rem, which protect against interference irrespective of interfering party's nature. These rights can be attached to movable or immovable property or form the basis for enforcing ownership claims. Rights in rem invoke third-party respect for property rights, underlining the basis that ownership entails the right of exclusion on the part of others. Rights in rem are central to legal controversy, as where they are violated, legal remedies become callable upon affected parties. Notably, the effectiveness of rights in rem rests upon an intelligent legal basis in aid of enforcement, such as registration and public recordation. In the majority of the jurisdictions, the evolution of these rights is an indication of conflicts between personal claims and interests of the community more broadly, evidencing dynamic property law (Sari et al., 2024). Ultimately, having knowledge of the types of property rights is key to comprehending how they impact personal agency and governance at the social level (Figure 7.1).

7.1.1. Movable versus Immovable Property

Property law regimes distinguishes and categorizes all types of property in a way that essentially differentiates between movable and immovable property. Movable property is what can be moved from a location to another, for example, vehicles, furniture, and personal effects. Immovable property, otherwise referred to as real property, includes land and any fixture permanently attached to it, for example, buildings and constructions. The distinction is important in that it affects ownership rights, transfer procedures, and legal regulations governing both types.

Figure 7.2. Shows movable versus immovable property.

Source: https://i.ytimg.com/vi/mSgoieesE8c/maxresdefault.jpg.

For instance, the law controlling the sale and transfer of immovable property has a tendency to require formalities like a written document and registration, which are not as stringent for movable property. This regulatory distinction is an expression of a wider appreciation of ownerships intricacies and the need for further protection when the assets involved are immovable due to their fixity and greater value in society. Upon analyzing property rights related to both sets of categories, it is clear that the effects of ownership far transcend possession. Law of immovable property usually contains rigorous regulations on limitations in uses, zoning, and the terms of changes or improvements. For example, laws on land use regulate how property owners can develop or utilize their land for purposes of promoting community planning and protecting the environment. Furthermore, the theory of adverse possession underscores the unique nature of immovable property, whereby long, continuous possession could vest legal title in a trespasser under certain conditions, as identified in various jurisdictions. This points to the intersection of law and time, rendering immovable property a subject of continuous legal scrutiny, especially where there are controversies of ownership among original and unacknowledged owners. In inheritance, how movable and immovable property is treated has a significant impact on the distribution of wealth. The two are most often differentiated in legal systems, as they are in Indonesia's plural inheritance law where multiple legal systems regulate the rules of distribution (Masriani, 2024). Fixed property would typically require supporting papers, such as land certificates and notarial procedures for transfer, which would not so much be strictly applied to movable assets. Moreover, partition of immovable property in inheritance may lead to strife because of the value it bears and the intricacies of ownership. The laws of rightful ownership formalized by mechanisms like the Certificate of Inheritance Rights (SKHW) are significant in ensuring clear transfer of title, particularly when there are multiple heirs and divergent legal views. Consequently, the dichotomy between movable property and immovable property is a significant consideration in determining property law systems and rightful governance of rights within society (Figure 7.2).

7.1.2. Public and Private Property Distinctions

Public property is typically regarded as that owned and possessed by the state in the interest of all citizens. This includes parks, roads, and government complexes, which are utilized for the benefit of community welfare, development, and administration. Private property, by contrast, refers to property belonging to individuals or firms, which can be used freely and sold at the pleasure of the owners. The rationale behind the differentiation is rooted in collective versus individual rights concepts, which then have implications for how legal systems establish and enforce property rights. Furthermore, control over public property is apt to involve some measure of regulation to balance public good against private interests, illustrating the subtlety of these distinctions. A consideration of state and private property also reveals conflicting interests between the state and individual rights, most notably where there are heirless estates and the state's interest as a legal heir. In a few legal systems, such as Georgia, the state claims the right to inherit properties with no heirs, raising significant questions as to what defines state ownership as opposed to the regime of private property rights. The juridical definition of the state as a successor given by Article 1343 of the Civil Code of Georgia gives rise to controversy over the need for public order in inheritance of property and the moral implications of interference from the state. This interaction is an expression of broader societal values on ownership and justice, particularly given that various jurisdictions are grappling with what the meaning of this interaction is within modern systems of property law, underlining the imperative for an equitable approach balancing public and private interests (Leonidze, 2025).

An exploration of public and private property convergence also elicits critical implications on gender and equity in property laws. The historical handling of women's property rights within national legal systems demonstrates the manner in which public and private ownership can reflect and reproduce the norms of society. As current legal discussions, such as those of feminist scholarship, elucidate, the dynamics of property ownership are intimately bound up in broader structures of privilege and power. The diminished access of women to private property during the long nineteenth century serves as a reminder of the way in which property laws can reinforce inequalities through public and private means. A reflection on these matters leads one to think about the state's role in regulating property rights and the necessity of reforms that remove historical inequalities as well as provide equal access to property for all regardless of gender (Mckenna et al., 2024) (Figure 7.3).

Private properties	Public properties
They belong to only one person or family.	They belong to everyone in society.
These are maintained by the respective owner(s).	These are maintained by the government.
These can be used only by the owner(s).	These can be used by everyone in a society.
Examples include houses and private vehicles.	Examples include parks, roads, and monuments.

Figure 7.3. The distinction between public and private property serves as a foundational concept within property law systems, influencing how rights and obligations are interpreted.

Source: https://i.ytimg.com/vi/IV-PNMCM27Y/hq720.jpg?sqp=-oaymwEhCK4FEIIDSFryq4qpAxMIARUAAAAAGAElAADIQj0AgKJD&rs=AOn4CLAKxrGmvRp-02Wk_0eG18Q1LddNkA.

7.1.3. Rights in Rem and Their Consequences

The complexities which surround systems of property law have a tendency to be founded on the relations which individuals form with tangible and personal property, leading to various classifications of rights. Among them are rights in rem, which are specifically used to describe rights which are enforceable against the world, as opposed to rights in person am, obligations owed to particular individuals. This differentiation is necessary in order to facilitate ownership and transmission of property, either immovable or movable. In practice, rights in rem confer a robust right over assets so that proprietors can assert their rights against any party who attempts to harm their property. The importance of this framework cannot be overstated, as it forms the secure platform for property exchange, fosters investor confidence, and preserves the integrity of legal systems (Figure 7.4).

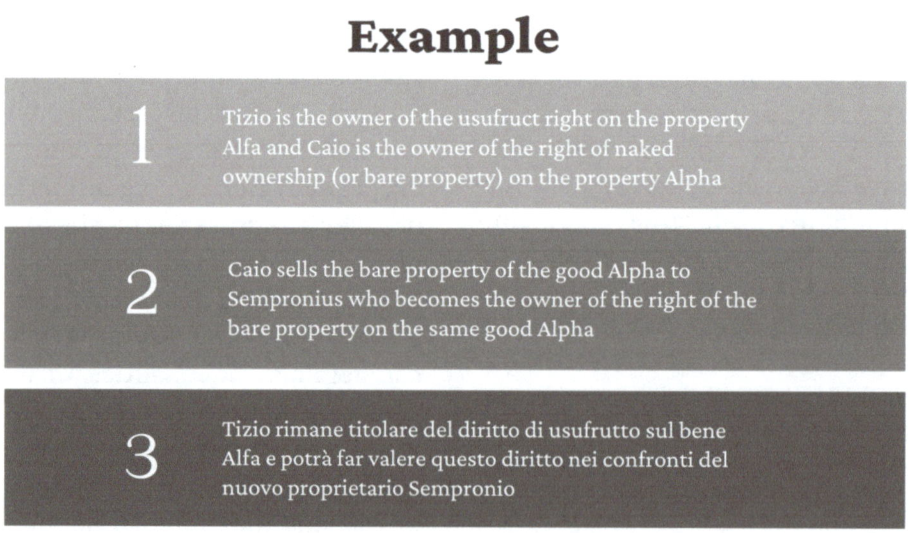

Figure 7.4. Shows Italian real rights (or rights in rem).

Source: The Legal Nook.

Consequently, understanding rights in rem is essential for comprehending the broader dynamics at play in property law and its influence on societal functions. Furthermore, the assertion of rights in rem demonstrates its critical relevance in cases of public and private property allocation. Public property typically conveys an inherent societal value, fostering community welfare and accessibility, while private property rights focus more on individual ownership and usage. The interplay between these two categories may lead to conflicts, particularly in urban environments where scarce resources are at stake. For instance, zoning laws often seek to mediate these tensions by regulating land uses, ensuring that public interests are balanced against private rights. This intersection reveals how rights in rem not only protect individual claims but also reflect societal values and priorities. Through a nuanced understanding of how these rights function within various legal frameworks, scholars and practitioners can explore potential reforms that address contemporary issues, such as environmental sustainability and equitable land distribution. In light of emerging challenges in property law, particularly regarding intangible assets such as intellectual property, the implications of rights in rem extend into newer territories. As advancements in technology redefine creative and innovative processes, the traditional categories of ownership come under scrutiny. For example, the development of artificial intelligence raises questions about the authorship and ownership of AI-generated works. Current legal frameworks often fail to accommodate these developments, as seen in the limitations of traditional intellectual property regulations, which necessitate human authorship. The discourse around these evolving definitions of rights in rem emphasizes the need for reform in property law systems to maintain justice and fairness while adapting to the unique challenges posed by technological advances. Legal scholars argue for new models that could reconcile the interests of creators with the necessity of broader societal access to innovations, thereby ensuring the relevance of rights in rem in the digital age (Gli Kściński, 2025; Pundir et al., 2025).

7.2. OWNERSHIP AND POSSESSION

Amidst the intricate framework of property law, differences and relationships between possession and ownership are of central importance. Ownership is a right conferred by law to possess and alienate an asset, while possession is the actual control or possession of the asset. This difference raises questions regarding the nature of property rights and how they can be enforced, especially where disputes can be anticipated. For instance, possession does not necessarily imply ownership; one may be possessed of land without being the owner. The procedures for title transfer through contracts and conveyances determine the formal means through which ownership is transferred. In this perspective, the doctrine of adverse possession is a focal lens; it allows a possessor to assert rights to ownership following persistent possession, thereby spotlighting the fine interaction between the ideas of ownership and the practical conditions of possession. The evolution of property law systems is adaptable enough to meet the need to respond to the nuances in ownership and possession.

Figure 7.5. Difference between ownership and possession.

Source: https://i0.wp.com/pediaa.com/wp-content/uploads/2015/12/Difference-Between-Ownership-and-Possession-infographic.jpg?resize=506%2C703.

There are various legal systems that have varying categorizations such as movable and immovable property, which influence the rights and obligations of possessors and owners. Movable properties, for instance, might involve less formalities in transferring ownership compared to immovable properties, which can involve huge documentation and regulation. Co-ownership, on the other hand, whereby multiple actors have claims to one single property, generates degrees of complexity in relations of ownership and power.

These various forms of property rights then mirror the various intensities of control, liability, and benefit between possessors and owners, demonstrating that ownership is not merely a label but instead a relational entity framed by law and custom. With technological innovations that continue to reshape societal interactions with property, particularly with technologies like the metaverse and blockchain technology, notions of ownership and possession are being put into question and reconstructed. The metaverse, as evidenced from research in recent years, presents a new landscape of ownership where digital assets can potentially be decentralized and challenge existing concepts founded on physicality and territoriality (Yogesh et al., 2022).

Similarly, blockchain technology promises a revolutionary approach to ownership through assured secure, transparent, and tamper-resistant transactions but raises issues of privacy as well as the extendability of existing legal frameworks (Pilkington, 2016). These emerging paradigms necessitate a rigorous examination of property law systems so that they can develop and adapt to the changing context of possession and ownership in a way that such law concepts can be applied in a more digitally driven world (Figure 7.5).

7.2.1. Title Transfer Rules and Procedures

Title transfer regulations are important in the study of property law systems since such regulations identify the legal process under which property ownership is transferred (Figure 7.6).

Figure 7.6. Title transfer involves numerous procedural steps designed to ensure that the ownership rights of both parties are accurately represented.

Source: https://imgv2-2-f.scribdassets.com/img/document/141258792/original/5343a74c8d/1?v=1.

Typically, this begins with a written contract that details the sale terms to be succeeded by signing a deed, a formal legal instrument whereby proof that ownership in property has been transferred. Additionally, the title must be thoroughly searched so that it is free from all encumbrances or third-party claims so that transfer to the new owner can proceed smoothly. This cautious governance gives assurance in property deals and is paramount in maintaining the honesty of property rights of ownership in the legal system under different jurisdictions (Gupta et al., 2025).

In addition to the deed and title search, there are certain jurisdictions that require recording the transfer of title in public records, again safeguarding against resultant disputes. This process of registration varies greatly from location to location, relying on historical legal traditions and statutes. For example, there are some states that observe a race system, where whoever first registers his deed is given preference, but other states may employ a notice system, offering protection to subsequent purchasers who acquire their interest without notice of prior claims. Aside from geographical differences, rules of title transfer may incorporate conditions affecting parties' rights, including communication time periods and disclosure requirements for material defects in property. These rules aim to minimize misunderstandings and foster openness in property transactions, thus facilitating efficient systems in property law (Abdulsamad et al., 2020). Furthermore, title transfer procedures are gradually affected by technological advancements which facilitate more efficient and secure transactions. Electronic filing systems and blockchain technology are examples, as these make the process of recording transfers easy and reduce fraud incidences. By creating an immutable record of ownership which is easily accessible and verifiable, these technologies facilitate the creation of trust within the property market as well as shielding the rights of new owners. But inclusion of these innovations must also factor in the legal implications of jurisdictional variability and regulatory compliance, highlighting the need for robust legal frameworks to accompany such innovations. As property regimes evolve, understanding historical as well as contemporary mechanisms of title transfer becomes increasingly relevant to legal professionals and property owners alike to grapple with the complexities of ownership and its implications in various contexts (Gupta et al., 2025).

7.2.2. Concept of Adverse Possession

This doctrine not only resolves disputes on boundaries between property but also economic utilization of land. By providing a legal avenue to a possessor who obviously and continuously holds land without the owner's consent, adverse possession plays a key role in curing imbalances in ownership. The aim of this legal principle is to promote the optimum utilization of land, discouraging owners from abandoning property. Thus, it emphasizes a cardinal foundation of property law: that possession of land, when accompanied by specified criteria, is adequate for establishing rightful ownership and hence redefining the context of definition of titles and rights to property in various legal systems. To have successful adverse possession, a party should generally establish open and continuous possession of the property for a specified period of time, together with exclusivity and intent to possess. Such factors have significance in distinguishing between permissible occupancy and unauthorized trespass. For instance, if one possesses land openly as his own in accordance with the local customs and the laws, it might lead to a valid claim if the possession persists over time. Surprisingly, this right of possession does not try to seek that the claimant holds a legal title and does not include any form of agreement on the part of the original owner of the land. This unique framework suggests that the law recognizes and compensates settled, established land use, which has the potential to lead to a better reallocation of resources, as explored in various paradigms of property law (Yogesh et al., 2022). Moreover, adverse possession challenges conventional notions of ownership by instilling a dynamic element into property rights. Courts usually have to deal with the difficult balancing exercise of setting the legal rights of the original owner against the interests of those in occupation of the land. Adverse possession is said to produce unfair consequences, particularly where landowners are unaware of the ongoing occupation of their land. However, proponents of this legal measure contend that the legal instrument ensures that property is still utilized, in accordance with the values of society towards stewardship and responsibility. In conclusion, the concept of adverse possession is a reflection of the complexities which are embedded within property law regimes, raising fundamental questions of entitlement, equity, and the evolution of land rights within contemporary society (Applbaum, 2010) (Figure 7.7).

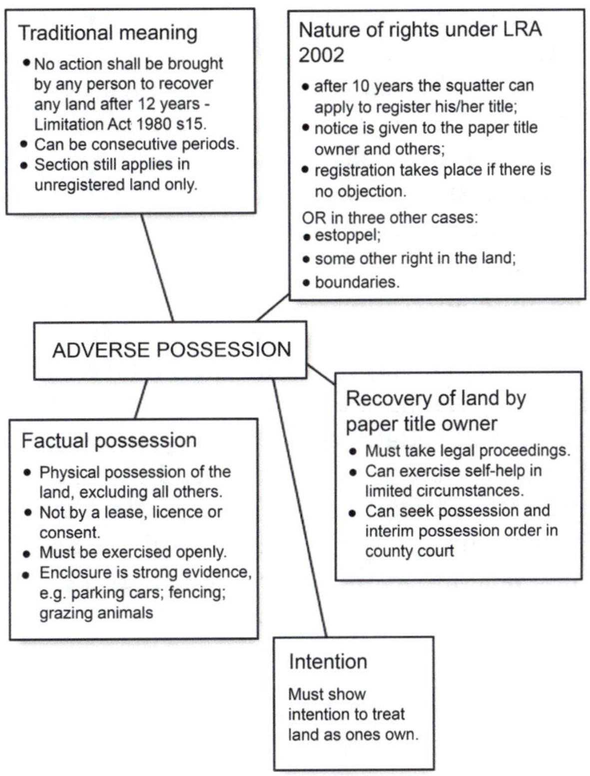

Figure 7.7. In the realm of property law, the concept of adverse possession emerges as a compelling mechanism through which individuals can acquire title to land under certain conditions.

Source: https://lawexplores.com/wp-content/uploads/2015/11/figu14_01.jpg.

7.2.3. Co-ownership Structures and Rights

The sophisticated nature of property law has a number of structures that allow for shared ownership, commonly known as models of co-ownership. These kinds of structures are also very important in dealing with a variety of interests of ownership where two or more people own an interest in one property. Co-ownership exists in different forms, that is, joint tenancy and tenancy in common, both having different legal consequences in regards to rights and obligations. For instance, joint tenants enjoy equal rights and right of survivorship, whereby when one owner dies, his/her interest automatically vests in the remaining co-owners. On the other hand, tenants in common can have unequal interests and alienate their interests without the consent of other owners. Their relationships are significant to comprehend, especially in places where there is evolving judicial interpretation and statutory regulation that attempts to provide clarity on co-ownership disputes and the rights thereto, as in most legal analysis of property law regimes. In most states, co-ownership structures meet with former and legislative settings influencing their enforcement and operation. In Romania, post-communist attempts at land restitution illuminate the complexities usually inherent in the law of property. Launched by means of Law No. 18/1991, such reforms aimed at restoring private right of ownership, both stressing the advantages and difficulties that co-ownership entails in a developing legal climate. The voluminous historical heritages of co-ownership provide intersecting claims and legal ambiguities subject to skillful negotiation of statute and custom. Furthermore, systematic schemes of property registration facilitate the enhancement of the legal certainty and security of co-ownership arrangements. Looking at the Romanian experience, it would appear that co-ownership management needs an holistic approach balancing past precedents and current regulatory frameworks to provide stability and promote co-owned property investment (Gherhe et al., 2025). The advance of technology, particularly with the inclusion of geospatial tools, is changing co-ownership structures in terms of how they are managed. Through employing new technologies like Geographic Information Systems (GIS) and Unmanned Aerial Vehicles (UAVs), property law regimes can improve their cadastral operations and promote transparency of ownership rights. For instance, such technologies can facilitate precise mapping and information sharing among co-owners and thus reduce boundary and use-related conflicts. Besides, as would be immediately obvious from ongoing debates regarding intellectual property rights in virtual environments such as the Metaverse, there exists a distinct need for adaptive frameworks that take into account evolving co-ownership scenarios (Limongelli et al., 2025). A fusion mechanism of adaptation through the law and technology advances is crucial to ensure co-ownership schemes continuity and efficacy across various property law contexts.

7.3. LAND USE AND REGULATION

With the strategic application of zoning regulations, cities are not only able to render their locations habitable but also induce economic stability and investment, thereby benefiting owners of property and the public at large (Khalfan et al., 2025). Apart from zoning rules, the concept of eminent domain is a significant vehicle with which governments address land for public uses. The practice allows seizure of private property, in the guise of the public good such as infrastructure expansion or urban regeneration schemes. Though application of eminent domain allows required development and expansion of public spaces, it also raises questions of legality and ethics concerning property rights and compensation. The question lies in balancing public interest with individual ownership rights so that owners of property are compensated appropriately. In most courts of law, the tension generates extensive legal examination, with property owners consistently challenging the rationale behind eminent domain actions. In this manner, awareness of the intricacy of eminent domain contributes to the research of land use regulations, with an emphasis on the ongoing negotiation between government authority and individual property rights in property law systems (Khalfan et al., 2025). Building codes are another critical land use and regulation element, attempting to ensure safety, usability, and visual harmony in construction practice. Building codes govern numerous aspects of building design and occupancy, covering everything from structural integrity to energy efficiency and environmental sustainability. Compliance with building codes is essential not only to safeguard public welfare but to maintain property value over the long term. As expansion goes on, adjustments to building regulations can keep up with evolving social norms and advances in technology, thereby subjecting them to continuous revision by developers and property owners. This interplay between regime regulatory powers and real estate development emphasizes the need for effective planning and management in regimes of property law. With local governments tweaking building regulations, the implications echo throughout property markets, influencing investor confidence and the nature of the urban landscape.

7.3.1. Overview of Zoning Laws

Knowledge regarding land use regulation is vital to know as one handles the legal framework of property law systems, particularly when referring to zoning laws. Zoning laws are a fundamental building block in land administration and urban planning, governing the use of land and orderly expansion in communities. By zoning land into separate zones—residential, commercial, industrial, and agricultural—they aim to minimize conflicts as well as enhance the quality of life of residents. But the enforcement of such laws can create tensions between property rights and collective interests, particularly when cities have more pressure for housing and commercial space. As highlighted in the new literature, growth of platforms like Airbnb has challenged traditional zoning laws, necessitating a re-examination of how local policy may effectively manage the resulting neighborhood transformations (Gurran et al., 2017) (Figure 7.8).

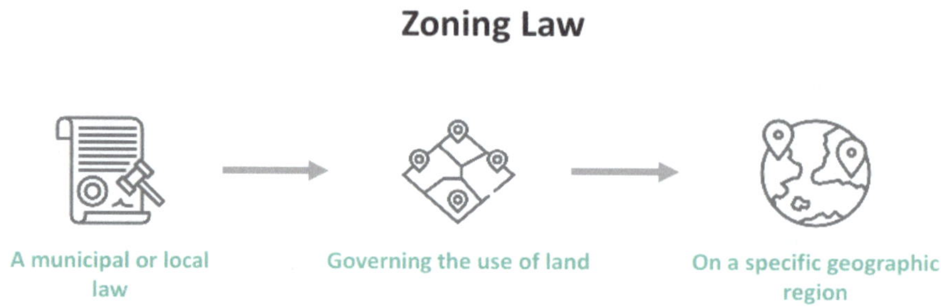

Figure 7.8. Illustrates zoning law.

Source: https://wallstreetmojo-files.s3.ap-south-1.amazonaws.com/2023/10/Zoning-Law.png.

The implications of zoning codes extend beyond basic land use, with socio-economic repercussions at the community level. In densely populated city centers, where housing demand has a tendency to outstrip supply, zoning needs can, by default, increase rental prices and produce housing shortages. This has been increasingly true in marketplaces with high rates of short-term rentals, eroding residential-commercial distinctions. The need for whole-scale tests of these effects has led to official inquiries in various jurisdictions, and as a result, policymakers have reacted by altering zoning laws favoring both the classic residential model and emerging trends in rentals and accommodations. Local planners are faced with the dilemma of balancing the benefits of short-term rentals, such as tourist income, against community disruption and lowered long-term housing supply (Gurran et al., 2017). The evolution of zoning legislation is a reflection of shifting societal trends and the necessity for environmentally friendly urban development practices. With urban expansion and population dynamics occurring, integrating nature-based solutions in land-use planning is now very common. These solutions not only address environmental concerns but also ensure holistic development of the community by triggering greenery and eco-friendly infrastructure. The intersection of environmental issues and zoning policies emphasizes the necessity for an integrated urban planning policy that emphasizes the significance of adaptive policies that respond to both social and environmental demands. Therefore, an equitable system of property law is dependent on the ability of zoning policies to adjust and react to the nature of contemporary urban challenges to eventually deliver robust and sustainable communities.

7.3.2. Understanding Eminent Domain

The doctrine of eminent domain illustrates the delicate balance between public and private property rights in property law systems. This state mechanism permits government authorities to purchase private property for a public purpose, so long as fair compensation is made to the owner of the property. The basis of the principles of eminent domain lies in the philosophy of utilitarianism, under which public goods accruing from something such as the improvement of infrastructure or urban renewal are given priority over private property rights. However, this exercise of power raises serious ethical and legal issues on the limits and extent of governmental power. Especially, reliance on eminent domain can lead to contentious disputes about the character of public use, an echo of the broader social debate over property rights and their evolution. Moreover, expressions of eminent domain extend beyond mere legal transactions, as they take in an extensive range of transaction costs that can potentially affect the allocation of property rights. Economic theory suggests that these types of transaction costs play a very large role in the mechanisms for how property rights are formed and enforced. For instance, when government action involves the use of eminent domain, the result is that things become problematic in real estate, influencing the value and desirability of surrounding properties. The relationship between these costs and property rights is an essential factor in the determination of how institutions evolve to meet economic efficiency as well as justice. Through an analysis of these dynamics, we can understand the historical development of property law and how it mirrors values and aspirations of society as well as priorities, in lieu of affirming that our systems today are determined by precedents in the past and transactional facts (Barzel et al., 2023).

Significantly, eminent domain language is also employed to describe the possible socio-economic imbalances that might arise when publicly supported developments displace marginalized communities. With accelerating urban sprawl and land requirements, public infrastructure needs to frequently conflict with marginalized communities' needs. The issue demands greater criticality for compensation, which is not always adequate to resettle individuals who have been displaced to their previous location. Supporters of property rights promote flexibility on the need for better protection to ensure justice in such processes. These supporters argue on behalf of mechanisms that promote protection of the rights of affected individuals and ensure transparency in government processes. Overall, the subject of eminent domain in the framework of property law systems is a critical analytical prism through which we examine the intersection of rights, public interests, and state power, thereby precipitating ongoing critical scrutiny of the theory and application of property law in the contemporary era (Nichols, 2020) (Figure 7.9).

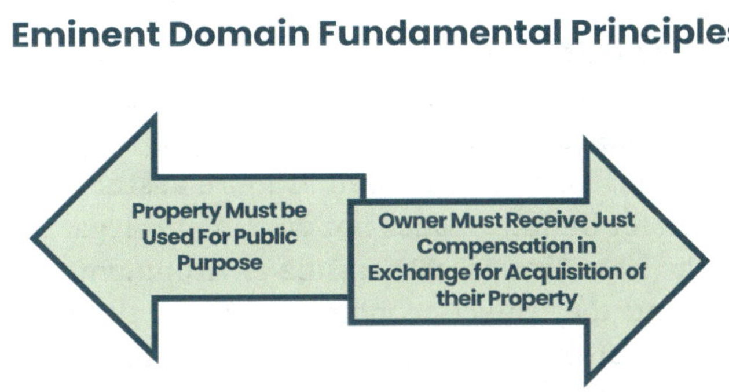

Figure 7.9. Eminent domain fundamentals.

Source: https://wallstreetmojocms.recurpro.in/uploads/Eminent_Domain_2c8af3dc39.png.

7.3.3. Role of Building Codes in Property Law

The interaction between building codes and property law is a complex tapestry of public safety, regulatory compliance, and property enhancement (Figure 7.10).

These codes address a variety of criteria, including stability of the structure, fire safety, accessibility, and energy efficiency, all of which are designed to safeguard occupants and the general public. Building codes as they exist are society's standards changing on issues of public welfare and health, abiding by the principle that law of property is not only concerned with ownership by individuals but also maintaining communal welfare. Thus, the interaction between building codes in property regimes law highlights that regulation is necessary for protecting individual and public interest.

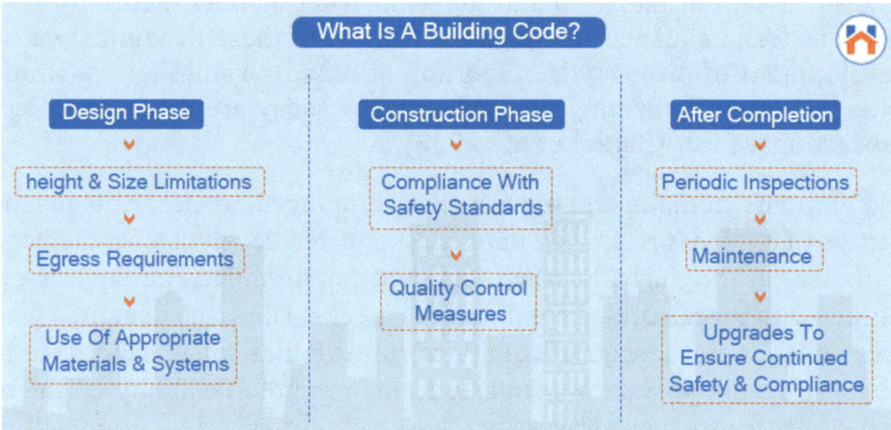

Figure 7.10. Building codes serve as fundamental regulatory frameworks designed to establish standardized construction practices and ensure that both residential and commercial properties adhere to safety protocols.

Source: https://homebazaar-blog.s3.ap-south-1.amazonaws.com/knowledge/wp-content/uploads/2023/06/15131216/What-Is-A-Building-Code-Final.jpg.

Additional analysis confirms that building codes have a wide impact on property value and market reaction and act as a catalyst for investor optimism. Compliance with these codes in proper language can serve to enhance the marketability of a property's, since prospective buyers will believe that compliant buildings are safer as well as more aesthetically pleasing. On the other hand, disobedience or disregard for building codes not only invites legal sanction but can also deter potential investors owing to the risks that go with unsafe environments. The role of building codes is thus greater than enforcement; they affect economic forces in the property market, creating a causal relationship between regulatory control compliance and financial outcomes. This dialogue is most apparent in urban development schemes, where compliance with building codes can lead to volumes of investment, thereby benefiting local economies as well as fostering sustainable development. Additionally, application of the building codes includes rigorous inspection and approval processes, which introduce new layers of complexity to the property law field. Local authorities and municipalities are usually the ones to assume the role of enforcers, tracking adherence to such codes and imposing fines for violations. This regulatory system ensures an equal application to different properties, eventually culminating in a structured and anticipated sense of predictability to real estate transactions. Complications in such codes are also feasible, though, that can be cumbersome to property owners and developers in handling the legalities of construction. Understanding specific building code requirements is essential to safeguard compliance and avoid costly litigation. Thus, the integration of building codes in property law not only enhances security but provides a systematic environment for the construction and management of property.

7.4. SECURITY INTERESTS

The hierarchical nature of property law accommodates various mechanisms designed to protect the interests of creditors, of which the security interests are a part. Liens and mortgages constitute a mechanism for security interests that serves as a means for creditors to secure their claims against debtors' assets. The mechanism not only allows lenders recourse in event of default by borrowers but also specifies a separate order of priority of claims over the assets (Figure 7.11).

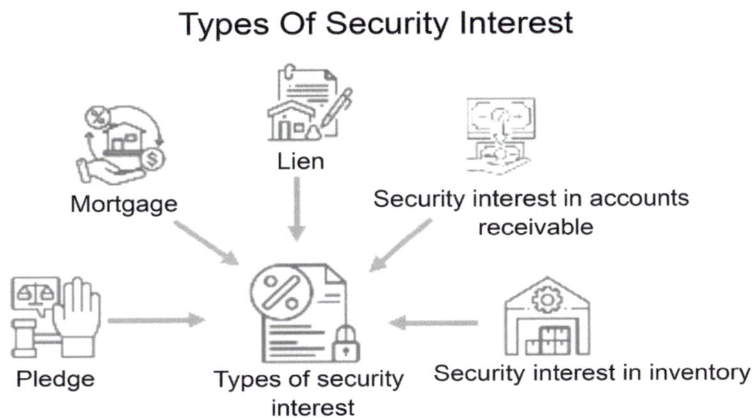

Figure 7.11. Types of security interest.

Source: https://wallstreetmojo-files.s3.ap-south-1.amazonaws.com/2023/03/Types-Of-Security-Interest.png.

Understanding the nuances of such interests contributes further to defining the needs and rights of parties to deals. A case in point is a mortgage, which entitles the financier to take over the property in case of non-payment, thereby necessitating due diligence in ascertaining the nature and extent of such interests in property law systems, emphasizing its role in facilitating economic transactions and market stability. Of key importance in security interests is the requirement for registration, which serves the interests of both parties by confirming openness and establishing priority. Registration of a security interest leaves behind a public document that advises potential creditors of existing claims over a property and thereby reduces the risk of lending. In the majority of jurisdictions, failure to register a security interest will lead to loss of priority against subsequent interests, thereby emphasizing the significance of adhering to practices of registration. Furthermore, the electronic revolution in record-keeping may enhance the efficiency of such a process. A future digital shared ledger, inaugurated by recent technological advancements, would make registering security interests easier, thereby enhancing existing property law systems and facilitating the effectiveness of trademark-backed finance schemes, as recent discussions on the topic reflect (Shaaban et al., 2024). The rules of priority with respect to security interests also indicate the complexity and importance of this section of property law. These rules regulate the order in which creditors may realize their claims out of a property's sale proceeds, determining lenders strategic planning. At default, secured lenders would generally have priority over unsecured creditors, and as such the understanding of these rules is crucial to effective risk management in financial transactions. In addition, the evolving status of the state in controlling interests unequivocally points to the necessity of a general framework ensuring economic activity and protection of individual rights. With mounting challenges in contemporary society, including hybrid conflicts and economic insecurity, the demand for properly organized legal mechanisms for guaranteeing security interests acquires even greater pertinence, epitomizing the compound nature of contemporary property law systems (Osaulenko, 2024).

7.4.1. Mortgages and Liens Explained

In real estate law, the intricate relationship between mortgages and liens is critical to the interpretation of security interests in real estate deals. Contracts that permit a lender to secure a loan by pledging the borrowers property are referred to as mortgages, establishing the property as collateral. Not only does it provide financing for prospective homeowners, but it also introduces intricacies into the players' obligations and rights. Conversely, liens are legal rights in a property that serve as security for debt or obligation payment, from tax liens to mechanic's liens. Mortgages and liens both play pivotal roles in establishing priorities between creditors, particularly where there are multiple claims on one property.

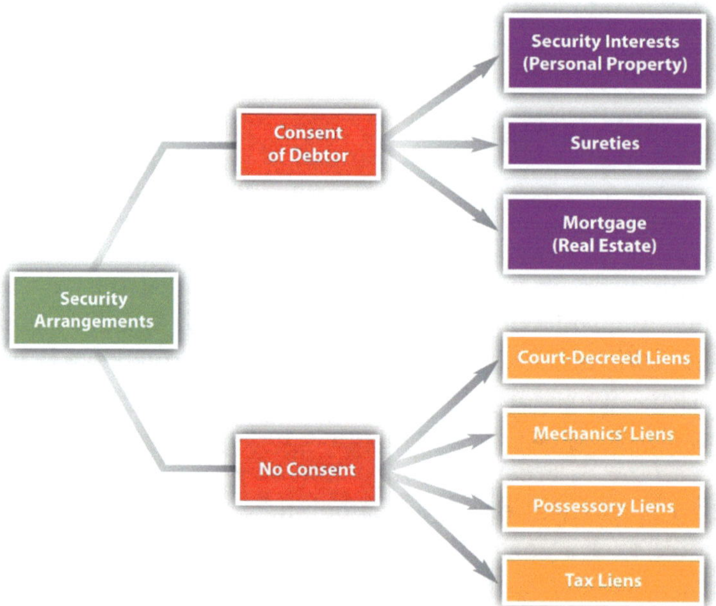

Figure 7.12. Mortgages and nonconsensual liens.

Source: https://saylordotorg.github.io/text_advanced-business-law-and-the-legal-environment/section_23/30b4c1201028809243cfd28b8370c28d.jpg.

Understanding how these interests function within varying regimes of property law contributes depth to financial transactions with regard to property. Mortgages and liens are significantly regulated by the overall regimes of property law in which they function. As noted, the numerus clauses principle restricts the creation of property rights to a quantifiable number of recognized interests and governs the formation and enforcement of security interests like mortgages and liens in both common law and civil law. In the United States and United Kingdom, the evolution of case law encourages a balanced perception of these interests and a reflection of shifts in ownership and obligation within society. Meanwhile, comparative analysis proves differential systemic implications; for example, the legal basis of Germany in relation to such matters seems to revolve around protection measures for property owners. This difference underscores the role of lawyers to see through how local context and principles govern the establishment and enforcement of mortgages and liens both in practice and theory, hence influencing the development of property law as a whole (Weil, 2024). Also, regulatory regimes' impacts on mortgages and liens add additional complexity to property rights questions. These interests are not only subject to legal recognition, but in some instances, even registration which shapes their enforceability. In the majority of jurisdictions, priority rules determination adds additional complexity to the order of claims upon sale or foreclosure of property. Successful operation of such systems in most cases will rely on an understanding of local laws and regulations, which can differ considerably across borders. Jurisdictions will also vary in their conflict of law approaches, particularly where they deal with foreign ownership of property or cross-border financial transactions by means of mortgages and liens. Such variations are even more reasons to adopt a holistic understanding of property law regimes, where it is recognized that mortgages and liens are not only transactional devices, but natural features of an evolving legal reality that shifts in character over time (Wyczik, 2024) (Figure 7.12).

7.4.2. Registration Conditions for Security Interests

A characteristic of property law regimes is the registration of security interests that operates to provide a formal record of lenders' claims over a borrower's assets. The process generally requires security interests to be registered in a public registry to establish priority over rival claims and provide notice to third parties. The registration acts as a shield, ensuring that all the parties are aware of crucial information regarding the responsibilities connected to various assets. In the majority of jurisdictions, non-registration can result in serious legal issues, making enforcement options against creditors cumbersome and undermining the financial stability of borrowers. Thus, effective registration not only generates transparency but also safeguards the interest of all the parties in property transactions, thereby improving the stability and integrity of the overall system of property law. Secondly, intricacies involved in requirements of registration can significantly vary with the character of the security interest concerned. Mortgages and liens on personal property, for instance, can have different procedural steps and timeframes of registration. Some jurisdictions can require additional paperwork or unique forms to be completed, while others can take the more direct path of registering security interests. This disparity likely arises from the disparity in legal traditions and economic environments that shape how rights over property are created and enforced. Additionally, in the new world of emerging technologies, considerations such as digital assets and blockchain technology are beginning to influence traditional registration practices. While these innovations promise efficiency and security, they also bring new regulatory problems which current legal systems have to deal with Yermack (2016).

Lastly, interaction of registration and priority rules plays a critical role in defining the sequence of claims over collateral. In the event where different creditors claim interests on the same asset, the order of registration will usually determine the priority of the claims, thereby establishing a hierarchy of the creditors. Such prioritization may be especially contentious in insolvency proceedings where the creditors are competing for limited resources. Borrowers and lenders alike should be aware of the nuances of such priority rules because mistakes in the process of registration can lead to unexpected consequences, including loss of collateral or diminished value of recovery in bankruptcy proceedings. The requirement for clear rules and consistent enforcement systems underscores the importance of systematic registration mandates in establishing a fair and equitable property law framework, ultimately advancing the predictability demanded by economic activity actors (Cöcker et al., 2017).

7.4.3. Priority Rules in Property Claims

In property law systems, priority rules are significant as they determine the hierarchy of claims against property, that is, in instances of competing claims by numerous parties over a single property. Complexity arises when differentiation among claims on the basis of different properties, for example, ownership and security interests, is required. Rules of priority order dictate the order under which claims are to be granted and implemented, in such a way that certain interests are realized before others. The system is most important where there are secured transactions and crops up in vehicles like mortgages and liens, where the first in time usually has a better right. Therefore, priority rules not only ensure predictable operation of property rights but also protect the interests of creditors and investors by clarifying the risk of securing interest over property. Moreover, the operation of priority rules becomes more sophisticated when it involves legal persons and limited proprietary rights. For instance, the theory of separate property highlights the relationship between limited rights in property and protection by claims of creditors and the implication that such rights have a bearing on segregation of securities and claims in a legal context. The silent functioning of such rules serves to delineate the liability of a legal entity to its creditors, particularly where it possesses not just property but also rights that may be restricted in nature. Generally, priority rules serve to delineate the ambit and limits of property rights and to guarantee that certain rights take precedence over others, thus delineating the ground on which property claims are established. This setting of coherent priorities serves as fundamental to maintaining economic stability and confidence in property markets. In addition, the interaction between tangible and intangible property in these priority rules raises extra challenges, particularly in jurisdictions such as Russia and Germany, where legal determinations regarding property acquisition need to take into account the unique nature of each category. Application of rules like bona fide acquisition and possession of prescriptions illustrates the way straightforward priority rules can illuminate the mystery of ownership of other forms of assets. Such regimes of law are intended to enhance the public credibility of property registers and render the mechanics through which the right can be vindicated or defected more simple. Interestingly, with new forms of property emerging, such as digital rights, applying these priority rules must be accomplished in overcoming them to remain applicable in the light of established principles. Legal systems accomplish this by taking and possibly reconfiguring existing doctrines to apply to these new property rights so that they receive equal fair treatment to other ownerships yet still uphold the coherence of the property law system overall (Ibragimov, 2024; Lorents, 2024).

7.5. LEASEHOLD AND TENANCY LAW

In dissecting the nuances of leasehold and tenancy law, it is worth noting the intricate tango between landlords and tenants, with a diverse set of responsibilities and rights. At the heart of this transaction is the process of lease agreements, which are contracts that bind the conditions under which property is rented. These contracts also specify the duration of tenancy, rental charges, and maintenance responsibilities, thereby safeguarding the interests of both parties. Legal doctrine for these contracts varies greatly from one region to another, depending on varying social norms for property rights. Dispute resolution mechanisms—for example, mediation or litigation—are also a key consideration for achieving balance in this relationship. These regulatory regimes are especially applicable to cities facing housing shortages, where heightened demand can heighten tensions over lease violations and tenant protection, highlighting the inherent importance of robust tenancy law in the broader framework of property law regimes. Termination procedures in lease agreements further characterize the complexity entailed in tenancy law, since they specify procedures for cancelling rental terms. Typically, a lease can be terminated with mutual agreement, expiration of the lease period, or breaches of either party's contract. It is crucial that landlords and tenants know the specific terms that outline termination—that is, notice period and circumstances for eviction—to avoid legal disputes. The repercussions of illegally performed termination may extend far past direct financial loss, that is, harm to both parties' credit scores and future leasing opportunities. Therefore, open communication and adherence to established legal procedures not only prevent clashes but also assist in the established fundamental principles of equity and stability in the rental housing sector. Thus, effective regulation of termination procedures is a key aspect of the legal story of leasehold and tenancy law. Rent control policies, typically instituted in response to prohibitively high rents and housing shortages, are a paradigmatic intersection of social policy and law of property. Such measures are adopted in an attempt to protect renters from excessive increases in rent, ensuring stability in housing and affordability in volatile marketplaces. But passage of rent control can be contentious, with landlords criticizing that such policy can lead to a decrease in housing quality and decreased incentive for property maintenance. Within these debates, the recent controversy surrounding rent control frequently returns to questions of fairness and availability of housing and reflects the necessity of equitable legislative approaches. particularly in those urban neighborhoods where real estate demand is so much greater than available supply, the association between rent control laws and tenant protection becomes increasingly entangled with other questions of economic justice. Thus, the creation of rent control legislation is not merely a matter of economic realism; it encapsulates the values of society, which mirrors the complex relationship between legal frameworks and human rights within the framework of property law frameworks (Watt et al., 2016; Saturnino et al., 2015).

7.5.1. Rights of Landlords and Tenants

The area of law that governs the rights of landlords and tenants is deeply intertwined in the texture of property law regimes, balancing between both parties' interests to a lease contract. Landlords are typically the owners of the property and have the right to allow the tenant to occupy and use the property in exchange for rent. This is governed by a number of laws and legal mechanisms that establish the responsibility and entitlements every party in such an arrangement has. While tenants enjoy the prerogative of enforcing lease terms and pay of rent, the same applies to the obligations of such as maintaining the dwelling in habitable conditions and effecting repair works. These regulations not only ensure the integrity of the investment of the landlord but also verify that tenants can live in their dwelling conditions with safety and comfort, which allows for harmonious cooperation necessary for efficient leasehold plans (Karapysh, 2025).

Rights Of Tenants VS Landlords Rights

Rights Of Tenants	VS	Landlords Rights
Right to privacy and peaceful enjoyment of the property	Right to Privacy	Right to enter the property for inspections, repairs, or emergencies with proper notice
Right to receive a copy of the lease agreement.Right to be informed about any changes in the lease terms.	Right to Information	Right to know the identity of the tenant and any other occupants
Right to request timely repairs for any issues affecting health and safety	Right to Maintenance and Repairs	Right to expect tenants to keep the property clean and not cause damage.
Right to be informed about the rent amount and any changes	Right to Rent and Fees	Right to receive rent on time as per the lease agreement
Right to proper notice if the landlord intends to terminate the lease	Right to Lease Renewal	Right to terminate the lease for non-payment
Right to get the security deposit back after the lease ends	Right to Security Deposits	Right to withhold part or all of the security deposit for unpaid rent.

Meanwhile, tenants possess a spectrum of rights that are designed to ensure their possession and use of the rented premises. These rights encompass areas such as privacy, protection against unfair eviction, and right to a decent living space. Rent control legislation in the majority of jurisdictions prohibits landlords from charging exorbitant rents or acting in retaliatory measures against those tenants that exercise their rights, ensuring equal access to homes. Further, tenants are also accorded the right to have repairs carried out in a timely manner, safeguarding their investment in the rental contract. In regimes of property law, such tenant rights are significant in preventing landlord exploitation and securing stable housing conditions for residents, ultimately leading to healthy communities and neighborhoods (Gupta et al., 2025). The overlapping of landlord and tenant rights is also exacerbated by legislative complexity, especially during periods of economic instability or legal overhaul. For instance, in the Ukrainian case, the evolution of leasehold law was influenced by broader transformations in property law and European integration processes (Karapysh, 2025). Reforms attempt to enhance legal protection of both landlords and tenants by updating antiquated rules and aligning national property laws with contemporary market trends. Moreover, under unusual circumstances such as the martial law regime, as experienced in Ukraine, the balance of rights is lost, and temporary measures shape eviction processes and controls on rent. The dynamic underlines the requirement for ongoing adjustments in property law regimes to accommodate changing needs and rights of owners and lessees (Gupta et al., 2025).

7.5.2. Procedures for Termination of Leases

The lease agreement processes are rather complicated, involving extensive knowledge of the termination procedures of leases. The property law systems allow termination to occur in certain ways, including by lapse of the term of the lease, mutual agreement between the parties, or breach of both parties. Expiry of lease term is the most direct method, where the lease conditions and terms automatically come to an end after the agreed period expires. Mutual consent, on the other hand, requires the consent of the landlord and the tenant in order to end the lease, typically resulting in negotiations that can reduce conflict. Breach of contract, on grounds like failure to pay rent or abandonment of the premises, provides a landlord grounds for filing termination proceedings, establishing the significance of compliance with lease covenants in developing healthy landlord-tenant relations. Where termination is sought, there are certain guidelines that must be followed in an effort to ensure that actions taken are constitutionally sound. Courts expect landlords to provide rightful notice to tenants before evicting them, as envisioned in tenancy agreements or law. The period of notice allows tenants sufficient room to rectify any breaches so that justice shall prevail in the process. The type of lease—residential or commercial—may also determine the procedure necessary for cancellation. In commercial leases, for instance, conditions may include additional terms in case of non-compliance, since companies prefer more formal contracts. Both landlords and tenants are supposed to understand such procedural nuances to navigate potential disputes and establish clear expectations that can minimize future litigation for lease termination. Legislative changes are able to play a major role in deciding termination procedures for property law regimes, which involves keeping a close watch by both tenants and landlords. Current developments, such as changes to prevent raiding in land lease agreements in Ukraine, show the need for adaptive law to safeguard parties rights against the complex context of land use (Ilkiv, 2020). As property law evolves, so does the lease contract environment, especially in rapidly developing fields such as renewable energy. With increasing demands for sustainability, the age and termination of leases for wind turbine assets present unique legal issues. Bargaining over lifetime extension of the assets indicates new regimes of law will need to address both economic and procedural aspects in order to facilitate efficient renewals and terminations of leases, bringing to the fore the interactive relationship between law and property management (Ziegler et al., 2017).

7.5.3. Impact of Rent Control Legislation

The relationship between rent control policy and housing markets profoundly influences urban space, both in regard to the supply of rental space and in impinging on the more general socio-economic processes within cities. As local governments implement rent control, supposedly to protect low-income renters from rent increases, the immediate effect can create a sense of security for renters. But these moves also have the potential to unintentionally discourage real property investment and reduce the incentive to renovate or upgrade existing buildings on the part of owners. The long-term effect is a drop in housing quality and a reduction in the overall amount of rental space available, as owners redevelop properties for other uses or remove them from the rental pool altogether. Lastly, the protections that rent control will provide can instead yield effects that exacerbate the lack of housing rather than alleviate it. Additionally, rent control legislation conflicts with the economics in general, and in particular, the theory of supply and demand. In extremely trendy city neighborhoods, where there is inherently upward pressure on housing price, the result of enacting rent controls is to bring about a mis-match in the housing market. Tenants have lower rent, but this protection can lead to abuse of rental housing, where long-term tenants, often at submarket rents, reside in houses that otherwise would be sold or rented at higher levels to new movers. These tendencies can take the housing market off track, leading to a frozen rental market where mobility is reduced and new movers are, in effect, shut out of gaining access to housing opportunity. This strict system also creates it hard to balance housing supplies, as the restriction can create a black market or an informal operation, making regulatory oversight and enforcement even more complex. Tacked on to this is the advent of platforms like Airbnb, which lays bare another facet of the rent control debate, and how localized regulation can run counter to globalized rental markets. With both the growth of Airbnb's and the curse of rent control, legislators are increasingly faced with the challenge of controlling short-term rentals without aggravating housing shortages. The tension between maintaining affordable housing for long-term tenants and accommodating short-term visitors is a special regulatory puzzle that many municipalities are struggling to solve. Research has indicated that the rapid growth of digital accommodation platforms will tend to erase the boundary between residential and tourist accommodations, resulting in a complicated intertwining of legal and economic effects on housing markets. It is necessary to understand this dynamic as policymakers struggle to craft rules that both address tenants' short-term requirements and avoid long-run economic dislocation in the housing market, making the sophisticated approach to systems of property law necessary (Gurran et al., 2017; Guttentag, 2013).

7.6. CROSS-BORDER PROPERTY OWNERSHIP

Handling the complexities of foreign property ownership presents unique challenges within systems of global property laws. Various jurisdictions have unique rules governing what rights and restrictions exist regarding foreigners or foreign entities wishing to own a property. For instance, countries will have foreign ownership restrictions, where they will delineate how much property a non-resident can own. Such limitations are intended to protect national interests, including economic sovereignty and indigenous land use. The environment then becomes multi-dimensional for potential investors. In addition, such limitation has the ability to create ambiguities in the law, especially when target purchasers lack knowledge of specific local legislation. That reality compels investors to be cautious, obtaining local legal expertise to satisfy compliance requirements and stay clear of cross-border property deal risks. The intersection of diverse legal systems also complicates cross-border property ownership, as conflicts of laws would arise. Every state has its own laws pertaining to ownership rights, rules of transfers, and mechanisms of disputing adjudication, which may result in conflicting lawful results. For example, a title of property that is valid in one country may prove ineffective in another, so that the owners are left with a dilemma under which they find it hard to enforce their rights abroad. The importance of title recognition cannot be overstated, as it affects not only the security of ownership but also the use of assets in property to collateralize transactions like mortgages or leases. Appreciating such variations, legal experts ought to facilitate the understanding of varied legal systems, navigating stakeholders through such nuances and achieving fair outcomes in the event of potential disputes. Legal safeguard and harmonization efforts play a great role in ensuring cross-border property ownership transactions. As business goes global, there is a requirement for robust treaties and agreements to address property rights. Organizations such as the United Nations and trade agreements have created forums to harmonize regulations and ensure cooperation in real property transactions. Such actions not only serve to encourage legal certainty but also facilitate the international movement of investments as well as the intensification of economic relations among countries. Nevertheless, fruitful cooperation is normally foiled by differing national interests as well as different regulatory systems, requiring successive dialogues between governments, legal professionals, and stakeholders. To achieve a more integrated system, understanding local legislation like (Syamsir et al., 2025) for state asset management and (Maharani et al., 2025) for ownership of personal data opens an understanding of the broader implications of property law, pinpointing the significance of detailed legal planning in cross-border ownership contexts.

7.6.1. Foreign Ownership Restrictions in Various Jurisdictions

With a more globalized economy, foreign ownership restrictions that are typical in most jurisdictions play an important role in determining the impact of property law systems. Such controls are typically formulated on grounds of national security, economics, or protectionism for the protection of indigenous industries from overseas competition. For instance, countries have imposed foreign investment restrictions in sensitive areas such as agriculture, telecommunication, or property. These restrictions can be either in the form of absolute prohibitions, where foreign ownership is categorically barred, or in the form of regulations that require a minimum percentage of national ownership, thus ensuring nationals have widespread control over key economic assets. The rationale of these rules serves to underscore the balance legal systems try to strike between encouraging foreign investment and safeguarding national interests. Within the sphere of property law, understanding such foreign ownership restrictions is of utmost significance for investors and lawyers alike. Nations adopt different approaches based on their legal cultures, economic goals, as well as their sociopolitical environments. For example, while some jurisdictions welcome foreign investment with incentives provided to foreign businesses to establish a presence, others lean towards protectionism. These imbalances can complicate cross-border transactions and require a general understanding of the domestic legal framework. Moreover, such restrictions are likely to force foreign investors to navigate complex regulatory regimes, which can include obtaining special permits, adhering to localization policies, or obtaining government approvals. Such regulatory complexity complicates foreign stakeholders' ability to undertake property transactions in limiting regimes. The foreign prohibitions of ownership have repercussions which reach into broader social and economic realms and influence the trends of investment, and encouraging the development of specialized property law traditions. Beyond immediate legal issues, these kinds of restrictions might affect the trends of the flow of capital, innovation, and the overall economic climate of a country. Furthermore, the adverse impact on foreign investment may lead to economic inefficiencies or suppress the technological advancements that foreign firms may bring. Moreover, as jurisdictions everywhere grapple with the implications of globalization, a growing debate over whether such curbs need to be reformed ensues. The majority of supporters favor a balanced strategy that preserves country interests while embracing beneficial foreign participation in national markets. This dynamic nature of the problem reflects constantly evolving property law systems and their accommodation of the complexity of cross-border holding of property and foreign investment.

7.6.2. Conflict of Laws in Property Transactions

Foraying into the complexities of property law is likely to untangle solemn stumbling blocks, particularly in situations that entail more than one jurisdiction. In such frameworks, theory of conflicting laws plays a crucial role, particularly in cross-border property deals. With accelerating globalization driving property investments around the world, legal frameworks are under pressure to standardize divergence in rights of ownership, transferability of assets, and usual practices, leaving space for misperception and contradiction. This divergence can be tremendous barriers to parties and entities that seek to enter cross-border property transactions. As varying legal traditions influence property rights—between codified enactments in civil law countries and customary practices in common law systems—it is crucial to distinguish how the differences impact the validity and enforceability of property transactions across borders. One of the common examples of this problem, worthy of note, is in the context of traditional systems of land ownership, for instance, in Malawi. The intertwining of kinship ties and land holdings here can lead to complex conflicts difficult to categorize under formal law. Customary laws may facilitate flexible transactions; however, they may also offer variability at odds with state-sanctioned formal property rights. According to research, these de facto systems are prone to breeding inequalities because marginalized groups are likely to oppose rooted legal orders that favor richer landowners (Takane, 2008). Hence, understanding the resolution mechanisms for such conflicts is essential in ensuring level property rights and more streamlined transactions across borders. Finding solutions to the dismembered nature of the law in property transactions necessitates a robust understanding of the connotations of diverse legal origins. Evidence exists for the correlation between the legal tradition of a country in the past and its current legal stability, ultimately affecting property rights and economic outcomes (Porta et al., 2008). Legal harmonization is imperative to minimize the drag caused by incompatible laws in property transactions, either through international treaties, agreements, or mutual understandings of countries. By fostering clarity in recognition of property and establishing uniform systems of resolving conflicts, jurisdictions can create more secure environments for investment in property and thus encourage economic development and social justice across borders.

7.6.3. Recognition of Titles Across Borders

In the complicated landscape of systems of property law, title recognition across borders plays a critical role in the enforcement of cross-border real estate transactions and investments. Various nations will have different standards and procedures in dealing with property rights, which present formidable obstacles to international owners in maintaining their titles in navigating various legal systems. For instance, a property title well established within one jurisdiction can be vague in another, and so lead to disputes undermining investment stability. Developing clarity and predictability of property title recognition is crucial to improving investor confidence, safeguarding investments, and promoting international economic cooperation. Furthermore, the lack of uniform procedures may provide grounds for conflict of laws, which may complicate disputes over ownership and hamper effective resolution of property rights issues, particularly in the era of globalization where cross-border transactions are increasingly common. Knowing the importance of title recognition requires an examination of the sociopolitical arrangements that hold water within different jurisdictions. Such frameworks tend to reflect larger societal issues, including power dynamics and long-term inequalities that underlie property law systems. Property title identification, therefore, is more than straightforward legal categorization; it involves complex narratives of ownership rights that may be shaped by intersecting sets of variables like race, class, and nationality. As explicated by Patrícia Collins (2015), identification of these intersections is important in determining the impact of property laws on social justice. Resolution of inconsistencies in title recognition is warranted not merely for the sake of effective legal adaptation but also to provide equitable access to property ownership across various sections and regions. Through resolution of these inconsistencies, stakeholders can progress toward an expanded property law regime accommodative of diversified interests from various nations. Coping with varying governmental attitudes and juridical conditions regarding foreign ownership is also an issue related to title recognition. Most nations impose protective restrictions for domestic interests, which may influence foreign investors' access to clear titles of ownership. These restrictions might be in the form of direct prohibition of foreign ownership or compliance requirements that are stringent and render it hard to make acquisitions. Thus, title recognition across borders is even more complicated since investors must reconcile their expectations with local law. This phenomenon calls for building policies that connect national legislations with international standards of property rights. As explained by Catherine et al. (2020), ownership and legal claim data need to be interpreted in a mindset that conceives broader implications in justice and equity. Finally, the promotion of an ordered system of title recognition will not only benefit investors but also foster a climate for fair property practices in the global arena.

SUMMARY

In outlining this process through property law regimes, it is evident that the complexities incurred in property rights have a huge impact on individual ownership as well as national administration. The difference between movable and immovable property and public and private ownership exhibits the diversified methods employed by legal regimes across the globe. Understanding these categories is crucial in understanding how rights in rem function and the resultant effects of title transfer rules. This is the core foundation of the wider property law debate, in which the battle between possession and ownership remains a central theme cutting across issues such as adverse possession and co-ownership. Last but not least, an appreciation for the subtle balance of rights helps explain the premises of legal systems that ensure equity and efficiency in property ownership and regulation.

Legal systems in different jurisdictions have not only accepted varying forms of property rights but have also established diverse structures of ownership transfer and rules of property use. The zoning ordinance case, eminent domain, and building codes example illustrates how states balance local rights to property with broader social interests. All legal systems are challenged in how regulatory regimes define land use and impact real estate market development, which illustrates the localized approach resonating across global property discourses. With increasing urbanization, more complex and dynamic property law is ever more crucial, protecting that expansion prioritizes both community and private interests. That regulatory dynamic affects not just individual ownership consequences but also the urban landscape as a whole, highlighting the significant role of property law in society. Findings on property law systems further indicate the pivotal role of courts to determine rights and translate legal principles within the limits of the numerus clauses principle. The principle operates with system effects that are effectuated differently across jurisdictions such as Germany, England, and the United States, influencing how courts resolve disputes over property and legal reasoning. This macro-comparative study illustrates that while most modern legal systems limit property rights, the implications of such boundaries differ. This difference enriches the discourse of property law, revealing possibilities for reform and renewal in defining property as an evolving and socially responsive concept. By examining these forces, practitioners and researchers can encourage more adaptable legal systems that recognize both individual and collective needs within their creation and enforcement, resulting in a property law environment that sustains both innovation and equity.

A LOOK TO THE FUTURE

THE FUTURE OF PROPERTY RIGHTS IN THE DIGITAL AND TECHNOLOGICAL ERA

The development of property law is closely tied to technological and social changes, paving the way for future directions that will transform how property rights are conceived and protected. As jurisdictions struggle with innovations precipitated by the digital era, creating legal frameworks for accepting virtual properties, like those in the metaverse, is becoming increasingly necessary. This change highlights the growing importance of concepts like digital identity and NFT rights in property, which need robust legal protection. The growing complexities around such digital assets also necessitate global cooperation among legal systems to effectively address judicial impediments. Thus, creating a uniform regulatory framework will be key to safeguarding consumer rights and ensuring digital assets retain value in an increasingly networked environment of online transactions (Chen, 2025).

Another indispensable trend reshaping the future of property law involves the integration of advanced biotechnologies and artificial intelligence into patent regimes. While these technologies revolutionize sectors such as medicine and conservation, they do so by also creating new intellectual property challenges. The landscape of property rights is becoming more complicated, with questions asked about ownership and innovation. For instance, how do property rights envelop medical innovations developed by AI? Moreover, existing legal frameworks may fail to keep pace with the unprecedented pace of innovation, and legislative updates are necessary to counter these dynamics. Jurisdictions are coming to appreciate the need for aligning legal infrastructures with scientific progress, highlighting the imperative for shrewd regulatory interventions that will raise the level of innovation while simultaneously protecting intellectual property rights (Raymond et al., 2025).

In the years to come, the intersection of property law and technology promises much in the way of fundamental transformation of security interests and enforcement instruments. Thanks to the advent of blockchain technology, smart contracts can be a game-changing solution for traditional property transactions, immensely streamlining transparency and efficiency. These computer programs can guarantee automatic enforcement of contracts that can eliminate uncertainty associated with title transfer and ownership disputes. Furthermore, the regulatory issues of broadening property definitions to digital assets—and the complexities involved—will necessitate a careful re-examination of existing laws that oversee ownership and tenancy. With continued international trade, the law has to adapt and ensure that property law not only reflects current realities but also future trends in what will shape the property rights regime (Chen, 2025; Raymond et al., 2025).

REFERENCES

1. Abdulsamad, H. M. S., Abaas, S., & Hussein, F. S. (2020). The fate of the partner's mortgage after division: A comparative analytical study in the Iraqi Civil Code. *Volume 7*, 1–18. https://www.semanticscholar.org/paper/9b9284abf608293d98a6c63c6ebb7f9eafb081f2 (accessed on 9th September 2025).
2. Angeler, D. G., & Allen, C. R. (2016). Quantifying resilience. *Journal of Applied Ecology, 53*, 617–624. https://doi.org/10.1111/1365-2664.12649 (accessed on 9th September 2025).
3. Applbaum, A. I. (2010). Legitimacy without the duty to obey. *Philosophy & Public Affairs, 38*, 215–239. https://doi.org/10.1111/j.1088-4963.2010.01186.x (accessed on 9th September 2025).
4. Barelli, M. (2012). Free, prior and informed consent in the aftermath of the UN Declaration on the Rights of Indigenous Peoples: Developments and challenges ahead. *The International Journal of Human Rights, 16*, 1–24. https://doi.org/10.1080/13642987.2011.597746 (accessed on 9th September 2025).
5. Barzel, Y., & Allen, D. W. (2023). *Economic Analysis of Property Rights*. https://doi.org/10.1017/9781009374712 (accessed on 9th September 2025).
6. Batko, I. (2023). Establishment and development of legislative regulation of industrial designs as objects of intellectual property law in Ukraine. *Visnik Nacional'nogo universitetu «Lvivska politehnika». Seria: Uridicni nauki*. https://www.semanticscholar.org/paper/745dbe6595ac460ad3f57b4f541db15aac57a730 (accessed on 9th September 2025).
7. Borras, S. M., Franco, J. C., & Monsalve Suárez, S. (2015). Land and food sovereignty. *Third World Quarterly, 36*, 600–617. https://doi.org/10.1080/01436597.2015.1029225 (accessed on 9th September 2025).
8. Chen, Z. (2025). Building a legal framework for the metaverse: Digital identity, NFT property rights, and global legal structures. *Digital Society & Virtual Governance*. https://www.semanticscholar.org/paper/7e8e7e8a017c6db847bd182e786da459d31d4abc (accessed on 9th September 2025).
9. Chung, K. (2025). Personal ownership regulation under the North Korean Civil Code revised in 2024–Focusing on the comparison of the provisions of the North Korean Civil Code before and after the amendment. *The Legal Studies Institute of Chosun University*. https://www.semanticscholar.org/paper/c506501f812fa9e7c339f2e8cf37346bdee67239 (accessed on 9th September 2025).
10. Collins, P. H. (2015). Intersectionality's definitional dilemmas. *Annual Review of Sociology, 41*, 1–20. https://doi.org/10.1146/annurev-soc-073014-112142 (accessed on 9th September 2025).
11. D'Ignazio, C., & Klein, L. (2020). *Data Feminism*. The MIT Press eBooks. https://doi.org/10.7551/mitpress/11805.001.0001 (accessed on 9th September 2025).
12. Demirgüç-Kunt, A., & Klapper, L. (2012). *Measuring Financial Inclusion: The Global Findex Database*. World Bank Policy Research Working Paper. https://doi.org/10.1596/1813-9450-6025 (accessed on 9th September 2025).
13. Didin, D. B., & Luo, Y. (2025). Acquisitive prescription/adverse possession: Turkish and

Chinese legal systems. *Yıldırım Beyazıt Hukuk Dergisi*. https://www.semanticscholar.org/paper/a746e63281c5f5bdec9466368ce8790738e3368a (accessed on 9th September 2025).

14. Dwivedi, Y. K., Hughes, L., Baabdullah, A. M., Ribeiro-Navarrete, S., Giannakis, M., Al-Debei, M. M., Dennehy, D., et al. (2022). Metaverse beyond the hype: Multidisciplinary perspectives on emerging challenges, opportunities, and agenda for research, practice and policy. *International Journal of Information Management, 66*, 102542–102542. https://doi.org/10.1016/j.ijinfomgt.2022.102542 (accessed on 9th September 2025).

15. Gherheș, V., Grecea, C., Vilceanu, C., Herban, S., & Coman, C. (2025). Challenges in systematic property registration in Romania: An analytical overview. *Land*. https://www.semanticscholar.org/paper/e84f16857c06b19401650c88a74e6e510fad1f1e (accessed on 9th September 2025).

16. Gliściński, K. (2025). Intellectual property rights as private rights: Implications of the theory of internally limited rights and incentive theory for reconstructing the normative content of rights in intangible goods. *The Journal of World Intellectual Property*. https://www.semanticscholar.org/paper/4d40927f93c51aae2c97187bb39b56202b305dec (accessed on 9th September 2025).

17. Gupta, N., & Arya, H. (2025). Land and real estate laws. https://www.semanticscholar.org/paper/fe976a4207db3c615b9e318bd4b127ccb6bc6a95 (accessed on 9th September 2025).

18. Gurran, N., & Phibbs, P. (2017). When tourists move in: How should urban planners respond to Airbnb? *Journal of the American Planning Association, 83*, 80–92. https://doi.org/10.1080/01944363.2016.1249011 (accessed on 9th September 2025).

19. Guttentag, D. (2013). Airbnb: Disruptive innovation and the rise of an informal tourism accommodation sector. *Current Issues in Tourism, 18*, 1192–1217. https://doi.org/10.1080/13683500.2013.827159 (accessed on 9th September 2025).

20. Huynh-The, T., Gadekallu, T. R., Wang, W., Yenduri, G., Ranaweera, P., Pham, Q. V., da Costa, D. B., et al. (2023). Blockchain for the metaverse: A review. *Future Generation Computer Systems, 143*, 401–419. https://doi.org/10.1016/j.future.2023.02.008 (accessed on 9th September 2025).

21. Ibragimov, K. Y. (2024). The problem of non-proprietary legal entities in the light of the theory of separate property. *Юридические исследования*. https://www.semanticscholar.org/paper/65d5c82bb011e9b93e098036cb9599f167cc515f (accessed on 9th September 2025).

22. Ilkiv, N. V. (2020). Інститут поновлення договору оренди земельної ділянки як засіб протидії рейдерству. *Юридичний вісник*. https://doi.org/10.32837/yuv.v0i1.1574 (accessed on 9th September 2025).

23. Intergovernmental Panel on Climate Change. (2023). *Climate Change 2022–Impacts, Adaptation and Vulnerability*. https://doi.org/10.1017/9781009325844 (accessed on 9th September 2025).

24. Kabisch, N., Korn, H., Stadler, J., & Bonn, A. (2017). Nature-based solutions to climate change adaptation in urban areas. *Theory and Practice of Urban Sustainability Transitions*. https://doi.org/10.1007/978-3-319-56091-5 (accessed on 9th September 2025).

25. Karapysh, B. (2025). Genesis of Ukrainian legislation on property lease relations in the sphere of land use. *Uzhhorod National University Herald. Series: Law*. https://www.semanticscholar.

org/paper/52340cfe7b13bff9523e523adcccdb37deb7db0b (accessed on 9th September 2025).

26. Khalfan, M., Al Amri, H., & Manahan, W. E. (2025). The effects of zoning regulations and land use planning on property values in Sultanate of Oman. *Journal of Information Systems Engineering and Management*. https://www.semanticscholar.org/paper/7b5fac902299872781620948c9eb739fc8f3997b (accessed on 9th September 2025).

27. Khan, M. K. (2025). Transforming libraries with blockchain technology: An overview of its potential implementation, benefits, and challenges. *Inverge Journal of Social Sciences*. https://www.semanticscholar.org/paper/ad7647f279f77db2a3e369bb90ec0b6538d68e09 (accessed on 9th September 2025).

28. Koohang, A., Nord, J. H., Ooi, K. B., Tan, G. W. H., Al-Emran, M., Aw, E. C. X., Baabdullah, A. M., et al. (2023). Shaping the metaverse into reality: A holistic multidisciplinary understanding of opportunities, challenges, and avenues for future investigation. *Journal of Computer Information Systems, 63*, 735–765. https://doi.org/10.1080/08874417.2023.2165197 (accessed on 9th September 2025).

29. Kristiyenda, Y. S., & Ramli, T. S. (2025). Implementation of intellectual property law awareness and cybersecurity technology against digital copyright violations in Indonesia during the 2024 elections. *Awang Long Law Review*. https://www.semanticscholar.org/paper/78186970c5616fb98db3391cd4fd71eac7888b37 (accessed on 9th September 2025).

30. La Porta, R., López-de-Silanes, F., & Shleifer, A. (2008). The economic consequences of legal origins. *Journal of Economic Literature, 46*, 285–332. https://doi.org/10.1257/jel.46.2.285 (accessed on 9th September 2025).

31. Lee, L. (2024). Examining the legal status of digital assets as property: A comparative analysis of jurisdictional approaches. https://www.semanticscholar.org/paper/f417b618aac4d9c9f23e1f38261a8100f845b869 (accessed on 9th September 2025).

32. Leonidze, I. (2025). State as an heir: Balancing public and private interests in Georgia and Europe. Part I: Comparative overview. *Review of European and Comparative Law*. https://www.semanticscholar.org/paper/7df9f45ca9adb8870fd308f36905fc076e55471a (accessed on 9th September 2025).

33. Limongelli, R., & Sposini, L. (2025). The (virtual) battle for intellectual property rights in the metaverse: The case of copyright, trademarks and the NFT technology. *Metaverse*. https://www.semanticscholar.org/paper/ee5a6d4ef4aa7100b6b394d759907e2c8c977b9b (accessed on 9th September 2025).

34. Lorents, D. V. (2024). Intangible property: Problems of bona fide acquisition and acquisitive prescription. *Vestnik Tomskogo gosudarstvennogo universiteta*. https://www.semanticscholar.org/paper/63f1b83939e19fe2ce300f99b79d4df0eb04d298 (accessed on 9th September 2025).

35. Maharani, D. P., Kusumadara, A., Widhiyanti, H. N., & Dewantara, R. (2025). Revisiting personal data: Ownership theories and comparative legal perspectives from Europe, Indonesia and the United States. *Journal of Data Protection & Privacy*. https://www.semanticscholar.org/paper/c4f0cb9c057bafc946128b1e90ba3d97e280475a (accessed on 9th September 2025).

36. Marchenko, V., Dombrovska, A., & Prodaivoda, V. (2024). Comparative analysis of regulatory acts of the EU countries on the protection of intellectual property in the conditions of the use of artificial intelligence. *Public Administration and Law Review*. https://www.semanticscholar.org/paper/32dd74fca0333e3aebe60532cbd138fb57677760 (accessed on 9th September 2025).

37. Masriani, Y. T. (2024). Penyuluhan regulasi dan aturan penggunaan harta waris dalam hukum Islam pada kelompok nasabah prioritas Bank Rakyat Indonesia. *Perigel: Jurnal Penyuluhan Masyarakat Indonesia*. https://www.semanticscholar.org/paper/9459964227ab94750f53803cf4f6d1b06c257f01 (accessed on 9th September 2025).

38. McKenna, M., & Arvidsson, M. (2024). Gendering public and private international law: Transversal legal histories of the state, market, and the family through women's private property rights. *AJIL Unbound, 118*, 12–17. https://www.semanticscholar.org/paper/e04a5c271e0291ef5bfd55f2c78aad92c4f6c4e8 (accessed on 9th September 2025).

39. *N/A*. (2022). Academic literature on compliance programs, ESG, corporate governance, fraud prevention, human rights, corruption, data protection, and SDGs. *Journal of Law and Corruption Review*. https://www.semanticscholar.org/paper/0ca212e17809a4295930314d2f37e012a44876c7 (accessed on 9th September 2025).

40. Nichols, R. (2020). *Theft is Property! Dispossession and Critical Theory*. https://doi.org/10.1215/9781478090250 (accessed on 9th September 2025).

41. Osaulenko, V. (2024). The state in the mechanism of law-formation as a subject of theoretical and legal knowledge. *Analytical and Comparative Jurisprudence*. https://www.semanticscholar.org/paper/afb363cf8a6f580d6fe8d7d0ac84e8a97187dc0e (accessed on 9th September 2025).

42. Pilkington, M. (2016). *Blockchain Technology: Principles and Applications*. Edward Elgar Publishing eBooks. https://doi.org/10.4337/9781784717766.00019 (accessed on 9th September 2025).

43. Pundir, D. S., Jindal, B., Ranga, P., Saini, V., Mahajan, N., Kusha, & Pandey, K. S. (2025). The rise of artificial intelligence in intellectual property law: Patentability and copyright issues. *Metallurgical and Materials Engineering*. https://www.semanticscholar.org/paper/d82e243ae8a898ae96aa188338d88826e10fe00e (accessed on 9th September 2025).

44. Sari, P., Yanuarto, T., Setyawan, E., & Prakoso, B. (2024). Comparison of legal in granting the rights of restitution to victims of sexual violence. *Pena Justisia: Media Komunikasi dan Kajian Hukum*. https://www.semanticscholar.org/paper/a969c0c570b320c56f47340fe2bf88128589f86f (accessed on 9th September 2025).

45. Shaaban, E., & Denoncourt, J. (2024). Capitalizing trademarks as security: The Canadian trademark finance perspective. *Laws*. https://www.semanticscholar.org/paper/f1a6bbb43be35ea1855e19b72b6722959be8c7e3 (accessed on 9th September 2025).

46. Sikes, R. S. (2016). 2016 guidelines of the American Society of Mammalogists for the use of wild mammals in research and education. *Journal of Mammalogy, 97*, 663–688. https://doi.org/10.1093/jmammal/gyw078 (accessed on 9th September 2025).

47. Stöcker, C., Bennett, R., Nex, F., Gerke, M., & Zevenbergen, J. A. (2017). Review of the current state of UAV regulations. *Remote Sensing, 9*, 459–459. https://doi.org/10.3390/rs9050459 (accessed on 9th September 2025).

48. Syamsir, Nuriyatman, E., Dhyta, N. B., Rahman, R. A., & Sitompul, M. G. (2025). Legal aspects of state asset management: International perspectives on implementing state-owned property law. *Journal of Law and Legal Reform*. https://www.semanticscholar.org/paper/118365090ce021395f0d750dd27611508b379a90 (accessed on 9th September 2025).

49. Takane, T. (2008). Customary land tenure, inheritance rules, and smallholder farmers in Malawi.

Journal of Southern African Studies, 34, 269–291. https://doi.org/10.1080/03057070802037969 (accessed on 9th September 2025).

50. Tikhonova, K. V., Burdova, D. V., Penko, V. V., & Chirva, E. A. (2024). Analysis of the law enforcement practices in regulating the territorial planning and forming the targeted land use criteria. *Economy and Ecology of Territorial Educations*. https://www.semanticscholar.org/paper/6b9fd4b6168e694695dd7117e1ca5b4693cc2e9a (accessed on 9th September 2025).
51. Tjandrawinata, R. R., & Budi, H. S. (2025). Future trends in biotechnology patents: Impact of nano-biomedicine and artificial intelligence on the patent landscape. *Journal of Law, Politic and Humanities*. https://www.semanticscholar.org/paper/88ce466ae9b9910c15971e5eed305d27118539e7 (accessed on 9th September 2025).
52. Vargas Weil, E. (2024). The numerus clausus and the governance of property law: A comparative approach to German, English and American legal reasoning. *European Journal of Comparative Law and Governance*. https://www.semanticscholar.org/paper/6260b17b82895d261d420604674e14af3a2e4c31 (accessed on 9th September 2025).
53. Watt, P., & Minton, A. (2016). London's housing crisis and its activisms. *City, 20*, 204–221. https://doi.org/10.1080/13604813.2016.1151707 (accessed on 9th September 2025).
54. Wyczik, J. (2024). Ownership in the 21st century: Property law of digital assets. *Information & Communications Technology Law, 34*, 187–206. https://www.semanticscholar.org/paper/6d83d609560968f2faea7aba69a44498b468a485 (accessed on 9th September 2025).
55. Yermack, D. (2016). Corporate governance and blockchains. *Review of Finance*. https://doi.org/10.1093/rof/rfw074 (accessed on 9th September 2025).
56. Ziegler, L., Gonzalez, E., Rubert, T., Smolka, U., & Melero, J. J. (2017). Lifetime extension of onshore wind turbines: A review covering Germany, Spain, Denmark, and the UK. *Renewable and Sustainable Energy Reviews, 82*, 1261–1271. https://doi.org/10.1016/j.rser.2017.09.100 (accessed on 9th September 2025).

Chapter
8

TORT LAW IN COMPARATIVE SYSTEMS

Contents

INTRODUCTION

The study of the axioms underlying tort law necessitates a firm understanding of its most fundamental ideas, each one rooted in various judicial understandings from courts globally. The duty of care is the cornerstone of tortious liability and forms the foundation upon which others become liable for their conduct. This maxim obliges individuals to exercise reasonable care so as not to cause harm to others, demarcating the boundaries of decorous conduct in society. In conjunction with the duty of care, breach and attendant causations are essential pillars on which negligence claims are made. Having a specific causative link between the breach and resultant damage is crucial since it not only supports a claim but also demarcates the extent of liability. A nuanced understanding of these factors is thus central to comparative reviews, particularly in addressing the way different legal systems conceptualize and implement tortious liability (Melnikova, 2025).

Imposition of strict and vicarious liability changes the dynamics of tort law because such doctrines address the cases where liability can be imposed even in the absence of negligence. Strict liability, especially found in product liability cases, attributes responsibility to manufacturers for defective products regardless of fault. This model of law prioritizes consumer protection and reaffirms the mandate of safety in commercial transactions, where it creates a drastic departure from conventional paradigms of negligence. Vicarious liability, conversely, clarifies the legal responsibility of employers over the actions of their employees conducted within the framework of their employment. These doctrines constitute the pillars of the argument about the liability of employers, particularly in industries where ventures that pose danger are the norm. From critical analysis of the doctrines comparatively, differences in safeguarding the public interest and administering justice in various systems of law can be seen (Bruna de Alc SMântara, 2025). In privacy tort and defamation law, the opening nuances reflect societys evolving standards of communication and human dignity. Protection of reputation and defamation by false statements are core social issues, especially during a time marked by rapid information spread through virtual media. Laws must discover a delicate balance between freedom of expression and protection of reputation, which leads to a series of statutory and common law remedies. Besides, emerging challenges in data privacy confirm the necessity of nimble tort codes that can evolve with technology, as with society's expectations. Through comparative analysis, such evolutions are demonstrated, and they cast more light on broad principles of personal injury, negligence, and compensatory systems used to reduce the loss incurred. Thus, a thorough introductory study of such complicated aspects of tort law is required to comprehend its intricacy and suitability in contemporary society, guiding the reader through a landscape full of legal significance (Melnikova, 2025).

8.1. GENERAL PRINCIPLES OF TORTIOUS LIABILITY

The tortious liability theory establishes core axioms that are central to the relationship between duty and breach. Central to this theory is the duty of care, which is a core principle that obligates individuals to act so as not to unreasonably harm other persons. This is cardinal jurisprudence in most legal systems since it is what defines standards of behavior in professional and social life. For instance, in both English and Taiwanese tort law, this duty encompasses avoiding foreseeable harm through negligence, with a need for close observation of the environment in both jurisdictions. The differences in the interpretation of this duty can lead to varying results for tort claims, particularly in fields like healthcare or product liability, where levels of safety and trustworthiness are high. Hence, a comprehension of the complexities of duty is essential in the comparison of tortious liability among different legal systems, as witnessed between North and South Korea (Lee, 2022). Breach of the duty of care owed gives rise to issues of causation and liability, which form the bedrock for the majority of tort claims.

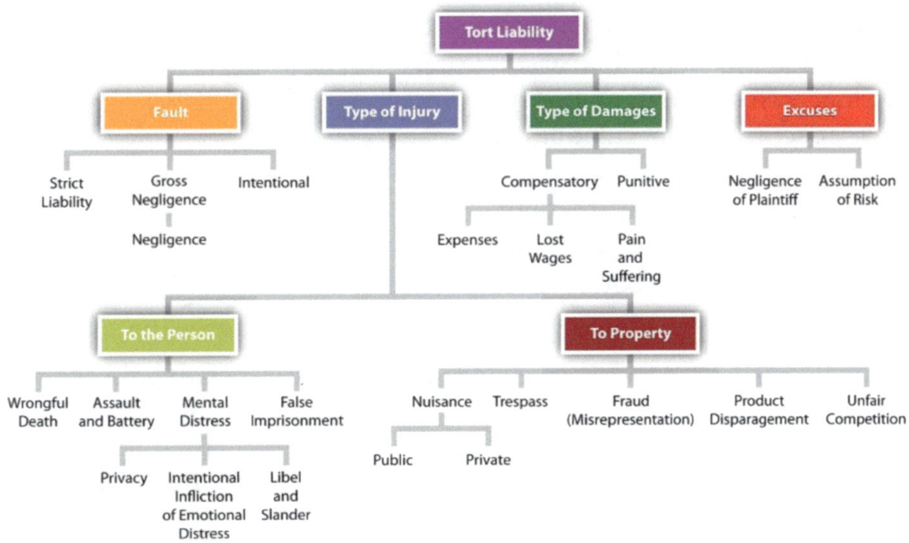

Figure 8.1. Tort liability.

Source: https://saylordotorg.github.io/text_legal-aspects-of-corporate-management-and-finance/section_10/cd8f4e4e35839374b889fff359ac50cd.jpg.

A plaintiff must not only establish that there was a duty owed but also establish the breach of that duty and the causing of immediate injury. This may prove complicated as jurisdictional differences may prevail in terms of the utilization of the 'but for' test or proximate cause and which will determine if the harm is a reasonably foreseeable consequence of the defendant's act. For example, English tort law specifically addresses negligent misstatements and negligent acts inflicting bodily injury, thus plugging gaps in conflicting tortious claims. In Taiwan, the same rules are augmented with others under the Consumer Protection Act and demonstrate a sophisticated handling of product liability (Dennis et al., 2021). It is the capacity to comprehend how causation functions in diverse systems that illuminates the different judicial philosophies behind tortious liability in comparative jurisdictions. Damage determination is the final component of the framework of tortious liability, and it attempts to make the plaintiff whole for the damage inflicted. Legal frameworks normally provide for compensatory damages as means of restoring the party harmed to the position in which they were prior to injury, accounting for tangible and intangible loss. Compensation levels differ considerably among jurisdictions, with variation in approach in each location to restitution and fault. South Korea, for instance, has a law of damages, including wrongful acts, which has an ordered approach reflective of its own legal traditions. Contrarily, the approach in North Korea, guided by ideological bases, is centered on doctrinal differences that impact awarded damages, specifically on culpability. These differences highlight the importance of understanding standard principles of tortious liability to understand the broader implications for tort law in comparative systems better (Lee, 2022) (Figure 8.1).

8.1.1. Duty of Care

Central to the determination that a tortious act occurred, Duty of Care establishes the relationship between the defendant and the victim. Duty of Care charges individuals and organizations to take an action that avoids harm to others that is foreseeable. The components of proving Duty of Care vary across jurisdictions, based mostly on societal, cultural, and legal norms. For example, within the common law tradition, Donoghue v. Stevenson demonstrates the evolution of this principle to set the precedent for contemporary ideas of negligence. It is crucial to see these nuances to comprehend how different judicial systems think about right action and liability. Comparative Duty of Care looks at Duty of Care within comparative legal frameworks and identifies profound differences in the use and interpretation of this principle. In other legal systems, the courts use a more conservative approach, closely adhering to earlier precedents established to define boundaries of care owed. In contrast, other systems show a trend towards liberal interpretations of rules that encompass broader social influences, reflecting current societal ideas of justice and responsibility. As seen in recent rulings such as Leghari v. Federation of Pakistan, incorporating Duty of Care into jurisdictional structures can stretch to new concerns such as climate change, with the judiciary accepting rights-based grounds in environmental negligence.

Figure 8.2. Navigating through the complexities of tort law, the principle of duty of care emerges as a fundamental concept that shapes how societies address negligence and liability.

Source: https://media.licdn.com/dms/image/v2/D4D12AQE1HqNLfabUJQ/article-cover_image-shrink_600_2000/article-cover_image-shrink_600_2000/0/1682962446712?e=2147483647&v=beta&t=3qRolJ-boHeoy8z3PiXOX2qK-HN89OUzA4axXo34i2s.

This evolving context confirms Duty of Care is not an absolute principle but a dynamic one to adapt to societal needs and moral demands, which further influences the manner tort law evolves globally. Secondly, the global implications of Duty of Care also fuel critical discourse around its ethical dimensions, particularly with emerging challenges like artificial intelligence and technology-led change. As AI applications are increasingly being integrated in numerous fields, there are concerns about who should take the blame when technology has injured an individual. The ethical consideration grows as such innovations bring not only utilitarian concerns of liability but also deontological obligations on safeguarding human rights. For instance, ethical debates over the use of AI highlight the establishment of clear, unambiguous standards of care between developers and users to mitigate possible harms pertaining to discrimination and privacy violations (Huang et al., 2022). This conflict between technical innovation and Duty of Care indicates the necessity for perpetual legal reform and ethical vigilance to adapt to the sophistications caused by modern-day societal problems (Peel et al., 2017) (Figure 8.2).

8.1.2. Breach and Causation

The complexity of tortious liability typically hinges on the related issues of breach and causation, which are focal points of the question of responsibility in various legal systems. Breach is a failure by an organization or a person to uphold a duty of care that one has to other individuals, resulting in harm. The failure can follow various paths, ranging from negligent acts to intentional wrongdoing. In tort law, establishing breach necessitates examination of the conducts and standards of care as they apply in the specific contexts.

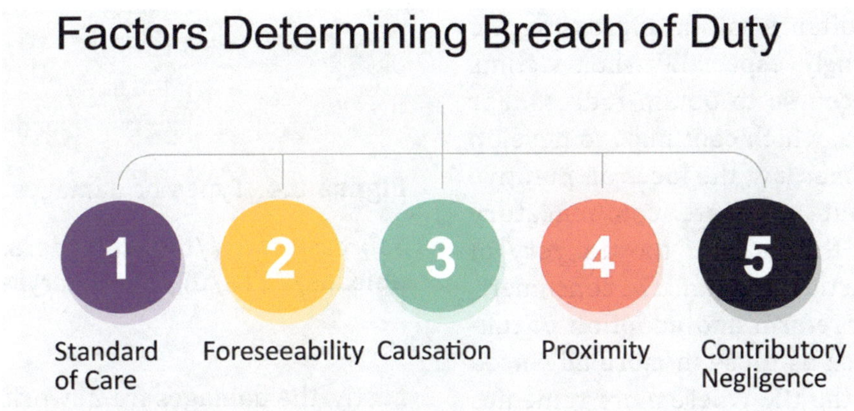

Figure 8.3. Factors determining breach of duty.

Source: https://fastercapital.com/i/Breach-of-duty--When-Duty-is-Breached--Unintentional-Torts-Explained--Factors-Determining-Breach-of-Duty.webp.

Comparative analysis manifests variance between legal systems; for example, in some legal systems, establishing breach could constitute an explicit breach of statutory law, whereas in others it could revolve around concepts of general reasonable conduct, thus manifesting different judicial interpretations and applications of the law of tort. Causation, on the other hand, needs an in-depth analysis of the relationship between the breach of duty and ensuing harm. In determining causation, courts typically utilize two distinct but complementary tests: factual causation, often ascertained through the but for test, and legal causation, which identifies whether the harm was a reasonable result of the breach. The variation between these tests is employed to improve the accountability of parties to tort claims. For instance, under comparative tort systems, varying legal standards of proof of causation may influence the disposition of cases significantly. In addition, jurisdictions may vary on the receptiveness of intervening factors, which would exonerate the initial tortfeasor if intervening factors turn out to be sufficient to rupture the chain of causation. The significance of breach and causation extends beyond legal wording; they play an important role in determining the remedies available to tortious behavior victims. Depending on the jurisdiction, remedies may vary from compensatory damages designed to restore the injured person to the position they occupied prior to the occurrence, or punitive damages meant to deter subsequent wrongful behavior. As reported in consumer protection problems under different systems of torts, regulating frameworks are often weak in addressing the breaches accordingly, especially when victims lack sufficient recourse to obtain redress. For instance, in Ghana, which continues to develop in terms of consumer law, the focus on punitive sanctions without adequate compensatory action identifies the gaps in the delivery of comprehensive justice to victimized consumers, and the need for reform and adoption of full-blown models such as those in more advanced jurisdictions like the UK, where more remedies for consumers have been provided to guarantee redress (Yidana, 2023) (Figure 8.3).

8.1.3. Damages

The grant of damages in tort law is a crucial mechanism in the quest for justice and compensation of victims for their loss. Primarily, damages aim to restore individuals to their pre-tort economic status, encompassing tangible and intangible losses. In comparative laws, the classification of damages varies significantly, mirroring ingrained legal axioms and cultural attitudes. For instance, whereas common law systems put great value on compensatory damages for wages lost and medical expenses, civil law systems also recognize non-economic damages for pain and suffering. This difference betrays a consequential aspect of tort law: balancing plaintiffs' and defendants' interests in the midst of the complexity of financial accountability (Figure 8.4).

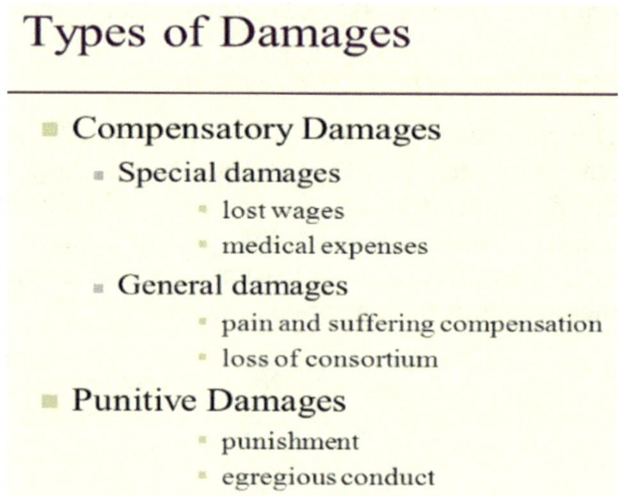

Figure 8.4. Types of damages.

Source: https://blog.ipleaders.in/wp-content/uploads/2018/07/BV-Acharya-12.jpg.

Lastly, the damages framework serves a crucial function of shaping personal responsibility and promoting the common good through appropriate compensation to affected parties. A significant exception in establishing damages is the rule of non-cumul, which prohibits parties from seeking simultaneous claims for tortious and contractual commitments. This principle has the effect of raising questions about the effectiveness and fairness of the system of torts, especially where victims have more to gain from compensation under law of tort than law of contract. In a system such as that in Hungary, where statutory frameworks are geared towards contractual priority, the relevance of this restriction is apparent. The critics argue that such limitations are unnecessary causes of ambiguities and have the potential to deter rightful claims, particularly where plaintiffs are obstructed in proving damages or navigating through complicated legal definitions. As has been elicited in recent analyses, the intersection of contractual and extracontractual claims creates critical questions about the proper method of compensation. Today's controversies around Hungary's Civil Code reforming reflect this underlying tension, as reformers balance the benefits of allowing concurrent claims and their probable impact on access to justice by victims (Ádám Fuglinszky, 2025).

Comparative tort law also considers the protective tools afforded to vulnerable parties, such as workers and victims of accidents, under different legal regimes. For example, the doctrine of vicarious liability shows how tortious damages can reflect various degrees of responsibility placed on employers across jurisdictions. In nations like France, the doctrine of non-option restricts pathways for pursuing damages, with a tendency to concentrate negotiations at contractual rather than extracontractual liability. Alternatively, Brazilian law has a broader approach by accepting vicarious liability even for contractual commitments. The comparative analysis highlights the way in which the policy of each system towards damages is not only to compensate the victim but to vindicate public policy goals, such as the safeguarding of public order and promotion of occupational safety. Such legal distinctions highlight the imperative to individualize damage awards according to society values as well as legislative intentions underlying tort law (Silva, 2025).

8.2. STRICT AND VICARIOUS LIABILITY

Uncovering the niceties of strict and vicarious liability illustrates the sophistication of difference in the application of tort law between varying jurisdictions. Strict liability, so commonly employed in cases involving activities dangerous per se or defective products, differs by a wide margin between systems. Liability in most jurisdictions is founded not on the negligent act of the defendant but on the risk inherent in the activity or product. This rule shields victims who may be harmed by hazardous situations, such as in product liability where producers are held accountable without negligence. Comparative frameworks focus on distinctions, particularly in civil law systems where model legislations are likely to prescribe the boundary and extent of strict liability and thus define how victims seek redress in tort law (Silva, 2025). Conversely, vicarious liability introduces a new dimension into tort law by imposing liability on the employer for the negligence of the employee carried out in the course of work. The doctrine is significant in that it acknowledges employers' control and supervision responsibility over the workplace environment, creating an inherent duty towards third parties (Figure 8.5).

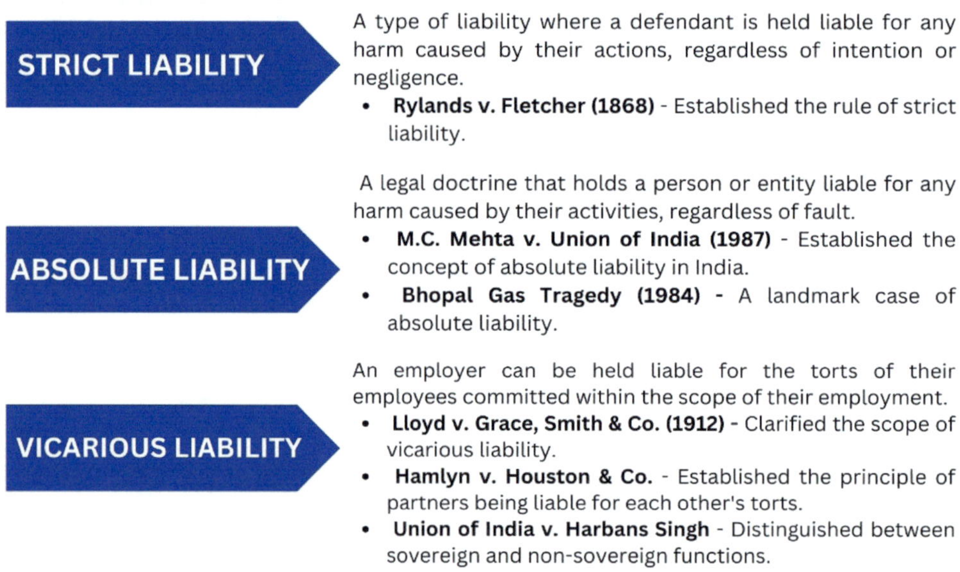

Figure 8.5. Strict and vicarious liability.

Source: https://thelawgist.org/wp-content/uploads/2024/12/Template-for-Mindmap-6.jpg.

Comparative analysis reveals jurisdictional differences in establishing vicarious liability; for instance, French law maintains a limited scope due to the non-option rule, which prioritizes contractual liability over tort claims. In contrast, many common law jurisdictions favor a broader application, reflecting a more victim-centric approach that facilitates claims against employers even in contractual relationships. This substantial difference underscores the importance of contextual legal frameworks in evaluating liability nuances (Silva, 2025). The evolution of tort law in response to emerging challenges, particularly with advancements in technology such as artificial intelligence, necessitates a reevaluation of liability frameworks, including both strict and vicarious liability. Recent studies indicate a growing legal ambiguity in addressing damages caused by AI systems. Existing liability structures may struggle to effectively govern the actions of autonomous machines, leading to calls for regulatory reforms that reflect the changing nature of risks. For example, the examination of civil liability in Saudi Arabia highlights significant gaps, with only 36% of provisions addressing fault-based liability for such systems. As jurisdictions work to refine these frameworks, embracing concepts like vicarious liability in tandem with innovations such as a Three-Tier Liability Framework could enhance accountability and better safeguard public interests across diverse legal systems.

8.2.1. Product Liability

In contemporary legal frameworks, the significance of product liability is underscored by its role in fostering consumer safety and promoting corporate accountability. Various jurisdictions adopt differing approaches to product liability, reflecting distinct cultural values and economic contexts. For instance, in Vietnamese law, product liability is seen through the lens of consumer protection laws, which impose strict liability on producers for defective goods. This regulatory stance aims to streamline the process for consumers seeking redress, alleviating the burden of proof typically associated with negligence claims (Figure 8.6).

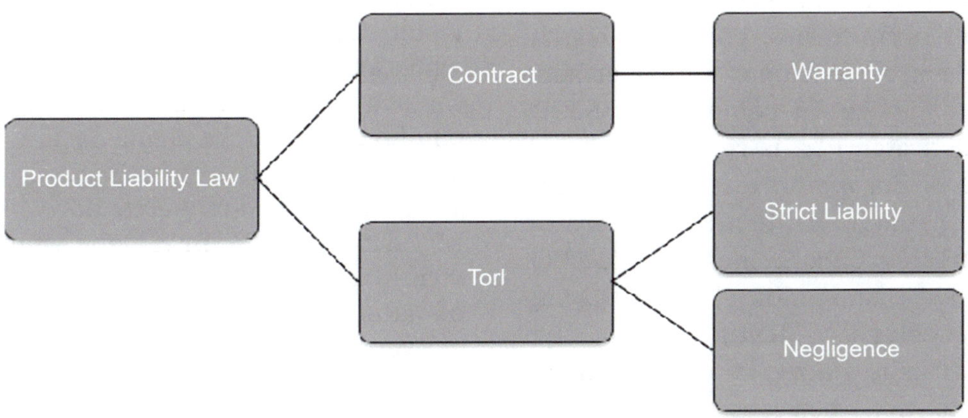

Figure 8.6. Product liability law.

Source: https://www.mondaq.com/images/article_images/974270a.jpg.

Conversely, similar to the system of the United States, other systems merge negligence and strict liability and allow plaintiffs to recover damages in effect, if within a complex legal regime dominated by tort reform initiatives to preclude frivolous litigation. The comparative analysis of product liability, therefore, projects the fine balance between protection of consumer rights and regulating commercial behavior. The varying degrees of liability bring into focus the complex relationship between tort law and consumer protection across jurisdictions. In Indonesia, the legal context is dominated by the Consumer Protection Law that gives priority to producer liability for injury caused by defective products based on Articles 19 and 27. The law gives priority to producers duty to ensure the safety of the products they bring to market in conformity with a stricter standard of care harmonized with international consumer protection principles. Despite this, there are barriers like the challenge consumers face in proving negligence due to a lopsided burden of proof. South Korea, however, has enacted the Product Liability Act (PLA) and thus serves as a model of active consumer protection. In this regard, producers are compelled to pay damages but rewarded with an incentive to enhance product safety and thus corporate responsibility is actively promoted. Further observation shows there are important ramifications for the enforcement of product liability legislation. In comparative perspective between South Korea and Indonesia, legislative structure differences highlight the problems of each system. Indonesia's Consumer Protection Law can ideally act as a foundation for consumer rights; however, its enforcement is often hindered by consumers' inability to deal with the law's complexities. This is indicative of a severe lack of consumer empowerment and access to justice. In comparison, South Korea's sophisticated PLA is representative of the influence of Europe on tort law, whereby extensive consumer protection generates incentives for safety enhancement and liability. A more detailed examination of these varying approaches enables the identification of best practices that can be utilized in order to inform legal reforms to strengthen consumer protection mechanisms in states like Indonesia. By such comparison, evolution of tort law in product liability is found to be marked by a direction towards more effective and just standards of liability that actually address consumer rights and safety.

8.2.2. Employer Duty

The concept of employer responsibility in tort law is an important topic that raises organizations' obligations to their employees and third parties. It is most precisely captured in the law of vicarious responsibility, by virtue of which employers are liable for employees' acts carried out in the course of employment. This doctrine is intended to address not only victim compensation but also the structural need for firms to maintain a healthy workplace. Various systems apply this doctrine differently; for example, the degree of liability imposed on employers can vary widely between jurisdictions. In some states, the requirement for clear-cut guidance setting the boundaries of employer responsibility arises as the law of tort adapts to the development of workplace practice and the expectations of society. This variety of interpretation adds to a general perception of how employer responsibility is defined in comparative systems. Not only must employers produce a safe workplace under the law of torts, but they must also implement policies that actually minimize the hazards for the employees and clients. Breaches of this duty would trigger major liabilities. For instance, when an employee hurts a third party during the course of his or her work obligations, the employer would be liable in law even if the employer himself is not negligently responsible. These features are particularly pertinent in regimes like the Brazilian, where there is vicarious liability against a less strict regime of liability, and thus emphasizing employers active role in risk management. In regimes where non-option principles prevail, employers might be subjected to limitations in claims for tort liability, as the tendency is to decide cases in terms of contractual schemata instead of delictual liability. These differences underscore the subtleties inherent in comparative employer responsibility studies. Public policy on employer liability develops in conformity with overarching trends and expectations within society, as well as in response to reforms in evidence in multiple legal systems. For example, the emerging new civil codes in Central and Eastern Europe introduced varied principles of employer liability, which were generally framed by a comparative methodology targeting the modernization of tort law. Above all, judicial recognition of non-pecuniary damages has made significant progress, as it offers employees and victims more reparation options in the case of workplace-related harm. Simultaneously, discussions around dualistic versus unitary regulations within tort law sciences point to a deeper inquiry into whether civil codes should encompass all civil liability aspects uniformly. Reform in progress signals growing acknowledgment of the worth of employer responsibility, and it is suggested that as tort legislation develops, so also should the frameworks that underpin employer liability in a more advanced jurisprudential setting (Silva, 2025; Baginska, 2025).

8.2.3. Dangerous Activities

In tort law, the categorization of activity as risky is central to determining whether or not there is liability. Risky activities tend to have stricter standards of care due to their nature of riskiness, and thus the issue of liability arises as soon as damage results. For instance, courts of law have a tendency to impose on an individual a duty of care proportionate to the magnitude of the risk inherent in the activity. In comparative schemes, risk liability for dangerous activity may vary significantly; jurisdictions apply different degrees of acceptable risk. Divergence is likely to affect post-injury analysis of breach and causation where the subtlety in evaluating foreseeability and reasonableness of conduct pursued can further complicate the adjudication process. Consequently, awareness of the legal framework supporting perilous endeavors is critical towards understanding overall implications of tort law in legal frameworks. In the discussion of perilous endeavors, a proper emphasis is placed on the use of strict liability. Under tort law, the doctrine holds parties liable for injuries resulting from perilous endeavors despite the absence of negligence or intent. For instance, industries that handle explosives, toxic substances, or handling hazardous wastes may be held strictly liable in the event of accidents. This helps in ensuring that the individuals who engage in highly hazardous activities are compelled to place utmost priority on overall safety practices and hazard minimization. These regimes make clear the extent of responsibility so that high levels of functioning practices are required. Different countries have different uses of this principle, both expressive of national traditions of law as well as cultural approaches to risk and responsibility. Consequently, variations can generate inconsistencies between jurisdictions in compensation for victims, presenting one of the most prominent areas of comparative tort law reform and harmonization. Furthermore, the consequences of engaging in dangerous activities also extend beyond strict liability, encompassing various degrees of employer accountability in the workplace. Employers can be held vicariously liable for employees' behavior where the activities being undertaken by employees pose significant risks to third persons or other employees. This is particularly relevant in high-risk sectors, such as building or manufacturing, where the risk of accidents is extremely greater. Comparative research shows the differences in employer liability approaches among various legal systems, ranging from more punitive towards others that are rehabilitative and preventive in nature. The efficacy of such measures may vary quite extensively; for example, the application of restorative justice may enhance safety mechanisms over time. Lastly, an understanding of the intricacies of tort law in relation to dangerous activities and employer liability is critical in developing equitable legal frameworks safeguarding society and people alike.

8.3. DEFAMATION AND PRIVACY TORTS

In the realm of tort law, the concepts of defamation and privacy torts serve as vital mechanisms for safeguarding individual reputation and personal rights (Figure 8.7).

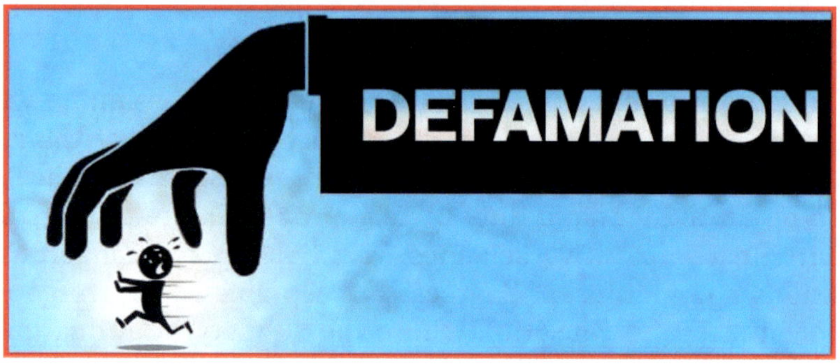

Figure 8.7. Defamation, characterized by false statements that harm an individual's reputation, encompasses both libel (written) and slander (verbal) forms.

Source: https://lawfoyer.in/wp-content/uploads/2021/05/defamation.jpg.

The idea of truth as a defense for defamation elements reveals the complicated connection between freedom of expression and individual rights. While nations such as the United States generally favor free expression, others, including the majority of Europe, are more facilitative in shielding reputational interests. The disparate definitions of what makes a statement harmful and how to establish fault, from negligence to actual malice, reveal various ways that regional approaches balance these competing interests within the law of torts. As outlined in a number of comparative studies, these differences illuminate the multifaceted legal contexts under which defamation cases are conditioned globally. Privacy torts such as intrusions such as abuse of personal information are yet another reflection of the ongoing evolution of tort law. Compared to defamation, which is reputation-oriented, privacy torts deal with someone's private space and integrity of information. Another characteristic of modern times is greater sensitivity towards privacy intrusions enabled by the emergence of digital technology and social media, prompting policymakers worldwide to revisit existing legal frameworks. In legal systems like those of the European Union, stringent data privacy laws center on individual control of personal data, a contrasting approach with other parts of the world with more open policies. This difference underscores the necessity of persistent reform and respect for sociocultural variables that inform privacy law. As the comparative studies indicate, the development of torts of privacy keeps pace with broader social values and technological innovations, pushing the legal systems to develop and guarantee citizens' full protection in the interdependent world today. The overlap of defamation and torts of privacy necessitates a critical examination of tort remedies and the implications of legal reform. Old remedies such as injunctive relief and compensatory damages restore privacy or reputation of the aggrieved party and avoid future abuse. Reforms on the new lines introduced in courts like France and China are a move in the direction of moving away from extensive schemas covering both punitive damages and extended definitional scope of emotional distress based on invasions of privacy and defamation suits. Such changes, as exemplified through recent legislative proposals, underscore the necessity of harmonized approaches to tort remedies responsive to changing social and technological environments. More recognition of the psychtic effect of privacy invasions also increases the need for effective legal remedies in addressing these invasions, as considered in comparative reviews of tort law reforms (Silva, 2025; Chen et al., 2025).

8.3.1. False Statements

In comparative tort law analysis across jurisdictions, the applicability of false statements gains more clear-cut significance in the context of liability and damages. False statements within a commercial setting can cause grave economic loss and, as such, necessitate an arrangement for accountability. There exist jurisprudential differences across the world in handling false statements, evident in the way various legal systems handle tortious liability. In a few of them, statements made in business transactions are subject to rigid standards of examination, while others will have less stringent requirements. The distinction reflects the need for a unified scheme of false statements as an idea of organization in tort law as a basis for imposing liability and demarcating the boundaries of permissible conduct that may involve payment for victims of misrepresentation or fraud. As is exemplified in the corporate responsibility context, namely in the form of false claims to sustainability reports, the scope of tort law may extend beyond particular immediate transactional contexts. The UK case of Vedanta is an example of the argument that companies, on the basis of public statements, can be under a duty to refrain from causing harm related to their operations or those of their subsidiaries. Such falsehoods not only hurt the reputation of a firm but also lead to legal liability under tort law when they cause actual harm. This expectation puts an effective accountability tool upon corporations, demonstrating that good-faith statements can have strong impacts. The discussion of duty and liability in such situations highlights the importance of fostering openness and credibility in corporate communications because their inability to uphold these principles leads to tortious liability. Further, comparative insights highlight the establishment of tort doctrines regarding false statements in securities markets, particularly with respect to market integrity. Since the redefinition of securities fraud laws across jurisdictions, an evident improvement in standards for the detection of differences in disclosures and implications of deceptive statements has been felt. In this regard, it is of particular importance that the amendment to the Peoples Republic of China Securities Law shows efforts at addressing the complexities relating to dates for implementing and making disclosures of such damages based on false statements. This comparative analysis not only shows an ongoing debate between legal writers on the theories of tortious liability but also sheds light on the prevailing shortcoming in regulatory policies. Lastly, understanding these trends is important for building an integrated answer to tort law that can effectively respond to the dangers posed by false assertions, with regulatory practice flexing in response to the changing face of business deals (Yang, 2025; Morgandi, 2024).

8.3.2. Reputation Protection

By examining the intricate dynamics of reputational harm, it is evident that tort law is one of the primary sources in upholding individual and organizational reputation. Reputation must be guarded in that individuals and organizations rely on their public image for social standing, trust, and prosperity. Within this environment, the laws of defamation, as part of tortious liability, serve as a vehicle for relief of false information that can significantly deteriorate reputations. By ensuring individuals can seek legal recourse when their reputation has been unjustly wounded, tort law captures the dynamic interplay between personal dignity and social interaction. The infringement of reputation thus invokes not just legal principles, but also social norms that enforce the value of truthful communication and morality in personal and business interactions. Secondly, the shifting communications environment, most notably with social media and internet sites becoming more influential, also complicates the reputation protection scene further. Here, speed of information diffusion and the volume of coverage can warp the impact of libelous content, causing permanent harm to one's reputation. The rigid application of the law of torts in addressing reputational damage signals commitment towards protecting individuals from suffering such suffocating repercussions. Legislative frameworks in various jurisdictions exhibit contrasting degrees of protection, and this in turn influences how reputations are conceptualized and maintained in such societies. In this sense, the operation of tort law measures hinges importantly on the acknowledgment that harm to one's reputation is not merely a personal complaint but a matter of societal concern that has the potential to affect public confidence as well as economic relationships. The complexity of reputation protection is even better explained when a cross-jurisdictional comparison is undertaken, particularly with respect to how various legal systems integrate reputation within their tortious frameworks. Comparative examination reveals that there are some legal systems, as they are prompted by cultural differences, considering reputational harm with varying degrees of seriousness, consistent with broader societal values regarding honor and personal dignity. For instance, in certain legal jurisdictions, strong protection of defamation ensures a sense of social stability and trust, which can be associated with economic wellness. Reflecting on these diverse approaches, it is evident that favorable protection of reputation is not a question of recourse through the law but is inseparably intertwined with the cultural and institutional mechanisms that regulate and mold public communication. In this regard, the codification of tort law principles is ensuring sophistication in the appreciation of reputation as a critical aspect of economic and social prosperity, concerning the importance of responsible governance in maintaining these standards in democratic institutions (Davidson et al., 2016; Powell et al., 2009).

8.3.3. Data Privacy

As technology develops at a great pace, the intersection of tort law and data privacy has gained increased importance. Problems related to transmission and storage of data raise significant duty of care concerns to be carried out on behalf of the individuals who handle personal data. Businesses need to have robust arrangements for safeguarding user information, but this information can become vulnerable in cases of negligence or intent. This concept has its roots in tort theory of law, under which a person or entity can be made liable if it fails to maintain the level of care, resulting in harm. A case in point is the commonality of data breaches, which reflects failures in guarding user data, an issue that can result in irreparable harm to reputation and cost. Therefore, legal frameworks must find ways to accommodate the nuances of data privacy, balancing an individual's rights and organizational responsibilities in the backdrop of a virtual world. In tort law, the breach of data privacy can be committed in various forms, specifically through defamation and torts of privacy. These principles of law are essential for the privacy of an individual's data from misuse and disclosure (Figure 8.8).

Figure 8.8. Privacy law.

Source: https://cdn.shortpixel.ai/spai/w_977+q_lossy+ret_img+to_auto/juristopedia.com/wp-content/uploads/2024/02/Privacy-Law-data-privacy-what-is-privacy-law-disclosure--scaled.jpeg.

Data privacy violations are being brought under existing tort law more and more frequently, as evidence of societys growing interest in personal rights in a ubiquitous technologies environment is revealed. Proving the causal link between such data privacy violations and resulting harm—either economic damage or emotional distress—is one of the serious problems. Additionally, the proliferation of artificial intelligence technologies makes identification of such tortious behavior all the more urgent. Studies are indicative that AI can potentially be a significant contributor to data privacy programs; however, regulatory structures in place to guide its use diverge profoundly between jurisdictions, complicating compliance with the right standards (Rabby et al., 2025).

Comparative theories of tort law reveal the broad divergence with which jurisdictions address data privacy issues, and they have important implications for international cooperation. In Europe, GDPR has a highly stringent emphasis on safeguarding individual data and mandates stringent compliance demands from organizations handling personal data. Asian jurisdictions, on the other hand, adopt a less stringent approach, modifying legislation like the PIPL in China to encourage technological advancement but with adequate privacy protections. This divergence then emphasizes the importance of harmonizing legal systems, as apparently divergent systems may otherwise inadvertently undermine attempts to cope with international data privacy challenges (Laksito et al., 2025). The specific implications of such regulatory divergences mean not only that frameworks ought to adapt to emerging technologies, but also that they must have the capacity to support collaborative approaches that foster data practice trust as well as robust protection of individual rights within an increasingly interconnected world.

8.4. PERSONAL INJURY AND NEGLIGENCE

The nuances embedded in negligence and personal injury create a fertile ground for legal debate, particularly when comparing tort law. Central to the doctrine of personal injury is the duty of care principle, which holds individuals to act in a manner that safeguards others from injuries. The various conceptions of duty of care in legal systems exhibit significant divergences; for instance, the United States tends to have a broader range than the more restricted conceptions of some civil law systems. These disparities provide the context for disputes regarding negligence, which entails both the breach of this duty as well as the resulting harm. In England and France, precedents in law significantly contribute to negligence interpretation, highlighting the role of case law in shaping tortious liability frameworks in the two systems (Huang et al., 2022) (Figure 8.9).

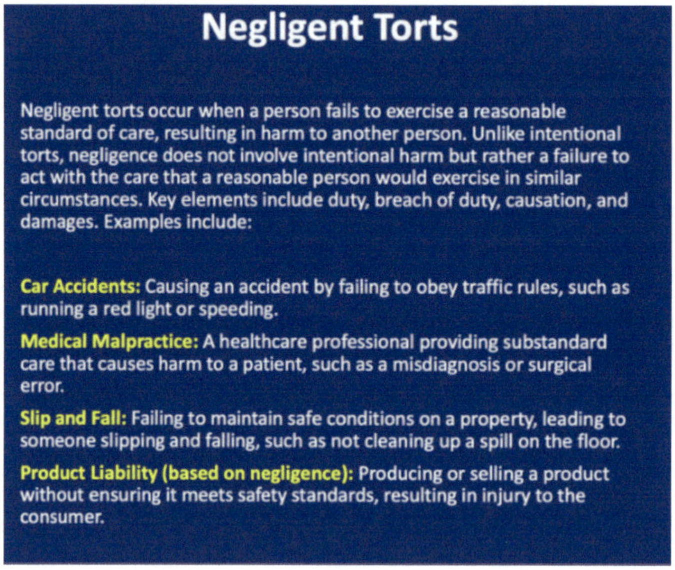

Figure 8.9. Negligent tort.

Source: https://pbs.twimg.com/media/GPlOspvWgAAudNO.jpg:large.

The evolution of medical malpractice as a field of personal injury law captures the intersection of professional capability and legal obligation. Under common law systems, such as those followed in the United States, establishing negligence entails demonstrating that a medical practitioner dropped below the standard of care for the community, resulting in patient harm. In contrast, civil law jurisdictions such as Germany place greater emphasis on codified norms, which can also inform adjudications in cases of medical negligence but do so in a more formalized legal framework. The contrast between these approaches serves to underscore the importance of appreciating the complex interplay between liability and professional ethics across countries. Aside from these differences, there is a similarity of purpose: to grant that the injured parties receive just compensation for their ordeal, illustrating the cross-cultural necessity for the implementation of justice and fairness in claims for personal injury (Huang et al., 2022).

The other most notable characteristic in the case of personal injury and negligence is that of traffic accidents, which are a serious issue in all legal frameworks. In the US, tort law predominantly addresses such accidents under the negligence principle, where fault is decided based on the behavior of the parties driving. Compared to this, countries like France have a hybrid system that includes both fault and strict liability elements, which often leads to different realities in awarding compensation to victims. The impact of regimes of strict liability has profound possibilities to alter the dynamics of recovery so that victims may recover damages even when negligence is not easily proven. In providing illumination on divergent means of responding to traffic accident personal injury claims, comparative analysis of the law of tort has the purpose of pointing to the global relevance of principles of negligence while clearly delineating the dynamic nature of standards of liability in an increasingly mobile world (Bussani et al., 2022).

8.4.1. Medical Malpractice

Duty of care is a fundamental principle in tort law, particularly when it comes to medical malpractice. Medical practitioners, such as doctors, nurses, and workers who work in conjunction with them, owe a statutory duty to exercise a standard of care that would be embraced by a reasonably prudent practitioner in the same situation. Duty of care has its origins in the common expectation that medical professionals will have the trust of their patients with respect to their health. Where this obligation is violated, leading to injury or harm to the patient, the legal principles of breach and causation are invoked. Proving causation requires a definite nexus between the breach of obligation and the resulting injury, which forces the courts to determine whether the claimed negligence was the immediate cause of the patient's negative outcome. This complex interplay is reflective of the complexities in medical malpractice cases, where proving liability demands careful legal and factual examination. Complications ensue when taking into account the varying legal frameworks that govern medical malpractice in various jurisdictions. In others, like the United States, a fault-based system of liability is prevalent, where plaintiffs have to prove negligence through exhaustive evidence. Other nations, however, have established no-fault compensation schemes that seek to simplify the process for those injured by medical errors. In Sweden, for instance, change has entailed a system in which compensation is paid without requiring proof of fault and in which victim support is prioritized over controversial litigation. Comparative systems provide valuable insights into balancing the need for accountability in healthcare with the obligation to deliver accessible remedy for harmed patients due to medical negligence. The varying approaches encourage legal scholars and lawyers to explore the most effective ways of safeguarding patient interests in addition to rectifying root systemic faults. The evolution of sophisticated technologies, such as artificial intelligence (AI), complicates the arena of medical malpractice further. As AI systems become more commonly deployed in healthcare settings, the issue is whether current fault-based models of liability can accommodate the unique challenges of such autonomous systems. Importantly, AIs growing role in diagnosis and treatment functions creates questions about responsibility in instances where errors occur. A comparative analysis reveals that although the fault principle will continue to provide protection to patients by virtue of current legislation, the imposition of the burden of proof is problematic, particularly in jurisdictions with stringent fault requirements. The situation points towards the necessity of legal reforms with regard to these issues in effective terms while keeping patient advocacy at the center of medical liability regulation advancements with regard to emerging technologies such as AI and their implications in health care settings (Dwike et al., 2025; Vasileios, 2024).

8.4.2. Traffic Accidents

The issue of road accidents is a poignant illustration of the complexity in tort law, especially when a comparative approach is taken. With increasing traffic flow as societies grow older, legal provisions for governing road interactions would have to catch up. In particular, Law Number 22 of 2009 on Road Traffic and Transport (UULLAJ) plays an imperative role in addressing illegal actions caused by road accidents. This law prescribes the obligations of drivers and has provisions for damages under Article 1365 of the Civil Code, which establishes the doctrine of tortious liability. The intricacy of traffic accidents not only poses issues of enforcement but also gives rise to pertinent issues on whether existing legal frameworks are sufficient to provide relief to the victims and ensure public safety (Sinaga et al., 2024). Aside from statutory systems, police discretion becomes a critical variable that affects the settlement process of traffic accident cases. Police investigators possess significant authority in determining the course of investigations, and these can, subsequently, impact the determinations that are made in liability evaluations. The extent of latitude provided to law enforcers tends to have the dual impact of ensuring efficiency and enabling fair resolutions that are responsive to public interests. However, inconsistency in discretion utilization may cause variation across cases and thus breach consistency in tort law principles. Systematic examination of policy papers explains the underlying principles for the decision-making of police in such environments, shedding light on the nexus between justice and rule compliance in traffic accident law enforcement (Nurhadinata et al., 2024). Lastly, the intersection of traffic accidents and tort law is a call to ongoing observation and future reform that will better address the needs of affected parties. While legislatures and judicial institutions struggle with the implications of high rates of traffic accidents, refinement in legal principles that oversee duty of care, breach, and causation becomes imperative. Policymakers are better positioned to improve compensatory mechanisms and better outline standards of liability by honing these principles. In addition, the imperative to balance protection of the victim against effective enforcement of road traffic legislation serves to point out the necessity of integrating multidisciplinary tort law doctrines, such as strict and vicarious liability, into legal praxis. With the combined effort including study of legislative systems and police discretion, a more equitable and effective response to road accidents can be attained, ultimately serving justice and public safety (Sinaga et al., 2024).

8.4.3. Professional Negligence

Professional negligence is a severe breach of the duty of care one is obligated to uphold as a professional in certain professions, presenting a quintessential overlap between law and ethics. Professional negligence involves a professional failing to exercise the quality of skill and care a reasonable professional in the same profession would have exercised, resulting in harm being incurred by clients or patients. In the majority of jurisdictions, the standard of care is not uniform and has a propensity to bring about great variations in legal decisions. Comparative examination of tort law regimes reveals that the sophistication of professional negligence has been addressed by multi-layered mechanisms within some professional fields like healthcare and finance. These paradigms emphasize that professionals must navigate the thin line between articulating client interests and upholding regulatory demands because failure to do this can precipitate catastrophic legal and financial repercussions. The evolution of tort law has seen ever more involvement of technological advancements, tainting the traditional models that dominate professional negligence. For instance, the use of artificial intelligence (AI) in the workplace necessitates that practitioners balance technical skills with ethical concerns. As more machine learning models are used, the matter of explainability and accountability arises. Professionals in fields like medicine and banking could be compelled by law to adopt explainable AI systems to minimize potential claims of liability. Consequently, professional duty of care can be stretched from adherence to approved practice to include the ethical use of new technology, refocusing professional responsibility in contemporary practice. It is a sign that professional education must be continuous regarding not just acceptable levels of practice but also the consequences of implementing innovative approaches in professional environments (Hacker et al., 2020). The effects of professional negligence do not only take legal form but have wider societal ramifications that extend to public confidence in different professions. The perception of negligence has the potential to discourage people from accessing basic services, especially in delicate areas like medicine, where high stakes are at play. By drawing on comparative legal studies, it is clear that jurisdictions with stricter standards of liability shape how professionals approach their duties. For instance, the financial implications of professional negligence claims under some systems compel practitioners to be more rigorous in practice, thereby enhancing accountability. Second, the role of tort remedies in addressing these infractions remains significant; remedial damages will mend harm while punitive action is a threat to prevent future negligence. Lastly, an understanding of professional negligence in the context of tort law evokes a long-standing debate about prudent practice, the ethical value of innovation, and the final responsibility of care owed to clients and society (Huang et al., 2022).

8.5. ECONOMIC AND PURE ECONOMIC LOSS

The distinction between economic loss and pure economic loss is of critical significance in tort law, particularly relative to other legal systems. Economic loss generally refers to financial injury that directly correlates with physical injury to a person or property. Pure economic loss results without accompanying physical injury, and in the process, the judicial system tends to face challenges responding to such cases favorably. For instance, the South African law shows nuanced handling of pure economic loss in its delict law, which has been the point of contention regarding whether individuals should be compensated for money losses caused by wrongdoing. In Sri Lanka, the current legal differentiation fails to adequately address pure economic losses, despite their increasing incidence, thus necessitating reform and a greater legal framework capable of better protecting economic rights for individuals subjected to such losses, particularly in a volatile economic climate, as was the case over recent years (Liyanage, 2024) (Figure 8.10).

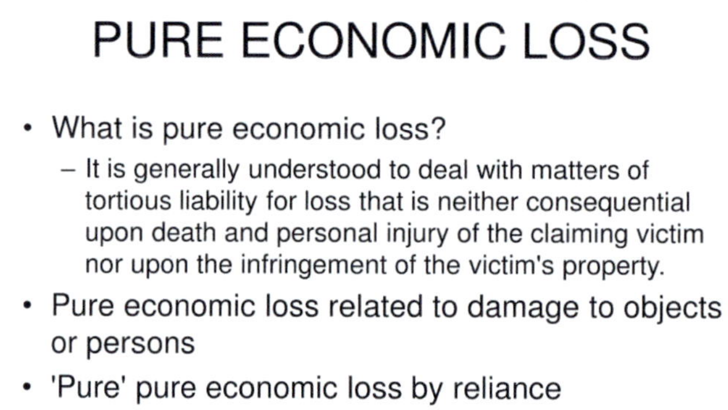

Figure 8.10. Pure economic loss.

Source: https://image1.slideserve.com/3002003/pure-economic-loss-l.jpg.

Economic loss rule of tort laws is a landmark principle, where plaintiffs can never recover pure economic loss damages unless there is physical injury. The rule varies by jurisdiction, with some jurisdictions providing exceptions to ascertain recoverability in specific situations. For example, English law often applies the principle of proximity in establishing a duty of care, which has wider implications regarding the admissibility of claims for pure economic loss. Comparative studies, however, reveal that West Western legal systems draw different interpretations of economic loss, which depend upon the different factors like socio-economic conditions and philosophies of the judiciary affecting legislative policies (Bussani et al., 2003). These inconsistencies underscore the need to engage more forcefully with the economic aspects of tortious conduct and the potential role of tort law in ensuring economic stability within plural societies. The policy implications of pure economic loss further complicate the tort law discourse, particularly in business torts and financial harm. The majority of jurisdictions grapple with trying to balance the protection of economic interests and the fear of unlimited liability that is likely to occur when courts permit pure economic loss claims. For instance, business transaction misrepresentation is likely to bring severe financial loss with no physical harm resulting from it; hence, courts should approach such claims with caution. Moreover, as jurisdictions wade into the complexities of economic loss, discourse on safeguarding economic rights is dynamic. The Sri Lankan legal system, although detailed in most aspects, is not equipped to address the modern-day challenges of pure economic loss claims, hence the need for legislatures to think about possible reforms that would accommodate these matters better (Liyanage, 2024). This could ultimately result in a fairer and effective tort system that can protect individuals' economic rights during an intricate global economy.

8.5.1. Business Torts

This branch of tort law primarily addresses economic-interest wrongs, which tend to cause economic damages rather than harm to the person. Examples include torts such as misrepresentation, fraud, and tortious interference that encompass a wide variety of business disputes where wrongful conduct of one party causes harm to another's economic interests. Here, the objective is to put the party that has been hurt in their position as if the tortious action had not occurred. While making these claims, the principles of duty of care and breach are becoming key maxims. Courts make determinations as to whether a party owed a duty of care to another and, if so, was that duty breached, which has a direct proportionality with the harm incurred in a business case. In tortious liability, vicarious and strict liability are critical in applying to the liability of agents and businesses. Vicarious liability doctrine establishes that employers have liability over the wrongdoings of employees if the acts are carried out in the course of employment. The doctrine encourages a responsible business environment that compels companies to ensure appropriate training, monitoring, and rules to manage risks. With shifting work arrangements—especially the spread of gig economies and distributed work setups—the application of vicarious liability becomes increasingly more complex. Businesses are compelled to rethink their regulatory frameworks to accommodate such fluid connections as well as adhere to changing regulatory demands. Consequently, an understanding of these liabilities assists organizations in safeguarding themselves against future legal disputes as well as highlight the importance of ethical business practices in the corporate world (Shukla, 2023). Emerging from the subject of business torts is the subject of economic loss, and with it comes the significance of determining the various means of harm.

Figure 8.11. Business torts plays a crucial role in navigating the complexities of modern commercial interactions.

Source: https://i.ytimg.com/vi/RbNF9AYACZM/maxresdefault.jpg.

Pure economic loss occurs when a business suffers financial loss without any concomitant physical injury. This results in intricate issues of law concerning the boundaries of recoverable damages. Illustratively, businesses can recover damages for negligent misrepresentation, whereby reliance on inaccurate information leads to financial loss. In addition, the principle of strict liability is now also taking center stage in product liability suits, which presses companies to pay close attention to making their products safe and effective in order to avert potential tort claims. With the growing globalized trade, business tort issues expand as well, necessitating robust legal systems that provide certainty and justice in addressing these intricate issues. Lastly, a thorough understanding of business torts is crucial to navigate the competitive culture while fostering responsibility and trust within commercial transactions (Aldmour, 2025) (Figure 8.11).

8.5.2. Financial Harm

The doctrine of financial harm has emerged as a core concern of contemporary tort law, particularly in relation to economic loss not resulting from physical harm. This aspect of tortious liability underscores the significance of determining damages that are caused exclusively as a result of financial loss, which can assume various forms such as lost profits, lost business opportunities, or loss of investment. As more economies become interwoven with each other and dependent on sensitive financial deals, the consequences of financial damage have become more critical. A comprehension of the subtleties of financial damage is needed for making claims under various jurisdictions, particularly given the different treatments accorded by legal systems to such damages as an expression of society's wider attitudes towards economic responsibility and accountability. Besides, financial harm conditions can be determined by comparative analysis of tort law across states. For instance, whereas some states have powerful provisions for recovering economic damages, others have stringent limitations that may undermine justice to victims. In nations such as Nigeria, economic loss is most applicable to youth delinquency where socio-economic factors are causative of criminality that can have negative impacts on business and society. As the comparative review of Nigerian juvenile delinquency observes, the socioeconomic concerns of young people propel an economic cycle of harm affecting not only specific families but the broader economy as well, illustrating the broader ramifications of tort actions outside of personal harm and into the economic mainstream of society (Osemuyi, 2025). Further, financial injury analysis should include a critical examination of tort relief that aims to provide relief to economic injury victims. While seeking justice in financial injury, the judiciary tends to traverse between compensatory and punitive damages, with the aim of guaranteeing that victims receive just compensation for loss. The disparity in the treatment of financial harm by various legal systems highlights the necessity for reform and harmonization in tort law. Financial harm in product liability and employer liability usually arises due to misrepresentation or negligence. As the law grows, effective remedies must maintain parity with the fundamentals of duty of care, breach, and causation, providing clarity and protection to victims claiming redress in tortious actions for financial harm (Okereke et al., 2025).

8.5.3. Misrepresentation

In law of tort, misrepresentation is a major area that impacts both contractual transactions and commerce. In various legal systems, misrepresentation is the act of providing false information which leads another party into acting to their own detriment. Misrepresentation is a concept that largely impacts the area of liability as well as remedy, which affects the way courts treat claims arising from false or misleading statements. Comparative analysis reveals that the standards and burden of proof in dealing with complaints of misrepresentation vary from negligent statements to outright fraud across nations. Importantly, the implications of misrepresentation are far-reaching in that they affect not just the parties involved but also the stability of the market as well as the market confidence, thus revealing the necessity for crystal-clear regulations and judicial precedents across various jurisdictions. The differentiation of the different types of misrepresentation is of utmost significance in the understanding of remedies under the law of tort. For instance, in the majority of the systems of law, a differentiation is made between innocent, negligent, and fraudulent misrepresentation, with each of these amounting to increasing levels of blameworthiness and attendant liability. Innocent misrepresentation, even though consisting of an involuntary untruth, can make possible rescission of a contract without further penalization. On the other hand, fraudulent misrepresentation exposes the perpetrator to damages since it is based on intent to deceive. This difference demonstrates the philosophical and practical challenges in attempting to locate equitable remedies for injured parties. Thus, the jurisdictions such as that under discussion in the context of tort law have developed complex frameworks to explain such distinctions and the resultant legal consequences, so that justice is served and deterrence is achieved efficaciously. Further, the economic dimension surrounding misrepresentation cannot be exaggerated, particularly in the context of economic loss. The presence of misrepresentation is generally accompanied by monetary damages which are more than mere breaches of contract, encompassing more-generalized concerns of market integrity in which trust is a core issue. In such instances, the economic loss rule takes center stage—whether damages arising due to misrepresentation can be recovered is an extremely subtle legal issue that varies significantly across jurisdictions. For instance, the distinction between direct loss and pure economic loss is significant because it determines the availability of tort remedies. The challenge of uniform application to misrepresentation in the law of tort indicates the need for careful understanding of legal rules and economic repercussions. These observations become extremely relevant in designing an integrated framework that guides parties to fair transactions and, at the same time, supports legal recourse legitimacy in preventing financial losses as a result of misrepresentation (Cheng et al., 2023; Bussani et al., 2003).

8.6. TORT REMEDIES

In the law of tort, a number of remedies are fundamental instruments for correcting and putting right damage caused by wrongful behavior. The most familiar form of relief is compensatory damages, which attempt to put the victim in as good a position as if they had not suffered the injury. By providing compensation for medical expenses, lost wages, and pain and suffering, these damages seek to make whole the injured party. The calculation of damages of this sort can differ considerably from place to place, showing cultural tendencies toward compensation and liability. Punitive damages, meant to punish the defendant and deter their behavior in the future, add a considerable degree of controversy to what is appropriate and effective in a system of torts. Compensatory damages are in line with the concept of restoring individuals to their former position, but punitive damages raise issues regarding the motivations of tort law and the interplay between deterrence and retribution under varied comparative legal systems (Wagner, 2021). The complexities associated with tort remedies persist in the scenario of the discussion of injunctive relief, where the offending party is compelled to cease offensive behavior or adopt measures that rehabilitate order. Injunctions are a crucial remedy not only for personal injury, but also in defamation and invasion of privacy, in which money damages will be an inadequate remedy to compensate for damage to a person's reputation or dignity. Injunctions emphasize the requirement of preventive measures to stop further damage. In some jurisdictions, injunctions are more sought after and utilized than in others, exemplifying how different jurisdictions appreciate immediate remedial action more than financial penalties. The interaction of these remedies with the overall context of tort law illustrates the different approaches employed across different legal systems to deliver justice and accountability (Wagner, 2021). Last, a look at tort remedies reveals a variety of legal philosophies and social values underlying application of these devices. Those regimes that embrace punitive damages as suitable remedy, such as those of the United States, generally grapple with their impact on fair outcomes and predictability in tort adjudication. Although countries that exclude or limit punitive measures, like Italy, favor a different combination of compensatory justice and public accountability, tort law has to keep evolving with globalization and discover a way to balance these disparate approaches and effectively resolve contemporary issues such as corporate liability for human rights violations. An understanding of how such remedies function across jurisdictions can illuminate broader debates about the efficacy and fairness of tort law in comparative regimes (Cappelletti, 2015).

8.6.1. Compensatory Damages

In tort law, the compensatory damages principle is the foundation for procuring justice and providing relief to the injured resulting from the wrongful act of another. The damages are intended to put the injured individual in his pre-tort position, including both tangible harm that includes the cost of medical treatment as well as damage to property and intangible injuries such as suffering and pain. Suitable remuneration is established significantly on the facts of a case, including the severity of the damage and the manner in which the tort was endured. This is a point of orthodoxy in the law of tort that emphasizes the need for definite provisions in law that control the awarding of damages, which varies across jurisdictions. While there are regimes that adopt a more formulaic approach, others accommodate judicial discretion, with implications for variable application of principles of compensation that make the predictability and fairness of the legal process uncertain. The determinants in computing compensatory damages are complex in that they are likely to be entangled with cultural conceptions of justice and moral fault. In comparative legal traditions, the definition of what is considered an actionable loss can be very different. For instance, there are some jurisdictions that are concerned with economic losses and others with non-economic losses such as emotional distress. Moreover, Bordalo et al. (2015) introduces the assumption that salient factors in a case could affect judicial decision-making. This suggests that the emotional meaning of some parts of a case can overly impact what damages are awarded, and the inconsistency of outcomes between comparable cases distorts comparative compensatory awards. These differences make the awards less comparable and represent underlying differences in society's harm and responsibility values. Lastly, the interaction of compensatory damages with judicial psychology reveals the intricate dynamics of tort litigation. As attested by variance in damage awards across jurisdictions, the subjective nature of harm's determination makes it hard to apply universally accepted legal principles. David (2018) highlights the importance of understanding how context will affect judicial outcomes and make it hard to predict compensatory damages in reality. This inconsistency can also set off arguments regarding fairness and equity and lead to calls for reform in the measurement and allocation of damages. Ultimately, the ongoing debate about compensatory damages is central to shaping tort law, challenging legal minds and practitioners alike to examine and refine the doctrines that govern tortious liability in comparative context.

8.6.2. Punitive Damages

In the law of torts, punitive damages are a necessary device used not only to punish bad behavior but also to deter wrongdoing in the future. Where a defendant's behavior is particularly culpable or malicious, garden-variety compensatory damages will at times be insufficient to satisfy society's interest in holding people accountable. It is in these situations then that punitive damages step in, so that simply compensating bad behavior can allow wrongdoers to sidestep accountability for what they have done. A clear demonstration of this axiom at work is the introduction of punitive damages into various jurisdictions, whereby it typically applies to malicious intent or gross negligence only. In placing the wrongdoer with substantial monetary burdens, such provisions in the law place importance on ethical conduct and serve as an incentive for avoiding similar behavior in the future. The imposition of punitive damages, however, varies significantly from jurisdiction to jurisdiction and relates to different worldviews of culture and law. For instance, according to American law, punitive damages can be awarded nearly at whim, particularly in consumer protection and civil rights tort suits, where the goal is as much punishment as restitution. Conversely, in countries like Saudi Arabia, the law is yet to be brought up with the ethical implication of punitive damages, especially on matters of artificial intelligence liabilities. Recent studies have shown that very little of Saudi civil law today provides for punitive action, which significantly means legal loopholes diverting from proactive adaptation to the present risks by autonomous systems (Aldmour, 2025). Such disparities reflect the broader problems faced by different systems of law in achieving a balance between punitive goals and the need for equitable justice. Further complication in punitive damages discussion is facilitated with the evolution of newer legal frameworks, such as China's newly implemented Civil Code reforms. The legislation of punitive damages in cases such as product liability indicates an increasing understanding of the requirement for strict liability provisions according to changing societal needs (Chen et al., 2025). In addressing the increasing demand for accountability with respect to economic harm and emotional distress, such reforms indicate a shift toward the acknowledgment of the broader implications of tortious conduct in the context of Chinese society. This comparison demonstrates a progressive trend in many jurisdictions to restructure punitive damages to accommodate contemporary ethical standards and technological developments. These trends indicate that punitive damages are not mere relics of punitive justice but, rather, an evolutionary component of tort law that must continually adjust to societal needs and technological demands.

8.6.3. Injunctive Relief

The sophistication that comes with tort law is not just about the simple apportioning of liability and awarding damages; it also entails a number of legal remedies, one being injunctive relief. Injunctive relief is a precautionary remedy aimed at preventing harm before it occurs. In contrast to monetary relief, which merely offers reparation to the harmed, injunctive relief operates in advance, hence eliminating issues and preventing future violations. Such remedies are most often sought in instances of ongoing harm or where a right is being jeopardized, reflecting an advanced understanding of how best to protect potential right violation across civil and common law jurisprudence. This preventative approach highlights the intrinsic difference in law philosophies among systems that stress prevention and those that stress rectifying past injustices. The application of injunctive relief varies significantly among jurisdictions, based on the respective connected legal traditions and legislative arrangements. In general common law jurisdictions, the issuance of an injunction is preceded by robust conditions, such as proof of irreparable injury and unavailability of a satisfactory remedy at law. Conversely, civil law jurisdictions are relatively more lenient, in that the courts' discretion can be expressed in wider coverage of injunctive orders. This divergence serves to underscore the degree to which culturally embedded legal norms direct the application of tortious remedies, thereby justifying comparative legal analyses. The comparison of these schemes also serves to underscore the relative strengths and weaknesses of each, as well as to provide an opening to systemic enhancements, most particularly to the harmonization of injunctive provisions to like protective objectives in various jurisdictions. An understanding of injunctive relief also means exploring its intersection with other areas of tort law, particularly in the areas of economic loss and actions in nuisance. For instance, where traditional remedies lag behind in acting in cases of economic torts, injunctive relief can bring speedy relief for dealing with ongoing losses from business conduct or competition. Their use in intellectual property and environmental law similarly illustrates their effectiveness and versatility in restricting harmful conduct from inflicting permanent damage. In contrast to the role of injunctive relief, it is clear that an overall resolution would reinforce protection measures such that judicial systems address modern challenges in tort law, where proactive remedies are more urgently required than reactive solutions.

SUMMARY

The analysis of the law of torts across different legal systems reveals profound similarities and significant differences that guide justice administration. With a study of the concept of duty of care, for example, it is apparent that different jurisdictions may share a common appreciation of the duty to refrain from causing harm but have differing extensive limits defining such obligations. The divergence between civil law and common law systems shows how contextual factors influence the determination of what a breach is. In countries with a well-established tort system, the notions of causation and breach go hand in hand in order to facilitate plaintiffs' ease in claiming their lawsuit. Consequently, the context within which every legal tradition is working is primarily accountable for sculpting the nuances of tortious responsibility, which consequently affects the resultant consequences for parties claiming indemnity for loss incurred in various environments, such as personal injury and economic damage. Refocusing on strict and vicarious liability, wide disparities occur not just between legal cultures but even within a particular legal reforms. The comparative Brazilian and French tort law shows that vicarious liability in France is significantly curtailed by the non-option rule, favoring contractual claims to tortious claims, reducing the scope of employer liability. Brazil, however, is more liberal in its approach towards the definition of vicarious liability and allows redress even in contractual relationships. Such distinctions highlight the dialectics between protecting individuals' rights and institutional interests. Furthermore, such models illustrate the dynamic character of tort law as reform proposals in both countries seek to reconcile principles with realities of the contemporary world. Such flexibility implies that tort law is not insular; it evolves as a response to the needs of society, which in turn influences legislative tactics and judicial interpretation. Finally, the inquiry into tort remedies reveals how various systems treat the compensation of the victim and the broader implications of tortious conduct. In analyzing compensatory damages, punitive damages, and injunctive relief, one gains insight into how different jurisdictions value accountability and deterrence. For example, while compensatory damages are more or less common in all legal systems, the rates for punitive damages typically reflect the cultural view of penalty and compensation. The forecasting value delivered through novel techniques such as artificial neural networks further substantiates the importance of understanding such complexities since they reveal subtle patterns between legal systems despite notable differences in tort definitions and applications. As law of tort evolves and grows, these conclusions reiterate that deep understanding of comparative systems of tort is extremely significant in an effort to ensure effective legal discourse as well as for enhancing safeguarding of individuals' rights throughout the world (Silva, 2025; Joshi et al., 2024).

A LOOK TO THE FUTURE

FUTURE DIRECTIONS IN COMPARATIVE TORT LAW

Legal systems worldwide are increasingly recognizing the nuance of environmental damage, and particularly in response to global concern regarding climate change and its effects on public health. This evolution of tort law is an indicator that the traditional model of liability must respond to new challenges. In countries such as China, the imposition of punitive damages on environmental torts has been a milestone that aligns practice with Anglo-American, providing a serious legal means to counterbalance immense ecological damage. The incorporation of such damages does not merely aim to compensate but even serve as a deterrent against violations in the future. Although the current system in China has tremendous potential, it is still plagued with challenges due to unclear application standards and norms to employ during the assessment of compensation. Overcoming these issues through comparative analysis would render tort law more effective and unambiguous in curbing environmental degradation (An et al., 2024). While populations grapple with long-term implications of history-making public health crises, implications for tort law are profound, particularly in the area of employer responsibility for liability in times of pandemic-caused harm. The case of so-called Long Haulers, or persons suffering ongoing health issues following COVID-19, underlines the need for tort reform that is sensitive to the rights and redress available to such persons. Employers can risk increased liability as employees demand increasingly healthy workplaces that benefit their well-being and safety. Effective corporate governance will likely become an integral part of organizational strategy; corporations which foster employee health by preventing illness may not only decrease their legal risk but also enhance workplace morale and productivity. The evolving dynamics of labor relations under such pressures hold the promise of a potential reconfiguration of how tort law addresses worker health and employer responsibility in the future (Julia et al., 2022).

Future tort systems of law can increasingly draw on lessons from environmental and public health crises, blending settled law with innovative solutions to compensation and liability. The comparative examination of other systems of law can offer useful comparisons regarding best practice and effective implementation for addressing emerging tort issues. For instance, as the punitive damages model gains increasing popularity across different jurisdictions, a more detailed appreciation of its application can facilitate a more equitable and efficient system of justice. Additionally, the increasing intersection between technology and health care necessitates tort law to adapt with the complexity of data privacy and electronic health records, a phenomenon which otherwise indicates society's slow drift towards openness and accountability. Lastly, such directives show a potential change in tort law, wherein both the need for exactness in legal provisions and the need for equitable outcomes for victims in every setting (An et al., 2024; Julia et al., 2022).

REFERENCES

1. Aldmour, R. (2025). Civil liability for damages caused by artificial intelligence in light of Sustainable Development Goals "SDG3, 9 & 16": A legal analysis within the Saudi Civil Transactions System. *Journal of Lifestyle and SDGs Review*. https://www.semanticscholar.org/paper/f5b815ecbb2a28ccbdffcf17baf494254459ea35 (accessed on 9th September 2025).
2. An, R., Zhou, Y., & Zhang, R. (2024). The development, shortcomings and future improvement of punitive damages for environmental torts in China—A reflection and comparative research. *Humanities and Social Sciences Communications, 11*, 1–12. https://www.semanticscholar.org/paper/b51718de10f48fef9d331f1d72f8a681674219c7 (accessed on 9th September 2025).
3. Baginska, E. (2025). Tort law reforms in Central and Eastern European countries. *European Review of Private Law*. https://www.semanticscholar.org/paper/16579ea367ff61b7999e0e918d4c06e3111d655a (accessed on 9th September 2025).
4. Bordalo, P., Gennaioli, N., & Shleifer, A. (2015). Salience theory of judicial decisions. *The Journal of Legal Studies, 44*, S7–S33. https://doi.org/10.1086/676007.
5. Broglio, S. P., Cantu, R. C., Gioia, G. A., Guskiewicz, K. M., Kutcher, J. S., Palm, M., & Valovich McLeod, T. C. (2014). National Athletic Trainers' Association position statement: Management of sport concussion. *Journal of Athletic Training, 49*, 245–265. https://doi.org/10.4085/1062-6050-49.1.07 (accessed on 9th September 2025).
6. Bussani, M., Palmer, V., & Parisi, F. (2003). Liability for pure financial loss in Europe: An economic restatement. *American Journal of Comparative Law, 51*, 113–162. https://www.semanticscholar.org/paper/de62edf776c05d8aa39bffd281245de1617aee70 (accessed on 9th September 2025).
7. Bussani, M., Sebok, A. J., & Infantino, M. (2022). *Common Law and Civil Law Perspectives on Tort Law*. Oxford University Press eBooks. https://doi.org/10.1093/oso/9780195368383.001.0001 (accessed on 9th September 2025).
8. Cappelletti, M. (2015). Punitive damages and the public/private distinction: A comparison between the United States and Italy. *Arizona Journal of International and Comparative Law*. https://www.semanticscholar.org/paper/cfa66b1d8072992640e913c1b2f5b172b6fcb299 (accessed on 9th September 2025).
9. Chen, L., & Wang, J. (2025). The tort law reform under the Chinese Civil Code. *European Review of Private Law*. https://www.semanticscholar.org/paper/3fe13988a7ce63b484da64cf5e853ff0edca829c (accessed on 9th September 2025).
10. Cheng, L., & Choi, W. (2023). Research on the copyright issues of SNS image: The problems involved in remake between Chinese and German. *Asia-Pacific Journal of Convergent Research Interchange*. https://www.semanticscholar.org/paper/3729a563dd7381b7def45af4618903dc66bcdea3 (accessed on 9th September 2025).
11. Davidson, S., De Filippi, P., & Potts, J. (2016). Economics of blockchain. *SSRN Electronic Journal*. https://doi.org/10.2139/ssrn.2744751 (accessed on 9th September 2025).
12. de Alcântara da Silva, B. S. M. (2025). French-Brazilian comparative law: Vicarious liability and tort law reform. *European Review of Private Law*. https://www.semanticscholar.org/paper/4362180b8db9407824a9add3249af74830c37bea (accessed on 9th September 2025).

13. Dorskaya, A. (2024). Evolution of the comparative method in Russian historical and legal research. *Journal of Foreign Legislation and Comparative Law*. https://www.semanticscholar.org/paper/f253030d0b5dcf93201081dd93328482b6184e3d (accessed on 9th September 2025).

14. Dwike, A., Efrila, E., & Prasetyo, B. (2025). Revisiting the legal implications of medical malpractice: A case study in Indonesia. *Ranah Research: Journal of Multidisciplinary Research and Development*. https://www.semanticscholar.org/paper/7d27f30d1c2a8a91c02730e4d14b4212d37840ec (accessed on 9th September 2025).

15. Engel, D. M. (2018). *The Oven Bird's Song: Insiders, Outsiders, And Personal Injuries in An American community*. Cambridge University Press eBooks. https://doi.org/10.1017/9781316979716.002 (accessed on 9th September 2025).

16. Fuglinszky, Á. (2025). Impeachment against non-cumul based on the Hungarian tort law recodification experience and some comparative hints. *European Review of Private Law*. https://www.semanticscholar.org/paper/d508a057df9127258df6ab0604235935dc0a7b34 (accessed on 9th September 2025).

17. Hacker, P., Krestel, R., Grundmann, S., & Naumann, F. (2020). Explainable AI under contract and tort law: Legal incentives and technical challenges. *Artificial Intelligence and Law, 28*, 415–439. https://doi.org/10.1007/s10506-020-09260-6 (accessed on 9th September 2025).

18. Huang, C., Zhang, Z., Mao, B., & Yao, X. (2022). An overview of artificial intelligence ethics. *IEEE Transactions on Artificial Intelligence, 4*, 799–819. https://doi.org/10.1109/tai.2022.3194503 (accessed on 9th September 2025).

19. Islam, M., Talib, M. F., Watto, O. M., Jubeen, S., & Yousaf, A. (2024). Women's rights and gender equality in Islamic and Western legal systems: A comparative analysis between Pakistan, the USA, and Europe. *Current Trends in Law and Society*. https://www.semanticscholar.org/paper/c11c59a6c3048bb2662b822eedf3b3548048208c (accessed on 9th September 2025).

20. Joshi, J. K., & Pandey, A. (2024). Predicting legal systems: An artificial neural network approach with statistical analysis for comparative study of civil law and common law countries. *Journal of Legal Studies, 33*, 22–37. https://www.semanticscholar.org/paper/415be2aae7e5559fcd5f75b2363e355f1a03dbc6 (accessed on 9th September 2025).

21. Khong, D. W. K., & Yeh, W. (2021). Liability from the use of medical artificial intelligence: A comparative study of English and Taiwanese tort laws. *F1000Research*. https://www.semanticscholar.org/paper/29cb9d7bd69fe0c0bb25a0bfb727c1ccfd881b21 (accessed on 9th September 2025).

22. Komissarova, E. G., & Volkov, A. V. (2024). French tort law in the context of national history, legal doctrine and case law. *Вестник Пермского университета. Юридические науки*. https://www.semanticscholar.org/paper/02b1d27b66be34021aeb27c3d33337e93fdc1457 (accessed on 9th September 2025).

23. Kondek, J. (2023). What do we owe to Romans? The Roman shift of the paradigm of thinking about law in the context European legal culture. *Journal of Security and Sustainability Issues*. https://www.semanticscholar.org/paper/dc52844001154e027c5dc279fe38ced300c7c7b1 (accessed on 9th September 2025).

24. Kryzhevskyi. (2025). Problems of the reception of contractual and tort obligations of Roman

law in the statutes of the Grand Duchy of Lithuania. *Uzhhorod National University Herald. Series: Law*. https://www.semanticscholar.org/paper/87715b9ea99e9f5febf1c7bb26b33baad35b6130 (accessed on 9th September 2025).

25. Laksito, J., Pratiwi, B., & Ariani, W. (2025). Harmonizing data privacy frameworks in artificial intelligence: Comparative insights from Asia and Europe. *Perkara: Jurnal Ilmu Hukum dan Politik*. https://www.semanticscholar.org/paper/cf6e9f5720046bbf3764aa91034241a22ec3e1d3 (accessed on 9th September 2025).
26. Lee, J. (2022). A comparative legal analysis of the institutions of non-contractual liability in the two Koreas. *Pravovedenie*. https://www.semanticscholar.org/paper/9cb5e9b3046c763e380c82c702ea9597aa871c5a (accessed on 9th September 2025).
27. Liyanage, U. (2024). The dilemma of pure economic loss: A critical legal analysis. *Sri Lanka Journal of International Law*. https://www.semanticscholar.org/paper/394d24e8e6f2b4d71047be7756d8e7c6d5a422d4 (accessed on 9th September 2025).
28. Maroudas, V. P. (2024). Fault–based liability for medical malpractice in the age of artificial intelligence: A comparative analysis of German and Greek medical liability law in view of the challenges posed by AI systems. *Review of European and Comparative Law*. https://www.semanticscholar.org/paper/c7751e95887be42528907746dc7c777e3b7c5e77 (accessed on 9th September 2025).
29. Melnikova, E. (2025). Principle of responsibility of the controlling person as approach to eliminating the "responsibility gap" for harm caused by AI systems and AI applications. *Moscow Journal of International Law*. https://www.semanticscholar.org/paper/6cde873b47ab01193fb17708446753ac6a2c1bc9 (accessed on 9th September 2025).
30. Mensah, G. B., Nyante, F., Akuffo, E. A., & Addy, A. (2024). Conducting a comparative analysis of medical negligence laws in Ghana's Courts Act 1993 (Act 459) and other African common law countries concerning artificial intelligence systems. *International Journal for Multidisciplinary Research*. https://www.semanticscholar.org/paper/d70beecc8146f4765dbc2402d1b0b4c923459179 (accessed on 9th September 2025).
31. Morgandi, T. (2024). Liability for greenwashing in company sustainability reports: A novel application of the English tort law doctrine of assumption of responsibility. *AJIL Unbound, 118*, 274–278. https://www.semanticscholar.org/paper/9fdb217968690ee187e2ea4dba6c36b9038fe0bd (accessed on 9th September 2025).
32. Nurhadinata, A., Wibowo, C., Harmono, H., & Dimyati, A. (2024). Law enforcement of police discretion to resolve traffic accidents at the investigation level. *Interdisciplinary Journal and Humanity (INJURITY)*. https://www.semanticscholar.org/paper/cf7bc9996f9346bd8963822aa78504ec5ca79ebd (accessed on 9th September 2025).
33. Nyitioseh, N. A. (2024). A comparative analysis of remedies and challenges in the protection of stakeholders' rights: OHADA vs. English corporate law. *Studies in Law and Justice*. https://www.semanticscholar.org/paper/5b4c9325a65909ed519735684a0685509d05a4d7 (accessed on 9th September 2025).
34. Okereke, O. N., Nnawulezi, U., & Adiyatma, S. E. (2025). Comparative analysis of gender discrimination in bail suretyship in Nigeria, Ghana and Kenya: A review of *Ken Nwafor*

v Economic and Financial Crimes Commission (2021). *Turf Law Journal*. https://www.semanticscholar.org/paper/93a8ed8a27502ab0995079254997fc464567b883 (accessed on 9th September 2025).

35. Osemuyi, O. C. (2025). Trends and comparative analysis of juvenile delinquency in Lagos and other states in Nigeria. *International Journal of Research and Innovation in Social Science*. https://www.semanticscholar.org/paper/df5e055819ffd2b84c2649db4ac4d3952df35ea2 (accessed on 9th September 2025).
36. Owen, R., Stilgoe, J., Macnaghten, P., Gorman, M., Fisher, E., & Guston, D. (2013). A framework for responsible innovation. https://doi.org/10.1002/9781118551424.ch2.
37. Parisi, F. (2001). Liability for pure financial loss: Revisiting the economic foundations of a legal doctrine. https://www.semanticscholar.org/paper/014311ee964d60fab2615e85f7993d6501cf1928 (accessed on 9th September 2025).
38. Peel, J., & Osofsky, H. M. (2017). A rights turn in climate change litigation? *Transnational Environmental Law, 7*, 37–67. https://doi.org/10.1017/s2047102517000292 (accessed on 9th September 2025).
39. Powell, E. J., & Staton, J. K. (2009). Domestic judicial institutions and human rights treaty violation. *International Studies Quarterly, 53*, 149–174. https://doi.org/10.1111/j.1468-2478.2008.01527.x (accessed on 9th September 2025).
40. Pribadi, I., Aquera, J., Dhiyaulhaq, M. N. S., Nurismawati, P., & Budi, Y. K. (2024). The tort of the breach of product liability principles: Comparative study between Indonesia and South Korea law. *International Journal of Law and Politics Studies*. https://www.semanticscholar.org/paper/7c9fec3342ced32ffa0bae6019ab8349eda6b74a (accessed on 9th September 2025).
41. Puaschunder, J. M., & Gelter, M. (2022). The law, economics, and governance of Generation COVID-19 long-haul. *Indiana Health Law Review*. https://www.semanticscholar.org/paper/33814c88e502f61e4388bfc4855255703f0170e2 (accessed on 9th September 2025).
42. Rabby, F., Chowdory, M. M. U., Al Mahmud, S. R., Sultana, M. M., Galib, D. A., & Barsha, B. R. (2025). Implications for law, ethics, and practice regarding AI's contribution in strengthening data privacy. *Journal of Computer Science and Information Technology*. https://www.semanticscholar.org/paper/4b8c43d5fe84f179e466bfb78b2a1d2e557a5407 (accessed on 9th September 2025).
43. Seliukov, V. (2025). The essence and content of administrative and legal (organisational and legal) principles of activity in a particular area in Ukraine. *Bulletin of Kharkiv National University of Internal Affairs*. https://www.semanticscholar.org/paper/fad0a1b9149c45591a5e0b3a5b7d1e0ed40e627c (accessed on 9th September 2025).
44. Shukla, P. (2023). Vicarious liability or liability for the acts of others in tort: A comparative perspective. *International Journal for Multidisciplinary Research*. https://www.semanticscholar.org/paper/e93d3440dc2215ab20656a92c31eeb38dd2fff4b (accessed on 9th September 2025).
45. Sinaga, C. D., Sigalingging, D. A., Garini, A., Isma, N. A., & Imran, S. L. E. (2024). Civil tort lawsuit against traffic accident cases. *Problematika Hukum*. https://www.semanticscholar.org/paper/a8716d9ddc4a6fa48e7c5d1baaa8e25413ce29fe (accessed on 9th September 2025).
46. Vashistha, S. (2024). Redefining juvenile justice: A comparative analysis of the United States, England, and India with UNCRC perspectives. *International Journal*

of Criminal, Common and Statutory Law. https://www.semanticscholar.org/paper/dacdd8e2c08d43fa33700d8989f6998a945d4973 (accessed on 9th September 2025).

47. Wagner, G. (2021). Tort law and human rights. *Interdisciplinary Studies in Human Rights*. https://doi.org/10.1007/978-3-030-73835-8_12 (accessed on 9th September 2025).
48. Yang, Z. (2025). The implementation date and disclosure date in China's securities false statements. *Lecture Notes in Education Psychology and Public Media*. https://www.semanticscholar.org/paper/baad33a1c6eb293678f3bac5ecf3f6c80080c4c1 (accessed on 9th September 2025).
49. Yidana, N. (2023). Regulatory remedies in the enforcement of product quality and safety standards in Ghana: A case for reform from a comparative analysis. *Business Law Review*. https://www.semanticscholar.org/paper/b7abe1c7586c47cf3bccdf9139dd26f99cfab82b (accessed on 9th September 2025).

Chapter

9

FAMILY AND PERSONAL STATUS LAW

Contents

INTRODUCTION

The intricacies of family and personal status law are a key part of legal systems everywhere, and an analysis which is historical as well as contemporary. Laws within these fields not only govern the primary connections between individuals—marriage and parentage, for instance—but also reflect broader societal norms and values. And as societies evolve, so too do legal frameworks that strive to accommodate multiple family forms and arrangements. In this multifaceted web of laws, issues of validity requirements, legal legitimacy, and annulment of marriages and civil unions have been a source of significant scholarly interest. Explaining these concepts is crucial, as they set the stage for the subsequent discussion on parental rights, child custody, and related topics in family law. The intricacies of dealing with these legislations roll out their substantial role in facilitating family stability and promoting equitability in relations among individuals. Also, applying family law provisions often overlaps with strongly entrenched culture and religion, potentially complicating legal proceedings. For Israel, controversy surrounding the codification of Islamic family law indicates the tension between customary practices and modern legal standards (Edres, 2025). The 2015 call for a new Muslim family rights law, launched by Palestinian Muslim feminists, speaks to the need for reforms that enhance women's rights in legal frameworks traditionally designed to reproduce patriarchal trends. By unpacking these political and legal narratives in the debates, what is apparent is that the discussion surrounding family law is not just about rights; it is about addressing systemic discrimination and ensuring a legal system that reflects the values of all stakeholders fairly. This is a three-dimensional understanding that must be addressed in order to develop inclusive family law practices that uphold human dignity and enable social justice. Furthermore, procedural challenges with regards to enforcement of family law, such as in the United Arab Emirates jurisdictions, emphasize the need for expert interventions in the law. The use of execution judges exclusively for personal status cases is an exemplary method of innovative management of family disputes in a way that is responsive to family relationships without a compromise on legal standards (Flayyih, 2025). This reform aims to maximize procedural effectiveness, but also raises legitimate concerns about judicial discretion and safeguarding power in sensitive family cases. As family life continues to evolve around the globe, examining legal practices that address the unique challenges posed by personal status law remains increasingly significant. Analyzing such developments can inform best practice and foster a legal culture that not only promotes respect for cultural settings but also safeguards personal rights and family cohesion.

9.1. MARRIAGE AND CIVIL UNIONS

The details of marriage and civil unions are rooted in the underlying legal frameworks that govern family and personal status law. Behind all these frameworks lies a demand of validity, one that prescribes conditions on which a marriage or civil union will be acknowledged by the state. Certain conditions, such as marriageable age, both's consent, and absence of previous marital responsibilities, are essential to legalizing such unions. There is also the need to consider cultural insensitivities and legal variations between jurisdictions that may impact such conditions. In some jurisdictions, for instance, gay couples are still excluded from access to legal sanctioning that heterosexual couples enjoy. These aspects occur together to create a sophisticated structure that calls for prudence when being handled by individuals seeking to legalize their unions under family law (Melnyk, 2023) (Figure 9.1).

Figure 9.1. Photo of marriage law.

Source: https://vajiramandravi.com/current-affairs/wp-content/uploads/2025/04/personal_laws_on_marriage_in_india.jpg.

Legal recognition is another significant aspect of civil unions and marriage that impacts people's rights and duties in the relationship. The distinction between marriage and civil unions typically depends on the legal status conferred upon each kind of union and its attendant benefits. For instance, while civil unions may confer some form of legal protection and social acknowledgment, they may not always be equivalent to conferring the same rights that marriage represents, such as tax advantages, inheritance rights, and social security advantages. This imbalance calls for basic questions of discrimination and fairness in legal treatment of various types of unions. The increasing public discussion of such issues has pushed lawmakers to research and potentially revise the existing legal framework, so that all unions—either by gender composition—are given equal treatment according to law (Woods, 2006). The dissolution regimes of marriage and civil unions provide another fundamental element of family and personal status law. The process of ending a marital union will typically be complex and emotionally taxing, especially in cases involving children. Dissolution in most jurisdictions will typically require judicial declaration, with provision for division of property, alimony, and custody of children. The significance of such mutual assents between the spouses cannot be overstated, particularly in cases involving young children, where amicable solutions take priority for the child's sake. Conversely, misunderstandings also arise where couples cannot come to terms with each other, leading to litigation that can turn out to be time-consuming and costly. Worth mentioning, such challenges are even compounded by external situations, such as social and political climates, that affect the forces of family dissolution and necessitate ongoing discussion and amendment in the legal sphere (Melnyk, 2023).

9.1.1. Validity Requirements for Marriage

In the examination of forms of family in family and personal status law, the validity of the marriage is central to sustaining many legal concerns. Historical legal recognition of marriage requires that there be a man as well as a woman, as provided under marriage codes. This differentiation is not merely ceremonial but also serves to substantiate the sanctity and purposes of marriage, including child bearing and child rearing. To continue to illustrate, Adzanu et al. (2024) posits that any such deviation from this essential criterion, including the creation of gender identity, has severe legal repercussions. These invalidations not only target the individuals involved but also question the legitimacy of legal institutions that have an obligation to control personal status. Legality of marriage has extensive implications in family law and civil rights as shown by registration provisions of marriage. In particular, legality is depreciated for unregistered marriages, which are legitimated as illegitimate by the state. As legally defined in María Rosalina (2020), if marriages are not legally registered, the children born through such unions encounter challenges of legal identity, which are classified under children outside marriage. The classification could have a huge impact on their civil status, eliminating them from inheritance rights as well as social entitlements. Thus, the requirement of marriage registration becomes a central aspect in upholding children's legal rights while demarcating legitimate family relations within the law. In addition, the effects of failure to satisfy the requirements of validity can extend to the socio-economic sphere, touching upon property rights and asset distribution in case of termination. In cases of marriages that are declared null and void, spouses revert to their pre-marital state with regards to properties and assets, as mentioned in Adzanu et al. (2024). This reversal underscores the importance of compliance with the law in guaranteeing equitable property regimes and the rights of individuals. Poor compliance with the validity requirements can trigger disputes regarding the ownership of assets and funds, to be preceded by further litigation—an unintended cascading effect of the lack of adherence to basic legal frameworks. Therefore, the legitimation of the marriage not only offers compliance with legal standards but also reinforces the legal institution consolidating family stability and protection (Figure 9.2).

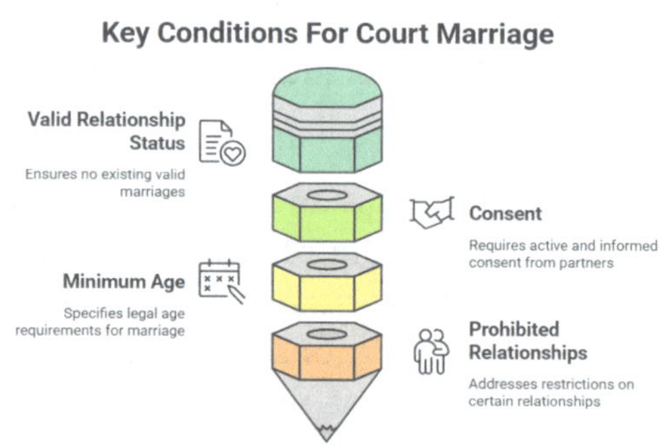

Figure 9.2. Key conditions for court marriage process.

Source: https://yourdoorstep.co/wp-content/uploads/2025/02/Key-Conditions-For-Court-Marriage-visual-selection.png.

9.1.2. Legal Recognition of Civil Unions

Legislative recognition of civil unions marks a turning point in Family and Personal Status Law, with far-reaching implications for the rights and social status of the parties involved. Since societies evolve, there is growing understanding that traditional forms of marriage do not capture varied patterns of relationships, and therefore this necessitates substitute legal form. Civil unions are a method by which couples, primarily same-sex, may gain similar legal rights and protection as married couples, and hence equality, as well as reduce discrimination. Validity for civil unions is generally akin to that of marriages, where the requirements may be such that they have to comply with certain legal criteria, perhaps such as mutual consent and no legally recognized barriers (Margaret et al., 2018). This parallel highlights the fundamental perspective that any relationships, regardless of their form, are entitled to be recognized by law and thus add to a tolerant society (Figure 9.3).

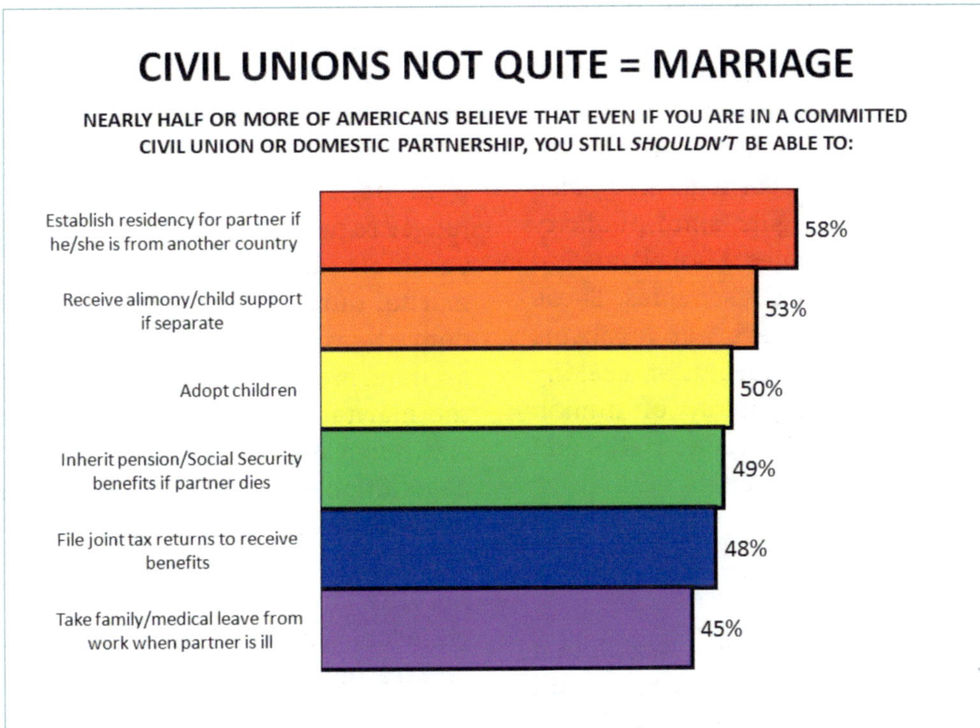

Figure 9.3. Civil unions and marriage are not a match.

Source: VeraQuest Research.

The legality of civil unions also encompasses gigantic equitable models in matters such as parentage rights, property rights, and right to inheritance. With the unions gaining legal status, couples within them are eligible for duties and benefits similar to those encountered in traditional marriages. This legal equality is crucial in protecting children raised within civil unions so that they enjoy equal advantages from the same legal rights and protection as those in married homes. The custodial dynamics of civil unions encapsulate the overall pattern towards expansive law that recognizes non-conventional family structures (Cho et al., 2013). Moreover, the seamless integration of civil unions into existing legal frameworks aims to eliminate intricacies often faced in dissolutions, fostering transparency and fairness in transitions. This recognition encapsulates the law's role to provide space for changing social trends and sustain family integrity. Besides, the social effects of embracing civil unions extend beyond legislative frameworks; they shape cultural stories and public opinion about relationships. As civil unions become more embraced, they compel individuals to redefine what partnership and marriage are, encouraging increased diversity in understanding family forms. This change inspires discussions about the worth of love and commitment over traditional definitions, encouraging a more expansive definition of what constitutes family. Legal legitimacy also generates calls for more rights, since publicity increases and society becomes more attuned to the different lives of civil union couples. These innovations in family law are not legalisms but signs of a slow cultural evolution seeking to encompass a widening array of human experience and therefore secure the rights and identities of all parties involved.

9.1.3. Dissolution Procedures for Marriages and Unions

Browsing through the landscape of dissolution processes of marriages and unions is full of serious legal complexities which vary extensively across jurisdictions. The divorce process typically begins with a court application, where one or both parties seek to bring about termination of the marital union. Residency requirements, grounds for divorce, and whether there are children involved may influence the procedure. In the majority of Western societies, no-fault divorce systems allow couples to end their marriages without allocating blame, which shows a trend towards the recognition of personal choice and individual autonomy. Moreover, dissolution of civil unions can be based on various state-defined criteria, outlining how legislative conditions and common law principles apply. Along with the evolving legal landscape, the intricate dynamic of inter-state laws and judicial interpretations still determines how dissolution is enforced, with a need for a keen sensitivity to distinctive regional statutes (Engin et al., 2017).

Underlying the procedure is the importance of matters pertaining to property division, spousal maintenance, and custody of children in dissolution. Upon the filing of a divorce petition, spouses are required to sort their assets and liabilities through the liquid interface of separate property and community property, with policies governing financial divisions. Judges regularly employ standards to determine equitable distribution, which may consider marital duration, economic contributions, and domestic roles not monetary. Spousal support, as determined by numerous factors such as the marital living standard and financial self-sufficiency upon dissolution, remains a focus for negotiation or judicial determination. Moreover, with children, custody is an essential factor of consideration, with the courts striving to provide arrangements most suited to the children. These factors contribute towards illustrating the magnitude of considerations contained in dissolution cases (Eekelaar et al., 2014). Legal issues are particularly observable in the instance of diverse family structures, such as same-sex marriages and cohabitations, which have gained prominence in a broad spectrum of jurisdictions. Dissolutions of such unions tend to raise new legal issues concerning property rights and parental responsibilities, necessitating an adapted treatment of legal codes that conventionally treated heterosexual relationships. Notably, changing society and norms for family arrangements are themselves being increasingly reflected in legislation, creating pressures for paradigmatic reform to correct errors in existing law. As lawyers and scholars grapple with such ongoing changes, dissolution processes must be analyzed not just on their procedural fairness but also on whether they help advance ideals of equality and justice. Such an evaluation ensures that all families, regardless of make-up, are accorded equality by law, therefore ensuring the integrity of family and personal status law in toto (Engin et al., 2017; Eekelaar et al., 2014).

9.2. PARENTAL RIGHTS AND CHILD CUSTODY

Custody arrangements often arise during divorce or separation, where the courts are tasked with determining the best interests of the child. This process involves evaluating various factors, including the emotional and developmental needs of the child, the ability of each parent to provide a stable environment, and the existing relationship between the child and each parent. Such considerations are not uniform and can differ significantly from jurisdiction to jurisdiction, leading to varying interpretations and outcomes. For example, while some courts may favor joint custody to promote ongoing parental involvement, others may prioritize a primary custodial arrangement that seeks to minimize disruption in the child's life. These standards reflect a delicate balance between ensuring parental autonomy and safeguarding the welfare of the child, a balance that can be increasingly complicated by cultural and societal norms (Asari et al., 2019). Support obligations also play a critical role in defining parental rights, influencing custodial arrangements and the financial responsibilities of each parent.

Figure 9.4. The intricate dynamics of parental rights and child custody are deeply embedded in the broader context of family and personal status law.

Source: https://encrypted-tbn0.gstatic.com/images?q=tbn:ANd9GcSnphTRZ393yS8ySDrRY7eBhg7z78xbadI-iuBxJ9RuLZGDYL4kiAgspHUNRWSpCo9YA-c&usqp=CAU.

Courts typically require non-custodial parents to provide child support, which is intended to cover essential expenses such as food, housing, and education. The specific calculations for child support can vary, often reflecting the income levels of both parents, as well as the child's needs. This financial aspect is paramount, as it underscores the importance of contributing to a child's upbringing, regardless of the living arrangements. Moreover, the enforcement of child support obligations can be contentious, particularly when one parent relocates or changes circumstances that affect their ability to fulfill these obligations. Ongoing communication and legal guidance are often essential in navigating these support obligations, contributing to the resolution of disputes while ensuring that the child's best interests remain at the forefront (Lena-Maria, 2018). In addition to custody standards and support obligations, the complexities surrounding relocation issues present further challenges in the realm of parental rights. When one parent wishes to move, potentially disrupting the established custodial arrangements, courts must carefully evaluate the implications of such relocation on the child's welfare. Parents seeking to relocate must demonstrate that the move serves the child's best interests, often facing scrutiny regarding the motivations behind the relocation. Factors such as job opportunities, family support systems, and educational prospects are frequently weighed against the potential emotional and social impacts on the child. Consequently, legal frameworks surrounding relocation emphasize collaboration and mediation to mitigate conflicts, encouraging parents to reach amicable agreements while adhering to judicial guidelines. This multifaceted approach reflects a growing recognition of the importance of stable environments for children while recognizing parental rights within the context of familial dynamics (Asari et al., 2019) (Figure 9.4).

9.2.1. Standards for Determining Custody

Determination of the custody of a child in the areas of personal and family status law needs to be carefully comprehended through multiple standards for the definition of the best interests of the child. In most cases, the courts weigh numerous factors like the emotional and psychological needs of the child, each parent's capacity to provide a stable environment, and the preference of the child if they are of sufficient age and maturity. This comprehensive procedure ensures that the legal standards do not merely operate on rigid customary norms but rather move to the particular situation in a given case. For instance, parental involvement, educational supply, and overall household environment are paramount areas of control over which the courts look to make informed choices in custody situations, hence attempting to promote family stability and protect the interests of children. In legal cases where jurisdictional conflicts arise, as in the case of the parents residing in different states or countries, standards for resolving custody face greater complexities. The best interests of the child criterion is a dominant foundation not only nationally but also globally in custody cases. As provided in recent studies, this principle gives a higher priority to the child's best interests over conventional legal categorization as nationality and domicile, thus enhancing a more effective reaction to custody orders. In courts faced with anomalies in legislation, for example, between Iraq and Kurdistan Region, the lack of a standard increases the complexity in determining custody and can hinder the achievement of family justice, as cited in Akrem et al. (2025). Close examination of these inconsistencies is a reminder of the necessity of harmonization under the law. Addressing the dynamic nature of custody standards is central because they are prone to blend with other topics of family law, including support responsibilities and relocation. Not only must legal systems create standards for custody decisions, they must make sure that these standards evolve in correlation with changes in society as well as with the diverse needs of families. This adaptability has the capacity to revolutionize judicial decisions, with courts observing how various legal systems approach the matter of custody and the protection of children. Notably, the comparative case example highlighted in research puts emphasis on using the child's best interest as a major driver in resolving conflicts, as is evident from Noria (2025). This unified effort aimed at giving priority to the welfare of children in custody cases eventually fortifies family stability and encourages fair legal outcomes.

9.2.2. Obligations for Child Support

Parental responsibilities rest deeply on the provisions of family and individual status law. Among the most significant elements in this system is the responsibility of child support that takes a paramount role in catering to the well-being of children once the relationships between parents have collapsed. Over the years, various jurisdictions have evolved over time in their understanding of such responsibilities, accommodating changing attitudes in society and economic conditions. In the majority of legal systems, child support is more than a financial transaction; it is a recognition of the permanent legal and moral obligations parents have to their children (Figure 9.5).

Figure 9.5. Factors that influence a court's determination of child support obligations.

Source: https://www.leadindia.law/blog/en/wp-content/uploads/2025/04/What-Factors-Influence-A-Courts-Determination-Of-Child-Support-Obligations.jpg.

This responsibility is basically connected to parental right and custodial order validity, which defines the level of financial support owed by each parent, irrespective of marriage status or relationship dynamic (Luchkovskyi, 2020).

In many instances, child support responsibility is distinguished by legislation between out-of-wedlock and in-wedlock children. This divide, often assumed to be unequal, affects the economic support offered to children and their stability overall. The tendency towards equalizing these support obligations increased in the later 20th century, driven by modifications in cultural attitudes towards non-marital relationships. As such, today's family law increasingly favors policies that reinforce the doctrine that all children, irrespective of the marital status of parents, are due adequate economic support. The development of child support standards in jurisdictions is an effort to address this disparity, such that relevant resources are made available to the child regardless of the configuration of their family (Walker, 2015).

Enforcement of child support often involves navigating a complex legal framework that varies significantly between jurisdictions. Enforcement measures are essential to foster compliance with such obligations, which can be either domestic or international law instruments, particularly where parents are resident in different states. The complexities of enforcement of support across borders have called for the creation of treaties and agreements meant to facilitate the enforcement of orders of support across borders. These frameworks not only make procedures easier but also result in a more streamlined approach to child welfare within family law. Ultimately, the ongoing evolution of child support obligations supports the overall aims of family and personal status law by promoting equal treatment of children as well as reinforcing the need for parental economic responsibility (Luchkovskyi, 2020).

9.2.3. Issues Related to Relocation of Custodial Parents

The relocation of custodial parents tends to raise complex emotional and legal issues more in family law. The decision on whether or not a custodial parent is permitted to relocate tends to rely on an approximated benefit from relocation versus the danger of disrupting a child's stability. Courts are likely to consider the matter through a two-pronged analysis by balancing the custodial parents right to alter his or her residence with the child's best interests. Such assessments may include the effect on the child's relationship with extended family and acquaintances, education, and overall emotional adjustment. These considerations then may render custodial relocation a war-of-the-wrocs case, where the custodial parent may be more likely to prioritize self or professional objectives and the non-custodial parent to focus primarily on not losing regular communication with the child and fostering established family connections.

Also, custodial parent problems of relocation tend to coincide with more generic socio-economic determinants that have a substantial impact on legal solutions. For instance, economic stability is a significant consideration for both parents' ability to manage relocation challenges effectively. If the custodial parent can achieve better employment opportunities in a different state, it can lead to reasoning in favor of relocation due to economy. Nevertheless, if the relocation would place financial burdens on the non-custodial parent, particularly where visitation schedules are involved, such matters would be of great significance to the court. In addition, the emotional effects of family disunity due to relocation can have long-term impacts on the child. The tension between the custodial parents desire and the non-custodial parents' rights is a hallmark of the complexity involved in contemporary family law cases, and they must often be skillfully navigated legally in order to reach fair outcomes. In analyzing custodial relocation, the legal community is also required to consider the possible ramifications of cultural and societal expectations that shape family life. Cultural values can be a significant force for a custodial parent's move decision, particularly if they seek to return to a community of relatives or support networks that offer cultural continuity. For African American custodial families, as discussed in the context literature, the intragenerational involvement from grandparents or extended family can be most significant, making relocation decisions more complex. Family and Personal Status Law will therefore need to take such underlying cultural forces into account when evaluating relocation requests, so that physical proximity to parents is not the sole criterion in the child's best interests, but also emotional bonding with a broader extended family. The alignment of family law with social realities and cultural forces remains an integral aspect of facilitating good child development amidst custodial relocation disputes.

9.3. ADOPTION AND GUARDIANSHIP

Adoption procedures encompass a complex array of legal requirements designed to secure the best interests of the child involved. These procedures often include assessments of prospective adoptive parents, background checks, and home studies, all aimed at ensuring a nurturing environment for the child. The ethical foundation of adoption is underscored by the principles of permanency and stability, as highlighted in recent literature, which emphasizes the importance of considering the child's needs and rights in legal frameworks. The nexus between these legal protocols and societal values is crucial in fostering a sense of belonging and security for adopted children, affirming the necessity of a comprehensive approach to family law that prioritizes the welfare of minors. Guardianship, distinct yet interconnected with adoption, presents a unique set of roles and responsibilities that are essential to the protection of vulnerable individuals, particularly children.

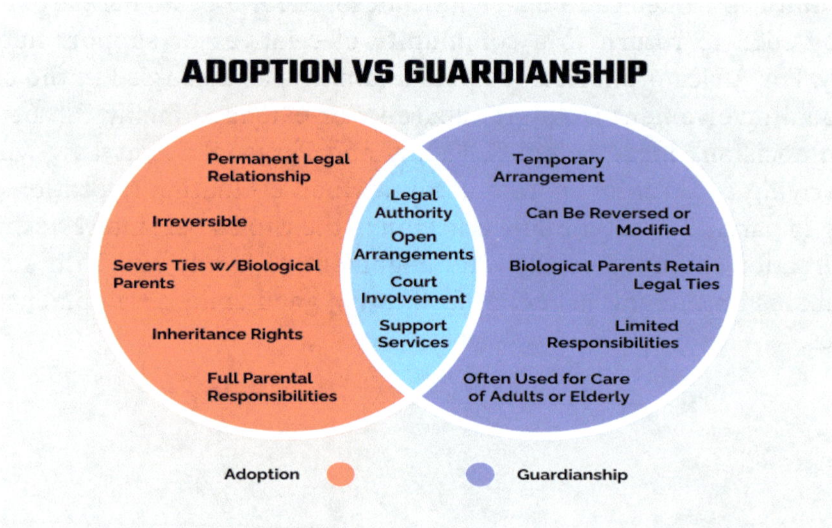

Figure 9.6. The intricate landscape of adoption and guardianship plays a pivotal role in Family and Personal Status Law, reflecting the societal commitment to ensuring the protection and welfare of children.

Source: https://inlawwetrust.com/wp-content/uploads/2024/04/Adoption-vs-Guardianship-Venn-Diagram-1.png.

Legal guardians assume a critical position within the family law spectrum, where they are entrusted with the care and upbringing of a child, albeit without the formal severance of parental rights. This arrangement provides an alternative for those unable to adopt, allowing for family structures to adapt to varying circumstances while ensuring that childrens needs are met. The implications of guardianship extend beyond immediate care, significantly impacting the child's development and stability, especially in cases where biological parents are unable to fulfill their roles (Walter et al., 2020). Thus, the guardianship framework serves not only as a legal mechanism but also as a vital support system within contemporary family dynamics. The evolving discourse surrounding adoption and guardianship increasingly emphasizes the necessity of aligning these practices with ethical standards and international conventions. As societal understanding of issues related to childrens rights and welfare advances, so too must the legal frameworks governing these domains. The call for adherence to ethical guidelines in adoption is particularly pressing, whereby officials and practitioners are urged to incorporate the principles of self-determination and respect for cultural identities into their practices (Walter et al., 2020). This holistic approach seeks to safeguard children from adverse experiences while promoting positive developmental trajectories post-adoption. Consequently, both adoption and guardianship must operate within a rights-based framework, ensuring that legislative responses reflect the complexities of familial relationships and the paramount importance of childrens best interests in all legal considerations (Figure 9.6).

9.3.1. Procedures for Legal Adoption

In the complex setting of family law, the procedure for legal adoption plays a significant role in establishing family bonds that endure longer than biological bonds. Legal adoption involves several steps that protect the child and follow established legal standards. The initial step involves adoptive parents-to-be undergoing a home study, which examines their home setting, economic status, and psychological readiness to be parents. This comprehensive assessment not only ensures the health of the child but also serves as a preventive measure to prevent inappropriate placement. Following the home study, prospective adopters are also asked to sign a series of legal documents, including an adoption application and biological parent consent forms if required. Thus, the comprehensiveness of these first steps underscores the importance of providing a safe environment for the adopted child, reflecting the values of family law in guaranteeing child well-being and stability. Upon completion of the initial assessment, the court becomes pivotal in the adoption process. After the home study is done and necessary papers are filed, a hearing is scheduled in which judges consider each case's unique situation. In this judicial procedure, the court assesses the adoptive parents' suitability and considers whether the adoption would be beneficial for the child, following the doctrine of paramountcy of children's rights. Hearings may involve testimonies from social workers, biological parents, and interested parties, emphasizing the participatory nature of the procedure. After approval, the court issues an adoption decree, formally legitimizing the relationship between the adoptive parents and child. This court oversight function is the secret to guaranteeing the integrity of the adoption process, safeguarding the observance of all norms of law, and safeguarding the welfare interests of vulnerable children in family law practice. Once an adoption becomes finalized according to law, various areas of life are considerably transformed, with far-reaching consequences for all parties involved. The adopted child also gains new family rights and duties, such as inheritance rights similar to biological children, thereby establishing them as a part of the family. Adoptive parents, too, gain full parental rights, which allow them to take important decisions regarding the child's upbringing, education, and healthcare. Such widespread integration into the family is an excellent illustration of legal recognition of the emotional bonds that are created through adoption, which is sometimes undercut by social perceptions of family relationships. Furthermore, the basis in legal procedures guarantees the resilience and stability of family settings of adoptions, thus optimizing emotional as well as social security for adoptive families. Lastly, the procedural framework that governs legal adoption provides a robust foundation for enduring family ties, expressive of the elementary principles of family and personal status law.

9.3.2. Role of Guardians and Responsibilities

The intricacies of guardianship illuminate an underlying aspect of Family and Personal Status Law, particularly with regard to protection and welfare of the incapable who cannot properly speak for themselves. Guardianship involves a wide array of responsibilities that extend well beyond custodial care, necessitating a devotion to the general welfare of the ward. Guardians are responsible for making significant decisions affecting their wards' day-to-day lives and future, ranging from healthcare to education and emotional support. Such a role calls upon guardians not only to negotiate with legal systems but also with interpersonal conflicts inherent in the care of vulnerable individuals, which puts into the limelight the ethical dimensions inherent in guardianship roles. Thus, the obligations of guardians assume a central position in protecting the interests and rights of the wards they represent within the jurisdiction of Family Law. Moreover, the regulation of guardianship varies throughout the globe as per the cultural ethos and social standards. Guardianship legislation in some jurisdictions is underpinned by a rights-based model, focused on the autonomy of persons, as seen in some legislative amendments (Zhao et al., 2014). These systems focus on the least restrictive alternatives, enabling people to the extent possible while ensuring guardians act in the best interest of the person. In contrast, traditional models leave great power in the control of guardians, thus limiting the ward's autonomy and freedom. This dual aspect of guardianship—teetering between authority and autonomy—is suggestive of tensions that face guardians in executing their mandate. As such, the dynamic nature of guardianship law calls for regular review so as to conform to human rights principles and protect personal dignity. Lastly, accountability lies at the core of the roles and responsibilities of guardians, particularly as legal and moral requirements surrounding guardianship escalate. Guardians are not only responsible for their immediate decisions but also for the long-term consequences of their decisions in their wards life. That not only encompasses their behavior but also an overall duty to advocate for appropriate resources and services that result in well-being and growth. For instance, the legal obligation to offer vital medical care represents both the ethical obligation and legal requirement that guardians have to uphold (Courson et al., 2014). The stakes are particularly high when looking at decisions relating to mental health intervention or treatment, in which good guardianship can profoundly shape the quality of life of those under guardianship. Therefore, existing frameworks in Family and Personal Status Law must provide for strict supervision and backstopping procedures, allowing guardians to carry out their dual roles as protectors and advocates without compromising the rights and freedom of whom they protect.

9.3.3. Legal Implications of Adoption and Guardianship

The intersection of adoption, guardianship, and legal penalties is critical in family and personal status law. Adoption is a serious legal procedure whereby parental responsibilities and entitlements are bestowed upon an individual or couple over a child who is not biologically theirs. It is governed by stringent legal procedures aimed at ensuring the best interests of the child, with an emphasis on permanence and stability in residency. As grounded, the child adoption entails an obligation to secure their highest interests under international conventions and national legislations favoring childrens rights (Jesús Palacios et al., 2019). Therefore, these procedures not only grant legal transmission of parents' rights but also confer critical obligations on adoptive parents, highlighting further the necessity for uncompromising adherence to standards of ethics as presented by child welfare policy. In addition to it, guardianship is another but related term in family law, specifically meant for care and control of individuals who are unable to make decisions for themselves, typically due to minority or incapability. The legal aspects of guardianship can be intricate, such as determining the fitness of the guardians and the rights of the wards in their protection. Guardianship can be temporary or permanent and can also include varying degrees of control and authority over personal and financial matters. Legally, guardianship is governed by stringent criteria to prevent abuse and to safeguard the rights of the concerned parties (Arstein-Kerslake et al., 2015). Each decision in matters of guardianship must walk a very fine line between providing sufficient protection without trespassing on the ward's independence, thus underscoring the delicacy and intricacies in such legal arrangements. The intersection of guardianship and adoption reveals other facets of legal intricacies, particularly where adopted people can later in life require guardianship. Practitioners in the field must examine how previous legal regimes intersect, specifically when the need for guardianship involves at-risk populations like people with disabilities or mental illness. The two-way examination requires a complete knowledge of both the interaction of the regimes and the rights children are granted or denied within them. Disposition of a child can have a huge impact on future guardianship orders, meaning these topics are integrally related. Essentially, navigating such intricate legal implications entails a detailed legal and ethical assessment to ensure that the universal goal of protecting and promoting the best interests of the individual is continually achieved.

9.4. SUCCESSION AND INHERITANCE

The intricate processes of inheritance and succession have far-reaching impacts on family life as well as the legal rights of individuals in a family environment. Understanding such processes is important in handling family legacies as it has direct bearings on the distribution of property upon death. In testate succession, people have control over the distribution of their property through court documents such as wills, which are personal preferences and typically family-oriented. Conversely, intestate succession happens when someone dies without a valid will, and their property is distributed according to statutory principles. These principles exhibit varying levels of cultural sensitivity, namely in gender and family ties, which ultimately impact survivors' lives. The intersection of private intent and public necessity in testate and intestate situations is a manifestation of the function of succession laws in ensuring family unity and enforcing fair distribution of wealth.

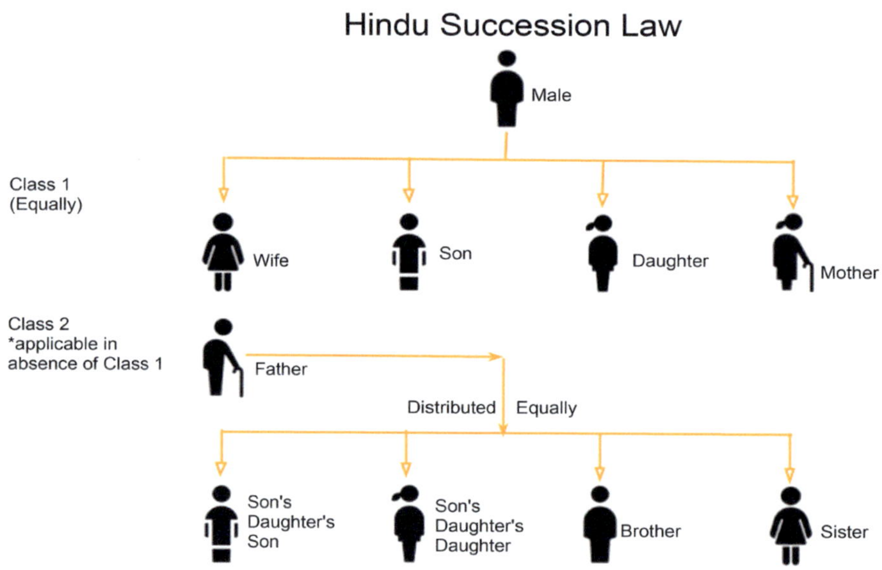

Figure 9.7. Succession and inheritance in Hindu law.

Source: https://ladderuptrustee.com/img/laws/Hindu-Male.png.

In addition, the principle of forced heirship also has major connotations in the law of inheritance under the law, generally demonstrating the pull between personal freedom and societal protection of familial interests. Forced heirship laws oblige certain heirs, typically descendants, to be granted a stated share of the estate irrespective of the testator's will. This provision is aimed at ensuring the economic security of close relatives and reflects universal cultural sentiments of family obligation and support. In those societies where forced heirship is practiced, its impact on rights in property can be appreciable, limiting the freedom of a person to dispose of their property in whatever manner they desire. Thus, their use results in important debate concerning the relationship between individual autonomy and social expectations, illustrating the intricacies involved in family and personal status law in resolving the sensitive issue of inheritance. In examining the relationship between gender and inheritance rights, one finds a dramatic improvement in legal systems over time. Historically, women outside formal wedlock had struggled to inherit, tied by social custom and legal philosophy in support of male successors. However, modern reforms, impelled by changing ideas about gender and equity, have made a decision to redress these disparities, promoting womens rights to inherit as in various cultural environments. As an example, transitions to greater political representation in conflict-affected countries have been linked to reconfigurations of womens rights law and thus enhanced legal status in succession and inheritance issues (Tripp, 2015). These phenomena represent an overall trend towards understanding gender equality as an issue within the ambit of family and personal status law, demonstrating how social change is able to rework inheritance norms and practices (Perry, 2013) (Figure 9.7).

9.4.1. Testate Succession and Wills

A key aspect of the law of family and personal status law is the domination and understanding of testate succession in the form of wills. In taking part in producing a will, one is exercising his or her right to decide post-mortem ownership of their wealth, thus ensuring a method by which personal desire and family equity may be achieved. Wills not only identify heirs but also provide specific bequests, pay debts, and satisfy obligations, including potential tax liabilities. Marriages, partnerships, and other familial relationships also figure prominently in the conceptualization and management of wills, as well as determining the enforceability of the documents and the rights of the parties. Thus, the will rules need to consider various social norms and individual circumstances to make them best reflect the testators' intentions without violating legal formalities of the jurisdiction. Validity in law of a will normally hinges on adherence to formalities which vary from jurisdiction to jurisdiction. Formalities generally include the ability of the testators to sign a will, the intention of distributing property, and accurate signing of the document. Shattering these formalities may create controversies or issues upon the death of the testators, bringing tension between potential inheritors and necessitating expensive and time-consuming suits. Furthermore, as is the case with so many legal situations, interpenetration of formal law and cultural customs can complicate the definition of testate succession. For instance, as quoted by Hassan et al. (2020), different accounts of systems of wealth dispersion can significantly affect enforcing wills, particularly in societies with specific notions of inheritance and property rights. Thus, the question of clarity and legal compliance is most fundamental in ensuring the protection of the testators' wishes. Also of greatest significance in testate succession vocabulary is that of forced heirship, whose objective is to protect the interests of specific members of the family, typically limiting individuals in completely disinheriting close family members. This doctrinal framework emphasizes the dynamic tension between family obligation and individual freedom, creating a paradigm in which wills must be written. The extent of forced heirship extends beyond its capacity to preserve family relationships; it also embodies broader societal expectations towards inheritance and the sharing of wealth, as seen in Elinder et al. (2018). Consequently, while testate succession can be conceptualized as an expression of individual choice, it is situated within a context of legal necessity and social convention. Understanding these factors underlies preparing wills that express personal wishes while honoring family entitlements and regulatory mandates.

9.4.2. Rules Governing Intestate Succession

Navigating the complexities of intestate succession includes acknowledging the unavoidable rules distributing a person's property in the event of their death without a valid will. These rules are the foundation for family and personal status law, reflecting societal values and granting equal distribution to potential heirs. Typically, the sequencing of inheritance is hierarchical: the immediate family such as spouses and children are prioritized first, followed by the extended relatives in the absence of direct descendants. This is an orderly attempt at preventing conflicts and honoring the decedents presumed desires on their properties. In the absence of a will, distribution becomes difficult and tends to cause conflict among the family members who may have different ideas about rightful claims. Hence, the law of intestate succession is thus a primary instrument in maintaining family harmony and providing orderly estate distribution, particularly within families that are under emotional turmoil. The complexity of intestate rules also illustrates the balance family and personal status law aims to achieve between autonomy and social norm. For instance, legal systems usually possess rules of forced heirship that ensure the delivery of minimum shares in the estate by certain relatives regardless of subjective decisions during the decedents' lifetime. This aspect reflects the legal system's recognition of family responsibilities and societal values regarding support and care within family structures. Such laws can be particularly strong in societies where social organization is decided by family relationships, and stability and care are ensured after the passing of a family member. In addition, the lack of a will can reveal existing problems in the family, and therefore the significance of the legal system even greater to maintain order during potentially unstable times. Besides, the law of intestate succession also alludes to broader socio-cultural trends, for example, the recognition of different forms of family in modern societies. In evolving societies, intestate succession laws must adapt to accommodate multifarious family arrangements, for example, cohabitation, blended families, and non-traditional relationships. These evolving legal standards attempt to reflect new realities without compromising on clarity in property division. This diversity enhances the call for holistic legal frameworks that can accommodate diversifying needs and expectations of varied family structures. In most situations, such revisions are called for in acknowledging rights of entities that cannot be defined in conventional terms as witnessed in recent reviews in reference to various community rights that promote womens positions within legal frameworks (Solomon, 2018; N/A, 2017). These advances represent a significant step toward the pursuit of equitable laws that are relevant to the everyday needs of modern families.

9.4.3. Concepts of Forced Heirship

In analyzing the personal and family status law dynamics, and in particular for purposes of inheritance, the topic of forced heirship emerges as being an extremely significant legal principle. Forced heirship mandates the inheritance by stated heirs, usually close relatives such as children and sometimes spouses, of a statutorily defined portion of a deceased's estate over the dead person's objection. This is a rule intended to protect the financial rights of the immediate family and an articulation of social norms concerning familial responsibility and provision. Compulsory heirship enforcement can be a source of conflict between someone's right to decide how to distribute their property and legal expectations in the interest of family provisions, being an involved balance between personal freedom and group-oriented cultural entitlements to inheritance. The effects of forced heirship are especially poignant in those jurisdictions that are strongly influenced by tradition. For instance, in some societies, the changing jurisprudential context for gender and inheritance rights has seen courts struggle with cases in which traditional practice will clash with contemporary notions of equality and justice. This convergence often requires careful judicial examination, as has been the case with the cases under review in accordance with international legal standards such as the ILO-169 and UNDRIP, which sometimes emphasize cultural rights at the cost of individual rights. Forced heirship can thus be both a symbol of collective family obligation and at the same time a source of conflict whenever personal desires concerning estate management come into conflict with existing legal norms (Rodrigo Céspedes, 2024). Besides, as society evolves, the rigidity of forced heirship laws is questioned and urged to be reformed. They argue that they be adapted to accommodate flexible family structures and arrangements to which contemporary life adapts, such as blended families and non-traditional roles in a household. These reforms may include provisions for equitable distribution and recognition of non-biological relations that impart familial support. In addition, arguments surrounding the reduction of rigidity in forced heirships may be even more general debates over gender equality since the practice of inheritance continues to increasingly cross into issues of social justice and fairness in other legal frameworks. As these debates evolve, players will need to balance the requirement to preserve the protective function of forced heirship with an acknowledgment of the importance of individual autonomy in family and estate matters (Adeola et al., 2023).

9.5. GENDER AND MARITAL PROPERTY REGIMES

In a study of complicated marriage property regimes, one will discover that these types of systems are inextricably linked to gender roles and economic agency within marriages. Classifying the property as community or separate property has a powerful effect on the financial autonomy of the spouses, particularly in situations where the marriage breaks down. In the majority of jurisdictions, the laws of community property ensure equitable distribution of assets that have been acquired during marriage to protect both the spouses' interests. The laws may knowingly or unknowingly reinforce patriarchal gender roles, wherein womens economic contributions are downgraded, so that economic disparities following divorce are reinforced. A closer look at the impact of unilateral divorce laws on savings and employment also lends support to this observation, revealing that an assumption of equal property division does not necessarily equate to equivalent money spent by both genders (Voena, 2015).

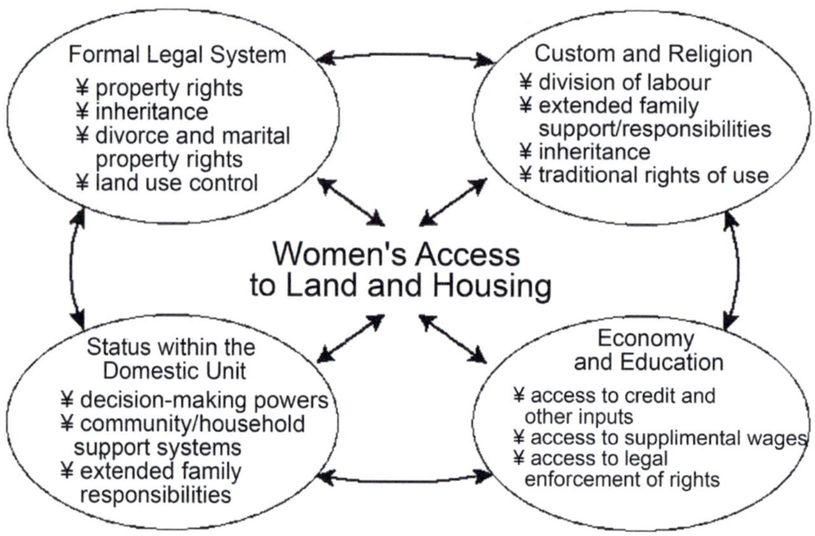

Figure 9.8. Why gender is an issue in access to land?

Source: https://www.fao.org/4/y4308e/y4308e00.gif.

The difference between community and separate property also shows how regimes of marital property can further help entrench gender differences. Where separate property is favored in jurisdictions, women are disadvantaged, particularly if they have dedicated years to domestic work while partners had command over financial means. The system has a tendency to generate asymmetrical economic power dynamics with women having fewer assets and less bargaining power in divorce or separation court proceedings. This can also be realized while studying women's economic status and partner violence. According to research, in conditions where women lack property rights, intimate partner violence is more likely to happen to them (Heise et al., 2015). Therefore, how the gender norms and property laws interact is crucial in addressing broader societal issues. With developments in marriage and personal status law, increasing amounts are being achieved regarding the need to reform property regimes so that they address these gender inequalities. It includes the promotion of prenuptial agreements and the valuation of non-monetary contribution to the household, which can redress the economic disadvantage faced by women upon divorce. By restructuring how marital property is classified and equitably shared, policymakers can enhance the safeguarding of vulnerable wives, promoting gender equality in legal frameworks. Issues of cultural norms that dominate such regimes are also important as they have a tendency to set the tone for perspectives toward womens value within the home environment. Last but not least, legal recognition of the economic and non-economic contributions of both spouses is essential in developing an equitable family law system that will be able to keep pace with the complexities of modern relationships (Figure 9.8).

9.5.1. Community Property Laws

Community property laws, in family and personal status law, are of fundamental significance to ascertaining the rights and obligations of the spouses as they apply to ownership and control of the marital property. Community property laws establish a legal presumption in favor of joint ownership of most property that is acquired during the marriage, given the assumption that both spouses contribute to the marriages economic foundation. These arrangements are meant to ensure equitable distribution of property at the end of marriage, thereby protecting the economic interests of both partners. Where states recognize community property, couples usually have the convenience of a simple rule that minimizes conflict when distributing property in the case of divorce, with a tendency to facilitate transition upon dissolution of marriage. This system becomes essential in the context of differences among diverse legal traditions, where common law might differ significantly in approach towards assets distribution, testifying to the need for informed legal awareness between spouses. The impacts of community property law extend beyond mere assets distribution; they also mirror sociocultural perceptions about marriage and partnership. The enforcement and adoption of these laws will often coincide with broader social norms, including gender roles and economic equality. By their very nature, community property laws negate the historical notion of individual ownership by upholding a collective understanding of marital assets. This shift can be particularly important to correct long-standing imbalances where one spouse was economically or socially disadvantaged. So, such communities which adopt or enact such laws are showing a shift in perspective towards marriage that encompasses mutual responsibility and accountability. So, analyzing the role of community property law in family law not only informs us about legal systems but also uncovers the underlying philosophies behind expectations of partnership in society.

Despite the preventive purposes of community property law, issues in its enforcement persist, particularly under current family structures. Issues in the characterization of property can inflate cases, especially when one of the spouses claims separate property or in the presence of blended families. More are the problems in jurisdictions with uneven standards for separate and community property. Additionally, as changing family norms increase with more diverse family formations, the recognition of the rights of non-marital partners is a potent legal concern. The interaction between these legislations and concerns of justice, equity, and equality underscores the necessity of ongoing legal reforms that are able to adapt to the reality of contemporary relationships without infringing on individual rights. Last but not least, community property legislation is the articulation of broader debates about sharing wealth and fairness in family relationships that indicate a need for continued dialogue in family and personal status law (Henrich et al., 2010; Java et al., 2007).

9.5.2. Distinctions of Separate Property

Among debates in today's family and personal status law, separate property is a most critical field to explore. The separation is a foundation of the laws governing marital relationships, particularly property ownership and financial responsibility. Separate property refers to property that still remains the exclusive ownership of one of the spouses, as contrasted with community property systems where the property is held in common. Separate classification of property can have critical implications on the division of assets upon divorce or judicial dissolution. It is important to understand under what circumstances property is considered separate because it might encompass properties that one acquires by inheritance, gift, or premarital ownership. These definitions and distinctions are crucial to sustaining personal economic autonomy within marriage and should be treated so that equitable legal protection is ensured for both parties. Furthermore, the legal definition of separate property varies significantly from jurisdiction to jurisdiction, as it does across more general cultural and economic contexts. In some legal systems, separate property can be defined rigidly, whereas in others there is allowance for more nuanced interpretations. This diversity necessitates additional examination of how courts impose these distinctions and with what budget planning implications on marriages. Particularly, statutory provisions regarding what occurs to separate property can impact couples' decisions regarding building wealth and controlling wealth within the marriage. This system not only draws attention to the legal complexities involved but also enlightens cultural attitudes towards individual versus shared holding within marriage. Knowledge of these differences is essential to an understanding of the intricacies that are revealed in family law, especially as couples confront the realities of divorce or death, which seems to require the equitable division of property. Additionally, the effects of separate property extend beyond mere labeling of goods; they impact general society attitudes toward marriage and economic independence. Based on literature already in existence, stigma can have an immense impact on individual decision-making processes, particularly in accessing legal consultation in the process of family breakdown. They can forgo invoking protection or rights on fear of stigmatization or perceived judgment, evidence for ongoing disconnection from services required (Patrick, 2004). Therefore, the argument regarding separate property not only calls for legal analysis but also requires a critical analysis of the socio-cultural thought that conditions behavior towards marital property and ownership of property. In the wake of altering public opinion, provisions for equal treatment and legal empowerment in family law become increasingly pertinent, leading to re-examination of conventions regarding marital property rights.

9.5.3. Entitlements of Spouses in Divorce

Dissolution of marriage raises difficult questions of law about the rights of spouses, many of which depend on prevailing family and personal status laws. Classification of marital property in many a jurisdiction is key to determining what becomes of assets upon divorce. Spouses' entitlements can depend upon whether a jurisdiction follows a separate property or a community property system. Systems of community property usually stipulate that any monies earned under the union be divided equally, hence equal division in the event of breakdown. Separate property systems, however, respond more to personal property, usually limiting access to property earned during the marriage. These variations in systems have such a significant bearing on negotiations and procedures in divorce agreements, illustrating the subtle interaction between law and personal realities. Besides property division, the relative entitlements position is also made more complex by duration of marriage, the couple's contributions, and other policy issues involved that can influence financial settlements. Spousal maintenance, or alimony, being an instance is provided on such considerations where a lesser earner of a couple might receive financial maintenance upon divorce. In all legal systems, the idea of alimony is to temper the economic disparities melodramatized by divorce, in order that both husbands and wives may establish financial stability once more. This premise is vital, particularly as social norms continue to shift, leading many jurisdictions to reconsider traditional means of offering spousal support. Consequently, spousal entitlements law is alive and kicking, reflecting broader social attitudes towards gender and economic equality. Given the numerous entitlements covered by family and personal status law, it can be seen that the effects of divorce extend far beyond the allocation of wealth in the short run. Legal barriers to womens economic participation have a tendency to worsen the issues to be addressed by spouses in divorce negotiations. Evidence suggests that factors like the right of inheritance and restrictions on property ownership are significant determinants of a woman's economic autonomy, which can lead to increased vulnerability in case of divorce (Gonzales et al., 2015). Being able to manage these legal complexities is vital, hence the significance of appropriate legal counseling. This discussion points out that subtle legislative reforms would be in a position to impart advantages on entitlements in divorce situations, thereby making the system more equitable for both parties, promoting the pursuit of gender justice and equality in family life.

9.6. NAME, IDENTITY, AND CITIZENSHIP

In contemporary legal terminology, the entwining of name, identity, and citizenship illustrates the complexity in personal status law. Names are not merely signs of persons but also become central in determining one's identity as well as being part of a nation. Legislative provisions to alter one's name reflect the social attitudes toward gender, ethnicity, and cultural identity, as seen in jurisdictions where individuals invoke personal significance in the names they choose to adopt. Moreover, the process of legally altering a name may be replete with bureaucratic entanglements, and it is informed by an understanding of the supporting legislative provisions. The effects of such legal recognition extend beyond personal will; they affect civil rights, social belonging, and in some cases, state services, which suggests the intense connection between one's name and legal self.

The subject of dual citizenship is another prominent view within the identity and citizenship frame. This experience explains how one can live multiple national identities as well as rights and duties in multiple countries. Dual citizenship is often a product of family circumstances, wherein individuals are capable of relating to cultural origins but enjoy the rights developed from the status of being a citizen in another political environment. However, the legality of dual nationality varies between states with consequences for the questions of military service and the legal complexities in family law, particularly parental rights and international custody cases. The consequences of the challenges reflect the necessity for advanced understanding of personal status law in the context of citizenship, particularly in the context of an interdependent world with complicated migration flows enriching the national populations. Personal status registers also conceptualize the interrelationship between name, identity, and citizenship more clearly, as official records that authenticate an individual's statutory status. The registers facilitate major life events such as marriage, divorce, and acknowledgment of parentage, all of which have tangible impacts on an individual's civic identity. The statutory regimes governing these registers are overwhelmingly variable across jurisdictions and decide an individual's entitlements and liabilities within their domestic family. For instance, discrepancies in the way registers update or recognize names can create problems during international arrangements, as occurred with the cases of Zambrano families during the Brexit talks, when non-EU parents' rights often found themselves lost in greater parliamentary controversies. Registers of personal status thus not only govern the central questions of family law but also condense a broader narrative on identity vis-a-vis citizenship rights.

9.6.1. Legal Processes for Name Changes

The process of going through the law regime that regulates name changes is often a process of balancing individual identity and legal formalities. Name change applicants must go through specific steps that vary between jurisdictions, as shaped by varying legal traditions and cultural environments. Typically, the process may begin with a petition or request presented to a court of law, in which the petition is scrutinized for its authenticity and adherence to established legal standards. Factors that affect approval can be the applicant's age, reasons for the name change—that is, marriage, divorce, or personal choice—and the lack of intent to commit fraud. Courts are concerned with preserving public order and individual autonomy by making sure that name changes are not used for nefarious purposes, including avoiding creditors or criminal responsibilities. On the filing of a petition for a change of name, the judicial process is generally a public notice to be published in newspapers, announcing the pending change of name. This publicity is to inform the public and give chance for objections so that any abuse of the name change through law can be prevented. Once the notice period has expired, a hearing takes place where the judge takes account of the petitioners rationale and any public opposition. The court issues an order declaring the new name legally valid in successful petitions, a notable accomplishment that demonstrates the ways in which attitudes towards personal identity are evolving in personal and family status law. Subsequently, the individuals must update their names on legal documents, such as Social Security records, driver licenses, and passports, further solidifying their new identity in official databases. Legal name changes have consequences that penetrate beyond personal identity; they drastically impact family life, social recognition, and legal rights. In the law of family and personal status, the ability to acquire a name through the legal process is at the core of the concepts of marriage and family unity. For instance, naming conventions will determine how the linkages of family belonging and descent are conceived in society. Moreover, because names influence personal status, special legal considerations can exist in relation to children born to families that are undergoing name change. Issues of inheritance, custody, and identity in the public documents arise, which require stringent compliance with legal procedures to ensure that names are a representation of the person's current identity and family ties, consistent with legislative frameworks that aim to safeguard personal status and family integrity (Figure 9.9).

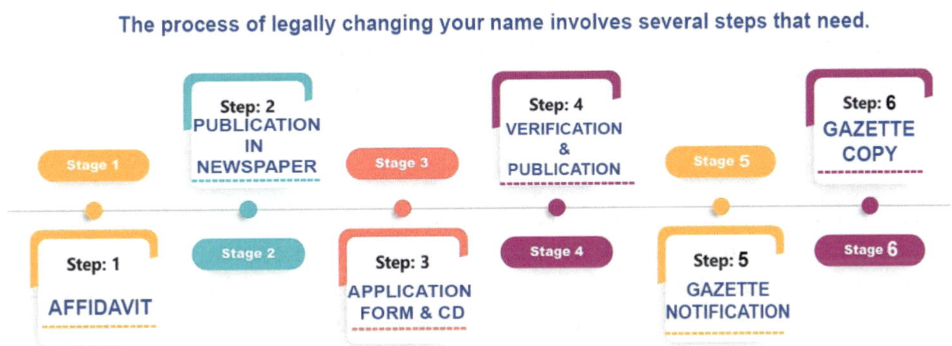

Figure 9.9. Shows name change process legally.

Source: https://www.mynamechange.in/images/NAME-CHANGE-PROCESS.jpg.

9.6.2. Issues of Dual Citizenship

The double implications of dual citizenship heavily intersect with family and personal status law, particularly as nations grow increasingly and increasingly comfortable with globalization and migration. Dual citizenship has numerous benefits that include increased rights and qualification for multiple welfare systems. On the other hand, it can generate complicated legal situations. One of the most central problems is the potential for conflicting allegiance and obligation to both nations, especially in areas of legal obligation under marriage, rights of children, and inheritance. Each nation might have divergent laws affecting these areas, and this raises an issue of which nation's jurisdiction takes priority in a conflict of law. Additionally, dual citizenship impinges on custody orders and liability for support among parents who may be citizens of two countries, forcing legal systems to navigate a tangled web of international law. As transnationality among families increases, the imperative for coherent legal structures becomes more pressing. Apart from legal conflict, dual citizenship distills intricate issues of belonging and identity that impact family life. Citizenship has a tendency to define the sense of self and family bonds of an individual, and affiliations with more than one nation can complicate this. The children of dual citizens are likely to experience special concerns regarding their identity, cultural identification, and social integration if their parents have very different points of origin. The stories behind dual citizenship also carry with them conceptions of loyalty and belonging, as those with the dual status can find themselves with conflicting duties to two nations. These conflicts can be felt in several different ways, such as the social effects of these identities and how others may see these individuals in both their two homelands. It is here, therefore, that the crossover between citizenship and personal identity reveals the intricacies at play for the families who travel this path. Moreover, the legal implications of dual citizenship cannot be disregarded, especially concerning succession and inheritance law. When relatives who possess dual citizenships pass on, their possessions could be liable to the laws of both countries, and could lead to disputes among heirs. Different countries generally have different laws regarding inheritance—like forced heirship, where certain portioning's of an individual's property regardless of what they desire—which could collide with one another. This conflict further indicates the necessity of legal certainty in cases of dual citizenship so as not to result in injustice and conflict in families. Additionally, the deliberation comprises how legislation on citizenship impacts other civil rights in general, opening for discussion about the best approach to handling the needs of such families under such dualities. As the citizens live their identities and obligations, calls for discussions about legal frameworks reforms become more urgent to address the needs of current family setups in the globalized world (Engin et al., 2017; Standing, 2014).

9.6.3. Importance of Personal Status Registers

In the very center of Family and Personal Status Law, the importance of Personal Status Registers cannot be overstated. They are source documents which authenticate individual identities and relationships and register in effect the significant milestones of birth, marriage, divorce, and death. Their authenticity is of vital significance because these documents not only facilitate legal recognition of relationships but also have profound effects on individuals' rights, entitlement to inheritance, and custody. For instance, when Personal Status Registers hold proper information, they ensure proper succession planning and protect heirs' rights, allowing for equitable property and responsibility distribution in accordance with family law. Margaret E Kruk et al., 2018 highlights that without good personal registries, personal status law is undermined, leading to increased controversies and legal complexities. Moreover, Personal Status Registers are an important mechanism for the safeguarding of the rights of individuals, particularly those of marginalized people. Correct recordation of identity and family ties is crucial in order to guarantee the exercise of access to legal protection and benefits, including social services and welfare aid. In nations where social issues, such as those of people with disabilities, are prevalent, the appropriate use of these registers can uphold rights and promote social inclusion. As noted in talks about the Convention on the Rights of Persons with Disabilities, improving the accessibility of Personal Status Registers has the potential to go a long way towards making these persons have full access to all rights guaranteed to them, creating an environment that is inclusive. N/A (2014) reports that initiatives aimed at improving the process of registration should focus on making these services accessible and reliable. The effects of Personal Status Registers extend beyond an individual's rights—they also reflect social norms and legal frameworks regarding marriage, custody, and inheritance. For most societies, the absence of an institutionalized record can potentially lead to conflict regarding the status of marriage, hence affecting the legitimacy of claims in divorce or child custody proceedings. Furthermore, when combined with sophisticated data-collecting systems, such registers provide valuable insights into population trends and social issues, facilitating informed decision-making for policymakers. Such synergy serves to illustrate that Personal Status Registers are not only administrative instruments; they are the key to the effective functioning of a fair and equitable legal system that is cognizant and sensitive to the observance of individual rights. The importance of these registers, therefore, then extends beyond convenience of personal and family legal transactions as well as looks to its greater importance towards societal values and governance of family law.

SUMMARY

The analysis of family and personal status law illustrates its constitutive significance in determining the norms of society and the rights of individuals. The confluence of jurisprudence regulating marriage, parental rights, and inheritance is central to creating a system that mediates family conflict and authenticates the status of individuals within the family structure. As is the case in most legal systems, establishing validity conditions for marriage and civil unions locks such unions in the eyes of the law, and stability and protection is provided for partners and children. The processes of dissolution bring forth the importance of equitable solutions taking into consideration the well-being of all members, particularly children, who are typically open in such cases. Thus, an integrated approach to family law as noted in codes and legislation is not just to regulate relationships but also to tighten the social fabric that binds persons under family bonds. The data on criminal liabilities on family law contracts show a vast present gap within existing legal systems. Indeed, the emphasis on making penal provisions precise mirrors the social impacts of illegalities, such as forced marriages, that desecrate people's rights to self-determination and threaten the welfare of society at large. The examination of forced marriages proves broader impacts of inadequate legal protection for vulnerable classes and calls for reconsideration of existing legislation. As seen in the comprehensive analysis of Iraqi law, the legislators' inability to address certain illegal marriage scenarios can lead to avoidance of responsibility on the part of abusers, and as a result, the development of abuse patterns and social tensions. It is obvious that the fight against such legal loopholes is important towards the development of a legal framework that protects violation of individual rights and upholds the integrity of family law. The complexity of family and home status law is further complicated by societal and cultural dynamics, particularly in religiously dominated contexts. The dilemmas illustrated by the proposed family rights law for Muslim women in Israel, for example, illustrate the way in which structural discrimination can shape womens rights discourse in the family. Feminist theory and campaign for legal reform seek to demystify such inequalities and advocate for women's fairer treatment. Through the study of the convergence of law, culture, and human rights, it is apparent that family law effective enough must not only be capable of adjusting to the realities of the law but be attuned to the differential experiences of various communities. Thus, ongoing controversy and evolution in this critical area of legislation are vital to the achievement of justice and fairness for all parties to the family structure, as the impact of the laws extends far beyond the boundaries of legal obligation into the realm of personal dignity and public health.

A LOOK TO THE FUTURE

FUTURE DIRECTIONS IN COMPARATIVE FAMILY AND PERSONAL STATUS LAW

With evolving times, so do the paradigms of family and personal status law, necessitating lawmakers and jurists to subject prevailing norms to critical scrutiny. The institution of civil union and marriage is one that can anticipate a radical overhaul, as evolving society's view of these arrangements must also evolve. The conditions of validity that presently envelop marriage, along with the enforcement of various forms of partnerships through law, will also receive a rethink. As non-traditional family structures become more mainstream, legal meanings may need to be expanded within their jurisdictions to encompass cohabitating couples, same-sex marriages, and polyamory. This impacts not merely validity requirements but dissolution processes as well, necessitating the establishment of fair and equitable systems able to accommodate diverse familial structures. All these adjustments are required to keep family law relevant and responsive to the times, fostering stability and security within the family, as discussed in similar debates under (Yogesh et al., 2022).

Parental rights disputes and child custody wars of the future also promise significant advancements, in line with broader societal concern for the protection of children. While families are becoming increasingly multicultural, standards of best interest applied today may have to essentially rethink what it is to be in the best interest of a child. Policy makers and legal practitioners will have to grapple with the issues of shared custody, alternative family role arrangements, and interstate relocation disputes. The inflexibility of the laws often prevents it from accommodating the intricacies of reality that face modern families, which can lead to intricate, confrontational proceedings. In calculating support obligations, the discussion will also need to consider equitable support formulas that do not unjustly prejudice lower-income parents, thus ensuring that the interests of children are met and fairness between custodial arrangements is maintained because these issues overlap with those in Margaret et al. (2018). Adoption and guardianship is yet another critical frontier in personal and family status law, particularly as social perceptions regarding child well-being and familial relationships evolve. The legal consequences of adoption procedures will likely evolve to address concerns like transracial and open adoptions, as well as the application of technology in promoting these types of adoptions. Increased awareness of the many types of guardianship, including extended family or non-relative guardianship, demands legal settings that facilitate and legitimize the arrangements. With guardianship law in review, there will be a need to ensure that legislation protects children's interests yet remains adaptable to accommodate shifting family structures. This new reality demands a multidisciplinary framework involving legal professionals, social workers, and mental health clinicians to create responsive models responsive to the complexity of today's familial settings that resonate with the ideas presented in Yogesh et al. (2022).

REFERENCES

1. Ademiluka, S. O. (2018). Patriarchy and women abuse: Perspectives from ancient Israel and Africa. *Old Testament Essays, 31.* https://doi.org/10.17159/2312-3621/2018/v31n2a5 (accessed on 9th September 2025).
2. Adeola, O., Evans, O., & Ngare, I. (2023). *Gender equality, climate action, and technological innovation for sustainable development in Africa. Sustainable Development Goals Series.* https://doi.org/10.1007/978-3-031-40124-4 (accessed on 9th September 2025).
3. Adzanu, M. D., & Zakaria, C. A. F. (2024). Penegakan hukum terhadap tindakan penipuan informasi jenis kelamin dalam pernikahan ditinjau dari Undang-Undang Nomor 16 Tahun 2019 tentang Perkawinan. *Bandung Conference Series: Law Studies.* https://www.semanticscholar.org/paper/87877c253980808f31588d6a2305425d728c952f (accessed on 9th September 2025).
4. Akrem, A. T., Ali, N. K., & Saeed, G. Q. (2025). The legislative disparity in questions concerning the implications of the marriage contract between the Personal Status Law of Iraq and the Kurdistan Region–A comparative study. *Journal of Legal and Political Studies.* https://www.semanticscholar.org/paper/051922376a94e8c8fe0ff79ba8df66952bdf7699 (accessed on 9th September 2025).
5. Andersen, R., & Newman, J. F. (2005). Societal and individual determinants of medical care utilization in the United States. *Milbank Quarterly, 83.* https://doi.org/10.1111/j.1468-0009.2005.00428.x (accessed on 9th September 2025).
6. Andrews, J. G., Buzzi, S., Choi, W., Hanly, S. V., Lozano, A., Soong, A. C. K., & Zhang, J. C. (2014). What will 5G be? *IEEE Journal on Selected Areas in Communications, 32*, 1065–1082. https://doi.org/10.1109/jsac.2014.2328098 (accessed on 9th September 2025).
7. Arstein-Kerslake, A., & Flynn, E. (2015). The general comment on Article 12 of the Convention on the Rights of Persons with Disabilities: A roadmap for equality before the law. *The International Journal of Human Rights, 20*, 471–490. https://doi.org/10.1080/13642987.2015.1107052 (accessed on 9th September 2025).
8. Asari, K., Makhtar, M., Abdullah Asuhaimi, F. B., & Pauzai, N. A. (2019). Compulsory childhood vaccination in Malaysia: Public health versus parental autonomy. *International Journal of Academic Research in Business and Social Sciences.* https://www.semanticscholar.org/paper/d87749e69534aa1eb629652cd5387ef96dd33025 (accessed on 9th September 2025).
9. Berger, R. (2013). Now I see it, now I don't: Researcher's position and reflexivity in qualitative research. *Qualitative Research, 15*, 219–234. https://doi.org/10.1177/1468794112468475 (accessed on 9th September 2025).
10. Bulska, E. (2024). From afar and from the inside: About the importance of ethics in the global world of science. *Brazilian Journal of Analytical Chemistry.* https://www.semanticscholar.org/paper/201a572f3cb68f4ece61c312d016c6117c9f0c77 (accessed on 9th September 2025).
11. Céspedes, R. (2024). Indigenous autonomy and justice for Latin American Indigenous women. *Revita CUHSO, 30*, 126–144. https://doi.org/10.7770/cuhso-v30n1-art2116 (accessed on 9th September 2025).
12. Cho, S., Crenshaw, K. W., & McCall, L. (2013). Toward a field of intersectionality studies: Theory,

applications, and praxis. *Signs, 38*, 785–810. https://doi.org/10.1086/669608 (accessed on 9th September 2025).

13. Corrigan, P. W. (2004). How stigma interferes with mental health care. *American Psychologist, 59*, 614–625. https://doi.org/10.1037/0003-066x.59.7.614 (accessed on 9th September 2025).

14. Courson, R., Goldenberg, M., Adams, K., Anderson, S., Colgate, B., Cooper, L., Dewald, L., et al. (2014). Inter-association consensus statement on best practices for sports medicine management for secondary schools and colleges. *Journal of Athletic Training, 49*, 128–137. https://doi.org/10.4085/1062-6050-49.1.06 (accessed on 9th September 2025).

15. D'Ignazio, C., & Klein, L. (2020). *Data Feminism*. The MIT Press eBooks. https://doi.org/10.7551/mitpress/11805.001.0001 (accessed on 9th September 2025).

16. Dwivedi, Y. K., Hughes, L., Baabdullah, A. M., Ribeiro-Navarrete, S., Giannakis, M., Al-Debei, M. M., Dennehy, D., et al. (2022). Metaverse beyond the hype: Multidisciplinary perspectives on emerging challenges, opportunities, and agenda for research, practice and policy. *International Journal of Information Management, 66*, 102542–102542. https://doi.org/10.1016/j.ijinfomgt.2022.102542 (accessed on 9th September 2025).

17. Edres, N. (2025). Changing personal status codes as a discriminated minority: Aspirations and pitfalls around the possibility to amend the 1917 Ottoman Law of Family Rights for Muslim Palestinians in Israel. *Arab Law Quarterly*. https://www.semanticscholar.org/paper/59214061d8b1aaa31711a4a41c4020fd609dbb00 (accessed on 9th September 2025).

18. Eekelaar, J., & George, R. (2014). *Routledge Handbook of Family Law and Policy*. https://www.semanticscholar.org/paper/095da930be12a2d47958acc111b12536746710c7 (accessed on 9th September 2025).

19. Elinder, M., Erixson, O., & Waldenström, D. (2018). Inheritance and wealth inequality: Evidence from population registers. *Journal of Public Economics, 165*, 17–30. https://doi.org/10.1016/j.jpubeco.2018.06.012 (accessed on 9th September 2025).

20. Flayyih, N. (2025). The specificity of execution in personal status matters: A study on the enforcement of national and foreign judgments before the execution judge. *Access to Justice in Eastern Europe*. https://www.semanticscholar.org/paper/3be723bf64923122acfcff80eb7e3b7e1b72e560 (accessed on 9th September 2025).

21. Gonzales, C., Jain-Chandra, S., Kochhar, K., & Newiak, M. (2015). Fair play: More equal laws boost female labor force participation. *IMF Staff Discussion Note, 15*, 1–1. https://doi.org/10.5089/9781498354424.006 (accessed on 9th September 2025).

22. Haji, N. K., & Ali, H. M. (2025). Penal responsibility arising from marriage in violation of the law in the Iraqi personal status law. *Journal of University of Raparin*. https://www.semanticscholar.org/paper/9f423e95702cc832b1b1133d23ecfe392647cf9d (accessed on 9th September 2025).

23. Hassan, R., & Mohamad Zaizi, N. A. (2020). The concept and application of *hibah* as a financial instrument from the Malaysian legal perspective: An analysis. *IIUM Law Journal, 28*, 227–252. https://doi.org/10.31436/iiumlj.v28i1.498 (accessed on 9th September 2025).

24. Heise, L., & Kotsadam, A. (2015). Cross-national and multilevel correlates of partner violence: An analysis of data from population-based surveys. *The Lancet Global Health, 3*, e332–e340.

https://doi.org/10.1016/s2214-109x(15)00013-3 (accessed on 9th September 2025).

25. Henrich, J., Heine, S. J., & Norenzayan, A. (2010). The weirdest people in the world? *Behavioral and Brain Sciences, 33*, 61–83. https://doi.org/10.1017/s0140525x0999152x (accessed on 9th September 2025).

26. Hochman, Y., Segev, E., Regev, I., Zafrani, Y., Sharfi, Y., & Elkayam, A. (2022). Bereaved mothers and widows' grief and their unfolding relationships: Implications for social work. *Journal of Social Work, 22*, 1323–1344. https://www.semanticscholar.org/paper/f4620286bfe72129ce4c17bdfd9beaad5b7e3b71 (accessed on 9th September 2025).

27. Isin, E. F., & Wood, P. K. (2017). *Citizenship and Identity*. https://doi.org/10.4337/9781788112376.00025 (accessed on 9th September 2025).

28. Java, A., Song, X., Finin, T., & Tseng, B. L. (2007). Why we twitter. https://doi.org/10.1145/1348549.1348556 (accessed on 9th September 2025).

29. Kruk, M. E., Gage, A., Arsenault, C., Jordan, K., Leslie, H. H., Roder-DeWan, S., Adeyi, O., et al. (2018). High-quality health systems in the Sustainable Development Goals era: Time for a revolution. *The Lancet Global Health, 6*, e1196–e1252. https://doi.org/10.1016/s2214-109x(18)30386-3 (accessed on 9th September 2025).

30. Luchkovskyi, V. (2020). Development of legal regulation of actual marriage relations under family law operated in Ukraine in the X–XXI centuries. *University Scientific Notes*. https://www.semanticscholar.org/paper/5ef9026c7fcc05516df4d16c348b5a033e14078f (accessed on 9th September 2025).

31. Melnyk, O. (2023). The issue of determining the child's place of residence after the parents' divorce during martial law. *Uzhhorod National University Herald. Series: Law*. https://www.semanticscholar.org/paper/4263981f6eedf8a1bfae2dcc148082acaafab9fd (accessed on 9th September 2025).

32. Möller, L. M. (2018). *Law: Modern Family Law, 1800–Present: Gulf States*. https://www.semanticscholar.org/paper/f8f004ed7943ac200b06c11a099a7632ffb8be56 (accessed on 9th September 2025).

33. N/A. (2014). Convention on the Rights of Persons with Disabilities. *Encyclopedia of Human Services and Diversity*. https://doi.org/10.4135/9781483346663.n124 (accessed on 9th September 2025).

34. N/A. (2017). Power and potential: A comparative analysis of national laws and regulations concerning women's rights to community forests. https://doi.org/10.53892/pmyv6840 (accessed on 9th September 2025).

35. Noria, C. (2025). The impact of the best interests of the child standard on resolving legal custody disputes. *Journal of Law and Sustainable Development*. https://www.semanticscholar.org/paper/27ef0c96e4d1722a6cfcdbabb5782d99098069ac (accessed on 9th September 2025).

36. Palacios, J., Adroher, S., Brodzinsky, D. M., Grotevant, H. D., Johnson, D. E., Juffer, F., Martínez-Mora, L., et al. (2019). Adoption in the service of child protection: An international interdisciplinary perspective. *Psychology Public Policy and Law, 25*, 57–72. https://doi.org/10.1037/law0000192 (accessed on 9th September 2025).

37. Pecheniy, O. (2024). Trends in the participation of legal entities in inheritance legal relations in modern realities. *Non-Governmental Organization "Civil Law Platform"*. https://www.

semanticscholar.org/paper/5248f054b4366ebc6642856b1228a03eb30469f6 (accessed on 9th September 2025).

38. Peek, S. T. M., Luijkx, K., Rijnaard, M. D., Nieboer, M., van der Voort, C. S., Aarts, S., van Hoof, J., et al. (2015). Older adults' reasons for using technology while aging in place. *Gerontology, 62*, 226–237. https://doi.org/10.1159/000430949 (accessed on 9th September 2025).

39. Perry, M. (2013). *Gender, Manumission, and the Roman Freedwoman*. https://doi.org/10.1017/cbo9781139628853 (accessed on 9th September 2025).

40. Rosalina, M. (2020). Akta kelahiran anak luar kawin sebagai hak perdata anak. *Bandung Conference Series: Law Studies, 1*, 175–184. https://www.semanticscholar.org/paper/1bc8041b0f3eafa29c82425411e1ad690aef50f4 (accessed on 9th September 2025).

41. Schmidt, M., Schmidt, S. A. J., Sandegaard, J. L., Ehrenstein, V., Pedersen, L., & Sørensen, H. T. (2015). The Danish National Patient Registry: A review of content, data quality, and research potential. *Clinical Epidemiology*. https://doi.org/10.2147/clep.s91125 (accessed on 9th September 2025).

42. Śmiechowski, M. (2024). O-181: It takes more than genes to build a family. *Human Reproduction*. https://www.semanticscholar.org/paper/2cc8ee2169e6c728cf09d1276651696f8469339d (accessed on 9th September 2025).

43. Solanke, I. (2020). The impact of Brexit on Black women, children and citizenship. *JCMS Journal of Common Market Studies, 58*, 147–159. https://doi.org/10.1111/jcms.13103 (accessed on 9th September 2025).

44. Standing, G. (2014). *A Precariat Charter*. Bloomsbury Publishing Plc eBooks. https://doi.org/10.5040/9781472510631 (accessed on 9th September 2025).

45. Tang, F., Jang, H., & Copeland, V. (2015). Challenges and resilience in African American grandparents raising grandchildren: A review of the literature with practice implications. *GrandFamilies: The Contemporary Journal of Research, Practice and Policy*. https://www.semanticscholar.org/paper/a62ff6fb9acc3b471a462ea8b10190283c8b6db4 (accessed on 9th September 2025).

46. Tracy, S. J. (2010). Qualitative quality: Eight "big-tent" criteria for excellent qualitative research. *Qualitative Inquiry, 16*, 837–851. https://doi.org/10.1177/1077800410383121 (accessed on 9th September 2025).

47. Tripp, A. M. (2015). *Women and Power in Post Conflict Africa*. https://doi.org/10.1017/cbo9781316336014 (accessed on 9th September 2025).

48. Vayezi, B., Khajeh Nori, Y., Saberi, M., & Tavana, A. N. (2024). Analysis of rehabilitation and treatment strategies for violent offenders in light of criminal psychology doctrines. *Interdisciplinary Studies in Society, Law, and Politics*. https://www.semanticscholar.org/paper/58a69060dc34c30724fd6b3d2c2c3544421a0117 (accessed on 9th September 2025).

49. Voena, A. (2015). Yours, mine, and ours: Do divorce laws affect the intertemporal behavior of married couples? *American Economic Review, 105*, 2295–2332. https://doi.org/10.1257/aer.20120234 (accessed on 9th September 2025).

50. Volpp, L. (2017). *(Mis)identifying Culture: Asian Women and the "Cultural Defense." Routledge eBooks*. https://doi.org/10.4324/9781351157728-18 (accessed on 9th September 2025).

51. Walker, L. (2015). *Maintenance and Child Support in Private International Law*. https://www.semanticscholar.org/paper/90266a31a9501570a51c99f7bd9e6aa3d1b2aa0b (accessed on 9th September 2025).

52. Walter, M., Kukutai, T., Russo Carroll, S., & Rodriguez-Lonebear, D. (2020). *Indigenous Data Sovereignty and Policy. Routledge eBooks.* https://doi.org/10.4324/9780429273957 (accessed on 9th September 2025).

53. Woods, P. (2006). Strange bedfellows. https://www.semanticscholar.org/paper/cf97d50037f1f6215b11f078aa7d2b0a55d9de3f (accessed on 9th September 2025).

54. Zhao, X., & Dawson, J. (2014). The new Chinese mental health law. *Psychiatry Psychology and Law, 21*, 669–686. https://doi.org/10.1080/13218719.2014.882248 (accessed on 9th September 2025).

Chapter 10

LABOR AND EMPLOYMENT LAW

Contents

INTRODUCTION

The intricate landscape of employment law is pivotal in shaping the relationship between employees and employers. The realm of concern entails a complex multitude of principles and legal frameworks that determine the way work relationships are formed, the rights and responsibilities of the parties, and the regulations that govern workplace culture. Understanding the fundamentals of labor and employment law is required, as it acts as a guide to manage various cases of disputes and safeguard working people's rights. The subtleties in the field are also brought out by the different classifications of work arrangements, that is, employees under a contract of service and independent contractors. These variations have significant connotations for labor rights, privileges, and obligations, which are critical in providing fair and equitable working conditions. As we move further into the domain of labor and employment law, several essential aspects become evident which are crucial in providing a healthy work culture. Working conditions, that is, regulation of hours, rest breaks, and occupational health, reflect the legal needs required for the purpose of ensuring employee welfare. In today's rapidly transforming work setting, telework policies have emerged as a major force, posing new legal meanings for employers and employees alike. The labor system underlying employee rights and entitlements such as minimum wage, paid leave, and termination pay constitutes the basis on which equitable labor practices are established. All the employees are entitled to be valued for their work and assured safe working conditions, with this highlighting the importance of possessing a keen understanding of these laws in practicing fair treatment in various situations of employment. Second, collective bargaining becomes a fundamental way through which employees can negotiate for improved terms of work and employment conditions, with an assurance of being heard. The power to bargain collective bargains and unionize empowers the workers, enhancing their bargaining ability for good wages and a working environment. Anti-discrimination provisions in labor laws provide vital safeguards, imposing equal pay, preventing workplace harassment, and establishing affirmative action which promotes inclusivity. In addition, effective mechanisms for the resolution of disputes such as labor tribunals and conciliation are also crucial in resolving disputes that may arise in the employment contract. The employment and labor law environment is not only at the heart of establishing workplace dynamics but also of fostering a system of upholding the rights and dignity of all employees required for a strong economy and society (Margaret et al., 2018; N/A, 2016).

10.1. EMPLOYMENT RELATIONSHIPS

The employment relationship profoundly impacts the employee-employer relationship, establishing a paradigm that determines rights and duties. At the center of this paradigm is the contract of service, determining the legal basis of employment and specifying the terms and conditions under which individuals operate within the organizational structure. This contract not only serves as a binding agreement but also establishes the expectations of compensation, work duty, and period of employment. Further, variations in employment status, for example, independent contractors and regular employees, create complexities to the employer-employee relationship because legislations may accord varying protections and rights (Figure 10.1).

Figure 10.1. Shows employer-employee relationship.

Source: ALP Consulting.

An in-depth understanding of these constructs is crucial to navigating and facilitating satisfactory employment relationships to base on the principles of fairness and respect in the workplace, which are fundamental elements of contemporary labor standards reflected in current legal standards (Eneh et al., 2024). In addition, probationary employment is a watershed moment within the employment relationship. This period of probation is a chance for employees and employers to review the viability of the work setup before inking a long contract. While probation may be useful in ascertaining staff performance and organizational culture, it also poses issues of job security and employee rights. Workers in this period may experience anxiety regarding future employment, so open communication and transparency by employers are essential. Organizations' ability to declare their review benchmarks at this initial point can foster a culture of morale and trust. It also offers a starting point in regard to viewing the broader issues of fairness and inclusivity within the employment practices and thus it is essential for labor law to create and respond to these emerging themes by the backdrop of employment relations (N/A, 2019). Finally, the restructuring of working relationships in light of contemporary patterns of work necessitates ongoing debate around rights and responsibilities in conventional and virtual workplaces. Telework, driven by technological developments, has transformed employers' responsibilities on occupational safety, work-life balance, and mental health provision. In this sense, compliance with labor law becomes a complicated process as companies try to accommodate new realities with the aim of maintaining employees' rights. Moreover, minimum wage issues, rights to leaves, and anti-discrimination clauses become more pertinent than ever before. All these factors put into context the role of legal frameworks that will be in a position to adequately respond to the evolving nature of employment relationships and safeguard the welfare of employees. As we observe these developments, we understand that labor and employment law has to continually change in order to capture the rich experiences and expectations unfolding in the modern workforce (Eneh et al., 2024).

10.1.1. Contract of Service

The Contract of Service is the focal point for an analysis that lies within the broader fabric of employment and labor law. The contract is what supports the relationship between employer and employee, determining rights, duties, and expectations of each. It will of course have essential ingredients such as wages, work hours, and job responsibilities that are important in fostering a harmonious workplace environment. Moreover, the law that governs the agreement also has a tendency of protecting workers' interests by providing rights that are significant in case of potential exploitation. As feminist labor law literature explains, the importance of the knowledge of these contracts extends beyond traditional borders, suggesting a call for introspection regarding issues like unpaid care work, which creates it difficult to implement normal employment conditions, thereby making lines between private and professional service relations blurred (Wimmer et al., 2014). The intrinsic complexities in the different forms of employment arrangements, such as agency work, have further implications for the Contract of Service. Agency workers, for instance, enjoy a unique status in the labor market whereby their rights and privileges can significantly differ from the direct hires. Legal ambiguities under the contracts of agencies create challenges, especially on the matter of job security and fair treatment. As in regulatory discourse, the laws currently in place tend to expose loopholes such that agency employees must not be subjected to discriminatory treatment solely on the basis of their employment terms. This disparity calls for scrutiny of what exactly constitutes equal employment in the current workforce and demands a reevaluation of legal definitions and safeguards (McGaughey et al., 2010). Referenced to the Contract of Service, there is a need to explore how various elements thereof evolve to fit the reality of present work arrangements. Contemporary discourses place into context the necessity of possessing a flexible legislative framework that adapts to the realities of the labor market today, for example, incorporating remote work arrangements and flexible working hours. These are not merely bureaucratic concessions, but a broader observation of different work arrangements that have been catalyzed by economic and social developments. By addressing these concerns through a holistic appreciation of labor contracts, legislators can provide a balanced and fair labor environment friendly to the rights of workers in a manner that permits more than one employment modality. Thus, the debate over Contracts of Service remains an essential part of building labor and employment law frameworks, with the need for constant engagement with new issues and trends.

10.1.2. Independent Contractor Status

The complexity of defining employment relationships in the context of modern labor markets necessitates a careful examination of various classifications, particularly the distinction between employees and independent contractors. This distinction is not merely semantic; it carries significant implications for liability, benefits, and workplace rights. Independent contractors, who typically operate under a contract for service rather than a contract of employment, often lack the protections afforded to employees such as minimum wage guarantees, health benefits, and collective bargaining rights. This classification has become increasingly contentious, especially as businesses seek to leverage gig economy models that prioritize flexibility and reduced overhead. As economic realities shift, so too must legal frameworks adapt to clarify the boundaries and responsibilities associated with independent contractor status, which calls into question longstanding assumptions about who constitutes a worker in the eyes of labor laws and regulations. The legal criteria for independent contractor status are multifaceted, often involving various tests that account for the nature of the work relationship. Factors such as control, the degree of independence, and the nature of the tasks performed play pivotal roles in determining ones classification. Courts frequently assess relationships based on whether the employer has the right to control not only the means but also the methods of accomplishing work. This examination can become convoluted when the tasks of independent contractors overlap with traditional employment roles, creating an ambiguity that may ultimately disadvantage these workers in claims against employers for benefits or protections. Consequently, legal interpretations have varied across jurisdictions, which has compounded the challenges faced by independent contractors, who often navigate a patchwork of laws that can hinder their ability to assert their rights effectively. Such legal ambiguities are exacerbated by the rapid developments in technology and labor practices, particularly with the increasing presence of the gig economy, which often relies on independent contractors for service delivery. This evolution raises critical questions regarding worker rights and protections in an environment where traditional labor models are being challenged. Moreover, the introduction of technologies may change the nature of independent contracting, introducing new dilemmas surrounding job security and the adequacy of existing legal frameworks. As articulated in ongoing discussions regarding generative AI and its impact on employment, there's a pressing need for a thorough investigation into how legislation can adequately protect these workers while still accommodating the evolving business landscape. Policymakers face the challenge of crafting laws that not only recognize the shifting definitions of work but also ensure fair treatment and protection for independent contractors within the broader context of labor and employment law (Budhwar et al., 2023; OECD, 2021).

10.1.3. Probationary Employment

One of the most significant aspects of the labor setting comprises the ways in which individuals transition from probationary to permanent positions, among them being probationary employment. This trial period offers employers time to assess the capability and fit of new workers with the organizational ethos, hence a more informed decision on full-time employment. During this period, the legal and moral obligations of both parties assume the greatest significance. Employers are thus not merely required to monitor performance but also to ensure adherence to relevant labor laws that protect the rights of the workers. These safeguards are pivotal in ensuring there is a fair and equitable working environment, particularly in light of growing utilization of various forms of employment, such as fixed-term and temporary work contracts, which tend to worsen the situation of workers to enjoy job stability and not worry about insecurity. Historical examination confirms that probationary work has evolved in line with patterns of the labor market more broadly, responding to shifting economic conditions and hiring practices. For example, during the severe macroeconomic downturn of the 1990s, prevalence of temporary employment quickened, with fixed-term contracts rising from 10% to 16% of total employment in Sweden. This shift in direction highlights the manner in which external pressures can affect recruitment practice, making employers increasingly likely to employ probationary periods as a risk-management strategy. Consequently, employees may find themselves in precarious circumstances, with a world in which work has become more conditional. The cyclical pattern of labor market dynamics necessitates strict attention to probationary terms to prevent them from becoming exploitative where employment shortage is the situation and workers are forced to accept adverse terms. Furthermore, the effects of probationary work extend beyond first-time recruitment procedures to affect employee rights as well as future career prospects. Employees frequently experience doubt regarding their rights during probation, particularly concerning termination benefits and performance assessment expectations. This uncertainty raises doubt over the adequacy of existing labor protection in safeguarding the interests of probationary employees. With the instability of labor markets growing and diversifying, concern for these employees' rights is vital; it serves to guarantee that they are not dealt with as disposable resources. The legislation governing probationary work must evolve to address such complex dynamics, and possibly draw lessons from other types of employment such as temporary work, where uncertainty and levels of turnover are similarly elevated (Holmlund et al., 2025). By building protections during probation, balances of power in employment relationships can be made more equitable, to create a healthier jobs market for all concerned (Figure 10.2).

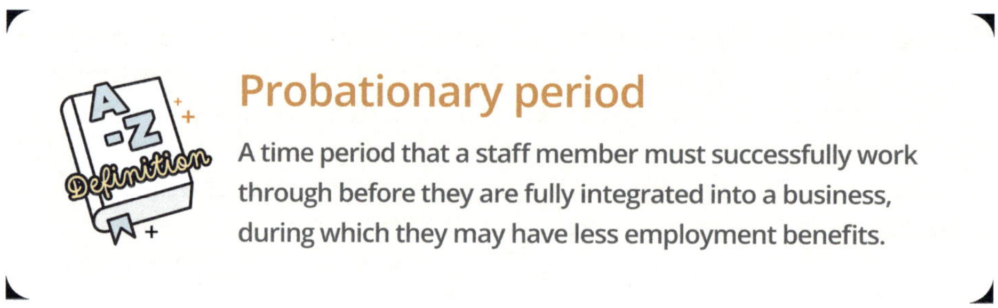

Figure 10.2. What is a probationary period?

Source: https://www.rocketlawyer.com/binaries/content/gallery/rocketlawyeruk/uk-infographics/probationary-period-definition-infographic.png.

10.2. WORK CONDITIONS

Creating a good working environment has many dimensions, including working hours and allowing adequate breaks. Working hours affect productivity and employees' welfare in a disproportionate manner. An overemphasis on productivity will lead to burnout, which undermines the health of workers and adversely affects their performance. In the context of labor law, regulations on mandatory breaks are an essential time of recuperation for employees, and hence enhancing overall productivity and morale. Secondly, the common phenomenon of telecommuting necessitates proper regulations on work hours and break times even more to enable workers' statuses to be linked without being disadvantaged. While labor laws are evolving to suit modern work practices, there is a necessity to consider the existing regulations that are geared towards shielding workers' health and safety as well as ensuring a balance in work-life incorporation. Occupational safety remains the priority in the discussion of working conditions, especially in dangerous industries where the rate of workplace accidents is greater. Good labor laws need to give priority to safety precautions in order to guarantee the safety of employees from harm. Compliance with some safety standards, for instance, as outlined in the Occupational Safety and Health Act, is crucial for minimizing workplace fatality and injury. The persistent disproportion in applying the regulations raises more questions about employers' role and methods of enforcement through which workers are safeguarded. Obligations outlined by labor jurisdictions are significant in the sense that they affect worker morale but also corporate atmosphere overall. This contention is further complicated with regard to online platforms, in which the lack of traditional regulation can exacerbate insecure work arrangements, and strong legal frameworks are required that provide for contemporary labor issues and the protection of workers' rights and welfare (Sitko, 2025) (Figure 10.3).

Figure 10.3. Legislation such as the Bangladesh Labor Act of 2006 exemplifies the ongoing efforts to rectify historical imbalances in working conditions and create a supportive employment landscape.

Source: https://textiletoday.com.bd/storage/uploads/2017/06/laborlaw.jpg.

By establishing comprehensive regulations related to job conditions and employee rights, this Act aims to ensure fairness in treatment and address the needs of vulnerable workers. However, the practical application of these laws often reveals significant disparities, particularly regarding employer discretion in hiring and termination procedures. Labor courts play an essential role in mediating conflicts and enforcing principles of equity in employment. Nonetheless, the intricate power dynamics between employees and employers raise critical questions about the effectiveness of the current legal framework. Revisions to labor legislation are essential to reinforce protections for workers, particularly as global economic trends continue to influence local labor markets, thereby requiring continuous evaluation and refinement of laws to uphold employee welfare and economic stability (Imran, 2025).

10.2.1. Hours and Breaks

The employers are generally obligated to adhere to certain norms of working hours, not only to avoid the depletion of workers but also to promote a better work-life balance. The legislative provisions vary across jurisdictions but generally ensure limited working hours and breaks compulsory so that the employees have sufficient time to recover. These regulations bring two advantages: they promote the health of employees and enhance productivity in the workplace. In the face of economic change and shifting work patterns, recent regional reforms reflect growing concern with the need for regulating the working day to ensure optimal working efficiency, as provided in employment law reform and adjustment discussion (Baker and McKenzie, 2013). The implications of break and hours policies extend well past mere compliance with the law; they overlap heavily with other employee protections and benefits.

Time Worked	Hour
8:00 a.m. to 9:00 a.m.	1st hour
9:00 a.m. to 10:00 a.m.	2nd hour
10:00 a.m. to 11:00 a.m.	3rd hour
11:00 a.m. to 12:00 p.m.	4th hour
12:00 p.m. to 1:00 p.m.	5th hour (break must be before the end of the 5th hour, i.e. 12:59 p.m.)

Figure 10.4. The regulation of working hours and breaks is a pivotal aspect that directly influences the well-being and productivity of employees.

Source: https://www.californiaemploymentlawreport.com/wp-content/uploads/sites/747/2018/06/Timing-of-meal-breaks.png.

The structure of work hours can have a direct impact on such things as overtime compensation, leave allowances, and worker satisfaction in general. For instance, the employer's inability to abide by prescribed break periods may lead to worker burnout and greater turnover. Moreover, Maternity Leave Directive debates not only indicate how such regulations might affect groups within the labor force, that is, parents and caregivers (Eurofound, 2015), but also that employers must not only implement structural policies but also craft an organizational culture wherein employee expectations of care are supported and placed in a priority position through reflective management of breaks and working hours. Moreover, break and hour legislations' compliance can be an essential preventive measure against accidents and workplace safety. If employees are overloaded with excessive working hours and lacking in breaks, their susceptibility to accidents and health issues compounds at an alarming rate. By following stipulated legal frameworks on breaks and working hours, employers can lower the risks of negligence and exhaustion. As stated in various employment law reforms, a policy to address these factors can assist in creating a stronger workforce as well as lowering liabilities associated with work. Thus, the acknowledgement of the importance of harmonizing breaks and hours not only synchronizes with legal obligations but also assists in organizational performance and employee morale in an economic labor market (Figure 10.4).

10.2.2. Occupational Safety

Occupational safety is part of labor and employment law, emphasizing the significance of the protection of workers in various environments. Legal systems that govern this subject are designed to enhance working conditions such that hazards are minimized and employees can execute their tasks optimally without being overexposed to risk. New trends in labor administration systems between countries, particularly in China, echo the greater focus on public services geared towards occupational safety. These improvements involve not only offensive inspection practices but also lengthy training regimes for the sake of boosting employees' safety consciousness. By implementing these measures, both employers and employees will have a better work environment in the long run, eventually translating to productivity and morale (Figure 10.5).

Figure 10.5. Code on occupational safety, health and working conditions.

Source: https://www.mondaq.com/images/article_images/1256990c.jpg.

Enhanced enforcement of safety standards ensures compliance and, consequently, a culture of accountability at the workplace (Casale et al., 2013). Moreover, consistent reforms take cognizance of the necessity of continuous adaptation in occupational safety standards, particularly in light of evolving workplace settings. While businesses evolve with respect to developments in technology and changing market demands, legal consequences attached to safety standards must also do so. The cross-jurisdictional observation presents a general overview of recent reforms and their projected contribution in the direction of employers, more particularly towards liability and compliance (Baker and McKenzie, 2013).

Not only do such reforms address usual workplace risks, but they also consider modern problems such as ergonomic challenges and mental health problems, which are becoming increasingly relevant in today's workforce. This comprehensive approach to occupational safety focuses on the importance of preventive measures that can eliminate risks from taking place before they show up as injuries or illnesses, making the workplace a safe place for all concerned parties. The success of occupational safety legislation relies significantly on collaboration between numerous stakeholders, including employers, workers, and regulatory bodies. Compliance with safety rules and regulations is not only a legal responsibility but also a major component of corporate ethics that can enhance the credibility and loyalty of a company towards its workers. Employee participation in safety initiatives makes them feel responsible and aware, and they take active actions to maintain a safe workplace. Furthermore, when safety laws are recognized as being a shared responsibility, it can lead to a more collaborative work environment and ultimately lower accidents and injuries. As labor law continues to evolve, the fusion of occupational safety with overall employment policies remains paramount to ensure that the rights of workers are protected while maintaining a sustainable labor market (Casale et al., 2013).

10.2.3. Remote Work Policy

In the past couple of years, debate on remote work policies has generated enormous momentum owing to shifting dynamics in the workplace and technological developments. The proliferation of digital communication tools has transformed organizations' modes of operation, allowing workers to accomplish their duties from locations distant from traditional office locations. This mobility, however, translates to legal concerns that need to strike a balance between the demands of employers and workers' rights. Specifically, employers need to develop integrated policies that address not only the mechanics of working at a distance but the health, safety, and overall well-being of their employees. Establishing guidelines that establish work hours, performance standards, and communication protocols becomes paramount to encouraging a healthy remote work environment that reflects broader trends in labor and employment law as reflected in the growing demand for transparency in employer-employee relationships. Remote work policies also have a wide effect on the rights of and benefits for workers regarding occupational safety and working conditions. The employers must extend beyond the working environment itself and cater to the remote work environments where their employees are undertaking their work activities. This means having the appropriate mechanism to ensure safe working environments as well as equipment required to conduct work activities effectively irrespective of the location. These are considerations that are crucial, since implications of remote work arrangements are such that they can result in variations in interpretation of labor rights and legislation across jurisdictions. In addition, as the OECD's emphasis on investment over the pandemic illustrated, there is a need to react to the demands of other categories of employees in putting in place effective remote work policies. Through removal of the legal cloud over telecommuting, companies can promote justice and resilience in workplace rules, thereby resulting in a more caring work culture. Secondly, constructing remote worker policies necessitates a proactive approach towards inclusiveness and sensitivity to changing workforce populations and needs. As an increasing number of employees, especially younger ones, come to the workplace with diverse expectations about work-life balance, businesses need to examine how these changes influence their working models. Interaction with employee communities can give important understandings about the problems of employees in remote locations so that policies are not like top-down orders but are instead collective efforts. Government intervention, based on various reports by various youth organizations, focuses on the aspect that integrating many perspectives is imperative in policy development. The aim is to achieve a flexible and equitable working environment that satisfies employee personal needs as well as fulfilling broader legislatory requirements, hence driving the future of labor and employment legislation toward remote work approaches (Gatta, 2022; OECD, 2022).

10.3. EMPLOYEE RIGHTS AND BENEFITS

The recognition of benefits and rights of employees is core to the formulation of equitable working conditions and enhancing employee satisfaction across various industries. As per modern labor laws, the minimum wage law plays a crucial role in offering equitable remuneration for labor to workers. Through the establishment of the minimum wage employers must adhere to, the law eliminates wage disparities and prevents worker exploitation, mainly by poor people. Aside from that, the application of the minimum wage laws can stimulate economic growth through increased purchasing power among the workforce, resulting in higher overall morale and productivity within the workforce. This system of law is required to maintain a just workplace because it directly affects laborers' level of living and economic well-being, ultimately showing societys commitment to the philosophy of just remuneration for labor. Leave entitlements are another important area of employee rights that greatly affect workers' general welfare and job satisfaction (Figure 10.6).

Figure 10.6. Workplace rights.

Source: https://images.cakeresume.com/images/37f02dd7-9d8f-45f5-ae7f-24a12b772429.jpg.

Accurate provisions for sick leave, family leave, and vacation time are essential in enabling employees to manage family and personal needs alongside work needs in an effort towards attaining a work-life balance. The need for such benefits arises from the fact that workers might be required to address unexpected situations that demand temporary absence from work. By extending certain entitlements of paid leave, employers not only strengthen positive organizational culture, but also improve employee loyalty and retention. Further, availing formal leave policies demonstrates a company's care for the health and happiness of its employees, which can prove a determining factor in high-level talent recruitment in competitive labor markets. Formalizing such benefits as a statutory right ensures the protection of employees' rights while promoting productivity and organizational commitment. Termination pay is an essential component of workers' rights that guards the economic welfare of workers upon termination. Workers are usually faced with financial insecurity following the termination, highlighting the importance of required severance pay, unemployment benefits, and retraining programs at work. Such arrangements help to moderate mechanisms of adjustment of dislocated workers, alleviating the adverse consequences of unemployment. Furthermore, the laws governing the termination benefits ensure that the process of redundancy and layoff is fair and so protects workers against arbitrary dismissal. Judicial practice in this case also enforces the right to be treated reasonably on layoff, focusing on notice to the affected workers and providing them with mechanisms of recourse in case their rights are violated. The systematic administration of termination benefits imposes the ethical obligations of employers and the principle of employment security, finally resulting in a more secure and stabilized labor market, as emphasized in the extensive discussion of employment contracts and labor law (Kniazkova, 2024) and the necessity to grant marginalized groups access to their rights (Polianskyi, 2024).

10.3.1. Minimum Wage

The complicated interaction of economic forces and legislative response defines the dynamics of minimum wage legislation in labor and employment systems. By establishing a floor wage, minimum wage legislation aims to protect workers against exploitation while promoting fair labor standards. Yet, such laws get mixed reactions from stakeholders, with proponents citing them as essential in providing a living wage and opponents claiming that establishing floors in wages will stifle job creation, especially in low-skilled labor markets. Such opposition exists as jurisdictions are adapting minimum wage requirements to their individual economic realities, resulting in a mosaic of protective laws that sometimes are inclined to protect employer welfare at the expense of employee rights. These disparities underscore the need for continuous review and modification of minimum wage policy to meet changing economic circumstances as well as to make a substantial contribution to the welfare of workers in the labor market. Another most important element of the minimum wage discourse is its enforcement, or at least lack thereof. Despite the enactment of minimum wage laws to protect workers, enforcement arrangements are frequently inadequate, resulting in extensive non-compliance by employers. This is further compounded in a number of economies where informal labor markets predominate, leaving numerous workers vulnerable to exploitation.

In a number of locations, for instance, whereas local minimum wages are set, they hardly reflect average living costs and therefore leave enormous gaps and undermine their protective role. This backdrop highlights broader systemic failure in compliance with labor law where de facto protections afforded to workers fall below legal standards. To this end, increasing enforcement mechanisms and imposing stronger penalties on noncompliance is crucial in breaking open the maximum potential of minimum wage law to secure workers in an internationalizing economy (Herd et al., 2010). Further, the role of social dialogue in the formulation of minimum wage policy cannot be downplayed. The International Labor Organization (ILO) points to the importance of engaging all interested stakeholders in deliberations that set regulations in the labor market. The participatory process strives to ensure consensus and to address the intricacies of setting and varying minimum wages. Policy decision analysis, such as that of past government worker relations in Nigeria, reveals a predisposition towards authoritarianism, which restricts genuine social discussion despite the global pressure for democratic governance (Onyeenoruket al., 2007). Giving listening space to workers in the discussion is crucial in formulating sustainable worker policies. It is only through an inclusive process that minimum wage law can change to accommodate the needs of a multifaceted workforce while remaining sensitive to economic conditions.

10.3.2. Leave Entitlements

The complexity of leave entitlements is a central aspect of employment and labor law, the social requirement to uphold work-life balance and worker welfare. Statutory leave entitlements in most jurisdictions comprise a range of provisions, ranging from annual leave to sick leave and parental leave. These guarantees play a crucial role in enabling workers to recover, care for family, or address personal matters and thereby enhance workplace productivity and morale. However, inconsistencies invariably arise by employment status, and independent contractors are all too frequently excluded from these valuable protections. This line creates great questions of fairness in the workplace, particularly as non-traditional forms of labor, such as gig work, become increasingly prevalent. Thus, the legal framework governing leave entitlements must be reformed in a way that all workers, whether employed or not, enjoy fair and equal access to such significant rights. In addition, leave is more than granting time off; it is a representation of respect for the dignity of workers and the right to health. The underlying logic of leave entitlement is a growing awareness that not only need employees be safeguarded in the workplace but also while they are away from work. As an example, sick leave entitlement has an important function of maintaining public health and preventing disease transmission and hence contributing to the welfare of society as a whole. In addition, parental leave is enforcing the rights of employees to care for family responsibilities without losing their jobs or incurring economic penalties. The only disadvantage, however, is that the rights are hardly made equal for all employment. As workers increasingly engage with various forms of employment regimes, for example, platform and contract labor, the inadequacy of full legal protection, as established in documents such as the Revised European Social Charter, points toward change in labor law to address these gaps in access to leave entitlements (Marian, 2020). In addressing employees' right to leave, particularly non-standard employment, emerging legislative frameworks must emphasize inclusivity as a primary objective. Right to rest is not only a fundamental labor right but also a measure of social justice in keeping with contemporary societal norms. As highlighted in the traineeship entitlement debates, many individuals, even without legal employee status, do labor under conditions that deserve similar protections (Staszewska-Koz, 2024). Expanding the definition of entitlement to leave can contribute to a more equitable labor market and protect vulnerable workers from losing out on necessary support. Law-makers are invited to consider these disparities in making laws, the evolving character of work and expanding scope of precarious work arrangements under their consideration. By confirming the right to leave across all types of work, labor law is better placed to safeguard personal health and uphold societal values that underpin an effective and fair labor force.

10.3.3. Termination Benefits

The intricacies involved in the process of employment termination have an important bearing on the entire scheme of labor and employment law. In this framework, termination benefits are an indispensable aspect that protects the rights of the employees during the process of ending their employer-employee relationships. Termination benefits aim to create a financial buffer zone for employees who lose their means of earning money as a result of termination. Such financial assistance may comprise termination pay, holiday pay, and other benefit packages, which help mitigate the economic loss of losing a job. Employers are required to satisfy statutory standards in such benefits in an effort to minimize legal ramifications accompanying unfair dismissal, since truncated benefits can lead to increased litigation and worker discontent, hence advocating for the importance of a strong regulatory system. Additionally, the application of termination benefits is considerably varied in various work settings, as dictated by contradictory legal requisites and industry conventions. Where workers hold permanent contracts, there is a requirement by law to apply certain benefits, whereas this can be less obligatory in the case of independent contractors. This disparity could result in a precarious environment whereby freelance workers, for example, lack adequate cover upon termination events. Their relative lack of explicit rules often works against them, according to research on legal protections for various forms of employment categorizations, such as those in Indonesias freelance market. The absence of legality in those contexts highlights the importance of ongoing legislative measures that not only promote workers' rights but also level terms for termination benefits, as discussed in debate surrounding employment law reform. Also, the debate about termination benefits acquires importance in light of international labor standards that can offer valuable lessons in best practices. For instance, countries with stringent labor laws typically ensure that the employees have wide termination benefits including severance pay and continuous health insurance coverage for a specified period. These practices not only maintain the dignity of the workers but also agree with provisions outlined in international labor conventions focused on guaranteeing equity in the process of termination. Despite some jurisdictions, such as in the case of Lithuania, grappling with the efficiency of current legal frameworks (Bartninkas, 2024), the need for fair termination benefits remains a concern in many legal systems. Hence, finding a balance between employees' protection and employer flexibility is crucial in advocating for labor standards and ensuring fair treatment in cases of termination, resonating across all sections of the workforce (Mu'adil Faizin et al., 2024).

10.4. COLLECTIVE BARGAINING

In the more globalized economy, collective bargaining's role cannot be overstated. Collective bargaining is a central channel through which workers, often unionized, negotiate with their employers on terms and conditions of work, including remuneration, terms and conditions of work, and security at work. Collective bargaining has played a historic role in setting the terms of work in the labor market to enable tremendous progress in workplace standards. These negotiations result in collective agreements that not only govern the immediate parties but also affect others beyond them, influencing the terms of non-union workers indirectly. As pointed out, the regime of collective bargaining is recognized in various international treaties and is the foundation of labor legislations of industrialized nations, pointing to its core element of industrial relations. Therefore, the efficacy of collective bargaining processes continues to be an important issue for labor law scholars and practitioners alike, especially in their quest to advance employee rights as well as equitable labor practices (Figure 10.7).

Figure 10.7. Collective bargaining objectives.

Source: https://media.geeksforgeeks.org/wp-content/uploads/20240419091925/Objectives-of-Collective-Bargaining-copy.webp.

The role of law in collective bargaining is more than the limited provision of frameworks; it is also to ensure that the parties negotiate in good faith and openness. Legal arrangements could be needed where voluntary agreements on bargaining processes fail, and states intervene for effective bargaining. Intervention could be in the form of establishing collective bargaining machinery to facilitate organized exchange of ideas between unions and employers. Furthermore, parties are obligated to uphold legal standards of conduct throughout the bargaining process, thus a promise that negotiations will be fair and just. The above legal framework not only enhances the credibility of the bargaining process but also offers assurances that reduce conflicts arising during the negotiation process. The legal foundations of collective bargaining are thus paramount to ensure good industrial relations and ensure that agreements reached are not merely symbolic, but also enforceable and effective (Law et al., 2013). As society evolves and the nature of the workforce evolves with it, the collective bargaining process itself also needs to evolve to deal with contemporary challenges. In regions such as the South Pacific, where local concepts of work are at odds with today's economic realities, imposing collective bargaining introduces unique challenges. As an illustration, the prior absence of codified labor legislation in these environments raises the question of how European judicial norms applicable to more developed economies can succeed or be relevant. Moreover, the process itself requires a refined understanding of local norms and practices that define work arrangements. This indicates the importance of comparative studies as practitioners and scholars try to examine the local impact of international labor principles in the context of indigenous practices. Analyzing how these forces work in different contexts is crucial in the broader debate within labor and employment law and serves to underscore the importance of collaborative, multidisciplinary approaches to understanding the complexity of modern labor relations (Law et al., 2013).

10.4.1. Union Formation

The unionization dynamics are central to understanding the broader context of employment and labor law. The core aspect of the process is the collective representation of workers wishing to enhance their bargaining power in relation to employment conditions. Workers come to understand that unionization provides a organized means of bargaining for higher wages, better working conditions, and additional benefits. Such group action is not only an alliance but also a strategic response to perceived injustice or disparity in the workplace. The legal framework that underlies the creation of unions, found in legislation and regulation, plays a significant role in defining the rights of employees to organize and the responsibilities of employers to adhere to these rights. Hence, knowledge of the social and legal dimensions of union formation is key to the knowledge of the impact of collective bargaining on labor relations. The theory of collective bargaining underlies successful union formation, wherein unions negotiate with employers on behalf of their members. This is often a reflection of the power dynamic in the workplace and can lead to collective agreements that explicitly define the terms of employment. For instance, in regions where law strongly encourages the formation of unions, the outcome of this negotiation often favors the employees with stipulations like minimum wages and safety measures. Conversely, areas with highly restrictive regulation of union activity might experience rampant wage disparities and wretched working conditions, making the case for legislative action in enforcing decent labor standards. Collective agreements resulting from this negotiation can establish standards on issues like strike rights and means of resolving disputes, further solidifying unions' role as central players in employment law. Finally, the consequences of union formation extend beyond immediate workplace conditions to impact more generic socio-economic principles. Unions do not merely fight for their constituents' rights but can also beg for policies impacting the public welfare, such as health care improvements or child care benefit systems. The high correlation of unionization with reduced economic inequalities has long been a target of labor research, though the issues facing unions in the current period, such as globalization and technological transformation, have a tendency to complicate their effectiveness. Furthermore, the changing landscape of work arrangements, with growing dominance of gig and independent contractor work, adds an additional layer of complication to the prospects for mainstream union forms. Thus, along with changing law in the sphere of labor and employment law come the need to adapt tactics by unions to remain effective and relevant in campaigning for workers' rights, as highlighted via the pressure of continuous policy-making and legal adaptation in this field (Gatta, 2022; N/A, 2019).

10.4.2. Strike Rights

The strike right remains a vital component in the paradigm of labor and employment law, being a core tool for employees to log protest and negotiate better working conditions. It has historically been seen as an integral part of collective bargaining, whereby laborers are able to organize and articulate their demands in the face of employer hostility. Yet the legal framework for strike rights tends to paint a confusing picture, subject to the pull of a number of statutes and provisions. For example, the effect of local laws can be quite dramatic from one jurisdiction to another, evidencing a patchwork approach towards recognizing and controlling strike actions. This discrepancy comes to the foreground particularly in the case of examples such as the Latvian summer 2017 strike of general practitioners illuminating the inadequacies of existing legal guarantees in granting equal access to strike rights to all employees (Bite et al., 2019).

The evolution of non-standard work arrangements in contemporary labor markets brings more complexities to the enforcement of strike rights. Since the workforce keeps including more freelancers, gig workers, and other workers outside conventional employment patterns, the existing rules supporting collective action can appear outdated. The existing restraints of this sort disproportionately harm such non-standard workers, limiting their access considerably to collective bargaining rights and the right to strike. In the majority of cases, such a shortage is incapacitating their ability to demand equitable work conditions. Thus, there needs to be an analytical critique to ascertain the degree to which the prevailing laws could be altered to accommodate the changing reality of work and uphold the underlying maxims of collective action as enshrined in the right to strike (Stefano et al., 2015). Resolution of these emerging challenges calls for re-casting current legal rules around strike rights. One of the most significant aspects of this transformation is the acknowledgment of the right to strike's transition from a mere tool of collective bargaining to a mass human right. The transition highlights the necessity that politicians take to revisit existing legislation so it can be fitting for prevailing socio-economic realities. Shifting the debate towards reform entails suggestions for modifying law amendments that expand on which workers have a right to strike. In doing so, the societies can promote the protection of the common interests and provide fair labor practices in accordance with global legal principles, thereby strengthening the need for strike rights as an integral part of modern labor law (Bite et al., 2019).

10.4.3. Collective Agreements

The dynamic landscape of the workplace and labor law necessitates a mechanism for managing the complex interrelationships between employers and employees. Collective agreements are at the heart of this mechanism, serving as central instruments in shaping the terms and conditions of employment. Besides articulating wages, working hours, and conditions of benefits, these agreements also regularize the grievance-redressal procedures in the workplace and safety regulations. Notably, collective agreements are products of collective bargaining processes, where unions negotiate on behalf of workers to gain fair working conditions and protect the rights of employees. Collective bargaining has also evolved to respond to emerging challenges and accommodate the needs of an evolving workforce and the emerging complexities introduced by technological change and globalization, as reflected by the OECD Employment Outlook (N/A, 2019). In collective agreements, union presence is indicative of significant developments in labor relations, especially with the growth of non-standard employment. Workers with varying employment statuses are likely to have varying challenges in collective bargaining rights, as legal classifications can compromise solidarity and bargaining power. For instance, the majority of workers in self-employment fall outside the coverage of collective bargaining protections as has been seen in some of the OECD countries where particular extensions of collective bargaining rights have emerged (N/A, 2019). The above situation underscores the need for legal measures to consider different forms of work while providing all workers with equal access to collective agreements, making the labor market a more inclusive and equitable one. Furthermore, the effectiveness of collective agreements rests on constant adjustments to the evolving needs of the labor force. With the evolving labor markets created by population change and emerging technology, the existing frameworks of collective agreements have to be adjusted likewise. Greater competition and innovation subject the unions and employers to greater pressure to seek flexible bargaining procedures that adapt to the realities of contemporary labor force. Such dynamism is particularly significant in addressing the issues of workers engaged in emerging industries or in undergoing employment transformation. The OECD emphasizes that further strengthening the institutions of collective bargaining is key to equipping workers with greater bargaining power and fostering partnerships for developing workplace security and adaptability in a changing economy.

10.5. ANTI-DISCRIMINATION PROVISIONS

As the workplace becomes increasingly diversified, the function of anti-discrimination provisions is a very important field of labor and employment law. The law systems assist in protecting individuals against discriminatory treatment for reasons of race, gender, age, disability, and sexual orientation. To this extent, equal pay is a fundamental anti-discrimination principle, not just a tool of economic fairness but a force behind broader social equality. Pay structures per se represent a contradiction of the norm of equal treatment, and comprehensive anti-discrimination law must be employed to correct such disparities. As has been reported in scholarly discussions, the relationship between collective bargaining systems and anti-discrimination laws further highlights the need for these regulations to be complete and binding in multiple workplace environments, enabling all employees to thrive without discrimination or prejudice (Blackett et al., 2002) (Figure 10.8).

Figure 10.8. Workplace harassment types and examples.

Source: https://www.canadasafetytraining.com/uploads/types-of-workplace-harassment.jpg.

The issue of workplace harassment accompanies the topic of anti-discrimination provisions because it is a blatant violation of employees' rights. Harassment comes in various forms, including verbal assault, unwanted advances, and discriminatory jokes, all of which contribute to a hostile work environment. In an effort to prevent such behavior, anti-discrimination provisions must mandate specific policies and training courses that are designed to sensitize employees to their duties and rights. Furthermore, effective reporting mechanisms must be established to empower victims and hold perpetrators accountable. As the conversation continues regarding the adequacy of existing provisions, it becomes evident that legislatures must adapt continuously to emerging challenges and societal expectations. By fostering a culture of respect and inclusivity, workplace harassment can be significantly reduced, thus ensuring a more equitable working environment for all (Lane et al., 2015). Besides answering immediate needs, positive actions are also a major approach in striving for workplace equality□□ under anti-discrimination legislations. Positive actions may be in the form of targeted hiring, mentorship programs, and ongoing professional training of previously disenfranchised groups. Implementation of positive action policies is contentious but an inconvenient truth that systemic barriers regularly block equal opportunity in the labor force. Anti-discrimination legislation must therefore meet with affirmative action to create a cohesive strategy towards equality. Supporters of such initiatives believe that they are necessary not only to balance the scales but to cut the yoke of past discrimination built into hiring procedures. By integrating these approaches in labor and employment law, societies can make actual progress towards diversity and inclusion, having workplaces that reflect the vibrant diversity of skills and experience in the community (Blackett et al., 2002).

10.5.1. Equal Pay

Equal pay rhetoric is both constructed by legal limits and social norms, often finding embedded in society deeply rooted social biases. In South Africa, legislative frameworks such as the Employment Equity Act offers a foundation for upholding equal pay claims. Section 6(4) of the Employment Equity Act demands that the distinctions that have been eliminated in terms and conditions of employment be stipulated, demonstrating the imperative that claimants are made aware of the nuance embedded in their rights. There being no clear description in regard to terms and conditions of employment complicates the larger landscape, rendering it essential for equal pay claimants to tread warily in this ever-changing landscape. By looking into domestic and international labor legislations, one can find out how the concepts are operationalized, revealing the potential loopholes that may arise in practice as complainants are confronted with such powerful institutional mechanisms that often enforce wage discrimination (Ebrahim, 2024). Moreover, assessing equal pay is not only a legal obligation; it is a moral effort towards gender equality and esteem at the workplace. The gaps in achieving equal pay reveal systemic issues involving gender discrimination as well as employment practices based on discrimination. In spite of significant advances to equate pay for individuals performing similar work, obstacles continue to be faced regarding the parental leave arrangements. Specifically, imbalanced parental leave arrangements are likely to reinforce economic disparities among women and men and sustain cycles of inequity connecting unpaid caregiving labor. The judicial interpretations of these issues emphasize the need for a review of the workplace policies to align them in harmony with the principles of equality under the Constitution, promoting a culture in which pay equity not only offsets current disparities but also recognizes the broader social implications of equitable treatment at work (Chitimira et al., 2024). In solving these pressing issues, collective bargaining becomes instrumental in amplifying the fight for equal pay for inclusive workforces. Employee unions' action of combating fair wages is inevitable since they serve as a link between workers' rights and policies of employers. Successful negotiation strategies can lead to more inclusive collective agreements that uphold the tradition of equal pay while addressing the sophistication associated with different employment relationships, including temporary and part-time work. Compliance with such agreements is crucial in upholding the respect and advancement of pay equity in different industries. Ultimately, where the convergence of legal frameworks, moral ideals, and collective bargaining is a multiplicative approach to real progress toward equal pay, it is one that is focused on the commitment to an equitable marketplace of labor characterized by just wages for all workers, irrespective of gender or organizational status.

10.5.2. Workplace Harassment

Workplace harassment is a significant branch of labor and employment law, as it directly impacts employee rights and general workplace culture. The phenomenon of harassment taking such forms as sexual abuse or bullying holds immense potential to undermine individual well-being and organizational morale. In all jurisdictions, there are legal frameworks that seek to provide protection to employees against such distasteful acts. For instance, countries have legislated giving victims legal rights, with a focus on the employers' responsibility to ensure a healthy workplace. It is vital that the laws are enacted; however, many organizations lack efficient means of reporting and handling harassment cases, leaving the employees to be exploited. It is evident that an active response is needed to expand these legal safeguards so that victims are guarded and the perpetrators held liable in an increasingly diverse workplace setting. Evidence of bringing in the explicit legal definitions against workplace harassment can be seen from the latest legislative moves toward tightening worker rights. For example, the passing of laws that target mobbing and bullying is proof that more parties increasingly acknowledge the negative effect of such actions against people and organizations. As posited in recent studies, the best legal provisions ought to include not only punitive action against offenders but also for employee education concerning their rights in the area of harassment at the workplace (Sereda et al., 2024). Legal safeguard mechanisms, such as the right to privacy, the right to a decent work environment, and protection mechanisms for victims, are required to minimize the risks of workplace harassment. There remain loopholes in application of these standards evenly, and hence continuous updating and alterations to prevalent laws are essential to offer thorough protection to all workers. Secondly, the value of employer responsibility in preventing workplace harassment cannot be ignored. Organizations must establish a workplace culture of respect and inclusivity through explicit policies and procedures that consider harassment in a comprehensive manner. Training courses and workshops to educate employees on how to identify, prevent, and handle workplace harassment are critical. Legal scholars argue that without an enlightened workforce that understands their rights and the avenues they have for recourse, the efficacy of laws designed to check workplace harassment is diminished significantly (Sugiharto et al., 2024). This is crucial in ensuring that all workers, regardless of where they stand in the company, feel confident reporting that they are being harassed without fear of repercussions. The provision of proper mechanisms for resolving disputes further ensures the seriousness with which complaints are handled and resolved, creating a culture of accountability within the organization.

10.5.3. Affirmative Measures

In the context of Labor and Employment Law, affirmative measures are crucial strategies that aim to reverse historical disadvantages faced by underprivileged groups in the working environment. Affirmative measures are designed to establish a more equitable labor market by actively promoting opportunities for underrepresented groups, thereby removing embedded prejudices. For instance, positive measures can be the offering of special recruitment or training schemes that specifically aim at increasing the number of women or racial minorities in the management levels. This is proactive action that sees the existing barriers and works towards eliminating them and promoting diversity and inclusion in the workplace. Therefore, organizations that implement such measures not only comply with legal standards but also establish a more vibrant and innovative working environment in which the interaction of different perspectives facilitates more effective decision-making and productivity. Of significance in ensuring measures are upheld is their alignment with anti-discrimination provisions aimed at eliminating discriminatory practices in recruitment, promotion, and remuneration. By including affirmative actions in legally mandated obligations, employers can become part of a comprehensive plan that endorses the value of equity as well as equality. Such provisions are particularly important in collective bargaining, as unions tend to resist attempts at affirmative actions that benefit their members. The pressure for equal wages, for example, is aggravated by affirmative measures that not only recognize wage discrimination but also recommend solutions to be implemented in order to correct them. Therefore, the complementarity of affirmative measures and anti-discrimination laws allows a climate of equity within the labor market to flourish significantly reducing the cases of discrimination and harassment at workplaces (N/A, 2021).

The implementation of affirmative measures, nevertheless, has some challenges that need to be approached cautiously. Organizations must balance the necessity for diversity against charges of reverse discrimination in which the members of dominant groups feel themselves discriminated against. This tension will require that there be proper communication of the objectives of affirmative actions and a rationalization in terms of the social merits of equality in the workplace. Proper monitoring of these efforts must be done periodically to ensure that these efforts find their target without engendering resentment in workers. Through adopting a comprehensive approach that involves stakeholder engagement and ongoing evaluation, organizations are better placed to include positive steps which make the workplace just while guaranteeing integration among their workforce (N/A, 2023).

10.6. DISPUTE RESOLUTION MECHANISMS

The complexity of employee-employer relations often gives rise to conflicts that necessitate effective dispute resolution mechanisms, a vital aspect of Labor and Employment Law. To manage these conflicts, jurisdictions typically implement a range of procedures that address grievances without resorting to litigation, thereby conserving resources and maintaining workplace harmony (Figure 10.9).

Figure 10.9. Labor tribunals serve a critical function within this framework, providing a structured environment where disputes can be presented and adjudicated by experts in labor law.

Source: https://external-content.duckduckgo.com/iu/?u=https%3A%2F% 2Fthf.bing.com%2Fth%2Fid%2FOIP.Kwj2gxE5w_NC2k9XtsY1fgHaE8%3Fr%3 D0%2 6cb%3Dthfc1%26pid%3DApi&f=1&ipt=c0c014ed019b6d96f2e95fb1e98e0fb642979babca546e6c9a947fe6a5be8b9a.

These courts are experts in hearing cases of employment, like claims for wrongful dismissal or compensation, so that both parties are accorded a fair hearing and judgments are passed as per the set laws. The establishment of these courts normally reflects a society's resolve to uphold employees' rights and preserve labor standards, fostering a balanced approach towards resolving labor disputes effectively. Aside from tribunals, arbitration and mediation are also forms of conflict resolution that are being gradually embraced within the field of Labor and Employment Law. Mediation involves a third-party individual who remains impartial and who brings the belligerent parties together so that they may address their conflicts peacefully. The process is centered on collaboration and is likely to result in resolutions that maintain current relationships, something that is particularly useful within the workplace. Conversely, arbitration forces a ruling by the arbitrator, whose decision is usually binding. The flexibility of both allows employers and employees to tailor the process of resolution to their own needs, perhaps achieving quicker, less adversarial resolutions. Collectively, the two highlight an evolving vision of dispute resolution consistent with contemporary notions of labor relations based on cooperation and conflict-prevention strategies (Campaign, 2005). Enforcement is a necessary part of any effective system of dispute resolution since the mechanisms for effectuating them have to be both available and credible if they are going to be effectively effective. Courts of general jurisdiction are most commonly utilized as a resort of last resort, allowing parties to seek judicial remedies when other avenues are not effective. These remedies can include reinstatement, wages in arrears, or damages, an indication of the degree to which legal systems take labor disputes. More significantly, the presence of robust mechanisms of dispute settlement ensures not only compliance with existing laws but also encouragement of compliance by inculcating a sense of respect for workers' rights and employers' responsibilities. The ability to resolve conflict peacefully decreases tensions among the workforce, resulting in a harmonious and effective workplace. This relationship between regulatory mechanisms, enforcement, and resolving conflict illustrates a broader dialogue on labor rights and governance that is essential in today's shifting work environment (Betcherman et al., 2025).

10.6.1. Labor Tribunals

Workplace conflicts are inevitable in employment relations, owing to varying contexts such as interpretation of the contract and work conditions. One of the principal avenues for conflict resolution is through labor tribunals, which are courts specifically instituted to hear employer-employee conflict cases. Labor tribunals offer a speedy process whereby both sides can ventilate their complaints and obtain a remedy effectively. This procedure is particularly valuable in areas of administration, such as claims for unpaid wages or wrongful termination, that may be cumbersome to pursue under regular court channels. The tribunal system is more likely to provide a calm environment where parties can interact face-to-face with adjudicators who possess specialized expertise in the field of employment law. By a singular focus on the specifics of labor disputes, tribunals guarantee the administration of justice at an accelerated pace, thus guaranteeing stability within the workforce and adherence to labor standards.

The operational efficiency of labor tribunals varies across different jurisdictions, as a function of the respective legal regimes and monies allocated to these institutions. Where there are large legal support mechanisms in jurisdictions, say some states located in Europe, tribunals play a role not just as judges but also as educators of the rights of workers and responsibilities of employers. For instance, countries that have large family policies complement working parents' employment strategies, an indication of a change where such policies engage with the decisions of tribunals. The emphasis on equitable resolution processes is brought out by the conflicting tribunal operations, with some embracing alternative resolution processes of disputes that minimize the judiciary workload and facilitate smooth agreements. The integration of mediatory practices into the tribunals' processes reflects the aspiration for peaceful resolution of disputes while maintaining the rights of all parties, which results in a harmonious work environment. Despite the advantages presented by tribunals of labor, there are challenges that can result in their effectiveness and acceptance of fairness at the workplace. One of the significant challenges is the accessibility of the tribunals, particularly for marginalized groups who could find complexities in the law or experience discrimination within the system. Additionally, tribunal case decisions are often uneven with divergent legal interpretations resulting in inconsistent judgments. Evidence indicates the retention of prejudices, in this instance, of vulnerable groups within the workplace, to suggest that fault lines in the system bring about discriminatory enforcement of labor laws. In an attempt to rectify the disparities, improved comprehension of tribunal functions as well as the inclusion of anti-discrimination law provisions will be essential. With evolving legal structures, the functioning of labor tribunals will be central to creating equitable employment practices by linking them with prevailing workforce developments and anticipations.

10.6.2. Mediation and Arbitration

Peaceful resolution of conflict within the ambit of labor relations demands understanding of mediation and arbitration as paramount processes. Both are alternative approaches to adversarial litigation, offering a more elastic and less adversarial resolution of conflicts arising between employers and employees. Mediation involves an impartial third party facilitating negotiations between warring parties with the expectation of coming to agreement. This is a process that promotes discussion and cooperation in that it affords the parties control over the outcome. Arbitration, on the other hand, is a more structured process in which the evidence adduced before an arbitrator determines a conclusive resolution. This reflects the different levels of control as well as formality involved in each of the processes that impact how disputes in labor are addressed and resolved. According to the framework of collective bargaining, these tools are fundamental in fostering effective relationships and fair employment practice at the workplace (N/A, 2019).

The applicability of mediation and arbitration also lies in their ability to adapt to the modern employment relationship landscape, particularly with regard to how they address matters of non-traditional forms of employment arrangements. The advent of the gig economy has introduced a complex context in which the basic definitions of employment status become increasingly slippery. As pointed out by recent research, the ambiguity surrounding gig workers very often dissolves traditional labor protection mechanisms, making the need for innovative solutions to uphold minimal standards imperative (Minter, 2017). Mediation can provide a channel for gig economy workers to raise concerns and negotiate fair terms of engagement with platform companies. Parallel to this, arbitration can serve a means of redressing disputes stemming from these new employment arrangements, holding everyone responsible to prevailing labor law and custom. For this reason, the implementation of these dispute resolution systems is essential in promoting inclusiveness and equity within contemporary labor markets. Furthermore, the efficacy of arbitration and mediation is derived from their capacity to maintain communication among social actors with a view to enhancing the collective bargaining process. With the workings of complex labor markets in constant flux, there is a new-found need for flexible frameworks that are capable of navigating emergent challenges with ease. Research emphasizes the pivotal role collective bargaining plays in responding to change such as globalization and automation, so that measures must be taken to protect the rights of employees (N/A, 2019). The inclusion of arbitration and mediation in collective bargaining enables participants to engage in fruitful negotiations with regards to the fluidity of labor relations. This collaborative approach, in addition to trying to resolve immediate conflicts, also positively strives to establish fair agreements that benefit both employers and workers in the long term, thus establishing an open and fair working environment.

10.6.3. Judicial Remedies

In the complex arena of employment and labor law, judicial remedies have a central role to play in compensating for infringements of statutory rights and terms of contract. Judicial remedies are all-important channels for the enforcement of employees' rights against unlawful employment policies. If employees are disadvantaged, such as by unfair dismissal or problems concerning pay, judicial remedies allow them access to the courts whereby their grievances are formally acknowledged. This type of legal remedy not only reinstates personal rights but also consolidates the rule of law by acting as a deterrent against misuse by employers. The ability of the courts to enforce remedies in this case is a reflection of the evolving needs of modern labor markets and the need for effective enforcement of protections generated through law. Each remedy provided must be appropriate in its context, thereby enhancing the judicial framework for cases relating to labor disputes. The efficacy of judicial remedies is contingent on the legal systems within which they function and can vary extensively from jurisdiction to jurisdiction. Some, for instance, will have heavy recourse to restorative forms, attempting to put the injured party back into its pre-transgression state, while others could have more recourse to punitive measures as a counter for future misconduct. These paradigms reflect the intricate interplay between codification of labor rights and judicial interpretation. It becomes necessary for courts to balance the requirement of ensuring the employees have good options for remedies and protecting employers' interests. In nations like the United States, judicial activism has been critical in shaping legal doctrine to address contemporary employment relations, particularly those non-standard conditions of employment, as identified by findings that explain system failures in different environments like China and France (Li et al., 2025). Furthermore, the courts' realm of remedy is also made complex by statutory and collective bargaining protections to which employees may be entitled. These statutory and collective bargaining employee tools can impact remedies provided, with other avenues available for resolution before turning to judicial recourse. Mediation and arbitration work quite effectively as reasonable alternatives, reducing the courts' workload while ensuring equitable resolution outcomes to affected parties. But where all these mechanisms fail, judicial remedies must step in as fail-safes that underscore the necessity of a robust legal recourse regime. Where such necessity is compounded by state intervention and regulatory agencies coming into play in tandem with private employment disputes, as in the case of emergent judicial frameworks in different nations and legal traditions (Smolenskiy, 2025), so much the more is this the case. The ongoing discussion surrounding such remedies paints a picture of the evolving nature of labor and employment law as well as its central mechanisms for protecting workers' rights.

SUMMARY

As Labor and Employment Law discussion comes to a close, it should be remembered that employment relationships underpinning modern workplaces are complex and dynamic. Legal frameworks that define these relationships, including contract of service and independent contractor, are pivotal in the determination of worker rights and obligations. In the recent years, the relevance of flexible working arrangements like teleworking policies has grown significantly, and thus there has been a reconsideration of traditional employment models. Amidst this uncertainty for workers and employers, emphasis must be placed on the intrinsic power disparities that typically emerge, ensuring legislation promotes fair treatment and similar working conditions, particularly in light of technological advances and globalization impacting labor markets. A sensitive understanding of the factors can help more efficient policies and practices that are respectful of all employees' dignity and rights. In taking into account employee rights and entitlements, the regime imposed by Labor and Employment Law is not just a tool of regulation but also the foundation of social justice in the workplace. Minimum wage laws, annual leave provisions, and termination pay are important in safeguarding the welfare of workers to enable them to achieve sustainable standard of life. However, according to recent assessments, inequalities in access exist for these benefits, largely among vulnerable segments and marginalized communities. These inequalities need to be addressed in coming up with an equitable labor market. Secondly, organizations must regularly discourse and negotiate together to maintain pace with evolving dynamics, whereby the rights of all employees are not just recognized but actively enforced. It is this integral strategy for worker rights that will ultimately result in a more just and equitable society. Finally, the large scope of Labor and Employment Law's mechanisms for resolving disputes serves to demonstrate the merits of accessible and effective channels through which workplace grievances can be processed. Forums such as labor tribunals, mediation, and arbitration are valuable instruments in facilitating dialogue and settlement between management and employees. As application of these mechanisms proceeds to encompass online platforms and other alternatives to conflict resolution, it is important that they are made available to everyone, particularly those who are in precarious employment conditions. The potential to struggle for one's rights through open and effective processes serves to enforce the measures of equality and justice within the workplace. As the discussion of Labor and Employment Law demonstrates, commitment to such values is priceless in creating an environment in which the labor force can thrive towards the overall goal of the well-being of society and economic stability (N/A, 2019; Margaret et al., 2018).

A LOOK TO THE FUTURE

FUTURE DIRECTIONS IN COMPARATIVE LABOR AND EMPLOYMENT LAW

As the dynamics of labor markets evolve, distinctions between conventional employment structures and non-traditional structures, including independent contracting, become increasingly significant. The advent of gig economy platforms has de facto transformed the character of how individuals engage in work and presents significant legal questions about worker classification. Regulatory frameworks must adapt in order to avoid eroding conventional protections as independent contractor work diffuses across the economy. This shift demands attention to service contracts and the effects of probationary work, as firms seek to navigate issues of flexibility and employees' rights. To address these challenges, it is necessary to create standards that reinforce the rights of workers but recognize the different paths of labor that contribute to the economy of today, as highlighted by research from institutions devoted to this discourse (School et al., 2008).

Furthermore, the future of employment and labor law must examine work conditions even more critically, especially with the more frequent practice of working from home as a constant element in most industries. The crisis has shown that there is a need for comprehensive policies for hours, rest periods, and work safety, and this has forced a redefinition of what constitutes a safe and productive workplace. Legal frameworks must evolve to incorporate remote work policies that are fair and maintain standards, potentially in the form of legislation to protect both mental and physical wellbeing. As organizations wrestle with productivity and employee well-being, legislatures will need to collaborate with stakeholders in order to establish guidelines appropriate to contemporary work arrangements. These innovative measures will be needed to guide rights and entitlements concerning multiple work forms, keeping the subject of labor law effectiveness abreast of a hybridizing world (Barbanchon et al., 2013). On the search for equitable labor relations, anti-discrimination and collective bargaining provisions will play a central role in shaping the employment law of the future. As workers seek to establish their rights and improve working conditions, the role of unions in mediating negotiations through collective agreements becomes more at center stage. Proposing a return of sorts of union formation, emerging trends show greater awareness of workers' rights during economic uncertainty. Meanwhile, anti-discrimination policies must adjust to guard against emerging prejudices in multi-racial workplaces. Equal remuneration, harassment in the workplace, and affirmative action must be advocated by the legal system to achieve equality. In an age of high-technology technological transformation and more diverse workplaces, labor law must remain sensitive to the changing landscape, offering equal treatment and protection for all employees (School et al., 2008).

REFERENCES

1. Akgüç, M., Jacquot, M., & Lopez-Uroz, N. (2017). Enhancing the effectiveness of social dialogue articulation in Europe (EESDA) Project No. VS/2017/0434: Social dialogue articulation and effectiveness: Country report for France. https://core.ac.uk/download/286731358.pdf (accessed on 9th September 2025).
2. Al Imran, H. (2025). The hiring and termination procedures for employees in Bangladesh under the Labor Act of 2006 and the role of the courts. *Asian Journal of Law and Policy*. https://www.semanticscholar.org/paper/51128684f919bf2f040b5c629f24783b94962c50 (accessed on 9th September 2025).
3. Baker & McKenzie. (2013). *The Global Employer: The Employment Law Reform Issue*. https://core.ac.uk/download/19958965.pdf (accessed on 9th September 2025).
4. Baker & McKenzie. (2015). *China Employment Law Update–December 2016*. https://core.ac.uk/download/219376821.pdf (accessed on 9th September 2025).
5. Bartninkas, M. (2024). Terminating an employment contract at the employer's will: Does expensive and simple mean safe? Lithuanian model. *Baltic Journal of Law & Politics, 16*, 47–63. https://www.semanticscholar.org/paper/ff48024e45a2d8ada6a02f1e1ddf8918ff17797e (accessed on 9th September 2025).
6. Betcherman, G., Luinstra, A., & Ogawa, M. (2025). *Labor Market Regulation: International Experience in Promoting Employment and Social Protection*. https://core.ac.uk/download/pdf/6314368.pdf (accessed on 9th September 2025).
7. Bite, K. (2019). Regulatory framework of strike and its problem in Latvia. https://core.ac.uk/download/480427079.pdf (accessed on 9th September 2025).
8. Blackett, A., & Sheppard, C. (2002). *The Links Between Collective Bargaining and Equality*. https://core.ac.uk/download/5129363.pdf (accessed on 9th September 2025).
9. Boje, T. P., & Ejrnæs, A. (2012). Policy and practice: The relationship between family policy regime and women's labor market participation in Europe. *International Journal of Sociology and Social Policy, 32*, 589–605. https://www.semanticscholar.org/paper/948ed645b652370c72a122695d0a17ccd5b17a59 (accessed on 9th September 2025).
10. Budhwar, P., Chowdhury, S., Wood, G., Aguinis, H., Bamber, G. J., Beltran, J. R., Boselie, P., et al. (2023). Human resource management in the age of generative artificial intelligence: Perspectives and research directions on ChatGPT. *Human Resource Management Journal, 33*, 606–659. https://doi.org/10.1111/1748-8583.12524 (accessed on 9th September 2025).
11. Casale, G., & Zhu, C. (2013). *Labor Administration Reforms in China*. https://core.ac.uk/download/18615785.pdf (accessed on 9th September 2025).
12. Chitimira, H., & Torerai, E. (2024). The right to equal parental leave rights for mothers and fathers in the South African workplace: An analysis of *Van Wyk & Others v Minister of Employment and Labor 2024 (1) SA 545 (GJ). South African Mercantile Law Journal*. https://www.semanticscholar.org/paper/84b256db0d87fe497f2eef59b3f169a813dc14cd (accessed on 9th September 2025).
13. Clean Clothes Campaign. (2005). *Clean Clothes Newsletter No. 19*. https://core.ac.uk/download/5122004.pdf (accessed on 9th September 2025).

14. Collins, H., Ewing, K., & McColgan, A. (2012). *Labor Law: The Right to Bargain Collectively*. https://www.semanticscholar.org/paper/1f4bd46b958e1c1178f497b887220b457e6b3fff (accessed on 9th September 2025).

15. De Stefano, V. (2015). Non-standard workers and freedom of association: A critical analysis of restrictions to collective rights from a human rights perspective. *WP CSDLE "Massimo D'Antona".INT–123/2015*. https://core.ac.uk/download/237467710.pdf (accessed on 9th September 2025).

16. Ebrahim, S. (2024). The ambit of terms and conditions of employment in equal pay claims under Section 6(4) of the EEA: Lessons from international labor law. *Potchefstroom Electronic Law Journal*. https://www.semanticscholar.org/paper/b2e0be7a3f6e14fd003b75cbc9cafe45c46e51df (accessed on 9th September 2025).

17. Eneh, N. E., Bakare, S. S., Adeniyi, A. O., & Akpuokwe, C. U. (2024). Modern labor law: A review of current trends in employee rights and organizational duties. *International Journal of Management & Entrepreneurship Research, 6*, 540–553. https://doi.org/10.51594/ijmer.v6i3.843 (accessed on 9th September 2025).

18. Eurofound. (2015). *Maternity Leave Provisions in the EU Member States: Duration and Allowances*. https://core.ac.uk/download/33611066.pdf (accessed on 9th September 2025).

19. Faizin, M., Zahra, D. T., Lutfina, L., & Riyandani, S. (2024). An analysis of employment termination for freelance workers: A justice approach from Islamic economic law. *ASAS*. https://www.semanticscholar.org/paper/53e82805efdac5b609b293ab55be4ad6a829806a (accessed on 9th September 2025).

20. Gatta, P. P. (2022). *The State of World Fisheries and Aquaculture 2022. FAO eBooks*. https://doi.org/10.4060/cc0461en (accessed on 9th September 2025).

21. Herd, R., Koen, V., & Reutersward, A. (2010). China's labor market in transition: Job creation, migration and regulation. https://www.semanticscholar.org/paper/7e5e85779a7806bea834999e5b73e8ab9821322d (accessed on 9th September 2025).

22. Hijdra, T., et al. (2023). The impact of overweight on employment outcomes: A review of the evidence. *The European Journal of Public Health, 33*. https://www.semanticscholar.org/paper/676683f25c23cad30734c3a9507ed53dab144dd0 (accessed on 9th September 2025).

23. Holmlund, B., & Storrie, D. (2025). Temporary work in turbulent times: The Swedish experience. https://core.ac.uk/download/pdf/6408631.pdf (accessed on 9th September 2025).

24. ILO, Office of the High Commissioner for Human Rights (OHCHR), & Irish Aid. (2008). *Sub-Regional Meeting on Disability Legislation: Decent Work for Persons with Disabilities in Asia, UN Conference Center, Bangkok, Thailand, 23–24 June 2008*. https://core.ac.uk/download/5130098.pdf (accessed on 9th September 2025).

25. ILR School, Cornell University. (2008). *ILR Faculty Publications 2007–08*. https://core.ac.uk/download/33597654.pdf (accessed on 9th September 2025).

26. Kniazkova, L. (2024). Some issues of the correlation of employment and civil law contract. *Vìsnik Marìupol's'kogo deržavnogo unìversitetu. Serìâ: Pravo*. https://www.semanticscholar.org/paper/b40bf09f69e87e9c3a234cf30730ca6ef7af4ce6 (accessed on 9th September 2025).

27. Kruk, M. E., Gage, A., Arsenault, C., Jordan, K., Leslie, H. H., Roder-DeWan, S., Adeyi, O., et

al. (2018). High-quality health systems in the Sustainable Development Goals era: Time for a revolution. *The Lancet Global Health, 6*, e1196–e1252. https://doi.org/10.1016/s2214-109x(18)30386-3 (accessed on 9th September 2025).

28. Lane, J., & Videbaek Munkholm, N. (2015). Danish and British protection from disability discrimination at work–Past, present and future. https://core.ac.uk/download/30731356.pdf (accessed on 9th September 2025).
29. Law, L., & Brooks, B. T. (2013). The significance of the South Pacific for comparative studies in labor. https://www.semanticscholar.org/paper/420f2d1bf834eebb5fe953745c0fb85f56ffd35a (accessed on 9th September 2025).
30. Le Barbanchon, T., & Malherbet, F. (2013). *An Anatomy of the French Labor Market.* https://core.ac.uk/download/16393437.pdf (accessed on 9th September 2025).
31. Li, C., Chen, J., & Shu, W. (2025). Comparative jurisprudential deconstruction of the modernization of the labor law system: A cross-border perspective on the logic of codification and the application of principles. *International Journal of Management Science Research.* https://www.semanticscholar.org/paper/107358a3e2ab79ffd2f8bf06799ab6444bcb8ed4 (accessed on 9th September 2025).
32. Luebker, M. (2008). *Employment, Unemployment and Informality in Zimbabwe: Concepts and Data for Coherent Policy-Making.* https://core.ac.uk/download/5131251.pdf (accessed on 9th September 2025).
33. McGaughey, E. (2010). *Should Agency Workers be Treated Differently?* https://core.ac.uk/download/17322.pdf (accessed on 9th September 2025).
34. Minter, K. (2017). Negotiating labor standards in the gig economy: Airtasker and Unions New South Wales. *The Economic and Labor Relations Review, 28*, 438–454. https://doi.org/10.1177/1035304617724305 (accessed on 9th September 2025).
35. N/A. (2016). *Millennium Development Goals Report.* https://doi.org/10.18356/98544aa9-en (accessed on 9th September 2025).
36. N/A. (2019). *Negotiating Our Way Up.* https://doi.org/10.1787/1fd2da34-en (accessed on 9th September 2025).
37. N/A. (2019). *OECD Employment Outlook 2019.* OECD Employment Outlook. https://doi.org/10.1787/9ee00155-en (accessed on 9th September 2025).
38. N/A. (2019). *The Capability Approach to Labor Law.* Oxford University Press eBooks. https://doi.org/10.1093/oso/9780198836087.001.0001 (accessed on 9th September 2025).
39. N/A. (2019). *The Heavy Burden of Obesity.* OECD Health Policy Studies. https://doi.org/10.1787/67450d67-en (accessed on 9th September 2025).
40. N/A. (2021). *A New Benchmark for Mental Health Systems.* OECD Health Policy Studies. https://doi.org/10.1787/4ed890f6-en (accessed on 9th September 2025).
41. N/A. (2023). *Toolkit for Mainstreaming and Implementing Gender Equality 2023.* https://doi.org/10.1787/3ddef555-en (accessed on 9th September 2025).
42. OECD. (2021). *Women in Infrastructure. Public Governance Policy Papers.* https://doi.org/10.1787/9eab66a8-en (accessed on 9th September 2025).
43. OECD. (2022). *Delivering for Youth: How Governments Can Put Young People at the Center of the*

Recovery. OECD Policy Responses to Coronavirus (COVID-19). https://doi.org/10.1787/92c9d060-en (accessed on 9th September 2025).

44. Onyeonoru, K. K. (2007). Social dialogue under globalization in Nigeria: Does democracy add value? *Volume (5)*. https://www.semanticscholar.org/paper/071d64fa7ca847b848ad57fe9d5e2b857ea7db09 (accessed on 9th September 2025).
45. Piercy, G. L. (2002). A 'third way' in industry training: New Zealand's adaptation of selected British policies. https://core.ac.uk/download/29198714.pdf (accessed on 9th September 2025).
46. Polianskyi. (2024). Regarding the employment of persons with disabilities. *Analytical and Comparative Jurisprudence*. https://www.semanticscholar.org/paper/b79753359cd79f82bba1993e41d168e4aafae956 (accessed on 9th September 2025).
47. Sereda, O., & Krasiuk, T. (2024). Preventing and combating harassment in the workplace social partnership. *Law and Innovations*. https://www.semanticscholar.org/paper/a7df1f222fe2ecdd50ee3bd387252a5ae907410a (accessed on 9th September 2025).
48. Simutina, Y. (2024). Challenges to the exercise of collective labor rights outside the employment relationship. *Uzhhorod National University Herald. Series: Law*. https://www.semanticscholar.org/paper/2ba56a91e1f4b6b419816d99bb3aec9789a15efd (accessed on 9th September 2025).
49. Sitko, N. (2025). Presumption of the employment relationship of digital workers and the protective function of labor law. *Z Problematyki Prawa Pracy i Polityki Socjalnej*. https://www.semanticscholar.org/paper/fe85dd556a6631cd6509a2667867c7a78d098a49 (accessed on 9th September 2025).
50. Smolenskiy, M. (2025). Preserving secrecy in the frame of labor relationships: Methods of secrets protection, analysis of the problems and proposals to improve the legislation. *Legal Order and Legal Values*. https://www.semanticscholar.org/paper/3bfc2fa75d60c4e13217bb917d4cdda989609fbb (accessed on 9th September 2025).
51. Staszewska-Kozłowska, E. (2024). The right to rest for participants in traineeships for the unemployed and graduate practices. *Roczniki Administracji i Prawa*. https://www.semanticscholar.org/paper/74da5db3751c2c7e96e76bbb14ce1f3239d79f95 (accessed on 9th September 2025).
52. Sugiharto, G., Shalihah, F., & Octivia, A. E. (2024). Sexual violence against female labor in the perspective of employment law and legal justice. *Substantive Justice International Journal of Law*. https://www.semanticscholar.org/paper/a9ce8de46fc82172c1d5bb25b8cd62a6959be4d4 (accessed on 9th September 2025).
53. Świątkowski, A. M. (2020). *Social Rights in Europe and Free Platform Work*. https://www.semanticscholar.org/paper/6c91f982cfff2e3c45ebff6b3577d119cfcecdfe (accessed on 9th September 2025).
54. Wimmer, A., Stewart, A., Davies, A., Picchio, A., Picchio, A., Renan Barzilay, A., Hochschild, A. R., et al. (2014). Feminist reflections on the scope of labor law: Domestic work, social reproduction and jurisdiction. https://core.ac.uk/download/30705215.pdf (accessed on 9th September 2025).

Chapter 11

COMPARATIVE ADMINISTRATIVE LAW

Contents

INTRODUCTION

Comparative administrative law plays a significant part to play in the examination of the similarities and differences between mechanisms of governance across jurisdictions. The discipline concerns itself with the way in which public powers make decisions affecting citizens' and firms' lives. In an age of increasing globalization and multinational transactions, a comparative study of administrative law gives scholars and practitioners a sense of what good governance practices are. The various approaches in exercising administrative actions, such as executive orders and agency regulations, reflect the diverse historical, social, and political contexts of the respective jurisdictions. Thus, the current essay shall not only discuss the central concepts of administrative law but also the intricate regulatory systems that typify various systems. Comparative Administrative Law describes how nations adapt to the complexities of administrative rulemaking in an attempt to be effective and accountable in public administration. During the thesis process, it will be important to analyze the regulatory norms that govern licensing and permitting processes across various legal contexts. These processes are central to state management, ensuring that economic and social activities conform to predetermined norms and policies. The divergence of revocation procedures and judicial review indicates the approach jurisdictions accord regulatory goals and protection of citizens. Analysis of these procedures sheds light on philosophies of administrative actions, from rigid conformity to adaptive case-by-case choice. Most importantly, an awareness of these distinctions contributes to a better appreciation of the way in which states balance the need for regulation with the need for commitment to upholding principles of justice. Comparative analysis in this way illuminates not only the process but also overall consequences for administrative justice and for public trust in official power. In addition to procedural justice and accountability mechanisms, the contribution of transparency in administrative law cannot be overstated. Public hearings, information access, and whistleblower protection are all critical components that foster trust between the governed and the powers. Observations of how each jurisdiction addresses these measures of transparency will provide hints regarding their commitment to citizen involvement and accountability. Variations in oversight bodies and their functioning indicate the various ways in which the states try to constrain abuses of power. These administrative systems are influenced by cultural attitudes towards state control and history of corruption. Accordingly, this essay will contrast and compare such systems in a comparative administrative law framework, explaining the manner in which different societies address the conflicts between discretion, authority, and citizens' rights in pursuit of moral government.

11.1. SCOPE OF ADMINISTRATIVE ACTION

In administrative law, administrative action range is pivotal in determining the power entrusted to governmental bodies and necessitates proper equilibrium among power and accountability. Executive orders are a classic example of an influential tool through which the executive can dictate organizational agendas and implement policies promptly. Strong as a tool, such must be subjected to legal frameworks to prevent misusage and preserve democratic ideals. Comparative analyses demonstrate varying approaches to the enforcement of executive orders, with some jurisdictions adhering more tightly to supervision to ensure legislative intent is upheld. Understanding how various juridical systems regulate the ordering and enforcement of executive orders is fundamental to an assessment of their effectiveness.

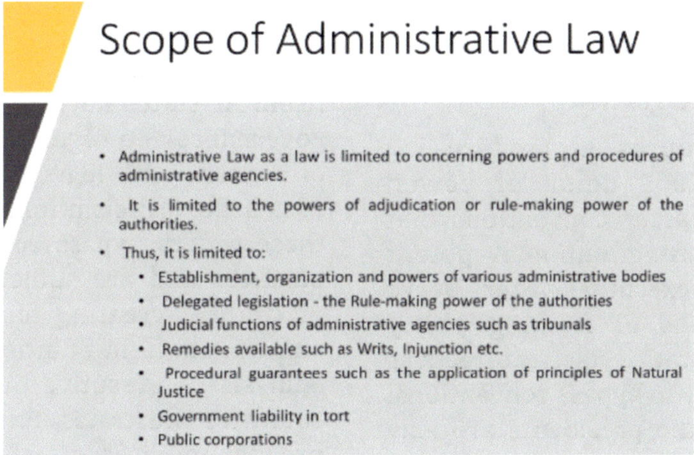

Figure 11.1. The scope of administrative action.

Source: https://www.slideshare.net/slideshow/nature-scope-and-development-of-administrative-law202204231634pdf/266036672.

Lack of a robust regulatory system renders such potential for abuse, necessitating transparency and checks in the administrative process. Administrative agency regulations also illustrate the scope of administrative action by setting parameters under which government agencies operate. These regulations will often be the product of a complex dynamic of statute and executive discretion, embodying principles of regulatory reform and efficiency. Regional decentralization allows local agencies in certain systems, as seen in Xu (2011), to adapt regulations to suit the particular economic environment, increasing flexibility but also variability and possible inconsistency. This dual effect of enhancing local governance while at the same time threatening fragmentation highlights the importance of harmonization among agencies. When bureaucracies grapple with the creation of regulatory standards, the balance between conformity and creativity is the norm of the day, and it is a test of administrative effectiveness and integrity in various legal regimes. The quasi-judicial power vested in administrative agencies best describes another dimension of their scope, spanning law and policy making while ensuring procedural justice. Such functions allow agencies to resolve controversies, interpret rules, and impose sanctions, and thus act at the boundary of policymaking and legal adjudication. Aggregation of such roles has a tendency to engender controversies over the legality and justice of administrative actions. For instance, the appeal mechanisms and judicial review, as discussed in Emerson et al. (2011), further clarify this scope by creating an avenue for surveillance and correction of potential overreach by the agency. The distinctive frameworks in which these quasi-judicial practices are pursued, combined with their procedural safeguards, ultimately shape public trust in administrative action and reflect broader social norms for governance and justice comparatively (Figure 11.1).

11.1.1. Executive Orders

Administrative procedures in modern-day governments illustrate a union of power, pragmatism, and regulatory conventions that guide their effective functioning. A potent tool in the executive, executive orders serve as a significant means of framing policy directions and administrative rule. As directives possessing the authority to bypass conventional legislative procedure, the presidents are able to institute sweeping reforms and respond promptly to emerging problems. In comparative administrative law, it is crucial to look at the way various states use executive orders as a way of addressing particular governance needs and in consideration of the risk of abuse and harmony between political authority and administrative effectiveness. A look at these orders illustrates the twofold role of the orders as political instruments and as tools that can pose a challenge to collaborative governance and democratic values (Murdoch, 2022). Further, the validation of executive orders may greatly vary across different jurisdictions depending on broader political and cultural settings. For instance, in the United States, executive orders have been the focal point of large-scale legal and political conflicts repeatedly defining presidential periods. Consequently, other nations may have more restricted or institutionalized use of such orders, upholding executive discretion through collective choice-making. This inconsistency is reflective of the interplay between administrative behavior and political processes, with the reaction of different systems of government to executive orders being reflective of the complexity of public administration itself. A series of case studies illustrates how these institutions operate and develop from executive determinations, applying the dynamic negotiation of power and duty in administrative law (Thelen, 2018). The ramification of executive orders also extends beyond immediate policy change; they influence the line of direction of administrative law itself. As states navigate the intricate webs of governance and regulation, their application is of concern with legitimacy and the possibility of misuse. Criticism follows particularly where these orders bypass conventional checks and balances and are subject to being taken out of context, creating fertile soil for criticism and litigation. In addition, as the comparative analysis of executive orders within different countries illustrates, an understanding of the broader implications of such actions requires careful examination of institutional settings and the legal frameworks coordinating them. Ultimately, executive orders reveal the delicate balance between authority and responsibility, confirming the need for firm safeguards against abuse of such powers within codified legal and ethical boundaries (Murdoch, 2022).

11.1.2. Agency Regulations

By examining Agency Regulations within the framework of Comparative Administrative Law, it is understood that such regulations play a pivotal role in shaping government interactions with citizens and other organizations. These regulations, implemented by executive agencies, seek to bring legislative requirements into life and respond to specific demands in society. The intricacy involved in agency regulations often reflects the unique political, cultural, and social circumstances of a nation. For instance, between Indonesia and Singapore, differences in the design and application of agency guidelines account for their distinct strategies toward improving public services. While Indonesia has the challenge of legal enforcement, Singapore trends are to depend on regulatory innovations based on technology to improve efficiency and openness, particularly in the provision of public services (Syafa et al., 2025). This comparative framework emphasizes the significant role of agency rules in maintaining well-ordered governance. Further, effective regulation requires a robust framework which not only circumscribes agency power but also emphasizes responsibility. Agencies are conferred with a large degree of discretion by most jurisdictions, which can lead to varying understandings and applications of the law. The need for clear guidelines and standards of agency discretion comes in to avoid any probable abuse of authority. The administrative law processes should ensure that all the regulatory decisions are accountable through adequate checks and balance. For example, under Indonesia's land redistribution, the legal and administrative concerns involved function to further emphasize the need for more inter-agency coordination as well as procedural clarity (Widowati et al., 2025). Without such frameworks, the danger of inefficient and implementation inconsistency remains an acute problem that draws away public trust in administrative processes. Finally, the comparative success of agency regulation entails their impact on citizens legal safeguards and conflict resolution. Given that agencies perform their role within the umbrella of a regulatory framework, their ability to redress grievances and resolve complaints is what comprises their overall effectiveness. These include the sophistication of bureaucratic processes, poor regulation, and the coherence of the regulations, which all have a major impact on the effectiveness of the regulatory responses. From the land redistribution policies case study, it is evident that how beneficiaries are often confronted with huge challenges through lack of legal certainty and lack of guidance in overcoming bureaucratic hurdles (Widowati et al., 2025). Consequently, a sound appreciation of agency regulations calls for an understanding of their critical function in facilitating high-quality public services and stopping discriminatory access to judicial protection in the administrative context.

11.1.3. Quasi-Judicial Powers

The advent of quasi-judicial powers represents a significant evolution within administrative law, impacting how governmental agencies resolve disputes and enforce regulations. These powers enable agencies to adopt roles that closely resemble judicial functions, thus allowing them to make determinations in an adjudicative manner. Unlike traditional courts, agencies exercising quasi-judicial powers may operate more efficiently, addressing specific regulatory contexts without the constraints of formal judicial proceedings. As observed in various jurisdictions, such adaptations help alleviate the burdens on formal courts, ensuring that minor disputes are efficiently resolved. The introduction of such mechanisms, especially in light of resource constraints, reflects a growing trend among administrative bodies to streamline processes and respond to the increasing complexity of regulatory environments, fostering both accessibility and efficiency in delivering justice (Figure 11.2).

In comparison, the structures governing quasi-judicial powers vary significantly between jurisdictions in accordance with the different historical and cultural backgrounds of each legal system. For example, the implementation of justices of the peace in Ukraine offers proof of how quasi-judicial roles can be incorporated into existing legal systems (Nishchymna, 2025). This scheme aims to resolve petty crimes and court cases in a system that alleviates the burden of higher courts while upholding essential juridical principles. Similarly, in Poland, the typology of acts imposing financial law highlights the nuanced application of quasi-judicial power to manage public finance, showing how various institutions function to impose compliance and ensure accountability (Ruśkowski, 2018).

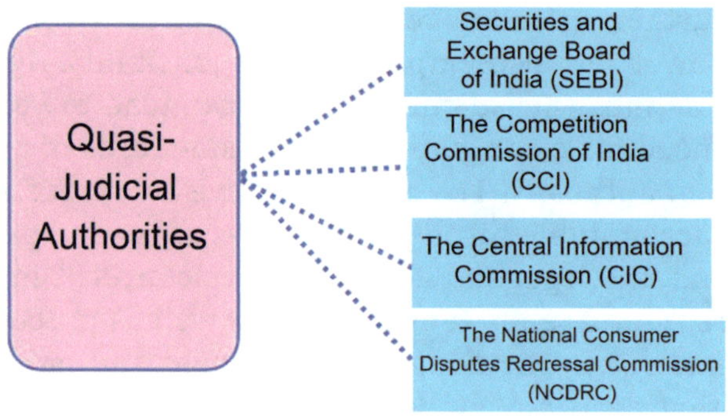

Figure 11.2. Quasi-judicial authority in administrative law.

Source: https://i0.wp.com/lawcafeindia.com/wp-content/uploads/2022/10/Quasi-judicial-Authorities-in-India-.jpg?fit=550%2C325&ssl=1.

Such comparative evaluations shed light on the efficacy and potential negatives of quasi-judicial regimes within different administrative systems. Successful use of quasi-judicial powers depends on maintaining procedural fairness and transparency, core components of safeguarding public trust and accountability. In practice, agencies must weigh their regulatory objectives against the rights of the individuals affected. The inclusion of procedural safeguards, such as the establishment of explicit appeal mechanisms and public hearings, is crucial in the pursuit of equitable outcomes. Moreover, apprehension of abuse of discretion underscores the necessity of oversight responsibilities that prevent arbitrary decision-making. As agencies increasingly exercise quasi-judicial power, adherence to international standards of judicial conduct becomes essential. Ongoing debate on these issues will go a long way in shaping the evolution of administrative law, how quasi-judicial powers are perceived and exercised within various legal systems.

11.2. PERMITS AND LICENSES

Under Comparative Administrative Law, the intricacies of permitting and licensing play a crucial role in the control of industries. Licensing is a government-approved legal authorization enabling an entity or individual to engage in some activity within prescribed terms. This regulatory tool is vital to ensure standards and foster public safety in healthcare, transport, and the environment industries. Still, the process of obtaining a license is normally complex and appreciably different in various jurisdictions. Every authority operates under its parameters, so there is a need of careful analysis and standardization so that licensing processes do not pose unnecessary barriers for entry but also effectively safeguard public interest, as highlighted in Welter (2011). In addition, the creation of new business models, such as the rise of platforms such as Airbnb, raises questions regarding the applicability and flexibility of existing licensing frameworks to the mechanisms of the present markets, as demonstrated in Guttentag (2013).

Along with the original licensure, even more crucial are the revocation processes. The power to revoke a license may be based on several factors, such as violation of provisions or fraudulence in the application process. Revocation processes should follow provisions of fairness and justice, so that parties affected are given a chance to dispute any claims before sanctions are imposed. The necessity of open revocation procedures cannot be over-asserted since they ensure the continued legitimacy of the regulatory regime and provide necessary checks against arbitrary discretion. Second, the proper dissemination of these procedures is essential to win public trust in administrative action. In this respect, the judicial review of decisions made by licensing authorities becomes a necessary tool for governing accountability and fairness in the administrative law, harmonizing with issues seen in Welter (2011), where contextualized entrepreneur is reliant on secure and clear regulatory environments. The jurisdiction of licensing is not confined to regulatory compliance but extends to broader economic and social contexts, and thus it becomes an essential component of comparative administrative systems. Licensing policies must balance the dual objectives of innovation encouragement and public interests safeguarding. In the face of a rapidly changing economic landscape, characterized by the transformation of new models of innovation, regulators must grapple with adapting to new approaches in response to evolving needs. Such flexibility serves to unlock the door to potential entrepreneurs who may be discouraged by inefficient or excessively restrictive permitting regimes. The interaction between administrative law and entrepreneurship is also complicated by regulatory frameworks which assist diverse industries and the unique complexity which they introduce, adding further to the debate about how administrative bodies can make their permitting and licensing more creative. This is also especially relevant as demonstrated in the phenomenal expansion of sites such as Airbnb, which has incited discourse on regulatory pertinence and responsiveness, as discussed in Guttentag (2013).

11.2.1. Regulatory Standards

Regulatory standards perform a foundational role in maintaining order and ensuring compliance at various administrative frameworks across various jurisdictions. These standards address a range of criteria governing the conduct of regulatory agencies, ranging from environmental protection to public health programs. Establishing open regulatory standards is essential towards achieving the desired outcomes of public policy as much as giving a platform where accountability can be structured. Effective regulatory standards not only guide the regulatory process but also put limits on administrative agencies' discretion, thereby creating a system of checks and balances. Here, the creation and application of regulatory standards serve as an example of good governance and contribute to establishing a stable administrative law environment that reflects society's values and needs. The relevance of regulatory standards is also brought out by their relation to the permitting and licensing processes, which are central to the functions of many sectors. To ensure integrity in such processes, regulatory standards prescribe the terms of obtaining permits, licenses, and approvals, so that entities comply with legal and procedural requirements before engaging in regulated activities. This not only guards public interests but also promotes fair competition and fosters higher market confidence. In the majority of instances, the use of regulatory standards is based on empirical evidence and data, which support policies responding to public matters appropriately. For example, pharmacoepidemiologic guidelines, as recent research indicates, provide a guideline on the assessment of the healthcare impacts of products, such that regulatory approaches are based on scientific awareness, (N/A, 2015). The regulatory standard difference across jurisdictions demonstrates the fertile landscape of comparative administrative law, with different legal traditions and governance styles influencing regulatory practice. The Worldwide Governance Indicators, for instance, show large differences along dimensions like Regulatory Quality and Rule of Law that affect how countries define their regulatory environment (Daniel et al., 2009). Such differences not only articulate the relative contextual circumstances of each regime but also raise basic questions regarding the effectiveness and responsiveness of regulatory regimes in an increasingly globalized world. While regulators and legislators struggle in harmonizing regulatory regimes, the worth of responsive but rigorous regulatory conditions is shown in promoting international cooperation, regulatory coherence, and protection of basic rights in diverse administrative settings.

11.2.2. Revocation Procedures

Effective governance necessitates adherence to established procedures, particularly in the realm of revocation, where the legalities surrounding the annulment of licenses or permits can significantly impact various stakeholders. Revocation procedures play a critical role in ensuring that administrative actions are both justifiable and transparent. Such processes can vary greatly between jurisdictions, reflecting differing supervisory philosophies and regulatory environments. In comparing these procedures, it becomes evident that the degree of procedural fairness afforded to affected parties often hinges on regional regulatory standards. For instance, the balance between swift enforcement actions and preserving the rights of individuals or entities is a persistent theme in comparative administrative law. A thorough examination of these dynamics underscores the necessity for consistent application of revocation standards to foster trust in regulatory agencies and enhance compliance across sectors. The principles that underlie revocation procedures are inherently linked to broader themes of accountability and due process within administrative law. Procedural fairness stipulates that parties facing potential revocation must be provided with adequate notice and a meaningful opportunity to contest the action. In many jurisdictions, this requires agencies to establish clear guidelines detailing the conditions under which revocation can occur, thereby minimizing arbitrary decision-making. Furthermore, stakeholders must be aware of the criteria that lead to revocation, which include violations of regulatory standards or failing to comply with established performance metrics. Such regulatory frameworks not only promote transparency but also serve to empower individuals and organizations to understand their rights and obligations. Ultimately, the integrity of revocation procedures is pivotal to maintaining public confidence in administrative systems. An additional layer of complexity arises when considering judicial review in the context of revocation procedures. The ability of an affected party to appeal a revocation decision plays a vital role in the system of checks and balances within administrative law. This process ensures oversight of administrative actions and helps to safeguard against potential abuse of power by regulatory bodies. By facilitating a transparent review mechanism, courts can assess the legality and fairness of revocation actions, thereby enhancing procedural legitimacy. In this regard, comparative studies of judicial review reveal significant variations in the efficacy of such mechanisms across different legal traditions. For example, some jurisdictions exhibit robust frameworks that enable timely appeals, while others may struggle with inefficiencies. Thus, understanding these nuances is essential for evaluating the comprehensive landscape of revocation procedures within the broader discipline of comparative administrative law.

11.2.3. Judicial Review

In considering the role of judicial review in comparative administrative law, there is evidently an intermeshing of different legal systems and how they intermesh in terms of administrative action. Judicial review is one of the significant mechanisms whereby legality and appropriateness of administrative decisions are ensured, especially where executive orders and agency regulations may be infringing individual rights. Judicial review procedure diversity in jurisdictions sheds light on the key phenomenon as courts address intricate principles like the administrative discretion and edges of executive power. In some national jurisdictions, judicial oversight is robust and enables comprehensive inquiry into administration action, but in others, it remains charted by legislative schemes that are more inclined towards efficiency than oversight. Consequently, these analyses of such differences reveal the higher stakes for democratic governance and accountability in comparative administrative law. Judicial review across various jurisdictions can be assessed against the processes of administrative adjudication. Courts are apt to tread a tightrope, balancing between requirements of procedural fairness and efficient agency operation. In the majority of legal systems, the development of quasi-judicial power facilitates a two-track mechanism of potential recourse—direct appeal to superior courts and administrative tribunals to resolve individual grievances. Problems still linger, however, since procedural arrangements to administer these problems can have an overarching effect. For instance, how much courts engage with administrative judgments varies quite greatly, with some jurisdictions nearly embracing total support for transparency and robust appeal mechanisms, yet others demonstrating deference in taking actions. These variations are traceable to opposing precedent history and prevalent pressures upon public administration. The development of public administration under the influence of globalization and New Public Management (NPM) ideals further adds to the complexity of the judicial review terrain. Findings suggest that conventional models of administrative law that focus on legality are being replaced by growingly managerial principles of efficiency and flexibility in response to these pressures. This transformation becomes a question of whether legal frameworks in place are adequate to address the need for legal accountability while confronting the practicalities of contemporary governance. As courts interact with these new paradigms, their role in the delivery of justice, transparency, and accountability becomes increasingly vital. Some national courts are beginning to adjust their tactics, particularly with respect to recognizing the need for judicial review of transnational administrative action in the integrated regimes of the European Union. This points towards the potential for harmonizing judicial approaches that can ultimately enhance effective judicial protection in various administrative contexts.

11.3. ADMINISTRATIVE ADJUDICATION

The role of administrative adjudication is pivotal in advancing fairness and accountability in the administrative law scheme. Administrative agencies, by virtue of their quasi-judicial powers, often engage in adjudicative acts that imitate judicial practice but vary in application. The tribunal and board system acts as an important framework for the adjudication of such cases as relate to compliance with regulation, licensing, and enforcement processes. This method not only permits specialized expertise to guide decision-making but also allows for a faster resolution of cases when compared with conventional court systems. Yet, the success of these adjudications significantly depends on the guidelines of procedural fairness that provide assurance that persons are entitled to a fair hearing and can put forward their case, thus promoting confidence in the administrative process. For administrative adjudication to be fair, procedural fairness must be uncompromisingly applied in the adjudicative organs. Pre-eminent among these precepts is the precept of due process, which insists that the persons against whom an administrative agency's exercise of adverse power is injurious are provided adequate notice and meaningful opportunity for hearing. This is not a cosmetic requirement but a fundamental rule that protects individuals against at-will decisions and thereby enhances the validity of administrative action. In addition, appeal mechanisms in such an arrangement must be accessible and efficient in order to enable affected parties to appeal unfavorable rulings effortlessly. These mechanisms provide accountability, where agency decisions are subject to scrutiny against established standards of law, based on comparative examinations of various administrative justice systems, such as those governing agricultural appraisals (Zhumataeva, 2024).

Finally, flexibility in administrative adjudication necessitates ongoing examination and amendment to fit changing social and regulatory contexts. Divergence in agency procedures across jurisdictions demonstrates the imperative to adopt best practices to facilitate efficiency and equity. For instance, the use of advanced technologies like geographic information systems can be effective in fostering transparency in the decision-making process, as illustrated in the assessment of agricultural land. Additionally, the initiatives towards obliterating inconsistency and maximizing legal clarity are essential in preventing the administrative cost to individuals and businesses. A holistic approach consisting of administrative adjudication, such as streamlining appeal procedures and ensuring equal access to justice, does not merely increase the efficiency of agencies but makes for a more informed and engaged public (Gaétan de Rassenfosse, 2025).

11.3.1. Tribunals and Boards

These tribunals are usually employed to settle certain disputes and issue rulings affecting people, business entities, and society. Providing a less formalistic option compared to conventional courts, boards and tribunals facilitate more open administration adjudication, often focusing on specialized areas such as labor, real estate, and environmental law. This learned determination can be reconciled with broad principles of comparative administrative law, acknowledging the diverse legal systems and traditions of jurisdictions, including those formed by treaties like the North American Agreement on Labor Cooperation (NAALC) (Banks et al., 2000). Thus, it is essential to familiarize oneself with the working and jurisdiction of tribunals and boards to ensure proper policy analysis and legal reform in diverse comparative contexts. Procedural models in the context of boards and tribunals form the basis of their function and legitimacy. Adjudication by administrations mandates adherence to the doctrines of procedural fairness, whereby the parties to a dispute are provided with a reasonable chance to present their cases. Detailed procedures specified for the institutions in most comparative juridical systems can also considerably vary, based on the culture and legal tradition of the jurisdiction. For instance, while some legal traditions would prefer greater leniency in the rules of procedure in order to quicken the resolution process, others would impart strict adherence to formal procedural norms. In this context, an understanding of the procedural requirements in a given context allows one to cherish more comprehensively how diverse legal traditions handle the resolution of administrative disputes (Scott et al., 2025). Aside from this, the transparency and consistency of such procedures also underscore their merit in ensuring public trust in the government. In the discussion of tribunals and boards in terms of administrative law, there should also be a consideration of appeal processes for dissatisfied persons with decisions rendered by these bodies. These appeal processes serve a critical function in maintaining checks and balances in the administrative system to ensure over-site of potential errors and injustices. Comparative administrative law highlights the importance of firmly established procedures through which parties aggrieved may seek remedy and appeal decisions. Especially, the possession of robust processes of appeal signals a broad intent to uphold fundamental democratic values and human rights in administrative rule. The comparative analysis of such mechanisms not only reveals variation across jurisdictions in terms of effectiveness and accessibility, but also sheds light on broader issues of accountability and transparency in public administration, towards a more informed discussion of best practice within the discipline (Figure 11.3).

Figure 11.3. The administration of justice within government frameworks often hinges on the functions of tribunals and boards, entities that serve a pivotal role in the realization of fair administrative law.

Source: https://encrypted-tbn0.gstatic.com/images?q=tbn:ANd9GcS_cDHE26uB-WbITY-xoPDXq4pOU-Th9n-0Gg&s.

11.3.2. Procedural Fairness

Ensuring fairness in administration is crucial to the validity of decision-making as well as protecting the rights of an individual. Procedural fairness in comparative administrative law captures the substance of the demands of transparency, due process, and stakeholder participation. Procedural fairness as a principle is applied variably across jurisdictions and impacts directly on how administrative organs interact with individuals and entities. For instance, in the UK, procedural fairness has its origins in common law traditions that put substantial premiums on the expectation of fair notice and opportunity to reply to administrative action. Within Sharia-principled jurisdictions, such as Saudi Arabia, procedural fairness could take on characteristics that are more attuned to the cultural context, which values very highly evenhanded treatment of creditor-debtor relations and hence reflects deeper social values. Thus, comparing such frameworks is insightful in identifying how procedural fairness drives administrative action and resulting credibility of administrative systems (Nasser, 2025). Procedural fairness has particularly been instrumental in the background of administrative adjudication, in which varying frameworks dictate procedure for dispute resolution. Administrative boards and tribunals, being decision-making bodies, are intended to provide the opportunity for individuals to present their cases. There is a need to ensure clear rules in such proceedings because ambiguity will lead to inconsistency and allegations of unfairness, which ultimately erode stakeholder trust. Furthermore, effective mechanisms for appeals must be put in place to address complaints as a consequence of administrative action. Analysis of procedures under different legal traditions, for example, protection of procedural rights, reveals significant variations. For example, while some jurisdictions will provide greater flexibility for administrative agencies in the exercise of discretion, others adopt stringent standards so as not to make arbitrary findings. These variations highlight the importance of procedural protections in serving the ends of fairness and integrity in administrative law (Lototskyi, 2025). Moreover, the procedural fairness principle is intricately linked with the transparency and accountability vehicles adopted by administrative agencies. In the UK as well as emerging legal regimes, access to information on the part of the public and the right to attend public hearings are paramount in promoting accountability. Once the agencies are forced to disclose information and justify their actions, there is developed an open culture that can help counter concerns related to administrative overreach or abuse of authority. Again, whistleblower protections serve as crucial deterrents, allowing whistleblowers to disclose abuses without fear of retribution. The comparative assessment of the frameworks calls out alternative approaches to making procedural fairness a concrete reality rather than an abstract concept to those whose conduct is administrative. By this comprehension of the varied applications of the principles of fairness, the stakeholders are well placed to navigate complex administrative settings, hence towards improved governance (Nasser, 2025).

11.3.3. Appeal Mechanisms

The processes under which the decisions of administrative agencies may be appealed are critical to the maintenance of accountability and the rule of law within public institutions. The structure of appeal systems varies considerably from jurisdiction to jurisdiction, reflecting diverse legal traditions and administrative cultures. For example, while some legal traditions place a strong emphasis on hierarchical ordering by which appeals rise progressively to higher levels of government, others might feature specialized tribunals that are optimally configured to deal with particular types of disputes. This diversity not only testifies to the comparative nature of administrative law but also attests to the applicability of procedural fairness and the right to a fair hearing as constitutive features of effective administrative processes. Such differences oblige policymakers to think about the efficiency and accessibility of these systems of appeal, guaranteeing they support the protection of individual rights and maintain transparency in administrative decision-making. In studying the value of appeal mechanisms in comparative administrative law, it is clear that such procedures need to adequately provide for efficiency and thoroughness in order to fulfill their intended function. The operations of these mechanisms can be hindered by issues such as lengthy procedural timelines as well as the complexity of legislations. For instance, in Ukraine, the high workload of the administrative courts has led to public demand for the implementation of alternative dispute resolution methods, which would help decongest courts as well as enhance the protection of taxpayers rights (Ugolkov, 2024). The institution of mandatory pre-trial appeals can close loopholes that presently arise, potentially offering a still more streamlined route for taxpayers to seek grievances short of a direct recourse to judicial review. Planning and implementation of appeal mechanisms, accordingly, must remain an evolving process, attuned to evolving needs of people and capabilities of administrative agencies. Moreover, the comparison of mechanisms of appeal sheds meaningful light on how different legal systems aim to find a balance between responsibility and authority. Analysis of administrative procedural codes in Europe and Vietnam draws attention to common devotion to values like lawfulness and justice but to different modes of implementation (Doan et al., 2024). It is only by recognizing such differences that knowledge-sharing and best practice development are feasible, ultimately giving rise to reforms that enhance the integrity of administrative procedures globally. Such reforms are not so much about reforming legal documents; they require a shift of culture towards one of accountability and public trust in government action. To resolve these values successfully across jurisdictions can lead to firmer legal frameworks that not only protect individual rights but also unite the legitimacy of administrative action in an increasingly interconnected world.

11.4. TRANSPARENCY AND ACCOUNTABILITY

The essential element of good governance from an administrative law perspective is the establishment of transparency and accountability mechanisms. The significance of these principles is that they generate public trust because government actions are subject to examination and intervention whenever necessary. For instance, access to information has evolved as a fundamental mechanism for enabling stakeholders to hold administrative authorities accountable for their decisions and actions. This process not only empowers citizens but also enhances the legitimacy of governmental processes. The existence of robust frameworks for information access eventually brings about an informed citizenry, which is essential for successful participation in democratic processes. In the shifting administrative law environment, transparency interventions are increasingly being solidified as milestones for public interest protection and discouragement of potential abuse of power, aligning with general governability principles infused in comparative administration studies (Molden, 2013). Public hearings are another important vehicle through which transparency and accountability can be solidified within administrative systems. These forums allow stakeholders, like affected communities and the public at large, to air their fears and sentiments regarding intended actions, policies, or rules by government agencies. Public hearings, through making free discussions possible, not only allow for multifarious perspectives to be considered in decision-making but also promote a culture of accountability among administrative agencies that must justify themselves publicly. Besides, the knowledge acquired through such engagements can lead to more enlightened policy-making that includes the needs and wishes of the people. In this sense, the process of conducting public hearings can be seen as a link between the government and the people with the impact of enhancing civic participation and a sense of collective responsibility in the ruling process (Emerson et al., 2011). Protection of whistleblowers is another vital element of the overall scheme of transparency and accountability in administrative law. Protection of whistleblowers is an important mechanism for protecting individuals who disclose abuse or malpractice in government institutions, thereby enabling the detection and corrective remedy of potential abuses of power. Protection of the safety and anonymity of whistleblowers induces would-be whistleblowers to report without fear of retaliation, which is of paramount significance in facilitating integrity in administrative action. This practice of putting into operation such safeguards not only discourages administrative officials from unethical practice but also increases the system's overall accountability by adding checks and balances. Where citizens can trust the institutions set up for the protection of their rights and interests, there is a high chance that an accountable and transparent administrative setup can be developed, reflective of the interdependence of these values amidst the broader theme of comparative administrative law (Molden, 2013).

11.4.1. Access to Information

The evolving regulatory landscape of administrative law highlights the significance of access to information for facilitating transparency and accountability in government bodies. Providing access to information is essential for allowing citizens to make administrative institutions accountable for their actions and enhancing decision-making participation. This democratization of knowledge operates at the core of modern administrative law, complementing various mechanisms aimed at facilitating a judiciary to enforce rights more effectively. The European Court of Human Rights (ECtHR) has elaborated upon the concept of access to information extensively within its jurisprudence, emphasizing particularly the enforceability of judgments within judicial proceedings. These trends, as evident from the reforms following such instances as Hornsby, emphasize the intersection of rights of access and the enforcement of court decisions, and therefore cast light on the pivotal role of the administrative judiciary in bringing about effective legal outcomes (Bruna et al., 2025). Additionally, access to information underlies the general rule of procedural fairness, in the absence of which the public cannot effectively engage in administrative proceedings. Through these mechanisms, one can consider the facilitation of access to information as tools that empower citizens to challenge administrative action effectively. Through the provision of information to citizens so they may understand the parameters and implications of regulatory decisions, administrative bodies promote better-informed citizens. Transparency becomes most significant in comparative administrative law, as variations in national practice reflect variations in orientations towards information accessibility. Different jurisdictions adopt different legal standards and institutional frameworks that mandate the extent to which information should be made available, but the common goal is one: promoting public participation and scrutiny of administrative proceedings (Ostrikova, 2022).

The conflict between access to information and the efficiency of operational regulatory methods is a unifying challenge to administrative law. While the requirement for openness necessitates the opening of information to administrative agencies, a balance is necessary in the implications against confidentiality and against bureaucratic efficiency. Policymakers must walk the fine line between responding to citizens' rights to information and maintaining sensitive operational information as confidential. As European governments enact reforms in line with the ECtHRs decisions, it is imperative to establish standards safeguarding not just personal rights of access but institutional effectiveness as well. Such reforms ensure that these are not only compliant with international law principles but also do not deprive regulatory agencies of discretion necessary (Bruna et al., 2025).

11.4.2. Public Hearings

The role of public hearings under administrative law cannot be overemphasized, since public hearings are fundamental tools for preaching openness and public participation in the government process. By inviting stakeholders to participate through public hearings, agencies provide the forum through which members of the public may voice opinions, objections, and suggestions regarding regulatory proposals. This is a central process in the establishment of a two-way communications channel between government and citizens to ensure that administrative decisions are not taken unilaterally. Above and beyond logistical involvement, the value of public hearings resides in being a commitment to procedural fairness, establishing an atmosphere wherein citizens have faith in their ability to challenge decisions and participate in decision-making about issues concerning their lives. Consequently, public hearings are an essential means by which responsibility within administrative frameworks can both be invoked and maintained in accordance with dominant democratic principles. Furthermore, the structure and effectiveness of public hearings will differ significantly across jurisdictions in accordance with nations' diverse conceptions of administrative law. Where inquisitorial processes are employed in those countries, the organization of public hearings might be an expression of the inquiring nature of administrative processes, attempting to acquire detailed and factual articulations of community interests. This can be observed in common-law systems like Canada and Australia, where mechanisms have been devised for enhancing public engagement and accountability in administrative decision-making. Hybridization of such processes justifies a convergence of adversarial and inquisitorial models, enhancing the quality of debate at hearings. Invoking more recent debates over administrative justice, jurisdictions increasingly attempt to employ innovative formats for public hearings with a view to maximizing stakeholder participation with efficiency and meticulousness, reasserting the integral role such forums play in modern systems of governance (Jacobs et al., 2016). Of note, public hearings themselves are called into question and debate, particularly concerning their effectiveness in really expressing public opinion. It is argued by critics that although procedural space is provided by way of public hearings, at times they end up being mere formalities, and hardly any real influence is retained on administrative decisions. The complexity of administrative rules can leave one in the cold and overlook submissions made by persons who are not necessarily experts or well-equipped. As seen in the comparison of administrative practice, it is necessary that the agencies develop public hearing procedures which not only solicit but also encourage broad dialogue (Jacobs et al., 2011). Thus, the evolution of public hearings must be addressed in the context of broader reforms of administrative law, ensuring that they are properly capable of fulfilling their function of ensuring accountability and embodying fairness and transparency in regulatory action.

11.4.3. Whistleblower Protections

In the last few years, the need to protect whistleblowers has arisen in comparative administrative law on the grounds of ensuring public governance to become transparent and accountable. Substantively core to this development is acknowledgement that individuals within organizations possess valuable information regarding maladministration or wrongdoing that, when brought into the public sphere, can lead to the necessary reforms and corrective steps. The legal frameworks for whistleblower protections vary widely across jurisdictions, and that influences the effectiveness of safeguarding those who disclose illegality. From their examination, one can more clearly see how systems of law distribute rights and protections to whistleblowers, thus determining the environment within which public administration unfolds. It is apparent that well-functioning whistleblower protections cultivate a culture of democratic responsiveness and accountability, and as such, there must be robust legal protections that encourage reporting of wrongdoing while not at the same time allowing threats of reprisal. The success of whistleblower protections relies not only on statutory regimes but also on the administrative culture that supports such provisions. Where there is a culture of transparency and support in those jurisdictions, whistleblowers are apt to come forth without fearing retaliation. Empirical research has established that administrative arrangements with political accounts of administration can further enhance these protections by recognizing the exchange among power relationships, civic engagement, and democratic accountability (Peters et al., 2022). With public administration striving to bridge the gap between bureaucratic practice and democratic ideals, a nuanced understanding of politics brings stronger whistleblower protections closer to reality. This perspective provokes not only legal protection but also the institutionalization of facilitative practices that provide individuals with autonomy to reveal abuse without fear of adverse consequences. Above all, the establishment of international institutions, such as the European Court of Human Rights, has increasingly had a pivotal role in shaping the national practice of whistleblower protection. Benchmarks set by such institutions can serve as a guideline for national legal systems to enhance their domestic legislations. Researchers have observed that the study of procedural matters and rules promulgated by such courts can inform us about best practices for incorporating whistleblower protection in public administration (N/A, 2021). Moreover, the nexus between these principles and domestic legal systems is fertile ground for comparative study to inform the dialogue regarding the good administrative practice. Through an analysis of these dynamics, researchers and practitioners can develop comprehensive methods that not only enhance whistleblower protections but also foster more administrative integrity and public trust.

11.5. DISCRETION AND CONTROL

The relationship between discretion and control under administrative law plays a critical role in their effect on the efficiency of the government. By granting a level of discretionary authority to regulatory agencies, governments attempt to enhance responsiveness to new social demands and economic realities. However, this discretion has the potential to lead to imbalances in power usage, which can result in arbitrary action contrary to legal standards. For instance, the delegation of power to subnational governments, such as in the case of China, illustrates how the regional government has considerable power over the economy in a highly centralized system (Xu, 2011). This balance between discretion granted to regional institutions and the overall control of the government raises fundamental questions regarding the limits of authority and the means by which administrative frameworks can be prevented from facilitating the abuse of power. Further, the idea of legal restraints on discretion is fundamental in the facilitation of administrative accountability. The restraints are essential in the prevention of agencies from going beyond their limits and consequently invoking a system that not only questions but also balances their authority. Judicial review is commonly employed in most jurisdictions to enforce these legal boundaries. One example is in British administrative law where institutions incrementally develop, reinforcing accountability by making dependency on established legal precedent more stable in the long run (Mahoney et al., 2009). This helps not only to mitigate potential abuse of discretion but also advances the culture of openness as well as public trust. Therefore, the learning of how varying legal frameworks exercise control over discretion presents a fertile source for learning comparative administrative laws implications. Finally, coping with the antidotes to excess is a vital component of controlling administrative discretion. Where administrative action transgresses laid-down limits, robust machinery should be in place to remedy such excesses. This includes both procedural remedies for redress and machinery through which people may be able to challenge administrative actions. For example, administrative boards and tribunals in most jurisdictions serve as irreplaceable forums wherein complaints are ventilated and decided, in the hope of ensuring procedural fairness within the ambit of bureaucratic decision-making. Inadequate remedies may not only instill arbitrary rule, but also disintegrate public confidence within administrative institutions. Therefore, research into how different regimes of regulation provide models of accountability contributes to our understanding of the broader issues of discretion and control within comparative administrative law.

11.5.1. Legal Limits on Discretion

In administrative law, discretion by public authorities is necessary but vulnerable to abuse unless strictly controlled by the law. Discretion allows administrators a degree of elbow-room in order to make decisions adapted to specific situations so as to be able to respond to individual situations. Unless there are well-established limits, discretion can nevertheless foster arbitrariness in decision-making at the cost of the rule of law and justice. Thus, the creation of legal frameworks for exercising discretion is essential in order to protect the rights of citizens while ensuring administrative effectiveness. To manage this dynamic, various jurisdictions have devised guidelines clarifying the limits of discretion whereby decision-makers make choices within a transparent and principled context. Balancing autonomy and accountability is an ongoing challenge, as reflected in divergent regulatory strategies between jurisdictions, highlighting the need for efficient oversight mechanisms (Kostin, 2025). The necessity for legal limitations on discretion is particularly acute where one considers the impact of administrative decisions on individual rights and public interests. In other academic arguments, specifically emphasized in Russian administrative legal theory, discretionary powers' effect has been decried for their ability to inflict significant harm on liberties and rights (Serkov et al., 2023). This criticism reveals the ethical dimensions of administrative discretion because unfettered discretion can lead to discrimination or rule that fails to meet democratic norms. Hence, institutions guaranteeing judicial review and procedural safeguard are essential. These systems not only grant redress to aggrieved parties but also serve as a constraint on the administrative agency's discretion. By being endowed with well-defined parameters, the law promotes an environment under which the decision-making process is justified as well as accountable to the public. Also, evolution of administrative law in the digital age raises new challenges and possibilities for legal limits on discretion. As government becomes online, the exercise of discretion may also change with the means, and attention must be given to existing frameworks. Discretionary powers must be revamped to respond to challenges built into the digital age, including transparency, data protection, and risk of algorithmic bias. Administrative reforms call upon legislatures to not only remake current policies but also value-based standards of newer realities without watering down the essential values of justice and fairness. Thus, the institution of legal constraints on discretion needs to be guided by different global experiences to ensure that optimal practices are borrowed in designing an administrative setup which is progressive as well as answerable (Kostin, 2025).

11.5.2. Abuse of Power

The subtleties of administrative law have the tendency to reveal the delicate balance achieved between governing authority and the rights of citizens. The subject, in this case, of potential abuse of power is a serious concern. Power, whether by executive order or agency regulation, has a facile tendency to ooze into overreaching when checks and balances are insufficiently enforced. In the past, this has been aptly illustrated by numerous uprisings, such as the ones that took place in the Arab Spring, which have highlighted how institution-building within both governments and militaries can affect the direction of civil rights and political protest. According to the comparative analytical model definition, knowledge about the distinct channels each government uses in exerting authority can provide valuable information about various types of power abuse, for example, the impact of military loyalty and desertion against state directives (Kraay et al., 2010).

Additionally, accountability is a crucial mechanism in avoiding potential abuses of power in public administration. Disconnection between the institutional mechanism and normative virtue of accountability becomes key. As a norm, accountability is concerned with the ethical obligation of public officials to be responsible and transparent. As a mechanism, though, accountability is the institutional arrangements on offer by which institutions can render different actors accountable for their conduct. This dualism not only clarifies what accountability is but further identifies its function to avert abuse of power (Bovens, 2010). A debate on procedural fairness in administrative adjudication, for instance, can illustrate how administrative agencies' operational dynamics can minimize or maximize the chances of power accumulation and discretionary abuse. Discretionary use in administrative acts makes power abuse even more complicated to discuss. Although regulatory measures impose some limitations, the procedure of administrative discretion can lead to significant variations in interpreting and enforcing laws. Legal control on this discretion is crucial for making the administrative situation equitable and fair. Along with this, mechanisms of recourse for handling instances of abuse, that is, appeals and revocation processes in the context of licensing, are essential components of any effective administrative framework. Without adequate mechanisms to correct excesses of power, the potential for abuse remains uncorrected, ultimately threatening the purity of governance. Shaping a whistleblower protection culture and transparent operations is required in order to ensure that not only abuses are identified, but action is also taken sternly, thereby increasing faith in administrative procedures (Bovens, 2010).

11.5.3. Remedies for Excess

When the complexity of government increases and the areas of administrative actions expand, the potential for abuse of discretionary power is a cause for concern. Administrative agencies wield enormous powers in issuing executive orders and formulating regulations that affect numerous areas. This authority raises significant questions about protection from bureaucratic abuses. Legal limits on discretion are one possible solution to check excess, so that the agencies' action remains within the permissible area of their statutory mandate. The requirement of transparent procedural rules, along with pre-established criteria for the cancellation of licenses or permits, is the complement to such legal checks. In the absence of these solutions, untrammeled discretion can lead to arbitrary decisions, and hence invalidate public faith in administrative institutions. Lastly, a balanced approach to agency autonomy and accountability is essential in order to minimize the risk of excess while ensuring fairness and justice within administrative law. Legal constraints are not the sole constraints which may be placed upon administrative remedies; judicial review can also be added as a necessary measure for checking excess. Judicial supervision can become the final check on administrative power so that the courts can decide whether the agency action was reasonable. By this judicial syncretism, citizens are protected against abuse, and rule-making procedures are caused to bend to the letter and spirit of the law. In this encounter between administrative agencies and courts, the importance of procedural justice in adjudication comes out, with citizens being able to appeal against judgments that may have unfairly prejudiced their interests. In light of the fact that people at times are faced with great imbalances of power against well-resourced agencies, the presence of efficacious remedies is most crucial. The issue presented by new technologies and approaches in administrative activity necessitates a system of checks and balances in place and includes the integration of corrective mechanisms against abuses, as has been underscored by recent work on AI and governance (Justin, 2019). Furthermore, with the advent of new technology such as artificial intelligence, another layer of complexity is added to remedy excess in administrative law. With bureaucracies increasing dependence on AI for informing decision-making, implications on discretion and with it the attendant risks of excess shift fundamentally. The interaction between human discretion and AI not only affects the landscape of decision-making but raises overarching ethical issues with regard to accountability. For instance, AI utilization in government must be weighed against openness because the algorithms used can conceal the rationale behind the decisions being reached. Additionally, innovations like autonomous vehicles usher in the requirement for regulatory frameworks and rules of fault to be revamped in light of the continued necessity to maintain pace with technological developments (Anderson et al., 2016). A survey of how administrative law evolves in response to these advances in technology illustrates the vital crossroads between innovation and application of accountability principles and underscores the need for remedies clearly established in meeting excess under conditions of sped-up change.

11.6. COMPARATIVE REGULATORY MODELS

The administrative legal regime is significantly shaped by the various comparative regulatory styles applied in various jurisdictions. The sectoral agencies are sites of convergence where specialist knowledge intersects with regulatory imposition and are therefore of particular significance to these regimes. In certain nations, the agencies are mandated and can respond quickly to sectoral problems, which can enhance efficiency and innovation in the government. However, the difference between regulatory philosophies raises issues of whether control is sufficient and whether power is appropriately balanced. Countries with stringent regulation models may grant better consumer protections, but may limit operational business flexibility, and this creates a paradox that must be examined in some detail. As governments continue to adapt to the imperatives of globalization and novel technologies, learning from such comparative regulatory designs is imperative in advancing effective administrative governance that strikes a balance between oversight and flexibility. The establishment of oversight institutions is essential to ensuring accountability in comparative regulatory designs. Such institutions are responsible for overseeing sectoral agencies' performance as well as ensuring compliance with stipulated standards and regulations. For instance, the formal evaluation by such monitoring institutions can mitigate corruption and abuse of power dangers, and therefore enhance public trust. Secondly, the effectiveness of oversight varies widely; in some countries, they possess robust institutions that promote transparency and public involvement, whereas others can be hindered by bureaucratic lethargy or low finances. Examining the working frameworks of oversight bodies can identify the ways in which they support both the efficiency and legitimacy of administrative law. Of note, the incorporation of citizen input into the regulatory process, in conjunction with active oversight, highlights a dedication to democratic governance that finds itself centered around public interest and rights. Interagency cooperation becomes an important aspect of comparative regimes for regulation, particularly in addressing complex, cross-cutting challenges that cross the jurisdictional boundaries of individual agencies. Effective interagency relations enhance regulatory coherence and enable improved allocation of resources, which may deliver a whole-of-government approach to matters such as environmental protection and public health. From case studies within various jurisdictions, one can observe various levels of success in interagency collaboration, which appear to differ based on the existing legal frameworks and institutional settings. The creation of Hybrid Dispute Resolution (HDR) systems, as indicated in existing appraisals, shows an overall trend towards the inclusion of diversified regulatory approaches for participatory governance promotion and the transcending of shortcomings related to traditional litigation strategies (Subrata et al., 2025). By bridging gaps between agencies, such models not only strengthen regulatory responses but also become more open, making room for a democratic process in public administration (Krasnohor, 2025).

11.6.1. Sector Agencies

The success of governance activities depends primarily on the existence and functioning of sectoral agencies, or specialized regulation institutions in administrative law systems. According to the comparative administrative model, these agencies are responsible for advancing and implementing specific regulation policies tailored for specific sectors such as healthcare, environmental preservation, and financial services. A defining feature of this regulatory model is the ability of sectoral agencies to exercise quasi-judicial powers, enabling them to determine cases in dispute, compel compliance, and punish by their own accord without requiring direct oversight by judicial institutions. The arrangement fosters a decentralized and nuanced regulatory framework, promoting sectoral expertise while maintaining efficiency. But at the same time, this technical expertise can also pose challenges in having well-coordinated interagency activities, which might lead to duplications or gaps in regulation enforcement (Abdulla et al., 2024).

Functional sectoral agencies also are the equivalent of robust licensing and permitting devices, which assist in producing regulatory standards and guidelines that form a part of agency operations. These requirements are essential for ensuring that organizations within a specific industry comply with established regulations, thereby raising accountability as well as public security. For instance, within the financial services industry, anti-money laundering and counter-terrorism financing programs are regulated by sectoral agencies in the hope of reducing the risks of illicit financial flows (Abdulla et al., 2024). It is important that such standards are implemented, because their lack of observance may lead to license revocation, undermining the agency's jurisdiction and regulatory objectives. In addition, an adequate revocation procedure must exist so that processes remain open and fair, as well as provide room for judicial review that can enhance overall confidence in the regulatory framework. The value of transparency and accountability in sectoral agencies cannot be overstated. Public hearings and open access to information are rudimentary mechanisms through which such agencies can extend a reach to stakeholders and elicit public trust. Furthermore, whistleblower protections are necessary to render it safe for individuals to report abuse or regulation violations without retaliation. Such degrees of accountability are essential in maintaining the integrity of sectoral agencies and enhancing their legitimacy among both the public and also the regulated organizations. In comparative administrative law, the success of sectoral agencies is not only in their regulating function but also in how accountable and open they are to the people (Rabin, 2005). As governance evolves, so too do the structures that oversee these agencies have to continuously adapt so that they can still manage new issues confronted by their rapidly evolving sectors.

11.6.2. Oversight Institutions

In the complex world of comparative administrative law, oversight bodies play a pivotal role in ensuring that the state and its powers do not supersede the rights of the people. Oversight bodies, including ombudsman agencies, regulatory commissions, and audit committees, are created to exert external control over government action, ensuring that it is transparent and accountable at all times. Their roles have evolved in response to challenges of governance, underscoring the need for institutions that can scrutinize executive orders and agency regulations effectively. In imparting meaning to the ideals of administrative justice, oversight institutions contest prevailing norms of bureaucracy, which requires a re-evaluation of public sector practices. Consequently, their impact is evident not only in law but also in reshaping governance culture with its emphasis on ethical values and public trust as constitutive cornerstone of democratic government. The evolution of New Public Management (NPM) principles has had an impact on the role of oversight institutions in different administrative systems as well. As public sector managerial paradigms based on efficiency become popular, regulatory agencies are often confronted with the dilemma of balancing flexibility and legal accountability. The evolving scenario has prompted these institutions to alter their roles to render their regulatory supervision effective but still remain vigilant about fundamental legal principles. For example, merging performance evaluation and accountability considerations reflects a change towards non-traditional administrative models, which raises issues regarding the dilution of protection for rights. The phenomenon indicates the necessity of firm legal mandates and institutional autonomy for oversight agencies to mitigate risks from managerialism and reinforce their role as protectors of public interest and administrative legality. In comparative regulation models, the capacity of oversight institutions varies considerably across jurisdictions and corresponds to prevailing political and legal culture. This variability implies that although common goals of promoting legality, equity, and public accountability are in place, the methods and results may vary according to structural designs and operating patterns. For instance, one may enhance the oversight powers with stronger legal foundations in some countries, whereas others will focus on public involvement and transparency mechanisms. Diversification does mean, however, also cross-jurisdictional learning possibilities where best practices in oversight are shared and locally adjusted. Lastly, it is essential to have an all-around realization of such institutions in comparative administrative law in determining paths towards effective administration upholding democratic values in addressing contemporary issues of administration and pressure (Zhyvko et al., 2025; Erraou, 2025).

11.6.3. Interagency Coordination

Effectiveness of administrative actions under various models of governance relies primarily on the interagency coordination ability. A critical element of Comparative Administrative Law, interagency coordination facilitates integration and coordination of multiple regulatory agencies that work towards common objectives. By coordination, strategies may be harmonized, and communication facilitated to solve complex problems that are hard for a single organization to solve on its own. The necessity for robust interagency collaboration is particularly urgent in addressing global health matters, where action must cut across sectoral silos. As observed in other studies, political will at the top level accompanied by consensus in issues comprehension among agencies significantly enhances interagency coordination. Such cohesion not only transcends bureaucratic fragmentation but also reinforces a systematic regulation system that is harmonized with strategic policy goals, thereby improving general governance outcomes. The intersectionality of the problems tackled by regulatory bodies further improves interagency coordination. For example, where there is public health, environmental protection, and social welfare at stake, overlapping jurisdictions that agencies encounter require joint mechanisms for coordinated policy application. Multisector collaboration constitutes an effective method in combating such intricate challenges, especially in low- and middle-income countries where institutions will likely struggle with capacity. The challenges to these agencies are not only the requirement of efficient utilization of resources but also the avoidance of competition as a result of disintegrated governance arrangements. The implementation of coordinated approaches requires deliberate efforts at developing trust and commitment among agencies that can lead to more efficient and distributive public administration outcomes, as highlighted by recent research on governance structures and their implications for interagency dynamics. Building an interagency coordination culture also enhances the legitimacy of public institutions by ensuring that a variety of stakeholders' perspectives is considered in decision-making. Youth, for example, have demonstrated their commitment to social cohesion by being actively engaged in a variety of activities for public welfare, as reported in recent reports. Not only does this demonstrate their resilience, but it also establishes the importance of intergenerational equity in governance. Effective interagency coordination ensures involving youth voices in policy-making and enhancing the trust of citizens towards the administrative institutions. With interagency collaboration, integrating evidence-informed practice and contributions of stakeholders, a more representative governance approach can be created, addressing the needs of all parties and reflecting the heterogeneity of society's needs, underscored by extensive work on multisectoral action (N/A, 2020; Bennett et al., 2018).

SUMMARY

The result of comparative research of the administrative law is the complex nature of theory and practice in the jurisdictions. Analyzing legal systems, one can observe that while some are more formalized by an administrative act, that is, in the CIS states, others are moving towards a more unified model. The development of administrative legal doctrine, particularly with regard to interactions with post-Soviet counterparts by the Russian legal system, emphasizes adopting new practices. The disparity between doctrine, legislation, and judicial practice evidences lagging regulatory frameworks in some jurisdictions, and the contemporary nature of judicial practice in Russia suggests potential for improvement and progress within the region. This comparative examination lastly recommends the adoption of successful provisions across diverse legal frameworks to aid administrative governance transborder (Davydov, 2024). A research into procedural institutions in administrative law, such as contractual forms under the Administrative Violations and Sanctions Act, also demands comparative examination in legal reform. The complexities of concluding such arrangements indicate the necessity of understanding procedural complexity and its impact on administrative penalties. Through the examination of the legal nature of these arrangements in combination with various procedural laws, the image of administrative penal procedural law is better understood. This comparative research not only contributes to the existing pool of knowledge, but also provides key information for policymakers and legal practitioners working towards enhancing procedural fairness and responsibility. The continuous evolution of such concepts illustrates the need to learn from one another since all jurisdictions worldwide are grappling with the same challenges in administrative rule (Nikolova, 2024). Given the core issues of transparency, accountability, and regulation of discretion, there is a timely need for universal standards in administrative law. With governments grappling with the intricacies of regulatory regimes, adopting principles that are universally accepted can enable improved interagency co-ordination as well as monitoring. Comparative study offers a model for governments that want to simplify their administrative systems. It will not only make administrative procedures more efficient but also improve public confidence in government policies. Interconnectedness of the legal systems continues to influence the canvas of administrative law, thus validating the argument that endless dialogues and adjustment are imperative towards more effective governance and justice in administrative systems (Davydov, 2024; Nikolova, 2024).

A LOOK TO THE FUTURE

ARTIFICIAL INTELLIGENCE AND THE TRANSFORMATION OF ADMINISTRATIVE GOVERNANCE

Future comparative administrative law scholarship is in need of an interdisciplinarity that brings political science, economics, and medicine knowledge together. By exploring the intersections of these bodies of knowledge, scholars can better see how comparative models craft regulatory practice and make administration more transparent. As the terrain of administrative law remains in a continuous state of change, academics should pay attention to the impact of executive orders and agency regulations within a regional environment, with special attention given to how differences in governance affect local compliance and enforcement. Studying quasi-judicial power and other routine legal procedures can shed light on the effectiveness of regulation and public influence, leading ultimately to best practices for sound government in a comparative context. Moreover, the emerging presence of artificial intelligence (AI) in administrative law holds significant future research implications. Even though uses of AI have begun to spread to a broad array of industries, including healthcare, administrative agencies have concerns that include transparency and accountability, particularly within decision-making. Interpretable outcomes of AI are urgently needed; otherwise, data-driven governance potential could be underutilized or mistrusted by the public. Taking into consideration the black-box character of machine learning algorithms is also necessary when guaranteeing that legal standards adapt to technological advancements efficiently without jeopardizing key rights. Research findings, such as those presented in Secinaro et al. (2021) and Tjoa et al. (2020), can help guide the establishment of standards for AI application balancing accountability and innovation in administrative mechanisms. Lastly, cross-jurisdictional implications of regulatory designs highlight the urgent need for comparative analyses considering domestic contexts and variations in cultural practices of administrative law. An exploration of how sectoral agencies and oversight institutions operate within distinctive legal systems can better inform us of effective regulatory coordination and cooperative governance. This comparative perspective can uncover rich lessons on balancing discretion and control in administrative conduct, thus guiding judicial review proceedings and the efficiency of remedies against excess. Future studies must identify the characteristics of effective administrative systems that are efficient and result in fairness, with the ultimate aim that comparative administrative law is dynamic in accordance with societal and technological advancements, as suggested by Secinaro et al. (2021) and Tjoa et al. (2020).

REFERENCES

1. Al-Kubaisi, H. A. R. A., Husain, F., & Ali, M. (2024). Charities or donations as a source of terrorism financing: Why does regulation fail in Pakistan? *Inverge Journal of Social Sciences*. https://www.semanticscholar.org/paper/191cbb651056e4f8607ce7c5475ed8ee245e52db (accessed on 9th September 2025).
2. Aldahmash, A. N. A. (2025). The petition for a liquidation procedure and the administrative liquidation procedure: A comparative analysis study in Saudi and UK insolvency law. *International Journal of Law and Management*. https://www.semanticscholar.org/paper/e4bf8ea00d48359c1b1e5cdb6603677cb58ca0ac (accessed on 9th September 2025).
3. Anderson, J., Kalra, N., Stanley, K., Sørensen, P., Samaras, C., & Oluwatola, O. (2016). *Autonomous Vehicle Technology: A Guide for Policymakers. RAND Corporation eBooks*. https://doi.org/10.7249/rr443-2 (accessed on 9th September 2025).
4. Banks, K., Compa, L. A., Lara, L., et al. (2000). *Labor Relations Law in North America*. https://core.ac.uk/download/5131456.pdf (accessed on 9th September 2025).
5. Bennett, S., Glandon, D., & Rasanathan, K. (2018). Governing multisectoral action for health in low-income and middle-income countries: Unpacking the problem and rising to the challenge. *BMJ Global Health, 3*, e000880. https://doi.org/10.1136/bmjgh-2018-000880 (accessed on 9th September 2025).
6. Black, E. (1976). Southern governors and civil rights: Racial segregation as a campaign issue in the Second Reconstruction. https://www.semanticscholar.org/paper/c18b0f0aefaee775671b29b0d4728486de9e4e87 (accessed on 9th September 2025).
7. Bovens, M. (2010). Two concepts of accountability: Accountability as a virtue and as a mechanism. *West European Politics, 33*, 946–967. https://doi.org/10.1080/01402382.2010.486119 (accessed on 9th September 2025).
8. Bullock, J. B. (2019). Artificial intelligence, discretion, and bureaucracy. *The American Review of Public Administration, 49*, 751–761. https://doi.org/10.1177/0275074019856123 (accessed on 9th September 2025).
9. Chiocchetti, E., & Ralli, N. (2011). *Legal Terminology and Lesser Used Languages: The Case of Mòcheno*. https://core.ac.uk/download/71976439.pdf (accessed on 9th September 2025).
10. Cotella, G., Janin Rivolin, U., & Reimer, M. (2011). Structure, tools, discourse and practices: A multidimensional comparative approach to EU territorial governance. https://core.ac.uk/download/pdf/11421882.pdf (accessed on 9th September 2025).
11. Davydov, K. V. (2024). The concept of an administrative act in the CIS countries: Comparative legal analysis. *Courier of Kutafin Moscow State Law University (MSAL)*. https://www.semanticscholar.org/paper/0eb39b8ccb98013fb41d21261b15d4620703f22b (accessed on 9th September 2025).
12. de Rassenfosse, G. (2025). The "strength" of patent systems. https://www.semanticscholar.org/paper/3cdfa94bdfb2dbe81807a20ae25d28a9bcd6014c (accessed on 9th September 2025).
13. della Cananea, G., & Andenas, M. (2021). *Administrative Procedure and Judicial Review: A 'Common Core' Research. Oxford University Press eBooks*. https://doi.org/10.1093/oso/9780198867609.003.0001 (accessed on 9th September 2025).

14. Doan, U. T. T., & Vu, T. V. (2024). In-depth comparative analysis of the principles of law on administrative procedures in Vietnam compared with that in European law. *InterEULawEast: Journal for the International and European Law, Economics and Market Integrations.* https://www.semanticscholar.org/paper/2fca8acb54c2944414161b1a546113db3e6251b4 (accessed on 9th September 2025).

15. Eliantonio, M., Klafki, A., & Lanceiro, R. (2025). Transnational judicial control in EU law: The practice of national courts. *European Public Law.* https://www.semanticscholar.org/paper/27baaa80506a8442619f3d2ecdedcccb91c18811 (accessed on 9th September 2025).

16. Emerson, K., Nabatchi, T., & Balogh, S. (2011). An integrative framework for collaborative governance. *Journal of Public Administration Research and Theory, 22,* 1–29. https://doi.org/10.1093/jopart/mur011 (accessed on 9th September 2025).

17. Erraou, M. (2025). Public administration and the evolution of administrative law: From institutional logic to organizational logic. *Dirasat: Shari'a and Law Sciences.* https://www.semanticscholar.org/paper/f7b4e0431d4d2a7d93ee0b8ca396acdd89c38ac7 (accessed on 9th September 2025).

18. Guttentag, D. (2013). Airbnb: Disruptive innovation and the rise of an informal tourism accommodation sector. *Current Issues in Tourism, 18,* 1192–1217. https://doi.org/10.1080/13683500.2013.827159 (accessed on 9th September 2025).

19. Hynes, M. (2021). The social, cultural and environmental costs of hyper-connectivity: Sleeping through the revolution. https://www.semanticscholar.org/paper/3cc6c3eed640ec32aa476dfe6b6706bdf6300f0d (accessed on 9th September 2025).

20. Jacobs, L., & Baglay, S. (2016). *The Nature of Inquisitorial Processes in Administrative Regimes: Global Perspectives.*

21. Jacobs, L., Baglay, S., Kwok, M., Mavrikkou, M., & Tay, K. L. (2011). *The nature of inquisitorial processes in administrative regimes: Global perspectives research workshop report. SSRN Electronic Journal.* https://www.semanticscholar.org/paper/e4bf8ea00d48359c1b1e5cdb6603677cb58ca0ac (accessed on 9th September 2025).

22. Kaufmann, D. E., Kraay, A., & Mastruzzi, M. (2009). *Governance Matters VIII: Aggregate and Individual Governance Indicators 1996–2008.* World Bank Policy Research Working Paper. https://doi.org/10.1596/1813-9450-4978 (accessed on 9th September 2025).

23. Kitchin, R. (2016). Thinking critically about and researching algorithms. *Information Communication & Society, 20,* 14–29. https://doi.org/10.1080/1369118x.2016.1154087 (accessed on 9th September 2025).

24. Koshel, A. S., Kuzminov, Y. I., Kruchinskaia, E., & Lesiv, B. (2025). In search of the regulatory optimum for digital platforms: A comparative analysis. *Legal Issues in the Digital Age.* https://www.semanticscholar.org/paper/965ca87da0aaf6a16ed50ba2a85e70eba71ff8d2 (accessed on 9th September 2025).

25. Kostin, S. (2025). Police discretion in the context of the digital transformation of public administration. *NB: Административное право и практика администрирования.* https://www.semanticscholar.org/paper/9b80dbe0bc3d5222de862a7a8df245566d549a03 (accessed on 9th September 2025).

26. Kraay, A., Kaufmann, D., & Mastruzzi, M. (2010). *The Worldwide Governance Indicators:*

Methodology and Analytical Issues. World Bank Policy Research Working Paper. https://doi.org/10.1596/1813-9450-5430 (accessed on 9th September 2025).

27. Krasnohor, O. (2025). Models of public and corporate governance in the development of e-notary systems: A comparative legal analysis. *Economic Scope*. https://www.semanticscholar.org/paper/60be84d56255d51fef09cd6e0250943cef4d14c6 (accessed on 9th September 2025).

28. Lee, L. (2024). Examining the legal status of digital assets as property: A comparative analysis of jurisdictional approaches. https://www.semanticscholar.org/paper/f417b618aac4d9c9f23e1f38261a8100f845b869 (accessed on 9th September 2025).

29. Lototskyi, M. (2025). Inadmissibility of abuse of procedural rights, as one of the basic principles of administrative justice. *Scientific and Informational Bulletin of Ivano-Frankivsk University of Law Named after King Danylo Halytskyi*. https://www.semanticscholar.org/paper/fc05d33d78b76330f7b4b84a433eca59f7c9261f (accessed on 9th September 2025).

30. Mahoney, J., & Thelen, K. (2009). A theory of gradual institutional change. *Cambridge University Press eBooks*. https://doi.org/10.1017/cbo9780511806414.003 (accessed on 9th September 2025).

31. Molden, D. (2013). *Water for Food Water for Life. Routledge eBooks*. https://doi.org/10.4324/9781849773799 (accessed on 9th September 2025).

32. Murdoch, Z. (2022). *5. Leadership of Organizations. Fagbokforlaget eBooks*. https://doi.org/10.55669/oa090305 (accessed on 9th September 2025).

33. N/A. (2015). Guidelines for good pharmacoepidemiology practice (GPP). *Pharmacoepidemiology and Drug Safety, 25*, 2–10. https://doi.org/10.1002/pds.3891 (accessed on 9th September 2025).

34. N/A. (2018). *Integrity for Good Governance in Latin America and the Caribbean*. OECD eBooks. https://doi.org/10.1787/9789264201866-en (accessed on 9th September 2025).

35. N/A. (2020). *Governance for Youth, Trust and Intergenerational Justice*. OECD Public Governance Reviews. https://doi.org/10.1787/c3e5cb8a-en (accessed on 9th September 2025).

36. N/A. (2021). *Theory and Practice of the European Convention on Human Rights. Nomos Verlagsgesellschaft mbH & Co.* KG eBooks. https://doi.org/10.5771/9783748923503 (accessed on 9th September 2025).

37. Nikolova, R. (2024). Conclusion of an agreement under the general and special administrative penal procedural order. *Law Journal of New Bulgarian University*. https://www.semanticscholar.org/paper/c7a0ab6d6cec1113a9f2dbd261ac55d7ad67a663 (accessed on 9th September 2025).

38. Nishchymna, S. (2025). The legal institution of justices of the peace: Feasibility and risks. *Economics. Finances. Law*. https://www.semanticscholar.org/paper/41a487de5058dd28971e508d63983c0dd373db8c (accessed on 9th September 2025).

39. Ostrikova, T. (2022). Legal origins and intersectoral regulation of AEO institution. *Lex Portus*. https://www.semanticscholar.org/paper/007a46cd288e7d27971e6d6bebd8200a83e95dbf (accessed on 9th September 2025).

40. Peters, B. G., Pierre, J., Sørensen, E., & Torfing, J. (2022). Bringing political science back into public administration research. *Governance, 35*, 962–982. https://doi.org/10.1111/gove.12705 (accessed on 9th September 2025).

41. Phelps, M. S. (2016). Mass probation: Toward a more robust theory of state variation in punishment. *Punishment & Society, 19*, 53–73. https://doi.org/10.1177/1462474516649174 (accessed on 9th September 2025).

42. Rabin, J. (2005). *Encyclopedia of Public Administration and Public Policy, First Update Supplement.* https://www.semanticscholar.org/paper/fa75c49c30472a681b353dbf7482d0498867452b (accessed on 9th September 2025).

43. Ruśkowski, E. (2018). Financial law enforcement acts in Poland. *Law Enforcement Review.* https://www.semanticscholar.org/paper/78b0574cc842d228070c159235057aa51c8e6346 (accessed on 9th September 2025).

44. Saputra, D., Maimun, & Susilo, E. (2025). Reevaluating leadership criteria in village governance: A comparative analysis of Law No. 3 of 2024 and Imam al-Mawardi's political thought. *Al-Risalah Jurnal Ilmu Syariah dan Hukum.* https://www.semanticscholar.org/paper/28816e7f9acd500fc44956f7cd827fbf560eff85 (accessed on 9th September 2025).

45. Scott, C., & Hardiman, N. (2025). *Ordering Things: The Irish State Administration Database.* https://core.ac.uk/download/pdf/6232260.pdf (accessed on 9th September 2025).

46. Secinaro, S., Calandra, D., Secinaro, A., Muthurangu, V., & Biancone, P. (2021). The role of artificial intelligence in healthcare: A structured literature review. *BMC Medical Informatics and Decision Making, 21.* https://doi.org/10.1186/s12911-021-01488-9 (accessed on 9th September 2025).

47. Serkov, P. P., & Solovey, Y. P. (2023). Administrative discretion: Questions and answers (Part 1). *Siberian Law Review.* https://www.semanticscholar.org/paper/c49174b1ad77f640179b75898de46d30a0c3bcc9 (accessed on 9th September 2025).

48. Subrata, R., Arifin, F., & Maarif, I. (2025). Hybrid dispute resolution in administrative law: Toward an integrated model for government conflict management. *Journal of Judicial Review.* https://www.semanticscholar.org/paper/5aa88d6cbd3dccc6314dc835784928fa89e3cb06 (accessed on 9th September 2025).

49. Syafa'i, I., & Megasari, I. D. (2025). Effectiveness of state administrative law: Perspectives comparative from Indonesia and Singapore in public service. *Journal of Scientific Research, Education, and Technology (JSRET).* https://www.semanticscholar.org/paper/462be775275230ffc8e1730de855f63d486797c6 (accessed on 9th September 2025).

50. Thelen, K. (2018). Regulating Uber: The politics of the platform economy in Europe and the United States. *Perspectives on Politics, 16*, 938–953. https://doi.org/10.1017/s1537592718001081 (accessed on 9th September 2025).

51. Tjoa, E., & Guan, C. (2020). A survey on explainable artificial intelligence (XAI): Toward medical XAI. *IEEE Transactions on Neural Networks and Learning Systems, 32*, 4793–4813. https://doi.org/10.1109/tnnls.2020.3027314 (accessed on 9th September 2025).

52. Ugolkov, E. O. (2024). Certain aspects of the introduction of mandatory administrative (pre-trial) tax conflict settlement. *Uzhhorod National University Herald. Series: Law.* https://www.semanticscholar.org/paper/d38c0f36cc2423befc76cf0773eb3dabdc7ad2b2 (accessed on 9th September 2025).

53. Welter, F. (2011). Contextualizing entrepreneurship—Conceptual challenges and ways forward. *Entrepreneurship Theory and Practice, 35*, 165–184. https://doi.org/10.1111/j.1540-

6520.2010.00427.x (accessed on 9th September 2025).

54. Widowati, A. R., & Kamil, A. I. (2025). Legal study of land redistribution policy as land reform object: State administrative law perspective. *Mendapo: Journal of Administrative Law*. https://www.semanticscholar.org/paper/2b1e212e44270128747d5bbc762464b47b6747ac (accessed on 9th September 2025).

55. Xu, C. (2011). The fundamental institutions of China's reforms and development. *Journal of Economic Literature, 49*, 1076–1151. https://doi.org/10.1257/jel.49.4.1076 (accessed on 9th September 2025).

56. Zhumataeva, M. (2024). Legal frameworks for the assessment of agricultural lands. *Eurasian Science Review: An International Peer-Reviewed Multidisciplinary Journal*. https://www.semanticscholar.org/paper/ff56add1c7b3de0d8d791ef1b4c27eb9af95108e (accessed on 9th September 2025).

57. Zhyvko, M., Dombrovska, A., & Kiblyk, D. (2025). The role of ombudsman institutions in administrative accountability: A comparative perspective. *Public Administration and Law Review*. https://www.semanticscholar.org/paper/6446c9ac103461cf3211740a61b7ebf34cb25c61 (accessed on 9th September 2025).

58. Žuber, B., & Majnik, T. (2025). Ensuring effective judicial protection in administrative disputes through the annulment power of the administrative judiciary. *Access to Justice in Eastern Europe*. https://www.semanticscholar.org/paper/4a354d650a9a6cc5e6a82288eec1e2a7d0c30c6d (accessed on 9th September 2025).

Chapter 12

LEGAL PROFESSIONS AND JUDICIAL SYSTEMS

Contents

INTRODUCTION

In contemporary society, the profession of law plays a very significant role in the realization of justice and maintenance of the rule of law. With its intricate hierarchy and branches, the profession of law provides a wide range of activities guaranteeing justice and accountability in judicial institutions. With the improvement of legal systems, arrangements of institutions supporting these professions also evolve, thereby emphasizing proper training, ethical standards, as well as public accessibility. The complexities of legal systems necessitate a clear appreciation of processes of judge selection and training, an appreciation that affects the efficiency of legal decisions. A properly trained judiciary, in association with robust legal practice environments, reflects the values that underlie justice, as the growing necessity for specialist legal interpretative services to support diverse groups within the system would imply, that is, the proposed Legal and Court Interpreting Service for Chicago's immigrant population (N/A, 2000). Central to the operation of legal professions are the formal organizations that make professional advancement among their members possible, notably through Bar Associations and boards of licensure. They both play a vital role in determining conditions for entry to the profession as well as providing support and facilities so that legal professionals can uphold ethical standards. The intricate nature of legal practice is attested to in its regulating framework, such as rigorous systems of licensure, regulation of the profession, and ensuring continuing education. Whereas legal settings continually change, the role of Bar Associations becomes increasingly important in tackling such change and making recommendations to both new and experienced attorneys. These systemic support frameworks not only enhance the credibility of the legal career but also the integrity of judicial systems in general, which are needed for the preservation of public confidence and trust in judicial proceedings (Buyanova et al., 1967). Efficient and precise court management becomes a key consideration in the pursuit of justice, encompassing many aspects of case administration, personnel, and the implementation of information technologies. With mounting caseloads and shifting needs, strategic management techniques become essential for optimizing resources and reducing delays. The incorporation of electronic systems in court operations has revolutionized traditional methods, promoting accessibility and efficiency in case processing. Furthermore, alternative conflict resolution methods such as mediation and arbitration are becoming increasingly popular solutions to conflicts, reducing the burden on court systems. Lastly, the coalescence of these components emphasizes the nature of public access to justice and the broader imperative for innovations in the legal practice and judicial system as a reaction to the demands of a diversified and evolving society. The convergence of these elements is vital in creating a fair legal system for all (N/A, 2000).

12.1. JUDICIAL APPOINT AND TRAINING

In questioning the intricacy of judicial appointment and training, one should understand that the selection procedures for judges differ. Such selection procedures may range from electoral systems to appointment procedures based on merit. One should understand that the efficiency of such systems has far-reaching implications for the judicial system. The intricate relationship between the traits of personality and decision types can affect the evaluation of criminal action by judges, as in recent studies. For example, the contribution of traits such as Machiavellianism indicates that judges, be they appointed or elected, bring their own psychological orientation to court, and their case verdict decisions are therefore affected (Caso et al., 2025). Finally, a close examination of these decision-making processes reveals not only the institutional steadiness of the judiciary but also the personal characteristics that can impact justice through their appointed or elected position. To top this off, the notion of a career judiciary also emphasizes the need for continuing education and training throughout a judge's career (Figure 12.1).

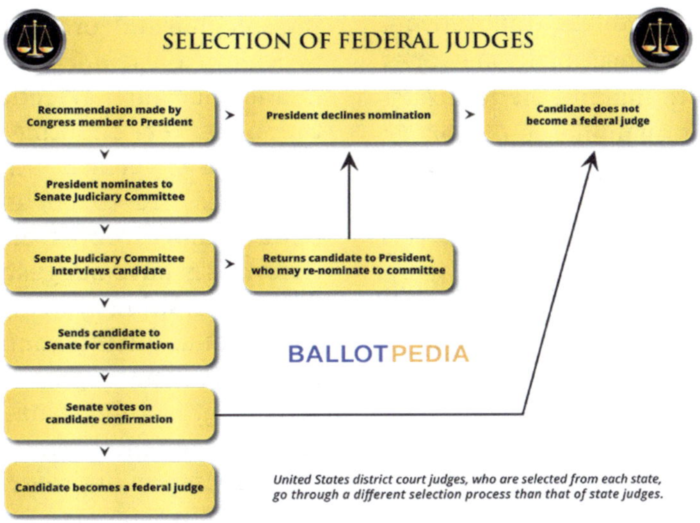

Figure 12.1. High court judge appointment process.

Source: https://ballotpedia.s3.amazonaws.com/images/a/a4/Selection_of_Federal_Judges_Flowchart.png.

A judge based on experienced individuals can substantially uphold fairness and impartiality tenets, required in facilitating public trust. Judicial training is imperative in the context of shifting legal processes and people's demands. Rigorous training programs can transfer essential skills to judges, thus reducing disparities in case evaluation and judgment. Introductory judicial education courses are but one of the ways in which potential judges are able to advance their qualifications and knowledge of the role of judges. These courses allow prospective judges to gain an understanding of both the ethical and practical aspects of their prospective duties, improving their competence and preparedness for the bench (Fisher, 2008). The focus on continuous professional education then aims to cultivate a judiciary that can keep up with the complexities of the law. Beyond that, specialized training is increasingly recognized as playing a central role in bridging holes in the selection process for judges. This approach responds not only to the demand for competent judges but also to the broader desire to cultivate a legal system representative of its populace. Surveys have repeatedly shown a disquieting lack of confidence in judicial fairness among minority communities, and this indicates the need for educational programs that make awareness and sensitivity to social issues greater. Judicial candidate programs can be used to build an awareness that extends beyond traditional legal studies. Through the encouragement of a responsive, representative judiciary that reflects the value of fairness, such education frameworks are critical in assisting in making the judiciary relevant to all citizens as an unbiased dispenser of justice. Creating an excellent foundation through training and appointment, therefore, is crucial to ensuring the promotion of the integrity of legal frameworks and enhancing public confidence in judicial processes.

12.1.1. Selection Procedures for Judges

The choice processes employed to select judges play a critical role in determining the integrity and effectiveness of judicial institutions. Various jurisdictions utilize varying choice processes, reflecting varying legal cultures and values. For instance, some utilize a merit appointment procedure that places high emphasis on qualifications and competencies over political loyalty. This is aimed at ensuring that judges possess both the legal wisdom and impartiality necessary for impartial justice. But it should be noted that such processes are often greeted with suspicion, with their opponents arguing that they can be far from really nonpartisan in outcome. Continuing debates regarding these processes themselves create a case for new reforms which create not only competence but also accountability in the selection process and eventually increase public confidence in the judiciary. In addition to merit choice, the political climate through which judges are elected also directly affects independence perceptions. Elections in most states are the typical methods by which judges are elected, another blurring of judicial and political domains. Elections have the potential to produce judicial bias anxiety and loss of impartiality through campaign pressures and financial influence. Besides, the efficacy of elections as a selection process also tends to reflect broader societal public perception about justice and governance. As such dynamics are considered, it is clear that there is an urgent need to balance democratic accountability and the safeguarding of judicial independence so as to achieve a just and equitable system of law. The nuances of such selection processes highlight the need for ongoing analysis and reform. Extensive experimentation in judicial selection processes has to be undertaken in order to build a more robust and transparent system. Reformists have suggested the application of a more diversified system, with elements such as educational qualifications for those aspiring to be judges. Opening up to such measures could provide greater legitimacy to judicial candidates and enhance the overall quality of the judiciary. Further, importing reforms that are responsive to consumer feedback and demand for legal services will underpin the construct of civil justice, enabling a more tailored experience for seekers of legal recourse. As set forth in recent dialogue regarding the civil justice system, there is significant potential for the cafeteria model, which would promote situational flexibility. As legal systems evolve, ongoing refinement of selection processes will contribute to the development of independent, accountable, and capable judges regardless of the selection method employed (Peacock et al., 2025; Bierman et al., 2002).

12.1.2. Career Paths Within the Judiciary

It takes expertise in various selection procedures and the trainings to be completed by those who are contesting to hold a judge's position. The contestants are normally from legal professions, with significant practice experience coming before the appointment. Judicial selection procedures play a key role in this career, and procedures vary across various jurisdictions. There are also elected judges and government-appointed judges, revealing the political and ideological biases that can dictate their tenure in office. The heavy focus on extensive training and education prepares judges to not only decide the law but also to understand the broader societal implications of their decisions, thereby dictating the judiciary's role in the legal system. This blend of professional education and choice processes underscores the paramount importance of ideology to decision-making in the judiciary implied by research on how such forces can determine outcomes in the courtroom (Allison et al., 2019). Moreover, the career trajectory for those in the judiciary can differ significantly according to gender, cultural background, and political environment, consistent with broader societal patterns of employment equity. In some locations, women judges have been able to ascend to mid-level leadership ranks, such as division chiefs, but are halted at obstacles that keep them out of the top brackets like court presidents. The phenomenon of dual-track promotion reveals how a prevailing masculine culture deters women from advancement in the judicial hierarchy.

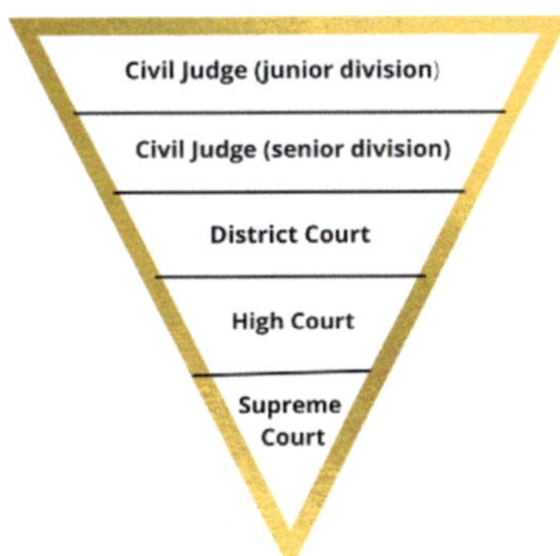

Figure 12.2. A career trajectory of civil judge in India.

Source: https://cdn.toprankers.net.in/images/career-trajectory-of-a-civil-judge-image-1--026025b409ebc.png.

Meanwhile, innovations like reverse attrition allow women to fill up vacancies left behind by male judges, thereby creating a dynamic in career mobility. This career dynamism not only attests to the complexities involved in gender in the judiciary but also shows the need for ongoing advocacy for equal opportunity in top judicial offices, as presented in the case of Chinese courts (Chunyan et al., 2017). One of the most important aspects of the judicial career debate is the role of institutional frameworks, including bar associations and licensing, which control the legal profession in a general sense. These kinds of associations have dual roles, not only fostering the professional development of judges but also establishing the code of ethics that they must follow throughout their careers. The balance between upholding the integrity of the judiciary and providing access to required training is critical in reinforcing public confidence in the judiciary. Additionally, with the introduction of computerized systems in court administration, candidates for judgeships need to learn new technologies that support case management and modernize operations. This adjustment underscores the necessity for ongoing learning and professional development so that judges can be competent and effective in their performances. It is essential to know these factors when learning about career development in the judiciary since they affect the career setting of judges (Allison et al., 2019) (Figure 12.2).

12.1.3. Importance of Judicial Education and Ongoing Training

In the complex landscape of the legal professions, the foundation for equitable and effective judicial systems is well-prepared legal practitioners and judges. The need for regular judicial education and training cannot be overemphasized, as it ensures that those who are in a position of authority remain up to speed with emerging laws, practice, and societal needs. Judicial education is not only designed to update knowledge but also impart critical thinking and ethical reasoning necessary for making sound judgments in court. The vibrant training environment equips judges to deal with contentious cases, where they possess necessary skills to efficiently interpret the law and apply it judiciously, which is the bedrock of upholding public confidence in the judiciary system. Also, continuous training promotes a professional and responsive culture within the judiciary. With the rapid pace of legal and technological innovation, continuous education allows judges to keep up with innovation such as electronic case management systems, which make procedures more efficient. Court staff who have undergone up-to-date training on technology such as this are in a position to complete their workload more effectively, leading to reduced delays and improved public access to justice. This flexibility is needed in an era where the expectations of society from the justice system are evolving. Through repeated training, judges can acquire methods to react to these demands as well as implement more effective case management practices that take into consideration the demands of modern society.

Finally, the provision for specialized training, particularly forensic psychology, underscores the need for multidisciplinary approaches within the judicial system. As attested to by the establishment of the Specialty Guidelines for Forensic Psychologists, effective judicial results necessitate an understanding of diverse specialties and methodologies (N/A, 2012). Judicial training must therefore span a broad range of topics, including matters relating to mental health as well as emerging subjects in law, in line with the complexities faced in modern courtrooms. Such general-based training not only enhances individual court performance but also to a more equitable and knowledgeable judicial system. Continuing education is therefore most critical in guaranteeing judicial experts are competent to perform their work effectively, establishing a system of justice which is just as well as reflective of contemporary societal ideals and moral practices.

12.2. LEGAL PROFESSION STRUCTURES

Legal profession organization is at the heart of making a court system as effective as it can be and determines everything from how cases are handled to public trust in legal proceedings. At the center of it all are bar associations, the governing bodies responsible for overseeing legal professionals and ensuring they are controlled. Bar associations establish professional standards of behavior, thus ensuring that members uphold professional standards. By promoting a sense of responsibility among lawyers, they contribute substantially to the maintenance of public trust in the legal profession. Apart from that, bar associations offer resources for continuing education and professional development, offering members access to information necessary to cope with a fast-evolving legal landscape. When the legal environment shifts, such connections have an important role to adapt training and accrediting processes to respond to new demands, thus adopting a robust legal framework that is suitable for today's societal needs, as noted in the analysis of law reforms in William (2009) (Figure 12.3).

Figure 12.3. Shows UK legal firm structures.

Source: https://a.storyblok.com/f/91079/1080x1080/7129240b69/blog-post-uk-law-firm-structure.png.

Another built-in component of legal profession structures is the accrediting and licensing process that works to regulate entry into the legal profession. Such step-wise path often includes rigorous exams as well as practice-based training provisions designed to assess lawyers preparedness for professional practice. Such processes provide a quality and competence sense within the legal profession by weeding out candidates who manifest inadequate knowledge or ethical ideals. Additionally, by undergoing the constant processes of accreditation, legal professionals are encouraged to continuously improve their skills and adapt to developments in law and jurisprudence. The professional enhancement is directly connected to the quality of the legal services provided to the public as well as the functioning of the judiciary. Therefore, the regulations imposed by licensing authorities are not bureaucratic mere formalities but integral parts in guaranteeing that the profession conforms to the changing expectations of society and thus maintains a just judicial system as noted in McCrudden (2008).

The structure on professional discipline is also fundamental to the legitimacy of the legal profession. Protocols for addressing misconduct, such as codes of conduct and formal complaint procedures, are minimum safeguards against unethical behavior. Where lawyers are in breach of professional standards, disciplinary bodies have the duty to investigate complaints and issue appropriate sanctions. This system acts not only to sanction aberrant practitioners, but also to deter others from following their example, encouraging compliance with ethical standards. In a world where public perception regarding justice matters so much, these disciplinary mechanisms increase the legal professions integrity. They ensure clients that their attorneys are being held accountable for their behavior, thereby fostering confidence in the court system. Public trust and the discipline of the profession are vital to ensuring that the rule of law is maintained and that the practices of legal professions are playing a beneficial role in an efficient working judicial system, as argued in the broader context of legal systems in William (2009).

12.2.1. Contribution of the Bar Associations Towards the Legal Profession

The extent of bar associations far exceeds mere membership; they are a linchpin of solidarity and control within the legal profession. As important intermediaries, bar associations enable legal practitioners to collaborate, ensuring their voices are heard in public policy and legislative forums. These organizations provide essential tools for legal training, instruction, and notification of evolving legal standards, all of which are required for practitioners wishing to be proficient in a continuously evolving world. Further, bar associations uphold ethical principles and professional norms, promoting the integrity of the law. Where access to justice is of great concern, such organizations call for initiatives like pro bono practice, so that the ethical mandate of the legal community to represent disenfranchised groups and respond to the broader objective of equitable legal representation is fulfilled, as in Nafzger (2019).

In other jurisdictions, bar associations are also at the core of the regulation and accrediting of legal professionals. By establishing standards and criteria for bar admission, they aim to ensure that only qualified practitioners are permitted to practice law. This gatekeeping function not only protects the public from unqualified practitioners but also builds a culture of accountability in the profession. By reviewing and accrediting legal education courses, bar associations have a direct influence on the quality of training lawyers-in-the-making receive and, in doing so, directly impact the effectiveness and credibility of the judicial system. Also, in the event of conflicts over the jurisdiction of the bar and its ethical standards, these types of organizations are inclined to be involved in constructive debate over their role and responsibility, according to the progressive development of legal practice and societal expectations placed upon it, as revealed by ongoing controversy over pro bono representation reported in Banakar et al. (2018). The presence of bar associations is particularly significant in jurisdictions where the independence of the legal profession is threatened. An example is in jurisdictions where government authorities attempt to exercise control over legal practitioners, for example, under the clerical state in Iran, bar associations strategically uphold their independence to maintain professional integrity. They seek to bring about legal reform and consolidate the profession against incursions from administrative powers, thereby establishing a balance within the judiciary. This struggle for independence is not an isolated local development; it reflects greater conflict between contending legal cultures, as when the local traditions and ideals of justice pursuant to international standards are in conflict. Consequently, the resilience of bar associations to withstand forces of government regulation is a testament to their significant role as champions of civil liberties and defenders of an impartial justice system, further enriching the context of legal professions and courts of justice, as argued by Banakar et al. (2018).

12.2.2. Licensing and Accreditation Processes for Lawyers

Within the legal occupations, the establishment of robust licensing and accreditation frameworks is key to guaranteeing the integrity and effectiveness of justice systems. These frameworks are meant to offer assurances that those admitted into the legal profession possess the knowledge, skills, and ethical standards necessary for effective practice. It is generally regulated by bar associations or licensing boards, and this organization includes stringent education requirements, examinations, and background checks in order to ascertain the competency of would-be lawyers. By mandating a standard path to licensure, the legal profession not only protects the public but also promotes confidence in legal institutions. Having taken such far-reaching steps is necessary, particularly in view of recent technological advancements that have introduced additional complexities to the practice of law and client relationships, emphasizing the need for a properly regulated legal system to progress well in overcoming prospective challenges. The accreditation and licensing procedures also play an important role in establishing the professional character and conduct of attorneys. These facilities normally incorporate provisions for continuing legal education to ensure lawyers remain current on emerging laws, technology, and ethical requirements. Furthermore, the inclusion of professional accountability measures, such as disciplinary action for unethical behavior, forms the foundation for ensuring the promise of ethical practice within the profession. Licensing authorities can punish lawyers from fines to disbarment, thereby ensuring public confidence in the self-regulatory ability of the legal system. This regulatory oversight becomes increasingly relevant as the legal landscape adapts to the development of new technologies and societal attitudes, rendering it ever more important to be proactive in guaranteeing justice and equitable access to legal representation, especially across jurisdictions and for underrepresented groups. The result of ineffective licensing and accreditation procedures is too high a cost, since it diminishes public trust and expands malpractice across the profession. Unless strictly regulated, incompetent and unethical legal professionals pose increased threats, which harm clients and the entire judicial system. More so, as technology remains to revolutionize the legal profession, there is a need to incorporate AI and other digital tools into the processes in order to enhance efficiency and transparency. Having algorithmic governance frameworks in place can provide data-driven information regarding the level of performance and ethics of lawyers, which promotes a more comprehensive evaluation system. The pressing need for effective controls arises from a broader societal interest in the implications of uncontrolled behavior to reinforce the demand for continuous advancement and adaptability in licensing and accreditation systems for providing the inherent basis of justice that is equitable and equal access (Truby, 2020; N/A, 2019) (Figure 12.4).

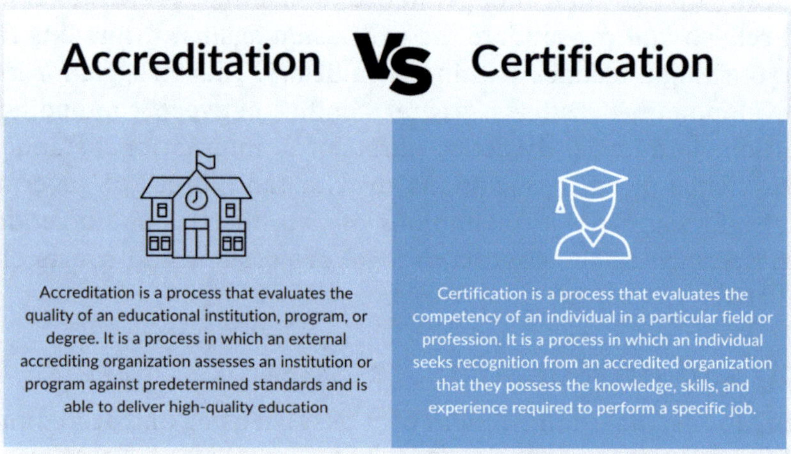

Figure 12.4. Accreditation versus certification.

Source: https://www.beaconlive.com/hubfs/Images%20for%20Blogs,%20Social,%20Content/Infographics/accreditation-vs-certification-understanding-the-difference.png.

12.2.3. Mechanisms of Professional Discipline and Accountability

The intricate matrix of professional responsibility and discipline in the legal profession plays a key role in maintaining the validity and credibility of judicial systems. The institutions established by bar associations and regulatory agencies not only function to uphold standards, but also to express the dynamic face of legal practice. With lawyers handling more sophisticated cases in their jurisdictions, models of professionalism get hybridized. These models merge established ethical principles with managerial influence that is necessitated, emphasizing that modern legal work demands a mixture of autonomy and ordered regulation. This blending is not a trend but rather enhances the accountability systems in practice, as attested to by extant practices that combine managerial doctrines with traditional professionalism. It is therefore important to have an understanding of the interplay between these dynamics in relation to how professional discipline adjusts to the changing social environment, while maintaining the rule of law and public trust in judicial processes (Noordegraaf, 2015).

Professional discipline mechanisms are central to not only resolving misconduct, but also in a culture of responsibility among legal professionals. At the heart of this paradigm are the codes of practice that define what is ethically acceptable in practice and behavior within the profession. The codes are backed up by clearly defined complaint procedures that allow clients and peers to complain about unethical behavior. The procedural controls guarantee fair and open investigations, and safeguarding public trust remains the overriding priority. Furthermore, the range of sanctions and remedies offered has the function of mirroring the profession's concern with upholding wrongdoing and also providing a vehicle for rehabilitation. These multi-faceted vehicles work not only to sanction bad practice but also to train and redirect practitioners back towards compliance in shifting legal environments, ensuring the collective quality and integrity of legal services provided (Tummers et al., 2015). In the face of rising pressures on front-line workers in the law process, from massive workloads to stringent demands for effectiveness, coping mechanisms are imperative. Lawyers often find themselves thwarted by rigid adherence to rules at the expense of the subtlety of their cases. This is a situation that calls for adaptive practice whereby judges and lawyers can stretch or reinterpret rules in order to deliver enhanced services to their clients, an articulation of the aspiration for effective justice. These adjustments, however, have to be done in caution so as not to reduce standards of ethics. A thoughtful analysis of how workload intersects with professionalism and discretion spells out the call for complementary frameworks that recognize the unique challenges of legal professionals. These institutions must allow for stressful environments while also enhancing discipline mechanisms to ensure that accountability is upheld and therefore safeguard the profession as well as the public (Tummers et al., 2015).

12.3. COURT ADMINISTRATION

Court administrative effectiveness is automatically attached to the case management principles, which concentrate on systematic handling of judicial cases from initiation to conclusion. Effective case management practices are required in curbing delay, which can undermine public trust in the judiciary. With the use of structured procedures, courts can handle resources better and assign cases on the basis of their complexity and urgency for quicker disposal. In looking at the international judicial landscape, it is apparent that the jurisdictions employing efficient case management systems realize increased adjudication speeds and reductions in backlogs. This is particularly pertinent, since delay can lead to significant stress for the parties and impact perceptions of the justice system's fairness. Balancing thoroughness with the need for efficiency is something that courts must constantly do, highlighting the value of innovative practices in case management to uphold the integrity of legal decisions (Ismaili et al., 2024).

Figure 12.5. Court administration.

Source: https://www.jud12.flcourts.org/portals/0/Images/Pages/generic/court-admin-graphic.png?ver=DyPMggmkpClP1wSKDGmU_g%3D%3D.

Court staffing is also a significant aspect of effective court administration, since the human resources of the judicial system determine whether its functioning will be catastrophic or successful. Courts require an array of staff including judges, clerks, administrators, and support staff, all of whom are responsible for making significant contributions towards the efficient operation. Staffed courts can ensure that cases are dealt with effectively and within the prescribed timelines, which is significant in protecting the rights of defendants and maintaining integrity within the judiciary. Appointment, education, and continuous professional development of court staff must be the priority to address evolving legal environments as well as technology change. By constant improvement in training, courts can enhance the proficiency of their staff, and therefore, facilitate more effective administration of justice, thus augmenting further public trust in legal processes (Singh et al., 2024). Technology has come to play a revolutionary role in the administration of courts, making operations much more efficient and accessible. Technology has streamlined many of the processes, from filing cases through scheduling hearings, making it easier to maintain an organized methodology for handling caseload. The application of electronic records and web portals has made it easier for legal professionals as well as the public to access the justice system with reduced ease, reducing the burden of paper-based documentation and improving communication. Furthermore, technology allows data collection and analysis, allowing courts to scrutinize their own operations and identify areas that need to be improved. The push for court digitalization is part of a broader commitment to modernization, enabling courts to respond dynamically to immediate needs while keeping administration of justice open, fair, and timely (Ismaili et al., 2024) (Figure 12.5).

12.3.1. Effective Case Management Strategies

Among the best practices is the implementation of automated file management systems, which significantly mechanize case-related document filing. By utilizing the technology, legal experts are able to access, transfer, and modify necessary information freely, hence reducing the incidence of manual documentation errors. The automation of a case scheduling system also simplifies court operations even further by minimizing double-booking to virtually none and ensuring appropriate time slots for the holding of cases. This not only increases clients' access to justice but also allows legal professionals to have greater control of their cases more proactively, which signals a move toward more systemic and systematic practice in the legal system as evident in the innovations presented in legal practice and education (Rindhiyaa et al., 2025). One of the most important elements of effective case management is the innovative communication networks developed for collaboration between legal professionals, clients, and judiciary officials. The use of electronic platforms facilitates more information interchange while encouraging transparency in all stages of the legal process. Such a move towards electronic technologies showcases a sector determined to remain responsive to evolving needs in society, especially in an increasingly interconnected world. In addition, such sites may also allow legal advocates to continuously interact with their clients and thus promote a model of open communication that enhances the attorney-client relationship. With these advancements, the judicial system not only enriches its process of operation but also gets closer to aspirations of modern standards of accessibility and accountability within the judicial system, even further establishing the growing importance of these strategies in enhancing the quality of justice (Gabani, 2025) (Figure 12.6).

Moreover, the overlap of artificial intelligence and data analytics presents a new horizon for handling cases in the law. These technologies not only provide insights into trends affecting case outcomes but also assist with anticipating potential challenges throughout legal processes. With the use of AI-based tools, legal professionals can study past cases and make suitable modifications based on their strategies in order to improve chances of successful verdicts. These technologies do need stringent regulatory frameworks for assisting in the protection of sensitive data and ensuring compliance with ethical principles. With the legal profession constantly evolving, the wise use of such advanced techniques goes to speak of the need to adopt a holistic approach that encompasses both the technological capabilities and good governance to enhance the efficiency of judicial practices (Rindhiyaa et al., 2025; Gabani, 2025).

Figure 12.6. In contemporary legal systems, the integration of effective case management strategies is critical for enhancing the efficiency of judicial proceedings.

Source: https://www.legalprod.com/wp-content/uploads/2024/02/Automatisation-des-processus-judiciaires.png.

12.3.2. Court System Staffing Needs and Court System Roles

In the complex environment of the legal process, quality staffing is crucial to the continuance of efficient legal proceedings and the administration of justice. The careers within the court system are not exclusive to judges and attorneys; there are a number of ancillary staff personnel, including clerks, bailiffs, and administrative assistants, all serving distinct yet connected purposes. Court clerks, for instance, manage case files, set up hearings, and maintain records of the court, all these being a prerequisite for the smooth running of legal processes. Furthermore, bailiffs secure the courtroom and assist in the execution of court orders. The complementary role of these various positions illustrates how a properly staffed court system is a component of judicial process that guarantees public trust in judicial bodies. Education and training are to blame for setting staff needs within the court system. Various selection processes ensure that individuals are adequately prepared to conduct their duties, particularly in the judiciary, where appointments have stringent qualification and ethical standards. Judges' education is not only required for judges but also for other court staff to cope with the sophistication of legal practice. Also, bar associations have a role in guaranteeing standards since they are responsible for controlling the process of licensing and accreditation, thereby establishing a foundation of professionalism that workers must adhere to. Such systematic staffing and training accompany the general goal of enhancing the integrity and ability of the judicial process, ultimately resulting in fair legal outcomes and citizen involvement in justice. As computerized systems are being used with greater frequency to manage cases and administrative tasks within courts, staffing needs track alongside these technological developments. Technological equipment necessitates workers to possess some level of technological skill, and this necessitates continuing professional training within the court system. This transformation does not only serve the efficient handling of cases but also handles public access matters through procedural simplification. Furthermore, as elaborated in the past researches, the incorporation of technology within the court system emphasizes the need to have staff that can respond and adjust to the evolving nature of legal administration. Therefore, training existing staff with funds as well as introducing technology-oriented individuals will be the solution to preventing future problems for staffing in courts, eventually strengthening the entire judicial system and making justice remain accessible to all members of society (Buber et al., 2009; Dong et al., 2003).

12.3.3. Implementation of Digital Systems in Court Operations

The development of court procedures through the application of computer systems is a significant shift in the legal professions' arena. In shifting from the traditional way to a greater amount of reliance on technology, enhanced case management and flow of communication are achieved. Computer systems enable efficient processes, which dispose of delays caused by paperwork and manual entry. Automated systems can produce case calendars, manage filings, and track court appearances, ultimately releasing court staff from burdens and expediting case resolution. This movement toward electronic filing and management systems is a component of broader judicial modernization efforts that keep legal systems viable and accessible to the public. Besides, the increased efficiency that accompanies these systems has a direct impact on the public's perception of how effective the justice systems are, which requires constant adjustment and evaluation of technologys place in legal proceedings. The implementation of computerized systems in court work has challenges as well as possibilities for court administrators and legal professionals. Providing equal access to technology to all parties involved in the judicial process is one of the greatest challenges. Courts must react to disparity in technological proficiency and access, particularly among vulnerable populations that might be left out of utilization of digital spaces. On the flip side, there is potential within the capability for bigger data aggregation and analysis to produce evidence-based decision-making and more effective resource utilization. Also, the adoption of online tools is going to transform the nature of representation being provided, with attorneys needing to adapt to new means of doing practice in an environment where everything is computerized. This can lead to a more consolidated manner of handling cases, as lawyers' teams make use of more collaborative online platforms to organize their activities harmoniously. Furthermore, the ethical and governing implications of integrating digital systems into court processes are top areas of concern. The implications of the European Commission's draft AI Act highlight the importance of a robust legal framework for overseeing the use of sophisticated digital technologies in the judicial system (Veale et al., 2021). These types of measures of regulation aim to address risks associated with algorithmic bias and maintain the integrity of the judicial process. Legal professionals must balance the risks with the traditional norms of conduct and transparency. The interface between law and technology thus calls not only for greater focus towards compliance and ethical concerns but also towards seeing that an inclusive and effective digital judicial system is developed. With collective effort from legal professionals, technology developers, and regulators, the potential for digital systems to enable court operations can be realized in a manner that enhances the values of justice and equity (N/A, 2019).

12.4. ALTERNATIVE DISPUTE RESOLUTION

In contemporary legal settings, the practice of resolving conflicts outside traditional courts has gained immense popularity. This owes primarily to increasing complexity and cost of litigation that deters parties from resorting to formal legal remedy. Alternative Dispute Resolution (ADR) encompasses several methods, most especially mediation and arbitration, which offer flexible and efficacious processes for conflict resolution. The inherent value in ADR is not just that it can accelerate the resolving process, but that it can assist in saving relationships between parties. Lawyers, once held up as advocates in combative settings, are now finding their roles change to facilitators and mediators, thus to align with a broader notion of legal practice based on peacemaking and cooperation. These developments highlight the need for revised ethical codes that acknowledge such new roles within the legal profession (Menkel-Meadow et al., 2002). While the controversy surrounding ADR rages on, it is evident that the institutional features of legal systems must adapt accordingly. The growing popularity of ADR channels calls for lawyers to be equipped with the proper skills and knowledge in order to navigate these alternative avenues effectively. This trend forces the jurisdictions to consider procedural reforms that will enhance the availability and effectiveness of civil justice. Where legal services are underutilized or not universally understood, the introduction of innovations such as cost capping and risk-sharing agreements can take great strides towards empowering clients and maximizing information dissemination about their options (Peacock et al., 2025). Through building a cafeteria-style system of civil justice that enables varying levels of dispute resolution, practitioners are able to represent competing client interests while promoting fairness and efficiency in the resolution. Moreover, the use of ADR within legal systems also necessitates reviewing the roles undertaken by legal professionals for building an equitable system of justice. The traditional perception of lawyers as only adversarial representatives does not encompass their role as constructive legal problem solvers. Organizations increasingly recognize the ethical significance of the lawyer's role in mediation and facilitative processes because these methods may not always be perfectly reconcilable with classical adversarial training. While the legal profession is grappling with this paradigm shift, the development of balanced training programs designed for ADR skills and best practices is of primordial importance. The search for a balanced theory of justice that embraces cooperation as well as competition is essential in developing a legal system that will benefit all parties equally (Menkel-Meadow et al., 2002).

12.4.1. Overview of Mediation Practices and Their Benefits

Within contemporary legal systems, the application of mediation techniques has emerged as a vital evolution in alternative dispute resolution (ADR). Mediation offers adversaries to conflict a formal but flexible method for resolving disagreements and translating potentially adversarial interactions into cooperative problem-solving forums. By facilitating an impartial third party to steer the process, mediation fosters dialogue and negotiation, as well as gravitates toward resolutions that are acceptable to all. This procedure not only instills a sense of empowerment between the participants but also gives rise to a climate of understanding and accommodation, thus reducing the likelihood of escalation to more adversarial legal battles. In increasing court caseloads, mediation is posed as a welcome ally in the effective management of conflicts with respect to the rights and interests of individuals to move about the world of law (Devi, 2025) (Figure 12.7).

Figure 12.7. The benefits of mediation practices extend beyond mere conflict resolution; they encapsulate efficiency and cost-effectiveness that are integral to modern judicial systems.

Source: https://viamediationcentre.org/images/categoryimages/1590360198med.png.

Mediation is usually quicker than regular court procedures, thus relieving the court docket burden and lessening judicial resource strain. Since parties can possibly reach a settlement within hours, not extend their cases for weeks or months as they would under litigation, time saved translates into less legal cost and attendant expenses. Additionally, mediation promotes the confidentiality that enables parties to present information freely without the threat of public dissemination, a luxury provided sparingly in court trials. This dimension of privacy not only inspires confidence in the mediation process but also protects the reputational interests of the participating parties. Such advantages make mediation a desirable option in intricate legal systems (Dawson et al., 2021). Furthermore, mediation processes contribute significantly to the provision of access to justice, which remains a concern of great importance in legal systems worldwide. Traditional litigation might be costly and inaccessible to the majority, thereby making access to justice a concern for marginalized communities. This is unlike mediation, which provides a less expensive and less intimidating alternative and, therefore, empowers individuals to engage directly in resolving their disputes. As mediations in the community become more prevalent, they bridge the gap in legal services and make certain that appropriate support is in place for individuals who may not otherwise have comprehensive legal representation. As technology is incorporated into mediation hearings, particularly in nations like India, access continues to rise with remote negotiations and online dispute resolution. By making conflict resolution mechanisms accessible to everyone, mediation practices not only increase judicial effectiveness but also adhere to the tenets of fairness and social justice and thereby support the integrity of legal systems (Devi, 2025).

12.4.2. Understanding Arbitration Procedures and Rules

In conflict resolution, arbitration serves as a major instrument through which parties may resolve conflicts outside the traditional court system. It is governed by established rules and procedures intended to ensure that the process will be fair and effective. Rules of arbitration typically stipulate the format in which disputes are to be settled, including basic things like appointment of arbitrators, hearing proceedings, and timelines for submission and determination. Further, rules of this nature often draw on settled legal canons and norms that lend credibility and enforceability to the arbitration process. The legitimacy of arbitration heavily depends on the observance of such procedural rules, which are there to safeguard the rights and obligations of each party. Knowledge about arbitration procedure is crucial not only for legal practitioners but also for parties to the arbitration process. Such procedures comprise preliminary processes like choosing between institutional and ad hoc arbitration, both with their respective distinctive set of rules and structures. Institutional arbitration, for instance, is regulated by entities that provide pre-established rules, which tend to lead to a more formalized process of resolution. Ad hoc arbitration, on the other hand, is less rigid, allowing parties to modify the rules according to their specific needs. Through such an understanding, legal practitioners are able to properly guide clients on the most suitable arbitration strategy and what the implications of such choices would be in the broader field of legal practitioners and judicial systems, mainly when it comes to professional integrity reflected in the roles which they play (Shaffer et al., 2012).

Moreover, legal practitioners' contribution to arbitration is not limited to representation; they even shape the environment of arbitration. In their role as lobbyists, lawyers interpret and enforce the relevant arbitration rules of practice, as well as engaging in the formulation of such guidelines by joining professional associations and lobbying. Drawing on their experience along with procedural know-how, these attorneys play a key role in institutionalizing best practices in arbitration. By advocating transparency and justice, lawyers are tasked with making society a place where arbitration can serve as an acceptable and proper way to settle disputes. This multifaceted role demonstrates how lawyers enable the inscription of rules of arbitration in broader institutional rhythms, grasping the tempo of professional field and institutional change (Suddaby et al., 2011).

12.4.3. Role of Ombudsman Institutions in Dispute Resolution

In contemporary court systems, the presence of ombudsman institutions is a new way of effective dispute resolution. These institutions are intermediaries that facilitate the resolution of grievances lodged by individuals against public agencies or private firms. Their role is naturally proactive, aimed at addressing grievances prior to their development into formal legal disputes. Informal procedures and the hosting of discussions enable ombudsmen to reduce the court workload so that the courts can deal with significant legal matters. It is a process that, not only offers swift results but also provides openness and accountability in public service institutions (Figure 12.8).

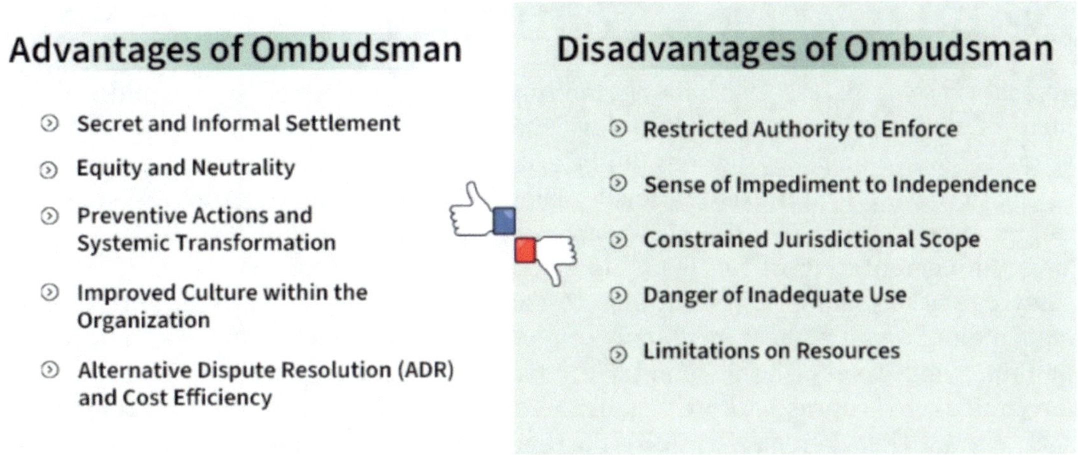

Figure 12.8. Advantages and disadvantages of ombudsman in dispute resolution.

Source: https://media.geeksforgeeks.org/wp-content/uploads/20240124172552/Advantages-and-Disadvantages-of-Ombudsman-copy.webp.

As countries begin to adopt these roles, examples of various implementations can be learned across the globe, just like creative steps taken by OECD countries in boosting public health adherence, implementing new mechanisms to ease congestion of the judicial system (Gostin et al., 2010). In addition, greater dependence on ombudsman institutions is an indication of trends towards alternative dispute resolution (ADR) systems that seek to construct more affordable and accessible justice mechanisms. The arrival of ADR has prompted many industries, including banking and health, to look at the level at which mediation and other non-judicial options can limit conflict. For instance, in the banking sector in Romania, mediation has been proposed to address increasing consumer complaints so that the matter is resolved quickly and to a higher degree of satisfaction (Bălan et al., 2010). With the incorporation of such practices, ombudsmen become communication facilitators and also educators about the rights of individuals so that public awareness and confidence in the justice process is enhanced. This growing appreciation is also a reflection of worldwide trends in professionalization of legal professions and encouragement of enlightened resolution of disputes. The success of ombudsman institutions as a means for conflict resolution can be quantified also in terms of being able to stimulate systemic change within the organization they serve. Often, the insights gained from one complaint lead to broader institutional reforms, improving processes and policies that may not have been considered previously. Through the examination of patterns of grievances, ombudsmen can recommend rectification of them to avoid future disputes and enhance overall quality of services. The step is aligned with the evolving expectations of legal institutions to not just resolve disputes but anticipate and prevent them as well. Consequently, with the process of modernization of judiciary systems, the ombudsman institutions become more and more pivotal in promoting a responsive and stronger legal system that is protective of citizens' rights and making the process of dispute resolution simpler (Bălan et al., 2010).

12.5. PUBLIC ACCESS TO JUSTICE

Access to justice remains a core challenge among the legal community and judicial institutions, particularly in the manner they provide legal aid services. Increasing costs and complexity of the legal processes remain key impediments to low-income and vulnerable populations in their pursuit of justice. Despite the existing legal structure endeavoring to promote equality, there are still systemic barriers and, therefore, it becomes necessary to value how legal aid can alleviate such issues. Implementation of full legal aid schemes is a must, not just to empower individuals so that they can assert their rights but also to render the judiciary system more credible for the masses. As highlighted by the recent concern with civil justice in England and Wales, reform aimed at improving access should similarly consider procedure innovations that may improve consumer choice over representation legally, hence advancing the perception that justice should be accessible to all (Peacock et al., 2025). Furthermore, the cost barrier and delay in the judicial system significantly erode the accessibility of justice to the public. Case delays, along with increasing expenditures, can breach public trust and discourage individuals from pursuing rightful claims. These inefficiencies are overcome by a critical examination of case management policies and the implementation of technology-based solutions that streamline the procedures of the court. Timely justice is more than just an administrative concern; it impacts the lives of those who pursue justice on a day-to-day level. Such an innovation as risk-sharing contracts among clients and their representative legal practitioners has the potential to usher in a new, consumer-friendly approach to access to the legal system, thereby relieving the economic burden for many who require legal services (Peacock et al., 2025). At the same time, community legal clinics are an essential mechanism in bridging the gap for individuals with difficulties in accessing the fundamental legal services. Not only do these clinics provide needed educational materials and assistance but also foster a feeling of community participation and empowerment. With emphasis placed on representation of minority groups, such programs can be life-changing for those undergoing the legal system without adequate provision. Moreover, the proposed establishment of services such as the Legal and Court Interpreting Service instills the importance of inclusivity within judicial systems, namely that of immigrant communities. By offering language support and ensuring equitable representation, such services can enhance public access to justice as a whole, enabling a more representative and equitable legal environment for all.

12.5.1. Availability and Relevance of Legal Aid Services

Access to justice remains a fundamental issue in the majority of legal systems, with legal aid services being at the heart of filling this gap. Legal aid plays a significant role in ensuring that individuals who are experiencing legal problems, particularly economically vulnerable individuals, can comprehend and access the courts. Without legal aid services, vulnerable members of society will most likely fail to assert their rights and, by extension, play a role in perpetuating social inequalities. Legal aid not only provides access to representation but also fosters public trust in the law as a fair institution by promoting fairness. As was emphasized during the United Kingdom's civil justice debate, there is a developing understanding that improving the supply and demand for legal services is at the heart of a fair society. This recognizes the demand for a facilitative legal system that caters to different needs of its citizens, and that is where the role of legal aid services is called for Peacock et al. (2025). Legal aid services are not only important at the case level, but they leave an imprint on the broader legal system and the democratic values. A robust and independent legal profession has been described as the backbone of a democratic state, which safeguards the rights of individuals against potential misuse of power. The criticism has been made that the legal profession at times defends self-interest at the expense of the general good, potentially undermining its status as a defender of justice, particularly for the poor (Kruuse et al., 2018). Legal aid services upend this dynamic by offering legal representation to all persons irrespective of their socio-economic standing. This ethos not only maintains the rule of law but also works to unsettle the status quo, triggering advocacy for systematic change that facilitates equal access to justice for all. Secondly, persistent delivery of legal aid services is imperative in ensuring that barriers to justice, such as unaffordability and long delays to legal procedures, are addressed. In the majority of jurisdictions, such barriers seek to dissuade prospective litigants from seeking legal redress, particularly those of low-income backgrounds. With the facilitation of affordable legal services, legal aid institutions can help overcome such barriers and empower individuals to seek their legal rights. Furthermore, community legal clinics and other initiatives have become important nodes of legal resource and education that foster a culture of legal consciousness and self-advocacy among poor communities. As attested to by civil justice system reform attempts, there is an urgent need for more innovative and responsive legal aid mechanisms to the changing needs of the public, which in turn help in support of a more equitable and inclusive judicial system (Peacock et al., 2025).

12.5.2. Barriers to Access: Cost and Delay Issues

Access to the law remains severely hampered by persistent cost and delay issues, which work against those seeking justice. Many would-be litigants are deterred from pursuing a lawsuit due to expensive lawyer fees and the expense of court proceedings in total. This intimidating financial barrier disproportionately harms marginalized populations who might lack the means to engage with the judicial system. Furthermore, the organization of legal professions as involuted processes of licensing and accrediting only serves to perpetuate such economic obstacles, since individuals may find that they need to run through a lengthy and costly process just to secure access to the legal counsel that they require. Such mechanisms also have a chilling effect whereby the prospect of incurring substantial costs will discourage many from seeking their legal rights altogether, thereby perpetuating inequalities within the judicial system. Aside from the hurdle of money, judicial delays worsen the plight of people who opt to pursue legal action. Uncertainly long court timelines, sometimes fueled by ineffective case management procedures, can turn ostensibly simple legal issues into long-drawn-out battles. If the parties get to wait for too long for resolutions, the effects can be far-reaching, especially in emergent situations in which prompt legal intervention is critical. These delays even deter others from making claims since the uncertainty of the decision as well as the time frame may lead to frustration and disillusionment. Also, the cost of prolonged litigation—such as additional attorney fees and lost income due to work absence—can discourage even persons of limited means from accessing the legal system, for which, therefore, reforming court administration and case management effectiveness is imperative. Overcoming cost and delay barriers is critical to expanding public access to justice, a bedrock tenet of democratic government. Legal aid plans and community legal clinics are significant elements in overcoming some of these access barriers by providing essential services and support to disadvantaged groups. But effectiveness is most typically reliant upon secure funding and political will to pursue equal access to legal representation. Besides, there should be an examination of current laws and procedural systems to identify areas where there can be improvement, especially in harmonizing procedures to avoid delays in cases. As there has been an advancement in legal systems, policymakers need to be concerned with innovative solutions in eliminating cost and delay burdens in order to foster a judicial climate that maintains fairness and justice for all members of society as emphasized by the recent emphasis on the worth of expeditious judicial processes and equal access to legal protection (Veale et al., 2021; N/A, 2019).

12.5.3. Function of Community Legal Clinics in Promoting Justice

The role of community legal clinics in advancing justice is multifaceted and irreplaceable within the context of the legal profession and judicial systems. They are essential tools for poor communities, bridging the gap between the population and the law. They do not only offer legal assistance but also important education on legal rights and responsibilities so that vulnerable communities can interact effectively with legal processes. This empowerment broadens a person's familiarity with the justice system, which is especially useful in jurisdictions where professional legal service is not easily accessible (Figure 12.9).

Figure 12.9. Community legal clinics mitigate the financial barriers that often hinder access to justice, making legal support more inclusive and equitable for all, regardless of socio-economic status.

Source: https://images.squarespace-cdn.com/content/v1/61c2f36a329cfe4aa53a49d7/0937bed5-ba70-4e4c-a058-f72facd24496/5E5A1973.JPG.

Community legal clinics tend to address issues of a systemic nature, dealing with issues of broad social justice in society. Their casework tends to reveal patterns of injustice, like discrimination and inequality in treatment by law, and calls for policy change on this basis. This dual approach not only works to help people in their specific legal problems but also fights for a fairer legal system by making legal reform proposals to improve the injustices observed in the system. Being community-based organizations, they can easily respond promptly to emerging problems, modifying their services to address new concerns in the community. Such responsiveness is imperative in settings where legal needs are created by specific social crises, thereby making justice not a static goal but a dynamic process that adapts to changing society's needs. The worth of community legal clinics also resides in their role in developing future legal professionals who continue to be devoted to public service. Some clinics engage law students actively in the delivery of hands-on clinical education, exposing them to worthwhile exposure and serving the legal needs of the community in the process. This experiential learning model instills social responsibility in law students and prepares them for future advocacy roles in justice. Through this encounter, clinics not only increase proximate access to legal services but also promote long-term reform in the legal community through an emphasis upon ethical practice and community engagement. Toward this end, such clinics become themselves living examples of the interdependent dynamic between legal education, community service, and the administration of justice, and they create a more active and engaged legal community.

12.6. PROFESSIONAL CONDUCT AND DISCIPLINE

To navigate legal careers involves strong adherence to established conventions and principles that govern professional conduct and discipline. They are essential directives governing lawyers' behaviors, which see them maintain ethical standards while arguing for clients and developing the law. The existence of effective codes of conduct makes it easier to uphold integrity, accountability, and trust that are essential pillars on which the legal profession can effectively and justly practice in society. Professional organizations, albeit bar associations more than any other, play a core mandate in formulating such codes and providing support materials for legal practitioners. Not only do these institutions establish moral standards, but also they focus on the importance of professionalism within judicial systems. This mutual dependence is very significant as it maximizes public confidence in legal institutions while simultaneously creating a safeguard against malpractice and misuse. To effectively regulate violation of such moral standards, an integrated system of complaint procedures is required.

Figure 12.10. Professional ethics for lawyers.

Source: https://media.licdn.com/dms/image/v2/D4E12AQFsIIqaw2yeQg/article-cover_image-shrink_600_2000/article-cover_image-shrink_600_2000/0/1678721588930?e=2147483647&v=beta&t=8DjldC4QlrvZjv6Oz9mhW_8XB96WLD4ERb3ZlIWaAjE.

Where lawyers cannot conduct their professional activities, the system for complaining and resolving such matters ensures accountability and transparency. An effective complaint process allows clients and also colleagues to complain against the behavior of lawyers to allow disciplinary action where appropriate. Such procedures typically entail initial questioning, hearings, and a right of defence for legal representatives, suggesting due process. Furthermore, having clear lines to report misconduct encourages legal professionals to uphold ethical standards because they know that failure to do so will have consequences. Not only do these processes address the cases of misconduct, but they also prevent the legal profession as a whole from being tainted by keeping offenders on their toes. The effects of the disciplinary actions in the court of law can have an extensive impact on individual practitioners and the judicial system as a whole. Sanctions and remedies imposed for ethical violations are designed to reiterate the necessity of upholding high standards of professional practice. The actions can range from as lenient as reprimand and fines to as extreme as suspension and disbarment, depending on the gravity of the violation. Thus, these efforts influence the behavior of legal professionals, which in turn influences their dealings with clients, peers, and the judicial system in general. The response to disciplinary issues is also in accordance with the concept of professional responsibility; it creates an environment where legal professionals are willing to practice more ethical methods. In this equilibrium, the legal profession not only responds to its own code but also, in the final analysis, responds to justice's and the public's interests, demonstrating the interconnected nature of professional conduct and judicial systems' performance (Figure 12.10).

12.6.1. Examination of Codes of Conduct for Legal Professionals

In the intricate context of legal professions, imposing codes of conduct is a central pillar for maintaining ethical limits and public trust. They mark out the professional standards of conduct of legal experts, prescribing their duties towards the client, the court, and society in general. Underlying these regulations are maxims such as integrity, confidentiality, and competence that seek to offer guarantees that legal professionals hold themselves in a manner that raises the dignity of the legal system. The formalization of these ethical standards not only facilitates standardization of practice but also operates as a shield against abuse, hence establishing a culture of accountability for the profession. This systematic system of ethical practice allows the legal profession to address possible conflicts of interest and increase transparency in all legal transactions. No less crucial is the enforcement system that accompanies such codes of conduct. Professional groups, such as bar associations, typically manage the enforcement and conformity with ethical standards through a variety of mechanisms, such as the establishment of complaint procedures. Such procedures allow clients, among other stakeholders, to report unethical behavior, and have complaints addressed in a clear and methodical manner. Such functions cannot be over stated of these associations, for not only do they serve as custodians of professional integrity but also direct legal professionals towards ethical behavior through continuous training and publications. By encouraging a culture within which ethical compliance is everybody's responsibility, such organizations enhance the reputation of the legal community and encourage public trust in the judiciary. Moreover, the consequences of breaking these codes are drastic, often culminating in professional disciplinary measures that may include reprimands, suspensions, or disbarment. Sanctions serve not only as a deterrent against unethical conduct but also reflect the commitment of the profession to upholding justice and protecting client interests. The interaction between ethical codes, enforcement mechanisms, and sanctions creates an equilibrium framework that is intended to regulate legal practice efficiently. Therefore, codes of conduct are not in place merely to discipline; they are included in the broader aim of ensuring that legal professionals act so as to support the rule of law and the public's confidence in the courts. Through such an organization, the legal profession is able to address new challenges as well as build up an ethical responsibility culture within its practitioners (Tummers et al., 2015; Zarzeczny et al., 2014).

12.6.2. Procedure for Filing Complaints Against Lawyers

Complaint resolution against legal professionals is a crucial part of the maintenance of integrity in the legal profession. Complain procedures against lawyers are usually governed by the ethical rules of the professional organizations, which provide a template for resolving cases of misconduct. The complainants should first articulate the specific reasons for their complaints ranging from breach of client confidentiality to misrepresentation and fraud. Having set the foundation for the complaint, the complainer typically must secure relevant documents and evidence to support their claim before initiating the formal process. This initial step not only gives the complaint greater strength but places the case in its proper context for review by the proper authority, frequently a state bar or regulating body. After satisfying the initial requirements, complainants are directed to a formal submission process, differing significantly from one jurisdiction to another. In most cases, the complaint will be required to be made in writing, detailing the alleged improper conduct in its entirety. That documentation will typically contain a description of how the lawyer's actions are deemed unethical, along with any attendant evidence, for example, contracts or correspondence. While these complaints are filed, they usually undergo initial screening to ascertain whether they have substance. Regulating agencies usually classify complaints according to seriousness and extent of impact, thereby ensuring that the most abusive uses of the system are addressed first. Transparency in the processes is also important because it promotes people to have faith in the ability of the judicial systems to hold legal professionals accountable for what they are doing, which is consistent with ensuring public confidence in the standards and practices of the law. Resolution of complaints may have various consequences, including dismissals up to severe sanctions, which points to the importance of the investigatory and adjudicative processes. Where a complaint proves to be meritorious, the penalties range from verbal admonishments and mandatory ethics courses to suspension or disbarment based on the severity of the misconduct. This multi-tiered system of response allows the legal profession to maintain high standards and, at the same time, offer attorneys opportunities for rehabilitation. The grievance procedures also offer appeal mechanisms, offering attorneys the ability to appeal findings they perceive as unjust. This interplay is as much about the strength of disciplinary measures as it is about the subtle dynamic between holding people to account and protecting the rights of legal practitioners within the justice system (Veale et al., 2021; Shaffer et al., 2012).

12.6.3. Types of Sanctions and Remedies for Professional Misconduct

The penalties for professional misconduct in legal practice demand a formal spectrum of punishments intended to both sanction inappropriate conduct and safeguard the integrity of the justice system. Punishments might include reprimand, suspension, or total disbarment, depending on the type of misconduct. A reprimand is often made as an official rebuke but without restricting the lawyers right of practice, thereby providing a warning rather than a punitive measure. In instances of more serious infractions threatening public confidence or the norms of the legal calling, suspensions may be a valuable tool to prevent further misconduct while allowing for possible rehabilitation. Lastly, these sanctions work only to the extent that they enforce professional responsibility and deter future abuses, so that the legal profession is preserved as an ethical and honored calling. In addition to deterrents, also considered should be the avenues of remedies for professional misconduct. Remedies normally include the reinstallation of a professional license, under which individuals who display remorse and dedication to professional practice are readmitted to the profession after a specified period. This approach not only restores an individual but also serves the greater public interest in qualified legal professionals. Supervision and ongoing education throughout the reinstatement process can also ensure compliance with ethical standards, enhancing public trust in the justice system. In addition, public disclosure of misconduct and resultant sanctions not only acts as a deterrent but as an educational tool for other practitioners, promoting transparency and ethical awareness within the profession. The sanction/remedy relationship reflects broader debates over the need for a robust regime of accountability in professional legal services. For example, providing clear codes of conduct and complaint procedures is essential to preserve professional integrity and enable complaints to be dealt with effectively. In addition, regulation of such conduct by bar associations is reflective of a desire to concentrate control and apply ethical compliance standards to colleagues. Because public enforcement systems are especially evident in such jurisdictions as Hong Kong, where regulatory agencies have extensive duties, it raises important questions about reconciling public and private enforcement systems (David et al., 2017). Hence, constant observation and sanctioning adjustments, remedies, and punishments are all necessary to sustain the credibility and effectiveness of legal professionals in creating an equitable society (Anna, 2018).

SUMMARY

In looking at the complexities of legal professions and judicial systems, it is evident that effective governance and accountability are of the utmost significance. The success of any legal system hinges not only on the sagacity of laws but also on the quality of judicial personnel responsible for enforcing them. Strict selection processes and continuous judicial training enable judges and legal practitioners to enforce justice effectively. Further, more sophisticated digital systems facilitate better court administration through improved case management and increased access to services. The innovations are central in curtailing delays that are typical in judicial process as an effort to more efficiently resolve disputes.

Moreover, the potential of alternative dispute resolution (ADR) processes to transform legal practice is crucial in addressing the mounting demand for access to justice. Processes like mediation and arbitration offer parties ways to resolve conflicts outside of the resource-wasting, adversarial courtrooms, which may become too common. Not only do these processes encourage cooperative solutions, but they allow participants to be active participants in their own legal proceedings, thereby resulting in a higher level of public trust in the legal process. The promotion of ADR highlights the necessity of constant adaptation in legal education and training, so that legal professionals are well equipped to function within these other streams of justice. Ultimately, the linking theme of legal professions and judiciaries is the need for reform and relevance in an increasingly dynamic societal context. The recognition of judicial precedent as being a significant source of law lends merit to ensuring consistency and precision in applying case law, which can serve to minimize the occurrence of miscarriages of justice (Bernaziuk, 2024). The examination of exemplary practices imitated across the globe reveals that the acceptance of overseas legal insight, while retaining an awareness of indigenous legal cultures, is crucial to improving judicial outcomes. While legal systems across the globe try to bridge tradition and innovation, continuous research and study of these dynamics will establish a more balanced and just legal sphere for future generations.

FUTURE OUTLOOK

The future of legal practice and justice is more likely to be redesigned by ongoing innovation in court administration and provision of legal services. Utilization of computer systems has already transformed traditional practices, enabling smoother case handling and remote access to legal materials. As courts evolve with technological innovations, it is critical to examine implications for disadvantaged groups who might be excluded from access to these resources. Enhanced digital access can have the potential to democratize legal service, but this also presents issues related to equity in adopting technology. For example, dependence on web-based platforms can increase inequities in access between users with digital literacy and those who lack it. Filling these gaps is crucial to ensure that these technological reforms are accessed equally by all citizens and thus enhancing the integrity of the overall justice system. Along with the establishment of online access, the establishment of services such as a Legal and Court Interpreting Service could transform underserved communities. Such a model as Heartland Alliances Medical Interpreting Services would facilitate communication within the justice system, particularly between language-barrier immigrants and refugees and the entire system. Offering essential legal interpretation, the service could not only improve direct access to justice by people but also raise overall confidence in the judicial process. The initiative underscores the ethical obligation to prevent language and cultural difference from blocking justice. Such services would require the collaboration of legal professionals, nongovernment organizations, and the government to develop an overall support structure to ensure pluralistic populations' access to the legal setting. Besides that, pre-sentence report policies and practices in the judiciary have other access to justice connotations. The research cited in Burns et al. (2008) illustrates the complex nature of how report writers intend and judges interpret, indicating that there is a potential gap that can undermine the intended aims of community penalties. As these reports gain significance, it becomes necessary to educate judges to identify and utilize these reports in an efficient manner but taking into account their partial nature. Future policymaking should ensure report quality and brevity to make judicial decision-making more effective towards balanced defendant representation. Synching the report writer's goals with judicial interpretation will guide the legal system closer to a fairer, knowledge-oriented, and more just sentencing procedure that ultimately benefits all parties.

REFERENCES

1. Ali, S., Abuhmed, T., El-Sappagh, S., Muhammad, K., Alonso, J. M., Confalonieri, R., Guidotti, R., et al. (2023). Explainable artificial intelligence (XAI): What we know and what is left to attain trustworthy artificial intelligence. *Information Fusion, 99*, 101805–101805. https://doi.org/10.1016/j.inffus.2023.101805 (accessed on 9th September 2025).
2. Bahoo, S., Alon, I., & Paltrinieri, A. (2019). Corruption in international business: A review and research agenda. *International Business Review, 29*, 101660–101660. https://doi.org/10.1016/j.ibusrev.2019.101660 (accessed on 9th September 2025).
3. Bălan, C. (2010). Alternative dispute resolution through mediation in Romanian retail banking. https://core.ac.uk/download/93378275.pdf (accessed on 9th September 2025).
4. Banakar, R., & Ziaee, K. (2018). The legal profession in the Islamic Republic of Iran. https://www.semanticscholar.org/paper/568df7064c972ae7ee41c7289d9b9e6cb43834ce (accessed on 9th September 2025).
5. Bernaziuk, O. (2024). Judicial precedent in the legal system of Ukraine: Modern approaches to the definition of the concept. *Uzhhorod National University Herald. Series: Law.* https://www.semanticscholar.org/paper/19b862b7729361d42a45181f28751110206884ad (accessed on 9th September 2025).
6. Bierman, L. (2002). Beyond merit selection. https://core.ac.uk/download/144229212.pdf (accessed on 9th September 2025).
7. Bosslet, G. T., Pope, T. M., Rubenfeld, G. D., Lo, B., Truog, R. D., Rushton, C. H., Curtis, J. R., et al. (2015). An official ATS/AACN/ACCP/ESICM/SCCM policy statement: Responding to requests for potentially inappropriate treatments in intensive care units. *American Journal of Respiratory and Critical Care Medicine, 191*, 1318–1330. https://doi.org/10.1164/rccm.201505-0924st (accessed on 9th September 2025).
8. Buber, M., Deák, D., Freidson, E., Ghoshal, S., Gulick, L., Honoré, A. M., Kasher, A., et al. (2009). The role of law and ethics in developing business management as a profession. https://core.ac.uk/download/12354840.pdf (accessed on 9th September 2025).
9. Burns, N., Halliday, S., Hutton, N., McNeill, F., et al. (2008). Assisting and advising the sentencing decision process: The pursuit of 'quality' in pre-sentence reports. https://core.ac.uk/download/9026344.pdf (accessed on 9th September 2025).
10. Butler, W. E. (2009). *Russian Law. Oxford University Press eBooks.* https://doi.org/10.1093/oso/9780199562220.001.0001 (accessed on 9th September 2025).
11. Buyanova, I., Chen, S., & Chen, W. (1967). Innovations and experiments in uses of health manpower—The effect of licensure laws. https://core.ac.uk/download/62555863.pdf (accessed on 9th September 2025).
12. Caso, L., Pergolizzi, G. R., Vitali, D., & Palena, N. (2025). The role of expertise, personality traits and decision-making styles in criminal case evaluation: A comparison among judges, law students and non-legal professionals. *Journal of Criminal Psychology.* https://www.semanticscholar.org/paper/028bffe752ff54dab9ca7ec0e01aacae89365dc0 (accessed on 9th September 2025).
13. Chen, B. M., & Li, Z. (2020). How will technology change the face of Chinese justice? *Columbia*

Journal of Asian Law, 34, 1–58. https://doi.org/10.7916/cjal.v34i1.7484 (accessed on 9th September 2025).

14. Chunyan, Z., Ai, J., & Liu, S. (2017). The elastic ceiling: Gender and professional career in Chinese courts. *Law & Society Review, 51*, 168–199. https://doi.org/10.1111/lasr.12249 (accessed on 9th September 2025).
15. Dawson, L., Di Maggio, R., McKinley, J., Di Capua, G., Peppoloni, S., & Pringle, J. (2021). A proposal for a white paper on geoethics in forensic geology. *Special Publications, 508*, 115–124. https://www.semanticscholar.org/paper/52b0ce5456b804b11d9874862ec3ecdfadb437ff (accessed on 9th September 2025).
16. Demir, F. (2025). *Ismāʿīlī–Fāṭimid Legal Education and Judicial Activities in Egypt. Dini Araştırmalar.* https://www.semanticscholar.org/paper/ece4a302e99a71d9811f9609ccd0c5245a33f179 (accessed on 9th September 2025).
17. Devi, S. (2025). The integration of technology in alternative dispute resolution process in India. *International Journal for Multidisciplinary Research.* https://www.semanticscholar.org/paper/827c5345782ddb514d60d0034cae46b138e85f2e (accessed on 9th September 2025).
18. Donald, D. C., & Cheuk, P. W. H. (2017). Hong Kong's public enforcement model of investor protection. *Asian Journal of Law and Society, 4*, 349–385. https://doi.org/10.1017/als.2017.9 (accessed on 9th September 2025).
19. Dong, W., & Isler, V. (2003). Combining professionalism, nation building and public service: The professional project of the Israeli Bar 1928–2002. https://core.ac.uk/download/144225639.pdf (accessed on 9th September 2025).
20. Dydikov, A. (2024). Comparative analysis of the resolution and prevention of judicial error in different legal systems. *Yearly Journal of Scientific Articles "Pravova Derzhava".* https://www.semanticscholar.org/paper/09a543ffd833937d346296f0f839ff781c1824c5 (accessed on 9th September 2025).
21. Ennis, S. (2019). Independent sector regulators and their relationship with competition authorities. https://core.ac.uk/download/293754858.pdf (accessed on 9th September 2025).
22. Fisher, K. (2008). Education for judicial aspirants. *Journal of the National Association of Administrative Law Judiciary, 31*, 3. https://www.semanticscholar.org/paper/57a5c172ad1cd6a1cd4265e3d8d7486cfe0f3db4 (accessed on 9th September 2025).
23. Gabani. (2025). International information in law enforcement: The role of digital technologies in cooperation between the legal profession and law enforcement agencies. *Uzhhorod National University Herald. Series: Law.* https://www.semanticscholar.org/paper/e1a8938e02c6973e9efc878e9e2f4913a07d4834 (accessed on 9th September 2025).
24. Gostin, L. O., Gupta, M. D., Levin, M., et al. (2010). Implementing public health regulations in developing countries: Lessons from the OECD countries. https://core.ac.uk/download/70373906.pdf (accessed on 9th September 2025).
25. Gulom, N., Dilbar, I., Ismoil qizi, O., Azamat, M., Abadovich, D., Zikirullaeva, N., et al. (2025). Key determinants of investment flow and fiscal health for data-driven policy decisions and information retrieval. *Innovation Science and Technology.* https://www.semanticscholar.org/paper/ca6ce18469cff8b1b3aed5214f65cc017ec22ac6 (accessed on 9th September 2025).

26. Harris, A. P., & Sen, M. (2019). Bias and judging. *Annual Review of Political Science, 22*, 241–259. https://doi.org/10.1146/annurev-polisci-051617-090650 (accessed on 9th September 2025).

27. Isaac, J. C. (2016). Political power and social classes. *Perspectives on Politics, 14*, 297–306. https://doi.org/10.1017/s1537592716000037 (accessed on 9th September 2025).

28. Ismaili, F., & Sulejmani, S. (2024). The right to trial within a reasonable time and the challenges of respecting it in the criminal procedure. *International Journal of Legal Sciences–JUSTICIA.* https://www.semanticscholar.org/paper/f03edd4ce548ca5d2ae4e38e83d20cef4c42a80f (accessed on 9th September 2025).

29. Kruuse, H., & Genty, P. (2018). The state's role in the regulation and provision of legal services in South Africa and the United States: Supporting, nudging, or interfering? https://core.ac.uk/download/216959177.pdf (accessed on 9th September 2025).

30. McCrudden, C. (2008). Human dignity and judicial interpretation of human rights. *European Journal of International Law, 19*, 655–724. https://doi.org/10.1093/ejil/chn043 (accessed on 9th September 2025).

31. Menkel-Meadow, C. (2002). The lawyer as consensus builder: Ethics for a new practice. https://core.ac.uk/download/70374047.pdf (accessed on 9th September 2025).

32. N/A. (2000). A study of the feasibility of establishing a legal and court interpretation service in Cook County, Illinois. https://core.ac.uk/download/71363756.pdf (accessed on 9th September 2025).

33. N/A. (2012). Specialty guidelines for forensic psychology. *American Psychologist, 68*, 7–19. https://doi.org/10.1037/a0029889 (accessed on 9th September 2025).

34. N/A. (2019). *Doing Business 2020: Comparing Business Regulation in 190 Economies*. Washington, DC: World Bank eBooks. https://doi.org/10.1596/978-1-4648-1440-2 (accessed on 9th September 2025).

35. Nafzger, J. (2019). Bring on the pettifoggers: Revisiting the ethics rules, Civil Gideon, and the role of the judiciary. *LSN: Rights & Liberties (Topic).* https://www.semanticscholar.org/paper/92e1a9d91fc7ad73d1cd2e5f302684a087bba391 (accessed on 9th September 2025).

36. Noordegraaf, M. (2015). Hybrid professionalism and beyond: (New) forms of public professionalism in changing organizational and societal contexts. *Journal of Professions and Organization, 2*, 187–206. https://doi.org/10.1093/jpo/jov002 (accessed on 9th September 2025).

37. Orel, V. (2025). Legal argumentation in the process of studying disciplines of legal history: Innovative approaches in the training of future lawyers in the context of legal education reform. *Visnik Nacional'nogo universitetu «Lvivska politehnika». Seria: Uridicni nauki.* https://www.semanticscholar.org/paper/74c926f86fbc7f018810fcf72e1d9402d3576d92 (accessed on 9th September 2025).

38. Peacock, A., & Main, B. G. (2025). What price civil justice? https://core.ac.uk/download/pdf/7068340.pdf (accessed on 9th September 2025).

39. Rindhiyaa, M., Sivaranjani, R., Jaivardhan, S., & Narendran, G. (2025). AI powered legal assessments: Evaluating advocate skills through scenario-based simulations. *International Research Journal on Advanced Engineering Hub (IRJAEH).* https://www.semanticscholar.org/paper/b05a01d61caa97c7c2cbd73f708094c4b49da99c (accessed on 9th September 2025).

40. Schmidt, S. K. (2018). *The European Court of Justice and the policy process. Oxford University Press eBooks.* https://doi.org/10.1093/oso/9780198717775.001.0001 (accessed on 9th September 2025).

41. Shaffer, G., & Ginsburg, T. (2012). The empirical turn in international legal scholarship. *American Journal of International Law, 106*, 1–46. https://doi.org/10.5305/amerjintelaw.106.1.0001 (accessed on 9th September 2025).

42. Singh, N., & Das, P. K. (2024). Impact of NARCO analysis on accuracy and reliability of evidence obtained in criminal investigation in India. *Frontiers in Health Informatics.* https://www.semanticscholar.org/paper/109e2e07700f609c4af2856394abae5766e55321 (accessed on 9th September 2025).

43. Śledzińska-Simon, A. (2018). The rise and fall of judicial self-government in Poland: On judicial reform reversing democratic transition. *German Law Journal, 19*, 1839–1870. https://doi.org/10.1017/s2071832200023257 (accessed on 9th September 2025).

44. Soelberg, D. C., Brown, R. E., Du Vivier, D., Meyer, J. E., & Ramachandran, B. K. (2017). The US opioid crisis: Current federal and state legal issues. *Anesthesia & Analgesia, 125*, 1675–1681. https://doi.org/10.1213/ane.0000000000002403 (accessed on 9th September 2025).

45. Suddaby, R., & Viale, T. (2011). Professionals and field-level change: Institutional work and the professional project. *Current Sociology, 59*, 423–442. https://doi.org/10.1177/0011392111402586 (accessed on 9th September 2025).

46. Truby, J. (2020). Governing artificial intelligence to benefit the UN Sustainable Development Goals. *Sustainable Development, 28*, 946–959. https://doi.org/10.1002/sd.2048 (accessed on 9th September 2025).

47. Tummers, L., Bekkers, V., Vink, E., & Musheno, M. (2015). Coping during public service delivery: A conceptualization and systematic review of the literature. *Journal of Public Administration Research and Theory, 25*, 1099–1126. https://doi.org/10.1093/jopart/muu056 (accessed on 9th September 2025).

48. Veale, M., & Zuiderveen Borgesius, F. (2021). Demystifying the Draft EU Artificial Intelligence Act–Analyzing the good, the bad, and the unclear elements of the proposed approach. *Computer Law Review International, 22*, 97–112. https://doi.org/10.9785/cri-2021-220402 (accessed on 9th September 2025).

49. Zarzeczny, A., Caulfield, T., Ogbogu, U., Bell, P. D., Crooks, V. A., Kamenova, K., Master, Z., et al. (2014). Professional regulation: A potentially valuable tool in responding to "stem cell tourism." *Stem Cell Reports, 3*, 379–384. https://doi.org/10.1016/j.stemcr.2014.06.016 (accessed on 9th September 2025).

INDEX

D

E